Doing Metaphysics in a Diverse World

ALSO AVAILABLE FROM BLOOMSBURY

An Introduction to Indian Philosophy by Christopher Bartley
Metaphysics by Jonathan Tallant
Doing Philosophy Comparatively by Tim Connolly

Doing Metaphysics in a Diverse World

How We Make Sense of Things Across Cultures

Edited by
Stephen Green

BLOOMSBURY ACADEMIC
LONDON • NEW YORK • OXFORD • NEW DELHI • SYDNEY

BLOOMSBURY ACADEMIC
Bloomsbury Publishing Plc
50 Bedford Square, London, WC1B 3DP, UK
1385 Broadway, New York, NY 10018, USA
29 Earlsfort Terrace, Dublin 2, Ireland

BLOOMSBURY, BLOOMSBURY ACADEMIC and the Diana logo are
trademarks of Bloomsbury Publishing Plc

First published in Great Britain 2025

Copyright © Stephen Green and Contributors 2025

Stephen Green and Contributors have asserted their right under the Copyright,
Designs and Patents Act, 1988, to be identified as Authors of this work.

Cover design by Louise Dugdale
Cover image © Wirestock/iStock

All rights reserved. No part of this publication may be: i) reproduced or transmitted in any form, electronic or mechanical, including photocopying, recording or by means of any information storage or retrieval system without prior permission in writing from the publishers; or ii) used or reproduced in any way for the training, development or operation of artificial intelligence (AI) technologies, including generative AI technologies. The rights holders expressly reserve this publication from the text and data mining exception as per Article 4(3) of the Digital Single Market Directive (EU) 2019/790.

Bloomsbury Publishing Plc does not have any control over, or responsibility for, any third-party websites referred to or in this book. All internet addresses given in this book were correct at the time of going to press. The author and publisher regret any inconvenience caused if addresses have changed or sites have ceased to exist, but can accept no responsibility for any such changes.

A catalogue record for this book is available from the British Library.

A catalogue record for this book is available from the Library of Congress.

ISBN: HB: 978-1-3504-0250-8
PB: 978-1-3504-0249-2
ePDF: 978-1-3504-0251-5
eBook: 978-1-3504-0252-2

Typeset by Integra Software Services Pvt. Ltd.
Printed and bound in Great Britain

For product safety related questions contact productsafety@bloomsbury.com.

To find out more about our authors and books visit www.bloomsbury.com
and sign up for our newsletters.

In memory of Alan Montefiore, who encouraged the editor in convening an inspiring group of colleagues to work on this project, many of whom would testify to his influence on their philosophical journeys.

Contents

List of figures x
List of contributors xi

Foreword A.W. Moore xiv

Introduction Stephen Green 1

Part 1

1 **Philosophizing while reading texts across cultures** Alex Samely 15

2 **Dao and the way – A comparative perspective** Xinzhong Yao 43

3 **Generative harmony: Origins and becoming in Confucian metaphysics** Chenyang Li 63

4 **The problem of the flying arrow: Comparing Hui Shi and Zeno of Elea using the method of sublation** Jana S. Rošker 79

5 **Xunzi and Maimonides: Language, metaphysics, governance** Nicholas Bunnin 97

6 **Metaphysics of normative values: Metaethical constructivism and Xunzi** Siufu Tang 115

7 **Spinoza and Wang Bi: Metaphysics of ethics** Nicholas Bunnin 131

8 **Personhood in Indian metaphysics: Touchpoints with other traditions** *Gavin Flood* 145

9 **Metaphysics of a Hindu goddess tradition and European phenomenology** *Gavin Flood* 167

10 **Brilliant darkness: Apophatic thinking in early Christian and Indian traditions** *Ana-Maria Pascal and Diwakar Acharya* 181

11 **Overcoming negative theology: Kūkai and Palamas on essence and energy** *Ana-Maria Pascal and Paulus Kaufmann* 199

12 **God without power: Kenosis and Tsimtsum as two paradigms of divine self-restriction** *Agata Bielik-Robson* 217

13 **Philosophy and African art: Léopold Sédar Senghor and the philosophy of emotion and rhythm** *Victor Emma-Adamah* 237

14 **The non-human in African metaphysics** *Elvis Imafidon* 259

15 **The divine names: The human role in the construction of the cosmos in the Maya *Popol Vuh* and Ibn ʿArabī's *Fusus al-Hikam*** *Alexus McLeod* 271

16 **Philosophy as a way of life: Metaphysics, ethics and spiritual exercises** *Sajjad Rizvi* 291

Part 2

1 **Suchness** *Lucia Dolce* 315

2 **Beyond, being and becoming**
   Agata Bielik-Robson 341

3 **Persons, selves and metaphysics**
   Ana-Maria Pascal and Gavin Flood 361

4 **Names, naming, unnamed, unnameable**
   Nicholas Bunnin and Sajjad Rizvi 379

Afterword: Continuing to do metaphysics in a diverse world *Stephen Green* 393

Index 395

Figures

1 *Kpélié* mask, Senoufo-Dioula, Côte d'Ivoire. Wood and pigment. Owned by The Art Institute of Chicago, Chicago. Reproduced with permission — 253

2 Mandala of Jūzenji and the Sannō deities of Hiei. Kamakura period (fourteenth century). Hanging scroll, colour on silk. Owned by Shinnyo-en Shinchōji, Tokyo. Reproduced with permission — 326

3 *Vegetable Nirvana*. Edo period (*c.* 1792). Hanging scroll, ink on paper. Formerly owned by Seiganji temple, Kyoto. Kyoto National Museum. Reproduced with permission — 331

Contributors

Diwakar ACHARYA is a Nepali scholar specializing in the religious and philosophical traditions of South Asia. He is Spalding Professor of Eastern Religion and Ethics at the University of Oxford and Fellow of All Souls College, Oxford. He has translated and written extensively on Indic texts.

Agata BIELIK-ROBSON is Professor of Jewish Studies at the University of Nottingham and Professor of Philosophy at the Polish Academy of Sciences. She works on philosophical aspects of psychoanalysis, romantic subjectivity and Jewish philosophical theology. Her most recent publication is *Derrida's Marrano Passover: Exile, Survival, Betrayal and the Metaphysics of Non-Identity* (2023).

Nicholas BUNNIN is Emeritus Director of the Philosophy Project, University of Oxford China Centre, and associate member of the Oxford Faculty of Philosophy. He co-founded with Qiu Renzong the Philosophy Summer School in China; co-authored with Yu Jiyuan *The Dictionary of Western Philosophy: English-Chinese* (2001) and *Saving the Phenomena: An Aristotelian Method* in Comparative Philosophy (2001).

Lucia DOLCE is Numata Professor of Japanese Buddhism at SOAS University of London and Chair of the SOAS Centre of Buddhist Studies. She has published extensively, in English and in Japanese, on the hermeneutical practices of East Asian Buddhist traditions and on the ritual and visual dimension of religion in Japan.

Victor EMMA-ADAMAH is Assistant Professor of Philosophy and Theology at the University of Austin, Texas, and Research Fellow at the Institut Catholique de Toulouse, France. His research interests are in metaphysics, philosophies of the subject in modernity and philosophical explorations of African religious traditions and aesthetics.

Gavin FLOOD is Professor of Hindu Studies and Comparative Religion at Oxford University, a Senior Research Fellow of Campion Hall, and the Piramal Dean of Academic Affairs at the Oxford Centre for Hindu Studies. Among his books are *Religion and the Philosophy of Life* (2019) and *The Truth Within: A History of Inwardness in Christianity, Hinduism and Buddhism* (2014).

Elvis IMAFIDON is Reader in African Philosophy and Director of the Centre for Global and Comparative Philosophies at SOAS, University of London. He is the author and editor of several books, including *African Philosophy and the Otherness of Albinism: White Skin, Black Race* (2019), *Handbook of African Philosophy of Difference* (2020) and *Handbook of African Philosophy* (2023).

Paulus KAUFMANN is Senior Lecturer at the Japan Centre of the Ludwig-Maximilians-Universität in Munich and at Zurich University's Institute of Asian and Oriental Studies. His research focuses on the writings of the Japanese monk Kūkai (774–835). His field of expertise is Japan's history of ideas with a special focus on early Japanese Buddhism and on the political discourse of the Edo period (1600–1868).

Chenyang LI is Professor of Philosophy at Nanyang Technological University, Singapore. His primary areas of research are Chinese philosophy and comparative philosophy. Author of *The Confucian Philosophy of Harmony* (2014), he has written extensively on Chinese philosophy in a comparative context, including over 100 journal articles and book chapters.

Alexus McLEOD is Professor of Religious Studies at Indiana University. His main areas of research are Mesoamerican, Chinese and Comparative Philosophy. His recent works include *An Introduction to Mesoamerican Philosophy* (Cambridge, 2023) and *Philosophy of the Ancient Maya: Lords of Time* (Lexington, 2017).

Ana-Maria PASCAL is Academic Director at SCIO and Member of the Common Room at St. Cross College, University of Oxford. She specializes in post-Kantian philosophy, the Patristic tradition and the Kyoto School. She wrote *Pragmatism and 'the End' of Metaphysics* (2009), *Multiculturalism and the Convergence of Faith and Practical Wisdom in Modern Society* (2017), and *Narratives and the Role of Philosophy in Cross-disciplinary Studies* (2018).

Sajjad RIZVI is Professor of Islamic Intellectual History at the University of Exeter. An intellectual historian working on the philosophical traditions of the Islamic East, he is currently writing a short manifesto on Islamic philosophy as global philosophy.

Jana S. ROŠKER is Professor of Sinology at the Department of Asian Studies of the Faculty of Arts at the University of Ljubljana. She is Chief Editor of *Asian Studies* and the author of numerous books, including *Confucian Relationism and Global Ethics: Alternative Models of Ethics and Axiology in Times of Global Crisis* (2023). For her extensive publications, see https://janarosker.academia.edu/

Alex SAMELY teaches Jewish Studies and philosophy at the University of Manchester, England. Trained at Frankfurt and Oxford Universities, he publishes on contemporary philosophical issues (*Reading and Experience*, 2024) and on the hermeneutics and literary genres of Jewish antiquity (*Forms of Rabbinic Literature and Thought*, 2007; *Profiling Jewish Literature in Antiquity*, 2013).

Siufu TANG is Associate Professor in the School of Chinese at the University of Hong Kong. His research interest focuses on early Confucianism (particularly Xunzi) and its modern relevance. He is the author of *Self-Realization through Confucian Learning: A Contemporary Reconstruction of Xunzi's Ethics* (2016).

Xinzhong YAO is Professor of Ethics in the School of Philosophy at Renmin University of China, Beijing, and Professor Emeritus at King's College London. His published books include *Chinese Religion: A Contextual Approach* (2010), *Wisdom in Early Confucian and Israelite Traditions* (2006, 2016) and *Reconceptualizing Confucian Philosophy in the twenty-first Century* (2017).

Foreword

I hope that it will not sound formulaic if I begin this foreword by saying what a pleasure and an honour it is to have been invited to write it. There is a distinctive conception both of metaphysics and of its significance that is embodied in the essays that follow, and writing this foreword has given me a welcome opportunity to associate myself with it.

These essays, as Stephen Green notes in his introduction to the volume, grew out of conversations among a group of academics that began in lockdown and that lasted for more than three years, ranging over some of the many ways in which different cultures make sense of things. The conversations were often based on early versions of these very essays. This gave the writers of the essays wherewithal to refine them, and it gave other members of the group something to write about in response. There is therefore a sense in which even the essays that are single-authored can be regarded as the results of collaboration.

This project clearly had the potential to be a fascinating and important one. That potential, it seems to me, has been admirably realized.

Before I proceed, I should like to make a couple of personal remarks. First, Stephen mentions in his introduction that it was a neighbour of his, the philosopher Alan Montefiore, who encouraged him to pursue the project. I am greatly saddened to note that Alan died between my finishing the first draft of this foreword and its publication. I knew Alan, both as a colleague and as a friend, for nearly half of the nearly one hundred years that he lived on this planet. I learned a great deal from him during that time, and I am indebted to him in countless ways. It is a pleasure to pay tribute to him in this context, albeit a pleasure combined with sorrow that he did not live to see my doing so. The second of my personal remarks is to note that I myself was party to some of the conversations out of which this volume grew, and I can attest to the excitement and sense of intellectual adventure that they generated.

Their subject matter, as I have said, was the many ways in which different cultures make sense of things. But what has that to do with metaphysics, to which I alluded at the outset and which appears in the title of the volume? The link is a definition of metaphysics that I have found helpful and in connection with which Stephen kindly references me in his introduction. Metaphysics, on this definition, is the most general attempt to make sense of things.

But if that is what metaphysics is, then I agree with Stephen that, 'like Molière's bourgeois gentilhomme and his prose, we have all been doing metaphysics all our lives'. Metaphysics is not the preserve of academic specialists, nor of intellectuals, nor of mystics, nor of the members of any other group. We are all metaphysicians. We all try to make sense of things, in the many varied senses of that phrase, and part of our doing so is our doing so at the highest level of generality. Metaphysics is one of the basic tools that we use to navigate our way around the world.

Two things, both of which Stephen highlights in his introduction, follow from this. First, metaphysics is not a private matter: the world that we use metaphysics to navigate our way around is a shared world. Secondly, metaphysics is as much a practical exercise as it is a theoretical one. Globalization is adding scale to the first of these. It is thereby adding urgency to the second. That is part of the rationale for what Stephen and the other contributors to this volume have undertaken. We need to reflect on how metaphysics pertains to our living in worldwide community with one another, and on what is required for its different manifestations to be involved in proper and fruitful dialogue rather than in conflict. One thing that is required is for those who are party to any of its different manifestations to have some basic familiarity with the others – precisely what the contributors to this volume have sought to provide. 'We have brought a variety of different perspectives to the conversations', Stephen writes in his introduction.

It is striking how the quotation continues: '... but [we] share three fundamental convictions' (emphasis added). I want to say a little about these three convictions.

The first two will come as no surprise given what I have already said. In fact they are reformulations of what I have already said. First, there is the conviction that 'people in all cultures do metaphysics and their metaphysics influence their lives'. Secondly, there is the conviction that 'the search for wisdom in inter-cultural dialogue is not merely an academic pursuit but matters to us all more than ever, in an increasingly connected but also fractious world'. The reference to fractiousness in the second of these is a reminder that mere familiarity with how other people in other cultures do metaphysics is no guarantor of a proper and fruitful dialogue with them. There are examples aplenty of how such familiarity can exacerbate conflict rather than alleviate it. Promoting such familiarity may be a necessary condition of attaining harmony; it is not a sufficient condition. What grounds are there, in that case, for optimism? Why think that such harmony is even attainable? This is where the third conviction is pertinent. The third conviction is that 'at some level there are common experiences of the world of life in all cultures and at all times, which mean that [the search for shared wisdom] is not in vain'.

Why think this? Are there any good empirical reasons to do so? Are there at any rate no good empirical reasons not to do so? Is it somehow *a priori*? What is its status? Does it serve as a working hypothesis? An article of faith? An object of hope? These are not only important questions in their own right; they are, as I see it, important metaphysical questions in their own right. Nor is it clear that all the contributors to this volume would answer them in the same way. But, however these questions should be answered, one thing about which all the contributors to this volume would agree is that the third conviction is pivotal.

What Stephen himself fastens on, when amplifying on the third conviction, is our shared humanity. He writes:

> [F]or all the translational and conversational challenges, there must be some level of commonality amongst humans. To deny this would be to deny that we are members of a single species, to deny ourselves a common humanity. To say that our perspectives are inevitably relative cannot be to say that we have nothing – or nothing that we can discover – in common … [W]e should surely never give up the search for wisdom in common, in an interconnected world. That is the motive for this book.

While this allows for variations in how we practise metaphysics, it is also intended to encourage the quest for commonalities in how we do so, the thought being that we can expect such commonalities simply by virtue of the fact that we are all human beings.

But can we? One reason for being sceptical about this is the threat of a kind of self-stultification. Metaphysics is inherently self-conscious. It forces us to question our ends as well as our means. In particular, it forces us to ask how far we ought to be defined by our humanity, or how far we ought to be beholden to our humanity, just as it has forced men in the past to ask how far they ought to be defined by or beholden to their masculinity. Is the very category of the human debilitating and restricting? Should our quest be, not for something that we are capable of sharing because of who we are, but rather for a new and broader conception of who we are, a conception that may (for instance) embrace various forms of artificial intelligence? And might this in turn force us to reconsider whether the shared wisdom whose desirability we have been taking for granted, rather like the shared wisdom among men whose desirability would once have been taken for granted (by men), is really desirable? I talk of self-stultification here, not because such questions cannot receive answers that would be conducive to the third conviction, but rather because the very posing of such questions – questions which, as long as we are engaged in metaphysics, will never go away – is disruptive. The shared wisdom that is proclaimed in the third conviction requires a certain self-confidence. Self-confidence and self-consciousness do not sit well together.

Moreover, I am painfully aware that, to whatever extent there really is a problem for the third conviction here, then simply drawing attention to it serves to aggravate it. And I use the word 'painfully' because I share the contributors' sympathy for the third conviction. To address this problem we need some way, in full spite of the problem, of maintaining our humanistic self-confidence. The essays in this volume, notwithstanding the fact that some of them are themselves self-conscious explorations of the very categories at work in the third conviction, are a significant contribution to that.

This is the chief reason why I am so enthusiastic about the volume. The contributors have managed to raise these questions without allowing their sense of the importance of their shared humanity – of our shared humanity – to be compromised. Although we must be open to the possibility that we shall one day adopt categories that disrupt that sense, for the time being it serves as a kind of framework for all our metaphysical undertakings and gives rationale to the third conviction, the conviction that our search for shared wisdom is not in vain.

I earlier raised the question of what status the third conviction has – whether it serves as a working hypothesis, an article of faith, an object of hope, or possibly something else entirely. Nothing in what I have just said helps to settle that. Indeed, as I indicated at the time, settling that is itself, in my view, a metaphysical task (and thus a further indication of how self-conscious the whole enterprise is). What I did not indicate at the time, but would like to emphasize now, is that it is another aspect of the enterprise to which what follows is a significant contribution. No doubt the status of the third conviction remains unsettled. That is only to be expected. The settling of this matter is an activity, not an accomplishment. I hope, and I anticipate, that the particular contribution to the activity that is to be found in these pages will continue well beyond them.

A.W. Moore
Oxford, July 2024

Introduction

Stephen Green

Philosophy is not a private matter, as Edmund Husserl noted towards the end of his life in the mid-1930s, when global storm clouds were gathering, as he was writing *The Crisis of European Sciences and Transcendental Phenomenology*.

It is not a private matter because philosophy is about the way we interpret our world and has implications for the way we live. And it is now a global matter. This book is the outcome of conversations among a group of philosophers and historians of ideas who have come together for over three years in that spirit. We have brought a variety of different perspectives to the conversations but share three fundamental convictions: that people in all cultures do metaphysics and their metaphysics influence their lives; that the search for wisdom in inter-cultural dialogue is not merely an academic pursuit but matters more than ever, in an increasingly connected but also fractious world; and that at some level there are common experiences of life in all cultures and at all times, which mean that this search is not in vain.

All three of these convictions could be problematized. But we believe them to be – at the very least – good working assumptions.

First, metaphysics is not just for those who are steeped in traditions of philosophical thought or religious practice. Sages have tended to regard metaphysics as their own preserve – a pursuit for an intellectual (and usually also social and/or clerical) elite. But we think a better assumption is that all people do metaphysics, if metaphysics means seeking to make sense of things, at least for the purpose of living their lives. We all have our perspectives on being, time and space, just as we have our logics and our ethics. The way we express such perspectives may be explicit, or it may be implicit in our stories or rituals – or just in how we act and relate. Our perspectives may be largely inherited or they may be subjectively and more radically determined. Our accounts may be inchoate and inconsistent; but like Molière's bourgeois gentilhomme and his prose, we have all been doing metaphysics all our lives.

Secondly, we inevitably do our metaphysics nowadays in a world which is increasingly interconnected, and thus more aware of its diversity. Not that we were ever wholly unconnected: Greeks, Persians, Egyptians and Indians influenced each other well before the Common Era; Xuanzang made his famous journey from China to India in the seventh century; medieval Christian Europe forged its intellectual identity under the influence of Islamic thought; early modern Europe not only renewed its acquaintance with its own classical Greek heritage but also discovered the thought worlds of India and China.

But the modern era interacts with a completely different degree of intensity. In consequence, the modern – indeed, post-modern, post-colonial, but above all increasingly urban and digitally connected – consciousness is shaping our world in wholly new ways. A large majority of humans now live in, or in the penumbra of, cities; urban life breaks down old social structures and attitudes, in a way that is both risky and exhilarating. It is changing every culture on the planet. Meanwhile, digital connectivity is transforming human life experience, and we are still in the early foothills of this change. This web of urbanization and interaction cannot be unravelled: there is no possibility of retreat to a simpler, less connected life experience (at least for the overwhelming majority of human beings).

Thirdly, therefore, we do our metaphysics in a complex, diverse, interconnected and rapidly changing world. This poses questions at the deepest level about who we are, both in community and in ourselves – and in our planetary context. The diversity is not just a colourful variety: the differences are fundamental. Thus, for example, Chinese perspectives have from time immemorial seen a world of flux in which harmony through a balance of forces is the natural order of things; Europeans saw a world of Aristotelian substance as a world of stuff to be worked. Both saw their principles as universal, with implications for the place of humans in the natural order: and both saw the human order within that natural order as shaped and governed by a universalizing principle which the Chinese called the 'mandate of heaven'. In recent centuries, both have been altered forever: China by its ideological upheavals and by one of the fastest processes of industrialization, urbanization and modernization the world has ever seen; Europe by the first industrialization, by rising secularism and by the gradual weakening of its ingrained sense of natural supremacy – the eventual consequence of empire and of its loss. In the world of thought, the result has been that each has been stealing some of the clothes of the other. China has learned from such seminal European thinkers as Karl Marx and Adam Smith about building a modern society; European thought has come to recognize the subtle relevance of the ancient Daoist sense that we live in a world of flux rather than substance – in a world that is non-binary.

We also recognize more clearly the subtle and profound issues posed by translation and conversation across languages, both across separate languages and within the same language tradition over time. Languages, widespread or not, represent thought worlds of whole communities, and they are not static. In fact, there can be no better indication of the sheer variety of human life experience than the plethora of several thousand languages still spoken around the world. (There is also no better indication of the challenge which modern interconnectedness represents than the rising extinction rate and the growing concentration on a few widespread regional and world languages.)

Yet for all the translational challenges, there must be some level of commonality among humans. To deny this would be to deny that we are members of a single species, to deny ourselves a common humanity. To say that our perspectives are inevitably relative cannot be to say that we have nothing – or nothing that we can discover – in common. We may find the commonalities difficult to define, and to call the commonalities universals may or may not be helpful. But we should surely never give up the search for common wisdom, in an interconnected world. That is the motive for this book.

The rocky but remorseless progress of interconnectedness

A generation ago, it looked to many as if an urbanized and connected world would usher in a brilliant new modernity in which individuals would be able to flourish as never before. Old restrictive norms and attitudes were weakening or being dismantled; old autocratic regimes were collapsing; new information connected people across the world; the international market would spread rational economic behaviour everywhere. This seemingly triumphant globalization brought new prosperity to hundreds of millions of people in just a few decades. It was recognized to be a work in progress, but it felt as though humanity was coming of age. It felt – to use a phrase which became a cliché – as though this might be the (Hegelian) end of history.

The world looks very different now. For nearly half a century after the Second World War, humanity had grown used to a world of two superpowers and a global conflict of two ideologies. Then China took its place on the world stage; there would still be two superpowers, it seemed – but henceforward it would be the United States and China, instead of the United States and the Soviet Union. But this would not be just a continuation of that postwar ideological contest. Communism as a controlling ideology has all but disappeared, in China as almost everywhere else. The nomenclature persists, but the reality is different from anything Marx, Lenin or Mao would recognize. And the liberal economic market of capitalism was shaken by a global financial crisis which exposed its weaknesses and shattered its self-confidence.

In fact, the new rivalry seems more like old-fashioned great power rivalry. Furthermore, the familiar post-war pattern of duopoly is now fragmenting: India has increasing momentum and is nobody's ally; the countries of the Arabian peninsula are more influential than ever; Russia remains a huge nuclear power which is not yet reconciled to the loss of empire; and the United States swings – as it has always done – between engagement and withdrawal from the international arena. In short, the world is becoming multipolar; what should keep us awake is the fear, not of a

Thucydidean trap, but of a chain reaction which echoes the way the twentieth century began its terrible course.

The fault lines are no longer primarily about economic systems; rather, they are manifest in the politics of identity in a whole series of globally significant countries. Meanwhile, the United States and the former imperialists of Europe are undergoing painful confrontations with the realities of their own pasts; and, partly as a result, populism is now a force to be reckoned with in much of the Western world. Perhaps above all, China is a very different place now, with its strident emphasis on 'socialism with Chinese characteristics' and its newly assertive regional and foreign policy.

So has the trend towards greater interconnectedness stopped? No. In fact, it cannot. Because this interconnectedness is not just the consequence of an economic system. Nor is it just the embodiment of a post-war order which owed its existence to the temporary dominance of the United States. Rather, it seems to be something much deeper; it is arguably a stage of human history which can no more be reversed than could the ancient shift from hunting to agriculture, or from fields to factories.

This new era brings tensions and challenges, the scale of which is wholly new. We know what at least some of those challenges will be: the virtual certainty of further pandemics; the dangers of nuclear proliferation; mass migration; the social impact of urbanization and digitalization; the promise and threats of artificial intelligence; and above all, environmental degradation and climate change.

What a change this is from all of human history up to the last century. Most fundamentally, never before has so much of humankind lived cut off from the natural world – on which we depend for our physical and perhaps also for our spiritual well-being. Never before have we uprooted and disconnected ourselves from our wider context in this way. When Kant wrote about the two things that filled him with more and more amazement the more he pondered them – the starry sky above him and the moral law within him – he could see the stars from the streets of Königsberg. Now, large numbers of people have never seen an unpolluted night sky. And as for Kant's moral law: we struggle with the question of human identity and with the question of universals – or commonalities – as never before.

The urgency of the conversation

Exploring the understanding of values to human beings cross-culturally is thus an imperative for our time. But values do not exist in a vacuum. Values imply metaphysics. So to explore values cross-culturally means to explore metaphysical contexts cross-culturally. As we do so, we must confront some new (but also clearly ancient) questions. At a nightmarish popular level, fiction writers will imagine a world in which creatures we have made take control of us in the dystopian cities of a burning planet. At a more reflective level, philosophers should worry about the human identity. What *are* we, we humans? What do we have in common with each other and with the rest of our world? How do we understand the diverse forces that shape us? What do the cultural traditions that have moulded us down the ages tell us about our place in a very different modern world?

We believe that such questions need to be explored – and nowadays can *only* be profitably explored – in cross-cultural conversation. Cross-cultural dialogue among philosophers will not, of course, make more than a marginal difference to the complexity and scale of our social and geopolitical challenges. But marginal differences matter; and we have come together as a group of professional academics, convened initially by an editor who is an amateur (in the original meaning as well as in the conventional use of the term), in conversation about metaphysics across cultures in order to see what we can learn. We do so in the shared belief that such conversation matters.

We are not alone in this, of course; nor would we want to be seen as doing something radical and distinctive. This book is the outcome of our particular conversations – a milestone on a conversational journey. By its nature, such a venture cannot be comprehensive; we are exploring a landscape which is limitless. We have not sought to be systematic; nor (other than in Alex Samely's and in Jana Rošker's chapters in Part 1) have we dwelt explicitly on methodologies of comparison or conducted any kind of comprehensive review of the growing literature on this topic. We have sought a de-centred perspective, not – as is still so often the case – a Western focus or starting point. What we mean by comparative metaphysics is an exploration of (and reflection upon) texts, themes and stories from diverse world traditions, which fit within a broad working definition of metaphysics, proposed by Adrian Moore, as the attempt by humans to make sense of things at the most general level. This includes the attempt to make sense of ultimate things or 'absolute' realities, in or beyond the world of experience.

This is not just an imperative born of modern geopolitics (though it is certainly that). It is also driven by a thirst for more knowledge about what matters. The objective is to deepen our understanding of ourselves and each other – and therefore of how humans can learn to live together and come together in the face of our common challenges in a connected world. In other words, the project is not just an intellectual enquiry but has an inevitable ethical commitment. Philosophy is not just a private matter.

This objective raises obvious questions: whom do we perceive to be 'the other' in their various degrees of alterity – our neighbour, the outsider, some ultimate Other? What voices do we hear? How do we learn to listen well?

Such musings pose in their turn the unavoidable question of language itself. In particular: what can't be translated – and yet must be? And, at an even deeper level, what can't be expressed – and yet must be? At one level, this is the familiar question of linguistics. All members of the group speak more than one language; at the same time all of us find ourselves confronting texts in languages we do not speak. We write in English as the world's current lingua franca. As we read and write, we face the question again and again: how best to translate? But what we are asking ourselves is also a deeper question: which of the ways in which I have learned to think about the world responds best to what the text is talking about? and how is my thinking changed by my engagement with the text?

This dialogue across borders means that we have to study the explicit or implicit understandings of ontology, epistemology and ethics (to use terms derived from the Greco-Abrahamic thought world) in what others write or say. We should not take for granted that understandings 'translate' easily, and yet key terms involved do seem to be recognized in some of the mirrors that cultures hold up to each other (as in, for example, the thought of Zhang Dainian). We should be alert to echoes – or 'family resemblances' à la Wittgenstein – and also to contrasts. The purpose is to take the risk of comparison, and to reflect on the significance of both the echoes and the contrasts for the dialogue which increased connectivity makes both inevitable and desirable.

Our conversations began as a pandemic lockdown project in 2020. The editor studied philosophy as an undergraduate and retained an interest in the way people think about things, all the way through a professional career in economics, finance and trade – a career which took him to live in America, in the Middle East and in East Asia. He then lived in the same street in London as Alan Montefiore, the distinguished retired Oxford philosopher, who encouraged him to pursue his idea of doing some methodical work on the way cultures approach making sense of things – and who put him in touch with other interlocutors and potential collaborators. The conversations fanned out and in the end it was a group of sixteen academics from around the world who came together to work on this project, most of whom have contributed chapters to this book.

We have met both virtually and in person over more than three years, to read texts, to reflect and learn from engagement with the texts and from each other, and to write in response – in some cases as joint authors of chapters, in others as 'conversationalists'. All our writing has been the subject of conversation, and has led to more writing and re-writing. It has been a journey for each of us, and the journey will continue. Parts 1 and 2 of the book demonstrate some of our learnings on the journey so far.

Part 1

Part 1 contains specific studies, chosen deliberately as examples (without claiming that they are *representative* of the whole of any tradition) to show how very different thought worlds can be brought into productive conversation. The examples come from Chinese, Japanese, Indian, Islamic, Jewish, European (Greek and Christian),

West and Southern African, and Mesoamerican traditions. Some bring two texts from very different cultural backgrounds into direct conversation; others look at one textual tradition and its touch points with others. There is no profound rationale for the order of the chapters – beyond a broad tendency to move from east to west around the world (if only to correct for the still prevalent tendency to start with Europe).

Chapter 1: Philosophizing while Reading Texts across Cultures. Alex Samely argues that basic processes of text reading can increase the chance that a reader will recognize an unfamiliar mode of discourse *as* philosophical. Readers are thereby able to *live through* meaning connections to which their own philosophical sub-culture might not have exposed them, and which might go beyond their habits of thought. The consideration of the processes of text reading therefore adds an important, hitherto neglected, dimension to the discussion of cross-cultural philosophizing.

Chapter 2: Dao and the Way: A Comparative Perspective. Xinzhong Yao shows how *Dao* is one of the most fundamental concepts in Chinese metaphysics and culture. It has been translated variously as the way, method, *noumenon*, truth, principle, nature, law or even God. However, none of these is a perfect fit for all its meanings. This chapter explores the origin and evolution of *Dao* in classical Chinese texts and especially in the different Daoist and Confucian interpretations, in order to clarify the commonalities with and differences from the notions of 'way' that play a role in Greco-Abrahamic contexts.

Chapter 3: Generative Harmony: Origins and Becoming in Confucian Metaphysics. Chenyang Li investigates and reformulates the conception of generative harmony as expounded by ancient Chinese thinkers. It provides an account of the role of generative harmony in the formation and evolution of the world in ancient Chinese cosmogony and metaphysics, and argues for its usefulness on the basis of reflections on modern scientific thought.

Chapter 4: The Problem of the Flying Arrow: Comparing Hui Shi and Zeno of Elea Using the Method of Sublation. Jana S. Rošker showcases a novel theoretical approach to transcultural philosophical comparison, the 'method of sublation'. She applies this method to two famous perspectives on the kinetic state of a flying arrow: those of the pre-Socratic philosopher Zeno of Elea from ancient Greece, and of Hui Shi, a prominent scholar of the Chinese School of Names, who were renowned for their contributions to Chinese logic. She shows how each perspective can be insightful for those who are prepared to 'sublate' them.

Chapter 5: Xunzi and Maimonides: Language, Metaphysics, Governance. Nicholas Bunnin explores the *Xunzi* and Maimonides' *Guide of the Perplexed*, focusing on how Xunzi and Maimonides employed approaches to language and metaphysics in order to provide context and justification for their proposals for governing their own societies. The chapter also demonstrates the importance of their accounts of language, metaphysics and governance as resources for our own times; in particular,

Bunnin questions John Rawls' claim that his theory of justice as fairness is political and not metaphysical.

Chapter 6: Metaphysics of Normative Values: Metaethical Constructivism and Xunzi. Siufu Tang argues that Xunzi's metaethical ideas are a version of constructivism – such that normative values and facts do not exist independently of human activities, but rather are brought into being through human practice, the core of which is living a good life in community. Such human practice has two aspects: the orderly satisfaction of the wants and needs of all people, and the establishment of a well-ordered society through distinctions which embody the meaning and significance of human life.

Chapter 7: Spinoza and Wang Bi: Metaphysics of Ethics. Nicholas Bunnin explores the grounding of ethics, in Spinoza's metaphysics of substance and necessity on the one hand, and in Wang Bi's metaphysics of change and possibility on the other. The chapter contrasts their metaphysical methods and concerns, and reviews the different outcomes of their thinking – about the relations between the world and God or *Dao* as the fundamental reality; about the natural world; about human thinking and acting; and about ethics and the implications for the stable governance of society.

Chapter 8: Personhood in Indian Metaphysics: Touchpoints with Other Traditions. Gavin Flood shows that Indian philosophy has been deeply concerned with metaphysics throughout its history, addressing similar sets of problems as in other civilizations. A long history of debate produced a range of arguments and positions about the nature of time and space, causation, what it is to be a person, the ontological status of the world, the existence of God, and what it is to live a good life. This chapter describes the main features of the metaphysical landscape of the medieval period in India, roughly corresponding to Scholasticism in Europe and to neo-Confucianism in China.

Chapter 9: Metaphysics of a Hindu Goddess Tradition and European Phenomenology. Gavin Flood examines a particular stream of metaphysical speculation in treatises and commentaries on the Tantras in early medieval India. These show a conceptual structure in which persons become open to the 'sky of consciousness' as the appearance of the Unnameable, the ineffable reality that undergirds all manifestation. Its themes of light, openness and awareness also suggest conceptual links to phenomenological thinking in the European tradition.

Chapter 10: Brilliant Darkness: Apophatic Thinking in Early Christian and Indian Traditions. Ana-Maria Pascal and Diwakar Acharya explore the nuances and implications of apophatic thinking in early Christian and Indian settings (roughly between the sixth century BCE and the sixth century CE). Their general typology of apophaticism opens the way to a mystical, rather than cognitive, approach aimed at establishing a personal relationship with God. The chapter explores the importance of the beyond and of the metaphor of divine darkness in both traditions, in conveying the notion that God, or the Absolute, can be known through mystical experience.

Chapter 11: Overcoming Negative Theology: Kūkai and Palamas on Essence and Energy. Ana-Maria Pascal and Paulus Kaufmann compare the Japanese Buddhist monk Kūkai (774–835 CE) and the Byzantine Greek theologian Gregory Palamas (1296–1359 CE), both of whom deny that we can make a sharp-cut distinction between an ineffable absolute realm and a world of phenomena. Both argue that the Absolute is not merely a static essence; it manifests in the phenomenal world. These manifestations or energies of the Absolute can be approached by human beings. This 'approach' is not an intellectual sort of cognition, but a spiritual and even bodily participation in practice.

Chapter 12: God without Power: Kenosis and Tsimtsum as Two Paradigms of Divine Self-Restriction. Agata Bielik-Robson addresses the question of the status of the divine power in monotheistic religions. She compares two models of divine self- restriction: the Christian *kenosis* and the Jewish-kabbalistic *tsimtsum*. These two notions did not develop in complete isolation from one another: following the kabbalistic logic of the primary divine contraction, Hegel introduces the concept of *kenosis* in creation, and attributes the kenotic self-humbling to the first person of the Trinity, the Creator, thus limiting His omnipotence from the start. Thus both kenotic Christianity and kabbalistic Judaism complicate the monotheist picture of an absolutist God.

Chapter 13: Philosophy and African Art: Léopold Sédar Senghor and the Philosophy of Emotion and Rhythm. Victor Emma-Adamah argues that Senghor's philosophy of African art is a philosophical endeavour opening new horizons for philosophy. Philosophy is seen as an account of the elemental, the originary movement of force expressed in e-motion and rhythm. This means that African philosophy involves an engagement with thinkers who are involved in any discourse – whether or not overtly philosophical – that is inspired by Africa and its heritage. In the very particularity of the tradition, something universal is demonstrated – because the artistic inspiration of African art speaks not only of Africans but of being.

Chapter 14: The Non-Human in African Metaphysics. Elvis Imafidon problematizes the dominantly human-centric focus of Western metaphysics, where humanness is bifurcated from thingness. Imafidon argues that African metaphysics provides a relational account of being and reality in which the non-human transcends thingness and is fundamental for the existence of the human. This metaphysics interweaves all beings in a fluid (not lineal) flow of time where the past, present and future are constantly intersecting. Imafidon explores the ontological relationality of being embedded in the concept of Ubuntu, and the fluidity in the way both humans and nonhumans can gain, lose or increase their status as persons.

Chapter 15: The Divine Names: The Human Role in the Construction of the Cosmos in the Maya *Popol Vuh* and Ibn 'Arabī's *Fusus al-Hikam*. Alexus McLeod shows how both the K'iche 'Maya text *Popol Vuh* and the Islamic mystic and philosopher Ibn 'Arabī's *Fusus al-Hikam* set out positions in which humans cooperate with nature, the gods or God, in the construction of the cosmos. In both the *Popol Vuh* and the *Fusus al-Hikam*, the positions ultimately depend on a kind of monism concerning the cosmos, paired with a view of a transcendent source of being with an essence which is wholly inaccessible to us.

Chapter 16: Philosophy as a Way of Life: Metaphysics, Ethics and Spiritual Exercises. Sajjad Rizvi explores the claim that philosophy is a way of life, not just an intellectual pursuit, and that it is broader than ethical concern for the self and self-cultivation. This chapter considers the work of Pierre Hadot on ancient philosophy (especially the Stoics and the Neoplatonists), and shows how it can be extended to the study of – among other traditions – Buddhist and Islamic philosophy. Rizvi argues that philosophy viewed as a way of life can constitute a productive approach to comparative metaphysics, which takes into consideration our embodiment and place in the cosmos and our mutuality with others.

Part 2

The studies in Part 1 are specific examples of how very different thought worlds can be brought into productive conversation. The texts, lore and art they focus on reflect their respective traditions, but they are nurtured in broad streams of expression full of cross-currents and eddies.

What these sources in all their variety show is that human beings have always wrestled with questions which can be considered metaphysical. Understanding the questions cross-culturally is itself a major challenge; we stand on shifting ground as we seek to understand and learn from each others' answers to their questions, unsure if the questions are even the same. But the ultimate denial of translatability or comprehensibility is ultimately a denial of our common humanity. And this we cannot accept.

So on the basis of the exceptionally rich and diverse landscape of Part 1, the authors in Part 2 reflect more thematically on some resulting questions of enduring human significance. Part 2 cannot be a comprehensive survey – any more than Part 1 could be. And yet, some questions seem to recur like a basso continuo of human experience: What is suchness? What is beyond the real? What is personhood? How do we order our world? How should we live?

Even on these questions, we offer only provisional reflections. But we hope that Part 2 will stimulate readers to find individual pathways in their own reflective metaphysical attempts to make sense of ourselves in our complex, increasingly connected, and puzzling world. Our exercises in comparative metaphysics will succeed to the extent that they encourage further creative explorations and conversations across cultures.

1. Suchness. Comparative philosophy has mostly unfolded as a history of ideas in a Western conceptual framework, with space provided for contributions from non-Western traditions. Few attempts have been made to focus on concerns which *originate* from a non-Western tradition. In this chapter, Lucia Dolce reconsiders some of the questions posited by the metaphysical pursuit, through the lens of a central idea which is indigenous to Buddhist metaphysics. The notion of 'Suchness' emphatically asserts this world and values the present, but is formulated in non-substantialist language that avoids both reification and apophaticism; it is non-dualistic and yet does not completely reject dualism. Recentring metaphysical discourse on such a notion is not only to move away from the centrality of transcendence as the model to approach ideas of reality, but also to set aside the certainty of distinct essences and to put ambiguity, paradox and fluidity at the core of metaphysical inquiry.

2. Beyond, Being and Becoming. Agata Bielik-Robson reflects on the concept of the beyond in relation to being and becoming. Following the theory of the axial religions (Weber, Jaspers, Eisenstadt), she focuses on the 'invention of transcendence' as a new way of approaching the metaphysical status of the beyond. The tension between transcendence and immanence varies from maximal to minimal in key axial traditions – Abrahamic, Indian and Chinese – but never disappears completely. In more static models, the immanent – time and becoming – tends to be reduced to a lesser significance. In more dynamic models, based on the contrary vision of the beyond as critical of and antithetical to the order of being, time and becoming tend to increase in value through a 'history of redemption'.

3. Persons, Selves and Metaphysics. Gavin Flood and Ana-Maria Pascal explore how the self (and its partial synonym, the person) is understood in Christianity, Hinduism and Buddhism, both in itself – i.e. the nature of a human person – and also in relation to the divine and the wider cosmos. The notion of such a link is present in all three traditions, albeit in different ways. The chapter explores the notion of human personhood in the context of the metaphysical search for foundations, and focuses on the role of the human in the hierarchy of the cosmos and on the model of ascent to the divine, which has become a symbol of human participation in the divine across many cultures.

4. Names, naming, unnamed, unnameable. Nicholas Bunnin and Sajjad Rizvi reflect on the significance of naming – in the realm of reality and in discourse about the transcendent. First, Bunnin surveys the uses of naming in Part 1 and reflects on his own journey of exploration into names. Then, Rizvi explores various approaches – cataphatic, apophatic and Neoplatonic – to the questions posed by naming the ineffable transcendent, with particular reference to Islamic traditions.

Part 1

1

Philosophizing while reading texts across cultures

Alex Samely

This chapter addresses the philosophical reading of texts across a cultural boundary. I undertake to show that basic processes of text reading can increase the chance that a reader will recognize an unfamiliar mode of discourse *as* philosophical. I will claim that readers build up their sense of a text by relating the meanings of sentences (or of similar units) to each other in a manner that is not deliberate but establishes coherence or else allows the encounter with incoherence. Readers are thereby able to *live through* meaning connections to which their own philosophical sub-culture might not have exposed them, and which might go beyond their habits of thought. The consideration of the processes of text reading therefore adds an important, hitherto neglected, dimension to the discussion of cross-cultural philosophizing.[1]

I begin by locating text reading as a key pathway by which philosophies meet across cultural boundaries. I then set out the mechanisms by which philosophical meanings are encountered when reading a text, including the role of a non-deliberate synthesis of the reader's experiences of the temporally dispersed text meanings (e.g. in sentences). I address the potential of conversations about a text, as well as the role of translations and of philosophical terminology. I examine the role of reading in recognizing the presence or absence of 'philosophy' across the cultural gap by exploring some widespread Western-oriented assumptions on what makes a discourse 'philosophical'. In an appendix, I provide an overview of text genres considered philosophical in a number of cultures.

Introduction: Appreciating the role of reading in cross-cultural philosophizing

How can reading a text constitute an opportunity for cross-cultural philosophizing? For a philosopher interested in learning from another culture's way of doing philosophy, the main path will almost always consist in, or at least include, the reading of texts produced in that culture. In the scenario here envisaged, a reader wishes to enrich their current practice of doing philosophy, but has no special or firsthand expertise in the other culture's cultural, historical or linguistic background. My main concern is thus not the philosopher who is equally or near-equally at home in two cultures, nor the scholar of two cultures who also philosophizes. Rather, the reader here envisaged is someone who needs to negotiate an initial and lasting lack of familiarity, and has no competence in the text's original language, but depends on translations and commentaries. They may be initially uncertain whether a particular text from another culture constitutes 'philosophy' at all, and if so, whether it speaks to their own philosophical concerns. And they may also think of a text from that other culture as 'religious', rather than as 'philosophical', or encounter it as written in an unfamiliar literary genre. In what follows, I will avoid relying on a categorization of genres as 'religious' versus 'secular', because the assumptions that accompany this dichotomy arise from specifically modern European – not universal – historical experiences, in which Christianity plays the role of a default 'religion' (see Sueki 2015: 639, for one instance of today's routine academic recognition of this). I will, however, distinguish texts which cite an earlier authority from texts that do not, a difference which is potentially relevant to the boundary between philosophy and non-philosophy.

The reflections which follow contribute to an ongoing discussion of methodological issues that arise in fields variously named inter-cultural, cross-cultural or comparative philosophy (cf. Angle 2010). Questions raised include in particular: Is cross-cultural understanding or comparison possible? If the answer is positive, can it be done – or can it be ethical – without accepting a position of 'relativism'? Two recent answers make use of the thought of the later Wittgenstein. Wong (2020), following Fleischacker, suggests viewing intercultural philosophical practice through the lens of diverging moral interests in terms of Wittgensteinian 'world pictures' (Fleischacker 1992, pp. 90–103 and passim). And according to Ma and van Brakel (2016), philosophers are able to expand their prior philosophical notions through an inter-cultural encounter because conceptual boundaries are malleable in the way of the Wittgeinsteinian 'family resemblance', in partial contrast to Davidson's 'conceptual schemes'.

Such approaches, promising as they are, tend to disembody the cross-cultural philosopher to some extent, by not taking into view the inter-cultural experience of text reading. Yet the practice of text reading – including the engagement with 'textual evidence' (cf. Cline 2013: 49–51) – will almost always be a basis for philosophizing across cultural boundaries, and barriers can arise from this very fact. For instance, how do readers address texts written in what, according to their own culture, is not a philosophical genre? This is acknowledged in Chakrabarti and Weber (2017: 27), Jenco (2007), MacIntyre (1985: 9, 14–15) and others. MacIntyre highlights the role which written canons play in the incompatibility of certain cultural outlooks, a question to which I will return.

In this context the link between text constitution and the articulation of 'systems' of thought is important. Thus Richardson's treatment of diverging ultimate ends (1997: 266–70) uses Quine and Davidson's 'principle of charity' to address conceptual 'systems' as concatenations of propositions that are capable of truth. This promising perspective, too, can benefit from a more detailed analysis of the reading process, because we encounter 'concatenations' primarily in texts. I will argue that the experience of text meanings, while making 'systems' possible, also renders conceptual content *fluid*. But if one thinks about the intercultural philosophical encounter without considering its reading practicalities, one is in danger of configuring it in static idealization. Chakrabarti and Weber illustrate this. Preparatory to advancing their favoured 'fusion' procedure (2017: 19–22), they envisage philosophers who engage with another culture as one pole of a relationship between two or more fixed poles. But for understanding text reading, temporality is paramount.

Furthermore, as soon as temporality is part of the consideration, the embodiment and materiality of the cross-cultural encounter also come into view. When cross-cultural philosophizing is merely discussed in terms of the (in)comparability or (in)commensurability of different ways of 'thinking', the thinker's basis in a perceived materiality (e.g. of reading) is ignored. Thus, in Tagore's view, world philosophy creates a link to the *possible* (2017: 536). This is in my view correct and highly important. But one cannot justify this claim without also considering the processes of reading, as involving perceived materiality. It is arguably the embodied engagement with meanings in the materiality of language – e.g. by perceiving signs on the page or screen, by listening to speech – that creates the room for an exposure to Otherness and to possibility. This exposure to Otherness, qua the possibility of a different Self, cannot be understood as arising in pure thought. I will show that text reading can be a key step in the openness of engagement.

For this openness, Stephen Angle has distinguished two modes, one 'rooted global philosophy' and one which he calls 'constructive engagement' (2009: 6–7, and 2010). Others, including Yu and Bunnin (2001) following Aristotle, have argued that there is intrinsic philosophical value in the very plurality of culturally diverging views. The exploration of such a philosophical plurality also constitutes, naturally enough, a recurrent theme in the chapters of this volume. Nick Bunnin himself presents two comparative case studies. In one, he links Maimonides and Xunzi with regard to language and politics; in the other, he explores Wang Bi and Spinoza for their views on ethics. A different but related way to gain philosophical insight from plurality is proposed by Jana Rošker, who places into dialogue the ways in which Hui Shi and Zeno of Elea conceptualized movement.

These comparisons of culturally diverse positions for gaining philosophical insight proceed at least partly on the basis of the careful reading of texts, and reading is, as I will show, a natural playground for philosophical diversity without one having to fall back on a claim that text interpretations are 'subjective'.

Some philosophically important texts have long been committed to memory, and memorization can be seen as a pathway for cross-cultural philosophizing. Thus Jenco 2007 and Kalmanson 2017 suggest to modify or supplement 'Western' philosophical and scholarly methods of inquiry by practices through which 'classic' texts become re-read and learned by heart. Prominent Chinese commentators, such as Zhu Xi and Wang Yangming, recommended such practices, and the same goes for many other cultures. Jenco and Kalmanson point to the wider embodied context of such recommendations, which can include valuing ritual, meditation, recitation, music, text transmission and other somatic habituations (cf. also Jenco et al. 2017; Sueki 2015: 640). Kalmanson speaks of these as 'processes in which we can trust' (2017: 409), and Jenco as possibilities of 'becoming' or 'conversion' (2007: 753–4). But if cross-cultural philosophizing is to adopt them, then the habituating effects of reading and memorization need to be placed into a wider research context.[2]

The present chapter will draw attention to some of the wider aspects of reading. I will summarize some of the results of a recent phenomenological investigation of the basic processes of text reading, as practised today in a, broadly speaking, Western context. As applied to the case of reading in Samely (2024), phenomenology involves a culturally anchored but systematic reflection on those aspects which make (everyday) acts of perceiving and reflecting meaningful experiences. It asks: What is unreflectively presupposed about how the world works for this to be *meaningful* to me? This procedure is related to what the phenomenologist Edmund Husserl called life-world, and his concept of *epoché* (e.g. Husserl 1970). The Greek word *epoché*, originally a suspension of judgement or a withholding, refers here to an act of bracketing of that which I, in a moment of lived life, presuppose as real. Bracketing what is taken as real allows reflecting on the content, structure and meaning connections of what it is that I have thus presupposed, thereby clarifying what kind of world I presuppose as I engage with that world. In this vein, Samely 2024 investigates text reading as an aspect of the reader's engagement with their world.

Recognizing 'philosophy' in texts across a cultural difference

In what follows, I will assume that the cross-cultural reader already has a strong, but not rigid, sense of what makes a discourse 'philosophical'. When reading a text that has by some route come to their attention as philosophical (e.g. by an expert in the culture calling it that), and after accepting this characterization initially, this reader may at any point in the reading process come to a realization that the text is, in fact, 'unphilosophical'. If, on the other hand, readers experience a text as indeed 'philosophical', then they will in due course form a view of it being (philosophically) stimulating or boring, illuminating or misguided, relevant to their concerns or not.

What constitutes a philosophical text in an unfamiliar genre is thus an open question. Seen outside familiar cultural parameters, any verbal entity may in theory constitute a philosophical text in some sense. Apart from discursive treatments of a topic, narratives and poems, being equally constituted through language, have often been treated as having such a potential. But even non-verbal products of culture can be seen as constituting philosophical expressions, so that textuality and reading (in a non-metaphorical sense of 'reading') do not constitute necessary conditions for 'philosophical' status.[3] Certainly, non-verbal products of culture have been treated as conveying or containing philosophy, from performative, plastic and visual arts to ritual and certain ways to manipulate material objects in order to interpret the world and define a space of action, as in the Chinese Y Ching and the Yoruba Ifà.[4] Addressing such topics, Victor Emma-Adamah's chapter in this volume analyses Léopold Senghor's interpretation of African art as constituting philosophy.

I am raising here again the question of materiality, for language in texts too involves materiality. Some twentieth-century philosophers point to the materiality (or exteriority) of language and texts as being inseparable from meaning. This diverges from a longstanding metaphysical tradition – and not just in 'the West' – which distances meaning in language from the material, and defines that which makes linguistic meaning possible as spiritual, mental or ideal. But like other manifestations of culture, text reading offers precisely an entanglement of meaning with materiality: written words are spatio-temporal objects, even if the reader does not objectify them as such when reading signs. And thus their reading also *takes time* – a point I will pursue presently.

While I assume that the reader of a culturally unfamiliar text has an idea or an inchoate *Vorverständnis* of what philosophy is, I also presuppose that they can change their mind.[5] According to my analysis of reading, one always lays oneself open to the possibility of being changed by what one understands, a possibility against which one cannot guard oneself effectively. The reason for this is that, as one progresses through a text, one affects oneself with meanings 'before' one can fend them off or place them at a distance.[6] While the source of my claim lies in a phenomenological analysis of reading in contemporary settings, it may be useful to note that many cultures assume that text reading can transform the reader. One illustration of this, which limits as well as values the potential of texts, is the following declaration by the Neo-Confucian thinker Zhu Xi:

> We rely on the classics to understand pattern-principle. Once pattern-principle is apprehended, there is no need for the classics.
>
> (Zhu Xi 2019: 75; §§2–3)

However, my claim about reading is in no way restricted to reading any classics. It is simply that, by reading any text whatsoever, one exposes oneself to the possibility of becoming changed in principle. This is relevant to philosophizing while reading a text.

Considering for a moment in particular the contemporary Western and Western-oriented reader, one key obstacle to their recognition of a work as 'philosophical' can be the text's tendency to quote earlier texts as philosophically authoritative, in the way Zhu Xi treats Confucian 'classics'.[7] While such a tendency was extremely common in Western philosophical discourses until modernity as well, it came to be rejected in the self-view of academic philosophy, as established in Western or Western-oriented institutions. That self-view defines the philosopher as standing in opposition to someone who holds beliefs without subjecting them to radical questioning first (see further below). In a philosophical engagement with traditional Indian texts (1988: 5), Eliot Deutsch summarizes this attitude by saying, 'We do not accept the authority of the Veda (or, for the most part, the authority of any other scripture)'.

So quoting earlier texts as if they carried philosophical authority can strike Western-oriented readers as *obviously* unphilosophical. Yet philosophical discourses in many cultures continue to incorporate precisely such references to earlier texts as authoritative,[8] even though they also tend to, less visibly to the non-expert, modify and update the scriptural meanings they apparently rely on. Examples of such texts treated routinely as authoritative include works like the Daodejing, the Analects, Vedic Upanishads, Biblical narratives and commandments, the Qur'an and the Lotus Sutra. As a consequence, openness to another culture's philosophizing may require that the reader appreciates, or at least does not become unduly sidetracked by, the author's inclusion into their philosophical discussion of references to earlier 'classics' or 'scriptures'.

The same is true from the opposite perspective. A reader who is used to seeing philosophical positions being developed through a sustained and explicit dialogue with prior cultural traditions taken as weighty (as was arguably also the habit of Aristotle, see Yu and Bunnin 2001), will initially miss this dimension in philosophical texts that present themselves as standing entirely on their own, or as making a new beginning without any reliance on substantial presuppositions, a well-known performative move in modern Western philosophizing. (Husserl speaks of the 'radicalism' of the 'new beginning' of the modern age in Europe; 1970: 14). The Appendix below marks this contrast through categories 1 and 3a.

My claim is that the very process of reading a text can weaken the effect of such cross-cultural impasses and misgivings. The core reason for this is that readers accommodate a text's multiple sentence meanings to each other's presence by virtue of a pre-reflective synthesis of experience. Husserl called such a pre-reflective synthesis of experience (in general), 'passive'. I too will use this adjective as a short-hand in what follows.[9] In my phenomenological analysis of reading, I came to the conclusion that one cannot really understand or misunderstand any text without receiving it as projecting a virtual whole which is both fuller and more interconnected than its articulated meanings could ever indicate. The notion of a 'passive synthesis' of text-meaning experiences names the role which associations of unmentioned details and unmentioned meaning connections play in understanding any text (Samely 2024). Of these non-deliberate but effective experiences of a world-like fullness which the text projects for the reader, some are accessible to reflection with hindsight. For these experiences of meaningfulness are unconscious (passive), but not in the sense of resisting in principle discovery by reflection. But only a small portion or dimension of passive synthesis can be the theme of thought, and almost always only with hindsight. They thus constitute an 'already' of experience, an 'already' of meaningfulness. Those that are reflected can become criticized with hindsight as well in re-thinking and re-reading, but the reader's understanding of some text parts may nevertheless remain indebted to such associative meaning experiences. For they may have motivated the reader's understanding of meanings elsewhere in the text, not just in the particular text location that has attracted the reflective retraction (Samely 2024: 118–20). For the current topic the upshot is that, through this dimension of passive synthesis, text reading contributes to the possibility that the reader undergoes meaningful (!) experiences that are not controlled in advance by the reader's initial philosophical convictions.

Reading a text in order to philosophize

So what does it mean to read a text in order to philosophize with it, or indeed against it? In the attitude here imagined, the reader appropriates what they experience the text to mean. As such a reader I am not a historian who seeks evidence for the reconstruction of some past.[10] I do not set out to eliminate from what strikes me as meaningful in the text everything that the original authors and readers might not have seen as meaningful. For my interest in reading the text is constituted by a live philosophical agenda, namely what I think matters philosophically. Along somewhat similar lines, Chakrabarti and Weber envisage the possibility of 'just doing philosophy as one thinks fit for getting to the truth about an issue' and, as a consequence, comparative philosophy losing 'its epithet comparative' (2017: 22; cf. Angle 2010: 110).

Reading in such an acquisitional mode is common and, if I treat the text as a unified text, pretty much unavoidable. Thus, when I read a sentence or some other text unit (e.g. a poetic line) as part of a text, I do not in a first moment reconstruct the wording's original or intended meaning, and thereafter evaluate, criticize, appropriate or creatively develop that meaning.[11] There is only one stage, in which both happen. I may devote distinct acts of *hindsight* reflection (or re-reading) to discovering facets of meaning which have already motivated my current understanding, and which if necessary I can now revoke if I think I have misread something. But 'working with' a meaning is always already involved in understanding a passage from the start. The philosophizing reader's most basic understanding of the meaning of a particular passage will often be embedded in their (philosophical) agenda in ways that hindsight reflection can recognize (but not thereby cancel).

Let us say that I am trying to understand a passage in one of the Kantian *Critiques*. As a reader interested in philosophical problems, my quest to find out, 'What *is* Kant's sense?', is not separated from my quest to find out, '*Does* this make sense?' (And normally the initial tacit assumption of text reading is that a passage makes sense *somehow*, which means, first and foremost, that it is connected to its neighbours in the text.) Only because this assumption is at work – albeit capable of being disappointed – can something said in the text make sense. It is by assuming *that* something is meaningful (i.e. connectible), that I am ready to encounter the *what* of it, as a content of meaningfulness. Even in a forensically hostile reading of a document, as when a prosecutor scrutinizes a criminal's statement which they already know to be unreliable (or an extremely suspicious historian reading a source), what allows picking the text apart for its contradictions are other dimensions of the text's meaning for which the reader has simply assumed text coherence, without deliberation.[12]

Let me apply these claims to the case of my reading a text from an unfamiliar cultural background. In this scenario too, I will have made associative non-deliberate connections, in the process of understanding a given passage's meaning, to other meanings that I experienced earlier (including earlier in the same text). Of course, I can thereby *misunderstand* a passage – but the possibility of discovering such a mistake comes later. In any case, the extent to which my understanding of what I take the text to say is a transformation of the text's original philosophical agenda, rather than something faithful to its original intent, would be unknown to me at that point.

In this regard there is little difference between a reader who stands outside the author's culture and a reader who lives later but shares the author's culture in principle (e.g. by being a native speaker of the text's language, or of a later stage of that language). There are important differences between these two types of reader, but both have to synthesize text meanings passively in order to understand what they read.

Text understanding in conversation

In order to engage philosophically with an unfamiliar culture, one will wish to draw upon scholarly literature, commentaries and annotated translations where available. This is no different from any other in-depth engagement which a philosophizing reader might undertake with documents that come from unfamiliar periods or languages belonging to their 'own' culture. The widespread use among contemporary Chinese speakers of renderings of the classics into modern Chinese and the need among educated modern Western readers for translations from ancient Latin, Greek or Hebrew are just two illustrations of this. They show clearly that 'inner-cultural' does not exclude a dependency on prior cultural and linguistic updatings or transpositions.

One advantage of dealing with a contemporary cultural difference, in contrast to a historical gulf, is that the reader has a chance to benefit from a conversation about the text with an expert member of the other culture. Such a conversation has the potential for unforeseen interpretative outcomes.[13] As an engagement with a text's meaning, a conversation differs significantly from a solitary reading of the same text. What my interlocutor says (and even what I say) helps to embed for me what I hear the text saying by reading it in ways that are, again, passively synthesized, and can only be partially disentangled by hindsight reflection. At times, I may find that my interlocutor has given voice to an unconscious meaning experience which I myself underwent during my prior solitary reading, and which I now discover motivated for me, as for the interlocutor, some aspect of my understanding of certain other passages in the text (Samely 2024: 198–203). In such a case, the conversation does some of the interpretative work that self-reflection might otherwise do. On the other hand, a conversation about the text can turn out to be frustrating for me, and not at all successful at producing a meeting of readerly minds. But the key difference from solitary reading lies in the fact that the latter allows a sustained thematization of my own experiences with the text, that is, an exploration of latent text meanings which proceeds *via an exploration of my self*, i.e., the earlier experiences *of mine*. There is, by contrast, often no opportunity for a reader to sustain such acts of self-exploration during a conversation, when face-to-face with another person.

Passive synthesis of text meanings and the ability to become surprised by the text

When reading the text with a philosophical or other concern in mind,[14] I may come to see it as not addressing that concern. If I look for the answer to a 'factual' question, say in a biology textbook, but do not find my question addressed, I may come to consider my question misinformed or erroneously framed. The very experience of the text not answering my question is capable of teaching me, of correcting me. In the case of a philosophical text read philosophically, 'textbook' is an inapplicable category, factual answers are not available, and books that look as if they treat 'the same' topic may offer entirely disparate and incompatible treatments of it. I can then disagree with the text about its way of framing the concern, or even acknowledge an insurmountable cultural gulf but withholding any value judgement (see below). If this is not my conclusion, however, then the experience of a non-answer of the text regarding my philosophical question can make me reflect on the possibility that my own framing of a topic is unfruitful or one-sided. In principle, I can 'learn' from the text's lack of connection to frame the question philosophically better. The lack of connection may teach me something I did not manage to learn from texts in my own cultural background. Yet after having learned it from a culturally unfamiliar source, I might then be able to see it in my own tradition (this is very common). It seems to me that it is the possibility of a significant re-contextualization of myself that makes inter-cultural philosophizing a compelling project.

Let me explore the idea of encountering a surprise in reading, from which any learning is likely to start. The reader does not have to assume a special attitude to 'allow' the text to surprise them: the most basic attitude of reading, observable in everyday and professional contexts, consists in such an openness to a possible surprise. It is the passive synthesis of the togetherness of text meanings as connected which allows the reader to encounter apparent or real contradictions in the text, and these often lead to self-examination by way of re-reading. In the process of such a self-examination the reader may discover either that they misunderstood an earlier passage or else that there is an inconsistency in the text. The form which a prompt to such a reflection tends to take is basically the surprise: something that the reader tacitly expected (protained) does not materialize in the next sentence they read. The tacit expectation of how the text will continue is integral to the reading process and therefore, so is the possibility of becoming surprised by the text and, on occasion, to learn from it as a result, without having sought to learn from it about *this* topic, *this* angle.

As the reader's latent sense of the text as a whole updates itself, every new sentence meaning is 'expected' before its meaning is actualized or understood. This happens by virtue of passive retention-connections of meanings the reader has encountered so far, and non-deliberate anticipations of meanings not yet encountered. Hence this 'expectation' is very largely not deliberate, in contrast to the acts by which the words or signs are integrated actively into a unity, such as a sentence meaning.[15] While readers integrate actively whatever they tacitly take to be the constitutive units of a text (such as the sentence), they do not need to integrate actively the *connections* between contiguous units in order to understand a text (there would never be an end to it, if reading a text depended on that happening).[16] But if a passively experienced relation between two neighbouring sentences differs from what was passively anticipated, thereby taking the reader by surprise, the acts of re-reading or reflection can be prompted. These acts then lift the relationship between two sentences (or other units) out of the obscurity of simply 'working' in passivity (Samely 2024: 82–94).

Meanings that surprise me are by no means peculiar to texts whose cultural background I do not share. They are a routine occurrence in all reading, although they are often low-key and easily repaired or not conspicuous enough to prompt reflection. If I find a text intellectually or artistically demanding, or simply unclear, then acts of reflection happening because passive synthesis does not 'work' anymore (i.e. cannot remain passive) will be more frequent. In reading any philosophical text, there are likely to be many passages at which I become surprised or puzzled, until I figure out their meaning (i.e. prominently, the way they fit together with other meanings), either learning something in the process or coming to the conviction that the author is in error.

In the encounter with 'strange' meanings in a text from an unfamiliar culture, I may identify surprises as indicating a somewhat wider range of phenomena: something exotic, archaic, philosophically unsophisticated or incoherent, for example. This is the case in particular if the text's genre is not 'philosophical' according to my prior experience. Alternatively, I may be charging an experience of surprise to my own otherness, my situatedness and limits, rather than to a lack of sophistication in the text. But either way, the reading may be experienced as not philosophically fruitful for me. The risk of finding the text ultimately not congenial, or indeed flawed, is inherent in all text reading. But in cross-cultural reading, my not 'connecting' to its way of doing philosophy is like not getting a joke, in the sense that, even if I believe the problem to be 'on my side' and I give the text the benefit of the doubt, I simply do not benefit from it philosophically.[17] It is important to acknowledge this as a possible outcome of a cross-cultural reading: 'I don't really benefit philosophically from this text.' Furthermore, this outcome must be seen as no less legitimate than when it happens within the reader's own cultural heritage, otherwise the cross-cultural project loses all seriousness and value.

The textual fluidity of technical terminology in passive synthesis

Terms in texts that may have a technical meaning can at times be taken to crystallize whole philosophical or cultural outlooks. Contemporary texts situated in the disciplinary context of academic philosophy usually strive to explicate the meaning of, and use consistently, important recurring concepts. In other genres, too, the text may present an expression as a technical term, or problematize a term's meaning while at the same time treating it as central. And even texts which do neither can nevertheless become read in later periods as employing certain terms in a somehow technical manner. The meaning of a putatively philosophical term can even be claimed to be impossible to define, as the Platonic *khora*, *dao* in the opening pages of the Daodejing, and *brahman* in the Kena Upanishad. Cross-cultural readers may then receive such a refusal to define key expressions as constituting a *philosophical* move in its own right. But this function of constituting a philosophical move, or its recognition, is far from guaranteed. A number of chapters in this volume explore philosophical views of the ineffable, the paradoxical or limitations of language more generally: Xinzhong Yao's chapter deals with the multiple meanings of *dao*, Ana-Maria Pascal and Diwakar Acharya examine apophaticism in Christian and Indian thought, Ana-Maria Pascal and Paulus Kaufmann compare Kūkai and Palamas, Nick Bunnin reflects on the way Maimonides and Xunzi see language and power, and Lucia Dolce (in Part 2) explores the 'paradoxes' of the central East Asian Buddhist notion of 'Suchness'.

Where expressions in a text are felt to carry a technical philosophical meaning, their translation promises to be an important access point for cross-cultural understanding. But, somewhat paradoxically, the effect of the passive synthesis of mutual sentence relations in text reading renders even explicitly defined word meanings fluid again for the reader. Any word that appears repeatedly in a text will have a new sentence environment (and a new wider environment) each time. If the expression refers to a spatio-temporal thing, this produces only small and almost unnoticeable variations in meaning (e.g. the case of the phrase 'kitchen table' mentioned in various connections). But the case of a philosophical term is different: every new usage is a significant confirmation, expansion or problematization of such a term's meaning. For, in the case of philosophical discourse, the scope of such a term's meaning is almost unknown when the reading begins, since it depends on how the author of the text 'uses' it (even if it has been used before by others). Often, its semantic content itself, that is, its meaning outside all use, is quite uninformative or highly ambiguous, e.g. 'way'. But in the reader's experience of the text, the meanings of sentences or other units usually show themselves (if the reader reflects on them) as not having been constituted in isolation from each other, but as being motivated by interconnectedness. (Notwithstanding the fact that most contemporary readers will not be able to recall the contents of earlier sentences *at will*.[18]) The non-deliberate interconnection narrows down the meaning possibilities of single words or phrases as well, and it happens all the time. That is why, for example, readers of the current paragraph are unlikely to have even considered the possibility that the word 'sentence' refers to a legal punishment.

If passively synthesized interconnections become problematical in the course of the reading ('surprises'), this prompts reflection. New perspectives on what I have *already* read are always possible ('It was all a dream!'; 'I am the murderer'). The ongoing mutual adjustment, and the openness of past text reading to future perspectives, includes the meanings of declared or implicit technical terms. Some of the passive associations that help to shape the reader's dynamic sense of the text can be encountered with hindsight in reflection, but many must be presumed to remain 'passive': effective, but never consciously entertained, thematized or scrutinized. Hence there is no full transparency to my consciousness of what meanings (from the same text) may have, at any given moment, already motivated my understanding of a given passage or of the text as a whole.

Texts are thus on the one hand crucial sites for the articulation of systems of thought and knowledge: their authoring an act of spatio-temporal materialization that pins down meanings and makes them coherent with each other, not just in philosophy but also in the sciences. On the other hand, texts harbour the deconstruction of systems. This potential for subverting systems of thought shaped into texts arises from the temporal dispersion of acts of understanding. It takes repeated and discrete acts to actualize one text local meaning (e.g. sentence) after another, and each of these meanings fades into the latency of passive synthesis as the reader actualizes the meaning of the next location. All the meanings of a text therefore come together first and foremost in the latency of passive synthesis. The totality of their detail is not simultaneously acute to the reader, even though we often misunderstand the reading process as making available such an acute totality of all sentence meanings.

Passive synthesis of technical meanings is not limited by what the text (or a commentator) may explicitly claim, or by an explicit precise definition, although repeated re-readings of any definitional passage can of course refresh the reader's retention of it. Nor can it be effectively circumscribed by a given term's semantic content in the original language or in a rendering (such as 'way', 'virtue', 'heart-mind' and 'form'). For passive synthesis includes passages across the text in which the term is actually employed, and employed in constantly varying syntactic-semantic environments. In this respect the reader who can understand the text in its original language and the reader who depends on a translation are in comparable situations, as long as the latter also has a way of tracking the recurrence of a term in the translation.[19] Indeed, if a translation offers an equivalent to the original text's plurality, identity and sequence of meaning units (such as sentence meanings), then its readers may live through passive syntheses which in certain respects 'parallel' the passive syntheses of readers of the original. (No two readers' passive syntheses in reading the same text, or even the passive syntheses of a single reader's reading the same text twice on two different occasions, can be said to be 'the same'.)

Passive synthesis only quasi-unifies the text, as it were. It constitutes merely a potential for some single act of reflection in which the reader explicates their sense of the text overall. As the basis of such a possible articulation, passive synthesis is under-determined before reflected verbalization, and the occasion of articulation, including its language and cultural context, determines the reader's selective emphasis.

The passive synthesis of text meanings and translational choices

So in the process of understanding a text, the meanings of individual expressions acquire fluidity. This has a bearing on the role of translations in cross-cultural philosophizing. Putatively technical expressions in philosophy often also possess a much wider societal significance. Examples include *dao*, *yin* and *yang*, substance, *conatus*, sensation, *Vernunft*, *eidos*, *praxis*, *logos*, ordinary language, *brahman*, common sense, reason and many more. The functioning of such terms in the original language tends to be impossible to replicate in translational equivalents. This is a well-known phenomenon in translation studies and related fields, and Xinzhong Yao's chapter in the present volume will explore this for the crucial case of *dao*; while Chenyang Li will examine the link of the Confucian notion of harmony to the meanings of the terms *yin* and *yang*, as a principle of being and becoming.

Yet this and other problems of translation are also alleviated by the processes of text reading. For the very same reading process which subverts statically fixed word and sentence meanings, also keeps the meaning nuances and connotations of technical terms open to dynamic and mutual determination, thus not making them depend on the semantics of the translator's choice for a key expression. In particular, if the translated meanings of the text's sentences (or other units) occur in the same selection and position as in the original, then the network of associative possibilities by which the technical term's meaning nuances are put into passive play will be as close to that of a reader of the original as one can imagine. Gaining translational access to the associative possibilities of the textual network of plural meanings is arguably central to understanding a text from another culture. As long as the translation avoids leaving out whole meaning units from the text (at least without acknowledgement), marks the recurrence of a putative technical term in the original somehow, even if the translations change (which may well be necessary), and avoids transposing the original's thought world wholesale into an existing philosophical position in the target culture – say, by rendering a Confucian text into a Kantian language or vice versa[20] – the differentials and limits between text meanings will be passively synthesized on the basis of textual togetherness.

It can also be beneficial for a translation to highlight certain aspects of the text's (anticipated) unfamiliarity in the target culture. Thus, the very unfamiliarity of a combination like 'heart-mind', as rendering of Chinese *xīn*, or 'pattern-principle' for *lǐ*,[21] directs English speakers away from an understanding which is merely based in ordinary English word semantics. Readers are shown that the term functions differently from the way either 'heart' or 'mind' would function in English discourse. This destabilizes the technical term's expected meaning, and may thus increase the reader's dependency on the associative synthesis of textual interconnectedness for their gaining a sense of the depth of the term's meaning. Leaving key terms entirely untranslated can also work, for the same reason.[22]

To sum up my argument so far:

- Reading a text philosophically involves recognizing the meaning of text units (e.g. sentences) by virtue of a passive synthesis of their togetherness with each other in the text, which synthesis also integrates them with the reader's own concerns, even if the reader is used to making a distinction between a text's original intent and their own philosophical agenda.
- Technical meanings of specific terms remain fluid, even if the text should explicitly define them.

That readers live through a largely passive synthesis of their experience of the plurality of meanings in a text provides the resource by which reflection, if prompted, can identify associations which have motivated their current sense of the text as a whole, of a particular passage, and of any putative technical term. All this applies in principle also to the reading of translated texts.

Western-oriented assumptions on what philosophy is; apodictic, narrative and poetic texts

What kind of written discourse may count as 'philosophy'? It is in connection with such a question that a text's genre may become a topic. In Western-oriented academic practice, philosophical texts tend to be distinguished not merely by striving to make true statements. They will also attempt to account in some fundamental way for the possibility (or impossibility) of true statements. Ancient Greece is sometimes credited with having achieved radical explication in Europe for the first time,[23] and the figure of Socrates is, as it were, the patron saint of such radicality, imagined as making the rounds in the *agora* discombobulating ordinary people by asking them what reason they have for a view they take for granted.

Philosophers from a variety of traditions have claimed, first, the importance of subjecting one's claims to explicit reflection rather than taking their truth for granted, that is, producing reasons in so many words; and second, the need to refuse tradition a voice in philosophical arguments. As Chakrabarti and Weber formulate it, philosophical arguments have to be able to 'stand independently of the sources they draw on' even if they are eclectic (2017: 27). These two aspects – the presence of reasons and the absence of appeals to authority – have thus become hallmarks of the philosophical text genre in many Westernized contexts. It may be useful to identify more generally some Western-oriented expectations of what constitutes a philosophical text, since such expectations can at times curtail the inter-cultural exchange.

I propose that Western-oriented philosophizing has long valued the following activities:[24]

1. reflecting on the conditions of its own knowledge claims; and, partly for that reason;
2. defining the meaning of its terms, and addressing the nature of concepts qua concepts;
3. giving reasons for claims, and separating descriptive from normative claims[25];
4. articulating a 'theoretical' content (see below) in a format that is discursive, rather than poetic or narrative;
5. striving for generalizations, rather than being interested in unique events or facts for their own sake, and generalizing by way of extension into an abstract dimension, rather than by way of analogy or metaphor;
6. radically questioning assumptions which are left unquestioned in one's culture (questioning as an ideal); also, moving beyond an already existing (school) understanding of a topic (i.e. being 'original');
7. taking up at least to some extent one of the recognized 'philosophical' questions, such as the nature of the real, experience, truth, the human condition, personhood; the nature of language and numbers, infinity; the conditions of knowledge/science, the possibility of a divine existent, standards of behaviour, and others.[26]

A number of chapters in this volume offer comparative perspectives on philosophical themes in this list. Siufu Tang explores the norm-fact distinction (point 3) in constructivism and Xunzi, while Sajjad Rizvi examines different cultural contexts for philosophy as praxis or as a way of life. Some of the topics in point 7 are taken up as well. Elvis Imafidon explores how some strands of sub-Saharan communitarian metaphysics configure the boundary between the human and the non-human; Gavin Flood's chapters provide a comparative view of Indian notions of personhood and of divinity, respectively; and Agata Bielik-Robson explores unacknowledged Jewish-Christian connections as motivating philosophical ideas of the limit of divine power in Hegel and Hans Jonas.

Perhaps the term *theory* gathers up many of the above strands under a single concept. Husserl claims that an ideal of 'theoretical philosophy … [as] absolutely free from prejudice' reaches us from Greek antiquity.[27] For Peter Ochs, 'theoretical thinking' goes beyond common sense in the following ways:

> The capacity to innovate imaginatively, which is in part to think associatively, anarchically and without concern for consequences; a complementary tendency to

think generally, or on behalf of any addressee about what is merely possible; and a complementary concern to define terms clearly, which also means without concern for any particular, existing addressee.

(Ochs 1998: 267)

This seems to capture well key aspects of what some dominant strands of contemporary Western or Western-oriented philosophy see themselves doing, including in particular their habits of de-contextualization (cf. Taylor 1985: 136–8). Those habits can lead to a side-lining of sense perception, the body, plurality and difference as philosophical topics, as well as of certain aspects of the everydayness of experience, historical situatedness and the temporal aggregation of experience: all these topics which have become championed by other strands of philosophy, on which more presently.

The points that strike me as particularly important in the above list are generalization (no. 5) and explicit, self-reflective argument (nos. 1 and 3), that is, 'giving reason', a modern transformation of the Greek *logon didonai*.[28] Generalization and self-reflection are assumed to establish a link from the meaning of a given claim on the one hand, to the real which that claim is *about* on the other.

They underlie one's ability to unify the knowledge of the real.[29] By terminology and origin, these ideals are potentially Eurocentric, that is, 'provincial' only, as opposed to universal. But even so, dispensing with the idea that philosophizing is concerned with the 'general' seems quite difficult. And what of self-reflexivity? If these moves are not to be considered as merely optional for philosophizing, then the recognition of culturally unfamiliar texts as philosophical hinges partly on the reader's recognition of them as somehow articulating or problematizing the possibility of general claims and as somehow supporting this by self-reflection.

Let us briefly address, by way of illustration, the format of Zhuangzi's 'Inner Chapters' (2009: 3–54). They consist of vignettes of narrated dialogical controversies, alternating with anonymous discursive or apodictic generalizations. In the dialogical vignettes, direct speech is attributed to characters, animals, mythical entities, etc., and sometimes there are extended responses, in effect expository speeches (e.g. Chapter 2, Zhuangzi 2009: 19–21). Stretches of text which contain generalizations may have a flavour, such as 'So no thing is not right, no thing is not acceptable'; or this claim: 'Hence, all things are neither formed nor destroyed, for these two also open into each other, connecting to form a oneness' (Chapter 2, Zhuangzi 2009: 13). The Inner Chapters also contain passages of self-questioning, such as: 'But is there really any waning versus fullness?' (Chapter 2, 2009: 15). A philosophizing reader who expects to encounter generalization and self-reflection may therefore easily find evidence for their presence in this text, even if they appear alongside other, starkly unfamiliar linguistic and textual structures.[30] (Among these are in this case and often, the fact that a text does not linger with and explain further some claims that the reader finds startling or important; hence, an experience of the text surface as 'aphoristic'.)

But what about texts which do not contain specific passages that can be recognized easily as explicit generalizations and self-reflections, not even in the disguise of narrative, poetry or reported dialogue? Readers in principle are able to recognize the implicit presence of generalizations in a text, generalizations which arise from the interplay of textual meanings, rather than from the content of a particular sentence. In other words, it is in principle possible for readers to test for a generalizing message by reflecting on their synthetic motivations for the sense they currently have of the text. A text may convey generalizing meanings, or generalizing meanings for certain topics, without containing bounded and explicit claims to that effect. The Western-oriented philosophical reader may therefore, upon reflection on their associative experiences, receive a text as conveying implicit generalization because this is required by what they experience (on reflection) as their *overall* sense of the text, or by their awareness of the literary context of a particular passage. A similar claim could be developed, mutatis mutandis, for the possibility of recognizing implicit self-reflectiveness in a text. And something like this can also apply to certain engagements with historical sources from the reader's own tradition, which may well be more implicit than contemporary habits of text making. Such moves of interpretation are possible because readers can encounter, in reflection, already-motivating aspects of their passive synthesis of the togetherness of the unit meanings.

If and when such readings take place, the reader could be said to recognize in culturally unfamiliar practices of text meaning the equivalent of more familiar ways to perform philosophical generalization or self-reflection. The reader might then even be moved to question any universal privilege attaching to these more familiar ways, e.g. (for Western-oriented readers) the propositional format of a generalization or self-reflection. They might then also wonder whether the conceptualizations of a 'generalization' and a 'self-reflection' which these very terms convey are as universally valid or neutral as they seem. Hence, some ordinarily privileged way to shape philosophical content, e.g. the proposition, might lose its tacit privilege for the reader, or at least lose the tacitness of that privilege.

If the reader has learned something philosophically valuable from a culturally unfamiliar text but has, as here envisaged, no historical and linguistic competence to reconstruct the relevant argument or meta-argument *on behalf* of the text, what is the way forward with regard to communicating the academic result? Philosophical experts in two relevant cultures can produce such engagements, have the authority to critique the two divergent viewpoints together (e.g. Sharf 2016), to embrace two viewpoints (e.g. Ram-Prasad 2002) or to criticize the one through the other (illustrated by some of the publications of Jitendra Mohanty). The current volume also contains a number of double-sided creative explorations, among which is the chapter in which Siufu Tang examines meta-ethical positions in Xunzi and the one in which Alexus McLeod discusses the Mayan *Popol Vuh* and Ibnʿ Arabī. But with regard to our main topic here, the philosophical reader who is not an expert in the other culture, yet has learned philosophically from one of its texts, can pay their debt only by explicating philosophically substantive, but philologically derivative, readings. Currently, such inter-cultural philosophical experiences have very low academic visibility, apart from certain specialized sub-fields of the philosophical-academic discussion, e.g. the discourse of the post-human (e.g. Braidotti 2019). Arguably, publication outlets in the philosophical mainstream should find a routine way to consider and judge their philosophical quality, submissions whose philosophical innovation arises from the engagement with texts from another culture by a self-declared cultural 'amateur' (who is otherwise a philosophical professional).

In the wider context of the humanities and social sciences, approaches have become common that try to avoid relying on concepts that arise from European historical experiences as if they were universal. The flagship fields of research in this vein engage with colonial,[31] racialized and gendered power matrices. But they have long had important thematic and methodological forerunners in the ethnography of ethnicity, economic life, socio-cultural affiliation and belonging[32]; in historical research that 'provincializes' the European experience[33]; in discourses of hybridity[34]; and in historiographic practices by which the present-day historian allows the categories in which they understand the past to become 'contaminated' by the perspectives of that past,[35] and more generally the investigation of historical sources not as evidence for reconstructing what the past 'was' but as evidence for how it was constructed or represented by contemporaries. Some of these academic developments respond to non-foundationalist approaches in philosophy, including the notion of a 'life-world' of the later Husserl[36] and the historicizing thought of Heidegger. The latter looked back to Nietzsche and was received with seminal academic consequences by Foucault. Wittgenstein's notions of 'forms of life' and 'language games' are also relevant, as are philosophical reflections on the history of science in the work of Quine, Kuhn and others,[37] and 'post-modern' practices, as in Derrida. What unites these, and the possibilities of cross-cultural philosophical reading explored above, is a discipline-critical and self-critical attitude that is open to the possibility that the sources/objects of study may contribute, or always have contributed, to the shaping of the very categories by which they are studied.

Much of this discourse takes place in the medium of 'global' English, a language which, even in its many international versions,[38] continues to carry usually unexamined Western philosophical baggage.[39] But alongside other originally European languages, English has also formed an integral component of many cultures of the Global South, through colonialism and other causes. Among philosophers from or in the Global South who do not see themselves as oriented (only) in Western habits of thought, and who are routinely multi-lingual, many have been active heirs to originally 'Western' notions, or have freshly reconstituted the meaning of such notions in new contexts, and Victor Emma-Adamah's chapter in this volume explores an important example of this phenomenon: Léopold Senghor's philosophical reflections on African art.

So while the non-European reception of Western thought has often been marked by a strong awareness of its entanglement in the projects of colonialism, slavery and other power inequalities,[40] Western categories have nevertheless often constituted, in the words of Gayatri Spivak, resources that need critiquing but that non-Western thinkers 'cannot "not" want'.[41] Hence, discursive practices exemplified in 'Western' works from Aristotle and Hegel to Bergson, Quine or Derrida, have on many occasions become transformed through traditions of Indian, Mayan, Chinese or Yoruba thinking, speaking, interacting, making and performing. In this context, Ogunnaike (2020: 13) speaks of 'Members of these older, non-Europhone traditions [who] have done and are doing sophisticated, compelling, and profound intellectual work that is worthy of academic attention'.

Given the imbalanced and one-sided realities of inter-cultural exchanges more generally, the 'directionality' of the flow of cross-cultural philosophizing is important. The burden of this chapter has been that some underlying mechanisms of text reading open up *by default* a space of inter-cultural learning, even, or perhaps in particular, for philosophers who belong to one of the dominant Western-oriented academic practices. I have presented text reading, as practised today in many everyday, professional and academic contexts, as a non-deliberate but potentially effective antidote against unwarranted narrowness in the cross-cultural encounter. It protects, sometimes even against a reader's unconscious prejudices, a realm in which it is always possible to learn from what takes one by surprise.

Appendix: Some philosophical text types in cultural diversity

In the body of the present chapter, I speak about the role of genre expectations in inter-cultural philosophizing. This appendix addresses one aspect of this in more detail, by suggesting distinctions of text types. Philosophical discourses themselves have on occasion engaged with the meaning of different textual formats, and sometimes placed philosophy into sharp opposition to some of them, for instance, 'myth'.[42] This raises the question of the authority of a society's cultural traditions more generally. While many philosophers have produced philosophical arguments that ascribe importance to communally revered texts in a great variety of genres, from narrative to poetic, mythical, mystical, dialogical or oracular formats,[43] other philosophers have found discourses philosophically suspect which ascribe any authority to earlier texts. The list below points to the variety of text types in which philosophizing has been claimed to happen, or in whose inner-cultural or cross-cultural reading it might still happen today:

1 Philosophical texts that present themselves as standing in relation to earlier texts while treating them as authoritative or foundational (this category is meant to allow overlap with 3.b and c. below):
   a by taking up the language of the earlier text: e.g. Xunzi in relation to Confucius' *Analects*, Zhiyi's use of the *Lotus Sutra* in his *Clear Serenity, Quiet Insight* (*Mohe zhiguan*), IbnʿArabī's *Bezels of Wisdom* in relation to the Qur'an, Maimonides' *Guide of the Perplexed* in relation to the Hebrew Bible and Talmudic literature
   b by addressing the wording of the earlier text in sequential or commentary format: e.g. Wang Bi's *The Structure of the Laozi's Subtle Pointers*, *Words and Phrases of the Lotus Sutra* ascribed to Zhiyi, Śaṅkara's Vedic Scripture commentaries, Zhu Xi's commentaries on the Confucian canon
   c by defining the language of the earlier text: e.g. Wang Bi's *The Structure*, Kūkai's 'Attaining Enlightenment in This Very Existence', Zhiyi's *Clear Serenity, Quiet Insight*, Maimonides's *Guide*
   d by problematizing the language of the earlier text: e.g. Maimonides's *Guide*, Wang Bi's *The Structure*, Zhiyi's *Clear Serenity, Quiet Insight*
   e by exploring the nexus between language and reality in the earlier text or in tradition, e.g. as a medium of societal formation in Xunzi, Maimonides's *Guide*.
2 Texts that consist of narrative or thematic exposition in prose or poetry, often presenting apodictic pronouncements, which later philosophical texts treat as somehow philosophically authoritative, and whose:
   a thematic discourse, exhortation, song or narrative addresses or problematizes the nature of language, possibly including its own language, in some prominent, repeated or sustained manner: e.g. Daodejing, Kena Upanishad; Parmenides's Poem
   b thematic discourse, exhortation, song or narrative does not, except incidentally, address language as such, or problematize its own verbal constitution: e.g. Popol Vuh, Genesis, Gospels, Sakha epic/Olonkho
   c reports of character speech or extended dialogue consist of thematic exposition, exhortation, song or narrative without, except incidentally, addressing language or problematizing their own verbal constitution (e.g. Pentateuch).
3 Texts that present an exposition of or a sustained discourse on a unified and general theme, and which provide:
   a no acknowledged dependency on the authority of earlier texts, regardless of how pervasive might be its quoted or unquoted connections to them:
      i Works of 'creative' philosophy from Plato to Wittgenstein
      ii Contemporary publications of Western-style 'professional' philosophy

    b an incidental or probative integration of quotations of, or allusions to, texts that have cultural authority or professional standing: e.g. Xunzi, Augustine, Zhiyi, Avicenna's *The Metaphysics of* 'The Healing', Maimonides's *Guide*, Al-Ghazali's *The Niche for Lights*, Mulla Sadra's *Wisdom of the Throne*, as well as works by self-identifying disciples in various philosophical 'schools' until the end of the nineteenth century (in Europe at least). Texts in this category may also fit under point 1

    c clusters of question-answer units or narrated dialogues, whether presented in a cohesive order or merely juxtaposed: e.g. Confucius's *Analects*, Zhuangzi, Wang Yangming's 'Questions on the Great Learning', Aquinas's *Summa Theologiae*, Platonic and Renaissance dialogues.

4 Texts consisting of the mere juxtaposition of (groups of) terse apodictic or proverbial maxims and propositions, whose mutual thematic relation or unity is not addressed[44]: e.g. Instructions of Amenemope, the biblical Book of Proverbs, Mishnah Avot, collections of Zen kōan.

5 Verbal entities that represent single, stand-alone apodictic or proverbial maxims (in contrast to point 4), often a reported utterance in a short narrative: gnomic utterance, oracular saying, proverb, apophthegm, chreia, kōan, and many more (transmitted e.g. as a pre-Socratic fragment, or in the *Lives* of Diogenes Laertius and in Hadith collections).

6 By contrast to the preceding text-based categories, it may be useful to mention at least also the following constellations: conversations that thematize concepts in everyday contexts, embedded in action and embedding action:

    a A spontaneous interpersonal utterance that problematizes or clarifies meanings and concepts without programmatic philosophical intent, yet is potentially 'philosophical' in nature

    b An ad hoc utterance that reflectively generalizes such situated clarifications of concepts, as implying dimensions of the speaker's 'ontology', 'psychology', 'logic', 'ethics', 'aesthetics' or 'metaphysics' (cf. Graeber 2015)

    c A non-verbal aspect of an action, a reaction and social behaviour which is capable of being embedded into verbal practices 6a or 6b by the acting person or by an onlooker – the implied 'ontology' of praxis (cf. Bourdieu 1977)

    d A primarily non-verbal 'artistic' performative or material practice, capable of being embedded into verbal practices 6a or 6b by artists and audiences

    e A ritual or other embodied performance, capable of being embedded into verbal practices 6a or 6b by performing agents, such as priests, shamans, participants and others.

Notes

1. For a partial overview of the field of cross-cultural philosophy, see Wong 2020, and for methodological considerations, see Cline (2013), Chakrabarti and Weber (2017), Smith (2017) and Ma and van Brakel (2016).
2. For the activity of learning texts by heart specifically, see now Samely (2024: 288–9 and 389–92).
3. For the role in cross-cultural philosophizing of non-texts, the non-textual contexts of texts or the non-textual use of texts, see Jenco (2007) and Kalmanson (2017).
4. For the latter, see in particular Ogunnaike (2020).
5. Cf. Heidegger (2010) and Heidegger (1998) (written in 1919). Gadamer (2004) takes such a position as his starting point.
6. Cf. Samely (2024: 183–7).
7. The expression 'Western-*oriented*' helps me address, albeit inadequately, a terminological difficulty while allowing me to avoid the term 'Westernized'. That the expression also evokes the semantics of 'Orient' is a gratefully received double entendre.
8. Mohanty (2023) addresses precisely this issue; cf. also Clooney (1992: 62–3).
9. Husserl (2001) and (1973). Husserl's notion of passive synthesis, which includes the aspects of protention and retention, was later developed and modified by Merleau-Ponty (e.g. 2012: 490–2), Levinas (1998), Deleuze (2014: 93–7 and passim) and others.
10. See the concise, if somewhat divergent, summary of this tension in Angle (2009: 5).
11. See Chakrabarti and Weber (2017: 18–19). With regard to historical accuracy, it is arguably the burden of Gadamer's (2004) argument that understanding a text does not involve such distinct stages even if the reader's goal is historical reconstruction.
12. Cf. Samely (e.g. 2024: 116–21). This effectively undermines any strict separation, as discussed in Angle (2010), between 'understanding' and 'developing' a philosophical tradition.
13. Rosenzweig (2000) made the point about unforeseen outcomes in the context of philosophical dialogue in particular ('speech thinking').
14. The concern which the reader finds in the text was helpfully analysed by Heidegger and Gadamer under the term *Sache*; cf. Gadamer (2004: 450–4), corresponding to Gadamer (1990: 462–6).
15. The unit which is actively integrated is often the sentence or its parts in Western languages, but it can also be a poetic line or collocations of words, and there are other possibilities. For the idea that differences in sentence structure between classical Chinese and Western languages led to the development of different ontological positions, see Graham (1989: 389–428); cf. Samely (2024: 176).
16. Indeed readers may read a text's units 'out of sequence' (or in selection), and still synthesize them passively in their *togetherness*, as meanings belonging to a single text.

17. Marcel Proust says, 'We laugh at what Molière says only to the exact degree we find him funny' (1971: 55).
18. The ability to recall specific wordings at will plays a very subsidiary role in text reading, at least in modern Westernized contexts (Broek and Gustafson 1999: 17; Gernsbacher 1985). Syntactic information is also very quickly lost to recall; cf. Radford et al. (1999: 394).
19. The reader's experience of the technical term's uses *outside* the text is also passively synthesized. This goes for the reader of the original (say, '*Dao*' in Chinese usage) as well as for the reader of its translation (say, 'way' or 'course' in English), creating the potential for wildly diverging cultural associations.
20. Cf. Chakrabarti and Weber (2017: 9).
21. For instance, Zhu Xi (2019); Angle translates it as 'coherence' (2009: 31).
22. Cf. Ma and van Brakel (2016: 173–7) and passim.
23. Husserl's words (1970: 8, 14) are typical in this regard: 'absolutely free from prejudice'.
24. There is a somewhat similar list in Ogunnaike (2020: 8, 12–13) and passim; and see Chakrabarti and Weber (2017: 13–14).
25. Notwithstanding the fact that the *nature* of that distinction is a theme of Western-oriented philosophizing. For a perspective on this from cultural difference, see Williams (1985: 141–6) and the literature cited in the first section above.
26. Ogunnaike (2020: 13) ascribes to 'traditional African philosophies … accounts of reality, the self, virtue, knowledge, and so forth', correlative to 'the ways of life they exemplify'.
27. Husserl (1970: 8); cf. the critique in Tagore (2017: 531–4). It is, however, important to take into view that Husserl treats theoretical acts as constituting a *praxis* (Husserl (1970: 111 and 181); see also Bourdieu (1977: 1).
28. Cf. Taylor 1985: 136–7. Heidegger (1991) offers a critique of this as a historically emerging Western attitude. For a somewhat simplified confrontation with non-Western, in particular Chinese, practices, see Kalmanson (2017). Platonic *logon didonai* is, historically speaking, less narrow than the translation 'giving reason' suggests; see Weiner (2012).
29. The link between knowing and unity has long been articulated in Western philosophical tradition; for two examples of many, see Kant (2000: 9); Husserl (1970: 31, 167–8) and passim.
30. Ziporyn (2022) provides a summarizing transposition of the English terms of his translations from the Chinese, into the English vocabulary of (certain) contemporary Western philosophies.
31. Appiah (1992), in particular Chapter 7, offers an exploration of the nexus between economy, colonialism and products of culture.
32. See, e.g. the definition of the boundaries of the field of 'Africana Philosophy' in Outlaw and Jeffers (2022); and the discussion of perspectives in Graeber (2015), Bourdieu 1977.
33. I have used the term 'provincialized', a borrowing from Chakrabarty, earlier already; for two examples of this, see Chakrabarty (2007) and Mitchell (1988).

34. An outstanding example of the discourse of hybridity, its 'practice' alongside its 'theory', is Glissant 2020.
35. Perhaps this is an outlook perhaps first practised by Benjamin (e.g. 1999b and 1999a: 470–81); cf. also the discussions on this in anthropology (e.g. Graeber 2015, where the Other is not a past but a present), and the methods of micro-history (e.g. Levi 1991).
36. See, e.g. Carr (2014: 141–72); cf. Tagore's use of the idea of 'world' in (2016: 537–8).
37. Kuhn (1982) is particularly relevant to the topic of reading, in that he explores the discontinuous intelligibility of scientific *texts*; and see MacIntyre (1985). Ma and van Brakel (2016: 149–56) explain the relevance of the position of Davidson (following Quine) on translatability and conceptual schemes for comparative philosophy, also touching on Kuhn.
38. See Crystal (2009).
39. Cf. Ma and van Brakel (2016: 27–8).
40. See Ma and Brakel (2016: 131–2) and passim; MacIntyre (1985), and Chakrabarti and Weber (2017: 10–14) and passim.
41. Sipiora, Atwill and Spivak (1990: 300).
42. Plato relies on 'myth' (e.g. in the *Timaeus*) and allegories (e.g. in the *Republic*), yet is hostile to representational arts; Derrida (1995) is instructive with regard to the former (*khora*).
43. Philo of Alexandria's allegorical readings of Hebrew Bible narratives are one of many examples.
44. For this and some other categorizations of texts here used or alluded to, see the concepts developed in Samely, Alexander, Hayward and Bernasconi (2013).

References

Angle, Stephen C. (2009), *Sagehood: The Contemporary Significance of Neo-Confucian Philosophy*. New York: Oxford University Press.

Angle, Stephen C. (2010), 'The Minimal Definition and Methodology of Comparative Philosophy: A Report from a Conference', *Comparative Philosophy* 1: 106–10.

Appiah, Kwame Anthony (1992), *In My Father's House: Africa in the Philosophy of Culture*. New York: Oxford University Press.

Benjamin, Walter (1999a), *Arcades Project*, trans. Howard Eiland and Kevin McLaughlin. Cambridge, MA: Harvard University Press/Belknap.

Benjamin, Walter (1999b), 'Theses on the Philosophy of History', in H. Zorn (trans.), *Illuminations*. London: Pimlico, pp. 245–55.

Bourdieu, Pierre (1977), *Outline of a Theory of Practice*, trans. Richard Nice. Cambridge: Cambridge University Press.

Braidotti, Rosi (2019), *Posthuman Knowledge*. Cambridge: Polity.

Broek, Paul van den, and Mary Gustafson (1999), 'Comprehension and Memory for Texts: Three Generations of Reading Research', in Susan R. Goldman, Arthur C.

Graesser and Paul van den Broek (eds.), *Narrative Comprehension, Causality, and Coherenc: Essays in Honor of Tom Trabasso*. Abingdon: Routledge, pp. 15–34.
Carr, David (2014), *History and Experience*. Oxford: Oxford University Press.
Chakrabarti, Arindam, and Ralph Weber (eds.) (2017), 'Introduction', in their edited volume, *Comparative Philosophy without Borders*. London: Bloomsbury, pp. 1–33.
Chakrabarty, Dipesh (2007), *Provincializing Europe: Postcolonial Thought and Historical Difference*. Princeton, NJ: Princeton University Press.
Cline, Erin M. (2013), *Confucius, Rawls, and the Sense of Justice*. New York: Fordham University Press.
Clooney, Francis X. (1992), 'Binding the Text: Vedānta as Philosophy and Commentary', in Jeffrey R. Timm (ed.), *Texts in Context: Traditional Hermeneutics in South Asia*. Delhi: Sri Satguru Publications, pp. 49–68.
Crystal, David (2009), *English as a Global Language*, 2nd ed. Cambridge: Cambridge University Press.
Deleuze, Gilles (2014), *Difference and Repetition*, trans. Paul Patton. London: Bloomsbury.
Derrida, Jacques (1995), 'Khora', trans. Ian McLeod, in his, *On the Name*, ed. Thomas Dutoit. Stanford, CA: Stanford University Press, pp. 89–127.
Deutsch, Eliot (1988), *Advaita Vedanta: A Philosophical Reconstruction*. Honolulu, HI: University of Hawaii Press.
Fleischacker, Samuel (1992), *Integrity and Moral Relativism*. Leiden: Brill, 1992.
Gadamer, Hans-Georg (1990), *Wahrheit und Methode: Grundzüge einer philosophischen Hermeneutik*, 6th ed. Gesammelte Werke, 1; Tübingen: Mohr.
Gadamer, Hans-Georg (2004), *Truth and Method*, 2nd ed., trans. revised Joel Weinsheimer and Donald G. Marshall. London: Bloomsbury.
Gernsbacher, Morton Ann (1985), 'Surface Information Loss in Comprehension', *Cognitive Psychology* 17: 324–63.
Glissant, Édouard (2020), *Treatise on the Whole-World*, trans. Celia Britton. Liverpool: Liverpool University Press.
Graeber, David (2015), 'Radical Alterity Is Just Another Way of Saying "Reality": A Reply to Eduardo Viveiros de Castro', *Hau: Journal of Ethnographic Theory* 5: 1–41.
Graham, Angus C. (1989), *Disputers of the Tao: Philosophical Argument in Ancient China*. Chicago, and La Salle, IL: Open Court.
Heidegger, Martin (1991), *The Principle of Reason*, trans. Reginald Lilly. Bloomington and Indianapolis, IN: Indiana University Press.
Heidegger, Martin (1998), 'Comments on Karl Jaspers's Psychology of Worldviews (1919/21)', in W. McNeil (ed. and trans.), *Pathmarks*. Cambridge: Cambridge University Press, pp. 1–38.
Heidegger, Martin (2010), *Being and Time*, trans. Joan Stambaugh. Albany, NY: SUNY.
Husserl, Edmund (1970), *The Crisis of European Science and Transcendental Phenomenology: An Introduction to Phenomenological Philosophy*, trans. David Carr. Evanston, IL: Northwestern University Press.
Husserl, Edmund (1973), *Experience and Judgment: Investigations in a Genealogy of Logic*, ed. Ludwig Landgrebe, trans. Spencer Churchill. Evanston, IL: Northwestern University Press.

Husserl, Edmund (2001), *Analyses Concerning Passive and Active Synthesis: Lectures on Transcendental Logic*, trans. Anthony J. Steinbock. Dordrecht: Kluwer.

Ing, Michael D. K. (2017), *The Vulnerability of Integrity in Early Confucian Thought*. New York: Oxford University Press.

Jenco, Leigh Kathryn (2007), '"What Does Heaven Ever Say?": A Methods-Centered Approach to Cross-Cultural Engagement', *American Political Science Review* 101: 741–55.

Jenco, Leigh, Steve Fuller, David H. Kim, Thaddeus Metz and Miljana Milojevic (2017), 'Symposium: Are Certain Knowledge Frameworks More Congenial to the Aims of Cross-Cultural Philosophy?', *Journal of World Philosophies* 2: 82–145.

Kalmanson, Leah (2017), 'The Ritual Methods of Comparative Philosophy', *Philosophy East & West* 67: 399–418.

Kant, Immanuel (2000), 'First Introduction', in Paul Guyer (ed. and trans.), *Critique of the Power of Judgment*. Cambridge: Cambridge University Press, pp. 3–83.

Kuhn, Thomas (1982), 'Commensurability, Comparability, Communicability', *PSA: Proceedings of the Biennial Meeting of the Philosophy of Science Association* 2: 669–88.

Levi, Giovanni (1991), 'On Microhistory', in Peter Burke (ed.), *New Perspectives on Historical Writing*. Oxford: Polity Press, pp. 93–113.

Levinas, Emmanuel (1998), *Otherwise than Being or beyond Essence*, trans. Alphonso Lingis. Pittsburgh, PA: Duquesne University Press.

Ma, Lin, and Jaap van Brakel (2016), *Fundamentals of Comparative and Intercultural Philosophy*. Albany, NY: State University of New York Press.

MacIntyre, Alasdair (1985), 'Relativism, Power and Philosophy', *Proceedings and Addresses of the American Philosophical Association* 59: 5–22.

Merleau-Ponty, Maurice (2012), *Phenomenology of Perception*, trans. Donald A. Landes. London: Routledge.

Mitchell, Timothy (1988), *Colonising Egypt*. Berkeley, CA: University of California Press.

Mohanty, Jitendra Nath (ed.) (2023), 'Indian Philosophy: Between Tradition and Modernity', in his, *Reason and Tradition in Indian Thought: An Essay on the Nature of Indian Philosophical Thinking*. Oxford: Oxford University Press, pp. 7–25.

Ochs, Peter (1998), *Peirce, Pragmatism and the Logic of Scripture*. Cambridge: Cambridge University Press.

Ogunnaike, Oludamini (2020), *Deep Knowledge: Ways of Knowing in Sufism and Ifa, Two West African Intellectual Traditions*. University Park, PA: Pennsylvania State University Press.

Outlaw, Lucius T., Jr., and Chike Jeffers (2022), 'Africana Philosophy', in Edward N. Zalta and Uri Nodelman (eds.), *Stanford Encyclopedia of Philosophy* (Fall 2022 Edition), https://plato.stanford.edu/archives/fall2022/entries/africana/.

Proust, Marcel (1971), *On Reading*, trans. and ed. Jean Autret and William Burford. London: Souvenir Press.

Radford, Andrew, Martin Atkinson, David Britain, Harald Clahsen and Andrew Spencer (1999), *Linguistics: An Introduction*. Cambridge: Cambridge University Press.

Ram-Prasad, Chakravarthi (2002), *Advaita Epistemology and Metaphysics: An Outline of Indian Non-Realism*. London: RoutledgeCurzon.

Richardson, Henry (1997), *Practical Reasoning about Final Ends.* Cambridge: Cambridge University Press.
Rosenzweig, Franz (2000), 'The New Thinking', in Paul W. Franks and Michael L. Morgan (trans. and ed.), *Philosophical and Theological Writings.* Indianapolis, IN: Hackett, pp. 123–7.
Samely, Alexander (2024), *Reading and Experience: A Philosophical Investigation.* Cham: Springer.
Samely, Alexander, Philip Alexander, Robert Hayward and Rocco Bernasconi (2013), *Profiling Jewish Literature in Antiquity: From Second Temple Texts to the Talmuds.* Oxford: Oxford University Press.
Sharf, Robert (2016), 'Is Yogācāra Phenomenology? Some Evidence from the *Cheng weishi lun*', *Journal of Indian Philosophy* 44: 777–807.
Sipiora, Philip, Janet Atwill and Gayatri Chakravorty Spivak (1990), 'Rhetoric and Cultural Explanation: A Discussion with Gayatri Chakravorty Spivak', *Journal of Advanced Composition* 10 (Gender, Culture, Ideology): 293–304.
Smith, Justin E. H. (2017), 'Philosophy as a Distinct Cultural Practice: The Transregional Context', in Jonardon Ganeri (ed.), *The Oxford Handbook of Indian Philosophy.* Oxford: Oxford University Press, pp. 56–74.
Sueki, Fumihiko (2015), 'Philosophical Literature: Japan', in Jonathan Silk, et al., (eds.), *Brill's Encyclopedia of Buddhism*, vol. 1. Leiden: Brill, pp. 639–52.
Tagore, Saranindranath (2017), 'On the Concept of World Philosophy', *Philosophy East and West* 67: 531–44.
Taylor, Charles (ed.) (1985), 'Rationality', in his *Philosophy and the Human Sciences: Philosophical Papers 2.* Cambridge: Cambridge University Press, 1985, pp. 134–51.
Weiner, Sebastian (2012), 'Platons "logon didonai"', *Archiv für Begriffsgeschichte* 54: 7–20.
Williams, Bernard (1985), *Ethics and the Limits of Philosophy.* London: Fontana.
Wong, David (2020), 'Comparative Philosophy: Chinese and Western', in Edward N. Zalta (ed.), *The Stanford Encyclopedia of Philosophy* (Fall 2020 Edition); https://plato.stanford.edu/archives/fall2020/entries/comparphil-chiwes/.
Xi, Zhu (2019), '*Poetry, Literature, Textual Study, and Hermeneutics*', trans. On-cho Ng, in Zhu Xi and Philip J. Ivanhoe (eds.), *Selected Writings.* Oxford: Oxford University Press, pp. 72–92.
Yu, Jiyuan, and Nicholas Bunnin (2001), 'Saving the Phenomena: An Aristotelian Method in Comparative Philosophy', in Bo Mou (ed.), *Two Roads to Wisdom? Chinese and Analytic Philosophical Traditions.* La Salle, IL: Open Court, pp. 293–312.
Zhuangzi (2009), *The Essential Writings: With Selections from Traditional Commentaries*, trans. Brook Ziporyn. Indianapolis, IN: Hackett.
Ziporyn, Brook (2022), 'Zhuangzi as Philosopher', https://hackettpublishing.com/zhuangziphil (Accessed 15 January 2023).

2

Dao and the way – A comparative perspective

Xinzhong Yao

'*Dao*' is a fundamental concept in Chinese metaphysics and culture, underlying the Chinese way of living, thinking, believing and behaving. In most English translations of Chinese texts, *Dao* is usually translated as the Way.[1] It does make sense to interpret *Dao* as a way or ways or the Way, since both *Dao* and the Way not only have similar meanings in their original forms, but are also used similarly in a range of extended references, for example, to 'method', the 'means' to do things, a 'manner' of doing something, or the 'road' to a final goal. More importantly, both *Dao* and the Way become used as a philosophical term for the truth or the principle that is believed to sustain the world, either metaphysical, physical or political and social. However, this is only a convenient translation; it does not mean *Dao* in Chinese and the Way in English are totally identical. To grasp their similarities and differences, we need to take a comparative approach to examine the usages of *Dao* in various texts. We need to focus on the origin and evolution of *Dao* throughout classical Chinese texts, and on the distinctive features presented particularly in Daoist and Confucian interpretations. This will enable us to clarify the differences from the use of the Way or ways in Greco-Abrahamic texts.

Focusing on the various Chinese uses of *Dao* underpins a comparative approach to this important concept as used in different philosophical traditions. This perspective provides a new lens through which to examine a term with a long and evolving history. It helps us highlight the different frameworks established by different Chinese schools.

Dao and 'methods'

The original meaning of *Dao* was simple. It was developed from a character with a simple reference into a complicated philosophical concept with multiple layered implications. The boundaries of *Dao*'s meanings are not easily drawn, as its uses in different texts are often diffused or ambiguous, and cannot be defined as clearly as those of the Way in English language contexts. It is therefore necessary for us to investigate where *Dao* originated and was applied, to gain a clearer idea about its original meanings and expanded applications and how they may be related to the Greek '*hodos*' or Hebrew '*derek*' – which in their primary uses also mean a road, route or pathway.

Dao comes originally from a pictograph of 'walking along the road'; one of its earlier references is 'way', pointing to the path (*dao*道) or the road (*lu*路). According to the earliest Chinese lexicon compiled by Xu Shen 許慎 (58?–147? CE), *Explaining Graphs and Analyzing Characters* (*Shuowen jiezi*說文解字), *Dao* is the path by which we walk (*suo xing daoye*所行道也) (Xu 2002: 111). The character of *Dao* in the bronze inscriptions of the Zhou dynasty (1046?–256 BCE) was composed of three parts, drawn as a picture in which a person (represented by the head) walks (represented by the foot) along a path (represented by the form of a street) (*Hanyu dazidian* 1993: 1608).

From this simple meaning as a 'road' or 'path', *Dao* evolved in subsequent ages into a philosophical concept with multiple meanings, gradually gaining a meaning in parallel with that of 'methodology' in Greek philosophy. The English word 'method', meaning 'a particular procedure for accomplishing or approaching something', is derived from the Greek word *methodos* which means 'the pursuit of knowledge', and comes from a combination of '*meta-*' ('with', 'across', 'after') and '*hodos*' ('way').

The meaning of 'method' is thus derived from the original '*hodos*', and it can also be drawn out from the Chinese character of *Dao*. As originated in the pictograph of 'path', *Dao* was easily extended to mean the 'method' of doing things (*fang*方)[2] or the 'skills' or 'arts' of accomplishing tasks (*shu*術).[3] In this sense, *Dao* seems to be similar to the Greek word '*methodos*' since it also refers to particular procedures by which an end can be reached (*yi da zhi wei dao* 一達之為道) (Xu 2002: 111) or to concrete ways of solving problems such as 'the art of war' or 'a way of acquiring property'.

Methodology is primarily concerned with the systematic development of methods and principles to foster knowledge. There is a long history of how deliberations on methodology develop various methods in ancient Greek philosophy. While Socrates (469?–399 BCE), holding that 'the unexamined life is not worth living', was engaged in the so-called 'Socratic dialogue' by using 'inductive arguments and general definitions', both of which are believed to have been the 'starting points of scientific knowledge' (Kenny 2010, 33, 37), it was Aristotle (384–322 BCE) who developed systematic methods for observation, classification and logical reasoning as primary tools in the search for truth (Bodnar 2023). This alerts us to the fact that methodology in the European context is not simply a term but a systematic way of using and developing intellectual means and tools, to deepen and expand our understanding of the world. When we examine *Dao* in its evolutionary process, we can clearly see that it functions in Chinese as 'methodology' in a more complicated way. *Dao* is certainly used to refer to the methods and skills of an intellectual enquiry in pursuit of true knowledge; but on the other hand – and more importantly – it often refers to the ways of practising virtue and cultivating a moral person, of fostering better conditions of community and of enhancing the management of the state. It is in these latter contexts where we find the difference between the two concepts in their respective applications.

The Chinese understanding of methodology tends to elaborate on how to practise *Dao* rather than how to intellectually study it. For example, the most famous Daoist text, *Daode jing*, differentiates the way to pursue knowledge from the way to pursue *Dao*: 'The pursuit of learning is to increase day after day. The pursuit of *Dao* is to decrease day after day' (*Daode jing* 48).⁴ Chapter 20 of the *Doctrine of the Mean* (*zhongyong* 中庸) lists five ways as the methods for 'being truly sincere'. These methods do include intellectual investigation but the most important of all is said to be how to practise it: 'Study it (the way to be sincere) extensively, inquire into it accurately, think over it carefully, sift it clearly, and practice it earnestly' (Chan 1963: 107).

Indeed, in the Confucian tradition, even more important than intellectual methods is the cultivation of one's virtue. In the *Analects*, Confucius praised the prime minister (Zi Chan 子產, ?-522 BCE) of the state of Zheng for his demonstrating four virtuous ways as a gentleman: 'Of the virtues that constitute the Way of the gentleman, he possessed four: in the way he conducted himself, he displayed reverence; in the way he served his superiors, he displayed respect; in the way he cared for the common people, he displayed benevolence; and in the way he employed the people, he displayed rightness' (*Analects*, 5.16). On another occasion, Confucius confessed that 'The Way of the gentleman is threefold, and yet I have not been able to achieve any aspect of it: A gentleman does not worry, the wise are not confused, and the courageous do not fear'. In commenting on these three virtuous ways, however, his disciple, Zigong (子貢 520–456 BCE), confirmed that 'the Master has in fact described himself' (ibid., 14.28).

This shows that while there are some commonalities between *Dao* in Chinese philosophy and 'methodology' in European classics, their differing extended applications mean that it is in general inappropriate to identify these two concepts. Since the meanings and implications of *Dao* go well beyond those of 'methodology' in a European context, the similarities *Dao* shares with 'methodology' are significant when and only when it is used on the way to a particular end. In fact, the reference to *Dao* cannot be limited to 'methods', means or procedures. In classical Chinese texts, *Dao* is often used in a much wider and more abstract sense, and by associating it with other characters, such as *tian* (天Heaven), *di* (地Earth), *wu* (無nothingness), *gen* (根 root), *shi* (始beginning) and *li* (禮ritual), it acquires meanings which can refer to metaphysical origins, ontological principles, the natural law, systematic ideology, political ideals or to the moral or ethical realm. In modern Chinese, by combining it with many other characters, there have emerged new terms or new meanings of old terms, such as 'road' (*dao lu*道路), 'reason' (*dao li*道理), 'morality' (*dao de*道德), ethical principle' (*dao yi*道義), 'knowing' or 'knowledge' (*zhi dao*知道), techniques (*men dao*門道), 'apologetics' (*dao qian*道歉), 'congratulations' (*dao he*道賀), as well as traditional terms such as 'Daoist philosophy' (*dao jia*道家), 'Daoist religion' (*dao jiao*道教), 'Daoist temple' (*dao guan*道觀), 'Buddhism' (*fo dao*佛道), 'Learning of the Way' (*dao xue*道學), 'the Middle Path' (*zhong dao*中道) etc. (*Matthews' Chinese-English Dictionary* 1966: 882–4). These old and new uses indicate that although it originated from the visual picture of a path, *Dao* was extended to refer not only to philosophical discussions of the background assumptions involved in all natural and human processes, but also to the mysterious substance that is behind all phenomenal existence, or the original power that is beyond the reach of human enquiry.

Dao, logos and *hodos*

To correctly present the meanings of *Dao*, some sinologists have attempted to relate it to two Greek words – *logos* (the Word or the reason) and *hodos* (the Way) – believing that both could serve as an adequate equivalent to *Dao* (Ching 1993: 88). An example of the former is the first sentence in St. John's Gospel, 'In the beginning was the Word (*logos*)', frequently translated into Chinese as '*Tai chu you Dao*' (太初有道). As an example of the latter, the Daoist founding text *Daode jing* (道德經) is typically translated as 'the *Classic of the Way and its Power*'. And it is worth noting that when Buddhism was introduced to China its doctrine of the 'Eightfold Right Path' was translated and interpreted as 'Eight Orthodox *Dao*' (*ba zheng dao*八正道). *Dao* was also translated by early Christian missionaries variously as 'God', 'Truth', 'Principle', 'Nature' or 'Law'.[5] What this shows is that a concept with such a complex culture and history as *Dao* is not really translatable. In translating, these translators tend to project their own world views and theological understandings onto the character of *Dao*, thus generating their own (new) images and twisting their original meaning, in order to suit a new cultural context. In short, this Chinese concept is impossible to be identified with any term in other languages, and it is undefinable by any concept from other cultural traditions without adding adequate qualifications.

The metaphysical implication of *Dao* is made clear in some of the classic philosophical texts. The Great Appendix of the *Book of Changes*, generally accepted as the work of the Warring States period (479–221 BCE), differentiates the metaphysical

Dao from the physical *qi* (器, vessel, the things of visible forms): 'What is above the form is called *Dao*; what is below the form is called "vessel".'[6] The thing which is antecedent to 'physical forms' sounds like something similar to the *idea* (ἰδέα) or *form* (*eidos*) (Plato used these two terms interchangeably) in Plato's philosophy,[7] and the pair of *Dao* and *qi* seems also to be close to that of '*noumenon*' and 'phenomenon' in modern Western metaphysics (Stang 2023). However, any comparison has limits. If we look at its other uses in the same text, it seems less apparent that *Dao* is the formless ontological entity or force or the thing that is itself, going beyond human sense knowledge, nor can it be placed in a clear contrast to formed physical entities or phenomena.

In the above-mentioned commentary, *Dao* is used thirty-one times. Some of these usages, such as the *Dao* of Heaven and the *Dao* of Earth, refer to the power behind or the principle enabling cosmic generations and regenerations (e.g. 'the Way of the Creative and the Way of the Receptive bring about respectively the male and the female'[8]). However, others are less clear in their meanings, such as in the context of 'the way of the superior man' versus 'the way of the inferior man' where *Dao* seems to be used to indicate different levels of moral quality possessed by different kinds of people. More importantly, *Dao* is used not only in the sense of the creative power or guiding principle, but also of universal forces that are constantly changing. *Dao* has been specified as the 'divine way' (*shen dao* 神道[9]) which is applied by the sage to give instructions (*jiao* 教) to the people so that the whole world might submit to him in peace. *Dao* here becomes a comprehensive guide for humans to lead a moral life: 'The *Book of Changes* contains a fourfold tao [*Dao*] of the holy sage. In speaking, we should be guided by its judgements; in action, we should be guided by its changes; in making objects, we should be guided by its images; in seeking an oracle, we should be guided by its pronouncements' (*I Ching or Book of Changes* 1989: 314). *Dao* is further embodied in the changes of the six lines that comprise a hexagram. As the lines are gendered as *yin* (broken) lines and *yang* (unbroken) lines, *Dao* is said to be none other than 'the alternation of *yin* and *yang*', or as Wing-tsit Chan translated, 'The successive movement of yin and yang constitutes the Way [*Dao*]' (Chan 1963: 266). In this sense, the nature of *Dao* cannot be determined except in and through the activities of *yin* and *yang*.

It seems clear that at least by the time of the Warring States period, the boundary of *Dao*'s references in Chinese contexts had been extended widely, ranging from the most profound source of the universe, the onto-substance, the natural law, the ethical principle that guides human as well as non-human living, and the noblest political course, to the concrete path or way by which a particular destination can be reached. Furthermore, these meanings in many cases are mixed up or used alternatively without being clearly defined or separated. From the textual fact that *Dao* is regarded as the original entity that gives rise to all subsequent existences, it seems apparent that *Dao* is more than *logos* and *hodos*, and that it has occupied multiple positions which are often taken for granted in ontological and methodological discussions in metaphysics, theology, epistemology, ethics, politics and education.

Dao as the 'mysterious entity'

Is *Dao* an entity? There is no definitive answer to this question. The difficulty in pinning down the exact meaning of *Dao* comes primarily from its uses in early Daoist philosophy. According to Chapter 25 of the extant version of the *Daode jing*, *Dao* is said to be 'Something' (*wu*物) that is undifferentiated and yet complete, born before Heaven and Earth (*xian tian di sheng*先天地生), and to be the source or origin of the universe. Because *Dao* is presumed to be the beginning of beginnings, it is considered as that by which the universe comes into existence and in which all beings acquire their lives. *Dao* as a 'thing' is said to be 'eluding and vague', and yet within it there are an image, a substance and an essence which have made it genuine (Chapter 21). Through all these mysterious terms, *Dao* is portrayed as the origin of all things. Paradoxically, as the beginning of all things, it logically cannot be 'something' but has to be 'Nothing' (*wu*無) from which 'something' (*you*有) can arise (Chapter 40).

The author of Chapter 25 confesses that *Dao* cannot be named, as it had already been there before all things that could be named, so much so that 'it is impossible to give it a name; hence I call it *Dao*; if forced to give it a name, it can only be named "Great" (*da*大)'. While admitting that *Dao* cannot be defined, this chapter does provide a hierarchical ladder for humans to trace back to the original *Dao*: 'Humanity follows Earth, Earth follows Heaven, Heaven follows *Dao*, and *Dao* follows nothing but its own nature.' *Dao* is from nowhere but from its own source, and arises from nothing but follows 'its own nature' (*dao fa ziran*道法自然).

The complexity of *Dao*'s references is already fully demonstrated in the first sentence of this text: 'The *Dao* that can be told (*dao*) is not the eternal *Dao*.' Here, '*Dao*' is used three times, each with a different reference. The first seems to refer to the metaphysical entity which is above all beings and existences. The second use might be said to be epistemological, referring to a human process of speaking and knowing; and the last (eternal *Dao*常道) to a transcendental sphere which human rationality and experiences cannot reach. This has effectively made *Dao* a mysterious entity, which is further mystified in Chapter 14: 'Look at it and fail to see: its name is "remote". Listen to it and fail to hear: its name is "diffuse". Feel it and fail to get anything: its name is "subtle" This threesome cannot be exhaustively probed for portents. Hence we blend them and deem them as one.'

Although admitting that *Dao* cannot be spoken of and is unknowable through human language and epistemic faculties, the author(s) of the text seem to be confident that they could grasp what it is. They do this through a number of metaphorical analogies illustrating the transcendental qualities of *Dao* that are beyond human languages. For example, *Dao* is likened to 'ancestor' (*zong*宗) in Chapter 4; or 'Dao is empty (like a cup *zhong*盅) – it may be used without ever being exhausted. Fathomless, it seems to be the ancestor (*zong* 宗) of all things' (Lau 1963: 8). *Dao* is said to have been the beginning of the universe (*tian di*天地). It is also said to be the 'Mother' (*mu*母) who is supposed to have given birth to the whole world, so that a kind of metaphysical genesis is presented.[10] *Dao* is also metaphorized as 'the spirit of the valley' which never dies, as the 'mysterious female' (Chapter 6) from whose gate the world comes out, or is likened to 'water' that is said to be closest to *Dao*, in the sense that water flows downwards rather than upwards, and in the sense that water, although the softest in the world, can conquer the hardest of all things in the world (Chapter 8).

Through all these metaphors, we can see that in the minds of early Daoists, *Dao* belongs to the sphere of the infinite or the unlimited that is beyond the reach of human rational knowledge and sense experiences. For them, human rationality is contrary to the nature of *Dao* and those who attempt to speak about *Dao* are therefore ridiculed as the ignorant or illusionary: 'One who knows does not speak; one who speaks does not know' (Chapter 56). The way for humans to know *Dao* starts with the abandoning of supposed knowledge and turning away from the so-called sagely teachings. This is what is recommended as 'exterminating the sage and discarding the wise', because only by 'exterminating learning there will no longer be worries' (Chapter 19). This sounds close to the ancient Greek maxim of 'knowing yourself' which Socrates uses in his project to dismiss those who claimed to possess wisdom. Only by confessing that one knows nothing can humans then move forward in their search of truth (Ryan 2023).

Instead of pursuing learning, Daoist philosophers seek to follow nature to achieve oneness with *Dao*. 'Being one with *Dao*' is not merely a perception but a strong belief held by early Daoist philosophers. For them, it is *Dao* that makes different things one (*dao tong weiyi*道通為一): 'things ribald and shady, or things grotesque and strange, the Way makes them all into one'.[11] For Daoists, the highest ideal or achievement is to be one with *Dao* (*yu dao heyi*與道合一), or obtaining *Dao* (*de dao*得道) which is sometimes termed as 'returning to the beginning' or the 'infancy' (*ying er*婴儿), the 'non-ultimate' (*wu ji*無極) or 'uncarved wood' (*pu*樸) (Chapter 28). In this context, *Dao* is both the end at which humans aim and the way by which humans can return to their own nature. Therefore, being one with *Dao* is a special process of returning, and returning is embedded in the original nature of all things. As this point is so crucial for our understanding of the Daoist reasoning, we quote Chapter 16 at length as follows:

> All things flourish, but each one returns to its root (*gen*根). This return to its root means tranquillity (*jing*静). It is called returning to its destiny (*ming*命). To return to destiny is called the eternal (*chang*常). To know the eternal is called enlightenment

(*ming*明). Not to know the eternal is to act blindly to result in disaster. He who knows the eternal is all-embracing ... Being one with Heaven (*tian*天), he (the true sage) is in accord with Dao. Being in accord with Dao, he is everlasting (*jiu*久) and is free from danger (*bu dai*不殆) throughout his lifetime.

(Chapter 16)

Dao is central to Daoist philosophy and religion, and underlies all Daoist beliefs and practices. In the second most important Daoist text, the *Book of Zhuangzi*, the character of *Dao* appears 368 times where *Dao* continues to be taken as the mysterious power or being, an entity that is the foundation of the world but is beyond human understanding and knowledge.[12] Sublime and profound as it is, however, *Dao* is also expanded to all fields close to human activities; thus, Zhuangzi (369?–286? BCE) talks not only about the Way of Heaven (*tian dao*天道), but also the Way of the King (*di dao*帝道), the Way of the Sage (*sheng dao*聖道),[13] and the Way of humans (*ren dao*人道). Thus, together with other usages mentioned above referring to the 'arts of *Dao*' (*dao shu*道術), we can see how Zhuangzi, at least in certain contexts, 'de-mystifies' *Dao*, as he shifts the emphasis from the metaphysical origin of all beings as prescribed in the *Daode jing* and uses *Dao* more frequently as 'concrete ways' which both the natural and the human world not only manifest but also follow.

The Confucian way

Dao is not an idea or ideal cherished and claimed exclusively by Daoists. Rather, it is the cultural symbol of traditional China and is indeed widely used by almost all Chinese schools, some of which may have used the concept of *Dao* much earlier than Daoist texts. Many of these usages are of a similar ambiguity but we can also see that different traditions often place different emphases on different aspects of its various meanings, drawing up different pictures of this profound idea.

In comparison with the *Daode jing* where *Dao* appears seventy-six times and is significantly mystified, the *Analects of Confucius*, where it is used eighty-nine times in its extant version, shares more similarities with the 'way' in the Greco-Abrahamic tradition. *Dao*, in some of these contexts, echoes the unknowable or the mysterious of Daoism. For example, while the disciples of Confucius learned many things from him, they seemed to complain that they did not hear their master talking much about the *Dao* of Heaven (*Tian Dao*天道). This fact could be interpreted as being simply because Confucius was fully aware of the difficulty in talking about it or because *Dao* implied something that would be beyond words. Interpreted as such, Confucius would appear to share the same concern as Daoists about the mysterious or transcendental nature of *Dao* when *Dao* is presented as the most profound cause of the world.[14]

Unlike Daoism, which discourages people from engaging the world and takes withdrawal as the way to personal salvation, the aim of Confucianism is to encourage people to engage in educational and political enterprises either personally or collectively for a better world. Pursuing *Dao* is taken as the only justifiable purpose for Confucian living, and it is often made synonymous to the moral high ground or the morally noble course in political debates. Realistic as Confucians were, they admitted that there was no consensus on what *Dao* was, and each might well claim that they were of, or with, *Dao*. Considering the huge influence Confucianism exerted in later Chinese history, we may say that this kind of admission underlaid the syncretic nature of Chinese culture and gave rise to a potentially tolerant attitude towards those whose political claims were different. In the Confucian context, *Dao* is both singular and plural, which highlights a need to accommodate different Ways. This point is made clear in the *Doctrine of the Mean* (Chapter 30) that 'All things are nourished together without their injuring one another. Multiple Ways (*Daos*) are pursued without any collision among them.' In this context *Dao* applies to both the natural world and the human world. The ontological parallel of the multiple and coexisting ways was the foundation of a syncretic culture in the past and continues to be used to enhance the importance of cultural diversity and ideological tolerance in today's intellectual and political discourses.

Unlike in Daoist philosophy where *Dao* is far beyond human reach, in the Confucian tradition *Dao* is both greater than humans *and* is within humanity. Confucius pointed this out when he said that 'it is humanity that makes *Dao* great, not the *Dao* that makes humanity great' (*Analects*, 15.29). The *Doctrine of the Mean* elaborates on this point: humans partake of the great *Dao* of Heaven by which humans can cultivate it in their own life. The text opens with the statement that 'What Heaven imparts to humans is called human nature. To follow our nature is called the Way (*Dao*). Cultivating the Way is called education. The Way cannot be separated from us for a moment. What can be separated from us is not the Way' (Chan 1963: 112).

Through these elaborations, the concept of *Dao* has been transformed from the mysterious and transcendental Way to the way which humans can follow, know and transmit. As a result, *Dao* has been widely accepted as both universal and particular, both immanent and imminent. Although some passages in Confucian texts retain the sense of the ontological substance that appears to be like the 'thing-in-itself', the origin of the universe or the first cause for the world that goes beyond human epistemological abilities, a large number of uses of *Dao* are in a common sense, serving to illustrate how humans can become perfect by learning and practising *Dao*. Confucian masters paid great attention to practices, elaborating on the way to unpack the power of *Dao* or to release the force of *Dao* in daily life. This helped shape not only the Chinese way of education but also Chinese religiosity in which the transcendental *Dao* is manifested as concrete paths, and can be therefore known through embodied experiencing (*ti dao* 體道), or through ethical cultivation or meditative learning (*xue dao* 學道).

The universality of the Confucian *Dao* also helped shape a unique popular culture and strengthened the belief in mutual transformation between the sacred and the secular (Fingarette 1972). It has become acceptable in all Chinese cultural traditions that everyone could become perfect, either as a God (*shen*神), Buddha (*fo*佛), an Immortal (*xian*仙) or a sage (*sheng*聖). This means that humans can transcend the secular and mortal worlds to enter the sphere of eternal or immortal *Dao*. Since it is believed that everybody or every sentient being is able to embrace and cultivate *Dao*, they are all able to become part of the indefinite or become sacred by themselves. This explains why the Chinese in general find no contradiction between the oneness of *Dao* and plural beliefs in the pantheon of gods, or between the oneness of the great *Dao* and the multiple paths that lead to it.

Moral teachings and political orders

Differentiated clearly from the focus of Daoist metaphysics, the emphasis of the Confucian *Dao* is placed on the moral, political and educational dimensions, using *Dao* to refer to the universal principle, the most profound knowledge and the highest ideal, for the full realization of which a benevolent person may even sacrifice his own life and well-being. Confucius made it clear that 'In the morning hear *Dao*, in the evening die content', and that 'The gentleman devotes his mind to attaining *Dao* and not to securing food' (*Analects*, 4.8, 15.32). At the same time, *Dao* is significantly moralized and politicized in the *Analects of Confucius* as the moral way or political legacy, such as the way of the Master (*zi zhi dao*子之道), the way of the father (*fu zhi dao*父之道), the way of the gentleman (*junzi zhi dao*君子之道), the way of the former Kings (*xian wang zhi dao*先王之道). These sayings indicate that the Confucian *Dao* as the human way can be known, experienced, learned and embodied, and should be transmitted to following generations. Thus, 'transmitting the Way' (*chuan Dao*傳道) has been characteristic of Chinese education theory, and is still regarded as the first priority for teachers in contemporary times.

Following the moral and political understandings of Confucius, the other three texts of the so-called Confucian Four Books – *Mencius*, the *Doctrine of the Mean* and the *Great Learning* – have enriched *Dao* with new elements and employed it as the Way to legitimize Confucian teachings. In the text of Mencius (372?–289? BCE), *Dao* is used to represent the Kingly Way (*wang dao*王道) and the foundation of the benevolent government (*ren zheng*仁政). For Mencius, *Dao* is the sagely teaching that is unified ('The Way is one and only one', 3A:1) and must be closely followed, for which he engaged in a fierce attack on the so-called heresies or excessive views, referring to the School of Mo Di (476?–390? BCE) and the School of Yang Zhu (395?–335? BCE); Mencius took it as the righteous way in order to safeguard the 'Way of the former sages' (Mencius, 3B:9).

In the other two texts, *Dao* also has a very prominent position. They go into detail about how *Dao* justifies Confucian understandings of human nature and human destiny. For example, the *Great Learning* starts with the sentence that 'The Way of learning to be great (*da xue zhi dao* 大學之道) consists in manifesting the clear character, loving the people, and abiding in the highest good', while the *Doctrine of the Mean* terms 'equilibrium' (*zhong* 中) as the great foundation of the world and 'harmony' (*he* 和) as the universal path (*tian xia zhi da dao* 天下之達道) (Chan 1963: 66, 86, 98).

Another important representative of Confucianism in the pre-Qin period (before 221 BCE) is Xunzi (313?–238? BCE), in whose text *Dao* is even more prominent, and is used nearly 400 times. Xunzi portrayed himself as the carrier of the Way of the Former Kings and took *Dao* as the sole criterion for justifying governing activities and institutions, in order to promote the Kingly Way (*wang dao* 王道) as his political ideal. Xunzi went one step further than his predecessors, by identifying *Dao* with human activities. For him, 'The Way is not the way of Heaven, nor is it the way of Earth. It is that whereby humans make their way, and that which the gentleman takes as his way' (*Xunzi* 荀子 2014: 55).

The Confucian uses of *Dao* in pre-Qin texts have laid a solid cultural foundation on which future Confucianists took it for granted that *Dao* is symbolic of the orthodox Confucian teachings. To fight against Buddhism, Han Yu (768–824) of the Tang dynasty (618–906) exalted the Way of the Confucian tradition to a sacred position and attempted to resume the transmission of the Confucian teachings from the earliest sages through Confucius to Mencius. Zhu Xi (1130–1200) of the Song dynasty (960–1276), the great master of neo-Confucianism, formally proposed a new paradigm concerning how Confucian teachings were transmitted from legendary sages to King Wen, the founder of the Zhou dynasty (1046?–256 BCE), to Confucius and Mencius, as the so-called the orthodox transmission line of the Way (*dao tong* 道統). Not only excluding Xunzi but also leaving out all important Confucian scholars in the Han and Tang dynasties, this orthodox transmission line was said to have been broken after Mencius, until the emergence of neo-Confucianism. Neo-Confucian masters considered themselves as the right inheritors and successors of Confucius and Mencius, and their elaborations were therefore named as the orthodox Confucian tradition, the learning of the Way (*dao xue* 道學). *Dao* thus became the highest moral principle for human beings and the sole source of all ethical and political justifications in China as well as across the Sinosphere.

The Way or the paradox?

Dao is not only a prominent concept in the Daoist and Confucian traditions, but is also central to the world views and political practices of almost all other schools and traditions, in particular, Mohism, Legalism and the Military Strategist School, in which *Dao* is used to refer both to the principles underlying the cosmic and social order – these are believed to be interdependent and interactive – and to the ways that can be used as technical means to sort out problems or in general to get things done adequately. Mozi states firmly that 'If rulers of the world today really want the empire to be wealthy and hate to have it poor, want it to be orderly and hate to have it chaotic, they should practice universal love and mutual benefit. This is the way [*Dao*] of the sage-kings and the principle of governing the empire, and it should not be neglected' (Chan 1963: 217). *The Art of War* of Sunzi (545?–470? BCE) highlights in its first chapter on 'Strategic Assessments' that there are five things any military strategist must appropriately measure and 'The five things are the way, the weather, the terrain, the leadership, and discipline' (Sun Tzu 2011: 1). As the first of the five, *Dao* is explained such that 'The Way means inducing the people to have the same aim as the leadership, so that they will share death and share life, without fear of danger' (Sun Tzu 2011: 2). The text further defines military strategy as the 'way of deception' (*bing zhe, gui dao ye* 兵者,詭道也), meaning that to ensure the success of one's operation a military strategist must employ various ways, or resort to any means, to deceive their enemies.

Legalism also makes good use of *Dao* to argue for enriching the state and strengthening the army. For example, in the *Book of Han Feizi*, *Dao* appears 242 times. While asserting that 'The Way is the beginning of all beings and the measure of right and wrong' (Chapter 5) (Han Feizi 2003: 15), Legalists place an emphasis on the governing skills of 'the enlightened ruler' (*ming jun* 明君) and the way of 'the worthy ruler' (*xian zhu* 賢主) who would employ the wise and the diligent to work for him. For Han Feizi, *Dao* implies a mysterious power behind governing: 'The Way lies in what cannot be seen, its function in what cannot be known. Be empty, still, and idle, and from your place of darkness observe the defects of others. See but do not appear to see; listen but do not seem to listen; know but do not let it be known that you know' (Han Feizi 2003: 16–17). However, the Legalist *Dao* is no longer the moral norm regulating people's mind and conduct. Instead, Han Feizi transformed *Dao* into different kinds of cunning or Machiavellian means for a powerful ruler to govern effectively.

A careful examination of how *Dao* is used in the texts of the Warring States period thus shows a change of emphasis. As the competition or clash between the states became more intense, *Dao* as the practical and technological way that helps people engage in all sorts of matters, from governing the country to launching a military campaign, increased its weight in comparison with earlier texts. Regarded as an effective means to achieve what is deemed an important goal, *Dao* was taken less as moral teachings than in earlier Confucian scholars or as a mysterious entity as in earlier Daoist philosophers. While remaining a kind of mystery in some contexts, *Dao* gradually reverted from a philosophized concept of the Way to its original meaning as a way (path) to reach the goal or as the means by which a task can be accomplished.

All these developments show that *Dao* is more like a paradox than a fixed object or entity. It is therefore better to preserve the Chinese character *Dao* as it is, not translating it as the Way or any other concept in other cultures. As a paradox, *Dao* includes many seemingly opposite interpretations and claims within itself. Metaphysically, it is both the 'Something' and the 'Nothing', both the origin of the world and its evolutional process, both the source and the function of power, both the universal and the particular. Epistemologically, it is both knowable and unknowable, both the learned experience and the *a priori* endowment, both concept and sensation. Ethically, it is both above humanity and within humanity, both the highest principle and the common experience, both the sublime ideal and the virtue each individual has to cultivate, both the primary guideline and concrete behavioural norms.

Paradoxical as *Dao* is, this further confirms that *Dao* is not merely a simple term or concept; rather it is the most profound way of life, at least for the majority of the Chinese intellectuals. In practice, *Dao* is the method or cluster of methods that are used for epistemological explorations of the truth. But more than that, it is also a profound belief in the cosmic order which guides believers in their way of life. This belief is deeply rooted in the minds and lives of the people who are determined to understand, manifest and follow *Dao*. It is seen in their thirst for the 'prevailing of the great *Dao*' (*da dao* 大道) in the political arena, and in their search for the realization of *Dao* under Heaven (*tian xia you dao* 天下有道) in reconstructing the world order. Just because of this belief, a large number of Chinese intellectuals were for most of Chinese history, and still are, fully convinced that the world is not merely what it appears to be but will become what it *should* be. This belief spurs an enthusiastic engagement in the intellectual pursuit of truth as well as in the search for ways to make a change for the better to the social and political reality of the world.

Concluding remarks: Contemporary applications

There remain many open questions concerning *Dao* and the Way in the twenty-first century. Should we read *Dao* as singular or as plural? Do historically different understandings of the Way point to the different aspects or dimensions of *Dao*, different ways to the same *Dao*, or to totally different '*Daos*'? If *Dao* is used as a plural rather than a singular word, what does this multiplicity of *Dao* mean? Would there be tensions between them which would further lead to conflict? Is this tension resolvable or can different ways be reconciled? These seemingly philosophical questions have a huge impact on how we lead our life in the contemporary world. Should we aim at the co-existence of different Ways? How should we deal with the tension that arises from the many Ways that are different or even opposite? In the time of Confucius, it was comparatively easier for him to say that human pursuits of *Dao* often lead to different paths, 'Those whose ways are different do not make plans together' (*Analects* 15.40). Today we might have to reverse this suggestion into an insistence that just because different people have different understandings of *Dao*, we must sit together, communicate and dialogue with one another, and be ready to make adjustment respectively. This is the importance of 'civilizational dialogue'. Mencius might have been right in his time to defend his belief in the oneness of *Dao* and to assert that if deviant views were allowed, the way of Confucius would not be made known, and that if the people were deceived by these incorrect doctrines, the *Dao* of humaneness and righteousness would be blocked. But today, we might have to rethink this fundamentalist position when not one but many diverse views, ideologies and philosophies prevail in different regions and among different peoples.

Despite certain hard expressions, Confucian discourses on *Dao* in general call for tolerance and sympathetic understanding towards cultural differences. While it is important to seek the oneness of different ways, their underlying idea is to accept and even encourage diverse manifestations of the Way in the world, and take it for granted that each of these manifestations has its own justification to run its own course. Derived from this understanding, a new form of '*Dao* metaphysics' is being revitalized as the ideological tool to support cultural diversity in an increasingly globalized and interconnected world where human beings take different paths to the common future. This means that we have to learn how to live together to avoid dying together, despite the fact that the latter scenario seems to loom larger than ever before, especially when we take into account such global challenges as climate changes, environmental disasters, ideological conflicts, violent and brutal wars, waves of pandemics, and AI technologies.

Finally, a comparative approach is implied by this '*Dao* metaphysics', because what is referred to as *Dao* varies from context to context in Chinese philosophical texts and daily conversations, either ancient or contemporary. In terms of modern Western disciplines, *Dao* is primarily used in the areas of metaphysics, ontology and ethics, but is also applicable in epistemology, politics and education, and the usages in these contexts may correspond to such English terms as 'being', 'principle', 'reason', 'law' on the one hand, and to 'ways', 'manners', 'methods', 'words', 'skills' on the other. In some texts *Dao* refers ambiguously to the beginning of beginnings or the cause of all causes, close to what might be termed as the first cause or first motion or first principle in Aristotle's *Physics*: '[I]f then everything that is in motion is moved by something, and the first mover is moved but not by anything else, it must be moved by itself,' and 'the first mover causes a motion that is eternal and causes it during an infinite time' (Aristotle 1991: 428, 446). In other contexts *Dao* seems to indicate specifically concrete ways or the means to get things done either naturally or consciously, in a similar sense to where it is said in the Hebrew Bible that in order to keep Adam out from the garden of Eden, God applied various *means* to 'guard the way to the tree of life' (Gen. 3:24) or to the sayings of the New Testament 'the way of the Lord' (Mt. 3:3), 'a way of salvation' (Acts 16:17) and 'the way of righteousness' (2 Pet. 2:21).

From a comparative perspective, we may conclude that while there are sufficient similarities between *Dao* and the Way, the metaphysics formed from them demonstrates obvious differences, even though these differences may be considered mutually supplementary rather than mutually exclusive. The differences may be summarized as threefold. First, the 'Way metaphysics' of Greco-Abrahamic thought starts with 'being' (God) from which time and space are generated, whereas apart from the mysterious uses in early Daoist philosophy *Dao* in general begins from 'doing' or 'acting'. This might explain why some contemporary Chinese philosophers argue that the first word of metaphysics is not the noun (being) but the verb (doing): in contrast with the Cartesian *cogito ergo sum*, they suggest a new dictum of *facio ergo sum* as the primary doctrine of the new metaphysics (Zhao 2023). Secondly, interpreted as principle, the Way implies cognitive knowledge or theological truth (*logos*) by following deductive logic. This diverges from the Confucian *Dao* that is focused on ethical guidelines and moral cultivation engaging the logic of inductive reasoning. From this we may understand why other Chinese philosophers stress the importance of 'affairs/things' (*shi*事) for a new type of 'concrete metaphysics' (Yang 2021). Thirdly, differing from the absolute and exclusive mentality concerning the Truth that took its initial form in the Greco-Abrahamic traditions and was further cultivated in the movements of Reformation and Enlightenment, a plural interpretation of *Dao* might open up new possibilities of an inclusive, flexible and comprehensive worldview. The more we look into the meaning, implication and philosophy of *Dao* and the Way, the more we find it urgent to cooperate and collaborate rather than to fight against one another. The insight to be gained from the metaphysics of *Dao* for contemporary times is that in the diversified cultures of the world, the only meaningful way to achieve well-being for humanity and sustainability of the earth may lie in a comprehensive understanding of *Dao* both as multiple ways and as the principle that transcends the division of the sacred and the secular. To ensure the common destiny of human beings as a whole, we must increase rather than decrease consensus on different ways to sustain biological and cultural diversity, and to protect the world from being torn apart by conflicting ideologies.

Notes

1. More recent English writers on Chinese philosophy tend to use its transliteration (*dao* or *tao*) rather than translations or interpretations, for example, Graham (1989), Hansen (1992), Kohn (ed. 2000), Meynard (2015). We will use the italic *Dao* with

the first letter in capital as a proper noun throughout this chapter to indicate that it is a special Chinese character containing multiple meanings and references of thought, of which Confucianism and Daoism stand out as the two most important ones.
2. 'The ability to take as analogy what is near at hand can be called the method (*fang*) of benevolence' (Confucius 1979: 85). In this context what Confucius refers to as 'the method of benevolence' is close to what is meant by the method of *Dao*, which can be seen more clearly in another saying of his that 'Wealth and high position are what men desire but unless I got them in the right way (*Dao*) I would not remain in them' (Confucius 1979: 3).
3. There are eight times when the 'art of *Dao*' (*Dao shu*) is mentioned in the text of Zhuangzi. In Chapter 6 people are compared with fish and are told to 'forget each other in the arts of *Dao*', while in Chapter 33 it is argued that because his contemporary people no longer 'perceived the purity of Heaven and earth, the great body of the ancients, "the art of the Way" in time comes to be rent and torn apart by the world' (Zhuangzi 2013: 50, 289).
4. All quotations with the numbers of their chapters in *Daode jing* are my own translations in light of D. C. Lau (1963), *Lao Tzu Tao Te Ching*. The same is also true for the quotations from the *Analects of Confucius*, unless referred to otherwise. However, the translations of Mencius mainly come from D.C. Lau's *Mencius* (1970), while those of the *Great Learning* and the *Doctrine of the Mean* from Wing-tsit Chan (1963). The *Doctrine of the Mean* mentioned above is one of the Four Books in the Confucian tradition, and is traditionally believed to have been composed by the grandson of Confucius, Zisi (子思, 483?–402? BCE).
5. For example, the Oxford Professor of Chinese, William Soothill translated *tian dao* 天道 as 'the Laws of Heaven' (Confucius 1910: 263).
6. James Legge translated this sentence as 'that which is antecedent to the material form exists, we say, as an ideal method, and that which is subsequent to the material form exists, we say, as a definite thing' (*The I Ching* 1899: 377). By adding a character for learning (*xue* 學), *xing er shang* (形而上, 'above the form'), Japanese scholars coined a new term for 'metaphysics' at the end of the nineteenth century, which has been since accepted as a standard term in modern Chinese philosophy.
7. For Plato, 'The form must be the same, but the material may vary' (*Cratylus* 2009: 389). Using as an example that blacksmiths make tools from iron, Plato explains why the forms are timeless and unchanging, physical things are in a constant change of existence, and why forms are unqualified perfection, while physical things are qualified and conditioned: 'different blacksmiths, who are making the same tool for the same type of work, don't all make it out of the same iron. But as long as they give it the same form – even if that form is embodied in different iron – the tool will be correct' (Plato 1997: 108).
8. Richard Wilhelm used 'the Creative' and 'the Receptive' to translate *qian* 乾 and *kun* 坤, and the Way to translate *Dao* (*I Ching or Book of Changes* 1989: 486, 285).
9. In the *Mathews' Chinese-English Dictionary*, *shen dao* is translated as 'the Way of God' (p. 883). This seems to be in tune with the Jewish and Christian uses of the

Hebrew word *derek*: 'To walk in the ways of God meant to live according to his will and commandments' (Deut. 10:12-13; 1 Kgs. 3:14). In Isaiah 'the way of the Lord' refers to God's provision of deliverance from enslavement or exile (Isa. 40:3; 43:16-19). *Derek* is also used to identify 'the overall direction of a person's life, whether righteous or wicked' (*Eerdmans Dictionary of the Bible* 2000: 1370).
10. In comparison with the creation account in the Book of Genesis, Daoist genesis is not personal but much more abstract: 'Dao gives birth to the One; the One gives birth to two; two give birth to three; and three give birth to the myriad things' (Chapter 42).
11. *Zhuangzi*, Chapter 2 (Watson 2013: 11).
12. *Zhuangzi*, Chapter 6. 'The Way has its reality and its signs but is without action or form. You can hand it down, but you cannot receive it; you can get it, but you cannot see it. It is its own source, its own root. Before Heaven and earth existed, it was there, firm from ancient times. It gave spirituality to the spirits and to God; it gave birth to Heaven and to earth. It exists beyond the highest point, and yet you cannot call it lofty; it exists beneath the limit of the six directions, and yet you cannot call it deep. It was born before Heaven and earth, and yet you cannot say it has been there for long; it is earlier than the earliest time, and yet you cannot call it old.' Watson 2013: 45.
13. *Zhuangzi*, Chapter 13. 'It is the Way of heaven to keep moving and to allow no piling up – hence the ten thousand things come to completion. It is the Way of the emperor to keep moving and to allow no piling up – hence the whole world repairs to his court. It is the Way of the sage to keep moving and to allow no piling up – hence all within the seas bow to him.' Watson 2013: 88.
14. For Edward Slingerland, '"human nature" and the "Way of Heaven" collectively refer to the range of things that are beyond human control, and the point is that the Master focused on what was within human control: commitment to learning and the Confucian Way' (Confucius 2003: 45).

References

Aristotle (1976), *Ethics*, trans. J. A. K. Thomson, revised with notes and appendices by Hugh Tredennick, introduction and bibliography by Jonathan Barnes, London: Penguin Classics.
Aristotle (1991), *The Complete Works of Aristotle*, The revised Oxford trans., ed. Jonathan Barnes, Volume 1 and Volume 2. Princeton: Princeton University Press.
Aristotle (1992), *The Politics*, trans. T. A. Sinclair, revised and re-presented by Trevor J. Saunders. London: Penguin Classics.
Bodnar, Istvan (stb@elte.hu) (2023), '*Aristotle's Natural Philosophy: Movers and Unmoved Mover*', Stanford Encyclopedia of Philosophy.
Chan, Wing-tsit (compiled and translated, 1963), *A Source Book in Chinese Philosophy*. New York: Columbia University Press.

Ching, Julia (1993), *Chinese Religions*. Houndmills and London: The McMillian Press.
Confucius (1910), *The Analects of Confucius*, trans. William Edward Soothill, published by the author, printed by the Fukuin Printing, Yokohama.
Confucius (1979), *The Analects*, translated with an introduction by D. C. Lau. London: Penguin Books.
Confucius (2003), *The Analects with Selections from Traditionary Commentaries*, trans. Edward Slingerland. Indianapolis/Cambridge: Hackett Publishing.
The Concise Oxford Dictionary (2001), 10th ed., ed. Judy Pearsall. Oxford and New York: Oxford University Press.
Dawson, Raymond (1978), *The Chinese Experience*. London: Weidenfeld and Nicolson.
de Bary, Wm. Theodore, and Irene Bloom (eds.) (1999), *Sources of Chinese Tradition*, 2nd ed., vol. 1. New York: Columbia University Press.
Eerdmans Dictionary of the Bible (2000), ed. David Noel Freedman (editor-in-chief). Grand Rapids, MI, and Cambridge: William B. Eerdman's Publishing.
Feizi, Han (2003), *Basic Writings*, trans. Burton Watson. New York: Columbia University Press.
Fingarette, Herbert (1972), *Confucius – The Secular as Sacred*. New York: Harper Torchbook.
Graham, A. C. (1989), *Disputers of the Tao: Philosophical Argument in Ancient China*. LaSalle, IL: Open Court.
Hansen, Chad (1992), *A Daoist Theory of Chinese Thought*. Oxford and New York: Oxford University Press.
Hanyu Dazidian 漢語大字典 (1993). Chengdu: *Sichuan cishu chubanshe* 四川辭書出版社.
The I Ching (1899), trans. James Legge, In the *Sacred Books of the East*, translated by various oriental scholars and edited by Max Muller, Volume XVI. Clarendon Press.
I Ching or Book of Changes (1989), The Richard Wilhelm translation, rendered into English by Cary F. Baynes, with a forward by C. G. Jung. London: Penguin Books.
Kenny, Anthony (2010), *A New History of Western Philosophy*. Oxford: Clarendon Press.
Kohn, Livia (ed.) (2000), *Daoism Handbook*. Leiden-Boston-Kohn: Brill.
Mathews' Chinese-English Dictionary (A Chinese-English Dictionary compiled for the China Inland Mission by R. H. Mathews, Shanghai: China Inland Mission and Presbyterian Mission Press, 1931), revised American Edition. Cambridge: Massachusetts, 1966.
Mernard, Thierry, SJ (2015), *The Jesuit Reading of Confucius–The First Complete Translation of the Lunyu (1687)*. Published in the West, Leiden Boston: Brill.
The New Oxford Annotated Bible with the Apocrypha (1973), ed. Herbert G. May and Bruce M. Metzger. New York: Oxford University Press.
Plato (1997), *Complete Works*, edited with introduction and notes, by John M. Cooper, Associate Editor, D. S. Hutchinson. Indianapolis, IN/Cambridge: Hackett Publishing.
Plato (2000), *The Republic*, ed. G. R. F. Ferrari, trans. Tom Griffith. Cambridge: Cambridge University Press.
Ryan, Sharon (2023), 'Wisdom', in Edward N. Zalta and Uri Nodelman (eds.), *The Stanford Encyclopedia of Philosophy* Cambridge. (Fall 2023 Edition), URL = https://plato.stanford.edu/archives/fall2023/entries/wisdom/.

Shen, Xu 许慎 (2002), *Shuowen jiezi xinding* 說文解字新訂. Beijing: *Zhonghua shuju*.

Stang, Nicholas F. (2023), 'Kant's Transcendental Idealism', in Edward N. Zalta and Uri Nodelman (eds.), *The Stanford Encyclopedia of Philosophy* (Winter 2023 Edition), URL = https://plato.stanford.edu/archives/win2023/entries/kant-transcendental-idealism/.

Tingyang, Zhao 赵汀阳 (2023), *Metaphysics on Verbs* 寻找动词的形而上学. Beijing: Sanlian shudian.

Tzu, Lae (1963), *Tao Te Ching*, translated with an introduction by D. C. Lau. London: Penguin Classics.

Tzu, Sun (2011), *The Art of War*, trans. Thomas Cleary. Boston, MA, and London: Shambhala.

Xunzi荀子 (2014), *The Complete Text*, trans. Eric Hutton. Princeton, NJ: Princeton University Press.

Yang Guorong 杨国荣 (2021), *Humanity and the World: Contemplating from the Perspective of Affairs*人与世界:以事观之. Beijing: Sanlian shudian.

Zhuangzi (2013), *The Complete Works of Zhuangzi*, trans. Burton Watson. New York: Columbia University Press.

3

Generative harmony: Origins and becoming in Confucian metaphysics

Chenyang Li

This chapter reconstructs an account of generative harmony as a concept of Chinese metaphysics. The first section outlines various conceptions of harmony and introduces generative harmony as an alternative. The second investigates and reformulates the conception of generative harmony as expounded by ancient Chinese thinkers. Thirdly, I provide an account of the role of generative harmony in the formation and evolution of the world in ancient Chinese cosmogony. The final section elucidates the role of generative harmony in Chinese metaphysics and argues for its plausibility on the basis of reflections on modern scientific thought.

Conceptions of harmony

There are various understandings of 'harmony'. The most common is 'harmony as concord'. In this understanding, harmony is an agreeable, friendly and philosophically unsophisticated state; in English and in other Western languages, harmony refers to the state of peacefulness and agreement. Rebecca Oxford has summarized the various meanings of 'harmony' in terms of four *a*'s, namely, *agreement, amity, attitude of calm* and *a pleasing arrangement*. In Oxford's analysis, *agreement* relates to *accord, compatibility* and *reconciliation*. Thus, *agreement* is connected to *amity*, which relates to meanings such as *friendship* and *collaboration*. Both *agreement* and *amity* can result in an 'attitude of calm'. Finally, 'a pleasing arrangement' includes a sense of *balance, proportion* and *coherence*, all of which are possible outcomes of the prior three themes in this cluster of meanings (Oxford 2022: 285). Thus, harmony is pure accord, freed from tension, opposition or conflict.

Such a notion has little value for philosophy. In her *Love's Knowledge*, Martha Nussbaum sees this sense of 'innocent harmony' as irrelevant to solving moral problems in real life:

> Moral objectivity about the value of a person (or, presumably, any other source of moral claims) requires, evidently, the ability to see that item as distinct from other items; this in turn requires the ability to see it not as a deep part of an innocent harmony but as a value that can be contrasted or opposed to others, whose demands can potentially conflict with other demands.
>
> (Nussbaum 1990: 131)

Innocence, as used in this sense by Nussbaum, suggests naivety. Obviously, people's moral encounters in real life include conflicts and dilemmas, which are far from this kind of harmony. The ideal of innocent harmony is unrealistic and can disempower us in solving moral problems. Hence, we should give up on the ideal of such harmony and be prepared to tackle conflicting and challenging issues in real life.

A different understanding is of 'harmony through conformity'. In Plato's idea of harmony Karl Popper sees a source of oppression and totalitarianism. Popper writes:

> Certain cogs will be virtuous, i.e. fit, only if they are ('by their nature') large; others if they are strong; and others if they are smooth. But the virtue of keeping to one's place will be common to all of them; and it will at the same time be a virtue of the whole: that of being properly fitted together – of being in harmony. To this universal virtue Plato gives the name 'justice.' This procedure is perfectly consistent and it is fully justified from the point of view of totalitarian morality. If the individual is nothing but a cog, then ethics is nothing but the study of how to fit him into the whole.
>
> (Popper 1945: 94)

In his reading of Plato, harmony is being 'perfectly consistent', and is to conform to a given order.[1] Popper argues that an essential feature of such harmony is the virtue of 'keeping one's place' as cogs in the great clockwork of the state. In doing so, one eliminates individuality and becomes part of a faceless and unified whole.

Like 'innocent harmony', 'consistent harmony' is also a common understanding. In contemporary China, 'harmony' or *he-xie* is often used in this oppressive sense. In its name, differing opinions are silenced into uniformity. Being harmonized, or *he-xie*'ed, means being forced to conform to a consistent state in society as prescribed by the government. In China's WeChat groups, for instance, group members often remind one another not to say certain kinds of things to avoid becoming *he-xie*'ed, that is, being shut down by the government for not conforming to a singular official voice.

Thus, in these understandings, harmony is either uselessly innocent and naive or seriously oppressive and detrimental to healthy society. Such concepts have no moral value in the contemporary world.

A third meaning of harmony, traceable to ancient times, is oppositional harmony. As Heraclitus famously claims, 'The opposite is good, and from opposing things comes the most beautiful harmony, and all things are generated by strife' (F8). Heraclitus' emphasis is on the role of tension and strife in harmony. For him, what is at variance agrees with itself, and harmony is an attunement of opposite tensions, like that of the bow and the lyre (F51). Thus, harmony is not free from tension; tension is intrinsic to harmony. In other words, harmony is a unity composed of conflicting parts (Kahn 1979: 200). Heraclitus' oppositional harmony should be understood in the context of his dynamic view, which sees the world as one of constant becoming, like fire. In such a world, oppositions are not permanent states of affairs. They get transformed and reformulated. It is in such constant becoming that harmony takes place. His conception of harmony, however, is underdeveloped. While insisting that oppositions are part of harmony, Heraclitus does not explain how opposite tensions can be incorporated or transformed into harmony. His theory, nevertheless, leaves room for philosophical imagination and exploration. Heraclitus provides good authority for us to think of harmony in ways different from the currently popular notions of 'innocent harmony' and 'consistent harmony'.

Drawing on studies of Confucian philosophy of harmony, Li-Ching Ho and Keith C. Barton have recently argued for a conception of 'critical harmony'. Contrary to the Platonic view of harmony as interpreted by Popper, Ho and Barton contend that 'harmony requires a sense of criticality that includes embracing conflict and tension, valuing difference and diversity, and striving for balance among divergent voices' (Ho and Barton 2022: 276–7). In their view, harmony must incorporate a critical dimension by valuing difference and diversity, managing conflict and tension, and striving for balance among divergent voices. Accordingly, tension that naturally occurs with the contestation of views is not problematic but is, instead, a generative element that can further contribute to the goal of harmony.

The above understandings of harmony do not exhaust its meanings in contemporary usage. They nevertheless give us a sense of the diversity of meanings and set a context for the discussion that follows. These theories, in contrast to Heraclitus' metaphysical reflections, focus mainly on the social domain. Ho and Barton, for example, argue that such a conception of harmony has an important role in civic education. I take this work as an indication that people have started to rethink and reimagine the concept of harmony in contemporary times.

In this chapter, however, my focus is on the metaphysical realm. Previously, I have argued that 'Confucian harmony is a dynamic, generative process' (Li 2014: 1). In what follows, I reconstruct a conception of generative harmony by drawing on ancient Chinese thinkers. In such an understanding, harmony is a process through which new things are produced, not a final, finished state of affairs; it is rather an activity that brings new states of affairs into existence and sustains their renewal.

Generative harmony

The Chinese character that we use in discussion of harmony is *he* 和, pronounced similarly to the syllable *ho* in *horizon*. The word in different characters originally means mixing together different things such as wine with water in a desired proportion, or mixing sounds to produce music.[2] The earliest attempt to give the word a conceptual definition was made by a scholar-minister and philosopher Shi Bo, who lived towards the end of the Western Zhou period and was active around 780 BCE. In the *Discourse on the States*, Shi Bo defines *he* as a productive process of gathering different things together to generate a new pattern of existence. Shi states:

> Harmony is generative of things. Homogeneity does not continue. When things balance one another it is called harmony. Consequently, they flourish and propagate.
>
> (Lai 2000: 746)

Shi emphasizes heterogeneity as the central feature of harmony. He states:

> A single sound is not musical, a single colour does not constitute a beautiful pattern, a single flavour does not make a delicious dish, and a single thing does not make harmony.
>
> (Lai 2000: 746)

In his view, if we use the same thing to complement the same thing, nothing is accomplished. He claims that ancient sage-kings were exemplars as they 'harmonized five flavours to befit the taste and the six measures of sounds to attune the ear, and, thus, they "achieved the highest level of harmony in society"' (Lai 2000: 746–7).

Later, another scholar-minister and philosopher Yan Ying (?–500 BCE) elaborated more on the meaning of harmony. The *Zuo Commentary of the Spring and Autumn Annals*, a Confucian classic text, records Yan Ying's articulation of the notion of harmony as follows:

> Harmony is like making soup. One needs water, fire, vinegar, sauce, salt, and plum to cook fish and meat. One needs to cook them with firewood. The cook needs to mingle (*he*) ingredients together to balance the taste. He needs to compensate for deficiencies and to reduce excessiveness. In eating [such balanced food], the virtuous person (*junzi*) achieves a balanced heart-mind.
>
> (TTC: 2093)

Yan Ying also made an analogy of harmony with making music:

> Sounds are like flavours. Different elements complete each other: one breath, two styles, three types, four instruments, five sounds, six measures, seven notes, eight winds, and nine songs. Different sounds complement each other: the clear and the thick, the large and the small, the short and the long, the fast and the slow, the sorrowful and the joyful, the strong and the tender, the lingering and the rapid, the high and the low, the

in and the out, and the close and the diffuse. The good person listens to this kind of music to harmonize his heart-mind.

(TTC: 2093–4)

These metaphors can be interpreted in different ways. The soup metaphor seems to rely on the cook, an external controlling agency, to harmonize the various ingredients. However, the music metaphor is clearly different; ancient Chinese musical troupes did not have a conductor. If we take Yan Ying to use both metaphors to make the same point, as he clearly intended, then external agency is not the point. Along the lines of Shi Bo's definition, Yan Ying maintains that harmony involves mingling various elements into a composite whole, as in making soup or in performing music. In such processes, each element with its own characteristics realizes its potential in contributing to the good of the whole.

In Yan Ying's conception, harmony involves heterogeneity, coordination and cooperation between diverse things that are in some kind of tension. Through such a dynamic process, each element transforms itself and becomes an organic part of the generated whole in mutual enhancement.

Anticipating the concerns raised by later thinkers such as Popper, Yan Ying specifically distinguished harmony from forced agreement or conformity. In a conversation with the duke of the state of Qi, the duke brags about the 'harmony (*he*)' between him and his minister Ju. Yan Ying counters that their relationship was mere homogeneity (*tong* 同, sameness) rather than harmony, because the minister always conformed to the duke's views. Unlike making a delicious soup by mixing a variety of ingredients, their relationship was like adding water to water and like repeating the same note in making music (TTC: 2094). Evidently, the duke holds dominance over the minister.[3] If their relationship can be called 'harmony', it is only 'consistent harmony' as in Plato as criticized by Popper. Yan Ying explicitly refuses to call their relationship *he*, because for Yan Ying *he* is generative harmony which requires diversity and creative tension. In the *Analects*, Confucius explicitly endorses such an idea when he says that 'virtuous people harmonize without becoming homogenized' (*he er bu tong* 和而不同, *Analects* 13.23). Confucian harmony as presented this way is not 'consistent harmony' that presses for uniformity and conformity.

The Confucian philosophy of generative harmony, as I have explained elsewhere, can be characterized as having the following features:

1. Heterogeneity. Harmony presupposes two or more co-existing parties. These parties are not uniform, and possess varied dispositions.
2. Tension. Various parties interact with one another. Tension at various levels arises naturally from difference.
3. Coordination and cooperation. While tension may result in conflict, it also places constraints on parties in interaction and generates energy to advance

coordination. In coordination, involved parties make accommodation to one another and preserve their favourable characteristics.
4   Transformation and growth. Through coordination, tension is transformed and conflict is reconciled into a favourable environment for each party to flourish. In this process, involved parties undergo mutual transformation and form harmonious relationships.
5   Renewal. Harmony is achieved not as a final state, but as stages in an ongoing process. It admits of degrees. A harmonious relationship is maintained through continuous renewal. (Li 2014: 9)

Such a concept of harmony is a complex one. Perhaps examples would help elucidate this feature. In his study of human knowledge, John Locke famously differentiates simple ideas and complex ideas. At the risk of oversimplification, these can be explained as follows: a simple idea results from a simple sensation, like the colour red; a complex idea is a collection of associated simple ideas. For example 'rose' is a complex idea as it is a collection of simple ideas, such as the colour red, fragrant smell, and a certain shape and size, etc. Locke's concept of complex ideas as a mere collection of simple ideas (plus substance) appears philosophically crude. It nevertheless points to an important difference between two kinds of ideas or concepts. A more philosophically complex idea is Hegel's notion of *aufheben*. Usually translated into English as 'sublate', the word means 'abolish', 'preserve' and 'transcend' at the same time. Thus, an entity can be seen as undergoing *Aufhebung* when it negates part of itself while transcending itself into a higher stage of existence, as when a seed grows into a sprout. Generative harmony, I propose, is a complex concept that contains several phases in this way. *Generative harmony presents a kind of unity that comprises diversity and tension. Yet, it is through diversity and tension that transformation takes place. Consequently, new states of affairs are generated in the process of the world's formation and re-formation.*

In the next section, I will investigate how this concept has been used in metaphysics by ancient Chinese philosophers.

Generative harmony and Chinese cosmogony

The philosophical significance of generative harmony should be understood in the context of Chinese metaphysics and cosmogony. Traditional Chinese metaphysical views of the world are grounded on the concept of *qi* 氣, an intangible material or energy that is self-generating and can take concrete forms of beings in the world. This concept provides the context for a dynamic metaphysical view of the world. In

Chinese cosmogenic theory, the primordial *qi*, whose original state is described as *hundun* 混沌, the formless and orderless, constitutes the world via an evolutionary process enacted through generative harmony.

The *Daoyuan* 道原 article of the Mawangdui Silk Texts describes the original state as a primordial 'One' (*yi* 一), the first natural number. It stands for the undifferentiated beginning. The text claims that, in the very beginning, 'all things were undifferentiated and unsubstantiated. The undifferentiated and unsubstantiated is the One' (Chen 2007: 38). This 'One' is the original whole of the *hundun* or chaos. The text explicitly designates the working of the One as harmony:

> Its name is One, its home is non-substantiation, its nature is effortless action, and its function is harmony.
>
> (ibid.)

Thus, the 'One' does not have a pre-given form. 'Effortless action' suggests that no effort is made through an external or independent agency. Because it carries the function of harmonization, the subsequently formed world is generated through a process of generative harmony. As shown by the study by contemporary philosopher Ding Sixin 丁四新,

> In the *Daoyuan* text, the idea of 'harmony' is not about harmonious relations among formed things. Rather it is the necessary and sufficient condition for generating the myriad things. Fundamentally speaking, without harmony there cannot be the generation of concrete things.
>
> (Ding 2015)

In a similar vein, the *Jing: Guan* 經-觀 article of the Mawangdui Silk Texts describes the beginning of the cosmos in terms of *hundun*:

> There was neither darkness nor brightness, neither *yin* nor *yang*. With *yin* and *yang* not being set, there is nothing to name for. Then it started to be divided into two, as *yin* and *yang*, and further divided into the four seasons.
>
> (Chen 2007: 210)

Darkness and brightness suggest night and day. The original *hundun* had no such differentiation or clarity at the beginning. It was even more primordial than the forces of *yin* and *yang*.

It would be helpful to compare this view with that of the *Book of Changes*, a text usually regarded as the first book among all the Confucian canon. According to the *Book of Changes*, the world is in perpetual evolution through change – so much so that Change (*yi* 易) is its primary concept and is embedded in the book's Chinese title *Yi-jing* (易經). Everything in the world is generated, both living and non-living, through the collaboration of the forces of *yin* and *yang*. The *Book of Changes* states:

The Change has its Ultimate Point. It generates the Two Wings. The Two Wings produce the Four Seasons; the Four Seasons then give birth to the Eight Hexagrams.[4]

(TTC: 82)

The Change refers to the fundamental characteristic of the cosmos as the text characterizes it. It is the Way/*Dao*. The Ultimate Point stands for the beginning. The Two Wings refers to *yin* and *yang*. The interaction of these forces propels the original state into the Four Seasons, implying the overall structure of our world. Within the Four Seasons, all other things are generated, which are represented by the variations of the Eight Hexagrams. The passage quoted above does not explicitly mention harmony; however, this discussion in the context of the *Book of Changes* should be understood in connection with harmony, as the central theme of the *Book of Changes* is how the interactive forces of *yin* and *yang* give rise to harmony through change (Yu 2006). *Yin* and *yang* are not concrete things; they are symbols of forces in interaction, tension, and coordination. Neither *yin* nor *yang* can exist on its own, nor can they act without the other. In any particular case, the forces of *yin* and *yang* may not be in perfect symmetry. However, on a large scale and over the long run, these forces are balanced. When they work together, they are in harmony. Harmony in such a cosmic process is evidently generative, as the driving engine for the world to renew itself by producing new things.

Such a changing world is characterized by the expression of '*sheng-sheng* 生生', doubling the word 'generating' to enforce its emphasis on the great creativity of such a world. The compound term is sometimes translated as 'creative creativity'. The *Book of Changes* claims that 'creative creativity is called the Change' (生生之謂易, TTC: 78). *Sheng-sheng* does not spring out of any mysterious force, but out of the process of creative harmony. If we use a Chinese expression, it is that *sheng-sheng ji he sheng* 生生即和生, namely, creative creativity is achieved through generative harmony. Unlike Henri Bergson's 'vital impetus' (*Élan vital*, Bergson 1998), *sheng-sheng* is neither confined to living entities nor driven by an unexplainable force.

Resonating with the *Book of Changes*, the author of the *Jing: Guan* claims that the harmonizing interaction of *yin* and *yang* leads to the generation of myriad things (Chen 2007: 210). Accordingly, the beginning of the cosmos as the undifferentiated One evolves when generative harmony makes its way in the world, and this originally formless One generates everything in the world through a process of generative harmonization.

Generative harmony in this sense can be characterized as 'deep harmony', because it does not presuppose an ultimate pre-set order in the world, whether in the form of an intelligent mind (the divine), Pythagorean numbers, or Platonic forms. In this conception of Chinese cosmogony, deep harmony is a self-generating harmony that reaches the most fundamental level of the world.

This harmony of *yin* and *yang* creating the world also finds its parallel in the *Daodejing*. Chapter 42 states:

> Dao generates One; One generates Two; Two generates Three; Three generates the myriad things. The myriad things carry *yin* and embrace *yang*, blending these types of *qi* in harmony.

The *Daodejing* is vague on specific definitions. One plausible interpretation is that Two alludes to the forces of *yin* and *yang*. The interaction of these types of *qi* results in the generation of the myriad things. Such a process is one of generative harmony.

This idea of generative harmony finds its strong advocate in the Song dynasty philosopher Zhang Zai 張載 (1020–77). In his landmark work *Enlightening the Ignorant* (*Zheng Meng* 正蒙), Zhang provides a more systematic account of generative harmony, which he calls the 'Great Harmony'. He writes:

> The Great Harmony is called the Way (Dao). It embraces the nature which underlies all counter processes of floating and sinking, rising and falling, and motion and rest. It is the origin of the process of fusion and intermingling, of overcoming and being overcome, and of expansion and contraction. At the commencement, these processes are incipient, subtle, obscure, easy, and simple, but at the end they are extensive, great, strong, and firm.
>
> (Chan 1963: 500)

These changes are driven by the forces of *yin* (坤 *kun*) and *yang* (乾 *qian*) acting in harmony. Zhang maintains that the Dao of the world is Great Harmony because the cosmos is in the process of fusion and intermingling like fleeting forces moving in all directions. For Zhang, understanding this fundamental idea of the operation of the cosmos is to understand the teachings of the *Book of Changes* and the Dao (Chan 1963: 501).

In Zhang's view, *qi* as the original state of the cosmos is absolutely tranquil, formless and orderless. It is called Great Vacuity (Great Void, 太虛, *taixu*) because it is the undifferentiated and unadorned One. There is no-*thing* in it yet. The primordial *qi* evolves to engender the two fundamental forces of *yin* and *yang*, and through integration of these forces gives rise to various kinds of being (Chan 1963: 506). Zhang writes:

> In its original state of Great Vacuity, material force is absolutely tranquil and formless. As it is acted upon, it engenders the two fundamental elements of *yin* and *yang*, and through integration gives rise to forms [*xiang* 象].
>
> (Chan 1963: 506)

The word translated as 'forms' by Wing-Tsit Chan is *xiang*. The word refers to concrete forms and appearances that *qi* takes in existence as various things in the world.[5]

Zhang specifically notes the role of opposition and tension in harmony, when he writes:

> As there are forms [of various things], there are their opposites. These opposites necessarily stand in opposition to what they do. Opposition leads to conflict, which will necessarily be reconciled and resolved.
>
> (Chan 1963: 506)

In Zhang's view, when various things are generated, their differences lead to tension and opposition. However, the word *bi*, which Chan has translated above as 'necessarily', is more accurately interpreted as 'must'. 'Must' can mean 'necessity', as in 'you must drink water to live'. But it can also mean being required by a need or purpose without a physical sense of necessity, as in 'you must pay taxes'. In the context of Zhang's saying, the statement should be understood as meaning that when opposition leads to conflict, conflict should be resolved by harmony because it alone can provide a satisfactory resolution.

In summary: Chinese cosmogony does not presuppose an external creator with a predetermined plan for the emergence of the cosmos. Instead, the formation of the world as we know it comes from an evolutionary process of the original orderless stuff. The evolution unfolds through a self-emerging process of generative harmony, which takes place in the interaction of the forces of *yin* and *yang*.

These ancient Confucian thinkers hold that harmony is the general trend of the world; it has evolved from the primordial chaos, which is neither good nor bad, into a world that is mostly good. This process of generative harmony is therefore a positive thing to be advanced and a positive value to be pursued.

Generative harmony and the metaphysics of becoming

In reference to the Big Bang theory of the universe, American astronomer and planetary physicist Robert Jastrow famously wrote:

> For the scientist who has lived by his faith in the power of reason, the story ends like a bad dream. He has scaled the mountains of ignorance; he is about to conquer the highest peak; as he pulls himself over the final rock, he is greeted by a band of theologians who have been sitting there for centuries.
>
> (Jastrow 1978: 116)

In other words, what scientists have come up with in their search finds its blueprint in ancient religious texts. To what extent the Big Bang theory confirms ancient religious views is debatable. Still more controversial is whether the theory supports the belief that the universe has a creator as Jastrow suspected. Nevertheless, it does appear that the ancient Chinese cosmogenic theory of *qi* and generative harmony is largely consistent with the Big Bang theory. Indeed, one could argue that Chinese theory is even more aligned with the Big Bang theory than is a religious view dependent on a divine creator.

Stephen Hawking, for example, holds that we cannot say anything about the time before the Big Bang because there is no time then (Hawking 2018: 37–8). This echoes the way in which Chinese thinkers have labelled the beginning stage the 'One' or 'Great Vacuity', of which little can be said. Whereas the Chinese have used the terminology of the forces of *yin* and *yang*, Hawking's scientific theory points to positive and negative energy. Hawking maintains that when the Big Bang produced a massive amount of positive energy, it also produced an equal amount of negative energy; there is a kind of perfect symmetry in the universe. This is, as Hawking describes it, like digging a hole to build a hill (Hawking 2018: 32). For Hawking, the balance of positive energy and negative energy is an important ingredient in our understanding of the subsequent formation of the universe. For ancient Chinese thinkers, it is the forces of *yin* and *yang* through generative harmony.

Through his study of time, the renowned physicist C. K. Raju discovered connections between spontaneity and order. In the physical world, spontaneous events will decrease entropy. A decrease of entropy is the same as the creation of order. This phenomenon shows creativity in the world without a central agency. In his essay entitled 'The Harmony Principle', Raju connects his theory of time and order to ethics. He argues that order, in the physical sense, is essential for biological survival. At the physical level, a human being is a vast collection of molecules that exist in a highly ordered state. Departure from this order entails illness and death; orderliness of the body is a must for the continued existence of a living organism (Raju 2013: 598). He relates such spontaneous natural order in the physical world to the positive human experience of it:

> The spontaneous creation of order is 'hardwired' to the deep sense of satisfaction one gets from a creative insight, the creative satisfaction that one gets from, for example, spontaneously arranging ideas, or musical notes, in a particularly interesting and novel pattern.
>
> (Raju 2013: 601)

Raju laments that there is no satisfactory English word for this phenomenon. The Western concept coming closest to such a notion of spontaneity is harmony (ibid.).

Raju's concept of harmony may not be the same as creative harmony discussed above. But in important ways his idea is analogous to creative harmony as reconstructed from Chinese thought: spontaneous events take place in the world without a predetermined plan, and with spontaneous events comes harmony which is a creative process.

The cosmogenic account of generative harmony illustrated in the previous section of this chapter only presents a vague concept, far from scientific. Modern scientific theories as represented above at most make generative harmony plausible, providing indirect support; they cannot of themselves establish generative harmony as a metaphysical theory. A metaphysical theory must be applicable to the world as we experience it in everyday life.

Aristotle famously uses four causes, or four senses of 'why', to explain the existence of things in the world, namely 'that out of which a thing comes to be, and which persists' (*Physics* 194b24). The first is material cause, which explains the aspect of things determined by the material that composes them; thus a house is made of bricks. The second is formal cause, which points to the form or pattern that makes material into a particular type of thing. It reveals the essence of a thing; thus the shape and design make a house a house rather than merely a pile of bricks. The third cause is the efficient cause, which is 'the primary source of change or rest' (*Physics* 194b30). The producer, for instance, is the efficient cause of the product. The fourth cause is the final cause. For Aristotle, the final cause is 'the end (*telos*), that for which a thing is done' (*Physics* 194b33). Health, for example, is the cause of walking, because someone walks in order to be healthy. These four causes provide explanations for the being of a thing in its different aspects and describe the 'why' of a thing's being.

By contrast with this Aristotelian framework, Chinese philosophy is not teleological. In Chinese philosophy, the question to address is more about 'how' than 'why'. If we take generative harmony as an answer to the 'how' question in Chinese metaphysical theory, what can be said about it?

I suggest that the mechanism of generative harmony enacting the formation and re-formation of things in the world can be understood in a way analogous to the role of evolution in explaining species in the world. Evolution is a process without teleology. It addresses 'how' rather than 'why'. On its account, mutations naturally occur. The living environment of a species and its own characteristics together determine its suitability or otherwise in the world. A viable species must fit its environment. But the species is also part of the environment as far as other species are concerned. In an important sense, there is mutual adjustment between a species and its environment, and a species persists if it has a fitting relationship with its environment. However, equilibrium between a species and its environment is temporary and transitional. Mutations in a species and changes in its environment pose tension between the species and its environment. Thus, evolution never ends. A species' fitness for survival has to be sustained through continuous renewal.

Generative harmony can be seen in a similar light. It is a process through which different things come together to form a new pattern of existence that is greater than the sum of the separate existences of each involved. Any existing thing is always in relation with some other existing things in its environment. It is a complex affair;

there is a sort of mutual dependence among coexisting things. As each existing thing tends to hold on to its own characteristics, there tends to be tension with other things. In their coexistence, different things need to adapt to the environment through mutual adjustment, mutual accommodation and mutual transformation. Through such processes, existing things renew their existence, new things are generated and new features are developed. This is generative harmony at work. Together, there is a kind of 'optimizing symbiosis', to borrow an expression from Roger Ames (Ames 2020).[6] Such optimizing symbiosis, however, is generative in character. In Xunzi's (third century BCE) words:

> *Yin* and *yang* undergo their great transformation, and winds and rain are broadly bestowed; their harmony enables them to live, and their nurturing helps the myriad things to strive.[7]
>
> (Hutton 2014: 176, modified)

The idea of generative harmony is also consistent with the Confucian ideal in the *Zhongyong*, one of the Confucian classic *Four Books*. Literally, '*zhong*' means the middle ground; '*yong*' means the common ground. Together, *zhongyong* has been translated as 'the doctrine of the mean'. A central theme of the *Zhongyong* text is harmony.[8] Indeed, if the driving force of world transformation is generative harmony as I have presented here, namely, things working with one another through a continuous process of mutual adjustment, mutual accommodation and mutual transformation, then the Way of *zhongyong* is generative harmony.

Like evolution, generative harmony can break down sometimes. When that happens, there is disharmony. When that happens in nature, nature has its way to restore harmony. When that happens in society, it is our moral duty to restore social harmony. Harmony in human society has a different dynamic than harmony in nature because human values are involved in social harmony.[9] So does harmony between humanity and the natural environment.[10] As in any processes of harmony, different participating components present different dynamic patterns and require different ways of harmonization. Since human beings uphold values, social harmony differs significantly from harmony in the non-human world. Discussing social harmony, however, is beyond the scope of this chapter.

In summary: there are various conceptions of harmony. A conception of generative harmony can be reconstructed by drawing on ancient Chinese philosophy. Generative harmony describes how different things join in creating a new pattern of existence in which participating parties form favourable relations through mutual adjustment, mutual accommodation, mutual transformation and mutual enhancement. Such a philosophy not only provides a meaningful cosmogenic account of the world, but also serves as a metaphysical theory for understanding the formation and re-formation of the patterns of existing things in the world.

Notes

1. For a different reading of Plato's idea of harmony, see Neville (2022).
2. For an etymological study of the characters, see Li (2014: 23–5).
3. For a discussion of domination, freedom and harmony, see Pettit (2022).
4. 易有太極, 是生兩儀, 兩儀生四象, 四象生八卦.
5. Ziporyn has offered a different but interesting interpretation of Zhang Zai. According to Ziporyn, Zhang's philosophy is a particular type of monism, there being only one thing. Ziporyn writes:

   > The model for the one is *qi*, which Zhang asserts to be identical to both 'the Great Void' (*taixu*, 太虛) and 'the Great Harmony' (*taihe*, 太和). *Qi* is chosen specifically because it is capable of providing an intuitive sense in which 'Harmony' and 'voidness' can be thought of as aspects of one and the same thing, a unity which inherently involves both the negation of any finite form (voidness) and the unity of all finite forms (Harmony).
   >
   > (Ziporyn 2015: 175)

   He further explains that, in Zhang's system, 'what all things really *are* is *qi*, but what *qi* really is is *also* the Great Void, and thus what both *qi* and the Great Void really *really* are is the Great Harmony' (ibid.: 175–6). Such a monist view is expressed in the form of 'Harmony-void-*qi*' (ibid.: 176). In such a reading, Zhang's harmony is substance, as are *qi* and the Great Void. Ziporyn's interpretation is more radical than Wing-tsit Chan's as quoted earlier. However, if we take it that the Great Harmony in Zhang is the Dao, the Way of being, and that both *qi* and the Great Void are also ways of being, then these 'ways' should not separate from one another. Therefore, the three are the same thing expressed in three different concepts.
6. For a more detailed discussion of harmony and revolution, see Chapter 1 of Li (2023).
7. 陰陽大化, 風雨博施, 萬物各得其和以生, 各得其養以成. (*Xunzi*, Chapter 17.3).
8. See Li (2004) for a discussion of the harmony theme of this text.
9. For a recent discussion of achieving harmony in society, see Wong (2020) and Li (2014).
10. For a discussion of Confucian environmental philosophy with respect to harmony, see Chapter 10 of Li (2014).

References

Ames, Roger (2020), *Human Becoming: Theorizing Persons for Confucian Role Ethics*. Albany, NY: State University of New York Press.

Bergson, Henri ([1911] 1998), *Creative Evolution*, trans. Arthur Mitchell. New York: Dover.

Chan, Wing-Tsit (1963), *A Source Book in Chinese Philosophy*. Princeton, NJ: Princeton University Press.

Dunkang, Yu 余敦康 (2006), 《周易现代解读》 *A Modern Interpretation of the Yijing*. Beijing: Huaxia Chubanshe.

Guying, Chen 陳鼓應 (2007), 黃帝四經今註今譯 *An Annotation, Interpretation and Commentary on the Four Classics of the Yellow Emperor*. Beijing: Shangwu Yinshuguan 商務印书馆.

Hawking, Stephen (2018), *Brief Answers to the Big Questions*. New York: Bantam Books.

Ho, Li-Ching, and Keith C. Barton (2022), 'Critical Harmony: A Goal for Deliberative Civic Education', *Journal of Moral Education* 51 (2): 276–91. DOI:10.1080/03057240.2020.1847053.

Hutton, Eric L. (trans.) (2014), *Xunzi: The Complete Text*. Princeton, NJ: Princeton University Press.

Jastrow, Robert (1978), *God and the Astronomers*. New York and London: W. W. Norton.

Kahn, Charles H. (1979), *The Art and Thought of Heraclitus: An Edition of the Fragments with Translation and Commentary*. Cambridge, England and, New York: Cambridge University Press.

Lai, Kehong 來可弘 (2000), 國語直解 *The Guoyu Explicated*. Shanghai: Fudan University Press 復旦大學出版社.

Li, Chenyang (2004), '*Zhongyong* as Grand Harmony – An Alternative Reading to Ames and Hall's *Focusing the Familiar*', *Dao: Journal of Comparative Philosophy* 3 (2): 173–88.

Li, Chenyang (2014), *The Confucian Philosophy of Harmony*. London/New York: Routledge.

Li, Chenyang (2023), *Reshaping Confucianism: A Progressive Inquiry*. New York: Oxford University Press.

Neville, Robert Cummings (2022), 'Harmony as a Virtue in Christianity', in Chenyang Li and Dascha Düring (eds.), *The Virtue of Harmony*. New York: Oxford University Press, pp. 229–52.

Nussbaum, Martha (1990), *Love's Knowledge: Essays of Philosophy and Literature*. New York: Oxford University Press.

Oxford, Rebecca L. (2022), 'Seeking Linguistic Harmony: Three Perspectives', in Chenyang Li and Dascha Düring (eds.), *The Virtue of Harmony*. New York: Oxford University Press, pp. 279–301.

Pettit, Philip (2022), 'Freedom and Harmony', in Chenyang Li and Dascha Düring (eds.), *The Virtue of Harmony*. New York: Oxford University Press, pp. 300–25.

Popper, Karl (1945), *The Open Society and Its Enemies*, 2 vols. London: Routledge.

Raju, C. K. (2013), 'The Harmony Principle', *Philosophy East and West* 63 (4): 586–604.

Sixin, Ding 丁四新 (2015), '本體之道的論說——論帛書《道原》的哲學思想 A Theory of the Dao of Reality: Philosophy in the Silk Text Dao-Yuan', in Ding's 先秦哲学探索 *Explorations in Pre-Qin Philosophy*. Beijing: Shangwu Yinshuguan 商務印书馆, pp. 330–55.

Thirteen Classics with Commentaries (TTC) (1985), 十三經注疏 *Thirteen Classics with Commentaries*. Beijing: Zhonghua Shuju 中華書局.

Wong, David (2020), 'Soup, Harmony, and Disagreement', *Journal of the American Philosophical Association* 6 (2): 139–55. DOI: https://doi.org/10.1017/apa.2018.46.

Ziporyn, Brook (2015), 'Harmony as Substance: Zhang Zai's Metaphysics of Polar Relations', in Chenyang Li and Franklin Perkins (eds.), *Chinese Metaphysics and Its Problems*. New York: Cambridge University Press, pp. 171–91.

4

The problem of the flying arrow: Comparing Hui Shi and Zeno of Elea using the method of sublation

Jana S. Rošker

This chapter showcases a particular approach to transcultural philosophical comparison by introducing a novel theoretical model, the 'method of sublation'. I aim to shed light on its practical application through a comparative analysis of two famous and distinct perspectives regarding the kinetic state of a flying arrow: those of Zeno of Elea, a pre-Socratic philosopher from ancient Greece, and of Hui Shi, a prominent scholar of the ancient Chinese School of Names, renowned for their contributions to Chinese logic.

The method of sublation

I begin by providing a concise yet comprehensive overview of the theoretical underpinnings of the method of sublation, followed by a meticulous dissection of its operational structure. In 2022, I introduced the basic features of the method of sublation in an article published in *Dao – A Journal of Comparative Philosophy* under the title 'Chinese and Global Philosophy: Postcomparative Transcultural Approaches and the Method of Sublation'. Since then, I have been continuously working on the improvement and development of this novel approach to transcultural philosophical investigation. Although that article describes the method in detail, I will give a brief introduction to its functional structure here for readers who are unfamiliar with it.

The term 'sublation' itself is, of course, derived from Hegelian dialectics, yet it diverges significantly from it in various aspects. In contrast to the conventional understanding where the second term negates the first while elevating it to a superior realm of existence (Spivak 1997: viii), this method assumes a distinct interpretation rooted in its etymological foundations of elimination, preservation and elevation.[1] These three fundamental notions are the sole connections between the post-comparative transcultural sublation and the Hegelian usage of the concept. The sublation method is rooted in dynamic paradigms of processual philosophy. It veers away from adhering to the formal laws of identity, contradiction and the excluded third. Unlike the conventional Hegelian model, it does not yield an entirely new, distinct, qualitatively different synthesis as the fusion of two opposing ideas engaged in dialectical interaction. Instead, the zenith of this process is a pivotal stage termed 'sublation', which is the core of the entire process. Although merely one among the eight constituent phases of this method, this stage is of paramount importance. It emerges from the tension inherent in the *comparata* and engenders a decisive shift, propelling our cognition towards fresh and innovative insights.

This method has been devised to address a range of concerns. Among other issues, it has been developed in order to find a distinct comprehensive approach to transcultural philosophical comparisons, avoiding the domination of Western standards and norms of evaluation, which – due to the colonial legacy of Europe – still prevail in the field of intercultural methodologies.[2] The problem manifests in the fact that in most traditional intercultural comparisons, the *tertium comparationis* was included in one of the *comparata,* namely (in the case of Western and Chinese comparisons) the Western one.

I aim to moderate, if not eliminate, this problem through stronger consideration of the referential frameworks which underlie both philosophical systems and ideas under observation. The method also aims to transcend the essential notion of cultures by basing the comparative inquiry on a discourse marked by a relational research question. This approach is rooted in the fact that in the framework of transcultural philosophy, all terms make sense only as relational, and not as essential notions describing fundamentally static and stable phenomena (Silius 2020: 274). The inherent relational quality of transcultural philosophical sublation manifests itself within the aforementioned referential frameworks which represent their paradigmatic foundations. These foundations are distinct forms of semantic relational networks interlinking the meanings and connotations of concepts, ideas and cognitive entities. As a result, the relational nature of the sublation method becomes evident through its role in interconnecting specific constituents that compose the assorted systems under examination. This interconnection imparts novel structural arrangements of information and comprehension to the overarching scaffolding of the study (Rošker 2021: 179).

Another distinct feature of the sublation method can be found in its basic goal to supersede the mere process of identifying, analysing and interpreting similarities and differences within two or more *comparata*. Rather, these are seen as inspirations for our own philosophizing, since the method is aimed at offering a novel approach to grasping new ideas or insights, by means of a fruitful dialectical interaction between the *comparata*. This interaction is not rooted in the mechanisms of comparing concepts, but in a process of conceptual comparison.[3]

Precisely within this context lies what could arguably be considered the most significant and decisive divergence that sets sublation dialectics apart from the Hegelian model. In contrast to traditional Hegelian dialectics, the sublation method is not a rigid apparatus that proceeds automatically, linearly and hierarchically from one stage to another. This process is not controlled by any transcendent or divine power like Hegel's absolute spirit. A significant characteristic of the sublation method is its subjective nature. The individual engaging with the method must maintain an open mind throughout the entire process. The methods, procedures and outcomes of the analyses are always subject to our own choices, as long as those choices adhere to a requirement for reasonable coherence.

In the following, I will briefly describe the operational mode of the sublation method, which consists of eight distinct phases:

1. In the first phase, we formulate a research question that is not merely fixated on comparing isolated concepts, but instead emphasizes the establishment of relationships between them.
2. After carefully selecting the *comparata* that deal with the chosen research question, our next step is to identify similarities in how these *comparata* address the question. Especially when engaging in transcultural philosophy, the concept of family resemblances allows us to focus on the similarities and interconnectedness of concepts in a broader, relational way, rather than attempting to find universal definitions or essential characteristics.
3. In the third step of sublation, we engage in the process of identifying differences within those broader similarities in our *comparata*.
4. We then establish connections between the identified differences within the treatment of the research question in different philosophies and the diverse referential frameworks that underlie the perspectives being compared, including the distinct paradigms by which they are defined.
5. Building upon this foundation, our next step involves identifying and examining the inadequacies present in each of the approaches we have investigated. These insufficiencies become apparent through a contrastive perspective that highlights differences and their connection to the referential frameworks underlying the philosophical theories under scrutiny.
6. Our focus then turns towards mutual complementarity, aiming to combine the preserved productive elements from each *comparatum* while simultaneously compensating for the eliminated elements, i.e. the particular insufficiencies of both comparata.

7 A significant shift now emerges: as these constructive elements of both (or all) *comparata* converge and mutually fulfil one another, a transformative process unfolds. This transformative phase can be understood as a form of sublation, which is the core of the entire procedure. This sublation phase is driven by the inherent tension between the synthesized unity of combined elements and the distinct perspectives and conceptual boundaries found within each individual *comparatum*. Rooted in the elimination of insufficiencies, the preservation of productive elements and their mutual fulfilment, this phase propels our thinking towards the discovery of new ideas or insights into the fundamental nature of the initial research question.

8 The sublation phase serves as the foundation for the eighth and final phase, which holds the potential for novel discoveries and the expansion of our intellectual horizons.

In the sections that follow, my aim is to elucidate the operational dynamics of the sublation method, by employing the above-described framework to facilitate a comparative investigation of a well-known philosophical problem. Through this framework, I will delve into a comprehensive analysis of two philosophers originating from contrasting cultural backgrounds in the ancient world, specifically China and Greece.

The primary focus of this contrastive dialectical analysis will be the nature of movement and stillness. We will explore their relationship through the thought-provoking 'flying arrow problem'. This seemingly simple question – whether a flying arrow is moving or not – holds profound implications. It was pondered by two ancient philosophers separated by vast distances – Zeno of Elea (*c.* 495–430 BCE), a pre-Socratic thinker from ancient Greece, and Hui Shi (380–305 BCE), an ancient Chinese logician and member of the School of Names.

We will compare and analyse the perspectives of Zeno and Hui Shi, shedding light on their unique approaches and their contributions to the understanding of motion and stillness. Despite their geographical, linguistic and cultural separation, their ideas share intriguing similarities, which are, however, embedded into two different views on the nature of reality. Hence, a contrasting analysis of their respective views through the method of sublation can offer us valuable insights into the complexities of philosophical thought across different cultures and epochs.

The School of Names and Hui Shi

The comparable developmental stage of technologies and similar modes of production in ancient Europe and China are undoubtedly intertwined with the questions that occupied their thinkers during their respective periods. Understanding these connections can shed light on the philosophical inquiries that emerged in both regions. Thus, a thorough exploration of the historical context will enhance our understanding of the philosophical ideas and their underlying motivations.

We begin by delving more deeply into the Chinese *comparatum* by providing a comprehensive introduction to the School of Names or the so-called Nominalist school, which was especially devoted to the study of classical Chinese logic. We do so because readers of this book are more likely to be acquainted with the ancient Greek philosophical tradition than with the intricacies of Chinese philosophical schools.

In pre-Qin China, logical reasoning was closely connected to language, especially with respect to semantic issues, and was determined by its tight relation to ethics (e.g. Mozi s.d., Jing xia, 155). However, this does not mean that in classical texts which are not immediately identifiable with metaphysical and ethical discourses there were not also forms of logical and methodological thought (Cui 2021: 105). Although Chinese philosophy developed in connection with ethical ideas and metaphysical concepts, there was a close relationship between moral and metaphysical thought on the one hand, and logical reasoning on the other.

The origins of Chinese logic can be traced back to the earliest known works, such as the *Book of Changes* (*Yi jing*), but its main development took place during the so-called golden age of Chinese philosophy, in the Warring States (*Zhan guo*) period (475–221 BCE). This period saw the emergence of the 'Hundred Schools of Thought', which include the most influential philosophical discourses, namely Confucianism, Mohism, Daoism and Legalism. This was a time of extraordinary intellectual development in response to political chaos and constant armed conflict between warring states. This period ended with the first unification of China and the rise of the totalitarian Qin Dynasty (221–206 BCE).

Traditional or classical Chinese logic generally refers to the logical thought developed in this era (Chmelewski 1965: 88). These discourses were established without outside influences: Chinese logicians were part of a small subculture, while logicians in India and Europe were part of the mainstream of intellectual development (Harbsmeier 1988: 7).

Classical Chinese logical thought never elaborated an explicitly systematic and comprehensive formulation of the laws of reason, nor did it produce a coherent system of symbols for abstract thought. Before the eighteenth and early nineteenth centuries, Chinese thinkers had rarely encountered a systematic and well-formulated logical work. But as Cheng Chung-Ying (1965: 196) points out, this does not mean that classical Chinese thought lacked logical depth or consistency.

Logical ideas, concepts and methods were developed mainly within the framework of two intellectual schools, namely the Mohist and the Nominalist schools of thought. During this period, issues such as the relationship between concepts or names (*ming* 名) and realities or objects (*shi* 實), the criteria of identity (*tong* 同) and difference (*yi* 異), or the standards of right/true (*shi* 是) and wrong/false (*fei*非) formed the objects of inquiry across the philosophical spectrum regardless of ideological orientation. Chinese interest in logical problems grew out of the methodology of debates or disputations. The earliest evidence of this interest can be found among the so-called dialecticians or debaters (*bianzhe* 辯者), whose discourses were primarily concerned with theories of names (*mingxue* 名學), which led them to become known as the 'School of Names' (Ming jia 名家). The leading figures of this heterogeneous current were Hui Shi 惠施 (c. 370–310 BCE) and Gongsun Long 公孫 龍 (c. 320–250 BCE), who is most famous for the logical defence of his white horse paradox, which claimed that 'white horses were not horses' (*Bai ma fei ma*).

These discourses made important contributions to logic, together with the works of the 'later Mohists' (*Houqi Mojia*), who – among other things – elaborated theories of argumentation (*bianxue*). They represented a current of the school of *Mo Di*, whose teachings were collected in the *Mozi* which includes a series of brief definitions and explanations outlining procedures for determining the validity of conflicting assertions, a theory of description, and an inventory of 'acceptable' (*ke*) links between consecutive statements.

I focus here on the work of Hui Shi, offering both a general introduction to his philosophical ideas and concepts and a more detailed analysis and interpretation of his theory of the flying arrow. But before we plunge into the deep currents of his logical thought, let us introduce the fundamental features and the social, as well as ideational, contexts of his life and work.

Hui Shi was a contemporary and friend of Zhuangzi; he was a minister in the government of the Song State. He was best known for his allegedly sophistical paradoxes, by which he attempted to express the absolute relativity of existence appearing in the mutual relations and shared contexts of absoluteness and relativeness. Hui Shi's teaching, which bears some similarity to Daoist philosophy, is rooted in a theory of relativity that extends a fundamentally atomistic view of space and time. However, if we consider its embeddedness in the dynamic frame of reference of Chinese philosophy and logic, this plurality of relative aspects of reality can be seen as part of an all-encompassing, unified absoluteness of existence. For similar reasons, he also modified the usual understanding of identity and difference by placing the two concepts within a dynamic, unified framework.

Hui Shi must have been a prolific writer, for Zhuangzi remembers him as 'very versatile, as his works could fill five carts' (Zhuangzi s.d. Tianxia, Za pian, 7). Unfortunately, most of those works have been lost; at the time of the Han Dynasty (206 BC – 220), according to the commentary in Liu Xin's encyclopaedia *Han shu*, only one chapter of the work bearing Hui Shi's name had survived. Today, only some fragments of his philosophical positions remain. The historiography of reception and interpretation of this undoubtedly extremely interesting philosopher are limited to his well-known '*Ten Postulates of all that exists*' (*Wanwu shi shi*) and a few individual sentences (mostly paradoxically constructed) without explicit context, preserved in the various commentaries of his contemporaries and successors (especially in the *Zhuangzi* and *Xunzi*).

From a transcultural perspective, it is most interesting that many of these fragments are strongly reminiscent of the sayings of Zeno from the Eleatic school, whose ideas represent the second *comparatum* of this chapter. This makes Hui Shi an interesting thinker not only in the context of classical Chinese logic, but also in terms of cross-cultural comparisons, especially – as we will see later – when we analyse the similarities between Zeno and Hui Shi from the perspective of transcultural studies, applying the method of sublation.

It is clear from his '*Postulates*' that Hui Shi derives his theorems from the assumption of the organic and structural interconnectedness of everything that exists. Within the framework of the holistic worldview already defined in the proto-philosophical classics and thus shared by most classical, especially Daoist, philosophers, Hui Shi focuses, among other things, on the relationship between time and space as an expression of the relativistic structured whole. Thus, for example:

> If we take a stick one chi's length and cut off half of it every day, we shall never come to the end of it.[4]
>
> (Zhuangzi s.d. Za pian, Tian xia, 7)

We find the same thought in Zeno of Elea's story of Achilles and 'the slower':

> The slower runner will never be overtaken by the swiftest, since the pursuer must first reach the point from which the pursued started, and so the slower must always be ahead.
>
> (cf. Lee 1967: 51)

Achilles can never reach the slower runner, because every time he reaches the place where the slower stood a moment before, the slower one has already moved a little further. This proposition is based upon the presumption that the real inseparability of pure time and space includes the implication that real motion independent of space and time is impossible. Indeed, this would imply that it should actually be possible to traverse an infinity of positions in a finite time (Philoponus, cf. Lee 1967: 47).

The apparent similarity of the theses of Hui Shi and of Zeno lies in the fact that the two arguments are both based on the assumption that spatial length is not reducible to minimal units, but is infinitely reducible. However, as we will see later, Zeno and Hui Shi wanted to prove different ideas by emphasizing such a relationship between finiteness and infinity, and also by their respective views on the relation between movement and non-movement.

Like Hui Shi, Zeno assumes the inseparable interconnectedness of everything that exists. But unlike Hui Shi, he sees this existential interconnectedness as the expression of an undivided and unchanging wholeness. This fundamental difference between the basic paradigms and the corresponding viewpoints of these two ancient thinkers can be demonstrated by a contrasting analysis of their respective views on the so-called 'problem of the flying arrow'. In what follows, I conduct such an analysis by applying the method of transcultural sublation.

The problem of the flying arrow: The eight phases of sublation

Sublation phase I: Relational research question

We begin our exploration by formulating a research question that expresses a profound philosophical dilemma, framed in a relational context. We seek to delve deeper into the enigmatic connection between movement and stillness, focussing on Hui Shi and Zeno and their interpretations of the state of a flying arrow, since they both grappled with the philosophical problem at hand through the lens of this question.

From their unique philosophical traditions, both offered captivating insights into the nature of reality; among other issues, both were interested in the paradoxical coexistence of movement and stillness, challenging the conventional understanding of the arrow's trajectory – although their approaches and arguments differ. Through their respective lenses, they attempted to understand the essence of a flying arrow and its profound implications for our comprehension of the dynamics of existence itself. Both philosophers invite us to reevaluate our intuitive notions of time, space and the vibrant nature of reality. As we route through the intricate webs of their philosophical ideas, we embark on a quest for a deeper comprehension of the fundamental forces that govern our existence and challenge our perception of the world.

The investigation of Zeno's and Hui Shi's views on the Flying Arrow problem can be seen through the lens of the concept of family resemblance. By understanding their views within that framework, we can appreciate the interconnectedness of philosophical thought across time and space. Despite the separation in culture and location, these thinkers were engaged in a similar exploration of fundamental questions about the nature of reality, change and motion. The family resemblance approach encourages us to look for shared patterns and themes in different philosophical traditions, fostering a more inclusive and comparative understanding of the human pursuit of knowledge and wisdom.

Sublation phase II: Similarities

Let us now take a closer look at the two famous theorems of Zeno and Hui Shi, in which they reveal their basic view on the problem. At first sight, they are very similar and both are concerned with the observation and mechanics of flying arrows, i.e. with the question whether they move or not.

We proceed from similarities. The two similar theses to be compared are, first, Zeno's assertion that a flying arrow does not move, and, second, Hui Shi's assertion that at a given moment in time a flying arrow does not move but does not stand still either. Zeno's assumption that there can be no motion led him to believe that the 'flying arrow is at rest' (Philoponus, cf. Lee 1967: 53). Hui Shi argues something that is, at first glance, quite similar: 'The problem with the tip of the flying arrow is that there is a time when it does not move, nor does it stand still'[5] (Zhuangzi s.t. Tianxia, Za pian, 7).

Actually, however, the similarity of the two statements is quite superficial: it rests only on the fact that both scholars aim to investigate the spatial, temporal and mechanical state of a flying arrow, and on the fact that their arguments differ from what we commonly assume about the state of flying arrows. But if the similarity is only apparent, where are the differences?

Sublation phase III: Differences

While Zeno and Hui Shi's theorems both revolve around the examination of flying arrows, their differences in philosophical approach, implications and cultural contexts highlight the richness and diversity of human philosophical thought. As we delve into these profound insights, we gain a profound appreciation for the various ways in which great minds have grappled with the profound mysteries of existence and perception throughout history.

Indeed, the parallel between Zeno and Hui Shi lies in their shared departure from the conventional belief that a flying arrow moves. But their negations of this prevailing notion differ significantly in complexity and scope. Zeno's approach is straightforward; he denies motion by suggesting that the flying arrow is not moving, for it exists in sequential states of stillness. On the contrary, Hui Shi's critique is multifaceted, going beyond a mere denial of movement and encompassing the rejection of stillness as well. Moreover, his nuanced perspective introduces the element of time, as he restricts his denial to specific moments in the arrow's trajectory.

Zeno's assertion that the flying arrow is at rest is both puzzling and provocative. By arguing that the arrow cannot move since, at any given moment, it occupies a single point in space, Zeno challenges our intuitive understanding of motion and time. His paradoxical reasoning invites us to reconsider the nature of time and the continuity of change, leading to profound implications for our perception of reality.

On the other hand, Hui Shi's critique navigates a more intricate philosophical terrain. In rejecting both movement and stillness, he delves into the realm of impermanence and constant transformation. His viewpoint captures the essence of change as a fundamental aspect of existence. By acknowledging that the flying arrow neither moves nor remains motionless in certain instances, Hui Shi embraces a dynamic worldview, where reality is in a constant state of flux.

Crucially, Hui Shi introduces the dimension of time, which distinguishes his stance from Zeno's. While Zeno's paradox implies a static arrow, devoid of temporal context, Hui Shi's perspective brings temporal moments into focus. He highlights the ever-changing nature of the arrow's state, revealing a continuous unfolding of different configurations as time progresses.

Sublation phase IV: Linking differences to referential frameworks and paradigms

The dissimilarity in their negations stems from their philosophical backgrounds and cultural influences. Zeno's Greek philosophical tradition emphasized logical reasoning and paradox as tools to explore the nature of reality. In contrast, Hui Shi's Chinese philosophical heritage, particularly from the School of Names, delved into the intricacies of language, meaning and ontology, guiding his nuanced analysis of the flying arrow's nature. The differences between the two arguments can be identified and explained by considering the referential framework in which each is embedded. Let us now take a look at the differences between the two propositions from such a perspective.

Zeno starts from a referential framework whose basic paradigm is the unchanging, i.e. static, nature of being. Hui Shi's paradox, on the other hand, is embedded in the dynamic framework of change.

Zeno thought that since every object or entity is a form of being identical with itself, they are all necessarily immutable and static. Zeno was a faithful disciple of Parmenides; he thus sought to confirm his teacher's theory that reality is one, indivisible and immovable. With this view Zeno explained the impossibility of change and motion. Thus, for any form of being in this totality, there can be neither a change in space nor a change in time. Therefore, the motion of the flying arrow is in reality the sum of innumerable static sections of space; it is not motion. In this way, Zeno actually denies the continuity of motion by dividing it into a series of successive, mutually isolated sequences of static space.[6] With this particular negation of movement and the absolute affirmation of immovable and immutable presence, Zeno's teacher Parmenides laid the paradigmatic foundations for Western metaphysics of Being. Parmenides' ideas profoundly influenced Plato, who studied under Parmenides' student Socrates, and was heavily influenced by Parmenides' notion of the eternal and unchanging forms (in Plato's philosophy known as Ideas). Plato's theory of ideas posits that there exists a higher realm of eternal, abstract and unchanging forms that serve as the true reality behind the ever-changing and imperfect world we perceive with our senses. This worldview had profound consequences for the later development of metaphysics in European philosophy, which was hence rooted in the idea of an unchanging and eternal substance, which, along with the distinction between being and non-being, became a central theme and fundamental premise of later philosophical inquiries.

For Hui Shi, on the other hand, every object or entity has a multifaceted nature and can change depending on the point of observation, which is always relative. Hui Shi's presumption is relativistic, which means that his basic paradigm, i.e. the paradigm of change and motion, is not absolute. It can only exist in a dialectical and complementary relation with stasis. According to the commentaries of Sima Biao (249–306) from the Jin Dynasty, Hui Shi proceeds from the two basic properties of the arrow, namely its form (*xing*) and its potential (*shi*).[7] While the form is fixed and unchangeable, and thus unmovable in the time and space of the flying arrow, its potential causes its movement. Hence, there is a time in which the flying arrow is at rest and, simultaneously, in motion.

Hui Shi's view on the flying arrow problem, along with his other paradoxes, resonates with key themes found in earlier and later Chinese philosophical discourses. These themes include the nature of change and interconnectivity (*Yi Jing*) and the limitations of language and fixed concepts (*Xuanxue* and other traditions).[8] While direct lines of influence may be difficult to trace, the enduring philosophical questions posed by Hui Shi and his contemporaries continue to reverberate through Chinese intellectual history.

Sublation phase V: Identifying insufficiencies

The insufficiencies and flaws in Zeno's and Hui Shi's respective views on the flying arrow become apparent when we critically examine their arguments and underlying assumptions.

As already discussed, Zeno's belief that every object is necessarily immutable and static stems from his adherence to Parmenides' theory of reality as one, indivisible and immovable. However, this view does not consider the complexities of the physical world. It is based upon an abstraction of a being-based substance, viewed as an independent, isolated entity. In empirical, actual reality, however, objects and entities exhibit change and motion, contradicting the absoluteness of Zeno's premise. But by dividing motion into a series of successive, mutually isolated sequences of static space, Zeno fails to address the continuity of motion. His notion of motion as an illusion due to the aggregation of static moments overlooks the interconnectedness and flow that we perceive in the natural world.

Hui Shi's presumption of relativism, on the other hand, introduces subjectivity into the understanding of reality, as it depends on the point of observation. While relative perspectives are valid in many contexts, they may not provide a complete and objective understanding of the flying arrow's motion. Besides, the distinction between the arrow's fixed form and its potential for movement seems like an oversimplification. Such a view does not take into consideration that any object's potential for motion arises from its dynamic interaction with the environment, and its form is not strictly unchangeable. Hui Shi's characterization of the arrow's form and potential as, respectively, fixed and changeable may overlook the nuances of physical phenomena.

Hence, both Zeno and Hui Shi seem to present extreme and rigid views. Zeno denies motion altogether, while Hui Shi appears to deny both motion and stillness at certain moments. Both perspectives overlook the middle ground and the nuanced coexistence of motion and stillness in reality.

While Hui Shi's view incorporates the concept of motion and potential, it does not adequately explain the continuous and smooth motion of the arrow throughout its trajectory. Hui Shi's approach may be seen as a partial explanation, but it does not provide a comprehensive account of the physical phenomenon of the flying arrow. Zeno's view, on the other hand, is limited by its absoluteness and inability to account for the dynamic nature of the world. Thus, both philosophers' perspectives offer intriguing insights, but both also fall short of providing a comprehensive understanding of the complex phenomenon of the flying arrow and its continuous motion.

Sublation phase VI: Mutual complementarity

While Zeno's and Hui Shi's views initially seem contradictory, they can be seen as complementary when considered from different philosophical perspectives and within specific contexts. Integrating their insights can lead to a more holistic understanding of the complex nature of reality.

Zeno's perspective challenges our intuition about motion by highlighting the paradoxes that arise when we analyse continuous movement as an infinite series of discrete moments. His approach serves as a thought experiment, inviting us to examine critically the nature of change and motion. In contrast, Hui Shi's relativistic perspective encourages us to recognize the importance of various viewpoints in understanding reality. Together, these views provoke a deeper conceptual exploration of motion, time and the relationship between change and stasis.

Zeno's paradoxical arguments also encourage us to question our common-sense notions of motion and stasis. When taken together with Hui Shi's view, we can appreciate that different contexts and frames of reference influence how we perceive motion in general. Hui Shi's relativistic approach reminds us that our observations are contingent upon our position and perspective, leading to a more nuanced understanding of the arrow's motion. Integrating Zeno's and Hui Shi's views enables us to embrace the complexity of reality. Zeno's emphasis on still moments and Hui Shi's acknowledgement of relative perspectives reflect the intricate nature of the world. The motion of the flying arrow involves a myriad of factors, including the arrow's physical properties, the medium it moves through and the observer's frame of reference. Combining these views, instead of understanding them as mutually exclusive, encourages us to avoid oversimplifications and appreciate the multifaceted nature of motion.

Last, but not least, both views invite us to engage in philosophical inquiry and question our understanding of existence. By integrating these inquiries, we engage in a more comprehensive exploration of the flying arrow's motion and philosophical concepts related not only to change, motion and stillness, but also to the basic constitution of our existence (or our being) in the world.

Sublation phase VII: Sublation as a shift

Now we proceed to the next phase of our reasoning, i.e. to the shift which is connected to the dialectic of eliminating and preserving particular aspects or views included in the two *comparata*. In this framework, Hui Shi's proposition includes and expands on Zeno's argument, but due to its insufficiency it also negates it. Zeno argues that the flying arrow stands still. In Hui Shi's view, it does not stand still, although it also does not move. What do we preserve and what do we eliminate in this dialectic of conflicting statements?

Indeed, from the viewpoint of form and potential, the flying arrow is continuously in its same form and thus is permanently at rest. However, it is also not at rest, because it is moving. In order to make room for a new understanding of the fundamental question of the existence and nature of motion, we decide to start from a processual view, which is closer to Hui Shi's theory, because dynamic flow is wider and leaves us more space for identifying new aspects of the question. A processual view can include both static and moving phases, whereas unmovable and unchangeable being cannot include any motion. In other words, the dynamic can include the static, but not vice versa. Thus, we eliminate Zeno's basic presumption that there can be no movement because entities of being that are identifiable with themselves cannot occupy different spaces. Instead, we preserve the processual presumption, according to which a flying arrow is moving from the perspective of its potential, but from the perspective of its form it stands still.

But this sublation phase also recognizes that the above-stated perspective of form and potential is not an exhaustive explanation of Hui Shi's flying arrow proposition, because he does not say that there is a time in which the flying arrow is simultaneously moving and at a standstill. Actually, he claims the opposite, namely that there is a time in which a flying arrow is simultaneously not moving and not standing still. There is tension between these opposing notions, and this tension can lead us to a shift, a sublation of the two arguments.

Based on the argument concerning form and potential, the flying arrow exhibits a simultaneous state of motion and stillness. From a perspective of form, it remains unchanged and therefore stationary, but it concurrently actualizes its potential for movement. However, as mentioned above, this is not what Hui Shi explicitly says, for he states the opposite. Yet it is clear that we might see a new perspective in Hui Shi's argument if we could explicitly connect the two perspectives of form and potential, i.e. of stillness and movement. Therefore, we sublate the argument of simultaneous movement and stasis in order to arrive at the opposite of Hui Shi's statement.

This can be done, for instance, when we contextualize Hui Shi's argument within Mohist philosophy, particularly its concept of antinomy. An illustrative example of this Mohist concept is a herd containing two kinds of animals: oxen and horses. Such a herd cannot be labelled as a herd of oxen or a herd of horses, as it encompasses both species simultaneously (Mozi s.d. Jingxia, 168).

Drawing on this formal type of antinomy, we can analogously assert that a moment in time with both movement and stasis is not solely determined by pure movement or pure stasis. In other words, when the flying arrow exists in a state of both movement and stillness, the reason it cannot be exclusively labelled as either one is precisely because it embodies both qualities. By acknowledging the coexistence of movement and stillness in this moment, we avoid reducing it to either one. Instead, we embrace its complex nature, where the interplay of both attributes leads to a unique and multifaceted understanding of the flying arrow's state. This perspective encourages us to appreciate the intricacies of motion, as well as the inherent limitations of rigid classifications in grasping the essence of reality.

Sublation phase VIII: New insight, new ideas, new theory

In this way, the use of the sublation method has led us to a new re-interpretation of Hui Shi's flying arrow paradox. This re-interpretation is based upon a threefold insight, structured as follows:

a) The apparent similarity of Zeno's and Hui Shi's flying arrow arguments is only superficial, because they are embedded in different referential frameworks.
b) The processual nature of Hui Shi's framework of reference leads us to the form and potential argument, which allows for simultaneous movement and stasis.
c) Simultaneous movement and stasis can be transferred into simultaneous non-movement and non-stasis by consideration of the Mohist concept of antinomy.

The second and third insights have made it abundantly clear that grasping Hui Shi's philosophy, much like Zeno's, necessitates understanding its tight connection to a broader context of various discourses that shaped and influenced the Greek and Chinese societies of the time.

By delving into Hui Shi's ideas in relation to other Chinese philosophical traditions, we uncover a deeper layer of meaning. The comparison with Zeno's insights illuminates the shared complexities and paradoxes in both philosophical perspectives; and this invites us to appreciate the intricate interplay between motion, stillness and change, which transcends the boundaries of a single philosophical school or culture. In addition, we have also shown that Hui Shi was a logician who was concerned mainly with the metaphysical foundations of logical discourses rather than with their purely formal principles.[9]

Through a comparative analysis of Zeno and Hui Shi, we can observe a shift in our perception of contradictions supposedly inherent in Hui Shi's viewpoint. This shift highlights that isolated propositions like form and potential, as well as stillness and motion, cannot exist independently in the dynamic reality of concrete life. Instead, the world is inherently relational and governed by continuous change. Though the ideas of non-movement and non-stillness are not directly manifested in the empirical world, they act as bridges connecting the immanent realm of perpetual change with the transcendent sparkles of our thoughts, ideas and imagination.

Conclusion

By juxtaposing the two philosophical perspectives, we gain a deeper appreciation for the complexity of reality and the interplay between seemingly opposing notions, but also for the limitations of language and conventional concepts, and for the importance of context and relationships in philosophical and scientific inquiries. The contrastive analysis also reveals that Hui Shi's viewpoint should not be viewed as a static assertion of non-motion and non-stillness existing simultaneously. Instead, it encourages us to see these concepts as interconnected and contextually dependent, embedded in the ever-flowing process of existence.

I hope this demonstration helps to improve our understanding of the meaning and process of the sublation method. The similarities identified go beyond the boundaries of the respective cultural contexts in which the two philosophies were originally developed. The identification of the differences proceeds not from the search for differences in the cultural backgrounds, but from different paradigms determined by the two frames of reference. In this way, it is possible to overcome static notions of cultures in which the philosophies being compared are embedded. In other words, the sublation method can help overcome the time and space that determine notions shaped by different cultural discourses.

Acknowledgement

The author acknowledges the financial support from the Slovenian Research and Innovation Agency (ARIS) as part of the research core funding *Asian Languages and Cultures* (P6-0243) and in the framework of the research project (J6–50208) *New Theoretical Approaches to Comparative Transcultural Philosophy and the Method of Sublation*

Notes

1. It is worth noting that the word 'sublation' emerged in nineteenth century English literature as a result of Hegel's and the Hegel School's use of '*Aufhebung*', which had a triple connotation of lifting up, preserving and eliminating. Hegel's translators sought an appropriate English equivalent for the term, which was not easy. Kai Froed (2021) points out that they 'looked to Latin (many English scientific words have Latin roots) and found the word "*sublatus*"; the Latin "*sublatus*" then became "sublation" in English'. It proved to be a very suitable word, for its original meaning covered all three crucial connotations of Hegel's *Aufhebung*.
2. This phenomenon is not inherently self-evident, given the well-known shift in economic and political power from Europe, and the so-called 'Western world' at large, to the East Asian regions, including China. Europe, along with its current political and economic structure, has become relatively inconsequential in the contemporary landscape of global decision-making. Given this state of affairs, it appears perplexing and even absurd to continue discussing Eurocentrism as a dominant guiding paradigm in philosophical inquiry and interpretation. However, we have to consider that contemporary globalization was largely shaped by the far-reaching impact of Western-style modernization that permeated global spheres through Europe's colonial expansion. This expansion went beyond mere economic motivations, encompassing ontological and metaphysical dimensions. As a result, it is no mere coincidence that today's globalized world is intricately bound by a universal axiology centred around Western values and norms, and that the *comparata* (in the case of Western and Chinese comparisons) are Western ones.
3. Comparing concepts is a highly problematic method, since the meanings (or the contents) of concepts are always highly contextual and changeable. Conceptual comparisons, however, are always relational, implying that conceptualizations – which are at the centre of interest in initial phases of the sublation process – are always products of a relation between given or perceived reality on the one side, and our cognitive or interpretive frameworks on the other. In this sense conceptual comparisons, which represent the fundamental epistemological tool of the sublation method, imply that the underlying research question itself and the (post)-comparative working procedure refer to the process of comparing general

conceptualizations or assumptions that shape or are a vital part of a particular cultural or philosophical tradition. These processes also involve comparing the fundamental structure or logic underlying and determining different concepts. To avoid the aforementioned problem of comparing concepts, the research question can be formulated in a relational way. For instance, instead of investigating the concepts of 'good' and '*shan* 善'in the Western and Chinese tradition, we can explore the general relationship between good and evil in both philosophies and theories under comparison. Instead of comparing the application and meaning of the terms 'time' and '*shijian* 時間', we can analyse the relation between time and reality in both (or all) *comparata*.

4. 尺之棰, 日取其半, 萬世不竭.
5. 鏃矢之疾, 而有不行不止之時.
6. This idea is linked to the view that the world of appearance, which we perceive through our senses, is illusory and deceptive. The apparent changes and multiplicity we observe are not genuine; they are merely manifestations of our faulty senses and opinions. In this view, Being is an eternal and immutable substance that does not come into existence nor pass away. It has no beginning or end and is not subject to change.
7. Sima Biao wrote: '形分止, 势分行;形分明者行迟, 势分明者行疾。目明无形, 分无所止, 则其疾无间。矢疾而有间者, 中有止也, 质薄而可离, 中有无及者也'. (Form denotes standstill, and force (tendency) denotes movement. When we cannot perceive the form of the arrow with our eyes because individual static sequences cannot be differentiated from one another, there is a problem of an absence of intermediacy. The problem with the intermediacy with the flying arrow is, again, that there are sequences of standing still in-between, which can be isolated despite their tiny duration. And this in-between is endless.) (Sima Biao cf. Wang Jisheng 2021: 1). This form and potential argument is reminiscent of Jin Yuelin's (1895–1984) ontology, because his interpretation of the ultimate cosmic principle *dao*道is likewise based upon a differentiation between form and potential, although he denotes the two ideas with different terms: While Sima calls form *xing* 形and potential *shi* 势, Jin denotes form *shi* 势and potential *neng* 能 (see Jin 1997: 186–239).
8. *Xuanxue* 玄学, also known as 'School of Mystery', was a philosophical movement that emerged during the Wei-Jin period in China (220–589 AD). It was characterized by its attempt to synthesize Daoist and Confucian thought, but was also influenced by certain elements of Buddhism. One of the notable attributes of *Xuanxue* is its evolution of classical Chinese logic. This philosophical approach advanced many traditional methods of reasoning, contributing to a deeper understanding of metaphysical concepts.
9. These metaphysical foundations were often incompatible with formal logic, in which antagonisms such as that between static and dynamic qualities are not valid (see Vrhovski 2021: 87).

References

Cheng, Chung-Ying (1965), 'Inquiries into Classical Chinese Logic', *Philosophy East and West* 15 (3–4): 195–216.

Chmelewski, Janusz (1965), 'Notes on Early Chinese Logic', *Rocznik orientalistycny* 28 (2): 87–111.

Cui, Qingtian (2021), 'Researching the History of Chinese Logic: The Role of Wen Gongyi in the Establishment of New Methodologies', *Asian Studies* 9 (2): 105–20. https://doi.org/10.4312/as.2021.9.2.105-120.

Froed, Kai (2021), 'Sublation (in German "Aufhebung")', *Hegel.net*. https://hegel.net/en/e0.htm. (Accessed 17 February 2021).

Harbsmeier, Christoph (1989), 'Language and Logic', in Joseph Needham (ed.), *Science and Civilization in China*, vol. 7. Cambridge: Cambridge University Press.

Lee, Henry Desmond Prichard (1967), *Zeno of Elea. A Text, with Translations and Notes*. Amsterdam: Hakkert.

Mozi 墨子 s.d. (Master Mo). Chinese Text project, pre-Qin and Han. Retrieved on 03 July 2023 from https://ctext.org/mozi.

Rošker, Jana S. (2022), 'Chinese and Global Philosophy: Postcomparative Transcultural Approaches and the Method of Sublation', *Dao – A Journal of Comparative Philosophy* 2022 21 (21): 165–82.

Silius, Vytis (2020), 'Diversifying Academic Philosophy: The Post-Comparative Turn and Transculturalism', *Asian Studies* 8 (2): 257–80. Retrieved on 03 July 2023 from https://doi.org/10.4312/as.2020.8.2.257-280.

Spivak, Gayatri Chakravorty (1997), 'Translator's Preface', in Jacques Derrida (ed.), *Of Grammatology: Corrected Edition*. Baltimore, MD, and London: The Johns Hopkins University Press, pp. ix–xxxviii.

Vrhovski, Jan (2021). 'A Few Important Landmarks in the Chinese Debates on Dialectical and Formal Logic from the 1930s', *Asian Studies* 9 (2): 81–103. https://doi.org/10.4312/as.2021.9.2.81-103.

Wang, Jisheng 王吉盛 (2021), *Zhongguo zhexiue mingti daquan.* 中国哲学的命题大全. (The Encyclopedia of Propositions in Chinese Philosophy). http://chinese.zhexue.org/philosophy/18292. (Accessed 15 January 2022).

Yuelin, Jin 金岳霖 (1997), *Jin Yuelin wenji.* 金岳霖文集. (Collected works of Jin Yuelin). Lanzhou: Gansu renmin chuban she.

Zhuangzi. 莊子 s.d. 'Chinese Text Project, Pre-Qin and Han'. (Accessed 03 July 2023) from https://ctext.org/zhuangzi.

5

Xunzi and Maimonides: Language, metaphysics, governance

Nicholas Bunnin

In this chapter I explore the *Xunzi* and Maimonides' *Guide of the Perplexed*, focusing on how Xunzi and Maimonides employed approaches to language and metaphysics to provide context and justification for their different proposals for governing their own societies. I also examine the importance of their accounts of language, metaphysics and governance as resources to broaden work in these areas in our own times. In particular, I conclude by questioning John Rawls' claim that his theory of justice as fairness is political, not metaphysical.

Both Xunzi and Maimonides use their accounts to contrast our ordinary use of language to talk about things and our use of language concerning the metaphysical grounds of reality. I investigate how Xunzi tests the boundaries of what we positively can and negatively cannot know and say of *Dao* and how Maimonides tests the boundaries of what we positively can and negatively cannot know and say of God. I examine their views concerning the role of Confucian sages and Jewish prophets who have degrees of knowledge beyond those of ordinary people. I then turn to consider the practical importance of their metaphysics of heart/minds or metaphysics of souls in dealing with the human tasks of governing and living together in a well-ordered society. In this way, both Xunzi and Maimonides provide cardinal examples of how metaphysics can return to the ordinary.

I am deeply influenced by Adrian Moore's broad, inclusive and non-doctrinaire conception of metaphysics as philosophical activity seeking to make sense of things and ourselves in what we take to be the ordinary world.

Xunzi

Xunzi (c.310–c.238 BCE) flourished over two centuries after Confucius and was born about two decades before the death of Mencius. The *Xunzi* is a Han-dynasty edited compilation of his writings, although some of the contents may have been produced by Xunzi's followers rather than by himself. Confucius, Mencius and Xunzi are the three great initial figures of Confucian thought, although until very recently Xunzi was excluded from accounts of Confucian tradition because of his attack on the views of Confucius's earlier followers and commentators, especially including Mencius. Xunzi's sharp critical attention extended to views of non-Confucian thinkers, from whom in some cases he also learned. Xunzi's student Han Feizi developed the legalist doctrines that framed the rule of Qin Shi Huang, who became the First Emperor of China nearly two decades after Xunzi's death. Xunzi's Confucian thinking thus provided pre-emptive criticism of doctrines he helped to inspire.

Central to Xunzi's account of language is his attention to correct naming, an elaboration of the claim ascribed to Confucius that his first action if in charge of governing would be to rectify names:

> If names are not rectified, then speech will not function properly, and if speech does not function properly, then undertakings will not succeed. If undertakings do not succeed, then rites and music will not flourish. If rites and music do not flourish, then punishments and penalties will not be justly administered. And if punishments and penalties are not justly administered, then the common people will not know where to place their hands and feet.
>
> Therefore, when the gentleman names a thing, that naming can be conveyed in speech, and if it is conveyed in speech, then it can surely be put into action.
>
> When the gentleman speaks, there is nothing arbitrary in the way he does so.
>
> (Confucius, Analect XIII, 87)

Xunzi's systematic reflections on naming and distinguishing things in *Xunzi* Chapter 22 'Correct Naming' begin with a general investigation into the diverse origins and later stable determination of correct names for things within a well-governed society:

> In setting names for things, the later kings followed the Shang in names for punishments, followed the Zhou in names for official titles, and followed their rituals in names for cultural forms. In applying various names to the myriad things, they followed the set customs and generally agreed usage of the various Xia states. Villages in distant places with different customs followed along with these names and so were able to communicate.
>
> (Xunzi, 236)

Here, correct naming and its proper application to things appear as a matter of legislation grounded in human custom and artifice, requiring neither origins nor standards beyond those determined by humans living in the natural world. According to a later passage, 'names have no predetermined appropriateness', 'no predetermined application to things', 'no predetermined goodness' before being set and further entrenched in custom.

The focus on the human is reinforced by Xunzi's turn to examining the different ways names apply to people. 'Human nature', 'feelings', 'emotions', 'thinking', 'choosing', 'acting', 'ability', 'understanding', 'work', 'virtuous conduct' and 'knowing': all these features, faculties, powers or capabilities are crucially ascribed to the human 'heart/mind'. The range and diversity of names cut across many boundaries of logical, linguistic, epistemological, metaphysical, ontological, pragmatic, ethical, religious and aesthetic categories. For him, distinctions such as those between fact and value, thinking and acting, reason and feeling, mental and physical, and inner and outer belong to patterns of mutual inclusion rather than dichotomous exclusion. This also applies to the distinction between correct naming and distinguishing things. For Xunzi, these are internally related aspects or phases of the same complex activity, not radically distinct activities somehow to be brought together. Correct names are both descriptive and evaluative, with distinguishing between like and different and between noble and base together determining their contents.

In other passages, 'true' is ascribed to things rightly bearing the correct names, such as true kings, rather than to names used in distinguishing things. Correct assemblages of names can extend where necessary the role of individual correct names in distinguishing the same from the different at an initial level; correct assemblages of names can ease groupings of like things at higher taxonomic levels of generality. But at any level, the danger is to use different names for the same or the same name for the different.

Xunzi next describes the harmonious workings of society when kings established and communicated through fixed correct names applied to properly distinguished human, social, ritual and natural things. Xunzi saw clear communicating in a rectified language used and understood in the same way by all members of society, whatever their social rank or degree of ethical development, as crucial for stable good order. He engaged directly with concrete saying and communicating rather than working at a theoretical removal that abstracts the said (or written) from the saying and abstracts communication from communicating.

In his view, this kingly order was threatened by undermining and obscuring the dynamic practice of clear correct communicating and acting by those frivolously and perniciously expounding paradoxes or by those otherwise unleashing destabilizing disputes and litigations by creating new names.

This wrongdoing was considered to be just like the crime of forging tallies and measures. Hence, none of their people dared to rely on making up strange names so as to disorder the correct names, and so the people were honest. Since they were honest, they were easy to employ, and since they were easy to employ, tasks were accomplished.

(*Xunzi*, 236)

In characterizing the populace governed by the late kings in this way, Xunzi offered his own analysis of the degradation and collapse of that order and provided the context for his proposal for reviving proper order in his own chaotic time.

Nowadays, the sage kings have passed away, and the preservation of these names has become lax. Strange words have arisen, the names and their corresponding objects are disordered, and the forms of right and wrong are unclear ... If there arose a true king, he would surely follow the old names in some cases and create new names in other cases.

(*Xunzi*, 237)

For Xunzi, new names created by the true king would not add additional strange names. Rather, the true king would follow the practice of earlier sage kings to create names which contribute to a restoration of clear accessible communication and good order by both distinguishing between noble and base and differentiating between like and unlike. There is much worth exploring in Xunzi's account of how the true king should proceed, but I restrict myself in this chapter to the metaphysical grounding of Xunzi's account of correct naming.

The mention of sage kings engages with the Confucian balanced combination of 'sageliness within and kingliness without' as needed for rulers to determine correct names. It also invokes the Confucian hierarchy of ethical and cognitive self-transformation and governance employing non-coercive virtue or power, by which sages create Confucian rites through attuning their heart/mind with *Dao*. A *junzi* (gentleman, excellent person) cannot create these rites, but has a heart/mind with the humane moral and cognitive capacity to exemplify these rites in all the *junzi* thinks and does. A *xiao ren* (petty person) has a heart/mind with a calculative cognitive psychology of perceiving one's own benefit and harm, rather than with a moral and cognitive psychology embracing virtue or power. *Xiao ren* accept their place in a harmonious governing order kept stable through communicating correct names. If they conform outwardly to virtuous behaviour, they do so without the ethical and cognitive inwardness of the *junzi*. In this account, the 'ethical and cognitive' are better understood as fused or mutually implicating rather than sharply distinct.

This static picture of the heart/minds of the sage, *junzi* and *xiao ren* needs to be set in motion, because the status of each individual is not fixed. The tortuous step-by-step upward path of self-cultivation and self-transformation of one's heart/mind is in principle open to all, both through education and through the radiating exemplification of virtue by sages and true kings. But although all people have heart/

minds, the sage's heart/mind and its engagement with *Dao* metaphysically anchor and legitimize Xunzi's whole account of naming. Recourse to metaphysics arises because *Dao*, without being a thing, is needed for making sense of things, correct naming of things and knowing things:

> When different forms make contact with the heart, they make each other understood as different things. If the names and their corresponding objects are tied together in a confused fashion, then the distinction between noble and base will not be clear, and the like and the unlike will not be differentiated. If this is so, then the problem of intentions not being understood will surely happen, and the disaster of affairs being thereby impeded and abandoned will surely occur. Thus, the wise person draws differences and establishes names in order to point out their corresponding objects. Most importantly, he makes clear the distinction between noble and base, and more generally, he distinguishes the like and the unlike. When noble and base are clearly distinguished, and like and unlike are differentiated, then the problem of intentions not being understood will not happen, and the disaster of affairs being thereby impeded and abandoned will not occur. This is the reason for having names.
>
> (*Xunzi*, 237)

Regarding human sensory knowledge in general through the five faculties (eyes, ears, mouth, nose and body), Xunzi states:

> The heart has the power to judge its awareness. If it judges its awareness, then by following along with the ears it is possible to know a sound, and by following along with the eyes one can know a form. However, judging awareness must await the Heaven-given faculties to appropriately encounter their respective kinds and only then can it work.
>
> If the five faculties encounter them but have no awareness, or if the heart judges among them but has no persuasive explanations [for its judgments], then everyone will say that such a person does not know.
>
> (*Xunzi*, 238)

Thus the general requirements of awareness and persuasive explanation justify the sage's knowledge of things. Furthermore, the heart/minds of sages exercise their power of reflexively judging their own awareness to create correct names for all the things they distinguish.

In all this, Xunzi attaches fundamental importance to the difference between knowing things and knowing *Dao*. If *Dao* were a thing, knowing *Dao* would be no different from knowing things, and the pull towards metaphysics would wane and perhaps vanish. The sage would create '*Dao*' as the name of *Dao* to distinguish it from other things, and '*Dao*' would have contents like other names. Puzzling through the place of *Dao* in the scheme of things would need no more than mundane exploration. But *Dao* is not a thing and '*Dao*' is not a name, so an account of knowing *Dao* would require exploring metaphysical issues of how the mundane world is possible.

According to *Xunzi* 'Discourse on Heaven', chapter 17:

> The myriad things are but one facet of the Way. A single thing is but one facet of the myriad things. Foolish people take a single facet of a single thing and think themselves to know the Way – this is to lack knowledge. Shenzi saw the value of hanging back, but not the value of being in the lead. Laozi saw the value of yielding, but not the value of exerting oneself. Mozi saw the value of making things uniform, but not the value of establishing differences. Songzi saw the value of having few desires, but not the value of having many desires. If there is only hanging back and no being in the lead, the masses will have no gateway to advancing. If there is only yielding and no exerting oneself, noble and lowly will not be distinguished. If there is only uniformity and no difference, governmental orders cannot be given. If there are only few desires and not many desires, the masses cannot be transformed.
>
> (*Xunzi*, 181–2)

Knowing *Dao* is neither knowing the myriad things as one facet of *Dao* nor knowing one thing as one facet of one facet of *Dao*. In each example, the 'things' mentioned are matters of acting, assessing and feeling, not just a matter of separate, persistent and individually identifiable objects: valuing hanging back rather than taking a lead, yielding rather than exerting oneself, making things uniform rather than establishing differences, having a few desires rather than many desires. For Xunzi, following any of these one-sided, narrow and mistaken claims to knowing *Dao* would have dire governmental and social consequences.

Reading this passage in terms of a metaphysics of change or flux derived from the Book of Changes rather than a metaphysics of substance or permanence, we see it in terms of the mutual inclusion of opposites characterizing the yin-yang approach to the metaphysical character of the natural world, and in terms of the metaphysical character of language appropriate for this world.

In *Xunzi* chapter 21 'Undoing Fixation' there are related passages on speaking of *Dao* as unchanging, yet covering all changes:

> Thus, if one speaks of it in terms of usefulness, then the Way will consist completely in seeking what is profitable. If one speaks of it in terms of desires, then the Way will consist completely in learning to be satisfied. If one speaks of it in terms of laws, then the Way will consist completely in making arrangements. If one speaks of it in terms of power, then the Way will consist completely in finding what is expedient. If one speaks of it in terms of wording, then the Way will consist completely in discoursing on matters. If one speaks of it in terms of the Heavenly, then the Way will consist completely in following along with things. These various approaches are all merely one corner of the Way. As for the Way itself, its substance is constant, yet it covers all changes.
>
> (*Xunzi*, 226–7)

The heart/mind's changing modes of attending and seeing in different ways should not be grasped as a progression from one fixed standing to another. The heart/mind and all the constituent features, powers and faculties known and named within it are facets of the world of flux. The heart/mind is both physical and mental, acting through the physical energy responsible for flux in the world; but the physical and mental are inclusively related rather than externally related and sharply distinct.

The claim that *Dao* is constant or unchanging yet covers or grounds all changes places *Dao* hovering in the vicinity of the boundary of the world of things and names and in some sense enabling the possibility of change. The question whether this grounding is a matter of metaphysical immanence or transcendence has led to serious debate over the contemporary Neo-Confucian Mou Zongsan's conception of immanent transcendence. At stake in this debate is how to relate wanting to name and say the unnameable and unsayable and the sense, if any, of succeeding in naming and saying the unnameable and unsayable.

Xunzi goes on to talk about the heart/mind knowing, approving and keeping to *Dao*:

> I say: the heart must know the Way, and only then will it approve of the Way. Only after it approves of the Way will it be able to keep to the Way and reject what is not the Way.
> (*Xunzi*, 227)

Taking 'then' to distinguish temporally ordered achievements can be challenged by taking 'then' as presenting a non-temporal priority among a fusion of mutually dependent aspects of complex agency. Xunzi addresses how the heart/mind knows *Dao*:

> How do people know the Way? I say: with the heart. How does the heart know the Way? I say: it is through emptiness, single-mindedness, and stillness. The heart is always holding something. Yet, there is what is called being 'empty'. The heart is always two-fold. Yet, there is what is called being 'single-minded'. The heart is always moving. Yet, there is what is called being 'still'.
> (*Xunzi*, 228)

Knowing *Dao* through emptiness, single-mindedness and stillness can be understood as attuning heart/mind with *Dao*. The reason for this is that *Dao* has these same features of emptiness, stillness and unity underlying the possibility of all change and hence of all things. Knowing *Dao* is knowing by an empty still centred unity communicated to the populace through exemplary energy rather than through the frantic agency of those misapprehending *Dao* by following narrow fixations or obsessions. For seeing, naming, knowing and following *Dao* are not seeing, naming and knowing an additional thing, but seeing, naming, knowing and following mundane things *in a new way* in terms of the ground of their possibility.

Placing *Dao* thus in the transitional vicinity of the limits of what can be said entails the practical activity of saying and cancelling and saying and unsaying, captured by rendering both *Dao* and the heart/mind as empty and filled; twofold and single, moving and still. A sage's heart/mind being thus attuned with *Dao* of nature enables sagely artifice to create the names and rites crucial to Confucian virtuous engagement with *Dao*.

Maimonides

Moses Ben Maimon (Maimonides) (1138–1204) was honoured in his lifetime and subsequently for his achievements as a Sephardic Jewish philosopher, ethical and legal scholar, rabbi, astronomer, physician and communal leader. His childhood was shaped by Torah study with his father within the tolerant Islamic Almoravid Empire in Andalusia, which accepted and encouraged a culture of mutual interchange among Islamic, Jewish and Christian thinkers. With the Almohad conquest of the Almoravids, this tolerance gave way to a choice for non-Muslims of conversion to Islam, exile or death. After a period of residence in different locations in Almohad Spanish and Moroccan territory, Maimonides and his family settled in Cairo, where his commentary on Oral Torah (Mishnah) was succeeded by a whole range of writings culminating in his masterwork *The Guide of the Perplexed*.

A fundamental aim of Maimonides' complex and many layered *Guide of the Perplexed* was to reconcile the doctrines of the written Torah and the oral Torah, expressed in the language of the common people, with a correct understanding of God, expressed in the language of Aristotelian metaphysics filtered through a commentarial tradition elaborating a notion of active intellect. Maimonides understood God to be the non-corporeal, simple, unified, active intellect governing the natural world and the Jewish community. Maimonides' own commentarial approach was embedded in that of major philosophers of Islam, who brought the same philosophical resources to bear in their interpretation of the Quran. Indeed, Maimonides composed the Guide in Arabic.

To understand Maimonides' account of language and its role in his metaphysics, we need to consider the main account of language and metaphysics that he contested. Maimonides rejected the views of rival metaphysicians more closely aligned with literal meaning and acceptance of analogical extensions from human attributes to those of God, especially those developed in the Islamic world by earlier Mu'tazilite theologians and their metaphysical followers of his own time. Following them would require Maimonides to accept at face value the extensive episodes of God as a character in biblical texts featuring human-like exchanges between God and humans, especially prophets, or divine companions. At stake were Maimonides' arguments for the absolute difference between God and the world, disallowing any likeness or relation between God and ourselves, providing only for the possibility of a negative metaphysical theology precluding our knowing, saying or thinking anything positive about the essential nature of God.

Maimonides began the introduction to the First Part of the Guide by stating 'The first purpose of this Treatise is to explain the meanings of certain terms occurring in the books of prophecy' (Maimonides, Part I, 5). Through the language of Moses and other prophets studied by Jewish sages, God seemingly provided laws by which earthly Jewish rulers could properly govern Israel. Maimonides saw the problem as being how to address those educated sufficiently in logic, mathematics, natural science and the legalistic study of religious law to be perplexed by the tension between faith and metaphysics, without destroying their faith and rendering them incapable of sincere leadership in the wider community.

Almost none achieving this level of education would, like Maimonides, find themselves caught up in such perplexity. Even for the few who were perplexed, including his disciple Rabbi Joseph, son of Rabbi Judah, to whom he dedicated the *Guide*, progress in learning would be slow. He proposed that their initial study be restricted to the chapter headings of the *Guide*, before gradually transitioning to the full content of the chapters under these headings. He cautioned each to retreat from their study if at any point it intensified rather than resolved their perplexity and confusion by seeming to be full of contradictions. He anticipated that circulation of his views to the well-educated but unperplexed would be met with dismissive mockery and attack. Even more important were his fears that if his views reached the uneducated wider community, their faith would be destroyed and they would become ungovernable.

The second purpose of the *Guide* was to explain the obscure parables occurring in the books of the prophets to show that they have an internal sense as well as an external sense. Maimonides' solution to solving the problem for the perplexed was to recognize that biblical accounts and commentaries are often figurative rather than literal. He saw the need for an apprehension of both figurative and literal use of language. The same words, phrases, sentences and passages can be equivocal or amphibolous, conveying more than one meaning to some or conveying different meanings to different readers. Maimonides reconfigured Aristotle's distinction between univocal and equivocal meaning of terms by interposing amphibolous meaning. For Maimonides, amphibolous terms were modulated according to attributes other than those constituting Aristotelian essential definitions, in a way that would be excluded from the explanatory metaphysical role that Aristotle accorded essential attributes in his taxonomical hierarchy. Maimonides was conservative regarding biblical language, but radical in expounding what he argued was the correct metaphysical rendering of the inner meanings of this language to contrast with and, for the right audience, to replace its literal outer meanings.

A crucial example of the importance of this distinction concerns the inner and outer meaning of worship. Maimonides employed Aristotelian distinctions between substance and attributes, essential and accidental attributes, and attributes and acts to reject any metaphysics leading to God as the object of idolatry: according to the inner meaning, God was solely worthy of the purely intellectual contemplative Jewish worship available to the learned. But according to the outer meaning, the learned could fully endorse and participate in the popular Jewish worship of God practised by the common people. Failure to endorse popular worship or revealing to the common people their own inner meaning of worship would destroy the ability of the learned to govern. The twin human faculties of *intellect* and *imagination* were to be employed in overcoming any error: intellect was central to the metaphysics of the perplexed, but they also required imagination to enter the lives and practices of ordinary people and to govern them successfully.

Maimonides intended the *Guide* to be a path for the perplexed to increase their skill in exploring biblical texts rather than a fully articulated systematic doctrine of biblical interpretation or an authoritative list of exhaustively complete examples of such interpretation. Maimonides warned:

> You should not think that these great secrets are fully and completely known by anyone of us.
>
> (Maimonides, Part I, 7)

But he also claimed:

> [T]o liberate that virtuous one from that into which he has sunk, and I shall guide him in his perplexity until he becomes perfect, and he finds rest.
>
> (Maimonides, Part I, 16–17)

This was the perfection of ease beyond perplexity, rather than a regress to the ease of the vulgar or to the ease of the educated unperplexed. It was the perfection of skilful interpreting rather than of humanly impossible perfection of full and complete interpretation.

Examples of interpretation are scattered through the chapters of the *Guide*. He instructed the perplexed to proceed by attending with extreme care to each chapter in its own place before gradually extending attention to the context of chapters containing similar parables and then to the context of the chapters in the *Guide* as a whole. Even at the first stage of reading each chapter, Maimonides instructed:

> when reading a given chapter, your intention must be not only to understand the totality of the subject of that chapter, but also to grasp each word that occurs in it in the course of the speech, even if that word does not belong to the intention of the chapter.
>
> (Maimonides, Part I, 15)

Maimonides wrote with appreciation of religious sages possessing knowledge of God, who spoke to those they instructed only in parables and riddles. For different texts, they stressed the beginning, middle or end of the same or similar parables to capture their significance. If the interpretative engagement between parts and parts or between parts and whole were rushed, apparent contradictions would be uncovered for the perplexed themselves and, more dangerously, for the educated and vulgar unperplexed if the views of the *Guide* circulated among them.

He explained these fears in a further Introduction which began, 'One of seven causes should account for the contradictory or contrary statements to be found in any book or compilation' (Maimonides, Part I, 17). Towards the end of these introductory remarks, he held, 'Divergences that are to be found in this Treatise are due to the fifth cause and the seventh' (Maimonides, Part I, 20). These two causes he expounds as follows.

His account of the fifth cause explains his propaedeutic strategy of leading students from a useful but inadequate initial engagement with obscure matters to a correct understanding of them:

> The fifth cause arises from the necessity of teaching and making someone understand. For there may be a certain obscure matter that is difficult to conceive. One has to mention it or to take it as a premise in explaining something that is easy to conceive and that by rights ought to be taught before the former, since one always begins with what is easier. The teacher, accordingly, will have to be lax and, using any means that occur to him or gross speculations, will try to make that first matter somehow understood. He will not undertake to state the matter as it truly is in exact terms, but rather will leave it so in accord with the listener's imagination that the latter will understand only what he now wants him to understand. Afterwards, in the appropriate place, that the obscure matter is stated in exact terms and explained as it truly is.
>
> (Maimonides, Part I, 17–18)

More fundamental to understanding the *Guide*, however, is Maimonides' account of the seventh cause dealing with very obscure matters:

> In speaking about very obscure matters it is necessary to conceal some parts and to disclose others. Sometimes in the case of certain dicta this necessity requires that the discussion proceed on the basis of a certain premise, whereas in another place necessity requires that the discussion proceed on the basis of another premise contradicting the first one. In such cases the vulgar must in no way be aware of the contradiction; the author accordingly uses some device to conceal it by all means.
>
> (Maimonides, Part I, 18)

After these introductory characterizations, Maimonides provided in his first chapter (Part I, Chapter 1) explanations of the meanings of two terms, *image* and *likeness*, that framed the whole of his project:

> Image (selem) and likeness (demuth). People have thought that in the Hebrew language image denotes the shape and configuration of a thing. This supposition led them to the pure doctrine of the corporeality of God, on account of His saying: Let us make man in our image, after our likeness.
>
> (Maimonides, Part I, Ch 1, 21)

For Maimonides, it was essential to interpret this correctly: refuting the doctrine of the corporeality of God was necessary to establish God's real unity and complete separateness from other things, including ourselves. The term 'form' (to'ar) in Hebrew scripture is applied to the natural and artificial shape and configuration of things *but never to the deity*. The term 'image' was equivocal or amphibolous, applying both to the sensory apprehension of shapes and configurations of natural bodies and also to the intellectual apprehension of non-corporeal God. We are like God because

> a 'very strange something', intellectual apprehension, is conjoined with us as corporeal selves, not because God is corporeal.
> (Maimonides, Part I, Ch 1, 23)

In his metaphysical account of the Garden of Eden (Maimonides, Part I, Ch 2, 23–6), Adam knew the false and the true through this intellectual apprehension – and acquired the ability to judge things as bad or fine only afterwards and separately (in the language of the common people, this development was marked by Adam and Eve eating the fruit of the tree of knowledge of good and evil).

For Maimonides, the non-corporeality of God required the rejection of all ascriptions to God of features applicable to natural things that can be measured against one another. He accepted the dictum of the philosophers that God is 'the intellect as well as the intellectually cognising subject and the intellectually cognised object, and that those three notions form in Him … one single notion in which there is no multiplicity' (Maimonides, Part 1, Ch 68, 162–3). For this reason, in a via negativa regarding knowledge of God, he interpreted the positive biblical description of God as being all-powerful in terms of a negative ascription to God of not lacking power. More generally, he rejected the claim that we can have true knowledge of the essence of God.

Maimonides focussed on the Prophecy of Moses in the gathering at Mount Sinai receiving and transmitting the Ten Commandments (Maimonides, Part II, Chapters 33–34, 363–7). In these and the following chapters, Maimonides distinguished Moses from all true prophets preceding or succeeding him. He held that Moses alone gained the contents of his prophecy solely through intellectual apprehension of God's active intellect, while the prophecy of other true prophets involved intellectual apprehension combined with imaginative apprehension through dreams and visions in which God appears and speaks in a humanly audible voice. For this reason, Maimonides exempted the account of Moses from his treatment of the biblical accounts of the others in terms of parable. Even so, he held that Moses expressed his intellectual apprehension of God's active intellect in human language. Maimonides held that 'the true reality and quiddity of prophecy consist in its being an overflow overflowing from God' (Maimonides, Part II, Ch 36, 369), although 'an overflow overflowing from God' might best be taken as an amphibolous phrase requiring disambiguation between the divine overflowing and the human apprehension of the overflow.

Comparing Xunzi and Maimonides and implications for our times

The accounts of language and governance by Xunzi and Maimonides were held by each to be crucial to initiating, maintaining or restoring stable and peaceful social order in their different societies ruled by those having knowledge and understanding beyond the level achieved or achievable by others, especially the common people. Both viewed their own societies as hierarchical, with common people placed as objects rather than agents of governance. This account, however, masks metaphysical differences grounding the explorations of Xunzi and Maimonides, making the comparison misleadingly straightforward.

For Xunzi and Maimonides, the learned acquire different knowledge according to different standards through different training. What their different common people lack in knowledge and understanding was also not the same. Both Xunzi and Maimonides tested the boundaries of what can and cannot be known and said of fundamental reality. Xunzi's emptiness, stillness and unity of *Dao* have resonances with Maimonides' negative theology, but *Dao* is not God. In their different societies, Xunzi accorded Confucian sages and Maimonides accorded the Jewish prophet Moses degrees and levels of knowledge and understanding to guide the learned in ruling and the ordinary people in accepting rule. Xunzi's heart/minds and Maimonides' souls have different metaphysical contexts. Would their solutions to the problems of maintaining political stability and peace, even if successful in their own societies, enhance or endanger the prospects of political stability and peace in the other's society? How can we assess the dangers of using the metaphysics of one to assess the solution of the other? It seems fanciful to expect that there is a universal standpoint that is neutral among all metaphysical approaches, although mutual influence remains possible without such a standpoint.

In our own times too, it remains important to explore the metaphysical grounding, if any, of accounts of language and governance, and more broadly of what it is to be human. My own concerns go back six decades to my own plunge into serious philosophical thinking through the work and personal example of John Rawls, my teacher and thesis supervisor when I was an undergraduate at Harvard. I remain overwhelmingly indebted to Rawls but have never lost my unease over his insistence that his theory of justice, developed within his fusion of the anti-metaphysical methods of analytic and pragmatist philosophy, was to be understood as being political, not metaphysical.

Many of the matters included by Rawls in the final Part Three of *A Theory of Justice* continue to strike me as in need of metaphysical investigation. If contemporary Western liberal democratic and individualistic political philosophy turns out to be metaphysical as well as political, the threads linking metaphysics to politics in conditions of modernity might show themselves more easily through comparative rather than internal examination. Comparison can be especially worthwhile if metaphysical commitments are completely or partly hidden in a prescribed methodology or contained in discoverable but unstated metaphysical presuppositions. In Chapter 6 of this volume, Siufu Tang compares Xunzi and Rawls regarding related issues.

Xunzi chose language with univocal meaning understood in the same way by the ruler, by those educated enough to assist the ruler and by the common people having their own skills but lacking the Confucian education central to Xunzi's approach. He proscribed innovations of language that would undermine this sanctioned clarity of communication. Maimonides chose equivocal or amphibolous language with an outer figurative meaning understood by the common people and an inner metaphysical meaning understood by the learned. To begin with, I follow Rawls by treating this question as 'political, not metaphysical', only later bringing metaphysics into the discussion. I focus on resonances between these two conceptions of language and the use of language in politics in contemporary societies.

Xunzi's approach helps to recognize the extraordinary value placed on repeating simple, direct slogans inspired by modern advertising practices in contemporary political life. Not surprisingly, hearing and repeating these chosen slogans can reinforce assent by partisan groups or whole societies, while at the same time evacuating the slogans of meaning. Xunzi also helps to understand attempts to suppress by censorship or rhetorical disdain political analyses and narratives using language outside the scope of preferred simplicity and directness. Both reducing discourse to slogans and suppressing alternative language of political discourse are currently dominant in democratic as well as authoritarian societies.

In contrast, Xunzi's account of correct naming as protection against the decay of harmonious well-ordered societies has positive value for our own times. His names are indivisibly descriptive and evaluative and are corrupted if inappropriately applied.

Whether this corruption is fundamental to the decay of harmonious societies or a symptom of more fundamental sources of decline is open to question. In either case, understanding corruption of language or the collapse of intelligibility of ethical and political language might require fusion of linguistic with sociological and anthropological examination that challenges the perspectives of contemporary philosophies of language in disciplinary isolation. If monitoring the correct application of names were controlled not by a 'true ruler' but formally by independent institutions or culturally through open intellectual debate, it might have greater acceptance in the circumstances of our current political life. Xunzi held that when a hegemon rather than a true king rules, the power to regulate names leads to disorder rather than harmony. Even current self-described liberal democracies pursuing ideals of popular education and commitment to equal citizenship commonly obstruct the realization of these ideals through the operation of entrenched hierarchies of power, wealth and influence. It is not clear what kinds of education and character in the whole society might maintain or renew a just harmonious order and guard against ongoing destructive descent into bitter and violent conflict. This question reflects current actual crises in many leading self-described liberal democracies; it is not just a matter of detached theoretical enquiry.

Xunzi's account of language and political order seems more directly applicable to what have been called illiberal democracies, where formal democratic institutions mask increasingly authoritarian practices of governance. Each illiberal democracy has its own complex history and character, but many have been initiated by leaders coming to power through fair competitive elections in states with recently established but not deeply entrenched democratic orders.

In terms of Xunzi's distinction, leaders of illiberal states have typically displayed the character he ascribed to hegemons rather than to true kings. Some significant leaders and their key advisors and supporters in crisis-ridden liberal democracies are currently attracted to models of illiberal democracy, where winning and maintaining power have displaced any ethical concerns that might otherwise have constrained their conduct. This is also true of some populist democracies in which power is maintained by attacking groups of minority citizens, sometimes genocidally, to spread and intensify support by the majority. The rulers of contemporary hierarchically ordered societies also seem open to assessment as true rulers or hegemons, although some apparently satisfy to varying degrees the criteria of both.

Maimonides' approach to language is more complex, with the same language open to having both outer common meaning and inner metaphysical meaning. Popularly accepted figurative tales of the Torah were written and understood in the language of the common people but were also open to the metaphysical understanding of the learned. His duality of outer and inner meaning has resonances with modern literary or poetic analysis in terms of the ambiguity of surface and depth, and with other investigations of interpretive complexity, including the language of politics and diplomacy.

A full study of the *Guide* might lead a suitably educated person to endorse Maimonides' method of distinguishing between outer and inner meaning but to question or reject some of his metaphysical renderings of biblical passages. With his metaphysics comes hermeneutics, including in our own time both Ricœur's hermeneutics of suspicion and hermeneutics of faith. Another legacy of Maimonides is the application of his rejection of literal fundamentalist readings of biblical texts to the reading of political texts, such as constitutions. In particular, he could be a source of measured criticism or the rejection of literalist and originalist readings of such documents.

A separate issue concerns how we might use the distinction between common outer and metaphysical inner meaning in contemporary metaphysical settings differing from that embraced by Maimonides. For this I return to Rawls to set out the possibility of reading his theory as metaphysical as well as political. The metaphysics Rawls rejected includes rigid speculative doctrines rather than the flexible activity of making sense of ourselves in a social and natural world. His task was to make sense of ourselves as citizens with notionally equal status and capability reflecting upon and acting freely within broadly fair liberal and stable democratic institutions. Rawls aimed to use his theory to bring order and perspicuity to political intuitions shared by members of such liberal societies.

> Whether justice as fairness can be extended to a general political conception for different kinds of societies existing under different historical and social conditions, or whether it can be extended to a general moral conception, or a significant part thereof, are altogether separate questions. I avoid prejudging these larger questions one way or the other.
>
> (Rawls, 225)

His representation of rational agents making choices behind a 'veil of ignorance' was shaped by economic rational choice theory modelling how individuals with intuitions shaped by membership in their liberal society would act if they were rational. Since then, behavioural economic theory using both economics and psychology has succeeded economic rational choice theory as the dominant model of how people act with economic rationality. In addition, Rawls did not attend to competing theories of social or anthropological rationality or to metaphysically grounded conceptions of rationality available in other contemporary settings, including those held by individuals and groups embedded in liberal societies. Any of these other theories of rationality would have challenged the adequacy of Rawls' rendering of the homogeneity of rationality in liberal societies.

Rawls' account of individuals making choices according to their different conceptions of the good has also encountered difficulties. He recognized that some of these goods were overwhelmingly important to individuals holding them but that pursuing them in public political decision-making could result in undermining the stability or even the existence of their liberal society. Rawls' solution was to distinguish between private and public goods in an individual's full conception of the good, with only the latter open to political pursuit in the public sphere. This solution is threatened if we focus on Rawls' expectation that living in a just liberal society would entrench stability in good part because the grounds of self-respect would increasingly become the basic good of greatest importance to members of society. But the grounds of human self-respect are not limited to matters in the public sphere, nor are the grounds of self-contempt or self-loathing with which self-respect can be contrasted so limited. I suggest that metaphysical reflection, as trying to make sense of ourselves and our human societies, can help assess the sources of stability and instability of just liberal societies. In particular, the distinction between pursuing public and private goods, so easy to see from a third-person overview, is often less secure in first-person accounts of one's own agency.

More broadly, Rawls sought to exclude metaphysics of the self from his theory of justice, but in the end his account of the interlocking capacities of equal democratic citizens to think, act and employ language seems to me to require metaphysical investigation to make sense. If rival metaphysical views are currently in play, a shared outer public meaning of language would potentially have a variety of inner metaphysical meanings, either hidden from other groups or at least distorted or partially unintelligible to them. This could undermine the stable peaceful legitimacy of a liberal political society through a withdrawal of mutual trust among its members.

Just as I asked earlier whether Xunzi's and Maimonides' solutions would enhance or endanger the prospects of political stability and peace in the other's society, I now ask whether in present circumstances the prospects of peace and stability within liberal democratic societies, so different from the hierarchical societies of Xunzi and Maimonides, are enhanced or endangered by considering political philosophy as political, not metaphysical. There are separate questions about the peace and stability of liberal democratic societies having relations with societies governed in other ways, only some of which aspire to a liberal democratic order. Finally, readers disquieted by my proposed metaphysical turn might find some reassurance in the use of metaphysics by my exemplars Xunzi and Maimonides to return to the ordinary.

References

Confucius (2007), *The Analects of Confucius*, trans. Burton Watson. New York and Chichester: Columbia University Press.

Maimonides, Moses (1963), *The Guide of the Perplexed*, translated and with an introduction and notes by Shlomo Pines. Chicago, IL: The University of Chicago Press.

Rawls, John (1985), 'Justice as Fairness: Political Not Metaphysical', *Philosophy & Public Affairs* 14 (3) (Summer): 198.

Xunzi (2014), *Xunzi: The Complete Text*, translated and with an introduction by Eric L. Hutton. Princeton, NJ, and Oxford: Princeton University Press.

6

Metaphysics of normative values: Metaethical constructivism and Xunzi

Siufu Tang

Normativity is ubiquitous in human lives. This chapter is primarily concerned with the metaphysical foundation of normative values, particularly in relation to the Confucian philosopher Xunzi荀子 (*c*. 310–238 BCE).

In general, there is no question regarding the existence of physical and biological entities. We know that they exist in the world, and there are reliable ways to perceive, examine and understand these entities and their various qualities. They are parts of the fabric of the world. However, there certainly are questions over whether normative values like goodness and badness, rightness and wrongness really exist, or if they are qualities objectively of the world. I use my eyes to see a red cup in front of me and fully perceive its redness, or I use my ears to hear the soft music of the bar; but what kind of faculty do I use to perceive the moral rightness of an action? How do I know that this is a morally right action?[1]

Yet we tend to believe strongly in there being right answers for moral questions. In everyday life we take seriously our moral judgement. When we are convinced that we have come to the right moral judgement and can see no convincing contrary arguments or evidence, we tend to think any contrary judgements mistaken and will argue accordingly with opponents when needed. Such beliefs in moral objectivity and the relevant moral phenomenon have provided a prima facie case for moral

---

The work described in this chapter was fully supported by a grant from the Research Grants Council of the Hong Kong Special Administrative Region, China (Project No. HKU 17604522).

realism, the position in metaethics that insists on the existence and objectivity of moral facts and values (Brink 1989: 14–36). Nevertheless, moral realism faces at least two daunting challenges.

First, moral realism has a difficult time explaining what kind of entities moral values are, or what kind of existence moral facts have. Essentially this is the argument of John Mackie, who points out that if there were indeed objective values, they have a very strange sort of existence, utterly different from other things in the universe (Mackie 1977: 38–42). Secondly, even if we grant the existence of objective values, moral realism still has difficulty explaining the motivating power of objective moral values; when a person sincerely holds a moral judgement, it is normally the case that there will be a motivation for the person to carry out the moral judgement in action. But if moral judgement is primarily a belief resulting from our perceiving or getting in touch with objective moral values or facts, as moral realism tends to suggest, why would people be motivated to act by a belief alone, since the primary task of belief as a cognitive state is to understand the world? There seems necessarily to be a gap between belief and motivation for action.

This is admittedly an over-simplistic picture of the relevant metaethical debates. However, my aim is not to provide a comprehensive survey of these debates, but to explain the theoretical background of metaethical constructivism. For it is precisely to the theoretical difficulties of metaethics that metaethical constructivism appears as a potential solution. In the following I employ metaethical constructivism as a perspective to explicate and, at some points, reconstruct Xunzi's understanding of and arguments for the Confucian normative order, with an emphasis on the metaphysical status of Heaven, human agents and normative values.[2] Such an explication can give us a better understanding of both Confucianism and metaethical constructivism.

Metaethical constructivism

Metaethical constructivism gained prominence through John Rawls' Dewey Lectures (Rawls 1980). Rawls himself is primarily interested in applying Kantian constructivism to political philosophy. Nevertheless, Rawls mentions that for Kantian constructivism, moral objectivity can be established without recourse to an independent moral reality. Indeed Kantian constructivism aims to explain the objectivity and normativity of morality as an alternative to the arguments of moral intuitionists and moral sentimentalists (Bagnoli 2013: 5–7). Moral intuitionism suggests that there is an independent moral reality and the role of a moral agent is to apprehend this moral reality and act accordingly. Moral intuitionism can explain the objectivity of morality, but it seems to have no non-circular way of explaining why a person is obliged to act in accordance with an independent moral reality. Moral sentimentalism, on the other hand, can explain the normativity of moral demands by construing them as conducive to the fulfilment of one's sentiments and desires, but it has difficulty in establishing universality and objectivity for morality, and in explaining the distinctive obligation of moral demands in contrast with prudential demands.

According to Rawls, the distinctive idea of Kantian constructivism is that 'it specifies a particular conception of the person as an element in a reasonable procedure of construction' (Rawls 1980: 516). While Rawls himself is mainly interested in establishing the first principles of justice, Kantian constructivism understood more broadly as a distinctive position in normative ethics and metaethics is concerned with normative values in general. There are three key elements of Kantian constructivism: a conception of the rational person, a hypothetical procedure of rational deliberation, and the resultant normative values and standards. It must be emphasized that 'construction' is used as a metaphor (Bagnoli 2022: 1), to underline that normative values are dependent on the conception of a rational person and rational procedure. Kantian constructivism holds that normative values and standards can only be established through a reasonable procedure of rational deliberation by rational agents who have the common aim of living a collective life in terms that are acceptable and justifiable to all participants. Rawls points out that 'moral objectivity is to be understood in terms of a suitably constructed social point of view that all can accept' (Rawls 1980: 519). In other words, Kantian constructivism does believe in moral objectivity and moral facts, but they are the results rather than the source of rational deliberation.

Sharon Street disputes a proceduralist characterization of ethical constructivism. She points out that the notion of a rational procedure is merely a heuristic device for drawing out the normative consequences of occupying a practical point of view in valuing. Instead she prefers a 'standpoint characterization' of constructivism where the emphasis is put on the relation between normative values and the practical point of view occupied by a valuer (Street 2010). Street also distinguishes a restricted constructivism from a thorough-going and metaethical constructivism. A restricted constructivism establishes certain normative values from a practical point of view with some pre-established values. For example, Rawls' principles of justice are established from the practical point of view of a valuer who accepts the public political culture of a liberal democratic society. On the other hand, a thoroughgoing constructivism attempts to establish normative values from a practical point of view understood in a purely formal way, without any commitment to substantive values. Christine Korsgaard is generally understood to be a representative philosopher who attempts to ground normative values in a formal conception of rational agency (Korsgaard 2008; Korsgaard 2009). Street suggests that while Kantian constructivism holds that moral values can indeed be established through such a formal practical point of view, Humean constructivism denies that substantive normative values can be established from a formal practical point of view (Street 2010: 367–70).

The major motivation for metaethical constructivism is thus to explain the foundation of normative values and affirm the objectivity of normative judgement without recourse to any dubious metaphysics, while at the same explaining the practical implication of moral judgement. 'Construction' is used as a metaphor to underline that normative values and facts are made and not discovered, as the results of particular kinds of human activities (practical reasoning), rather than having an independent existence that functions as the basis of human normative judgements. The major challenge for metaethical constructivism is to make good the promise of establishing normative values and facts that are dependent on human beings and yet are objective and universally binding for us. Andreas Müller points out that there are in general two alternative ways to do this. One is to emphasize that the normative facts and values are the output of a specific kind of human activity but nevertheless maintain that normative judgement is mainly a matter of perceiving and representing such facts and values. Another is to emphasize that normative judgement is primarily not a matter of perception or representation, but a kind of active response that we make to natural facts. In the latter interpretation, there are no normative facts independent of normative judgement (Müller 2020: 18–19). It seems to me that the two types of interpretation need not be inherently conflicting. It is possible to maintain on the one hand that there are no normative facts independent of normative judgement, yet on the other hand maintain that such normative facts can nonetheless be the targets of reflection and understanding, particularly in terms of social interaction, historical development and personal moral cultivation.

Some doubt if metaethical constructivism is really a distinctive position that can provide a global foundation for normative values (Enoch 2009), or if constructivism can be seen as a metaethical theory at all (Darwall et al. 1992; Hussain and Shah 2006). We cannot delve into such debates in this chapter, but it is obvious that metaethical constructivism is a blossoming development in philosophy. It is an open question whether metaethical constructivism can provide an adequate answer to the foundation of normative values, but it has at least a promising chance. It is in this spirit that I will attempt a Xunzian version of metaethical constructivism. In the following sections, I shall explicate why and how Xunzi's Confucian answers to moral foundation should be seen as a version of metaethical constructivism. The primary aim is to argue for a justifiable interpretation of Xunzi's metaethics, rather than to explicitly defend Xunzi's metaethical constructivism against potential critiques.

Zhuangzi's critique of Confucianism

To understand the intellectual context of Xunzi's metaethics, we should first consider Zhuangzi莊子 (late fourth century BCE). Zhuangzi wrote in the second chapter (*Qiwu lun* 齊物論, 'Discourse on Equalization of Things') of the *Zhuangzi* that there is an essential link between our normative judgement (*shifei*是非, literally 'this is the case and this is not the case') and the accomplished heart-mind (*chengxin*成心).[3] What Zhuangzi intends to convey is that normative judgement reflects not what the world is like but is rather the result of certain established ways of perception, understanding and evaluation of the world. Zhuangzi believes that there are many different ways of perception, understanding and evaluation, and there are no independent standards by which to judge which established way is better or worse. Zhuangzi points out that Confucianism and Mohism have contrasting ways of *shifei*, and each tends to affirm what the other denies. Their respective *shifei* do not represent the *Dao*道, the ultimate standard of the world.[4]

Chad Hansen suggests that one of the targets of Zhuangzi's arguments is Mencius 孟子 (*c.* 372–289 BCE). While Mencius believes that the Confucian cultivation allows the cultivated heart-mind to pick out the uniquely correct way of normative judgement as intended by the Heaven (*Tian*天), Zhuangzi suggests that the so-called correct way of normative judgement represents only the Confucian version of the accomplished heart-mind and argues that it has no external authority and priority over the competing Mohist version (Hansen 1992: 277–80).

If Zhuangzi is successful in his arguments, then Confucianism is in trouble. For then Confucianism cannot claim normative superiority for its teachings and will have difficulty answering the Mohist challenges. Xunzi荀子 took up the challenge to reply to Zhuangzi and argue for the normative superiority of Confucian teachings, in a way that is different from that of Mencius.

In the texts of the *Xunzi* Zhuangzi is mentioned only once, where Xunzi criticizes Zhaungzi for being concerned with *Tian*天 (Heaven or Nature) only and for not understanding matters regarding human beings: 'Zhuangzi is beclouded by Heaven and does not know human beings. … If one speaks of the Way in terms of Heaven, then it consists completely in following the natural course' (*Xunzi* 21.103.15–18).[5] Xunzi is not of the opinion that Heaven is unimportant. Indeed Heaven represents one facet of the true Way (*Dao*道). The problem with thinkers like Zhuangzi, Xunzi suggests, is that they take one corner of the Way to be its totality. It is in this sense that they are beclouded (*bi*蔽). From Xunzi's point of view, only Confucianism is able to comprehend and put into practice the totality of the Way.

Xunzi would probably agree with Zhuangzi that human beings' normative judgement is not part of the natural order. For Xunzi, Heaven represents what things are naturally, including the natural course of development of the world. Xunzi points out that 'Heaven moves in a constant way. It does not survive because of the Sage King Yao, nor perish because of the tyrant Jie' (*Xunzi* 17.79.16). Xunzi also suggests that order or disorder is not due to Heaven (*Xunzi* 17.80.21–24). Given that Xunzi defines good partially in terms of order, and bad partially in terms of disorder (*Xunzi* 23.115.1–2), Xunzi would probably also agree that good or bad is not due to Heaven either. However, Xunzi disagrees with Zhuangzi's claim that normative judgement is consequently without any universal standard. Xunzi points out that Zhuangzi fails to consider the case of human beings themselves. Even though normative judgement is not a part of the natural world and does not come from Heaven, this does not mean that there cannot be universal normative standards for all human beings. Xunzi insists that the way of the former kings is true and good for all human beings; Confucian ritual and appropriateness (*liyi*禮義), the key Xunzian notion of Confucian normative standards, as the embodiment of the way of the former kings, should be the guidance for human beings.[6] The way of the former kings is indeed not the way of Heaven nor Earth, but it is the way of human beings (*rendao*人道) (Xunzi 8.28.15–16).[7]

Thus, Xunzi suggests that order or disorder, and consequently good or bad, come not from the constant movement of Heaven, but are rather the result of human responses (*ying*應) to natural circumstances. Xunzi's position can obviously be interpreted in two different ways. First, it might be the case that although order or disorder, good or bad, comes through human responses and actions, the evaluative fact that such responses are orderly or disorderly is not determined by human responses, but is so rather because it corresponds to an independent normative framework. It might be the case that normative and moral values simply exist in the world,[8] as part of the 'fabrics of the world' (Mackie 1977: 15). The sage king Yao's responses were orderly because Yao successfully tracked and complied with the normative order of the world. The tyrant Jie's responses were disorderly because Jie failed to do so. Such an interpretation puts Xunzi as a normative objectivist and realist.[9] Secondly, it might be the case that when the sage kings like Yao responded to natural circumstances in order to fulfil human needs, they were at the same time creating or constructing the normative standards of good and bad. This second interpretation suggests that normative standards do not exist in the world independently of human activities. It is of course a further substantial question how normative standards and values can be constructed through sagely activities. Without directly arguing against the first interpretation,[10] in this chapter I shall follow the second interpretation and explore whether a viable account of metaethical constructivism can be given in respect of Xunzi's ideas.[11]

Normative judgement as human artifice

Xunzi thinks that Confucian ritual and appropriateness represent and instantiate order, while states of affairs contrary to ritual and appropriateness represent and instantiate disorder (*Xunzi* 3.10.12). He also explicitly suggests that ritual and appropriateness were created by the sage kings.[12] He suggests that human beings' inborn nature (*xing*性) is bad and cannot become good by itself,[13] and the sage kings created ritual and appropriateness to transform the chaotic inborn nature of human beings and achieve order and morality (*Xunzi* 23.113.10–12). Xunzi insists that ritual and appropriateness do not come from the human *xing* which is the totality of natural endowments from Heaven. Instead, they are the results of human artifice (*wei*偽) as conscious and intentional exertions. Xunzi uses the analogies of pottery and carpentry to illustrate how the sage kings created ritual and appropriateness: just as the potter creates earthenware from clay and the carpenter creates wooden utensils from wood, the sage kings created ritual and appropriateness from accumulated thoughts and accustomed practices (*Xunzi* 23.114.8–11; *Xunzi* 23.115.20–2): human creativity enables craftsmen to create useful utensils from various materials and the same is true of the sage kings' creation of ritual and appropriateness.

However, ritual and appropriateness, and normative standards in general, are not merely tools or instruments for pre-existing desires or aims. If this were the case, then even though there might be instrumental normativity, it would be unlikely that there would be moral demands able to govern and even override human beings' existing desires and wants. Xunzi suggests that an essential part of human artifice is deliberation (*lü*慮) on natural feelings. Such deliberation and its consequent action form the basis of human artifice (*Xunzi* 22.107.23–4); natural desires by themselves do not determine human actions. It is the heart-mind's approval (*xin zhi suo ke*心之所可) that prompts human actions (*Xunzi* 22.111.4–12). Xunzi also makes an important distinction between natural desires and the heart-mind: natural desires by their very nature know nothing of propriety and are constituted of crude seeking for objects that are simply deemed to be achievable and appropriate. It is the faculty of understanding (*zhi*知) of the heart-mind that is responsible for judging if and which objects of desires should be achieved and guiding our actions accordingly (*Xunzi* 22.111.14–15).

On what basis does the heart-mind make its approval and guide human actions? Xunzi tends to say that the ultimate basis for our approval and action is the Way, the actual contents of which are likely the human way (*rendao*人道) (*Xunzi* 22.111.20–3; *Xunzi* 21.103.25). But how do we know the Way? Xunzi suggests people must be in specific epistemic states that he calls emptiness, unity and tranquillity (*xu yi er jing*虛壹 而靜) in order to know the Way. Put simply, by emptiness Xunzi refers to the state where a person is not hampered by what he already knows and is thus receptive to new ideas and new information; unity refers to the state where different ideas held by a person do not conflict with one another but can co-exist in a coherent way; tranquillity refers to the state where the heart-mind is not engulfed by its various conscious or subconscious activities but can maintain a firm grasp on proper understanding (*Xunzi* 21.103.25–104.9). Such an emphasis on knowing the Way through specific epistemic states might give the impression that for Xunzi the Way refers to the totality of independent normative facts, the perception of which tells us what is right or wrong. Such an impression might be further strengthened by taking into consideration the analogy of the heart-mind and a pan of water. Xunzi points out that just as a pan of water when still and clean is able to clearly reflect things, the heart-mind will also be able to clearly distinguish what is right or wrong when it is not misled by external things and become slanted (*Xunzi* 21.105.5–9).

However, there is no clear indication in the texts exactly how the analogy between the heart-mind and a pan of water should be interpreted. It is clear that Xunzi thinks there is a direct relationship between the heart-mind in a proper state and right judgement. But it is less clear what kind of relationship this is. While it is highly plausible that Xunzi thinks that when the heart-mind is in a proper state, it can clearly perceive some facts, it is less plausible that Xunzi also thinks these are independent and objective normative facts. First, Xunzi does not say that the heart-mind in a proper state knows (*zhi*知) what is right or wrong. Instead he says that the heart-mind determines what is and what is not the case (*ding* shifei定是非), and decides what is doubtful (*jue xianyi*决嫌疑). The use of words like 'determine' and 'decide' strongly suggests that there are not independent normative facts to be readily known by the heart-mind. Secondly, contrary to Mencius who tends to think that when the heart-mind activates its function of thinking (*si*思) it will never fail to get the right answer (Mencius 6A.15),[14] Xunzi is less optimistic. Xunzi points out that thinking and deliberation (*silü*思慮) must be accumulated in order to give rise to ritual and appropriateness (*Xunzi* 23.114.10–11), which suggests that there is not an immediate link between thinking and correct normative judgement. Thirdly, Xunzi also suggests that it is the Way that is the proper balance for weighing fortune and misfortune and as such the Way is the proper guidance for people's action, for not following the Way will surely bring about disaster (*Xunzi* 22.112.1–2). At another place Xunzi explains in more detail the kind of weighing involved: weighing the desirable and the undesirable, and what is worth adopting and what is worth rejecting:

> When something is found to be desirable, then you must deliberate if there is anything undesirable about it before or after. If something is found to be beneficial, then you must deliberate if there is anything harmful of it before or after. Only after inclusive weighing and thorough calculation do you determine whether it is desirable or undesirable, worth adopting or worth rejecting.
>
> (*Xunzi* 3.12.6–7)

It should be noted that Xunzi does not say that the Way, as the ultimate normative standard, is only for determining fortune or misfortune, though this is certainly one aspect of it. Thus, I am not suggesting that the weighing of the desirable and undesirable, and of what is worth adopting and what is worth rejecting, by itself constitutes the normative standards. What I aim to show is that such weighing, as an important aspect of the normative standards, shows that for Xunzi, the normative standards are unlikely to be independent entities waiting for the heart-mind's perception, but are more likely the results of certain activities of the heart-mind.

From artifice to Confucian ritual

To better understand Xunzi's conception of normative standards, we need to investigate Xunzi's explication of Confucian ritual. Xunzi explains the origin of ritual as follows:

> From what did ritual arise? I say: human beings are born with desires. If what they desire is not obtained, they cannot but seek for it. If there are no measures and limits on their seeking, then they will inevitably fight with each other. Fighting leads to disorder, disorder leads to destitution. The former kings disliked such disorder, so they designed ritual and appropriateness to make divisions, so as to nurture people's desires, and to provide for their seeking. They saw to it that desires never wanted for goods and goods were never exhausted by desires. Desires and goods were sustained by each other and developed. This is the origin of ritual. Thus ritual is nurturance.
>
> (*Xunzi* 19.90.3–6)

Xunzi thinks that an essential aspect of Confucian ritual is nurturance (*yang*養) of natural desires. Nurturance is not the satisfaction of natural desires whatever they happen to be. First, '*yang*' is a developmental concept. To nurture something is to cater to its needs in such a way that it will grow into a desirable state.[15] Nurturance of desires therefore refers to the process of catering to people's natural needs and wants so that they have a happy and meaningful life. Secondly, '*yang*' is a cultural answer to disorder and destitution. Xunzi points out elsewhere that human beings are social animals. As a species we live in groups, and we need regulations and standards to maintain a proper order of social life (*Xunzi* 9.39.9–16). Nurturance through ritual is given as a partial solution to the chaos and disorder that will result if there are no proper measures to cater to people's natural needs and wants.

Nurturance is a partial solution because it is just one aspect of ritual; another aspect is differentiation (*bie*別). By differentiation Xunzi refers to the proper ranking of noble and lowly, the proper disparity of elder and youth, and the matching treatment of poor and rich, humble and eminent (*Xunzi* 19.90.10–11). It is obvious that Xunzi believes in a hierarchical society, where people occupy different ranks that carry different privileges and opportunities, from the Son of Heaven down to the ordinary people. Xunzi believes that such a hierarchy is justified and necessary for a proper social order, at least in his times. He argues that different ranks must be arranged in such a way that virtues are matched with positions,[16] positions matched with emolument, and emolument matched with uses (*Xunzi* 10.43.2). In other words, the different ranks of status are designed to match the actual qualities of people and their needs. But Xunzi also makes it clear that hierarchy is a means and not the end. Xunzi points out that if people are of the same power and authority, then no one will obey the other's order and direction, and there will not be social unity, and similarly there will not be ample supply for everyone's equally high demand for material goods (*Xunzi* 9.35.22–36.3). 'Precisely equity demands inequality', Xunzi claims (*Xunzi* 9.36.3).[17] Nor are hierarchical and differential arrangements meant to serve the lavish enjoyment of the powerful; rather, they are necessary for a proper social order that serves everyone's interests. As long as such differential arrangements are enough to serve their social and ethical functions, then there should be no more extravagance (*Xunzi* 10.43.9–19). Xunzi explicitly points out that such a social order is meant to enable everyone, including the Son of Heaven and ordinary people, to have an enjoyable life and have their talents and aspirations fulfilled (*Xunzi* 12.60.1–4). Moreover, Xunzi suggests that when such a proper social order is in place, then everyone under Heaven understands that the social divisions are not aimed at differential treatment, but at establishing a proper order which is sustainable over ten thousand generations (*Xunzi* 12.60.5–6). Xunzi seems to value transparency highly and to believe that a proper order and its normative standards are justifiable to and understandable by everyone, including less educated ordinary people.

Xunzi believes that Confucian ritual plays the double role of nurturance and differentiation. Yet these two functions are actually different aspects of the same normative order, and nurturance is precisely realized through differentiation. Now if differentiation as a reasonable and justifiable social order can explain normativity at the societal level, to what extent is it also justifiable at a personal level? This is a question asked not from the perspective of a person as a member of society, but from the perspective of a person as a rational and self-interested individual. It seems that the social order and its constitutive normative standards are not part of the 'fabrics of the world' that inherently command moral allegiance. Rather they are seemingly only a social construction for solving human practical problems. Could such normative standards command more than instrumental allegiance, particularly given the possibility of free-riding? Xunzi does have an answer for such a potential challenge. He suggests that Confucian ritual actually grants meaning and value to human life, and the corresponding normative values are also constitutive of human agency.

Xunzi argues that what makes human beings human is not the natural desires we have; our human essence lies rather in our having distinctions (*bian*辨) (*Xunzi* 5.18.13–15). He also suggests that of distinctions, none are greater than social divisions, and of social divisions, none are greater than ritual (*Xunzi* 5.18.17). In other words, Xunzi believes that through ritual we exemplify human essence. As an illustration Xunzi points out that while animals also have the biological relationship of parents and offspring, only human beings have and care about the affection (*qin*親) between father and son; only human beings have and care about the differentiation (*bie*別) between male and female (*Xunzi* 5.18.16–17). When Xunzi suggests that only human beings have parent-child affection, he is not primarily referring to the parental care for the child, for animals also care for their offspring; he has in mind the filial respect (xiao孝) of children for parents, and correspondingly the parental love for children. Similarly, by differentiation of sex and gender Xunzi is not primarily referring to the differential treatment of male and female, but rather the reflective awareness of and value attached to sexual and gender differences. I suggest that Xunzi is referring to the distinctive human activity of *investing meaning and value* into natural differences and responses.

We can use the example of funeral ritual to illustrate what kind of activity this is. Xunzi points out that birth is the beginning of human life while death is the end, and the completion of the human way lies in making both the beginning and the end good and valuable (shan善).[18] Ritual is reverent over both the beginning and the end. And the nobleman (junzi君子) maintains the same respectful attitude towards life from the beginning to the end (*Xunzi* 19.93.6–7). In what way does ritual make life good and valuable? A partial answer is given through the way we treat the deceased. Xunzi suggests that if we treat a person well when he is alive but neglect his corpse when he dies, we are not truly reverent towards him. Our previous respect is only dependent on the person's awareness of our attitude. Xunzi calls such behaviour vile and treacherous (*Xunzi* 19.93.7–8). Our respect is a kind of calculated attitude to please the person and to gain benefits for ourselves. Our respect for a person should be true and sincere. Such respect is an exemplification of our care and love for the person. Xunzi argues that all sentient beings in the world care for their fellow beings; even beasts and birds mourn over the loss of a member of their family. Human beings are the most sentient of all living beings, and so it is no wonder they have lifelong love for their parents (*Xunzi* 19.96.10–13). It is a central idea of Confucianism that love and respect for parents (qinqin親親) are both the beginning and the core of the Confucian virtue of humaneness (ren仁).[19] Xunzi admits that our love for parents is natural, but how is such a natural love transformed into an essential part of the ethical virtue of humaneness? And what role is played by the Confucian ritual? Xunzi suggests:

> Nature is the original basis and the plain materials. Artifice is the grandeur and flourishing of culture and ordered pattern. Without nature then artifice has nothing to improve upon. Without artifice then nature cannot beautify itself. Only after nature and artifice have been conjoined is the title of the Sage achieved, and the merit of uniting the whole world fulfilled.
>
> (*Xunzi* 19.95.1–2)

Xunzi makes it clear in this passage that artifice as conscious human endeavour does not work independently of people's inborn nature. Instead the aim of artifice is to improve upon inborn nature which is ugly and chaotic by itself, making it beautiful and part of a flourishing life. Earlier we have seen that the heart-mind's approval is needed to guide chaotic desires and feelings: there must be holistic weighing of the desirable and undesirable, as well as the need to nurture desires through differentiation, so as to build a unified, harmonious and fulfilling society. All these are different aspects or considerations of a holistic normative order.

Besides calling such an order the Way or the human way, Xunzi also calls it culture or cultural form (*wen*文). It is *wen* that Confucius vowed to carry forward as his life mission (Confucius 9.5). *Wen* as the cultural project of Confucianism can be understood as the process of understanding, interpreting and structuring natural needs and wants, feelings and desires of human beings so that we can live a flourishing life together. Xunzi calls such an ideal social state harmonious and unified life in community (*qunju heyi*群居和一) (*Xunzi* 4.17.2; *Xunzi* 19.97.4). Normative standards, including ritual and appropriateness, are essential elements of *wen*. These standards are normative and ethically binding because they are constitutive of the cultural and social life, and by extension, human agency which is constituted by language and culture. Noncompliance with these normative standards is of course possible but it is parasitic upon general compliance and norm-abiding.

Wen transcends the usual distinction between the social and the individual, the rational and the emotional, and the ethical and the prudential. Its very indistinctness in these aspects is its advantage. Xunzi suggests that ritual subtracts from what is excessive and supplements what is insufficient so that there are the cultural forms of love and respect, and beauty and perfection of appropriateness (*Xunzi* 19.94.8). For example, we need to learn how to behave and take care of ourselves as a child; how to return in love and gratitude the love and care we receive from parents; how to take care of elderly parents in need; how to make friends and nurture friendship; how to love our husband or wife and maintain a happy marriage; and how to treat fellow human beings. Confucianism tends to believe that what is quintessentially ethical is exemplified in daily human relationships. Within such an ethical model the altruistic sacrifices that are typically associated with morality in contemporary times are rather seen as the extension of daily relational requirements. We have always been mutually responsible to others ethically because of the relationships we are in and the common life we share. Most of the time such ethical requirements are part and parcel of a flourishing human life. Sacrifices are called for mostly because of exceptional circumstances. Normative standards are thus value frameworks we employ to articulate and express our understanding of humanity and human life. It is also through such value frameworks and normative standards that we transcend the momentary existence of immediate desires and feelings and achieve cross-temporal human agency that has a past and a future. Xunzi calls a person who loses himself in the continuous pursuit of objects of desires someone who enslaves himself for external things; it is only when a person understands the values of life that he can employ things to nurture himself and he is then someone who treasures himself and enslaves external things (*Xunzi* 22.112.9–21). There are indeed ethically right and wrong answers regarding human actions. There are also normative facts regarding which of our normative statements are true or false. However, such normative facts do not exist prior to and independently of human activities. Normative facts are constituted by and constitutive of human beings' self-interpretation of our native conditions, humanity and values of human life. As such, normative values are not entities of the world in a strict sense and thus not a part of the 'fabrics of the world'.

Conclusion

We can now summarize what we have gained through an explication of Xunzi's metaethics from the perspective of metaethical constructivism. Metaethical constructivism is a metaphysical position: it holds that normative values and facts do not exist independently of human activities, but are rather brought into being through specific kinds of human practice. According to my interpretation, Xunzi's metaethical ideas should be understood as a version of metaethical constructivism.[20]

Xunzi agrees with Zhuangzi that normative values do not come from the natural order of the world. But he disagrees with Zhuangzi that normative values are consequently without objectivity. Xunzi suggests that normative values and facts are established through and constituted by human artifice, the core of which is the human practice of living a good life in community. There are two mutually related aspects of such human practice. One is to bring about an orderly satisfaction of the wants and needs of all people, another is to establish a well-ordered society and relationships through distinctions which at the same time embody an understanding of the meaning and significance of human life.

For Xunzi Confucian rituals are the objective answers to the practical task of living a good life in community. Confucian rituals are established through human artifice that aims to solve the double task of providing for human wants and needs, and bringing about orderly and unified community. There are three roots in Confucian rituals: one root lies in Heaven and Earth which endow us with our biological nature; a second root lies in human ancestors who are the origin of our life and history; and the final root is rulers and teachers who bring about order and community (*Xunzi* 19.90.2–22).[21] Confucian rituals aim to establish order and community that allow for good life for all. There are no normative values and facts independent of our quest for order and community. Normative values and facts are established through our understanding and interpretation of our biological nature, history and humanity.

The resultant normative values and facts are nonetheless objective because not every kind of understanding and interpretation works equally well for the double tasks of satisfying wants and establishing a unified community. Xunzi is confident that Confucianism has already established the right answers to the practical task of living a good life in the community. He allows that changes in circumstances might bring about certain alterations to Confucian rituals, but he maintains that the core of rituals remains the same through generations (*Xunzi* 17.82.20–1). This is the case because humanity remains more or less the same. Whether Xunzi's confidence in Confucianism is well founded is of course open to debate, but I think he is right in insisting on there being objective answers to normativity. And just as we should be able to determine which school of thought within a civilization provides a better answer to the practical task of living a good life in community, so we should also be able to ask which of two civilizations, if either, provides a better answer. This is surely not an easy project. But in my opinion, instead of denouncing others as utterly wrong and evil on the basis of our own moral intuitions, metaethical constructivism provides a better description of the nature of our moral conflict, and a more promising chance of finding a common answer to living together.

Notes

1. In this chapter, I simply assume that moral values are a kind of normative values and do not make a clear distinction between moral values and normative values, as this is not a major concern of the chapter. I freely switch between normative values and moral values in accordance with contexts. Such a move is also partially motivated by the lack of sharp distinction between normative values and moral values in Confucianism.
2. By explication, I refer to the explanation and elaboration of the original texts of the *Xunzi*. Reconstruction is the process of the articulation of certain ideas based on indirect textual evidence that I believe are either implicitly held by Xunzi or should be held by him, even though there is no direct textual evidence.
3. There are debates over the relation between the historical figure, Zhuangzi, and the texts of *Zhuangzi*, particularly regarding the question of to what extent the texts were the products of the historical Zhuangzi. In this chapter, I assume the dominant scholarly opinion that the inner chapters of the texts can be attributed to the historical Zhuangzi.
4. It is an open question whether Zhuangzi himself believes that the *Dao* is directly accessible to human beings, and if so in what way. We cannot tackle this issue in this chapter.
5. All citations of the *Xunzi* refer to the ICS Concordance Series Edition (Xunzi 1996). Citations are in the form of chapter/page/line numbers. The English translations are my own, though I have consulted translations by others, including Hutton (2014) and Knoblock (1988–94).
6. *Li* 禮 of Confucianism is an important yet complex concept. There are two aspects of this concept: First, *li* is an all-encompassing concept of propriety, referring to all appropriate standards and norms, indeed including any proper behaviour, relationships or states of affairs. Secondly, *li* is also expressive and is embodied in various forms. The word 'ritual' is meant to convey that for Confucianism there are established codes of behaviour that are also part of the cultural tradition.
7. The exact term '*rendao*' does not appear in the passage but can be inferred. *Rendao* as a term appears six times in the *Xunzi*.

8. Normative values refer to what are good or bad in general, while moral values refer to what are morally good or bad. Moral values are normative values, but there are normative values which are nonmoral. In this chapter, I tend to use the more inclusive term 'normative values'.
9. Objectivity is one criterion of normative realism, but not the only one. Cognitivism is another criterion.
10. Wong has made a very helpful comparison of the realist versus constructivist reading of the *Xunzi*, and points out that textual evidence for either side is quite evenly balanced (Wong 2016).
11. By taking up the second interpretation I am not thereby suggesting that Xunzi is a normative conventionalist. If by normative conventionalism we refer to the position that normative standards are merely the results of social convention and do not have universal applicability beyond the relevant social circle, then in my opinion Xunzi is not a conventionalist. Rather I am exploring the possibility of Xunzi being a value cognitivist without a commitment to ontological value realism. I agree with Alexus McLeod's observation that Xunzi's view does not fit well with the standard picture of realist versus conventionalist (McLeod 2016: 86). David B. Wong also suggests there are limits in classifying Xunzi in terms of Western contemporary metaethical terms (Wong 2016: 157–8).
12. There are debates over whether the sages 'create' or just 'articulate' the ritual (McLeod 2016: 92). Here I use the word 'create' in a general sense and leave open the question of what sort of creation it is.
13. '*Xing*' is not equivalent to 'human nature' and refers only to natural qualities that become so without human conscious effort, particularly natural feelings and desires.
14. I follow the standard section number of the texts of the *Mencius*, as in, for example, Mencius 2003.
15. Some examples are nurturance of livestock, and the healing process from illness, both of which are described by the character *yang*.
16. It is a key belief of Confucian virtue politics that the Son of Heaven and officials must be in possession of ethical virtues.
17. The Chinese characters are '*wei qi fei qi*維齊非齊'. Here Xunzi quotes from the *Book of Documents* and is playing with the different connotations of the same character '*qi*齊'.
18. The same character '*shan*善' is also used to describe what is ethically good. So presumably by using this character Xunzi is referring to a life that is not just good in a general sense, but also good in an ethical sense.
19. For example, Mencius suggests that *qinqin* is *ren*, and the fulfilment of the virtue of *ren* lies in extending the same love and respect to the whole world (Mencius 7A.15).
20. Xunzi does not use the same notions as those of contemporary metaethical constructivism, nor does he make a sharp distinction between ethical and metaethical concerns. But this does not prevent us from presenting his position as a version of metaethical constructivism as a way of explication and reconstruction.
21. I thank Chenyang Li for alerting me to the relevance of the three roots of Confucian rituals to my interpretation of Xunzi's metaethics.

References

Bagnoli, Carla (2013), 'Introduction', in Carla Bagnoli (ed.), *Constructivism in Ethics*. Cambridge: Cambridge University Press, pp. 1–21.

Bagnoli, Carla (2022), *Ethical Constructivism*. Cambridge: Cambridge University Press.

Brink, David O. (1989), *Moral Realism and the Foundations of Ethics*. Cambridge: Cambridge University Press.

Confucius (1992), *The Analects*, 2nd ed., trans. D. C. Lau. Hong Kong: The Chinese University Press.

Darwall, Stephen, Alan Gibbard and Peter Railton (1992), 'Toward Fin de Siecle Ethics: Some Trends', *The Philosophical Review* 101: 115–89.

Enoch, David (2009), 'Can There Be a Global, Interesting, Coherent Constructivism about Practical Reason?', *Philosophical Explorations* 12 (3): 319–39.

Hansen, Chad (1992), *A Daoist Theory of Chinese Thought: A Philosophical Interpretation*. Oxford: Oxford University Press.

Hussain, Nadeem J. Z., and Nishi Shah (2006), 'Misunderstanding Metaethics: Korsgaard's Rejection of Realism', *Oxford Studies in Metaethics* 1: 265–94.

Hutton, Eric L. (trans.) (2014), *Xunzi: The Complete Text*. Princeton, NJ: Princeton University Press.

Knoblock, John (1988–94), *Xunzi: A Translation and Study of the Complete Works*, 3 vols. Standford, CA: Stanford University Press.

Korsgaard, Chrsitine M. (2008), *The Constitution of Agency: Essays on Practical Reason and Moral Psychology*. Oxford: Oxford University Press.

Korsgaard, Chrsitine M. (2009), *Self-Constitution: Action, Identity, and Integrity*. Oxford: Oxford University Press.

Mackie, John L. (1977), *Ethics: Inventing Right and Wrong*. London: Penguin.

McLeod, Alexus (2016), *Theories of Truth in Chinese Philosophy: A Comparative Approach*. London: Rowman and Littlefield.

Mencius (2003), *Mencius*, rev. ed., trans. by D. C. Lau. Hong Kong: The Chinese University Press.

Müller, Andreas (2020), *Constructing Practical Reasons*. Oxford: Oxford University Press.

Rawls, John (1980), 'Kantian Constructivism in Moral Theory: The Dewey Lectures 1980', *Journal of Philosophy* 77 (9): 515–72.

Smith, Michael (1994), *The Moral Problem*. Oxford: Blackwell.

Street, Sharon (2010), 'What Is Constructivism in Ethics and Metaethics?', *Philosophy Compass* 5 (5): 363–84.

Wong, David B. (2016), 'Xunzi's Metaethics', in Eric L. Hutton (ed.), *Dao Companion to the Philosophy of Xunzi*. Dordrecht: Springer, pp. 139–64.

Xunzi (1996), *A Concordance to the Xunzi*, ed. D. C. Lau. Hong Kong: The Commercial Press.

7

Spinoza and Wang Bi: Metaphysics of ethics

Nicholas Bunnin

This chapter explores the grounding of ethics in Spinoza's metaphysics of substance and necessity and in Wang Bi's metaphysics of change and possibility. Each has a depth, complexity and brilliance that fundamentally transformed the philosophical understanding of their different traditions. I contrast their metaphysical methods and concerns and the different outcomes of their thinking about the relations between God or *Dao* and their accounts of the natural world, human thinking and acting, conceptions of ethics and implications for stable governance in society.

Baruch Spinoza, who died at the age of forty-four in 1677, and Wang Bi, who died at the age of twenty-three in 249, employed radically different methods of grounding their metaphysical pictures of the world and of human knowledge and action. Both were born in periods of profound political, cultural and intellectual crisis, when long-settled views of what to believe and how to think and live were open to fundamental re-examination. Spinoza's family had moved from Portugal to Amsterdam, where they could openly practise their Jewish faith. Spinoza himself was born during the final stage of the calamitous Thirty Years' War. Wang Bi was born just after the decaying Han Dynasty collapsed into chaos. Spinoza and Wang Bi responded critically to the philosophical methods, views and terminology of the ancient progenitors of their traditions and to those of their contemporaries. In our times, Spinoza has been lauded as a principal initiator of radical Enlightenment thought, and Wang Bi has been understood as crucial to the metaphysical exploration of both Confucian and Daoist thought.

Spinoza's Method of Geometrical Demonstration gave priority to theoretical reason over practical reason. He began his *Ethics* with an account of God and proceeded through what he held to be rigorous demonstrative argumentation to consider the human mind as comprising intellect and affect: as affect, the powers of emotion and feeling place us in human bondage through what he called inadequate ideas, and the power of intellect frees us from this bondage through knowledge. In doing so, he employed technical terms derived from Aristotle and used by both medieval predecessors and Descartes, to reject their very different metaphysical and theological claims. Spinoza's thinking, although starting with his understanding of God, can also be taken as yielding a natural and human metaphysics of substance and necessity.

Wang Bi's Method of Commentary gave priority to practical reason over theoretical reason. He was inspired by earlier metaphysical commentary on the *Yijing* (Book of Changes) ascribed to Confucius, and expounded a complex multi-layered metaphysical interpretation of the sixty-four hexagrams of the *Yijing*, taking them to offer an exhaustive structure of the kinds of situations in which human agency and its outcome can occur. He employed technical terms drawn from Confucian and Daoist predecessors but used them to overcome the rigidly textual claims of Confucian metaphysics flourishing in the Han dynasty. In his commentary on *Laozi* Wang Bi discussed empty *Dao* that made possible the existence and features of the myriad things, but his focus in his commentary on the *Yijing* was human *Dao*, exemplified by sages (*sheng*) and guiding the agency of excellent persons (*junxi*). Wang Bi's thinking yielded a natural and human metaphysics of change and possibility.

Each of these texts contains a multitude of insights; but I have selectively aligned their most fundamental commitments to focus my comparative metaphysical exploration, crossing important contextual boundaries of time, language, culture, method and orientation. I hope readers will be drawn to explore the metaphysical grandeur of the primary texts for themselves. My aim is to preserve metaphysical insights I find in Spinoza and Wang Bi rather than to use the insights of one to defeat those of the other. This is in accord with the method Yu Jiyuan and I devised to extend the Aristotelian method of Saving the Phenomena to comparative philosophy. Like Aristotle, we saw truth to be many-faceted and had the aim of retaining and integrating facets of truth worth preserving in the diverse opinions (phenomena) we examined, as a way to situate and contribute to our own active philosophical thinking.

In this chapter, I set out what seems worth comparing rather than driving through to any of potential integrative results. In this way, it contrasts with the achievement of Jana Rošker in Chapter 4. I hope my personal waystation will have value for those in our own times turning with fresh philosophical sensibilities to Spinoza or to Wang Bi or for those who for other reasons find questions of necessity and possibility to be fundamental to their own metaphysical task of making sense of the world.

In discussing necessity and possibility, I recognize a deeply puzzling mutual interdependence among formal logic, philosophical logic and metaphysics. But I also take each of these three domains as having a significant measure of autonomy.

Reducing the problems, methods and conclusions of the three to those of any one of them can lead to overwhelming philosophical difficulties. My attention to this issue of appropriate methodologies for different domains is inspired by 'The Discipline of Pure Reason in Its Dogmatic Employment' in *Critique of Pure Reason* (Kant, 630–43) where Kant distinguishes the metaphysical grounds and methods appropriate for mathematics from those appropriate for philosophy, in order to forestall following Spinoza who had used a standard of mathematical rigour rather than the standard of philosophical rigour that Kant employed in dealing with the philosophy of nature.

Thus, in this chapter I explore the possibility of endorsing the peculiar character and claimed priority of metaphysical questions as fundamental to philosophy. Of course, the investigative or systemic choice of metaphysics as first philosophy – the philosophy that orders and renders intelligible investigations in other philosophical domains – risks frustration as much as insight; but that risk seems at least as great for any proposed alternative for the status of first philosophy, such as logic, philosophy of language, epistemology, ontology, science or ethics.

Spinoza: Substance and necessity

Spinoza sets out definitions of substance and of freedom and necessity as he begins 'Of God', the first Part of the *Ethics*, thus starting a metaphysical exploration culminating in the last Part 'Of Human Freedom' that finally justifies the title of the work as a whole:

> Definition 3: By substance I understand what is in itself and conceived through itself, that is, that whose concept does not require the concept of another thing, from which it must be formed.

> Definition 7: That thing is called free which exists from the necessity of its own nature alone and is determined to act by itself alone. But a thing is called necessary, or rather compelled, which is determined by another to exist and to produce an effect in a certain and determinate manner.
>
> (Spinoza, 85-6)

Substance is a thing, but it becomes apparent that for Spinoza substance is neither a thing among a multiplicity of things counting as substances, like those of Aristotle, nor things existing in two kinds, material and mental, like those of Descartes. Substance in some sense exists in itself rather than wholly or partially in anything else. Indeed, substance is defined not only as existing in itself, but also as being in some sense conceived through itself.

If a thing existing in itself could not be conceived through itself, then in Spinoza's definition it would not be substance. More radically, if it did not fall under a concept at all, it might be nothing rather than a thing. If no concept were to be independent in the required way, and every concept required the concept of another thing or things, there would be no substance. If there were no substance, the infinity, unity, necessity and stability of reality would be undermined. Also at stake would be the stability of the meaning or employment of terms Spinoza used to account for what is in substance, especially attributes, affections, modes.

Spinoza brought himself and his understanding into play in many of his initial definitions, as seen above in his definition of substance. Later, Spinoza accounts for the nature of ourselves as finite modes of substance; on this basis, he describes our intellect and affects, and our progress from the inadequate ideas of imagination and reason to adequate knowledge available to us solely through intellectual intuition. If there were no substance, this depiction of ourselves and our knowledge would be at risk.

Furthermore, he distinguishes being in substance from being a part of substance, rejecting the latter as an account of how we are related to God. He argued that as infinite substance God has no parts.

I turn now to Spinoza's definition of freedom and necessity: a thing is called free only if it exists from the necessity of its own nature alone. Its freedom thus involves necessity, rather than excluding necessity. A second condition of its freedom is that it is determined to act by itself alone. Here again, freedom involves determination. But this leads to the question of whether there are differences of meaning or differences in employment of the term 'necessity', when contrasting necessity regarding a free thing and a thing that is not free. Are there two distinct meanings or uses of 'necessity'? Or is the term univocal and/or unifunctional? Is the necessity of things as determined by God the same as the necessity of things determined by finite things (which for Spinoza required something partially in common between cause and effect for cause to compel effect). And how does Spinoza's metaphysical necessity of things relate to other claimed necessities? to logical necessity? mathematical necessity? natural necessity? practical necessity? ethical necessity? aesthetic necessity?

Spinoza's arguments famously concluded that there can be and is only one unique substance, which is infinite, which alone among things exists through its own essence, which has infinite and finite attributes, affections and modes, and which is in essence simple without parts. For Spinoza, substance is God and contains within itself the whole of our natural world. God is intelligible to us through two modes of substance, thought and extension, but has an infinity of other modes that are beyond what we can conceive.

For Spinoza, God and nature must be considered in two ways. First, God is the free cause of the natural world:

> [B]y Natura naturans we must understand what is in itself and is conceived through itself, or such attributes of substance as expressed an eternal and infinite essence, that is … God, insofar as he is considered as a cause.
>
> (Spinoza, 104-5)

> [B]y Natura naturata I understand whatever follows from the necessity of God's nature, or from any of God's attributes, that is all the modes of God's attributes insofar as they are considered as things which are in God, and can neither be nor be conceived without God.
>
> (Spinoza, 105)

In this way, Spinoza's rephrasing of an ontological argument for the existence of God is, or is on the edge of, an ontological argument for the existence of the natural world. The temptation to see these as a single argument is intensified by the single addition of the phrase 'Deus sive Natura' [God or Nature] to the Latin translation of the Dutch text of the *Ethics*. There is perhaps a question as to whether the two terms are interchangeable or not; but in any case, would an ontological argument for the existence of the natural world fare any better than an ontological argument for the existence of God?

Two further points follow. First, God as a free cause acts out of the necessity of his own essence, rather than acting teleologically. God's creativity is thus a matter of necessity rather than a matter of intention and choice. Although not the same, Spinoza's God has echoes of Plotinus' constitution of reality through emanations grounded in the intellectual self-contemplating of the One. Secondly, Spinoza ascribes both the persistent existence of finite things, including ourselves, and the mutual power of finite things to destroy one another, to their sharing material *conatus* or striving to preserve their being. Thus *conatus* is used to explain both persistence and change.

Spinoza's contrast between infinite and finite requires us to understand his account of how finite things, including ourselves, are related to infinite God. If God were not an actual simple infinite thing, then there would be no substance. Yet we understand finite things through the division of their parts, while the unique infinite thing is indivisible and hence without parts. For Spinoza, the question of how infinite and finite things are related to one another is thus a facet of the question of how a simple thing and things with parts are related to one another. Because for Spinoza an infinite thing, unlike finite things, is beyond measure, this is also a question of how the immeasurable and the measurable are related.

Let us now turn to Spinoza's assessment of our human selves, not as substances but as finite modes of substance entirely governed like all finite things in nature by causal necessity. He rejected the Cartesian dichotomy between mind and body and, with it, human freedom of the will and any explanation of our agency as involving intentions.

He ascribed these rejected views of human freedom and agency to inadequate ideas of imagination that can be overcome by adequate ideas of intellect.

Spinoza thus focused on our finite intellect, drawn from God's infinite intellect, as the human mental power that allows us to achieve knowledge, including ethical knowledge of how to live. However, Spinoza viewed our intellect, as the greatest part of our minds, to be internally challenged by our affects or passions, as the smallest part of our minds. Affects trap us in human bondage. Intellect on its own, being distinct from affect, had no causal capacity to free us from this bondage, because only an affect could causally defeat or control an affect. But in one case alone human intellect is not on its own. For human intellect and affect fuse together in our knowledge-and-love of God, purely grounded in our *intellectual intuition* rather than in our imagination or reason and allowing us to cure our sickness of mind and to free ourselves from bondage. This, rather than freedom of the will, constitutes human freedom for Spinoza.

I conclude this section by noting some continuities between Spinoza's *Ethics* and his political writings in *Theologico-Political Treatise* and *Tractatus Politicus*, where he presented his proposal for the stable and peaceful governance of society. He argued for a rational politics of tolerance, peace and freedom under the law, grounded on philosophical truth rather than on tyrannically strife-ridden religious authority.

Tolerance would be available to all religious bodies, granting priority over their doctrinal differences to a shared minimal agreement to which widely diverse religious believers could subscribe. In principle, this agreement would provide crucial political space for his own radically heterodox account of God and humanity. Perhaps Spinoza hoped that a more general acceptance of his own religious knowledge through adequate ideas would supplant diverse affect-driven religious doctrines confined to inadequate ideas at the level of imagination. For him this would both enable and justify stable political peace by eliminating major grounds for tyranny.

Wang Bi: Change and possibility

Wang Bi's *Commentary on the Yijing* (*Book of Changes*) provides metaphysical grounding for guiding people seeking to achieve their aims in the natural world. This world is one of flux and possibility: things (including people), situations and choices for acting, all form and dissipate rather than remaining permanent, uniform or fully predictable. General, not universal, principles or patterns of change can usefully be discerned, but none of these patterns are guaranteed to be permanent or universal.

The natural world is governed by cosmic *Dao*, the source of all things but not itself a thing. Cosmic *Dao* is not to be understood as outside the world or as dependent on anything outside the world. For Wang Bi, sages both discovered cosmic *Dao* and formed and ordered the sixty-four hexagrams of the *Yijing* which exhaustively structure and encode the possibilities of change in the world. Each hexagram is a pattern of six unbroken and broken lines formed by placing one trigram of unbroken and broken lines above another.

Wang Bi criticized those taking the texts as primary rather than reading them as inadequate renderings of what had been said in speech. Indeed, he sought to reach even beyond what was said by the great figures who inspired him; he held that their speech was inadequate to render their thinking. He preferred Confucius – whose thinking exemplified not only *Dao* but also *you* (being), *wu* (nothingness) and *wuwei* (non-action) – to Laozi, whom he criticized for speaking endlessly of such matters without embodying them. Wang Bi's aim to drive beyond texts and speech to thinking was focused specifically on what he took to be mysterious or dark matters. For him, relations among thinking, speaking and writing raise questions for philosophical scrutiny.

In their thinking, the sages grasped *Dao's* mysterious power to create, constitute and regulate the workings of the natural world. In the Confucian tradition, thinking involved all the capacities of the human *xin* (heart/mind), including reason, desire and emotion, rather than reason alone. For Wang Bi, the thinking of the sages is better grasped in terms of the shifting inclusive unity and changing balance of *yin* (negative principle) and *yang* (positive principle) ascribed to the *xin* (heart/mind) in attunement with *Dao*, rather than in terms of concepts ascribed solely to the intellect. Furthermore, not only *Dao* but Confucius as a sage are mysteries that can be apprehended but not defined, and the thinking of sages requires the highest cognitive and ethical achievement of *de* (virtue or power).

The metaphysically understood cosmic *Dao* of heaven and earth and its creation of the myriad things in the natural world frames Wang Bi's commentary. Things come into being through the interaction of *yang*, which provides the active flow of *qi* (vital energy) and *yin*, which provides the receptive *li* (forms) which *qi* temporarily consolidates into things, including persons. Wang Bi's primary orientation, however, is repeatedly shown to be the metaphysics of human *Dao*, grounding how a *junzi* (excellent person) in risky and unstable natural and social circumstances can choose and act with successful outcomes in a world of change and possibility.

The hexagrams model not only a world of possibilities, but also a world of changing probabilities of human success and failure according to the aims, characters and placement of human agents in different kinds of natural and social situations. Wang Bi's commentary seems to embody something like a dynamic probabilistic analytical and predictive modelling of interactive human agency in contrast to a model of interactive human agency organized in terms of universal causal laws.

Turning to the metaphysical roots of Wang Bi's *Commentary*, I draw on his discussion of hexagram 1 ䷀: *qian* (pure *yang*) and hexagram 2 ䷁: *kun* (pure *yin*), guided by his citation of the saying of Confucius: 'Qian and Kun, do they not constitute the two-leaved gate into the Changes? *Qian* is a purely *yang* thing and *Kun* is a purely *yin* thing.'

Wang Bi's commentaries regularly included a 'commentary on the judgement', discussing the body of the hexagram as a whole and clarifying its chief controlling principle. Clarifying here seems to be a matter of making evident rather than of definition; the 'controlling principle' identifies inherent tendencies of things, situations and human characters, and perhaps can be compared to 'potential', 'power' and 'disposition'. He also typically includes a commentary on the image (the means to express ideas), on the words of the text (the means to explain such images), and on phrases included in the so-called Ten Wings (*shiyi*) – traditionally ascribed to Confucius – to give injunctions guiding human action in view of the good and bad fortune involved.

There are similarly ordered commentaries on the component trigrams and their place in the hexagram, and commentaries on each line of the hexagram and its place in relation to the other lines. Of special importance are lines 2 and 5, the central lines of the trigrams, clarifying their controlling principles. In effect, the sixty-four hexagrams are transformed into immensely fine discriminations to analyse and predict changes in the natural world and to guide human action in the natural and social world.

We might ask whether and in what sense such a finite model, however refined, might be adequate to deal with an infinity of different circumstances, a question drawn from a crucial concern in the philosophy of mathematics. But Wang Bi's grounding for his attempt to bring some pragmatically useful order of understanding and action in a world of change and possibility without being overwhelmed by chaos is better seen as metaphysical rather than mathematical.

Wang Bi inherited a traditional ordering of the sixty-four hexagrams: each, except the first, was naturally led into by its predecessor and, except the last, naturally led into its successor in a fixed and intelligible progression. But aside from the crucial pairing of the first two hexagrams that metaphysically ground the whole system of changes, he held that in orienting and guiding action the circumstances under one hexagram could change the circumstances under any other hexagram, depending on the outcome of the action taken in the context of the initial hexagram. In some cases, therefore, including the initial two hexagrams, his commentaries were accompanied by discussions providing the sequence of the hexagrams and the hexagrams in irregular order.

In the *Yijing* the judgement for hexagram 1 *qian* [pure *yang*], in which all lines in the trigram above and trigram below are unbroken lines, is:

Qian consists of fundamentality [*yuan*], prevalence [*heng*], fitness [*li*] and constancy [*zhen*].

(Wang Bi, 129)

Wang Bi's commentary on this judgement begins:

How great is the fundamental nature of *Qian*! The myriad things are provided their beginnings by it, and, as such, it controls Heaven. It allows clouds to scud and rain to fall and things in all their different categories to flow into forms.

(Wang Bi, 129)

In his commentary on the words of the judgement text, he writes:

> 'Fundamentality' is the leader of goodness [*shan*]. 'Prevalence' is the coincidence of beauty [*jia*]. 'Fitness' is coalescence with righteousness [*yi*]. 'Constancy' is the very trunk of human affairs.
>
> (Wang Bi, 130)

In this way, virtue or power [*de*] was embedded in Wang Bi's fundamental metaphysics of change and possibility. Wang Bi immediately goes on to characterize the *junzi* (the gendered noble man) as sufficiently embodying the virtue or power [*de*] of humanity [*ren*] 'to be a leader of men', with the beauty in him 'sufficient to make men live in accordance with propriety [*li*]'. He engenders 'fitness in people sufficient to keep them in harmony with righteousness, and his constancy is firm enough to serve as the trunk of human affairs' (Wang Bi, 130). There was thus an easy transition of focus from the *Dao* of heaven to human *Dao* and its application to governance in a well-ordered society:

> In the *Yijing*, the judgment for hexagram 2 *kun* (pure *yin*) is: Sublime success, Furthering through the perseverance of a mare.

Wang Bi explains:

> The mare is a metaphor for the Earth, for it travels the earth without limit. [T]he noble man who sets out to do something, if he takes the lead, will be in breach of Dao, but if he follows and is compliant, he will find his rightful place.
>
> (Wang Bi, 130)

In moving from *qian* to *kun*, *Dao* of heaven becomes *Dao* of heaven and earth, to complete its expression in the myriad things. Without this expression through the vital energy [*qi*] of *qian* taking on the earthly forms of *kun*, there could not be things, including humans, and the existence of *Dao*, heaven and earth would all be uncertain.

Moreover, this would be metaphysical, and not just epistemic, uncertainty. Finally, the discussion of *junzi* in *kun* again involves a change of focus from cosmic *Dao* of heaven and earth to human *Dao* and its application to governance – which should not be hegemonistic but grounded metaphysically in the natural and social world of change and possibility.

Comparing Spinoza and Wang Bi: Implications for our times

I begin with the framing methods of Spinoza and Wang Bi. If Spinoza's method of demonstration in geometric order is merely a matter of propaedeutic exposition, it can permit his metaphysical insights to be extracted for independent scrutiny. But if we take the geometric ordering as carrying with it a compelling standard of proof drawn from geometry, we can question the extension of a method suitable for geometry and mathematics to employment in metaphysics, which might have its own appropriate methods of justification. We can ask similar questions about Wang Bi's metaphysical commentary on the *Yijing*. The priority he accorded to thinking over speaking and writing might warn us against taking his apparent method as determining his own metaphysical insights and standards.

Underlying questions about the framing methods of Spinoza and Wang Bi are questions about their different priorities regarding reason. I claimed earlier that Spinoza's metaphysics gave priority to theoretical reason and the workings of the natural world, while Wang Bi's metaphysics, at least in his *Yijing* commentary, gave priority to practical reason and human agency in the natural world. I am deeply suspicious of reducing practical reason to theoretical reason and of reducing theoretical reason to practical reason. For me, both are needed in dealing with the most fundamental philosophical questions about ourselves in the natural world, where both Spinoza and Wang Bi, with their different understandings of the natural world, placed us. We should not presume that we have a neutral notion of the natural world from which to judge the views of Spinoza and Wang Bi.

I surmise, however, that Spinoza would have seen Wang Bi as confined to affect-determined inadequate ideas and in need of liberation through an intellectual love of God, and that Wang Bi would have seen Spinoza as lacking an adequate appreciation of agency in those sufficiently educated in knowledge and virtue to recognize their circumstances and act well. Although Wang Bi was not supporting a religious doctrine of freedom of the will, the rich moral psychology of his heart/mind would conflict with the austere moral psychology endorsed by Spinoza. At stake are the roles of intellect and affect in the moral psychology of human thought and action. Can humans think and act with the resources of intellect alone or do we require the additional resources of desire, emotion and imagination somehow entangled with intellect for us even to make sense of finite human intellect?

I now turn to compare Spinoza's God and Wang Bi's cosmic *Dao* of heaven and earth. A crucial difference is that for Spinoza God is a thing, but for Wang Bi *Dao* is not a thing. We can ask 'What is it then?', but if that question is reserved for things, it would be inappropriate to ask it about *Dao*, which is not a thing. Wang Bi understood *Dao* as an emptiness making possible the existence of things. Our question would be appropriate if an emptiness were a thing, but then we would seem to be asking about a thing which is not a thing. Perhaps we could turn to mathematics where zero or nothing is a number without quantity, but the methods and standards of mathematics might not be appropriate for metaphysics.

For Spinoza, God is not only a thing, but is the only thing that is a substance, on which the existence of all non-substantial things depends. We might be tempted to listen to the echoes back and forth between the texts and to claim that Spinoza and Wang Bi had the same or very similar insights about God and *Dao*, masked by differences in articulation. This seems to me too easy to be true, but the echoes still beckon me.

Thus, there seem to be plausible converging claims of immanence rather than transcendence in the cases of both Spinoza's God and Wang Bi's *Dao*. European Enlightenment thinkers towards the end of the eighteenth century, for example, condemned Spinoza and Chinese philosophy together as sources of heretical pantheism on the grounds of their rejection of the transcendence of God or *Dao*. Spinoza's escape from this charge relies on his view that human knowledge of God is based on only two of God's infinite modes, thought and extension, with the infinity of God's other infinite modes being beyond our power to conceive. We could conjecture that these alternate infinite modes might be conceived by alternative finite beings in the natural worlds inconceivable to us that they inhabit. But how could they conceive anything if the infinite modes forming their natural worlds did not include thought? And how then could they possibly conceive their worlds through a metaphysics of substance and necessity, as Spinoza proposes for us?

Spinoza's discussion of the conceivable and inconceivable can be compared to Wang Bi's embrace of the dark or mysterious in his claim that thinking cannot be adequately captured by writing or speaking. It is a matter of scholarly controversy whether Wang Bi analysed what we write and say in terms of concepts. But if thinking is in some sense pre-conceptual or non-conceptual, then any account of thinking as saying in the heart becomes suspect; and we might also ask how pre-conceptual or non-conceptual thinking might become conceptualized. Is this a matter in which we are agents or passive? Or are we better understood as being variably placed on a continuum of agency and passivity in the conceptualization of thinking?

The immanence of Wang Bi's cosmic *Dao* appears to be more straightforward than Spinoza's, so long as transcendence is ascribed to things that exist beyond the limits of the world and are nevertheless required for the world and for the things it contains to exist as the things that they are. Wang Bi's cosmic *Dao* is not a thing and is the, or a, limit of the world rather than beyond the limits of the world. Nevertheless, as the limit of the world enabling the multitude of things to exist, it has a special status comparable in some ways to the role of Spinoza's God.

Earlier I suggested that questions about Spinoza's account of relations between the infinite and the finite, the simple and the many-parted and the immeasurable and the measurable can be taken as facets of the same question. There are certainly questions also about the relations between Wang Bi's empty cosmic *Dao* of heaven and earth as the ultimate metaphysical grounds of possibility and the myriad things, and about the dynamic interaction between *Dao*'s active creative power of *yang* and its passive receptive capacity of *yin*. Although *Dao* is constant or eternal in the sense of unchanging, it is perhaps better understood as being boundless, but without the implication of being infinite. If *Dao* of heaven and earth is simple and immeasurable, it is not a simple and immeasurable *thing*. The questions of its being simple rather than having parts and being immeasurable rather than measurable might be open to rejection – rather than being answered 'no' – because *Dao* is outside the scope of its appropriate application. But this is an issue to puzzle over rather than a conclusion to reach.

In comparing Spinoza's metaphysics of substance and Wang Bi's metaphysics of change, I focus on Spinoza's *conatus* and Wang Bi's *qi* in their different accounts of the workings of the natural world. *Conatus* can be rendered as material striving and *qi* can be rendered as material energy. Although this partial convergence of translation places the two terms in shouting distance, the assumption that they are identical can be challenged by investigating their differing intellectual trajectories and relations with differing clusters of associated terms. Spinoza confined *conatus* to the natural world; Wang Bi introduced *qi* at the more fundamental level of *Dao*. At that level *qi*, rather than the successive forms it assumes, is the key to understanding the workings of the world.

In any event, accounting for change seems to be the main problem for Spinoza's metaphysics and accounting for persistence seems to be the main problem for Wang Bi's metaphysics. Without *conatus* Spinoza's natural world would be both immobile without change and empty without enduring worldly things having a natural tendency to persist. Without *qi* Wang Bi's natural world, characterized by change and explaining persisting things as temporary consolidations of energy, would be impossible.

In contrasting the fundamental place of necessity in Spinoza's metaphysics and of possibility in Wang Bi's metaphysics, contemporary discussions often give priority to necessity and possibility in systems of formal logic. But any necessity-based logical system can be shown to be equivalent to a possibility-based logical system. And in any case, if we are concerned with the contrasting metaphysics of necessity and of possibility, it is not at all clear that formal logical equivalence determines metaphysical equivalence. Thinking about Spinoza and Wang Bi might encourage contemporary philosophers to explore a metaphysics-first approach to necessity and possibility. If the task of metaphysics is one of making sense of ourselves and the world, we can turn to contrasting what it is like to make sense of living in Spinoza's world of necessity with what it is like to make sense of living in Wang Bi's world of possibility. Here we reach the human nub of the alternative reflective understandings of ethics available to Spinoza's mind and Wang Bi's heart/mind.

Spinoza's mind and Wang Bi's heart/mind are both physical and mental and are in different senses relational. Causal interdependence with other natural things is one reason for Spinoza to deny that human selves are substances and assert that they are finite modes of substance. It is not clear whether being finite modes leans more towards being the Cartesian substantial 'I' that he rejects or more towards not being an 'I' at all. The issue is intensified by Spinoza's rejection of any understanding of our human selves as acting through intentions involving both affect and intellect. He held this understanding – which is arguably crucial to understanding agency and practical reasoning – to be based on inadequate ideas at the level of imagination. He replaced this intentional account with a causal account of action, with the potential for knowledge based on adequate ideas being drawn from intellect alone. This ascription of intellectual intuition to finite human minds is open to question, however. Kant classically and perhaps decisively restricted human minds to sensible intuition rather than extending it to intellectual intuition and he contested Spinoza's dismissal of imagination as a corrupting source of inadequate ideas.

Relational interdependence of heart/minds was for Wang Bi a source of our potential to move towards being fully human rather than a demotion of the status of what it is to be human. Rather than causal, his functional interdependence was based on the Confucian relations between human beings in family and society. In addition, Wang Bi examined different levels of knowledge – those achieved by petty persons, excellent persons and sages – but this progress involved at each stage the reciprocal engagement of intellect, passion and desire. This can be understood as a single intellectual and ethical virtue, where virtue is understood as exemplifying material power or *qi*. For Wang Bi the transformative path to achieving fuller humanity was human *Dao* devised by sages rather than the cosmic *Dao* of heaven and earth; and indeed, some heart/minds surpass taking human *Dao* as a written or spoken recipe for progress by embracing *Dao* in the fluidly creative depths of their thought.

I have already discussed continuities between Spinoza's concerns in his political writings and in his *Ethics*. The whole of Wang Bi's commentary on the *Yijing* can be construed as a guide to governance because it focused on the choice and timing of appropriate actions of the *junzi*, those capable of governing. To what extent, if at all, would Spinoza's governors have the resources for agency that Wang Bi required to govern successfully in a world of possibility? To what extent, if at all, would Wang Bi's governors have the resources for dispassionate intellect that Spinoza required to govern successfully in a world of necessity?

The metaphysics of both Spinoza and Wang Bi have implications for our times, and the significance of each can be enhanced by thinking about them together. I conclude this chapter by suggesting some starting points that I especially value.

Of special interest are the implications of Spinoza for contemporary investigations of structural necessity and the implications of Wang Bi's focus – well before Pascal – on the calculation of probabilities. Both are important themes in contemporary political and social discussion.

Contemporary philosophers of physics could explore Wang Bi's *qi* and Spinoza's *conatus* as contrasting precursors linking the fundamental roles of material energy in quantum and standard physics, respectively.

Some contemporary philosophers of religion might benefit from comparing Spinoza's God as a fundamentally infinite, simple and immeasurable thing and Wang

Bi's Cosmic *Dao* as unlimited emptiness that is not a thing, both with each other and with their own committed views. For those framing their thoughts on measuring infinity by Georg Cantor's proof that there are mathematical infinities of different sizes, it is important to recall that Cantor himself refused the extension of his proof to what he took to be the immeasurable metaphysical infinity of God.

Contemporary philosophers exploring human reasoning and agency might engage with the implications of the priority of theoretical reason in Spinoza and of practical reason in Wang Bi, and of Spinoza's causal and Wang Bi's intentional accounts of action. This exploration has obvious relevance to contemporary investigations of theory and practice, as do the contrasting moral psychologies and understandings of what it is to be or to become a human self in Spinoza and Wang Bi.

These are starting points addressed to contemporary philosophers pursuing their different specialities, but my real hope is that some philosophers and other readers will continue to find their own ways through a wider range of issues addressed in this chapter. Some might find their way to a single integrative metaphysical position incorporating elements drawn from Spinoza and Wang Bi. Others might embrace a metaphysical pluralism celebrated as a source of continuing reflection about how to make sense of ourselves and our world. In either case, I invite readers to share my sense that serious metaphysical investigation is both extremely difficult and an extraordinary delight.

References

Kant, Immanuel (1998), *Critique of Pure Reason*, trans. and ed. Paul Guyer and Allen W. Wood. Cambridge: Cambridge University Press.
Spinoza, Benedict de (1994), *The Ethics in a Spinoza Reader*: *The Ethics and Other Works*, ed. and trans. Edwin Curley. Princeton, NJ: Princeton University Press.
Wang, Bi (1994), *The Classic of Changes*: *A New Translation of the I Ching* as interpreted by Wang Bi, trans. Richard John Lynn. New York: Columbia University Press.

8

Personhood in Indian metaphysics: Touchpoints with other traditions

Gavin Flood

There is no Sanskrit word that directly translates 'metaphysics', but Indian philosophy expressed through the medium of Sanskrit, along with pre-philosophical scriptures and commentaries, has been deeply concerned with metaphysics from its earliest beginnings. It has a long history of debate about the nature of time and space, causation, what it is to be a person, the ontological status of the world, the existence of God, and what it is to live a good life. This chapter maps some of this diverse landscape, taking concrete examples from the philosophical situation in the medieval period, roughly corresponding to Scholasticism in Europe and to neo-Confucianism in China, and identifying touchpoints with other traditions.

India did not explicitly make the Greek distinction between *logos* and *mythos*, reason and story, but it nevertheless held reason to be a way of knowing, and rational arguments between schools were undertaken mostly in the form of commentaries on scripture, a mode of inquiry similar to Scholasticism in medieval Europe. In this chapter, I will focus on the idea of the human self as a central theme in relation to the idea of transcendence, along with the soteriological understanding of the human person that addresses questions about the predominance of action or cognition and knowledge.

Different systems had distinct views about the nature of the self, and about how the broader question of reality as the unity of a single substance or a pluralism of distinct substances impacted upon this question. Although it is difficult to incontrovertibly establish the history of philosophical texts,[1] there are philosophical themes in the very early literature of the founding revelation, the *Ṛg-veda*. Here a famous hymn at the foundations of Indian philosophy, possibly dating back to as early as 1200–1000 BCE, posits an ontological question about the very nature of life and the relation of being to nothingness. In the very beginning, what was here? Was there something or nothing? Perhaps even the highest deity does not know.[2] Apart from the paradoxical idea of there *being* nothing, this suggests that the ontological question about the relation of being to nothing was posited at the very foundations of Indian philosophy in this pre-philosophical text. Heidegger's claim that the ancient Greeks raised the ontological question, the question of the Being of beings,[3] could also be applied to this ancient Indic source. The questioning theme is taken up by the *Śvetāśvatara-upaniṣad* ('the esoteric treatise of [the sage] with the white mule') which opens with several speculative metaphysical questions about the nature of time, the cause of an absolute power, and the foundation upon which the world is established.[4]

Brahmanical thinking[5] formed from the revelation known as the Veda. This scriptural body developed over a long period of time, the earliest layers being hymns to a variety of deities that would have been used liturgically to accompany the central Vedic rite of sacrifice. The body of literature called the Upaniṣads from about 800 BC offered symbolic interpretation of earlier textual material, and philosophical schools unfolded from this, notably the school of Vedic exegesis, the Mīmāṃsā, and a school of philosophical substantivism called the Vedānta. These schools were partly reacting to Śramaṇa traditions such as Buddhism and Jainism, which did not accept the authority of the Veda, were generally atheistic, and claimed that suffering and reincarnation could be overcome through meditation and asceticism. The Mimamsa defended the Vedic sacrificial model and the Vedānta brought ideas of reincarnation, renunciation and liberation within the remit of Vedic thought.[6]

Here I will focus discussion on metaphysical systems as they had developed in the early medieval period from the fourth to eleventh centuries CE, at a time when the philosophical systems had clarified their positions in relation to each other. The dominant mode of philosophical engagement was to clarify differences rather than reach consensus.[7] By the early medieval period religions focussed on the deities Śiva, Viṣṇu and the Goddess were emerging with their own scriptural revelation, engaging with each other and with the ambient philosophical discourse. I will examine the question of the self in relation to transcendence as presented in five systems: the Mīmāṃsā school of exegesis, the Advaita Vedānta (also known as the Later (Uttara) Mīmāṃsā), the Sāṃkhya dualists, the Buddhist impersonalists and the Śaiva idealists. Finally, no discussion of Indian metaphysics would be complete without some acknowledgement of the theistic philosophies that developed and their arguments for the existence of God.

The Mīmāṃsā philosophy of action

For the Mīmāṃsā, the most significant characteristic of human reality is that we act: action is more important than cognition, because action has consequences in the world. As action is a defining hallmark of persons in modern Existentialism, so action is central to the Mīmāṃsā understanding of person. But this is no existentialist discourse, because the philosophy is about *ritual* action, the sacrifice, along with the language used to command. As human beings we need to be concerned with the ritual action enjoined by scriptural revelation. The ritual act for the Mīmāṃsā, namely the sacrifice, is performed not to achieve a specific purpose such as going to heaven at death (even though this is a consequence), but because it is enjoined by scripture. We should act in conformity to *dharma*, truth or duty; the founding text of the school, Jaimini's *Mīmāṃsā Sūtra*, opens with the statement: 'Now the inquiry into Dharma.'[8] We must perform ritual action because of *vidhi*, injunction, and these injunctive sections of the text have greater importance than other statements that simply commend those injunctions.[9] Thus in its emphasis on bringing about transmundane desires, the Mīmāṃsā is primarily a study of Vedic texts and the science of language to discern the meaning of the unauthored, infallible body of injunctions and prohibitions.[10] The purpose of the Vedic revelation is injunction which is the heart of dharma, and such injunction has a productive force (*bhāvanā*) that brings about the result of the ritual act performed as a consequence of the injunction. This unseen effect (*apūrva*) inheres in the soul of the patron rather than in the sacrifice itself, although the purpose of the injunction is not the human consequence but simply the fact of its being commanded by scripture.

Much of this literature, such as Mahādeva Vedāntin's ritual manual, is concerned with precise ritual detail and procedure rather than abstract speculation; for example, the injunction to sacrifice a cow entails that a goat is not sacrificed. We need to pay attention to the detail of what is required, which remains sufficient for the performance of correct action. In this philosophy we are not defined by abstract purpose, but by our correct ritual action. The performance of sacrifice produces a transcendent power (*apūrva*) that ensures the results of sacrifice, particularly heaven (*svarga*) after death (rather than liberation). Somewhat akin to the idea of accumulated merit as the result of good action, *apūrva* is a force that operates only within a single lifetime, as the accumulation of sacrificial merit for the sacrificial patron (*yajmāna*).

Thus the sacrifice is metaphysically significant and its performance forms the person. We are constructed by ritual act, which is substantiated by the common Hindu notion of rites of passage or *saṃskāra* in which the person is formed from birth to death. *Saṃskāra* is that which is made, put together or constructed; and the destiny of the metaphysical principle of the person, the *ātman* or life essence that continues after cremation of the body, the last sacrifice (*antyeṣṭi*), is determined by ritual action. While the later tradition accepted reincarnation, this seems to have been absent from Mīmāṃsā's origin where there is a sense of continuity into the realm of the ancestors (*pitaraḥ*) but not of return to the world. We perform ritual not to go to heaven but simply because it is a Vedic injunction and so is regarded as a good in itself and thus might be seen as a kind of celebration – an act in which personal desire and intention are minimized in celebration of the act itself.

This philosophy of ritual action presents the human person in a distinct light. Human desires and purposes are quite irrelevant to the performance of ritual for it is injunction that counts. There is a 'de-centring' of the human, to use Clooney's term,[11] such that the objectivity of sacrificial rite takes precedence over personal reward. The ritual itself almost has an ontology that takes precedence over the performer, who must be defined in terms of their suitability (*adhikāra*) to perform the rite. So only Brahmins can perform it; women, lower castes and imbeciles are forbidden from participating.

The idea of a human purpose (*puruṣārtha*) is superseded by the idea of the sacrificial purpose (*kratvārtha*). The importance of this Mīmāṃsā insight has perhaps been underestimated in histories of Indian philosophy, as this is a clear articulation of sacrificial religion that was arguably the core practice through the medieval kingdoms to their demise with the ascendancy of Mughal and then British rule.

Because of the emphasis on dharma, the philosophy of correct ritual action, the Mīmāṃsā extended its inquiry to other areas of philosophical concern. The fundamental structure of the primacy of ritual, almost a kind of ritual agency, led to its implications being worked out in other areas of philosophical inquiry, especially language. Through analysing the sentence and arguing for its syntactic unity completed by the expectancy of the reader, the Mīmāṃsā philosophers showed how Vedic injunction functions and how sacrificial purpose impacts upon a human community of qualified practitioners.[12] Related to the analysis of language are epistemological questions; the Mīmāṃsā accepted all six traditional modes of knowledge[13] to establish the reality of the world and thus rejected the idealism of rival traditions, particularly Yogācāra Buddhism. For the Mīmāṃsā the world is real, and objects of knowledge can be known because they contain substance (*dravya*), quality (*guṇa*), action (*karma*) and non-existence (*abhāva*), along with sub-categories. This aligns the school with the other major realist philosophy, the Vaiśeṣika.[14]

This de-centring of the human and the privileging of impersonal sacrificial act as the fulfilment of revealed injunction becomes overlaid by other discourses that, in complete contrast, put the self at the centre of philosophical concern. The Mīmāṃsā emphasis on ritual action made a claim about textual revelation itself: the sections on ritual act (the *karma-kāṇḍha*), for the Mīmāṃsā, are considered to be the most important, in contrast to sections on knowledge (*jñāna-kāṇḍha*), namely the Upaniṣads, which they regarded as mere elaboration and extension (*arthabhāva*) of the injunctive material. The later Mīmāṃsā or Vedānta, by contrast, claimed the exact opposite: the scriptural sections on knowledge are most important and reveal the true nature of the self and its relation to cosmic Being.

The Vedānta philosophy of Being

In contrast to the Mīmāṃsā where action defines who and what a person is, the Vedānta is concerned with how Being defines the person. The central term here is *brahman*. This word meant power in the earliest scripture, the *Ṛg-veda*: the power underlying the chants in the sacrificial rite,[15] but by the first millennium CE has come to mean an absolute, all-pervading reality that sustains the cosmos, with which, in one view, all beings are identical. I render the term *brahman* here as 'Being' because it is the power in the Upaniṣads that sustains and upholds all appearances, including the esoteric connection (*bandha*) between different realities, such as the sunrise and the Vedic ritual of the horse sacrifice. The term *brahman* is characterized in the later literature as 'Being' or *sat*, that which exists, along with consciousness (*cit*) and bliss (*ānanda*).

Whether *brahman* can be translated as 'Being' is contentious, but it is arguably justified on the grounds that as 'Being' is the foundational ground of all 'beings', so *brahman* is the foundational ground of all existents, both sentient and non-sentient.[16] It is the power that pervades the cosmos as sap pervades wood or salt pervades water.[17] The term occurs throughout the Upaniṣadic literature such as the *Kena* upaniṣad where *brahman* is the power that surpasses all the other gods (see Chapter 10). The semantic range of *brahman* is wider than the English 'Being' because it comes to contain within it the idea of transcendence, of the source and sustaining power of the universe that is not simply immanent, although it is that too. With the early Upaniṣads such as the *Bṛhadāraṇyaka* and *Chāndogya*, *brahman* is used in the sense of a total reality with which the individual self (*ātman*) is identical.[18] Thus some of the earliest metaphysical speculation is monistic with the identification of all beings with Being. This is conceptualized as the cosmic sound OṂ which pervades the universe and is identified with *brahman*, the world, and the self in the *Māṇḍūkya-upaniṣad*.[19] In these early, pre-philosophical texts, metaphysics is drawn from earlier reflections on Vedic ritual, from the idea that there are hidden connections between the cosmos and the sacrifice. *Brahman* is a cosmological concept and the principle of creation or generation in the sense that all things come from *brahman*: 'in the beginning this world was only *brahman*, only one'.[20] So *brahman* designates the sustaining power and ground of existents and the source to which all returns. And yet, the reality of *brahman* is ineffable and ungraspable and can only be designated negatively by the phrase 'not, not' (*neti neti*).[21] The semantic range of *brahman* is thus broader and more active than that of 'Being' and this does raise the question of whether, in fact, the onto-theological question about the being of this sustaining reality ever actually arose in the Brahmanical context: its functions of creation, sustenance and destruction are simply identified with its being.

The Upaniṣads are the 'end of the Veda' (*vedānta*), and this becomes a tradition flowing into Non-dualist or Advaita Vedānta and later forms. The most famous exponent of this was Śaṅkara (c. 788–840 CE),[22] who tried to maintain a strict non-dualism, arguing for the identity of the self as *ātman* with this absolute reality. While this reality is non-dual, a monos, Śaṅkara inevitably uses dualistic language to refer to it. The highest goal of the human person is to realize their identity with this absolute, to wake up to the truth that we misperceive the cosmos because of ignorance (*avidyā*), not through our action, which is ultimately illusory.[23] Once we realize our identity with absolute Being, we are freed from the apparent suffering of reincarnation (*saṃsāra*). Śaṅkara introduces the idea in his commentary on the foundational or root text of the tradition, the *Brahma-sūtra* where he speaks of human ignorance due to superimposition (*adhyāsa*) of the self on to what is not the self. Our knowledge of the world is distorted by this superimposition that inhibits and prevents us from directly perceiving our true nature as the absolute reality. To perceive the true nature of ourselves, we must develop discrimination (*viveka*) to distinguish the true self from what is not the self, and true perception from mistaken perception – as when somebody sees a snake in the house which turns out to be a rope. Thus, perceptions are different cognitive experiences in which faulty perception can give way to correct perception, while the object that gives rise to the perceptions remains the same, as Mandanamiśra, an older contemporary of Śaṅkara, observes (in terms that Husserl could almost have used).[24] In an independent work attributed to Śaṅkara, the *Upadeśasāhasrī*, he extols the virtues of the teacher who should teach the definition of absolute reality (*brahman*) as taught in primary and secondary revelation, presenting a list of quotations:

> And in secondary revelation '[*brahman*] is not born and does not die', 'it is not affected by anyone's sin, just as [air] is always established in the ether', 'know me as the knower of the field', 'it is called neither being nor non-being because [it is] beginningless and without qualities', 'the same in all beings', [and] 'the supreme person is other [?]'. All these support the definition given by primary revelation and prove that the innermost self is beyond transmigratory existence and that it is not different from brahman, the all-comprehensive principle.[25]

These citations indicate the ineffable nature of this absolute to which Śaṅkara refers that is identical to the self. The problem is that we project features of the not-self – the apparent objects of awareness – onto the self and features of the self – such as awareness – onto what is not the self. Once superimposition (*adhyāsa*) is removed, we realize the self to be identical with *brahman*, which is also the witnessing subject (*sākṣin*), so liberation (*mokṣa*) is achieved in this life (*jīvanmukti*) and reincarnation is at an end. The correct understanding of scripture has been attained and the great sayings of the Upaniṣads, the *mahāvidyās*, have been realized.

This raises more questions, perhaps, than it answers and it seems to me there are inconsistencies in the system, in particular the idea on the one hand that the self is identical with *brahman*, 'you are that' (*tat tvam asi*) as the *Chāndogya-upaniṣad* states,[26] while on the other that the self is a witnessing consciousness (*sakṣin*) that presents a different model of the person. On the one hand, we have a pure monism in which the status of the many, of differentiation, is unreal, while on the other we have a view in which the self is a detached witness to the world, more consonant with a dualist model. Śaṅkara seems to get around this confusion by claiming that there are two levels of truth and apparently dualistic language is but a lower level of thinking,[27] a distinction that also emerged, probably first, in Buddhism with Nāgārjuna (see below).

So far we have two models or metaphysics of the human person presented, first with the Mīmāṃsā an understanding of person as transactional, born within a network of relationships with other people, with the ancestors, and with the gods. Secondly, we have the Vedānta tradition that lays emphasis on the knowledge sections of scripture rather than sections about action. In the non-dualistic version, the Advaita Vedānta, the highest value of life is to correctly perceive the self to be the absolute reality. Here the notion of person is deeper than the personality, deeper than the bearer of language and the limited first-person pronoun; the truth is that all selves are ultimately one and all distinction is due to ignorance. But there is a third position regarding the self that emerged in this early period, namely the view, diametrically opposed to the Advaita, that the self is quite distinct. This is the view of the Enumeration school of philosophy or Sāṃkhya.

The Sāṃkhya philosophy of isolation

Very early in Brahmanical thinking, there developed ways of understanding the universe involving the introduction of different classifications of what we might call ontic levels. As in ancient Greece, we have the classification of the elements, earth, air, fire, water and space/subtle element, and the analysis of the constituents of the human person, such as the five senses, bodily functions and capacities for action, and mental faculties such as intelligence and sense of 'I'. We find this kind of thinking in the Upaniṣads[28] as well as speculation about the absolute. Such reflection occurs in later literature too, of particular note being the presence of Sāṃkhya categories in the *Bhagavad-gītā*.[29] This way of thinking was also associated with the non-Vedic – and anti-Vedic – traditions of wandering ascetics, the Śramaṇas, particularly with classifications we find in early Buddhism.[30] So while various parts of the Upaniṣads are proto-Sāṃkhya, it is not until Īśvarakṛṣṇa composed the *Sāṃkhya-kārikās, Verses on Enumeration*, probably in the late third to early fourth century CE that we find the development of a system of classification combined with a metaphysics of the self. Indeed, like the first truth of the noble one in Buddhism, the text begins with the idea that life is suffering (*duḥkha*); but unlike Buddhism, the way to end suffering is not the realization of no-self (*anātman*) but rather the realization that the real self (*puruṣa*) appears to be entangled with matter (*prakṛti*) and the highest human purpose is to free the self from this entanglement. The condition of liberation thereby achieved is a state of isolation (*kaivalya*).

We are all numerically distinct selves which are infinite in number, entangled in matter from beginningless time but we can extricate ourselves from this entanglement through the discrimination of the self from matter, which is a kind of cognition in which the self realizes that it is not really tied to matter but distinct, perceiving matter as a spectator perceives a dancer.[31] This philosophy is not dissimilar to the Neo-Platonism of Plotinus's *Enneads* where the spirit needs to be freed from the confines of matter to rise through the cosmos to its true abode.[32] While this is a dualism, it is not the dualism of Descartes because the 'mind' is included within the category 'matter'. Indeed, the human, embodied person is a consequence of the unfolding or evolution of matter from a quiescent, unmanifested state to a manifested state. What is particularly interesting about the unfolding of these categories or ontic levels (levels of existence) is that they combine an individual psychology with a cosmology. The ontic categories are both constituents of a person and levels of cosmic unfolding. Briefly, this unfolding takes place according to a pattern: from matter (*prakṛti*) evolves what might be translated as 'intellect' or perhaps 'higher mind' (*buddhi*), from which emerges the ego, the sense of 'I' or 'I-maker' (*ahaṃkāra*), from which emerges the mind (*manas*), along with the five senses and their objects, the five motor functions or organs of action, and the five subtle and then gross elements (namely earth, air, fire, water, and space).[33] This is a very thorough classification of the person in a vertical hierarchy whose different dimensions are controlled by three qualities that emerge in *prakṛti*, namely the qualities of light (*sattva*), darkness (*tamas*) and passion (*rajas*).[34] This becomes a pan-Hindu system for classifying propensities of the personality as well as types of food.

The importance of Sāṃkhya for Indian metaphysics is not so much the philosophy itself, but that the classification it introduces finds its way into many systems of Indian philosophy. Sāṃkhya is the metaphysical backdrop behind Patañjali's yoga system; it is found in the *Bhagavad-gītā;* the Vedānta uses it in its account of the (illusory) universe we experience; and it is fundamental to tantric philosophies which add their own categories to those of the Sāṃkhya. The dualism it presents is fundamental to the system and is interesting in not being a philosophy of the person in a Cartesian sense, because the features of personhood – such as sense of the empirical I, intellect and mind – are classified as being within matter. The only quality of the self is that it is conscious in contrast to unconscious matter. So once the self is freed, it is only conscious of itself and no longer conscious of matter, which had been a perception that kept it bound in a condition of suffering. There is no God in this system to become one with in mystical union, nor to praise in ontological distinction, although the sixteenth-century Sāṃkhya philosopher Vijñānabhikṣu does introduce a putative theistic reality into his thinking, combining Sāṃkhya with Vedānta, in which distinct selves along with matter participate in the Being of the absolute *brahman*.[35] This dualism is different from that of Descartes where mind and matter are distinct substances. For Sāṃkhya, what Descartes characterized as mental substance, the sense of an 'I', is still within matter. The true subject, the self or *puruṣa*, is beyond the empirical I.

Sāṃkhya's metaphysical dualism is important in the history of Indian philosophy, but questions remain concerning the coherence of the category of the self and its relation to matter. The question of how the self originally became entangled with matter is not addressed, nor is the precise nature of the self-defined other than as numerically distinct selves. There is some incoherence to this idea in the sense that it is not the *puruṣa* who is the subject of first-person predicates, but the empirical I, the *ahamkara*, yet the *puruṣa* provides the animating consciousness to the empirical I. There is also some incoherence to the Sāṃkhya view that selves are numerically distinct and unique and yet also have the quality of all-pervasiveness. One might question the efficacy of the category of the *puruṣa* and its explanatory force, as it seems not to be needed in the analysis of person and world; and this is precisely what the Buddhists did, abandoning any notion of unchanging essence.

Buddhist impersonalism

The abiding theme of Buddhism from its early inception in the teachings of the Buddha (d.c. 400 BCE) through to the later development of the Mahāyāna and Vajrayāna has been the idea that reality can be characterized as having three characteristics, namely suffering, impermanence and no-self (*anātman*). We suffer because we are attached to situations that pass away and the passing away of all phenomena is a characteristic of the person. There is no permanent self but rather a stream of constantly changing moments due to causes and conditions.[36] The philosophy of no-self came to be explicitly attributed to the world as well with the Mahāyāna development of the doctrine of emptiness (*śūnyatā*). Not only is the person empty of any essence, but so is the world and our experience in it. Through Buddhist analysis of the ways in which experience arises and passes away, such as can be achieved through meditation, we can gain insight (*vipaśyāna*) into the nature of the world as being empty of essence, an insight that has soteriological consequence in freeing the empirical person from rebirth. As with the Vedic traditions, with Buddhism we have the scriptural revelation or *sūtra*, and the philosophical reflection or *śāstra*. It was the Perfection of Wisdom scriptures and the school or Prajñāparamitā that followed from these scriptures, that developed the idea of emptiness, and its most famous exponent and articulator of its philosophy is Nāgārjuna (c. 150–250 CE) although the philosopher Dharmakīrti (c. 530–600 CE) is perhaps the religion's Aquinas.

Nāgārjuna provides a searing critique of the notion of essence. In his key work, the *Mūlamādhyamika-kārikā*, *Verses on the Fundamentals of the Middle Way*, he criticizes the earlier Buddhist philosophy of the Abhidharma that maintained that reality is a causal chain or stream of time made up of discrete constituents, each of which is only a momentary consciousness (*cittakṣana*). Each of these comprises an essence or own-being (*svabhāva*) that arises and passes away. The Nāgārjuna critique is that this is incoherent because something with essence cannot cause something else with essence, for they could never have contact due to the discrete nature implied by the notion of essence. This is similar to Hume's critique of causation. Let us take a passage from Nāgārjuna's text:

> 15.1. The coming into being (*saṃbhava*) of own-being (*svabhāva*) is not possible from conditions (*pratyaya*) and causes (*hetu*). Coming into being from conditions and causes would be that own-being has been constructed (*kṛtaka*).
>
> 15.2. So how can own-being that is said to be constructed come into being? Own-being is not constructed for it is not dependent on another [thing].
>
> 15.3. If there is the non-existence of own-being, from whence does other being arise? For the own-being of other-being is called other-being.
>
> 15.4. Again, how can there be an existing thing (*bhāva*) without own-being and other-being? For if there is an existing thing, it is established due to [there being] own-being and other-being.
>
> 15.5. If of an existing thing there is no proof [then] a non-existing thing (*abhāva*) cannot be proved, for people speak about the non-existence of an existing thing [as] the non-existence of another [existence].
>
> 15.6. Those who see own-being and other-being, and existence and non-existence, do not see the truth in the teachings of the Buddha.[37]

The argument is dense but clear. If own-being and other-being are characterized as having an essence, then they cannot have been constructed or brought into existence from causes and conditions, for something with an essence cannot have been caused.

So, if we cannot prove an existing thing because we cannot prove the essence of anything, then a non-existing thing cannot be proved either. Of course, non-existence cannot 'be', so a non-existing thing is impossible. Nāgārjuna's terse argument has the force and provides the intellectual backbone of the Mahāyāna Buddhist philosophy and the justification of emptiness. Although the Madhyamika position rejects the notion of essence and self (and also God) – and so is in one sense anti-metaphysical – the emptiness that it posits as real is metaphysical, even though the tradition tries to circumvent this by speaking about the emptiness of emptiness: even the category emptiness is empty of substantiality. Whether this is a form of nihilism has been open to debate,[38] but there is a clear difference here from substantialist, Vedic metaphysics.

The history of debate has been a history of the substantialism of the Vedic schools clashing with the non-substantialism of the Buddhist Madhyamikas. This is an impersonalist philosophy and a reductionism in which human life – which is essentially suffering – is perceived through insight to be empty of essence. This perception, as we have seen with the Vedic philosophies, is salvific and ends rebirth once understood at a deep, existential level.

Yet there is another story to tell in the history of Buddhist metaphysics that lays stress on consciousness. Arguably the understanding of emptiness emerges from the fundamental teachings of the Buddha about suffering, impermanence and no-self, and from insight meditation. There is another kind of meditation, calmness (*śamatha/ samatha*), that develops absorbed states of consciousness (*dhyāna/jhāna*) and which emphasizes the state of meditation as luminous (*prabhasvara/pabassara citta*).[39] Arguably this strand of Buddhist meditation develops into the Yogācāra (the practice of yoga) school which comes up with the philosophy of consciousness only (*vijñānavāda*). This philosophy denies the reality of the empirical world and holds that reality comprises only mind. This idealism in time becomes merged with the Madhyamika in a joint school and both are regarded as necessary in Vajrayāna or Tibetan Buddhism.[40] Both Yogācāra and Madhyamika reject the scriptural revelation of the Vedas and there is a history of rigorous debate between these competing metaphysical positions. Often the Vedic philosophies simply reject the Buddhist view a priori, but arguments are also presented for the notion of a substantial self as well as for the existence of God. One metaphysical system that developed in the ninth and tenth centuries was that of non-dualistic Recognition school (Pratyabhijñā) within the tradition focussed on the deity Śiva. This critically engaged with Buddhism and was not unsympathetic to Buddhist idealism, although regarding itself as presenting a superior truth.

The recognition of Śiva

From around the ninth century a school of philosophy developed stemming from the scriptural revelation of Śiva, the non-dualist Tantras, and strongly influenced by the Grammarian school, which called itself the Recognition school because the central claim is that the self, characterized by limited consciousness, is in fact the absolute consciousness which is Śiva. In recognizing ourselves as this absolute consciousness, we realize the truth of scriptural revelation and achieve salvation from the cycle of reincarnation. Although perhaps not the most original voice in this philosophy, the most famous exponent was Abhinavagupta (*c.* 975–1025 CE) in Kashmir. His last, mature work is a commentary on his grand teacher Utpaladeva's *Verses on the Recognition of the Lord* (*Īśvarapratyabhijñākārikā*) in which he presents arguments for the absolute consciousness of Śiva and for the existence of the self against Buddhist impersonalism.

Abhinavagupta's *a priori* assumption in his scriptural exegesis is that there is a single reality of consciousness only. This is what the theistic language of Śiva, the equivalent to 'God', really means. Individual consciousness is identical with this absolute consciousness; the perception of plurality and distinct beings is due to our ignorance that is corrected by true recognition of what we really are.[41] While this is an idealism perhaps in some respects consonant with Buddhist idealism, it is not a denial of the reality of the world as with Advaita Vedānta, but rather a metaphysics that identifies the world with absolute consciousness that is dynamic and characterized by power (*śakti*). It is not as if the world does not exist, but rather that the world is in fact consciousness as dynamic vibration (*spanda*). This is not dissimilar to the idealism of Fichte in which 'I' and 'other', subjectivity and objectivity, are reduced to the transcendental-I, absolute subjectivity, and are co-constituted within a single absolute reality.[42] (Indeed, one reason perhaps for European Romanticism's engagement with Indian thought is a resonance between these worldviews.) Our sense of self, the empirical I, is really a contraction of God's absolute subjectivity or I-ness (*ahantā*), which has occurred because of the spontaneous freedom of God (*svatantrya, svachanda*) that conceals itself through a process of contraction (*saṃkoca*), which is the cosmological hierarchy of ontic levels. These ontic levels add further Śaiva levels to the Sāṃkhya categories already described.

In his argument against Buddhism, Abhinavagupta says that our ordinary human experience, the experience of the empirical I, is a limitation of absolute consciousness due to the powers of knowledge (*jñāna*), memory (*smṛti*) and exclusion (*apohana*)[43] These constrictions are necessary conditions for experiencing a world. Knowledge (or perhaps 'cognition' might be a better rendering of *jñāna* here) allows us to experience a world and to know the world we experience as apparently distinct. Memory allows us to know ourselves as a process of continuity through time. The term *smṛti* has a wider semantic range than the English 'memory' and has the connotation of awareness and bringing something to mind, while *apohana* is exclusion, where experience of one thing entails the exclusion of something else.[44] The power of exclusion is the force that particularizes our experience into what it is and is a necessary constraint that allows us to experience our own lives within an apparently distinct world. In order to make sense of experience, we need the idea of a permanent self. Abhinavagupta writes:

> So, even spatial succession appears in the limited self whose nature is circumscribed, as one's own self, body (and the experience of) emptiness and so on (as in the statement) 'I am standing here'. And it appears in existents also in relation to oneself as in 'what is in close proximity to me is near and what is otherwise is far'. To the unlimited reality

of consciousness whose nature is free from constraint, objects appear as one's own self, the existence of 'I', so as such are perfect. Their nature is such that it is unconstrained. Such is the reality that is his own self.[45]

We need the idea of a permanent self to make sense of experience. The Buddhist claim is that our sense of continuity between the child and the old person is simply due to traces (*vāsana*) in memory, but there is nothing permanent in this series.

Abhinavagupta argues, by contrast, that traces are insufficient to account for experience because they are qualities that need a receptacle to hold them, namely the unchanging self. The flow of experience constituted through the powers of cognition, memory and exclusion, is undergirded by a permanent self, which is identical to absolute consciousness. This consciousness is self-luminous and although the objects of consciousness or experience – such as the experience of a pot or mat – might change, this self-luminous awareness never changes. While within the flow of experience one perception might correct an earlier perception, as when the perception 'this is silver' is corrected by the perception that it is mother of pearl, even here the 'relation of contraries' (*bādhyabhādhakabhāva*) is within the flow of experience that must rest on a subject, the permanent self.[46] Even everyday actions such as raising one's hand and letting it fall establish the permanent self. This is because *action* is actually *time* that is only perceivable in movement: the movement of the sun, being born, and in different flowers seen in summer and winter.[47] While the Buddhists might be on to something in their analysis of the changing objects of consciousness, they fail to take account of the unchanging self-luminosity of the permanent self, the unchanging 'I', who is also God, that allows us to experience the continuity of experience.

But why is this? Even if we are permanent selves, why do we experience the flow of time and experience in this way? Abhinavagupta says it is because the Lord wills to rule, shine and to move, just as we, as distinct persons, might have a desire 'let me cook' which leads to a succession of movements within which the desire remains unchanged.[48] All of this action, which is time, thus occurs within the unchanging I-consciousness of Śiva, our true identity.

Arguments for the existence of God

Abhinavagupta uses theistic language, as above, in speaking about the will of the Lord, although ultimately this *theos*, or rather *deva*, is identical with the self, characterized as pure consciousness. The non-dualists were not completely averse to theistic language and Utpaladeva, the grand teacher of Abhinavagupta, presents an argument for the existence of God, although ultimately to abandon this to the higher non-dual synthesis.[49] These arguments that arose mostly during the ninth and tenth centuries were rational justifications for the existence of God, intended to be persuasive without recourse to scriptural revelation.[50] The most important arguments for the existence of God were from Nyāya philosophers, the Logicians, against the Mīmāṃsā and Buddhist atheists, even though the Mīmāṃsā accepted the revelation of the Veda. The fundamental Nyāya argument is that the universe is an effect and all effects have causes, and we can infer that the cause of the universe is God. The Nyāya philosopher Udayana (late tenth to early eleventh century) combines the force of logical argument from the Nyāya with the metaphysical categories of the Vaiśeṣika, into a realist and pluralist philosophy.[51]

In his *Bouquet of the Flowers of Logic* (*Nyāyakusumañjali*) Udayana offers proofs for the existence of God, most notably a version of the cosmological argument that the universe has the nature of an effect, so its cause must be an intelligent creator whom he names Īśvara, Lord or God. Something that has a cause must have an intelligent being as its cause, as we see with a chariot where the chariot is the effect of an intelligent maker.[52] Another argument is that the universe comprises a combination of atoms (*aṇu*), which is the fundamental Vaiśeṣika philosophy,[53] but these atoms are unconscious and so there must be a conscious agent who arranged them. This agent is God, omniscient and unchanging.[54] The universe is a specific arrangement (*sanniveśaviśeṣa*) and so we must infer an intelligent, non-material cause, because no material cause could account for this arrangement. This is a sophisticated argument that lays down a gauntlet, as it were, to the Mīmāṃsaka and Buddhist atheists to account for the apparent harmony and interlocking specificity of the cosmos. Because of such complexity, we must infer an intelligent agent, who must be omniscient and omnipotent in order to arrange and control that complexity. The Mīmāṃsā counter-argument is that if the specific arrangement that is the universe demands that we infer an intelligent agent or creator God then there is an analogy here to the creation of a pot. But the pot, the Mīmāṃsaka reasons, is either the product of the potter or the product of God, if the latter, the arrangement that is the pot is not proof of an imperishable creator because the pot perishes. If God is compared to the potter, then God must perish as does the potter. But Udayana offers further arguments. We can also infer the existence of God from revealed scripture whose nature is knowledge (*veda*). It must have been revealed by an intelligent agent, and the acceptance of this scripture by a large number of people proves that it is not a secular or worldly text (*laukika*). People would only believe the word of a trustworthy person (*āpta*) and that person is God.[55] Sentences in the Veda are intelligent and so we must infer an intelligent author according to the Nyāya, in contrast to the Mīmāṃsakas who claim that any reference to an author in the Veda is simply a discourse upon an injunction (*vidhi*) and is merely elaboration (*arthavāda*), a position that, of course, Udayana rejects.

There are clear parallels with the cosmological argument developed in Christian theology by Aquinas and the *kalam* argument in Islam.[56] It is possible that Udayana's argument reached Europe, but the more likely explanation is that Brahmanical, Muslim and Christian discourse developed parallel ways of thinking.

We can see from these debates that there was rich engagement between a variety of metaphysical positions articulated through the philosophical schools of the early medieval period. Philosophers such as Abhinavagupta and Udayana were pressing the frontiers of knowledge and inquiry into the nature of the human and the nature of the world, developing distinct metaphysical positions and sharing a discourse and common philosophical language in debate. The heyday of this pan-Indic discourse was more or less at an end by the thirteenth century; then the Śaiva kingdoms declined, the Delhi Sultanate (1206–1526) arose and the Buddhists left.

Concluding reflections

We close our survey in the eleventh century, although much was yet to happen in the history of Indian metaphysics. Many of the traditions fade away – there is no Buddhist response to Abhinavagupta for example – with the rise of the Mughal Empire and then British imperialism. We might note the development of Nyāya, the school of logic, into a new school, Navya Nyāya in Bengal in the sixteenth century – a development with Ragunātha Śiromoṇi[57] that parallels the paradigm shift in European philosophy a hundred years later with Descartes and the rise of rationalism. Theological engagement with Moslem Sufis took place among the Sants[58] and devotion to a putative theistic reality became normative Hinduism, with Vaiṣṇava Gosvāmins speculating theologically on the nature of Kṛṣṇa, along with the aestheticization of religious experience[59] from the sixteenth century. But the impact on education of British rule meant that philosophy departments became less metaphysically focussed in the twentieth century, although some thinkers continued to think metaphysically, such as Aurobindo who developed an Indo-Hegelian metaphysics.[60]

While this has been inevitably a selective survey, the issues that have arisen are important in the history of Indian metaphysics – and beyond. Although there is variety, certain metaphysical questions are shared: the transcendence/immanence relation, universalism and particularism, impersonal power and personal deity, and the centrality of cognition or action. We have focused on the question of what humanity is, or more precisely 'Who am I' (*ko'ham*)?' For the Mīmāṃsā we are above all ritual actors who fulfil the Vedic injunction. By contrast the Vedānta wishes to reveal the self as ontologically identical with a pan-cosmic Being, the cognition of which has soteriological consequence in freeing us from the apparent cycle of reincarnation. The Sāṃkhya dualist response to the question is to posit a strict dualism between the eternal self and transient transformations of material substrate (itself eternal in essence). It is the constituents of the material substrate that constitute the person and the empirical I, which must be transcended to realize the deeper self. By contrast Buddhism rejects any substantiality: the person is constructed through causes and conditions without a permanent self in an impermanent world. And responding to these earlier positions, non-dual Śaiva metaphysics argues, against the Buddhists, for a transcendent and immanent deity who is identical with our true nature as light and consciousness.

The Śaiva and Vedānta systems are theistic in the sense that they posit a transcendent God who is the ultimate source of life and the universe, but the non-dualist versions of these traditions that we have seen here subsume any theistic language within what they perceive to be the higher truth of metaphysical identity. But there were debates about the metaphysics of deity within these traditions, and Nyāya and Śaiva philosophers formulated arguments for the existence of God. The later Vedānta is also strongly theistic, with philosophers such as Rāmānuja (traditional dates 1017–1137 CE) arguing, against Advaita, that God's transcendence is his essence (*svarūpa*) but his body is the universe and the beings that inhabit it, while the dualist theologian Madhva insists on the unbridgeable gap and distinction between the self and God. Similarly, Śaiva Siddhānta maintained the three distinct realities of transcendent God (*pati*), universe (*pāśa*) and bound soul (*paśu*), which the non-dualist Pratyabhijñā rejected in favour of its metaphysics of consciousness and light. But all agree, even the Buddhist systems, that the empirical 'I' is not the truth of the self and that ontological identity is deeper than we think. So a wide range of positions emerged during this history. Notably absent are philosophies of history, partly because there is a view of time as cyclic, in which history itself has no telos. While individuals are saved, there is no collective salvation or shared eschatology. There was some historiography in India, notably Kalhana's *Chronicles of the Kings of Kashmir* (*Rājataraṅgini*) but not much, and this again indicates a lack of concern with history. It is not the changing truths of our changing world that are metaphysically important but the unchanging truth of cosmic transcendence.

Lastly, we might like to consider echoes and resonances with other metaphysical systems. On the one hand we have philosophies that have placed importance on worldly transaction and duty, such as the Mīmāṃsā, in contrast to philosophies that have placed emphasis on transcendence and going beyond worldly concerns, such as the renunciate tradition of Advaita. This echoes Chinese metaphysics where Confucianism placed great stress on the importance of correct relationships and correct comportment to the social and political order, in contrast to Daoism that sought a wider truth, beyond purely human transaction. Indeed, Confucianism was disparaging of monastic Buddhism with its celibate monks seeking a truth beyond the social order, beyond the family and ordinary responsibilities. Thus, we have metaphysical systems that wish to accommodate social values of duty, human love and worldly prosperity, and we have those that wish to transcend social values. Traditions such as the Mīmāṃsā, along with theistic Hinduism such as the worship of Kṛṣṇa in the *Bhagavad-gītā*, generally have a positive attitude to worldly transaction, reconciling the aspiration for personal redemption with the fulfilment of worldly duty. By contrast, renunciate traditions are gnostic in orientation, arguing that transcendence of worldly life is our ultimate goal, a reunion of our deeper self with its source in an absolute reality – a position very close to Plotinus' journey of the alone to the alone. Furthermore, we might contrast the worldly affirmation of Chinese Confucianism or dharmic Brahmanism with the gnostic transcendence of Daoism or renunciate Brahmanism – or with the metaphysics entailed by modernity.

Especially since the nineteenth century, the rationalism of Descartes and the empiricism of Hume have been incorporated into Indian philosophical reflection. While there are still traditional institutions that teach the systems of philosophy described above, much Indian metaphysics now takes place in modern university settings through the medium of English. The older metaphysical systems still echo in the modern world but will inevitably be transformed in the contemporary Indian context and the new political reality of India as a major player on the world stage.

Notes

1. Sanskrit texts were not dated until the medieval period. There is an inevitable vagueness about dating the earlier levels of Indic thinking. One benchmark is the redating of the death of the Buddha to around 400 BCE. Brahmanical texts that contain Buddhist influence can therefore be dated later. Conversely, texts such as the early Upaniṣads that seem to contain no knowledge of Buddhism must be earlier. The sequence of texts can often be established by demonstrating the influence of one text upon another. See Oberlies, 'Die Śvetāśvatara Upaniṣad: Einleitung-Edition und Übersetzung von Adhyāya I', *Wiener Zeitschrift für die Kunde Sudasiens*, vol. 39, 1995: 61–102; Oberlies, 'Die Śvetāśvatara Upaniṣad: Edition und Übersetzung von Adhyāya IV–VI (Studien zu den "mittleren" Upaniṣads II – 3. Teil)', *Wiener Zeitschrift für die Kunde Südasiens*, vol. 42, 1998, pp. 77–138. On the difficulty of dating early Sanskrit texts along with a report of progress in this field, see the essay by Oliver Hellwig, 'Dating Sanskrit Texts Using Linguistic Features and Neural Networks', *Indogermanische Forschung*, 2019, DOI: 10.1515/if-2019-0001.
2. *Ṛg-veda* 10.129. Jamison and Brereton (2014: 1609): '1. 'The nonexistent did not exist, nor did the existent at that time. There existed neither the airy space nor the heaven beyond. What moved back and forth? From where and in whose protection? Did water exist, a deep depth? … 7. This creation – from where it came to be, if it was produced or if not – he who is the overseer of this (world) in the furthest heaven, he surely knows. Or if he does not know … ?'
3. Heidegger (1959: 95–8).
4. *Śvetāśvatara-upaniṣad* 1.1.Olivelle (1998: 415): 'People who make inquiries about *brahman* say: What is the cause of brahman? Why were we born? By what do we live? On what are we established? Governed by whom, O you who know brahman, do we live in pleasure and pain, each in our respective situation? 2. Should we regard it as time, as inherent nature, as chance, as the elements, as the source of birth, or as the Person? Or is it a combination of these?'

5. I use the adjective 'Brahmanical' rather than 'Hindu' because that term only occurs as a term of self-description from the fifteenth century with the Kashmiri historian Śrīvara. See Alexis Sanderson, 'Tolerance, Exclusivity, Inclusivity, and Persecution in Indian Religion during the Early Mediaeval Period', p. 156, in Makinson (2015: 155–224). 'Brahmanical' indicates a style of discourse through the medium of Sanskrit as the shared language of philosophical discourse and generally learned topics such as poetics. On the power of Sanskrit as a uniting, ideological force in the formation of polities as well as literatures, see Pollock (2006).
6. This is inevitably a simplified picture of a controversial theme. Some scholars regard ideas of liberation from the cycle of reincarnation, along with the practice of asceticism and yoga, as coming from a different region to the development of the Vedas, namely Greater Magadha as Bronkhorst argues (Bronkhorst 2007), whereas other scholars, such as Jan Heesterman, regard these ideas as developments from within the Vedic worldview (1985: 40).
7. This idea was developed by John Clayton who presents Indian discourse (saṃvāda) as concerned with difference in contrast to the Enlightenment model of philosophy where consensus is sought. While one might have concerns about this characterization of Western philosophy, the overall point is well made. See Clayton (2006: 16–57).
8. Jaimini, *Mīmāṃsā sūtra* 1.1.
9. Clooney (1990: 119).
10. James Benson (2010: 27).
11. Clooney, *Thinking Ritually*, 163.
12. For a fine account and analysis, see Raja (1963: 151–73).
13. The six means of knowledge or *pramāṇas* are: perception (*pratyakṣa*), inference (*anumāna*), verbal authority (*śabda*), analogy (*upamāna*), presumption (*arthapatti*) and non-apprehension (*abhāva*). Nicholson (2010: 148–54).
14. Halbfass (1992: 70–2).
15. Elizarenkova (1995: 97); Signe (2008: 47).
16. E.g. *Śvetāśvatara-Upaniṣad* 4.4.
17. *Chāndogya-upaniṣad* 6.12–13.
18. E.g. *Bṛhadāraṇyaka-upaniṣad* 1.4.7 and *Chāndogya-upaniṣad* 6.12–13. In Olivelle, *The Early Upaniṣads*, 47–9, 255–7.
19. *Māndukya-upaniṣad* 1–8. In Olivelle (1998), *The Early Upaniṣads*, 475–6.
20. *Bṛhadāraṇyaka* 1.4.11.
21. *Bṛhadāraṇyaka* 1.3.4. See Diwarka Acharya (2013), 'Néti Néti. Meaning and Function of an Enigmatic Phrase in the Gārgya-Ajātaśatru Dialogue of Bṛhad Āraṇyaka Upaniṣad II.1 and II.3', *Indo-Iranian Journal*, vol. 56, 2013: 3–39.
22. On Śaṅkara's dates, see Isayeva (1993: 69–91).
23. Arapura (1986: 74–86).
24. Dasgupta (1975: 94–7).
25. Śaṅkara, *Upadeśasahasrī*, translated by Swami Jagadananda (Mylapore: Sri Ramakrishna Math, 1979) (translation modified).
26. *Chāndogra-upaniṣad* 6.12.13 etc.
27. Isayeva, *Shankara*, 192–3.

28. E.g. the *Chāndogya-upaniṣad* 7.25; 6.24 where a singular (*eka*) being (*sat*) produces fire, which becomes water, which becomes food. The text also contains the idea of self-identity consonant with the Sāṃkhya view of the ego (*ahaṃkāra*).
29. The *Bhagavad-gītā* 7.4 describes Kṛṣṇa as having an eightfold nature of earth, water, fire, wind, ether, mind (*manas*), intellect (*buddhi*) and ego (*ahaṃkāra*), which are Sāṃkhya categories.
30. See for example Gethin (1992).
31. Larson and Bhattacarya (1987: 162).
32. Plotinus, *Enneads* III.3.1. A. H. Armstrong (trans), *Plotinus: Porphyry on Plotinus*, Loeb Classical Library 440 (Cambridge, MA: Harvard University Press, 1966).
33. Larson, *Sāṃkhya*, 158–9.
34. Larson, *Sāṃkhya*, 158–9.
35. Rukmani (1981: 9–12).
36. Gethin (1992: 19).
37. Nāgājuna, *Mūlamadhyamika-kārikā*. (My translation.)
38. Westerhoff (2009: 1995).
39. Shaw (2008: 27–32).
40. Harris (1991: 63–83).
41. Isabelle Ratié, *Le Soi et l'Autre: Identité, différence et altérité dand la philosophie de a Pratyabhijñā*. Leiden: Brill, 2011: 680–2.
42. Neuhouser (1990: 66–116).
43. This is a summary of a more detailed account of Abhinavagupta's argument in my *The Truth Within*, 143–54.
44. *Īśvarapratyabijñāvimarśinī* 1.4.4; Ratié (2011: 174–83).
45. *Īśvarapratyabijñāvimarśinī* 2.1.7, 22. Translation by R.C. Dwiwedi, K.C. Pandey and K.A. Subramania Iyer, *Bhāskarī* 3 vols. (Delhi: MLBD, 1986).
46. IPV I.7.6.
47. IPV 2.1.3.
48. IPV 2.1.8.
49. Isabelle Ratié, 'Utpaladeva's Proof for God: On the Purpose of the Īśvarasiddhi', in Rafelle Torella and Bettina Bäumer (2016: 257–340).
50. Dasti (2011: 1–21).
51. I present a more developed discussion in Flood (2020: 38–44).
52. Udayana (1972: 87–8).
53. Halbfass (1992: 269–70); Tachikawa (1981).
54. Udayana (1972: 90); Also Moise (2020: 67–9).
55. Udayana (1972: 100).
56. Reichenbach, Bruce, 'Cosmological Argument', *The Stanford Encyclopedia of Philosophy* (Fall 2022 Edition), Edward N. Zalta (ed.), forthcoming https://plato.stanford.edu/archives/fall2022/entries/cosmological-argument.
57. Jonardon (2011: 44–50).
58. Vaudeville (1971).
59. Stewart (2010).
60. Heehs (2010).

References

Abhinavagupta (1986), *Īśvarapratyabijñāvimarśinī*, trans. R. C. Dwiwedi, K. C. Pandey and K. A. Subramania Iyer, *Bhāskarī*, 3 vols. Delhi: MLBD.

Acharya, Diwarka (2013), 'Néti Néti. Meaning and Function of an Enigmatic Phrase in the Gārgya-Ajātaśatru Dialogue of Bṛhad Āraṇyaka Upaniṣad II.1 and II.3', *Indo-Iranian Journal* 56 : 3–39.

Arapura, John G. (1986), *Gnosis and the Problem of Thought in Vedanta: Dialogue with the Foundations*. Dordrecht: Martinus Nijhoff.

Benson, James (ed.) (2010), 'Introduction', in *Mahādeva Vedāntin Mīmāṃsānyāyasaṃgraha: A Compendium of the Principles of Mīmāṃsā*. Wiesbaden: Harrassowitz, pp. 11–50.

Bronkhorst, Johannes (2007), *Greater Magadha*. Leiden: Brill.

Chemparthy, George (1972), *An Indian Rational Theology*. Vienna: de Nobili.

Clayton, John (ed.) (2006), 'Thomas Jefferson and the Study of Religion', in *Religions, Reasons and Gods: Essays in Cross-Cultural Philosophy of Religion*. Cambridge: Cambridge University Press, pp. 16–57.

Clooney, Francis (1990), *Thinking Ritually: Rediscovering the Pūrva Mīmāṃsā of Jaimini*. Vienna: De Nobili Research Library.

Cohen, Signe (2008), *Text and Authority in the Older Upaniṣads*. Leiden: Brill.

Collins, Steven (1998), *Nirvana and Other Buddhist Felicities*. Cambridge: Cambridge University Press.

Dasgupta, S. N. (1975), *A History of Indian Philosophy*, vol. 2. Delhi: Motilal Banarsidass.

Dasti, Matthew (2011), 'Indian Rational Theology: Proof, Justification, and Epistemic Liberality in Nyāya's Argument for God', p. 1, *Asian Philosophy* 21 (1): 1–21. DOI: 10.1080/09552367.2011.536631.

Elizarenkova, T. Y. (1995), *Language and Style of the Vedic Ṛṣis*. Albany, NY: SUNY.

Flood, Gavin (2013), *The Truth Within: A History of Inwardness in Hinduism, Buddhism and Christianity*. Oxford: Oxford University Press.

Flood, Gavin (2020), *Hindu Monotheism*, Cambridge Elements. Cambridge: Cambridge University Press.

Ganeri, Jonardon (2011), *The Lost Age of Reason: Philosophy in Early Modern India 1450–1700*. Oxford: Oxford University Press.

Garfield, Jay (1995), *The Fundamental Wisdom of the Middle Way*. Oxford: Oxford University Press.

Gethin, Rupert M. L. (1992), *The Buddhist Path to Awakening*. Leiden: Brill.

Halbfass, Wilhelm (1988), 'India and the Romantic Critique', in *India and Europe: An Essay in Understanding*. Albany, NY: SUNY Press, pp. 69–83.

Halbfass, Wilhelm (ed.) (1991), 'Vedic Apologetics, Ritual Killing, and the Foundations of Ethics', in *Tradition and Reflection: Explorations in Indian Thought*. Albany, NY: SUNY Press, pp. 87–129.

Halbfass, Wilhelm (ed.) (1992), *On Being and What There Is: Classical Vaiśeṣika and the History of Indian Ontology*. Albany, NY: SUNY Press.
Harris, Ian (1991), *The Continuity of Madhyamaka and Yogācāra in Indian Mahāyāna Buddhism*. Leiden: Brill.
Heehs, Peter (2010), *The Lives of Sri Aurobindo*. New York: Columbia University Press.
Heesterman, Jan (1985), *The Inner Conflict of Tradition: Essays in Indian Ritual, Kinship and Society*. Chicago, IL: University of Chicago Press.
Heidegger, Martin (1959), *An Introduction to Metaphysics*, trans. Ralph Manheim. New Haven, CT: Yale University Press.
Hellwig, Oliver, 'Dating Sanskrit Texts Using Linguistic Features and Neural Networks', *Indogermanische Forschung*, September 2019. DOI: 10.1515/if-2019-0001.
Isayeva, Natalia (1993), *Shankara and Indian Philosophy*. Albany, NY: SUNY Press.
Jamison, Stephanie W., and Joel P. Brereton (2014), *The Rigveda: The Earliest Religious Poetry of India*, vol. 3. Oxford: Oxford University Press.
Larson, G. and R. S. Bhattacarya (1987), *Sāṃkhya: A Dualist Tradition in Indian Philosophy*. Delhi: MLBD.
Moise, Ionut (2020), *Salvation in Indian Philosophy: Perfection and Simplicity for Vaiśeṣika*. London: Routledge.
Nāgārjuna, *Mūlamadhyamika-kārikā*. E-text: Version: 0.1a. Last updated: Sun Feb 9 17:44:00 NZDT 2003. Original text input by Douglas Bachman. Revised text input by Richard Mahoney: r.mahoneyācomnet.net.nz.
Neuhouser, Fredrick (1990), *Fichte's Theory of Subjectivity*. Cambridge: Cambridge University Press.
Nicholson, Andrew J. (2010), *Unifying Hinduism: Philosophy and Identity in Indian Intellectual History*. New York: Columbia University Press.
Oberlies, Thomas (1995), 'Die Śvetāśvatara Upaniṣad: Einleitung-Edition und Übersetzung von Adhyāya I', *Wiener Zeitschrift für die Kunde Sudasiens* 39: 61–102.
Oberlies, Thomas (1998), 'Die Śvetāśvatara Upaniṣad: Edition und Übersetzung von Adhyāya IV–VI (Studien zu den "mittleren" Upaniṣads II – 3. Teil)', *Wiener Zeitschrift für die Kunde Südasiens* 42: 77–138.
Olivelle, Patrick (1998), *The Early Upanishads*. Oxford: Oxford University Press.
Plotinus (1966), *Enneads* III.3.1. A. H. Armstrong (trans.), *Plotinus: Porphyry on Plotinus*, Loeb Classical Library 440. Cambridge, MA: Harvard University Press.
Pollock, Sheldon (2006), *The Language of the Gods in the World of Men: Sanskrit, Culture and Power in Premodern India*. Berkeley, CA: University of California Press.
Potter, Karl H. (1981), *Encyclopedia of Indian Philosophies: Advaita Vedānta up to Śaṅkara and His Pupils*, vol. 3. Delhi: Motilal Banarsidass.
Raja, Kunjuni (1963), *Indian Theories of Meaning*. Madras: Adyar Library.
Ratié, Isabelle (2011), *Le Soi et l'Autre: Identité, différence et altérité dand la philosophie de a Pratyabhijñā*. Leiden: Brill.
Ratié, Isabelle (2016), 'Utpaladeva's Proof for God: On the Purpose of the Īśvarasiddhi', in Raffele Torella and Bettina Bäumer (eds.), *Utpaladeva: Philosopher of Recognition*. Shimla: Indian Institute of Advanced Study, pp. 257–340.

Reichenbach, Bruce, (forthcoming), 'Cosmological Argument', *The Stanford Encyclopedia of Philosophy*. (Fall 2022 Edition), Edward N. Zalta (ed.), URLhttps://plato.stanford.edu/archives/fall2022/entries/cosmological-argument.

Rukmani, T. S. (1981), *Yogavārttika of Vijñānabhikṣu*, vol. 1. Delhi: Munshiram Manoharlal.

Sanderson, Alexis (2015), 'Tolerance, Exclusivity, Inclusivity, and Persecution in Indian Religion during the Early Mediaeval Period', p. 156, in John Makinson (ed.), *Honoris Causa: Essays in Honour of Aveek Sarkar*. London: Allen Lane, pp. 155–224.

Śaṅkara (1979), *Upadeśasahasrī*, trans. Swami Jagadananda. Mylapore: Sri Ramakrishna Math.

Shaw, Sarah (2008), *Introduction to Buddhist Meditation*. London: Routledge.

Staal, Frits (1989), *Rules without Meaning: Ritual, Mantras and the Human Sciences*. New York: Peter Lang.

Stewart, Anthony (2010), *The Final Word*. Oxford: Oxford University Press.

Tachikawa, Musashi (1981), *The Structure of the World in Udayana's Realism: A Study of the 'Lakṣaṇāvalī' and 'Kiraṇāvalī'*. Dortrecht: D. Reidel.

Udayana (1972), *Nyāyakusumañjali* in George Chemparthy, *An Indian Rational Theology*. Vienna: de Nobili.

Vaudeville, Charlotte (1971), *Kabir*. Oxford: Clarendon Press.

Westerhoff, Jan (2009), *Nāgārjuna's Madhyamaka: A Philosophical Introduction*. Oxford: Oxford University Press.

9

Metaphysics of a Hindu goddess tradition and European phenomenology

Gavin Flood

The early medieval period in India witnessed the development of new metaphysical speculation that emerged in texts of revelation called Tantras and that found articulation in philosophical treatises and commentaries on those scriptures. Texts focused on the deity Śiva in various forms were the scriptural backbone of the public religion known as the Śaiva Siddhānta but there also developed more esoteric forms of the religion focused on the Goddess. This new form of tantric religion attracted royal patronage and became the central state religion for kingdoms of South and Southeast Asia from around the tenth to the thirteenth century.

Some of these new forms of religion were transgressive and challenged Brahmanical purity rules in the belief that shattering Brahmanical inhibition was salvific in facilitating the recognition of the self as divine and allowing the cultivation of supernatural power. One of these transgressive cults was focused on the ferocious Goddess Kālī in one of her emanations. This cult was called the Krama, which means 'gradation' or 'system', and worshipped Kālī in cycles of emanation and contraction. This religion was transgressive in advocating erotic worship of the deity, while at the same time presenting a striking metaphysics in which transcendence is conceptualized as light and awareness as the deeper meaning and purpose of tantric revelation.

The Goddess in Hinduism was regarded as the power (*śakti*) of God or Śiva, but was sometimes worshipped on her own as the supreme deity. The Krama was a sect that worshipped the Goddess as supreme, and so is classed as a Śākta tradition[1] because it focused on *śakti* or power as the ultimate reality. Two texts are regarded as the scriptural revelation of the religion, the *Kālīkulapañcaśataka* ('Five Hundred Verses on the Power of the Goddess') and the *Kālīkulakramasadbhāva* ('The Essence of the

System of the Power of the Goddess'), which predate the famous Śaiva philosopher Abhinavagupta (c. CE 975–1025); there is also a body of post-scriptural literature, in particular three texts named *Mahānayaprakāśa* ('The Illumination of the Great System'), one of which, authored by Arṇrasiṃha, summarizes the system; and a work of Śrīvatsa called the *Cidgananacandrikā* ('The Moon in the Sky of Consciousness') composed sometime between CE 1100 and 1300.[2]

This chapter describes this system and draws out from it a phenomenology that has echoes elsewhere and that has contemporary relevance. I focus on the concept of the 'sky of consciousness' (*cidvyoma, cidganana*) and discuss a philosophical articulation of this idea in the Śākta-Śaiva philosopher Kṣemarāja (c. CE 1000–1050).

The sky of consciousness

One of the key features of the Krama is that there is a level of description that is impersonal and a use of language not in terms of a Goddess but in terms of consciousness. There is a realm of human experience that the tradition speaks about as the expansion of consciousness as non-dual awareness, using the metaphor of 'the sky of consciousness' (*cidvyoma, cidgagana*) that it regards as a more accurate account of our knowledge of absolute reality than the personal language that speaks about the Goddess. Here is the opening of Śrīvatsa's *Cidgananacandrikā*, who himself is summarizing, as Sanderson shows, an earlier poem to Kālī by Arṇasiṃha. The opening verse reads:

> The sky of consciousness is an ocean of milk, like the full moon, a glittering wave, an expansive sound, a garland that is an undulating wave of drops of flashing and spreading light. Its own nature which is the primal vibration spreads out like the juice from an elephant's temples as the syllable OṂ. May this Gaṇeśa, born from the Goddess (*śaktijanmā*), forcefully calm difficulty.[3]

Although identical with one's innermost self, the Goddess is difficult to behold:

> You are the eternal shining light that consumes the universe, although difficult to behold, you are the habitation of truth, you are the cremation ground, dwelling in the heart of the spiritual hero, without fluctuation, to be honoured in the Karavīra cremation ground.[4]

For Śrīvatsa this is not simply a description of a metaphysical truth but has soteriological implications in so far as the Goddess calms the fires of suffering and transmigration,[5] and she does this through a range of powers or goddesses that are her emanations. Śrīvatsa continues:

> Those powers/goddesses who are your instruments, who open [themselves] to the condition of externality (*mukhabāhyapada-*), move in the sky whose nature is consciousness, O Goddess, for you stand on the elevated path.[6]

These powers of the Goddess, the movers in the sky of consciousness, are 'open to the condition of externality', which means that the apparently external universe is actually an appearance of the inner reality of consciousness that is the Goddess. This is the inner truth of consciousness whose emanations are described as the movers in the sky. The essence of the Goddess, 'where she is established' (*yatra sā saṃsthitā*), is calm or tranquillized consciousness,[7] which is also the real identity of the self. Indeed, the practitioner who recognizes or realizes this innate tranquillity becomes a mover in the sky of consciousness and has attained the highest human achievement. The earlier scripture, the *Kālīkulapañcaśataka*, adds a statement about the emanation and contraction of the cosmos:

> 1.48: He who suddenly finds [that level of tranquillised consciousness] becomes a mover in the sky of consciousness. [So] the entire immeasurable universe is consumed again by the play [of the Goddess]. 7.49. There is no one equal on the earth to that practitioner. He stands supreme in the three worlds in his power, like the Lord. 7.50 The supreme power of consciousness has been told to you, O three-eyed one. This is the supreme secret which cannot be named, the system of the Goddess.[8]

The cosmos itself is an emanation of the Goddess who also 'consumes' it over and over again and this is a kind of play (*līlā*). There is no inherent telos to cosmic emanation other than it being the nature of absolute reality to manifest and consume the cosmos. Nevertheless, the Goddess has great beneficence (*mahālakṣmī*) even though she is addicted to consuming the universe (*viśvagrāsaikalampaṭām*)[9] The adjective *lampaṭā* to describe the Goddess is curious for the term implies covetousness or lustfulness and when used in a compound means 'desirous of or addicted to'.[10] The theological implication here is that the Goddess who is the source of the cosmos actually needs her creation and consumes the experience she creates as a kind of necessity. This image of consumption is important in the tradition, although it always accompanies the calmer metaphor of the Goddess as the sky of consciousness. The Goddess is the source of emanation followed by contraction, and contraction is the delight of consumption.

But the theological implications are not worked out. In the religion of Śiva, God is transcendent and without need; but in the Goddess tradition, there is a sense in which the Goddess creates out of necessity. I wonder whether this is a doctrine that develops from the central practice of sacrifice in mainstream Goddess or Śākta religion where the Goddess demands blood, although with the Krama this may have become metaphorical.

The Krama expresses the idea of emanation and contraction in a system of four categories or 'cycles' (*cakra*), namely the creation of the cosmos, its maintenance, its destruction and the cycle of the Nameless (*anākhya*). The creation, maintenance and destruction of the cosmos are standard functions of a theistic reality: the last cycle, the Nameless, expresses the ineffable nature of the transcendent reality of the Goddess. In this last cycle, the tradition expresses the emanation and contraction of the Goddess in thirteen forms, thirteen Kālīs, with the thirteenth as the Nameless one.

Alexis Sanderson has plotted the history of these thirteen emanations and has shown how the Krama cosmological understanding is given a 'psychological' account in Abhinavagupta, for whom the emanation and contraction of the Kālīs are the emanation and contraction of consciousness itself. Consciousness emanates its objects externally and then contracts, erasing all trace of objectivity in pure reflexive awareness or awareness of its own destruction.[11] This final self-absorption of consciousness is called 'The Nameless', yet is also named as Kālasaṃkārṣiṇī, she who destroys time or death.

This is not, in my view, a pure idealism but rather an emanationism in which the cosmos is conceptualized as an outer expression ('facing outwards', *bahyamukha* …) of the inner truth of universal consciousness. A pure idealism might claim that any differentiation between subject and object is mistaken, there being no such differentiation in truth. That would certainly be a metaphysics promoted within the Recognition (Prayabhijñā) school of Śaivism. In this philosophy, the objects of consciousness are constituted only within consciousness (they are not external to it).[12] But the tradition also uses a more common language of emanation or manifestation, such that the cosmos and individual persons are appearances of absolute consciousness. According to this philosophy, the cosmos is a solidification of the subtle substance of consciousness. The Krama system is consonant with this view. The Recognition School as expressed by Kṣemarāja is a philosophy that adopts the Krama system but incorporates it into its non-dualist metaphysics. Kṣemarāja was an important philosopher in this school, the student and nephew of Abhinavagupta, who was deeply influenced by the Goddess tradition of the Krama. He uses the Krama categories such as emanation, maintenance, destruction and the nameless to interpret the Recognition philosophy and to promote his non-dualism, a view that was rival to the dualist philosophy of the Śaiva Siddhānta that maintained three distinct realities of God, soul and matter. For Kṣemerāja these three are united in a shared or absolute consciousness as their metaphysical ground.

The interpretation of the recognition school

Adapting the Krama terminology, Kṣemarāja tells us that universal consciousness (*cit*) becomes particularized in individual consciousness (*cetanā*) and that recognition (*pratyabhijñā*) of absolute consciousness as our real identity is liberating. He opens his succinct summary of the system with the following statement:

> Verse 1: Consciousness, due to her own freedom, is the reason for the actualisation of the universe.[13]

Absolute consciousness (*citi*) is impersonal language for the reality of the Goddess who manifests the cosmos: there is no inherent telos to the cosmos other than the spontaneous expression of the Goddess's freedom, which is also the spontaneous expression (and self-limitation) of absolute consciousness. Limited consciousnesses are free, undifferentiated and self-luminous. In his auto-commentary on the verse Kṣemarāja writes:

> 'Of the universe', means from the level beginning with [the god] Sadāśiva to the earth [i.e. the entire cosmic hierarchy comprising the ontic levels]. 'Actualisation' (*siddhi*) means the production, illumination, maintenance, and destruction [of the universe], which comes to rest in the highest subject. 'Consciousness' (*citi*) means the Goddess (*bhagavatī*) whose nature is absolute power (*parāśaktirūpā*). 'Freedom' (*svatantrā*) refers to the one comprising highest awareness who is non-distinct from Lord Śiva, and 'reason' (*hetuḥ*) means cause (*kāraṇam*). Thus, the universe opens out (*unmiṣati*) in its diversity, continues, and closes down (*nimiṣati*) with its destruction. One's own experience (*svānubhavaḥ*) is a witness (*sākṣī*) in this matter.[14]

Here Kṣemarāja identifies the term 'universe' with the totality of the cosmic hierarchy from the highest level (the first manifestation that is the deity Sadāśiva), to the level of the earth. Kṣemarāja identifies absolute consciousness as the Goddess who creates, maintains and destroys the cosmos and also illuminates it. The identification of the Goddess with consciousness and with light is a striking feature of this system: the personal language of a *theos* or *deva* is identified with impersonal language of awareness and both descriptions are regarded as true. Kṣemarāja continues:

> Verse 5: That very consciousness, descended from the level of [universal] consciousness, [becomes] limited consciousness contracted to [the form of] its objects.

In his auto-commentary, Kṣemarāja tells us that this universal consciousness is, in fact, the Goddess herself. Hiding her own nature, she manifests as contraction and this contraction appears as the manifested cosmos. Limited consciousness is characterized by its conformity to its objects, which means that our consciousness takes the forms of its objects. Limited consciousness is from the level of universal consciousness and at this lower level is characterized by being distinguished from its objects. At the restricted, human level, we are always conscious of something, which is what Husserlian phenomenology calls intentionality. In Kṣemarāja's phrase, consciousness faces its objects and grasps them; there is a facing or intentionality towards the objects of consciousness.[15] I interpret this phrase, which might be rendered literally as 'facing upwards (*unmukhī*) towards the grasping (*grahaṇa-*) of an object (*artha-*)', in the phenomenological sense of intentionality as 'consciousness of'. From undifferentiated consciousness the Goddess manifests as subjects and objects of consciousness and so self-limits in contraction, simply as spontaneous freedom which in its essence is self-luminous (*svaprakāśaḥ*). This identification of consciousness with light is a characteristic of this system which Kṣemarāja interfuses with the Krama tradition of the Goddess in his analysis of human experience and the possibility of transcendence.

One of the features of this philosophy is that human experience recapitulates the cosmic experience of the Goddess. For Kṣemarāja, individual consciousness is universal consciousness in a state of contraction, and because of this contraction we wander through the universe in repeated incarnations. While contraction is a limitation, the limited life of the human person still reflects the actions of the Goddess, namely creation, maintenance, destruction, concealing and revealing. Such recapitulation occurs in everyday life. Going about one's business reflects or repeats in a limited way the divine acts of creation and destruction. Even concealing and revealing are human functions that reflect the way the Goddess manifests through grace and conceals through human ignorance. The reason for this ambiguity of concealing and revealing is not addressed but Kṣemarāja goes on to elaborate the five acts recapitulated in individual lives through introducing a new set of categories from the esoteric Krama. He states:

> Verse 11: These are illumination, delight, awareness, revealing the seed, and dissolving.

Kṣemrāja's auto-comment proposes a subtle understanding of the five cosmic acts recapitulated in the person. Here illumination (*ābhāsana*) refers to the manifestation of objects of consciousness and is equivalent to creation; delight (*rakti*) or the experiencing of objects of consciousness is equivalent to maintenance; and awareness (*vimarśana*) refers to supreme consciousness that is revealed at the dissolution of the universe and so is equivalent to the act of destruction. Revealing the seed (*bījāvasthāpana*) is the unfolding of manifestation and so is equivalent to the concealing of pure consciousness, while dissolving manifestation (*vilāpana*) is equivalent to the revealing of pure consciousness. The principle seems to be that the opening out of manifestation, the experiencing of our limited world, is simultaneously the closing in of awareness of cosmic expanse; conversely, the closing down of limited experience is the opening out of cosmic expanse. The systole and diastole of cosmic emanation and contraction are the opening and closing of eyes of the deity. Kṣemarāja tells us that this gradual expansion refers to the goddesses of the senses (sight and so on) who withdraw awareness of objectivity, which is a wonder (*camatkāra*) because it entails the opening out of the sky of consciousness. The seeds of becoming – the seeds of future reincarnations – are burnt up by the reality of the fire of consciousness (*cidagnisadbhāva*). The seeds of becoming that are planted within the self through interaction with world, with the objects of experience, unless they are destroyed in the fire of absolute consciousness, will grow again into future experience and karmic force that prevents the person from realizing their true nature as the Goddess and source of personal and cosmic manifestation.

In this theology, the Goddess is the source of both liberation and bondage. We wander through the cycle of reincarnation deluded by our own powers (*svaśaktibhir vyāmohitatā*), ignorant of the fivefold act of the Goddess.[16] Freedom from ignorance is the realization that the Goddess is the true actor (is there a distant resonance with Spinoza here? – see Chapter 7). In his auto-commentary, Kṣemarāja states this theology succinctly in an extensive passage:

> And again, the Goddess who is the power of consciousness, called Vāmeśvarī because of her nature as being against path of transmigration and due to her emitting the universe, appears at the level of the bound creature. [Here] she manifests the entire [cosmos as] the 'Goddess who moves in the heavens' (*khecarī*), the 'Goddess who moves in the sky' (*gocarī*), the 'Goddess who moves in the directions' (*dikcarī*), and the 'Goddess who moves over the earth' (*bhūcarī*). [These powers comprise] the essence of the subject of experience, the inner-instrument, the outer instrument, and external objects. Resting in the condition of emptiness, she appears as the limited agent who consists of the (limited) powers of authorship (*kalā*) and the rest [namely, limited knowledge, passion, limited time, spatial constraint]. She conceals her supreme reality as the essence of the Goddess who moves in the sky of consciousness (*cidgaganacarī*) by means of the circle of the Goddess who moves in the heavens (*khecarīcakra-*). She appears in the form of the Goddess of the inner instrument whose primary function is mental activity that ascertains difference and self-referentiality. She conceals the true nature of the supreme reality, which is the ascertaining of non-difference, through the circle of the Goddess who moves in the sky. She manifests in the form of the deity of the outer senses whose primary function is the perception of difference. She conceals the true nature of the supreme reality whose nature is non-difference through the circle of the Goddess who moves in the directions. She appears as objectivity characterized by particularized appearances everywhere, through the circle of the Goddess who moves on the earth, concealing her essence as the universal self and deluding the hearts of bound creatures.
>
> But at the level of the Lord she manifests as the Goddess who moves in the sky of consciousness, whose nature is the power of universal agency along with other powers. She appears as the Goddess who moves in the sky, whose nature is the ascertainment of non-difference; as the Goddess who moves in the directions whose nature is the perception of non-difference; and as the Goddess who moves over the earth as objectivity, whose essence is non-dual like one's own limbs. These shine forth in the heart of the Lord.[17]

There is a lot of technical terminology here, but the central idea is that the Goddess who is the power of consciousness appears as the Goddess who moves in the heavens, in the directions, and over the earth and who appears within the person as the functioning of ordinary awareness, through the instruments of awareness such as intellect, mind and ego along with the senses and their objects. In the first paragraph, the Goddess conceals her true nature through these functions. The truth that she animates all experience is hidden from us most of the time. She conceals her true nature (the reality of non-difference and undifferentiated awareness) through the goddesses who govern the senses at our lower level. In this metaphysics, when we interact with the world through the senses, this is regarded as the operation of the Goddess in the mode of concealment. It is the Goddess who empowers all interaction in what appears to be an objective world. Our ways of interacting with the world through the senses, along with our structures of mental interaction, are appearances of the Goddess. Conversely, in the mode of revealing, the Goddess is the ascertainment of truth that begins with non-difference (*abhedaniścayādi*). At the supreme level, the Goddess is the single, true agent and animating force of persons who think of themselves as possessing agency. In all the realms where the Goddess appears, in the sky, in the directions, over the earth, her true nature is non-dual awareness.

The exoteric understanding that individual actions reflect the five cosmic actions of God goes only so far in understanding the nature of the cosmos and human action within it; but the further esoteric understanding that the Goddess manifests and consumes experience within the person is a deeper truth. The language of Śiva is supplanted by the language of the Goddess, and the surface understanding of the human person as reflecting the five acts of God is replaced by the deeper understanding of the person as reflecting the all-consuming act of the Goddess who is supreme consciousness: she creates experience through the senses, she tastes that experience, and she consumes that experience in an act that destroys it. At the same time, this opens out experience of transcendent awareness. The closing down of restricted human experience through the senses is the opening out of unrestricted experience of the sky of consciousness. Conversely, the closing down of unrestricted, cosmic experience is the opening out of limited, sense experience.

The phenomenology of cosmic expanse

There are some notable features of the Krama system that resonate with a number of other metaphysical systems and this kind of thinking is not alien to Western metaphysical moves. One might think of the Lurianic Kabbalist idea of God contracting part of himself (*tsimtsum*) to project creation from himself into that nothingness (see Chapter 12) or even of Spinoza's non-dualism that identifies God with nature (*deus sive natura*), although the Krama is ambiguous here in sometimes seeming to maintain transcendence beyond immanence. But there are particularly interesting conceptual links that can be made to the phenomenological thinking of the European tradition.

In making a comparison with phenomenology, which of course itself is not monolithic, I would not wish to claim that they point to the same metaphysical reality. But it is striking that there are parallel forms or strategies of thinking, which in my view are not random but point to a realist metaphysics that entails historical change.[18] In particular, I would like to identify three parallel themes found in both the Krama and phenomenology, namely light, openness and awareness.

(a) *Light*. Historically in India and Europe, and possibly elsewhere too, consciousness is identified with light. This is something that can be traced in Ancient Greek philosophy; Heidegger notes that the meaning of *phainomenon* is something that shows itself and the verb *phaino* means bringing something to the light of day, the stem *pha* being connected to *phos*, light.[19] In the texts cited above, consciousness is a transpersonal quality identified with cosmic expanse (the sky of consciousness) and with light. This is a striking similarity that could be coincidental but is arguably a discovery of something fundamental to human self-awareness. Heidegger's phenomenology makes the connection between appearance and light as does the Krama. But Heidegger would not go down the route of emphasizing consciousness as transcending world as the Krama does at times. In the Krama metaphor the sky of consciousness, the realm of light (*prakāśa*), is above and beyond us, while yet also being our true nature.

(b) *Openness*. We have seen the use in the Krama of the term 'openness' as orientation to cosmos. This sky of consciousness indicates transpersonal reality apprehended in openness. The Krama texts use the term *vijṛbana*, an opening (as in a yawn), but figuratively to indicate openness to cosmic expanse. Openness is a characteristic of the 'movers in the sky of consciousness' (*khecarāḥ*) but also of persons who apprehend that reality. This metaphor of openness to cosmic expanse resonates with phenomenology in laying emphasis on human apprehension of consciousness as light and on openness as human freedom in its apprehension. The sky of consciousness might be understood as a metaphor for expanded awareness that encompasses something universal in human experience and that identifies human freedom as openness in its apprehension. Such apprehension is non-linguistic, and posits a direct encounter prior to cultural significations. Or perhaps more accurately, the Krama claims that cultural configurations of reality are limited, and inhibition prevents us from apprehending the truth of the Nameless, which is cosmic reality. Such openness is a new apprehension of being, and is in many ways paralleled in Heidegger's notion of openness (*Offenheit*) and a clearing (*eine Lichtung*). The clearing is that which illuminates being and grants us access to what we are; it is the open space (*das Offene*) within which beings show themselves.[20] Both Heidegger and the Krama seem to be pointing to a mode of human receptivity to a reality best characterized as being or becoming open.

(c) *Awareness*. There is a phenomenology in the Krama texts that describes the structures of human awareness. We interact with the world, with objects of perception, through the senses and through the innate structures of intellect (*buddhi*), mind (*manas*) and ego (*ahaṃkāra*) that are the conditions for interacting with a world. But under this surface phenomenology lies a deeper theological structure in which human modes of interaction are animated and governed by the transhuman power of the Goddess that is our deeper identity. Couching this in different language, the Krama asks implicitly whether our experience possesses immanent structures, in the phenomenologist Claude Romano's terms.[21] Its answer is that they do and that such immanent structures are outside of cultural construction. The sky of consciousness is not the product of culture or social formation but is an ontological reality that spontaneously manifests in human awareness. Indeed, it is almost as if this truth manifests itself despite cultural formation and the construction of persons in particular endogamous social units or castes, despite the social restriction of dharma. The Krama holds that there is a pre-linguistic order or pre-predicative experience which, while being accessible to phenomenological description, exceeds linguistic, and therefore cultural, formulation. More real than the lower cosmic levels, the ontological structure of the sky of consciousness as expanded awareness is described as 'a mass of consciousness' (*cidghana*) or 'mass of consciousness and joy' (*cidānandaghana*).[22] This is semantically dense: it transcends mere social identity or stage of life and is integral to the higher identity of person with cosmic expanse that is simultaneously the Goddess. To use Romano's phrase, there are certain givens that are inherent in the structure of human experience, rather than being simply added by consciousness to purely amorphous givens.[23]

Concluding remarks

The phenomenology of expanded awareness proposed by the Krama is striking in its being a kind of verticality outside of usual practices of ritual for, as Sanderson observes, the Krama advocates no ritual, no initiation and no visualization,[24] none of the usual practices that make up a religious tradition. This is unusual in the sense that gnostic forms of religion are difficult to maintain through the generations without ritual practices that support them (although the Krama does seem to have advocated occasional transgressive, anti-Brahmanical practices that serve to underline how the tradition went against the grain of normative adherence to social mores).

This was never to become a major philosophical tradition but is significant in the history of Indian metaphysics in the power of its description. Although it is impossible to assess the numbers of adherents, the Krama was not a mainstream tradition in contrast to the Śaiva Siddhānta, even though it has a substantial body of literature. But given the social and political conditions in which these texts were being produced, it is a remarkable achievement in its discovery of cosmic expanse. The medieval period – as in other civilizations of Europe and China – would be characterized by a feudal hierarchy with a dominant, Brahmanical ideology of conformity to *varṇāśramadharma*, duty regarding caste and life stage. At a horizontal level of social engagement, there would be a high degree of conformity to Brahmanical social mores; and the conformist, central tradition of Śaiva Siddhānta regarded such conformity as a necessary condition for further spiritual advancement through Śaiva initiation.[25] The Krama challenges such conformity and while it may not be socially transformative in its theology, it posits a new metaphysics of expanded, cosmic awareness that it claims goes beyond mere social conformity. There is a verticality in the structure of persons becoming open to the sky of consciousness that is identified with light and awareness as the appearance of the Unnameable, an ineffable reality that undergirds manifestation, so the tradition claims. We might posit this as a discovery that offered an insight into a transcendental structure of human awareness discovered despite prevailing social and cultural conditions: an example of human communities going beyond themselves to elevation and aspiration to a higher reality.

Notes

1. Also known by various other names, notably the Mahānaya, Mahārtha, Devīnaya and Kālikula, Rastogi (1979: 10–30).
2. Sanderson's dating, 'Śaiva Exegesis', 412.
3. *Cidgaganacandrikā* 1.
4. *Cidgananacandrikā* 82. Karavīra is a famous cremation ground in Uḍḍiyana. See Sanderson, 'Śaiva Exegesis', 276.
5. *Cidgananacandrikā* 3: 'May the Moon Goddess in the sky of consciousness cool the heat of the fire of cyclic existence for us'.
6. *Cidgananacandrikā* 3.
7. *Kālīkulapañcaśataka* 7.46ab: 'where the Goddess is established is the level of tranquilized consciousness'.
8. *Kālīkulapañcaśataka* 7.48–50.
9. *Kālīkulapañcaśataka* 2.68cd.
10. Monier-Williams, *Sanskrit Dictionary*, 897.
11. Sanderson (1986: 169–207). The Krama system is found at the esoteric heart of the religion of the Trika in Kashmir. Sanderson notes: 'The innermost power of the maṇḍala of final initiation into the Trika is then this quintessential deity group of the Krama, Kālasaṃkārṣiṇī mirrored in the twelve Kālīs of the Nameless as all-pervading, all-devouring non duality in the dynamic cycle of the object, act and agent of cognition' ('Maṇḍala and Āgamic Identity', 198).

12. Ratié (2011: 37).
13. *Pratyabhijñāhṛdaya* by Kṣemarāja, E-text, Encoded by: Dott. Marino Faliero, Dipartimento di Studi Orientali, DSO – Sanskrit Archive, July 1998.
14. Kṣemarāja, *Pratyabhijñāhṛdaya* 1, auto-commentary.
15. Kṣemarāja, *Pratyabhijñāhṛdaya* 5, auto-commentary.
16. *Pratyabhijñāhṛdaya* 12: The condition of being a wanderer is being deluded by one's own powers in ignorance of that [fivefold act].
17. *Pratyabhijñāhṛdaya* 12, auto-commentary.
18. This is beyond the remit of this chapter, but I develop this in *Naming Invisible Light: A History and Phenomenology of Holiness* (Oxford: Oxford University Press, forthcoming), chapter 8.
19. Heidegger (2005: 4).
20. Heidegger (2002 [1950]: 30). *Holzwege* (Frankfurt: Vitorio Klostermann, 1972. [1950]): 40.
21. Romano (2011: xi).
22. *Pratyabhijñāhṛdaya* 8, auto-commentary.
23. Romano, *At the Heart of Reason*, 460.
24. Sanderson, 'The Śaiva Exegesis', 260–1.
25. Sanderson, 'The Śaiva Exegesis', 231, citing Nārāyaṇakaṇṭha, *Mṛgendravṛtti, Vidyāpāda*, 63.

References

Primary Sources

(All translations are my own, although in the case of previously translated texts, namely the *Pratyabhijñāhṛdaya*, I have been guided by those of Jaideva Singh. Scholarship on the Krama has been opened up by Alexis Sanderson and is now being continued by Diwakar Acharya.)

Cidgaganacandrikā by Śrīvatsa alias Kālidāsa, E-text copied from Arthur Avalon series. Tantrik texts; 20. Published in Calcutta: Sanskrit Book Depot; London: Luzac, 1937. Data entered by the staff of Muktabodha under the supervision of Mark Dyczkowski. Revision: 30/11/2005.

Kālīkulapañcaśataka. Muktabodha Digital Library. Data entered by the staff of Muktabodha Indological Research Institute, also known as ***devīpañcaśatikā,*** edited by Mark S. G. Dyczkowski. Muktabodha Indological Research Institute.

Mahānayaprakāśa (anon.) edited by K. Sāmbaśiva Śāstrī (Trivandrum: Trivandrum Sanskrit Series, 1937).

Mahānayaprakāśa of Arṇasiṃha, edited by Mark S. G. Dyczkowski from NAK ms no. 5–5183 (called kālikākulapañcaśatakam) śaivatantra 157 NGMPP A/150/6, folios 26–33.

Pratyabhijñāhṛdaya by Kṣemarāja, edited by J. C. Chatterji KSTS vol 3 (Srinagar: Research Department, Jammu and Kashmir State, 1911). English translation, Jaideva Singh (Delhi: MLBD, 1963). E-text, Encoded by: Dott. Marino Faliero, Dipartimento di Studi Orientali, Sanskrit Archive, July 1998.

Secondary Sources

Acharya, Diwakar, 'Kenopaniṣad' in this volume.
Heidegger, Martin (2005), *Introduction to Phenomenological Research*, trans. Daniel O. Dahlstrom. Bloomington, IN: Indiana University Press.
Heidegger, Martin, 2002 [1950], 'The Origin of the Work of Art', in *Off the Beaten Track*, trans. Julian Young and Kenneth Hayes. Cambridge: Cambridge University Press, pp. 1–56; *Holzwege* (Frankfurt: Vitorio Klostermann, 1972 [1950]).
Rastogi, N. (1979), *The Krama Tantrism of Kashmir*. Delhi: MLBD.
Ratié, Isabelle (2011), *Le Soi et l'Autre: Identité, différence et altérité dand la philosophie de a Pratyabhijñā*. Leiden: Brill.
Romano, Claude (2011), *At the Heart of Reason*. Evanson, IL: Northwestern University Press.
Sanderson, Alexis (1985), 'Purity and Power among the Brahmins of Kashmir', in Michael Carruthers, Steven Collins and Steven Lukes (eds.), *The Category of the Person*. Cambridge: Cambridge University Press, pp. 190–216.
Sanderson, Alexis (1986), 'Maṇḍala and the Āgamic Identity in the Trika of Kashmir', in André Padoux (ed.), *Mantras et Diagrammes Rituels dans l'Hindouisme*. Paris: CNRS, pp. 169–207.
Sanderson, Alexis (2007), 'The Śaiva Exegesis of Kashmir', in Dominic Goodall and André Padoux (eds.), *Mélanges Tantriques à la mémoire de Hélène Brunner*. Pondichéry: Institut Français, pp. 231–582.
Sanderson, Alexis (2009), 'The Śaiva Age', in Shingo Einoo (ed.), *Genesis and Development of Tantrism*. Tokyo: Institute of Oriental Culture, pp. 41–350.
Sanderson, Alexis (2012–13), 'Śaiva Literature', *Journal of Indological Studies* 24–5: 1–113.

10

Brilliant darkness: Apophatic thinking in early Christian and Indian traditions

Ana-Maria Pascal and Diwakar Acharya

There are different kinds of apophatic thinking in both Christian and Indian traditions. Some have become more prevalent than others, but all entail an element of mystery in relation to perceptions of divinity (or the Absolute), from the unsaid, unnamed or inexpressible, through the incomprehensible, to the utterly unknown, either only knowable through non-cognitive means, or simply inaccessible by any means. Each of these represents a somewhat different stance on the nature of, and our relationship to, the Absolute. So we begin with a typology of apophaticism, before exploring some of the core conceptual nuances of the possibility of knowing God, in the two traditions.

In Christianity, apophaticism is usually associated with the desert fathers' spirituality – roughly, the period between the first and the fourteenth century, which is sometimes described as 'mystical', because of the monks' focus on contemplative prayer; this is important, because, as we shall see, apophatic thinking is directly linked to the notion that God may be known through non-cognitive means, such as contemplation.

The early centuries are dominated by what is often referred to as 'gnostic intellectualism', a combination of Greek philosophy, neo-Platonism and early Christian faith, which can be found in the works of Origen and Clement of Alexandria. It is, indeed, difficult to separate these traditions; one can detect apophatic elements in Plato's *Parmenides* and in the neoplatonic Proclus' commentary on it (Proclus 1987). The distinctly Christian version of apophatic theology is present in Maximus the Confessor and John Damascene, but the terms are first used by Pseudo-Dionysius the Areopagite (cf. Louth 1989: 87).

While the typical definition draws a distinction between positive and negative theology, each of the two terms has a wider range of nuances than this binary approach implies. In what follows, we explore these nuances, and the respective paths to the divine that each of them entails.

There are different ways of knowing – some of which allow for the possibility of naming God, others that don't; some even allow for a degree of uncertainty; one can talk of the possibility of both knowing and not knowing God; finally, one can speak of the possibility of a union with God (through prayer, or mystical contemplation) that constitutes a different kind of knowledge – non-cognitive, and all the deeper for that. In this view, God may be 'seen' (albeit, in an unnatural way), rather than known; He is accessible to us in a mysticism of light – or indeed in a theology of darkness (Merton 1951: 25).

There are equivalent non-cognitive options in Hinduism. Brahman, the soul of the universe, or the Absolute, is in everything – and yet beyond any understanding (*Brihadaranyaka* Upaniṣad (BAU) 4.3.29; Olivelle 2005: 117); but he can be attained in moments of intense experience (Ib. 4.3.21; Olivelle 2005: 117), similar to the Christian union with God, or while asleep (*Chandogya* Upaniṣad (ChU) 6.8.1–4; Olivelle 2005: 251), cf. Goodall, 1996: xvii.

In the Indian thought-world, one can detect a similarly complex range of nuances of apophatic thinking. Although India has many gods, Indian mystics and thinkers posit one and the same Brahman, the ultimate entity or the Supreme Self that is capable of infinite faces and forms but ineffable in itself lying behind all gods, all beings and all things, omnipresent, omniscient and omnipotent.[1] The notion that one and the same God is invoked by various names is already attested in the philosophical hymns from the tenth book of the *Rigveda* (*c.* 1200–1000 BCE). These hymns rhetorically ask the unanswerable question of who is that One whom we worship; and a kind of apophatic thinking is already evident in one such hymn that describes the primordial One, often called 'Song of Creation':

> The nonexistent did not exist, nor did the existent exist at that time. There existed neither the airy space nor heaven beyond.
> What moved back and forth? From where and in whose protection? Did water exist, a deep depth?
> Death did not exist nor deathlessness then. There existed no sign of night nor of day. That One breathed without wind by its independent will. There existed nothing else beyond that.
> (Jamison & Brereton 2014: 1607: *Rigveda* X.129.1–2)

This ontological apophaticism is complemented by an epistemological one, which comes at the end of the hymn – 'who knows truly? (…) whence is this emanation?' and the final suggestion is that only God – and perhaps not even He (God) – knows.

Cosmogonic accounts of the Brāhmaṇas and the earliest Upaniṣads (*c.* seventh century BCE), as they expand the Vedic ideas, present the ultimate Being of Brahman as the Primordial Person who wishes to multiply, and in so doing, creates every entity and becomes manifest in it. These texts describe the Ultimate Being of Brahman or the Primordial Person in both cataphatic and apophatic ways but identify the apophatic method as superior.

Typology

Apophaticism is commonly described as 'negative theology' – namely, an attempt to approach divinity by *negation*, highlighting what or how the divine is not. However, apophatic thinking is often more nuanced, and not all apophaticism entails a purely negative approach. Some texts do indeed use negation to indicate something *unnamed* or *unknown*; but others embrace *uncertainty*, acknowledging that God is known in some sense and unknown in another; yet others aim to *transcend* both affirmation and negation, in an attempt to reach a different kind of experience than the cognitive.

The unnamed God

At the root of this theology is the belief that there are no words to describe God's perfection. There is an element of this in Christianity, drawing on God's name YHWH in the Hebrew Bible, 'I am who I am', interpreted as implying 'without a name' – either because God's name is too holy to pronounce or due to His ontological status (too high above creation to be contained in any created words).

Several references in the Christian New Testament indicate that if we did name God, we would have to use created names, inherently limited, whereas 'His name is above all names' (Philippians 2.9), and this will stay so – 'above all rule and authority and power and dominion, and above every name that is named, not only in this age but also in the one to come' (Ephesians 1.21). Such cataphatic elements – and the accompanying knowledge they bring – are associated with God's features or His manifestations in creation, never with His core nature which remains utterly incomprehensible. The distinction between God's unknown nature and His manifestations in the world was to mark various stages in Christian theology – the *ascetic* (fourth to sixth centuries CE), the *Christological* (sixth to eighth centuries) and the *pneumatological* (from the eleventh century onwards).

In the Indian thought-world too, some esoteric mantras are recited only mentally, and names of certain deities are not pronounced. However, Indian theologians do not claim that any of God's names is too holy to pronounce. Instead, they argue that any one name can describe only one aspect of the Ultimate, or even the truth of any being; it can only be 'a verbal handle' (cf. ChU 6.4.1). Any name will place the Ultimate in a certain perspective, such that it would no longer be the Ultimate. This applies to all terms used to denote the Absolute, such as Brahman, *Puruṣa* and *Ātman* (or God, the Ultimate etc.) Therefore, after denying all attributed names, the BAU describes 'the reality of reality / the truth of the truth' (*satyasya satyam*) as 'a way of naming' the Ultimate, the essence of everything. This reminds us of the notions of 'suchness' (*tathatā/dharmatā*) and the reality 'as it is' (*yathābhūta*) found in early Buddhist discourse. Truth can only be experienced in a deep meditative state, and as soon as our mind conceptualizes it, it dissipates; language alters it.

We can already begin to see two rather different types of apophatic approach – one related to language (and the impossibility to *name* God), the other about ontological status (and the impossibility to *know* God, due to His utterly otherworldly nature). Each of these can be split into two further categories. The ontologically unknown God may be either *utterly unknown*, or unknown in His nature but known in His manifestations – hence, an *approximative* God. The unsaid God may be both unsaid and unknown, that is incomprehensible, or just unsaid but possibly known (or experienced) through lived experience, like a *personal* God. This last option opens the way to mystical union. Let us consider these views, in some detail.

The unknown God

One classical apophatic approach holds that not only we cannot name God, we cannot know Him at all. By definition, the Creator is unknown to its creation. In this view, God is not only ineffable; He is also utterly incomprehensible, both in His essence and in His attributes.

Such a view can be found in many Upanisads. The Ultimate Self cannot be grasped intellectually alone, even by great teaching and learning; only those chosen by the Ultimate Self can grasp him (cf. *Kaṭha* Upaniṣad 2.23; Olivelle 2005: 387). And mind alone cannot behold the Ultimate Self (cf. BĀU 4.4.18,19; Olivelle 2005: 125). 'Sight does not reach there; neither does thinking or speech. We don't know, we can't perceive, how one would point it out. It is far different from what's known. And it is farther than the unknown – so have we heard from men of old, who have explained it all to us' (*Kena* Upaniṣad 1.3–4; Olivelle 2005: 365).

Early on in the second century CE, Clement of Alexandria helped establish the negative way within Christian theology. In his amplest work, *The Stromata*, whose full title is 'Miscellanies Notes of Revealed Knowledge in Accordance with the True Philosophy', he aims to show that real knowledge is not rationalized but revealed.

Commentators see him as 'a key link between the earliest Christian theologians who applied negative predicates to God, notably Justin Martyr (died *c*. 165) and the Cappadocian fathers, eminently Gregory of Nyssa …' (Franke 2014: 135). Indeed, one of the chapters in part V of *The Stromata* is titled 'God Cannot Be Embraced in Words or by the Mind'. And earlier in the book, he announces that 'knowledge of ignorance is (…) the first lesson in walking according to the Word'. The next stages in this process are detailed in Chapters 11–13, where Clement argues that 'true knowledge of God' requires a pure mind (one that draws nothing from the senses) and grace coming from God, through the Son; and is therefore 'a divine gift' (The Stromata, in *Ante-Nicene Fathers*, vol. II). This opens the door to the mystical route taken by later theologians, also confirmed by the fact that Clement cites the same biblical references (to the Book of Exodus) that Pseudo-Dionysius and Gregory of Nyssa would later use, about Moses' ascent for holy contemplation of God in brilliant darkness.

This 'via negativa' became the established view in the fourth century, when the Cappadocian[2] Fathers, especially Gregory of Nyssa, insisted on God's radical unknowability. In his *Life of Moses*, Gregory interprets the episode of Moses seeing God in a dark cloud thus:

> '… leaving behind everything that is observed, not only what sense comprehends but also what the intelligence thinks it sees' because there 'it gains access to the invisible and the incomprehensible (…). This is the true knowledge of what is sought; this is the seeing that consists in not seeing, because that which is sought transcends all knowledge, being separated on all sides by incomprehensibility as by a kind of darkness. Wherefore John the sublime, who penetrated into the luminous darkness, says, *No one has ever seen God*, thus asserting that knowledge of the divine essence is unattainable not only by men but also by every intelligent creature. When, therefore, Moses grew in knowledge, he declared that he had seen God in the darkness, that is, that he had then come to know that what is divine is beyond all knowledge and comprehension, for the text says, *Moses approached the dark cloud where God was.*'
>
> (Nyssa 1978: 113)

This is the classical expression of apophaticism, understood as unknowability of God, one that uses the metaphors of the cloud and luminous darkness, as well as the distinction between seeing and (cognitive) understanding. We return later to the multiple meanings of divine darkness.

An Indian equivalent of this unknowability of God can be found in the early Upaniṣads: 'It has no sound or touch, no appearance, taste, or smell; It is without beginning or end, undecaying and eternal; when a man perceives it, fixed and beyond the immense, he is freed from the jaws of death' (*Kaṭha* Upaniṣad 3.15; Olivelle 2005: 391). Again, the suggestion is that a man might be able to 'perceive' the Ultimate through other means than knowledge.

The incomprehensible God

Another Cappadocian, St Basil of Caesarea, highlights a different nuance of apophaticism – the sheer incomprehensibility of God (1930). This is close to the utterly unknown, but not quite the same, for it suggests a sense of mystery, more than a total barrier. John Chrysostom, bishop of Constantinople and contemporary with the Cappadocians, refers to this in his sermons on the incomprehensibility of God, where he argues for the compatibility between knowledge and incomprehensibility: 'For I know that God is everywhere and that he is everywhere in his whole being. But I do not know how he is everywhere' (1982: 57–8). Chrysostom uses a range of adjectives to describe this mystery, from 'inscrutable' to 'unsearchable' and 'indescribable'. 'This incomprehensibility, however – as Andrew Louth explains – is not merely a sense of the limitations of reason; it is rather a matter of fear and awe (Hollywood and Beckman 2012: 138), which has practical consequences for the way people live.

This sense of mystery or inexplicability has an equivalent in the Indian tradition – where the Ultimate beyond is neither known nor unknown; it is known to not knowing bhaktas, and unknown to knowing sophists. The philosophy of transcendence and immanence (*bhedābheda*) in Vedanta is relevant here; it states that the individual self is both different and not different from the ultimate reality. Also, the sense of unknowability and submission is explicit in popular devotional prayer such as 'I do not know the truth of your nature, o Great God! My homage to you in whichever form you may exist'.

The approximative God

As the previous interpretation suggests, there may be a way of knowing God, not in His essence, but through His presence in His creation. This would constitute an approximation of God from His attributes and manifestations. One can find this cataphatic route in Pseudo-Dionysius' *Divine Names*, where the Areopagite attempts to give his disciple Timothy 'an explication of the divine names (…) "not in the plausible words of human wisdom but in demonstration of the power granted by the Spirit" [1 Corinthians 2.4] to the scripture writers' (1987: 49) – thus acknowledging the role of divine inspiration in the very attempt to approach God.

Names (and language more generally) play an important role in Pseudo-Dionysius' work. They constitute a stage in the spiritual ascent, before that of silent contemplation. Indeed, *The Divine Names* comes before *The Mystical Theology*, because 'via affirmativa' is a stage on the way to achieving that kind of understanding which is beyond knowledge with the mind – as Dionysius says, referring to Moses' experience on the mount. Cataphatic knowledge is, by nature, imperfect, as it relies on words and expressions, which inevitably limit their object. To say of God that He is perfect, all-encompassing and all-knowing is limiting, because, like all such attempts at describing Him, who is larger than any description, it is doomed to fail. All affirmations are limiting – but they help guide the beginner's mind in her attempt to approach the divine – until, that is, she becomes confident enough to abandon all tools (linguistic and epistemological) and embrace a different type of approach. This is indeed possible because, by the power of the Spirit, 'in a manner surpassing speech and knowledge, we reach a union superior to anything available to us by way of our own abilities or activities in the realm of discourse or of intellect' (1987: 49).

On the other hand, the view that recognizing the presence of God in His creation *does not* amount to any knowledge of the divine is yet another form of radical apophaticism – radical, because it still entails negation. God and His features remain unknown to us; He is beyond both being and intellect. But although unknown, He can still be accessible to us – in His manifestations, and through His grace; the result may be some form of mystical union, ecstasy or communion. It is this third option – of 'knowing' God through experience rather than cognitive or linguistic methods – that occupied the minds and hearts of many church Fathers. Let us briefly explore their understanding of how to relate to this unknown, unnamed God. The focus, here, will be on *what follows* from their negative theology, because they do not stop here; they seek a relationship with God. And it is that *lived experience*, that level of apophaticism that goes beyond both the positive and the negative routes, that captures our imagination.

The personal God

The shift from dogma and intellectualism to an increased focus on monastic practice (mainly mystical contemplation), which is noticeable from the fifth and sixth centuries onwards, brings us to another type of apophatic thinking, which constitutes an attempt to go beyond the positive/negative duality. This is, in a sense, the natural next step for those who are more interested in religious practice – its contemplative side, based on prayer and meditation. Theologians like Pseudo-Dionysius the Areopagite take the view that God is neither known, nor unknown; in fact, our relationship with Him is both, or none, depending on whether we consider practical experience a kind of knowledge. The aim is not to 'know' God and be able to describe Him, but to have a relationship with Him, which is to 'know' Him differently – with one's heart.

Some describe the striving to experience divinity as an ascent towards union with God.[3] John Climacus' *Ladder of Divine Ascent*, written in the early seventh century, is arguably the most elaborate description of this process. This reminds us of Dionysius' description of a true believer's attempt to leave everything behind and seek union with God through silent prayer. Indeed, both Climacus' and Dionysius' ascents end with a clear indication of an apophatic stage, which is beyond (rather than opposed to) things and language – *hesychia* (stillness) in Climacus, and silence in Dionysius. For both theologians, writing was a form of spiritual practice, aimed at conveying to their disciples that to know God is to become united with Him in prayer. Their books are not scholarly, but experiential; their purpose is soteriological.

Maximus the Confessor, a Christian monk from the sixth/seventh century, showed great interest in the kind of apophatic approach embraced by Dionysius. He makes this explicit both in his *Scholia to The Mystical Theology* (one of Maximus' major early works, little known in English language literature due to the lack of a full modern edition), and in his later works. In the Scholia (Areopagitus 1996: 251–4), he provides valuable insights on the notion of brilliant darkness, which he equates with 'total infinite (nonunderstanding)'; on the mount of Moses' ascent, which Maximus believes to be the very place where God had been before him, and as such, the ultimate place of all knowledge and understanding ('the top of all things seen and understood'); on what it means to contemplate divine darkness – viz., to know God through not knowing; and on transcending both affirmations and negations, in this striving for knowledge. The underlying reason for overcoming dualism is that both affirmation and negation show the greatness of God; in Him, they are not opposite, because He is beyond both (see below).

Several centuries later, St Gregory Palamas goes to some length to explore this kind of non-cognitive understanding, which transcends knowledge and instead relies on prayer in silence (Palamas 2002). For more on Palamas, see Chapter 11. The hesychast tradition was centred on the notion of *hesychia*, a term introduced by Gregory of Nyssa, in his *Life of Moses*, and often used to describe silent contemplation. The purpose of this monastic practice was to achieve the same kind of union with God that Dionysius was talking about in his *Mystical Theology*, as the aim of the mystical ascent. The difference is that, all those centuries later, with the hesychasts, the 'method' is more clearly articulated. It consists of a continuous 'prayer of the heart', which, given its brevity and repetition, works like a mantra in Hindu meditation – and there have been attempts to compare the hesychastic prayer with yogic practices (see, for instance, Chapter 6 in Mangala Frost 2017).

Practice is key in the Indian tradition too, where a strikingly similar typology to the Christian one can be detected. To begin with, the Upaniṣads state *cataphatically* that Brahman is the self within all; it is cognition and bliss; it is Being/truth, awareness and infinity (cf. e.g. *Taittiriya* Upaniṣad 2.1.1; Olivelle 2005: 301). Also, the Upaniṣads metaphorically refer to the Sun, the moon, the space, etc., as Brahman. All these positive descriptions, however, are meant to facilitate meditation on a particular quality or representation of the Ultimate. In each of these forms, He is accessible to us and we can engage with him. Thus, the cataphatic description is relational and contextual, so it can only suggest one aspect of reality at a time. According to this view, the Ultimate can be approached or venerated effectively, and in infinite individual ways, invoking one name (or form) or another; but if one wants to awaken oneself to the all-accommodating nature of the Ultimate, and feel his ineffable infinity, one needs to resort to apophatic methods. As long as the Ultimate is limited to one particular aspect, if one clings to any one particular form and the name attached to that form, one has an incomplete understanding. Therefore, if one wants to understand the reality in its entirety, one must deny each of its fragmented identities or approximations. With this apophatic approach, all boundaries of specification collapse, and the series of negations is automatically terminated. It becomes clear that one and the same truth/reality is everywhere, in the form of the essence of each entity, though it appears differently in different places. Thus, apophatic thinking leads the seeker to the highest level of understanding, where he or she abandons all fixed names and follows ways of naming the ultimate, such as 'the reality of reality' (cf. BAU II.3.11), which cannot be formalized and attached to one aspect or another.

The BAU, one of the earlier Upaniṣads compiled before the time of the Buddha, formalizes the apophatic method using *neti neti* (neither so nor so) as the best method of knowing the truth of the truth. It argues that 'neither so nor so' is there anything else beyond the Ultimate, that is the Sacred Fire in the ritual context and the ubiquitous Person (*puruṣa*) in the context of an inquiry about the essence of the world and being. However far or near, high or low, one may go, there is the Ultimate, which remains concealed under its context-specific names and forms. Unless one negates these, one is unable to understand the complete truth. Thus, early on, the Upaniṣadic apophatic method highlighted the ultimacy of the Ultimate, beyond which there is nothing else, which itself is beyond all names, forms and human quests. But it also demonstrated that, thanks to its ubiquity, it is everywhere, here and now, but one can only understand this when one is awakened to its truth apophatically.

Once thus articulated in the BAU, the apophatic method is subsequently applied in other Upaniṣads.[4] Apophatic statements from the Upaniṣads describe the truth of the Ultimate, the purest essence in the body and the universe, and its experience, proclaiming the nondual unity of the Ultimate. The original spirit of the BAU teaching was holistic; every one-sided claim was critically negated, relativized and adjusted as an aspect of the single, all-pervasive whole. What followed was a transcendentalist interpretation, advocating that the Ultimate was that which remained at the core of everything.

In Vedanta (where Upaniṣadic ideas are elucidated), the apophatic method is regarded as the best one leading to the truth of Brahman,[5] the Ultimate. Beyond the Upaniṣads and Vedānta, apophatic thinking can also be found embedded in the Epic Sāṃkhya's concept of *avyakta*, the unmanifest, which refers to the source of everything, both consciousness and matter, in its primordial state. The concept of *avyakta*, the unmanifest that exists without name or form in the beginning of creation, is apophatic in nature.[6]

Beyond the canonical texts, as philosophical systems begin to formalize, the quest is no longer limited to divinity, but is extended to truth or being in general. Buddhist philosopher Nāgārjuna (*c.* 150 CE) and Jain monk Samantabhadra (seventh century CE) both apply the apophatic method in their thinking. Following the Buddha's middle path, Nāgārjuna uses it to build his dialectic edifice of tetralemma (a type of argument that he often uses to reject not only thesis and antithesis, but also their conjunction and disjunction); and to describe the dependent origination of all phenomena by negating two extremes such as eternity and transiency.

Analogously, the Jain doctrine of *anekānta* denies all unilateral views, in order to arrive at the complete truth of the complex unity of diverse reality. And they render this apophatic truth in seven steps: the truth as known; as unknown; as known and unknown; as inexplicable; as known but inexplicable; as unknown and inexplicable; and as known and unknown and inexplicable.

Bhartṛhari (the fifth century CE philosopher of language) and Gauḍapāda (fifth/sixth century, Vedanta) also draw on both Upaniṣadic and Buddhist sources, to apply the apophatic method. In later centuries, followers of the Buddhist, Jain and Upaniṣadic Vedanta schools continue to apply and refine apophatic methods.

Apophatic methods aim at exhausting the intellect and forcing it to see truth holistically. To know that the ultimate is unknowable is true knowing. As the BAU 4.5.15 rhetorically puts it, 'by what means would one know the knower!'. The knower, the self, is the Ultimate himself, and he is the source of all knowing, but himself remains beyond knowing. His attributes are knowable and describable, but given the limitations of human intellect, it cannot know all attributes. When we realize this, God/Truth/the Ultimate is graciously revealed to us. There are two ways of experiencing the Ultimate methodologically. The first is the path of devotion, where one surrenders oneself to God, in whichever form one is worshipping him. Surrender will help him receive God's grace, so one can be in the presence of (or in union with) God. Another way is the heroic path of training oneself through meditation to experience within oneself the all-present consciousness seen as the Ultimate/God who is the sole being in the world and beyond. Thus, one can directly experience Him within oneself but cannot know or explain Him (cf. BAU 3.4.1). This is similar to the mystical experience of the Christian monks discussed above.

The Christian God is comparable to the One Universal Person/Self of the Upaniṣads. One can know Him to some extent – namely, by seeing Him in every being and within oneself. As the *Kaṭha* Upaniṣad teaches, 'As the single fire/wind, entering living beings, adapts its appearance to match that of each; so the single self within every being, adapts its appearance to match that of each; yet remains quite distinct' (KaṭhaU 4.9–10; Olivelle 2005: 397). However, one has to transcend both the physical and the mental, to really see Him. For, 'Higher than the senses are their objects; Higher than sense objects is the mind; Higher than the mind is the intellect; Higher than the intellect is the immense self; Higher than the immense self is the unmanifest; Higher than the unmanifest is the person' (KaṭhaU 3.10–11; ibid., 389).

In sum, the multiple approaches of apophaticism in both Christian and Indian traditions can be categorized as: the unnamed God; the unknown God; the incomprehensible God, or the Ultimate beyond, *neither* known *nor* unknown; the approximative God, both known (in His manifestations) and unknown (in His nature); and the personal God. While the first four types of apophaticism entail a degree of knowledge, the fifth transcends all cognition. There is only presence in it; meditative practices transcend the subject-object divide that characterizes any cognitive rapport. Key elements in this last stage are: the notions of brilliant darkness, silence, contemplative prayer or meditation, and the beyond. In what follows, we shall explore the role played by the first and the last of these notions – brilliant darkness and the beyond – in both traditions.

Brilliant darkness and the beyond

The last category in the typology – 'knowing' through non-cognitive means – is perhaps best described using the phrase 'beyond' (*hyper*), as it transcends both affirmation and negation. This led some commentators to call it a 'hyperphatic' approach, to distinguish it from the cataphatic and apophatic (Conway-Jones 2021: 13). Let us explore the nuances of this approach, both with respect to the absolute itself, and the process of reaching it.

A good starting point is Dionysius' *Mystical Theology*,[7] which can be viewed as a guide on what it means to go beyond language and intellect – indeed, beyond the world and everything in it, beyond the perceptible and the conceptual, and ultimately beyond transcendence itself – to attempt actual union with God. The text encapsulates the key elements of apophatic thinking understood as spiritual practice rather than cognitive effort, starting with the key term from the opening prayer –'beyond' (*hyper*), which is repeated ten times. Translations in some languages, for example the Romanian (Areopagitul 1996), retain this repetition. In English, translators prefer to avoid repetitions, so the word 'beyond' is in many instances replaced with other idioms, like 'higher than', 'up to' and 'overwhelming'. In the Romanian text, by contrast, most occurrences of '*hyper*' are translated by the particle '*supra*': *supra-naturala, supra- divina si supra-buna* (higher than – or beyond – any being, any divinity, any goodness); *supra-necunoscuta si supra-stralucitoare* (beyond unknowing and light); *intunericul supra-luminos* (darkness beyond light – or, as in the English translation, brilliant darkness); *supra-stralucind in chipul cel mai supra-luminos* ('more than shining in a way that transcends brightness'); and *straluciri supra-frumoase* (super-beautiful sparkles).

The advantage of repeatedly using the particle 'hyper' in this way is that it stresses the importance of transcendence both as a feature of the divine and as a movement of the soul, as it seeks to reach that place of brilliant darkness where God dwells – to experience the presence of divinity which is inaccessible to the intellect alone. This can therefore be described as 'negative' metaphysics in the same sense that apophasis is considered a negative theology. Indeed, one of the instances where the particle is used by Dionysius refers to what happens to the mind searching for God: the bright darkness that is the divine presence 'fills up' the mind engaged in contemplation: 'they [the mysteries of God's word] completely fill our sightless minds / with treasures beyond all beauty.' The mind is 'sightless' not because it cannot see, but because it has chosen to see beyond that which obscures the divine; the mind, therefore, is in a state of blessed 'blindness', in the contemplation of God who dwells in 'brilliant darkness'.

The metaphor of 'divine darkness' is used to convey apophatic notions in both Indian and Christian tradition. It features in the title of *Mystical Theology*'s very first chapter – a good indication of its prominent role in the text. Neither 'darkness' nor 'brightness' is taken in their literal sense; figuratively brought together, they indicate a *place*, rather than a feature; a way (or mode) of being – that of the divine, which transcends all others. Dionysius confirms this at the start of Chapter 2: 'brilliant darkness' is above (or beyond) light, and that is where we should aim to ascend, in order to meet God.

Biblical references used in this section also support this reading of darkness as a place, rather than a feature: the first refers to God as 'he who has made the shadows his hiding place' (after Psalm 18.11). Others recall the episode of Moses' ascent on the mountain: he leaves behind all things, to enter 'the darkness where, as scripture proclaims, there dwells the One who is beyond all things' (after Exodus 20.21; 19). Once there, says Dionysius, Moses 'contemplates not him who is invisible, but rather where he dwells'; Moses 'breaks free (…) away from what sees and is seen, and he plunges into the truly mysterious darkness of unknowing (…) Here, being neither oneself nor someone else, one is supremely united to the completely unknown.' This union is the very aim of the practice in which Dionysius is instructing his disciple. The contemplative soul united with God 'knows beyond the mind by knowing nothing' – yet another expression of *via negativa*, which is in fact the mystical experience.

And yet the repetition of the term 'beyond' somehow also reminds us that Dionysian apophasis is more than *via negativa*. 'We should not conclude that the negations are simply the opposites of the affirmations, but rather that the cause of all is considerably prior to this, beyond privations, beyond every denial, beyond every assertion' (Chapter 2, paragraph 2). Dionysian apophasis, then, is that *practice* which is beyond cognition and language; it is that *via mistica* which takes the soul into the silence where God abides. And it is because of this prominence of practice over knowledge that one can talk about *The Mystical Theology* as a soteriological text. Its function is neither epistemological nor educational; it is practical – namely, it is there to help Dionysius' disciples advance in their spiritual quest and save their souls.

The key elements of this (mystical) type of apophasis have clear equivalents in the Hindu framework. Indeed, darkness as a metaphor for the primordial state where nothing is yet formed has a long history in the Indian tradition. For example, the Creation Hymn from the *Rigveda* (X.129.3) states:

> Darkness existed, hidden by darkness, in the beginning. All this was a signless ocean. What existed as a thing coming into being, concealed by emptiness – that One was born by the power of heat.
>
> (Jamison & Brereton 2014: 1609)

Furthermore, the Ultimate itself in this original state is sometimes described mystically and poetically in cosmogonic accounts of the Brāhmaṇas as the Non-existent.[8] For example, the *Jaiminīya* Brāhmaṇa (III.360–1) explains that:

> When this Non-existent (*asat*) was there – not a thing was there, then the cosmic order (*ṛta*) endowed with light emerged floating, truth (*satya*) endowed with light emerged floating, ardency (*tapas*) endowed with light emerged floating.

Thus, a special kind of darkness (or the non-existent) is the seed of everything that exists, and it is often described as the primordial ocean where everything occurs. This kind of apophatic description of the Ultimate implies that in the original state, 'it' cannot be seen, perceived or described in any way. There is no knowing, knower or known. Again, it is important to note the ontological implications of this framework – in particular, the non-existence of the Ultimate itself, and how striking the link is between this and apophatic epistemology.

A similar correspondence between ontological and epistemological (indeed, mystical) levels can be detected in Dionysius' theology. His *Letters* are particularly helpful in this regard, as they connect the notion of divine darkness with both God's unknowability and His 'non-existence', understood in the sense that the absolute is even beyond being and transcendence. In his first letter (to monk Gaius), he writes:

> Someone beholding God and understanding what he saw has not actually seen God himself but rather something of his which has being and which is knowable. For he himself solidly transcends mind and being. He is completely unknown and non-existent. He exists beyond being and he is known beyond the mind. And this quite positively complete unknowing is knowledge of him who is above everything that is known.
>
> (Areopagite 1987: 263).

The similarity with the Upaniṣadic text is remarkable. Mystical apophaticism has both ontological and epistemological connotations, and it centres around the notion of union with God – beyond all determinations.

The 'ascent' as mystical experience

The soteriological purpose mentioned above explains the abundance of practical elements in the texts, aimed at attaining union with God and salvation of the soul. Such practical elements include mental askesis (watchfulness) and silent contemplative prayer. This will develop into a full regime of meditation, in the hesychast tradition, based on the 'prayer of the heart'[9]; its counterpart in Hinduism could be yogic meditation practices, particularly the *ajapā* prayer 'without muttering' in which inhalation and exhalation turn into prayer in the constant presence of the Absolute in the form of one's chosen God or Goddess.

At the core of this practice lies the attempt to rid one's mind of all worldly impressions and raise one's soul towards God. That this is the very aim of the *Mystical Theology* is clearly indicated right from the outset: 'Timothy, my friend, my advice to you (…) is to leave behind you everything perceived and understood, everything perceptible and understandable (…) and (…) strive upwards as much as you can towards union with him who is beyond all being and knowledge' (Areopagite 1986: 135).

One of the theologians who refers to this ascent as a purpose of all Christian knowledge and practice is Maximus the Confessor (who played a key role in spreading Dionysius' teachings). Maximus explicitly builds on the Areopagitic approach, to develop his own negative theology, especially in his 'Four Hundred Chapters on Love'. Here, the very fact of knowing nothing about God 'is to know beyond the mind's power' (1985: 46).

Another major theologian who theorized the mystical ascent is Gregory Nazianzus, a fourth-century Archbishop of Constantinople and one of the Cappadocian fathers. He is best known for his doctrine of the Trinity and the knowledge of God as illumination (Beeley 2008). The subtle link between the incommensurability of God and the way in which Christians gain knowledge of God (i.e. though union with Him, or participation in His presence) is explored using the same biblical episode – of Moses' ascent on Mount Sinai (see the Theological Oration 28 in Nazianzus, 2002). And it is telling that Maximus refers to Gregory, alongside Dionysius, when he describes the way in which Christians 'know' the unknowable. A key pre-requisite of the ascent, in Gregory's view, is purity of the soul:

> If any are from the multitude and unworthy of such a height of contemplation – if they are altogether impure (αναλνος) – let them not approach at all, for it is not safe. If anyone is purified (ηγνισμενος), at least for the time being, let him remain below and hear only the voice and the trumpet, the bare words of piety; and let him behold the mountain smoking and lightning – at once a terror and a marvel for those not able to ascend.
>
> (28.2)

And what the purest of the souls can hope to see, up there, is only the back part of divinity.

This is, as far as I know, God's majesty that is manifested among the creatures that he has produced and governs (…). For these are the back parts of God, which he leaves behind as tokens of himself, like the shady reflections of the sun in the water, which show the sun to our weak eyes because we cannot look at the sun itself.

(28.3)

This is how the Cappadocian plants the seed of what would later become the theological dogma of the distinction between God's essence and His manifestations in the world.

The fact that Dionysius and Gregory choose the same biblical episode to illustrate the Christian spiritual experience does not necessarily mean the nature of that experience is the same; indeed, the way in which the two theologians describe it is rather different. Dionysius chooses to focus on one out of several stages of the biblical ascent, while Gregory refers to the whole episode; this helps the former describe the mystical experience as union with God, whereas the latter sees it as a continuous journey (Conway-Jones 2021). Therefore, the ascent becomes a metaphor for different kinds of epistemological pursuits – one linear, aiming at knowledge, the other dialectical, of a rather mystical nature. Indeed, the ascent can be seen as a representation of the various types of apophaticism, from the cataphatic to the mystical.

It is in the context of this mystical theology that other key terms occur, which are common to the early Christian and Indian traditions – namely, contemplative prayer and silence, its sine-qua-non. We do not have the space to address them here, but the former is discussed in Chapter 11. For our purposes here, suffice it to say that union with what dwells beyond all affirmation and negation, achieved through purification, silence and contemplation, is the ultimate aim of both Christian and Hindu spirituality. And this striving to transcend cognition entails a whole set of practices (combining mental and physical elements) and an openness to receive the divine gift of non-cognitive understanding. The 'ascent' is right at the core of this framework – just like 'darkness' and the 'beyond'. Together, they form a distinct and suggestive veil of communication about that which is better left unsaid, in both Christian and Indian traditions.

Conclusions

There is no 'proper' (i.e. linear and systematic) way to approach apophaticism. What we have attempted to do in this chapter is more like a meandric approach to the topic – following the ebb and flow of suggestions from different Christian and Upaniṣadic texts, to approximate the way in which apophaticism is understood and practised in the two traditions. As we have seen, there are important commonalities in these practices as well as points of divergence. But at the core of it, the apophatic approach in both traditions strives to be a way of *living with* God, of experiencing the ineffable Ultimate, more than a theory, or even a set of rituals.

Notes

1. In theist systems Brahman is the supreme God, but in more metaphysical ones, Brahman is the ultimate principle that evolves in every form of existence.
2. Saints Basil the Great, Gregory of Nyssa and Gregory Nazianzus – the three founding theologians of Greek Christianity – are collectively referred to as 'the Cappadocians' because they came from the Cappadocia, a region in modern-day central-eastern Turkey, which was the largest Roman province at the time. The area included the cities of Caesarea Mazaca, Nyssa and Nazianzus, where the three Fathers came from, respectively.
3. This is indeed the case not only in Christianity, but also in other mystical traditions – like Sufism, for instance. There, prophet Muhammad's ascent through the heavens is considered the prototype of the mystic's spiritual ascension, one that brings the believer, through prayer, into the immediate presence of God (see Schimmel 2011: 27, 148 et al.).
4. For details, see Acharya (2013: 4–5).
5. However, although the ancient Upaniṣads contain both cataphatic and apophatic elements, they do not explicitly contrast these methods, or describe one as better than the other.
6. Beyond Vedānta and Sāṃkhya, no other Brahmanical/Hindu school of thought uses the apophatic method to describe the ultimate. Rather, it is applied in transcendentalist and also in pluralist, relativist philosophies of the Buddhists and Jainas. For a detailed discussion of the philosophy of being and non-dualism in Vedanta, see Chapter 8 of this volume, on 'Personhood in Indian Metaphysics'.
7. It is important to note that this is the last book in the *Corpus Dionysiacum* (and the briefest one). The ones that precede it – *Divine Names* and the two *Hierarchies* (Celestial and Hierarchical) – are cataphatic in both content and style, and the purpose of *The Mystical Theology* is to go beyond all affirmations, towards contemplation of divine silence and brilliant darkness.
8. See Acharya (2017) for details.
9. See Chapter 11 of this volume.

References

Primary sources

The Areopagite, Pseudo-Dionysius (1987), *The Complete Works*, trans. Colm Luibheid. New York: Paulist Press.

Areopagitul, Sf. Dionisie (1996), *Opere complete si Scoliile Sf. Maxim Marturisitorul*, trans. Pr. Dumitru Staniloae. Bucuresti: Paideia.

Basil of Caesarea (1930), *The Letters*, vol. 3, trans. Roy J. Deferrari. Cambridge, MA: Harvard University Press.

Chrysostom, John (1982), *On the Incomprehensible Nature of God*, trans. Paul W. Harkins. Washington, DC: The Catholic University of America Press.

Clement of Alexandria, *The Stromata*, in Rev. Alexander Roberts and James Donaldson (eds.), *Ante-Nicene Fathers: Fathers of the Second Century*, vol. 2, available at https://ccel.org/ccel/schaff/anf02/anf02.i.html.

Climacus, John (1982), *The Ladder of Divine Ascent*, trans. Colm Luibheid and Norman Rusell. London: SPCK.

Confessor, Maximus (1985), *Selected Writings*, trans. G. Bethold. New York: Paulist Press.

Goodall, Dominic (ed.) (1996), *Hindu Scriptures*, trans. Dominic Goodall. London: J. M. Dent.

Nazianzus, St. Gregory of (2002), *On God and Christ: The Five Theological Orations and Two Letters to Cledonius*, trans. F. Williams and L. Wickham. Crestwood, NY: St Vladimir's Seminary Press.

Nyssa, Gregory of (1978), *The Life of Moses*, trans. A. Malherbe and E. Ferguson. New York: Paulist Press.

Olivelle, Patrick (ed.) (2005), *The Early Upaniṣads: Annotated Text and Translation*, trans. Patrick Olivelle. Oxford: Oxford University Press.

Palamas, St Gregory (2002), *The Triads in Defence of the Holy Hesychasts*, vol. 1, trans. Robin Amis. New Hampshire: Praxis.

Proclus (1987), *Proclus' Commentary on Plato's Parmenides*, trans. Glenn R. Morrow and John M. Dillon. Princeton, NJ: Princeton University Press.

The Rigveda: The Earliest Religious Poetry of India, trans. Stephanie W. Jamison and Joel P. Brereton. Princeton, NJ: Oxford University Press, 2014.

Secondary sources

Acharya, Diwakar (2013), 'Neti Neti: Meaning and Function of an Enigmatic Phrase in the Gargya-Ajatasatru Dialogue of *Brhad Aranyaka Upaniṣad*', *Indo-Iranian Journal* 56: 3–39.

Beeley, Christopher (2008), *Gregory of Nazianzus on the Trinity and the Knowledge of God: In Your Light We Shall See Light*. Oxford: Oxford University Press.

Conway-Jones, Ann (2021), 'Exegetical Puzzles and the Mystical Theologies of Gregory of Nyssa and Dionysius the Areopagite', *Vigiliae Christianae* 75: 1–21.

Franke, William (2014), *On What Cannot Be Said: Apophatic Discourses in Philosophy, Religion, Literature, and the Arts*. Notre Dame, IN: University of Notre Dame Press.

Hollywood, A., and Patricia Z. Beckman (eds.) (2012), *The Cambridge Companion to Christian Mysticism*. Cambridge: Cambridge University Press.

Louth, Andrew (1989), *Denys the Areopagite*. Wilton, CA: Morehouse-Barlow.

Mangala Frost, Christine (2017), *The Human Icon: A Comparative Study of Hindu and Orthodox Christian Beliefs*. Cambridge: James Clarke.

Merton, Thomas (1951), *The Ascent to Truth*. New York: Harcourt, Brace.

Schimmel, Annemarie (1975), *Mystical Dimensions of Islam*. Chapel Hill, NC: University of North Carolina Press (anniversary edition 2011).

11

Overcoming negative theology: Kūkai and Palamas on essence and energy

Ana-Maria Pascal and Paulus Kaufmann

The reader might wonder what an eighth-century Japanese Buddhist could have in common with a fourteenth-century Greek monk. And yet, Kūkai and Palamas do indeed have some striking similarities – from their life circumstances to their religious thinking. They were both born in aristocratic families close to imperial courts; they both received an excellent education and were set up for successful careers, but decided to become monks instead, around the same time in their life. And they both wrote a lot.

Kūkai and Palamas were both interested in the esoteric and ritualist side of their respective traditions, which they placed at the core of their theology/buddhology. At a metaphysical level, they both grappled with the challenges of transcendence – and came up with similar solutions to it, using a conceptual distinction between God's/Buddha's *essence* and His *energies* (or manifestations) in the world. This opens a horizon of possibilities at both philosophical and theological levels, which the two religious thinkers explore in remarkably similar ways, emphasizing the holistic aspect of participation in God/Buddha. In what follows, we explore the extent of these similarities, together with the nuances that set them apart, and suggest possible areas for further research.

Kūkai

Background

Kūkai was born in 774 CE as a member of the Saeki clan on the Japanese island of Shikoku. According to his autobiography, he first entered the Confucian State College to become a bureaucrat. He then converted to Buddhism, after being impressed by a Buddhist scripture promoting the recitation of mantra and other esoteric rituals. He left the College and joined the Buddhist order. He led an austere, meditative life in the midst of nature (TKZ 7.41), drawn by the powerful ritual practices of Buddhism. In his later years, Kūkai became one of Japan's most original and influential Buddhist thinkers, creating an impressive theoretical system. His initial fascination with Buddhist practice is still present in his mature theories. In fact, all his theoretical efforts can be seen as explaining and defending Buddhist practice. He promoted, in particular, the rituals of esoteric Buddhism that were already in use in Japan, but without theoretical underpinning. So Kūkai aimed at theoretically defending esoteric practice and showing how it could have the powers it was believed to possess.

In his early years, Kūkai was probably associated with the Sanron School of Buddhism (Fujii 2008: 27–9). The Sanron School is based on the Chinese Sanlun School, which originated from the Indian Madhyamaka movement, hearkening back to Nagarjuna (see Chapter 8). Generally speaking, Madhyamaka thinkers adopt an apophatic approach, arguing that we can only speak negatively about the absolute. Human ways of thinking and speaking are so fraught with ignorance that we can use reason and language only to reject opinions about ultimate reality. There are no affirmative answers to metaphysical questions, and the mere act of asking such questions expresses our illusory worldview. Kūkai, however, was not content with this purely negative approach to reality. In 804 CE he travelled to China and learned about the new Esoteric Buddhist movement, promoted by his Chinese teacher Huiguo. This new school did not embrace an apophatic Buddhology; instead, it offered a sophisticated system of powerful practices. From then onwards, promoting this form of Buddhism in his native country became Kūkai's lifelong project.

Behind the practical project of establishing a new school of Buddhism stands a philosophical question regarding the nature of the Buddha. Kūkai agreed with Sanron/ Madhyamaka that the Buddha is, in essence, a being beyond human intellect and language. But he was also convinced that sentient beings can participate in the Buddha's grace. But how is participation in a transcendent being possible? In its emphasis on specific practices, Esoteric Buddhism offered the answer. Kūkai came to argue in his writings that sentient beings cannot grasp the Buddha intellectually, but they can participate in his activities through ritual practice.

The nature of the Buddha

To understand Kūkai's position, we should recapitulate earlier Buddhist discussions about the nature of the Buddha. The Buddhist message was first taught to the world by Siddhartha Gautama, an Indian noble from the Śākya clan who lived approximately 400 years BCE in North-Eastern India. Through his relentless quest for spiritual insight and his practical efforts, he awakened to the truth of Buddhism. He thus became an 'Awakened One', a Buddha, and started teaching. During his lifetime, he attracted a group of followers; after his death, this movement grew and nowadays comprises around 500 million people. Although Siddhartha Gautama is currently seen as the historical founder of this religious movement, in the past he was considered just one buddha in a line of previous and subsequent buddhas (Bond 1982: 6). Moreover, the appearance of a buddha on earth came to be seen not only as a recurring event, but also as the mere manifestation of a supramundane (*lokottara*) and genuine Buddha (Steinkellner 2000: 259–61). This supramundane Buddha exists eternally and unchangeably, and only temporarily manifests in human form in order to save sentient beings from ignorance.

In Mahāyāna Buddhism, a tripartite buddhology developed: the so-called *dharmakāya* ('body of truth') is the Buddha in his ultimate, supramundane form of existence. As ignorant beings, we can only experience *manifestations* of this *dharmakāya*, the so-called *nirmanakāya* ('transformation body') and the *saṃbhogakāya* ('enjoyment body'). These manifestations appear as human beings and parts of the phenomenal world. Siddhartha Gautama was one such manifestation. The *dharmakāya* is the source of these manifestations, but it remains eternal, unchanging and not subject to conditions. It cannot be experienced directly by sentient beings.

The Madhyamaka school of Buddhism developed this negative approach to the *dharmakāya* into a comprehensive negative theology. It criticized all attempts to spell out positively what the Buddha and his teaching amount to. The Buddhist teaching is brought to the world by manifestations of the Buddha, but the *dharmakāya* remains transcendent, beyond human intellect and language. However, despite the popularity of the apophatic solution, not all Buddhist schools were content with merely negative assertions.[1] Some schools in China, especially Huayan and Tiantai, used a more constructive method to interpret the ineffability of the absolute and the mystery of its interaction with the phenomenal world.[2]

Kūkai's idea of an active Buddha

Kūkai followed a cataphatic route; he challenged the traditional view and identified the dharmakāya with the Buddha Vairocana. In the esoteric *Mahāvairocana Sutra*, the Buddha Vairocana is characterized as a cosmic Buddha, whose body comprises the whole universe: 'I am freely ruling everywhere, pervading all kinds of beings, the sentient and the non-sentient' (T848.18.38b27–28). Another paragraph of the same sutra reads: 'The Buddha's body has the nature of the cosmos' (T848.18.36b18; Giebel 2004: 147). Kūkai adopts this idea of Vairocana and identifies him with the supramundane Buddha, the *dharmakāya*. So Kūkai, in contrast to Madhyamaka, sees the *dharmakāya* itself – not only its manifestations – as a bodily being. However, this somatic interpretation of the *dharmakāya* does not render it more accessible to sentient beings. Kūkai still stresses that the Buddha is too vast to be perceived or intellectually grasped by humans or other beings. So, even the materially omnipresent Vairocana remains transcendent.

Kūkai also diverges from traditional understanding of the Buddha in that he emphasizes the *dharmakāya's* being *active*. This leads him to his notorious claim that the '*dharmakāya* teaches the dharma', *hosshinseppō* (法身説法) in Japanese. Kūkai is aware that this doctrine contradicts the traditional understanding of the Three-Body-Theory (trikāya), according to which only the *nirmanakāya* and the *saṃbhogakāya* act and teach, whereas the *dharmakāya* always and eternally remains motionless and silent (TKZ 3.103). The other schools agree that the 'dharmakāya neither expounds nor reveals the Dharma' (TKZ 3.77); Kūkai disagrees with this common position and defends the view that the Buddha teaches in all his states of existence.

In Kūkai's view, *teaching* consists of a *change of mind through words*. Since the *dharmakāya* himself teaches with words, then language cannot be just a means of communication with the unawakened; it must be a genuine expression of buddhahood. However, the Buddha's language is not the same as our everyday language. It comprises ordinary languages that human beings use, but is not restricted to them. The Buddha's language consists of all material, sonic and mental processes in the world. The claim that the *dharmakāya* teaches implies that reality consists not only of matter, but also of mind and language. Therefore, matter, mind and language should not be understood as static entities, but as activities of the *dharmakāya* Buddha. In this view, Kūkai adopts the traditional idea that the Buddha's acts are acts of body, speech and mind (*sangō* 三業). But in Kūkai's theory, these kinds of acts become three cosmic activities beyond human understanding, the three mysteries (*sanmitsu* 三密). The cosmos consists of these somatic, sonic and mental activities:

> These three omnipresent activities pervade the whole cosmos, they are eternal und unchanging.
>
> (TKZ 3.35)

The Buddha's activities thus comprise all changes and transformations that make up the universe. Unfortunately, sentient beings can only perceive an evanescent section of these transformations; thus, Kūkai and the esoteric tradition call them 'mysterious acts' (see, e.g. TKZ 3.25).

Kūkai considers these mysterious activities of the *dharmakāya* to be 'teachings'. This does not mean that the supramundane Buddha intentionally addresses an audience and is constrained by its needs or capacities. The Buddha does not act to communicate with sentient beings. His activities are instead compared by Kūkai to the act of singing: singing expresses one's inner thoughts and feelings without addressing a specific audience. The Buddha enjoys the bliss of dharma through such an intonation; his utterances are moved by an inner spontaneous impulse, and not by a desire to communicate with sentient beings. Therefore, the three mysterious activities of the *dharmakāya* Buddha are non-intentional, spontaneous, self-sufficient and uncreated.[3]

The mysterious activities of the Buddha are nevertheless beneficial to the suffering beings in the world. This is because the Buddha's singing does not consist of a single incomprehensible voice but of the voices of all beings that have reached buddhahood. Kūkai's description of this choir entails a functional distinction between different sorts of buddhas. The Buddha as the so-called *mind king* is the eternal foundation from which other buddhas emerge. The emerging buddhas are seen as the virtues or *mental functions* of this foundation. The mind king is eternal and beyond individuality; it is the *essence* of buddhahood. The mental functions appear in time and have individual features. They can be interpreted as *energies* of the Buddha.

Participation in the Buddha's activities

The three mysterious activities become a teaching not because they enable a *rational understanding* of the Buddha and his insights on reality. They are teachings because they elicit another kind of participation; they can be emulated in ritual. Concretely, the Buddhist practitioner may imitate the Buddha's mysterious activities by making mudra gestures, reciting mantras and contemplating or visualizing features of reality.

Although the *dharmakāya's* activities are mysterious to us, we can participate in them when we perform esoteric practices. This participation is possible because esoteric ritual acts – mudras, mantras, visualizations – are understood as microscopic correspondents to the Buddha's macroscopic activities.

It is one of the central tenets of esoteric Buddhism that a practitioner of its powerful rituals can manipulate the world according to his wishes, while also achieving new insights that gradually lead him to awakening. Esoteric sutras thus speak of the two *siddhi*, the twofold result of esoteric practices.[4] Mantras, in particular, serve both as means of spiritual progress and as tools to achieve healing, rainmaking, protection from evil spirits and other mundane goals. One ritual text attributed to Kūkai emphasizes that the practitioner of esoteric rituals achieves 'great wisdom'[5]. This cognitive state is symbolized by the practitioner's emission of light or fire. Practitioners achieve such great wisdom by visualizing their identity with the cosmos (*dharmadhātu*), i.e. with the cosmic Buddha Vairocana. The performer of the rite thus experiences a transgression of the boundaries of his inborn condition. The concomitant expansion of the mind is metaphorically expressed as a bursting light illuminating the whole cosmos. The acquisition of wisdom through practice is possible because each practitioner hears the message he needs to hear for his spiritual development. This, in turn, is possible because the 'teaching of the Buddha' is actually a choir of numerous buddhas intoning their individual insights; this polyphony produces a fitting message for every practitioner.

Buddhist practices change the world, but they also initiate a transfiguration of the practitioner. In Kūkai's eyes, different sorts of practices lead to different levels of insight. Fasting and alms giving help to overcome egoism. Meditation changes the mind and leads to new and deeper insights. Esoteric rituals are the highest form of practice because they directly imitate the Buddha's activities. They culminate in a ritual union with the Buddha. All these practices make the practitioner a new kind of person. In Shingon Buddhism – for which Kūkai's teachings laid the foundations – this transformation is symbolized by a multi-stage initiation procedure.

Kūkai was philosophically motivated by the question of how participation in the Buddha's grace is possible. As we have seen, in many Buddhist traditions that emerged after the death of Siddharta Gautama, the Buddha was understood as an eternal, supramundane being. In Kūkai's eyes, this negative approach did not answer the question about the possibility of participation in the Buddha's insights. The Buddha is indeed too vast to be grasped by the minds of ordinary sentient beings, but ritual practices emulate the activities of the Buddha and trigger the same insights that he awakened to. Thereby Buddhist practices enable participation in the Buddha's grace and eventually guide the practitioner to awakening.

Gregory Palamas

A man of his time

Born in an aristocratic family in Constantinople, in 1296, Gregory Palamas was raised in the proximity of royals and received an excellent education; around the age of twenty, he decided to become a monk and entered Mount Athos, where he practised the hesychast discipline centred on prayer. The second half of his life was marked by the controversy around hesychasm, which he assertively defended against the Latin humanists – especially Barlaam[6].

At the centre of the debate was the nature of the light in which Christ showed Himself transfigured to the apostles on Mount Tabor. Barlaam claimed it to be a material light (a created, atmospheric phenomenon), whereas for Palamas, this was the uncreated light of God's energies. Between 1340 and 1360, Palamas spoke at several synods[7] dedicated to clarifying the dogma on the possibility of seeing God and on associated issues – including the nature of the taboric light and hesychastic practice. His theology was endorsed at three major councils in Constantinople; thus, he is regarded as a key figure in one of the major religious disputes between the Byzantine and the Latin branches of Christianity. Because of him, the hesychast tradition of contemplative practice became accepted doctrine.[8]

Palamas was also ahead of his time in the interdisciplinarity of his work. One of his major works, *One Hundred and Fifty Chapters*[9], deals with natural and theological science, as well as ethics and the ascetic life. His teachings combined the theoretical and the practical: he addresses the issue of God's knowability or unknowability, while also dealing with prayer and the whole spiritual discipline of the hesychasts. These two threads are not merely deeply interconnected; they are essential to one another, and together point towards the notion of communion with God, which is for Palamas the very goal of Christian life. This is particularly evident in his *Triads* – aimed at defending the hesychasts, but focussed on the role of philosophy, the nature of apophatic theology and the notion of *deification*, which is intricately related to incarnation and the distinction between the essence and energies of God.

It is not by coincidence that Palamas brings all these topics together; the link between the practical and the theoretical is deeply significant both to Palamism and to the Christian view of the very purpose of Christian life. This may well be a key reason why Palamas' theology is often referred to as a synthesis of the patristic tradition, for it encapsulates – in a coherent whole – dogma, trinitarian theology and mystical practice.

The light of apophaticism

To start addressing the theoretical side of this edifice – the (un)knowability of God – we can pick up a thread from Chapter 10 above: the 'cloud of darkness'. By this, as we have seen, earlier Christian thinkers meant something more (or different) than a negative stage in the ascent of the soul to God; they meant a *presence* – not unlike that of God on Mount Sinai, when He reveals Himself to Moses. And this is exactly what Gregory Palamas takes from apophaticism – the prospect of a union with God, which however entails a different kind of knowledge than the intellectual one. 'The ascent by negation is in fact only an apprehension of how all things are distinct from God'; beyond this negative phase (the 'stripping away of things'), there is a presence to be felt – and the possibility of communion with God, through contemplation. That is why apophatic darkness is described as 'brilliant' or 'dazzling', for 'it is in this dazzling darkness that the divine energies are given to the saints' (Palamas 1983: 36). It is the locus of a mystical encounter, rather than a mere darkness denoting the impossibility of knowing God at all. Apophaticism is, therefore, a stage towards the practical purpose of union with God, beyond knowledge or lack of knowledge: 'God is not only beyond knowledge, but also beyond unknowing', says Palamas in his second Triad, titled *Apophatic Theology as Positive Experience* (Palamas 1983: 32). Thus, apophaticism understood as mystical experience transcends both positive and negative theology.

Palamas and Barlaam, in fact, agreed on one aspect of apophaticism – namely, as an expression of God's transcendence, illustrated by the cloud He surrounded Himself with, when speaking to Moses on Mount Sinai. But while Barlaam's interpretation dwells on the negative, Palamas moves to emphasize – just like Dionysius and Maximus before him – the positive aspect, which is the presence of God in that cloud. What we have there, on the mountain, is not an empty darkness, but a brilliant one, full of God's manifestation, His energies. And true knowledge of God is indeed possible, through a complete transfiguration of man.

Palamas' focus on a trinitarian theology helps him explain how this transfiguration is possible – namely, through the grace we receive from the Holy Spirit, after the incarnation. Man is capable of transcending his fallen nature, due to 'an organ of vision' that is 'neither the senses, nor the intellect' (Palamas 1983: 35). Thus, apophaticism describes a state, beyond any conceptual process, where God reveals himself to the spiritual senses as 'light' and a 'source of deification' – which is to say, God as manifestation in the form of light makes human participation in God possible. And in doing so (becoming manifest in a way that grants us access to Him), He also keeps His essence – in its pure, transcendent form. Indeed, the fact that God manifests Himself through His energies allows Him to remain 'more-than-God' and 'more-than-Principle' in His essence; and it allows us to overcome our nature and 'see' God, become united with Him through His grace and our spiritual practice. Thus, the very purpose of the Palamite distinction between the ultimately transcendent, unknowable *essence* of God, and the uncreated *energies* through which man enters in communion with God the Unknowable is to solve the problem of God's transcendence, and allow us to 'know' Him – not in His essence, but in the way He becomes manifest in the world.

In the context of this trinitarian theology, one can ask what we should make of the Taboric light of the transfiguration of Jesus[10]? Since early Christianity (perhaps under the influence of Neoplatonism), contemplation of God was conceived as a luminous vision. According to Barlaam, everything must be understood as a symbol; so, this light *tells us* about the divine nature of Christ. For Palamas, in contrast, the Taboric light is more than a symbol; it is an actual manifestation of God's essence. To explain this, he introduces the doctrine of the divine energies (*energeia*), or *uncreated* manifestations of God, which make our communion with Him possible. We do not have access to God's being, but we can aspire to communion with Him through prayer, which brings body and soul together through the Holy Spirit – God's presence in the world. But the focus of Palamas' notion of the transfiguration of Jesus was an insistence on the *uncreated* character of divine light, which signifies the very divinity of Christ.

This light is uncreated, and thereby divine, just as Jesus is one of the three hypostases of God. What the apostles saw on Mount Tabor was the uncreated light, which is to say God's own manifestation (Evdokimov 1995/1988: 76). This is the point of his distinction, which makes sense in the context of trinitarian theology: a key aspect of this framework is the fact that our imperfect contemplation – aided by the work of the Holy Spirit – is an alignment with the eternal contemplation of the Father by the Son.

At a metaphysical level, the distinction between God's being (or essence) and His energies is an ontological (rather than temporal) one. There was never a time when God was without His manifestations. But there is a difference of ontological level between them and His being. This reminds one of Aristotle's *Metaphysics*, where the meta-level of *hyperousia* (designated with the verbal form *einai*, the being of being) is intended to be distinct from (and indeed, beyond) that of the actual essence of things (*ousia*).[11] The former is seen as something unmoved, absolute and beyond all knowledge; the latter is the essence of something specific, that exists; it is the 'substance' from the *Categories*.[12] This distinction, between the infinitive-based absolute Being (*to einai*) and the participle one, the first substance (*to on*)[13], is important from two points of view. First, it introduces the notion of ontological hierarchy – whether we adopt a Platonic, Aristotelian or Neoplatonist reading of it; and secondly, it opens the path to a different kind of knowledge (or experience), namely the mystical one, which was to bear fruit in apophatic theology. This is a possible source of inspiration for Palamas' distinction between the transcendent being (or essence) and those manifest in the world – and it is also how Meister Eckhardt uses it, with the same purpose of allowing for an apophatic way of knowing God.

In this metaphysical context, the metaphor of light becomes a symbol of the dialectic between the different levels of being – a hypostatic light, which makes deification (*theosis*) possible, not just symbolically but in actual fact, due to the incarnation (and then transfiguration) of Jesus. The word actual (as opposed to symbolic) is key here, because – according to Palamas and a whole Eastern tradition – after the incarnation we can actually participate in God, not just intellectually (through some 'vision' of a disincarnated mind), but with our soul and body united in prayer. So, the taboric light – as symbol of our participation in God, due to the transfiguration of Jesus – is not only linked to the distinction between God's essence and His energies; it also highlights the key role of prayer, where body and mind (or soul) are united, in the ascent to God. The whole point of the Christocentric prayer[14] is a transfiguration of the human being (as a whole person), not a disincarnation of mind, or merely a ritual. Indeed, for Palamas and the tradition he represents, this possibility of knowing God is not related to any conceptual system; rather, it is an expression of how we *experience* God – as mysteriously perceiving the presence of God in our soul.

Withdrawn in His essence, present in His energies

Before turning to the practical aspect of Palamite teaching, let us consider one more aspect of his theology – the issue of the possibility to know God. To address this, Palamas introduces the distinction between uncreated essence and energies, in the third *Triad*:

> there is only one unoriginate essence, the essence of God (…) and the essences other than it are seen to be of a created nature'; but also 'the divine powers (which the Fathers often call "natural energies") (…) [and] some works of God are without beginning.
>
> (1983: 93)

By 'works of God', Palamas means 'His foreknowledge, will, providence, contemplation of Himself, and whatever powers are akin to these', as well as virtue, existence, holiness, goodness, immortality, etc. Following Maximus, Palamas insists that such virtues belong essentially to God, but they are also participable: 'Created beings participate in them (…) but they themselves are works without beginning' (94–5).

But there is yet another, more mysterious aspect of Palamas' theology, which goes beyond the essence/energies distinction, towards a third level – that of the transcendent *superousia*, 'the Superessential One', which transcends all energies, as well as 'place, time and nature' – and in that sense, 'it is nowhere' (1983: 96–7).

Palamas stresses the point by quoting a number of earlier Christian teachers – from Basil the Great and John Chrysostom to Dionysius and Maximus. He uses Dionysius' phrase 'the superessential Mystery' to reiterate the notion of God's transcendence, which is unoriginated and beyond essence itself. Indeed,

> When God was conversing with Moses, He did not say, "I am the essence", but "I am the One Who is". [Ex. 3.14] Thus it is not the One Who is who derives from the essence, but essence which derives from Him, for it is He who contains all being in itself.
>
> (98)

Furthermore, Palamas invokes Maximus to stress that God transcends all participable virtues, both created and uncreated. Not only does God's essence transcend everything in the created order; it also transcends His uncreated energies (or works), including that of being or essence.

This indicates two things. First, there is the explicit notion of God's transcendence – the fact that He is beyond everything, including 'being' and 'essence'. Secondly, the rather more implicit idea of a God beyond the essentialist language of philosophers. It is – as Meyendorff puts it – a 'living God, ultimately indescribable in the categories of essentialist Greek philosophy' (Palamas 1983: 21).

There seems to be little appetite for speculation on that third level that Palamas refers to, among commentators. Perhaps that is because the theological message about the possibility of participation in God is clear, whether we see it as a dualism, or as allowing for a further level of *superousia*, as indicated above.

Paul Evdokimov considers the distinction between God's inaccessible being and His energy, which we can participate in, to be similar to that between the Being and hypostases of God – the core of trinitarian theology. Neither affects the simplicity and unity of God; they are just different ways of divine being and presence, within and without Itself. The distinction – he argues – was already present in the early Fathers and indeed in the Hebraic tradition, which distinguishes (without separating) the transcendence and immanence of God. And he quotes Palamas saying that it is Being that comes from He who is, not the other way round (Evdokimov 1995/1988: 76).

Rowan Williams offers an interesting interpretation of the essence/energies distinction, in his commentary to Maximus' *Centuries of Love*. He sees it as a symbol of our knowledge of the world and everything in it: 'To know the 'essences' of things is simply to know their meaning in relation to God's action in the universe' (Williams 2021: 16). Seen this way, the distinction serves not only as a facilitator for our communication with God (through His energies), but also as a key to unlocking the meaning of the world. Thus, the distinction

> is not primarily a solution to a metaphysical problem (…) but a way of codifying this vision of a world in which all meanings rest on a divine act whose own meaning can never be specified with reference to anything else.
>
> (Williams 2021: 17)

Finally, the distinction has a soteriological role, which Flanders (2020) and others comment on: it aids our own deification (rather than just being a philosophical argument); the use of the term 'uncreated light' provides an illustration of the way in which the body is deified. The goal of Palamism is to safeguard true union with God.

Theosis – Participation in God, body and soul

A major theme in Palamas is defining the role of the body in prayer, i.e. the spiritual practice leading us to transfiguration. The latter is seen as a unity of spirit (from the mind, down into the heart) and body, in the act of prayer. Palamas explicitly focuses on the role of the body in his first Triad, where he refers to it as the natural 'temple of the Holy Spirit which is in us' (1 Corinthians 6.19) (1983: 41). The point of highlighting the connection between human body and one of the hypostases of the Holy Trinity is to stress the possibility of communion with God, through a transfiguration of the human person. This he calls deification (*theosis*), involving both body and soul – a crucial point that goes to the core of the Christian experience as a whole – neither intellectual knowledge, nor physical or mystical vision; God's presence is not the simple result of natural efforts, but the gift of personal divine communion (deification, *theosis*) that transcends all creatures, because

> those who possess not only the faculties of sensation and intellection, but have also obtained spiritual and supernatural grace, do not gain knowledge only through created things, but also know spiritually (…) that God is spirit (…) It is therefore by this mystical knowledge that divine things must be conceived.
>
> (1983: 69)

This knowledge beyond knowledge, this effective communion with God – through our transfiguration (body and soul) and through God's grace present in His energies – is the very aim of Palamas' theology. That is why the debate with Barlaam is so important – because it addresses the very notion of the possibility of 'knowing' or 'seeing' God (through His uncreated works), despite His ineffable nature. Through the coming of Christ, God enters into real, immediate community with humanity. This is the meaning of the doctrine of uncreated energies, which is rooted in the Christological doctrine of 'hypostatic union'. Hence, the possibility to affirm simultaneously the transcendence of God and His immanence in the free gift of communion in the Body of Christ, as Meyendorff points out (1983: 22).

Furthermore, deification understood as communion between divinity and humanity does not mean confusion (or merging) of the two natures; rather, it is a union that maintains the distinction (like that between the three hypostases of the Holy Trinity). This is not to say it is just symbolic; it is a '*real* communion between the Uncreated and His creature, and real deification – not by essence, but *by energy*' (1983: 19).

A related theme is the focus on the notion of wakefulness or watchfulness (*nepsis*) in the Patristic tradition: indeed, the *Philokalia* is often referred to as the collection of the Neptic Saints, because of the role of inner watchfulness in spiritual growth:

> [T]he term used in Orthodox ascetical and mystical theology for this experience of waking up in Greek is *nepsis* … which means sobriety, watchfulness, alertness.
>
> And this experience of *nepsis* is indicated in the original Greek title of *The Philokalia*. It is called '*Philokalia ton Hieron ton Neptikon*' which means 'Philokalia of the Holy Neptic Fathers' or 'The Fathers Who Taught Wakefulness'.
>
> (Ware 2011)

Similarly, Williams explains (following Hesychios) that, just like watchfulness, the Jesus prayer brings together action and contemplation. Indeed,

> [T]he Jesus Prayer is an 'inscription' of watchfulness in the rhythm of the human body. (…) the invocation of the Name is the activity through which the intelligence is held and stabilized when all images and concepts of God have been laid aside.
>
> (Williams 2021: 27–8)

At the core of this unifying activity is the body, 'understood as that which connects us to the world, as that which speaks and symbolizes the truth that is being realized in the spirit (...) a proper instruction in Christianity 'should start with the body' (Williams 2021: 27).

The body is part and parcel of the spiritual practice, as much as the mind and the heart is; for it is the body, gathered in meditation, which helps quieten the mind, so it can dwell in a constant invocation of Jesus' name. Palamas quotes John Damascene's description of the hesyschast as 'one who seeks to circumscribe the incorporeal in his body' (p. 45) and he details the mechanics of this process, with all its nuances – from the way mind is hosted in the heart,[15] to the actual attempt to 'recollect the mind not only within the body and heart, but also within itself' (44). The presupposition of this latter stage is that 'the essence of the mind is one thing, its energy another' (44), so it is possible for the mind to *return* to itself, having been *dispersed* abroad, in external observation. Palamas refers to this circular movement, as 'the most excellent and most appropriate activity of the mind, by which it comes to transcend itself and be united to God' (44). And this is the very purpose of contemplation – deification, union with God.

Williams explains how the embodied experience relates to the theological framework in which the early Christian thinkers operate – one that is no longer dominated by dualisms (body/soul, mind/matter, intellect/emotion), but allows humanity to be infused with grace: 'a restored humanity must be one in which bodily experience is given meaning (...) Restored humanity is humanity properly embodied, and this embodiment includes the freedom to relate to the things and the persons of the world as they are in relation to God' (Williams 2021: 29).

In sum, the elements of the Palamite framework – the essence/energies distinction, the emphasis on prayer as the practice that brings us closer to God, and the role of the body therein – point towards the doctrine of deification. Palamas – often seen as a theologian of hesychasm – synthesizes the elements of apophatic theology from the early Fathers, with those of Christocentric theology, to formulate a trinitarian theology aimed at helping us achieve this deification – the purpose of Christian life.

Conclusions

There is a special kind of beauty in discovering unexpected commonalities between thinkers from such different times and places as Kūkai and Palamas. These range from their life circumstances to their choice of method, and the issue they grappled with the most: how to reconcile human participation in the divine with absolute transcendence, and their respective solution to it – a certain form of practice. This is esoteric ritual in Kūkai and hesychastic prayer in Palamas. Their respective practices also have common features: repeated recitation, fixed bodily positions and mindful attention to breath; they involve body and mind, and culminate in a union with God/Buddha.

The relational aspect of the self and world is a common feature of their philosophy[16]. The analogy between the mind transcending and returning to itself, and the world being infused with God's/Buddha's energies, is a key similarity between Palamas' views and those of Kūkai. Mental attention (in Christian spirituality) and ritual (in Kūkai) are at the core of this analogy; and the result – a dynamic and relational, rather than static, view of the world – is a remarkable common thread.

Each of these themes can be further explored with a view to better understand both the scope of commonality between the two visions, and where (and how) they differ. Indeed, if there is intellectual beauty in discovering the common ground, exploring nuances of difference can also bring sublime insights. We shall mention just two such areas of divergence. First, there is an important focus on cognitive knowledge in Kūkai's notion of union with Buddha (a kind of *teaching* by the Buddha himself), which is not there in Palamite theology (or the Patristic tradition as a whole). The nuances of the link between knowledge and union with (or participation in) God / Buddha are certainly worth exploring, with especial focus on understanding what kind of knowledge is envisaged by the two religious thinkers.

Secondly, Kūkai stands in the non-dualistic tradition of Mahāyāna Buddhism. Like many other thinkers in this tradition, he seeks to overcome the dichotomies of our thought – even that of *Nirvāṇa* and *Saṃsāra*. The rejection of dualism is mainly reflected in Kūkai's buddhology. Thus, he understands the Buddha – even in his highest manifestation – as materially present in the world. The Buddha is identical with the creative natural processes that continuously bring forth the cosmos. In this view, the Buddha is precisely not transcendent, ontologically speaking. Because of its inconceivable dimensions, it transcends human perception and intellect, but it is also present in its essence in the human world.

What these differences do for us here is to emphasize the key message in the two theological/buddhological frameworks, about the role of direct participation (body, mind and soul) in the quest for the transcendent. Whether this is made possible through love and grace, as in Palamas, or through some kind of teaching by the transcendent itself – it is a powerful message about the possibility of a live experience of the absolute.

Notes

1. See also Gimello (1976: 117–36).
2. Zhiyi uses the term 'constructive' (*jianli* 建立) to set his own approach in contrast to the destructive (*qiandang* 遣蕩) method of Nagarjuna's *Middle Treatise*; see

T1911.46.1b27. Discussions about the validity of positive statements also took place within the Madhyamaka tradition; see, e.g., Della Santina (1986); and the contributions in Dreyfus and McClintock 2002.
3. T1796.650c14-18; quoted in TKZ 2.321.
4. See e.g., T848.18.17b17-c20, and T865.18.208b25-c20.
5. TKZ 5.119 and 5.121.
6. In 1339, this Calabrian philosopher attacked the hesychasts, criticizing their notion of 'spiritual knowledge' and their method of prayer, which required a participation of the body in the continuous practice of the Jesus Prayer in order to achieve the very reality of communion with God (Meyendorff, Introduction to Palamas 1983: 8). Barlaam also accused the hesychasts of mesalianism, a heresy that advocated the possibility of seeing God materially and considered all teachings (as well as baptism, fasting and other forms of Christian discipline) to be useless, while only continuous prayer mattered.
7. The Synods were not anti-Latin; rather, they represent a synthesis of the Patristic tradition, from the Capadoccians to John of Damascus. They confirmed hesychasm as a perfectly orthodox spirituality, in line with the Patristic tradition. (See Evdokimov 1995/1988.)
8. See Meyendorff (1974).
9. The English version referred to in this paper is the one published in the fourth volume of *The Philokalia* (2020) as 'Topics of Natural and Theological Science and on the Moral and Ascetic Life: One Hundred and Fifty Texts' (346 – 417).
10. See Mt. 17.1-9; Mk. 9. 2-9; Lk. 9.28-36; 2 Pet. 1.17-
11. In chapter VII of Book Delta, Aristotle distinguishes between being *per se* and being by accident.
12. In chapters I–II of Book Epsilon in his *Metaphysics*, Aristotle reminds us that there are four ways in which we talk about being, or 'the thing that is', and that philosophy is concerned with this whole range of meanings. These are – accidental (temporal) being; being as truth; being as substance; and being in actuality v. potentiality. The third meaning – that of substance, or *ousia* understood as a prime category – is investigated in Book Z, through questions such as 'What is that which is?', or 'What is substance?'. Although the discourse is completely different here from that in the *Categories*, the starting point is the same – namely, the key position that being-as-substance occupies among categories and within Aristotle's philosophy as a whole. In paragraph 5 of the *Categories*, he adopts a negative approach: 'A substance – that which is called a substance most strictly, primarily, and most of all – is that which is neither said of a subject or in a subject' (Barnes 1998, vol. II: 4). Substance is the subject itself. And Aristotle insists on this individual aspect of 'something in itself', in its essence (*tode ti*): 'Every substance seems to signify a certain "this"' (Barnes 1998: 6). In *The Metaphysics*, this is referred to using the longer phrase *to ti en einai* (usually translated by essence), the 'what it is' of a thing, or 'what-it-is-to-be-that-thing' (Barnes 1998, vol. I: 1626).
13. According to Pierre Hadot, this is but 'a creative misunderstanding' that arose out of a Neoplatonist interpretation of Plato's *Parmenides* (see Hadot 1987: 14–34).

14. The hesychast prayer reads: 'Jesus Christ, our Lord, son of God, have mercy on me, the sinner'. The abbreviated version is simply a reiteration of the divine name – 'Lord Jesus Christ', which monks are meant to repeat mentally, until it becomes a continuous chant within their heart.
15. We (…) know exactly that our rational part is not confined within us as in a container, for it is incorporeal, nor is it outside of us, for it is conjoined to us; but (…) our heart is the place of the rational faculty, the first rational organ of the body (…) that 'body' most interior to the body, which we call the 'heart' (Palamas 1983: 42–3).
16. Williams highlights the relational aspect of the self, extrapolated to the whole creation: '*Hesychia* and mindfulness dissolve the fiction that the world is constituted by a solidly boundaried self confronting solidly boundaried objects that must be catalogued and filed. They insist that we see the self as never outside relation, never the source of life and meaning as an individual, separable entity' (Williams 2021: 44–5).

References

Primary sources

Barnes, J. (ed.) (1998), *The Complete Works of Aristotle: Revised Oxford Translation*. Princeton, NJ: Princeton University Press.

Junjirō, Takakusu 高楠順次郎 and Watanabe Kaigyoku 渡邊海旭 (eds.) (1931), *Taishō Shinshū Daizōkyō*大正新修大蔵経. Tōkyō: Taishōissaikyōkankōkai, (abbreviated as 'T').

Kūkai (1991–97), *Teihon Kōbōdaishi Zenshū* 定本弘法大師全集, ed. Mikkyō Bunka Kenkyūjo Kōbō Daishi Chosaku Kenkyūkai 密教文化研究所弘法大師著作研究会. Kōyasan: Mikkyō Bunka Kenkyūjo, (abbreviated as 'TKZ').

Nikodemos of the Holy Mountain and St. Makarios of Corinth (2020), *The Philokalia*, trans. Christina, vol. 5., Redbank Plains, Queensland: Virgin Mary of Australia and Oceania.

Palamas, Gregory (1983), *The Triads*, trans. Nicholas Gendle. Mahwah, NJ: Paulist Press.

Secondary sources

Bond, George (1982), *The Word of the Buddha*: *The Tipitaka and Its Interpretation in Theravada Buddhism*. Colombo: Gunasena.

Cheng, John (1998), 'The Distinction between God's Essence and Energy: Gregory Palamas' Idea of Ultimate Reality and Meaning', *Ultimate Reality and Meaning* 21 (1): 56–75.

Della Santina, Peter (1986), *Madhyamaka Schools in India: A Study of the Madhyamaka Philosophy and of the Division of the System into the Prāsaṅgika and Svātantrika Schools*. Delhi: Motilal Banarsidass.

Dreyfus, Georges B. J. and Sara L McClintock (eds.) (2002), *The Svatantrika-Prāsaṅgika Distinction: What Difference Does a Difference Make?*, Studies in Indian and Tibetan Buddhism. Boston, MA: Wisdom Publications.

Evdokimov, Paul (1995), *Cunoasterea lui Dumnezeu*, trans. Vasile Raduca. Bucuresti: Christiana, (after original French edition, *La connaissance de Dieu selon la tradition orientale*: *L'enseignement patristique liturgique et iconographique*, Desclée de Brouwer, 1988).

Flanders, Timothy (2020), *Palamas, Aquinas, and the Metaphysical Wordwebs of the Athenians*, 10 October 2020. https://meaningofcatholic.com/2020/10/10/palamas-aquinas-and-the-metaphysical-wordwebs-of-the-athenians/.

Fujii, Jun 藤井藤井 (2008), *Kūkai no shisōteki tenkai no kenkyū.* 空海の思想的展開の研究, Tōkyō: Transview.

Giebel, Rolf W. (2004), *Shingon Texts*. Berkeley, CA: Numata Center for Buddhist Translation and Research.

Gimello, Robert M. (1976), 'Apophatic and Kataphatic Discourse in Mahayana: A Chinese View', *Philosophy East and West* 26 (2): 117–36.

Hadot, Pierre (1987), 'Théologie, exégèse, révélation, écriture, dans la philosophie grecque', in Michel Tardieu (ed.), *Les règles de l'interprétation*. Paris: Le Cerf, pp. 14–34.

Meyendorff, John (1974), *Saint Gregory Palamas and Orthodox Spirituality*. Crestwood, NY: St. Vladimir's Seminary Press.

Steinkellner, Ernst (2000). 'Buddhismus: Religion oder Philosophie? Und vom Wesen des Buddha', in Andreas Bsteh (ed.), *Der Buddhismus als Anfrage an Christliche Theologie und Philosophie*: *Studien zur Religionstheologie*. Mödling: St. Gabriel, pp. 251–62.

Ware, Kallistos (2011), 'Word and Silence in the *Philokalia*', Lecture delivered at North Park University in Chicago in February 2011, available at https://www.ancientfaith.com/specials/kallistos_lectures/word_and_silence_in_the_philokalia.

Wilkins, Jeremy D. (2003), 'The Image of This Highest Love: The Trinitarian Analogy in Gregory Palamas's *Capita 150*', *St. Vladimir's Theological Quarterly* 47 (3-4): 383–412.

Williams, Rowan (2021), *Looking East in Winter*: *Contemporary Thought and the Eastern Christian Tradition*. London: Bloomsbury.

12

God without power: Kenosis and Tsimtsum as two paradigms of divine self-restriction

Agata Bielik-Robson

It is commonly assumed that the passage from polytheism to monotheism implies concentration and intensification of the divine power: from the plethora of rival gods emerges a single God who rules the universe. According to Hans Blumenberg – who in his understanding of the monotheistic theology followed the nominalist school's defence of theological absolutism – the monotheistic God is granted *potentia absoluta*: an absolute power which comprises his infinite will, infinite potency and total control over the created realm. In the correspondence between Blumenberg and Carl Schmitt – a political theologian from the Nazi era – on the issue of the Christian Trinity, Schmitt argues in favour of the Cappadocian doctrine of the *stasis* (conflict), in which the three trinitarian powers remain in constant tension.[1] Blumenberg, however, rejects this concept as nonsensical and quotes the famous line of Goethe:

> *Nemo contra deum nisi deus ipse* [...] Goethe believes that 'A god can only be balanced by another god. *That power should restrict itself is absurd*. It is only restricted, in turn, by another power.'
>
> (Blumenberg and Schmitt 2007: 42)

According to this view, the monotheistic God cannot but possess absolute power. Blumenberg agrees thus with Franz Kafka who illustrates the monotheistic logic of power in one succinct aphorism: 'The German word *sein* signifies both "to be there" and "to belong to Him"'.[2] God's *potentia absoluta* leaves no room for any other manifestation of will or agency; the only logical outcome of the monotheistic regime is an equally absolute quietism. The creature is nothing compared to its Creator. His is all the power and the glory – but also being. As Simone Weil put it, following the absolutist-quietistic logic of the monotheistic faith: 'Only God has right to say "I am." "I am" is for ever and only God's unique name' (Weil 1957: 72).

But does this logic truly reflect the essence of monotheism? In this chapter, I argue that it is not necessarily the case: that, from the very beginning – that is, from the first emergence of the Jewish concept of one and unique (*ehad*) God – divine power manifests itself as *originally restricted*. The Hebrew name for this originary restriction is *tsimtsum*, meaning God's self-contraction, self-limitation, self-retreat, or – in the most extreme cases, as in the Lurianic kabbalah – even self-negation. When conceived under the aegis of *tsimtsum*, monotheism emerges not as a theological doctrine of absolute power – or, in the nominalistic terminology, *potentia absoluta et inordinata* – but as a theology of a power that proves itself precisely in self-limitation. On this view, the self-limitation, dismissed by William Ockham as a mere *potentia ordinata*, a secondary form of power, would in fact determine the specific distinctiveness of monotheistic faith as it emerged in Judaism. This is the precise reverse of the Blumenbergian praise of polytheistic 'diffusion of power' as opposed to the monotheistic concentration of all *potestas*: while the so-called pagan gods may be worshipped as full of infinite vitality, the proper Mosaic distinctiveness lies in the God who restrains his wrath so that the world can evolve to stand on its feet as an autonomous entity (as in the Book of Isaiah), contracts his presence to make it endurable for humans (as in the Ark of Covenant), or 'diminishes his lights' in order not to overshadow the last sphere of emanation which is our world (as in the kabbalistic thinkers).[3] According to the paradigm of *tsimtsum*, therefore, the idea of the self-restricting power is not only not absurd, but remains definitive for monotheism also in its later developments – most of all Christianity which sports its own variant of the divine self-limitation: *kenosis*. In his commentary on the kenotic self-humbling of Christ, Origen points to the divine self-restriction as the source of a new higher glory that surpasses simple absolute power:

> One must dare to say that the goodness of Christ appears greater, more divine, and truly in the image of the Father, when he humbles himself in obedience unto death – the death of the Cross – than had he clung onto his equality with the Father as an inalienable gift, and had refused to become a slave for the world's salvation.[4]

In this chapter, I trace affinities between *tsimstum* and *kenosis* as two paradigms of divine self-restriction, in order to disprove Goethe's saying *that power should restrict itself is absurd*. But there are also significant differences between them; while the Christian *kenosis* (as well as the notion of Trinity) operates within the Neoplatonic metaphysics of presence and participation, the Jewish *tsimtsum* eventually breaks with the Neoplatonic continuum of being and paves the way towards an alternative metaphysics of absence and separation. To elucidate this difference, I will reverse the historical order and treat *kenosis* first; this will put *tsimtsum* into sharp relief as a notion harbouring revolutionary metaphysical potential which began to manifest only in the modern appropriation of Isaac Luria's sixteenth-century variant of the kabbalah.

Kenosis: Death of Christ versus the Trinitarian Life

According to Gregory Nazianzus, the Trinity is in the state of *stasis*: 'The One is always in rebellion against itself [*stasiazon pros heauto*].' In Carl Schmitt's interpretation, which cuts across Gregory's assurance that the trinitarian structure constitutes the most successful formula of plurality in unity, the Trinity is static/stable only by being constantly at war or at variance with itself: for Schmitt, this has a dangerous parallel in the equally static instability of modern democracy, permanently in a crisis of legitimacy and prone to fall into misrule (which he wishes to replace by an absolutist model of unrestricted mono-power).[5] But why the *stasis* within the Trinitarian life? The reason for this permanent conflict is precisely *kenosis*: the self-humbling of Christ, the second person of the Trinity, who, in Origen's depiction, 'humbles himself in obedience unto death – the death of the Cross'. How can this death be reconciled with the eternal life of the hypostatic union? How much *reality* should one attribute to the 'tragedy of the Cross' if the triune God, a perfect plurality in unity, is to remain an eternal infinite being which can suffer no harm? How much self-restriction is to be introduced into the very essence of Christian divinity?

The notion of *kenosis* derives from Paul's Letter to the Philippians 2.5-11. The first lines of Paul's Philippian hymn famously describe Christ as simultaneously *deiform* and *cruciform*:

> Let the same mind be in you that was in Christ Jesus, who, *though* he was in the form of God, did not regard equality with God as something to be exploited, but emptied himself, taking the form of a slave, being born in human likeness.

This translation (from the New Revised Standard Version) renders the Greek *hyparchōn* as *though* (where others use the more open phrase *being in the form of God*), thus reflecting the Cappadocian insistence on the element of *stasis* – tension, perhaps even conflict – within the Triune God. According to Michael J. Gorman, however, *hyparchōn* can also be interpreted causatively, which would lead to a completely different meaning: '*because* he was in the form of God' (Gorman 2009: 16–29).

Translation as *though* presents kenosis as a *skandalon* – a shocking negation of the infinite divine nature; translation as *because* presents it as agreeing with God's essence which then appears as *cruciform*, always already taking the form of Christ dying on the Cross:

> One implies that Christ's condescension was a contravention of his true identity, while the other implies that it was the embodiment of his true identity [...] God, we must now say, is *essentially kenotic*, and indeed *essentially cruciform*. Kenosis, therefore, does not mean Christ's emptying himself of his divinity (or of anything else), but rather Christ's *exercising* his divinity, his equality with God.
>
> (Gorman 2009: 26; 28)

One way of reconciling the stasis, therefore, would be to follow the second person of the Trinity in his downward movement of *kenosis* and see it as the defining self-restricting moment of God who, instead of maintaining the prerogatives of absolute power and potency, humbly takes the cruciform shape of vulnerability.[6]

Another way of reconciliation is shown by Rowan Williams who defines *kenosis* not as an act of divine descent into the lower regions, but rather as an act of lifting the finitude of the created world to a possibility of relation with the infinite. Without Christ's *kenosis*, the creaturely realm, immersed in its finitude, would indeed be *nothing* in the face of the eternal God, as in Simone Weil's formulation. Without the mediating activity of Christ, the world, when confronted with the divine infinity, could only be annihilated:

> God makes the world to be itself, to have an integrity and completeness and goodness that is – by God's gift – its own. At the same time, *God makes the world to be open to a relation with God's own infinite life that can enlarge and transfigure the created order without destroying it* [...] And all this is summed up in our belief in a *Christ who is uninterruptedly living a creaturely, finite life on earth and at the same time living out of the depths of divine life* and uninterruptedly enjoying the relation that eternally subsists between the divine Source or Father and the divine Word or Son. It is in this sense that we can rightly speak of Jesus as the heart of creation, the one on whom all the patterns of finite existence converge to find their meaning. While the relation between Jesus and the eternal divine Word – the 'hypostatic union', which is an *uninterrupted continuity of distinct, self-identifying, active life between the Word and Jesus* – is unique, it can only be understood in connection to a general conception, a metaphysical model, of how the finite and the infinite relate to one another.
>
> (Williams 2018: xiii; emphasis added)

The *stasis*, therefore, is merely an appearance which results from the application of the human logic, unable to contemplate the paradox of 'a Christ who is uninterruptedly living a creaturely, finite life on earth and at the same time living out of the depths of divine life'. When committing *kenosis*, the second person of the hypostatic union, who 'humbles himself unto death – the death of the Cross', does not contradict the Trinitarian Life which goes on eternally and uninterruptedly:

[T]he significance of what is (following Phil. 2.7) regularly called the *kenōsis*, the self-emptying, of Christ is *not that it involves a sort of collision between divine action and human action, such that one or the other element must be denied, qualified or diminished*, but that a certain mode of finite life (self-sacrifice, other-directed love) is so attuned to the eternal mode of divine action that it becomes the occasion and vehicle of that infinite agency within the finite world.

(Williams 2018: 56; emphasis added)

In William's rendering of *kenosis*, the main reason behind the Cappadocian *stasis* – the real death of Christ on the Cross – is visibly downplayed: *kenosis* is rather an occasion to raise finite life to the plane of an encounter with the infinite which then informs finitude with 'the eternal mode of divine action'. Here, instead of God becoming cruciform, the World gets a chance to become, at least partly, deiform. But can *kenosis*, this extreme variant of the divine self-restriction, resulting in the 'tragedy of the Cross', be so easily glossed over? In the next section, I will ponder this issue in reference to Hegel for whom the death of Christ constituted *the most real* event in the history of the world. At the same time, however, Hegel proposes his own version of the reconciliation (*Versöhnung*) of the *stasis*, which – prima facie surprisingly – puts him in the close vicinity of the heritage of *tsimtsum*. An ardent reader of early modern esoteric theosophy – from Jacob Böhme and Angelus Silesius to the Rosicrucian Kabbalah – Hegel will emerge here as a pivotal thinker in whom Christian *kenosis* and kabbalistic *tsimtsum* meet and clash simultaneously.

Hegel's speculative Good Friday

All the models of the hypostatic union, both hetero- and ortho-dox, centre around the *crucial* question: how *real* was the death of Jesus Christ, the Man-God, on the Cross? Did he *really* suffer and die (as Tertullian claimed, inaugurating the line later on called *deipassionistic*) or did he merely *seem* to suffer and die (as Gnostic Christianity assumed, taking the position of *docetism*)? This is indeed the crux/cross of the matter called Incarnation, the true novelty of the nascent Christianity which challenged the Platonic dualism of the infinite and the finite, but which, having no access to Aristotle's *Metaphysics* and its hylomorphic solution, wandered *nolens volens* into Neoplatonic language and its strongly dualistic metaphysical scheme. Thomas Aquinas is regarded as the first scholastic Aristotelian, yet, as John Milbank has recently demonstrated, his *analogia entis* (analogy of being) belongs firmly to the Neoplatonic arsenal of concepts: it maintains a strong asymmetry between the divine and the worldly which exists only thanks to participation in the transcendent subsistence.[7] It is only Duns Scotus, Aquinas's rival and nominalist champion of the alternative principle of *univocatio entis* (univocity of being), who begins to think about Incarnation in a truly Aristotelian manner: for Scotus, God-Man is a synthetic hylomorphic 'overlapping of two individuals' that cannot exist without one another and are thus both destined to die with the death of the material component.[8] These two principles, therefore – *analogia* versus *univocatio* – circle around the most fundamental problem of the kenotic tradition: the ultimate *realness* of the tragedy of the Cross. Thinkers choosing the Thomist *analogia* have a tendency to downplay the scandalous reality of the cruciform God and thus risk falling into the Gnostic heresy of docetism; thinkers engaging with the Scotist *univocatio*, which takes the death of God for real, fall perhaps into the opposite trap of deipassionism which fixates so strongly on the divine demise that it gradually dissolves into atheism, no longer capable of retaining even the most vestigial idea of infinity.

Rowan Williams, who prefers Aquinas's *analogia*, answers the fundamental question in the negative. No, the death of God *as such* is not possible; God cannot die in the manner of a finite being; God who became flesh can suffer death, but he cannot die as we do; just as God exists differently, he also dies differently. His death on the cross may be analogical to the death of human being, but can never be identical. Analogy allows for the *communicatio idiomatum* or the exchange of properties between transcendence and immanence, but resists the implication of mutual transformation: immanence can be changed by transcendence, but transcendence stays unaffected and immutable. The finite experience can be communicated to the infinite, but the latter will register it 'analogically'. For Thomists, therefore, the *real* death of Christ on the cross and his descent to Hell is unthinkable, since finite experience is felt differently by the divine being; for the Scotists, on the contrary, it is not only thinkable but absolutely fundamental to Christianity. In its Reformed version, *communicatio idiomatum* must be full and accepted with no provisos: it must be a total univocal 'overlapping' of all properties, infinite and finite alike. Hence the Lutheran focus on the 'tragedy of the Cross' and his famous meditation on the Paschal hymn which contains the ominous phrase: *Gott selbst ist tot*, 'God *himself* is dead'.[9]

Martin Luther's emphasis on *selbst*/*himself* explicitly touches on the very nature of God: no longer a deiform Absolute, now decidedly cruciform, defined by the painfully real moment of his death on the Cross. While reflecting on Luther's sentence, Hegel writes:

> *God has died, God is dead* – this is the most frightful of all thoughts, that everything eternal and true *is not*, that negation itself is found in God. The deepest anguish, the feeling of complete irretrievability, the annulling of everything that is elevated, are *bound up* with this thought.
>
> (Hegel 2006: 465; emphasis added)

According to the partisans of *analogia entis*, such a deipassionistic accent inevitably leads to heresy, because it challenges the perfect eternal arrangement of the Trinitarian Life, where God the Father is *ever-living*, God the Son is *ever-dying* and God the Spirit is *ever-resurrecting*. For Nicene Christianity, this is the highest Paradox. It can be poetically contemplated but never understood intellectually: the *perichoresis,* the constant dance of God living-dying-resurrecting, always dead and alive simultaneously, constitutes the ultimate mystery of eternity of which our world is merely a Platonic 'temporal copy'. Within the flawed temporal imitation of the Trinity, life, death and resurrection can occur solely in a sequence, but this forms merely a distorted image of the truly eternal Trinitarian Life. For modern post-Scotist Christians, however, temporality of the material world is no longer a distorted image of the Trinitarian eternity: the Incarnation itself announces a break in the Trinitarian continuous 'dance', by adding matter and time, now to be taken fully seriously, to the metaphysical picture. From the point of Trinitarian orthodoxy, they are thus in danger of succumbing to what the Catholic church defined as the Joachimite heresy: the vision of the Trinity based not on a timeless 'dance', but on historical succession. God the Sovereign Creator *himself* dies, so the Son can step to the fore with the Word of Love – but he *himself* must die too, so the Spirit can resurrect *within the world* and thus complete the work of creation. The first age is the time of Judaism, the second of Christianity and the third of modernity, here conceived as *nova era* or the Age of the Spirit.[10] When conceived as a temporal sequence, Trinity proceeds *ad extra*: instead of remaining an eternal Platonic paradigm for the merely 'analogical' worldly existence, it enters the creaturely realm to transform it from within. The infinite wanders into the finite; the sacred migrates into the profane.[11]

For Hegel, therefore, the measure of the *seriousness* of reality is the 'tragedy of the Cross' extrapolated in the ontological mode of becoming as the constant historical 'tarrying with the negative' and 'abiding in death': this is the final test of true reality and possibly the strongest intuition of the Real in the whole history of Western philosophy. *Experimentum mundi* is thus also an *experimentum crucis* in the double sense of the word *crux*: literally, the 'cross' – and, figuratively, the 'crux of the matter', the crucial point through which Word becomes Flesh, or the divine Spirit leaves the realm of absolute freedom and enters the realm of actualization, where it takes on itself all the laws and limitations determining the material Kingdom of Necessity, including death. Having become material in the act of *kenosis*, the Spirit does not die differently or analogically: it dies the death of all finite beings, it goes the way of all flesh. 'God himself *is* dead', Hegel repeats after Luther, this time putting an emphasis on the actuality/*Gegenwart* of God's ordeal of the cross as the ongoing historical process. Hence his own definition of modern philosophy as a 'speculative Good Friday' that should assist Christ's kenotic wrestling with death and hopefully look forward to the universal Good Sunday, the day of the ultimate victory of life and freedom over necessity and death. It is then up to the End of History to see if the Word manages to resurrect and recognize itself – its original freedom – in what it became as a Flesh.[12]

Tsimtsum in Kabbalah

The importance of Hegel lies in the hybrid nature of his thought. Poised between theology and philosophy, Hegel's borrowing from kabbalistic lore did not go unnoticed by Protestant theology. In his widely discussed essay, 'God's Kenosis in the Creation and Consummation of the World', Jürgen Moltmann praises Hegel for creating an innovative 'account of Christian and Jewish kenotic theology', which consists in a fusion of kenosis with *tsimtsum* (Moltmann 2001: 137). God the Father is no longer imagined as the Creator making being out of nothing by his absolute infinite power, but rather as the First Notion/Word which undergoes a self-limitation in order to create the world as its Other (*Anderssein*). Creation, therefore, is not an expression of the divine omnipotence; it is a self-limiting kenotic activity of 'the self-knowing Spirit [who] knows not only itself but also the negative of itself, or its limit: to know one's limit is to know how to sacrifice oneself' (Hegel 1977: 493). The self-restraint is no longer reserved for the second person of the Trinity; it is now elevated to the main principle of the whole Trinitarian life, which is *Autoopferung*: a willing self-sacrifice.

Before Moltmann, however, it was Gershom Scholem who spotted the affinity between the Lurianic doctrine and the Hegelian notion of *kenosis* in creation. In one of his numerous works on the kabbalistic tradition, Scholem postulates a strong connection between the sixteenth-century theosophic kabbalah of Isaac Luria and German Idealism, Hegel especially. He adds that he cannot prove a direct influence (a rather improbable hypothesis), but suspects that Hegel was exposed to the so-called Christian Kabbalah which fused the kabbalistic divine manifestations, called by Isaac Luria *partsufim*, into the Christian trinitarian context of The Father, The Son and the Holy Spirit[13]

According to Scholem, *tsimtsum* is a truly novel concept which has a potential to revolutionize Western metaphysics, breaking with the predominant Neoplatonic pattern which privileges continuity over difference and participation over separation. Nonetheless, he admits that all kabbalistic writings are marked by a certain appropriation of the Neoplatonic idea of emanation. God is imagined here as *yitron*, the Hebrew equivalent of *superessentia*, *Ein Sof*, the Infinite or 'without limits', as well as *'Ayin*, 'nothingness'. This divine source, hidden from any knowledge and approached only through strictly negative theology, emanates through circles of reality forming a metaphysical hierarchy. This hierarchy is based on ten pillars of creation called *sephirot*, standing in two columns, left and right, from the highest (*'Ayin*) to the lowest (*Malkut*, kingdom). The divine light, overflowing from the hidden source of being (*Ein Sof*), flows through the channels formed by the *sephirot* and thus becomes differentiated, eventually creating a variety of beings in the realm of Kingdom. The lower it flows, the less perfect it becomes; the principle of emanation sees the matter and the evil that pertains to material being as the result of deprivation and distance from the origin. In Scholem's view, this quite traditional Neoplatonic account of the chain of emanation ends with Isaac Luria's invention of *tsimtsum*.

Scholem always insisted that, in Jewish theology, the act of creation is primarily a *separation*: that is, a creation of something emphatically and truly other than God. Kabbalah offers two versions of creation out of nothing, which constitute opposing answers to the fundamental question concerning the nature of the first *sephira*, *'Ayin* (nothingness): does it belong to the *Ein Sof*, the Infinite, or is it already something separate from God? The earlier solution, beginning with the speculations of Moses de Leon, which decides for the participation of *'Ayin* in *Ein Sof*, is, in fact, a very sophisticated variation of pantheism in disguise, which, as Scholem rightly points out, troubles all Neoplatonism, whether Jewish, Christian or Islamic: it claims that 'nothingness' is a secret name of the Infinite which is beyond being as we know it, and thus is a *superesse*, a hyper-being which can be known to us only as *nothing*. According to this logic, creation is not at all separate from the nature of God, for it continuously participates in 'the fountain of all life'. *Creatio ex nihilo* becomes then merely a cover for the mystical theory of emanation: 'In this way the theory of identity is given a pantheistic spin: the creation out of nothingness becomes only an encrypted code for the essential oneness of all things with God' (Scholem 1976a: 268). In another place Scholem adds: 'We cannot find here an *authentic nothingness* which would break the continuity of the chain' (Scholem 1991: 99; emphasis added). As it was put by one of the Spanish Kabbalists from around 1500, Joseph Taitatzak, in a poetic formulation: 'Everything lives in the palace of Nothingness' (Scholem 1991: 102).

Only the later solution, created by Isaac Luria, according to Scholem, gives true meaning to the notion of *creatio ex nihilo* as radical separation. Luria did not invent the term *tsimtsum*: the word had already existed in rabbinic commentaries and then in the kabbalistic context. The first to introduce the midrashic concept of *tsimtsum* into the arcana of kabbalist Neoplatonism was Isaac Luria's older contemporary: Moses Cordovero. For Cordovero, *tsimtsum* is an act of God's hiding, in which God withdraws into his secret and unknowable nature, choosing to show only his attributes of creative agency, i.e. the Tree of *Sephirot* which form the emanative backbone of the worldly reality. God, therefore, reveals himself in concealment: these two agencies are strictly parallel and cannot be dissociated from one another. We could thus call it an *aspectual* theory of *tsimtsum*, where God changes aspects between his secret in-dwelling and his revelatory/ creative action. But is it enough to give us 'an authentic nothingness which would break the continuity of the chain'? Or is creation only a different aspect of the Godhead which constantly oscillates between *'Ayin* and *Ein Sof*, nothing and everything, as if leaping from one to the other side of the Möbius strip? Perhaps it is precisely to secure 'authentic nothingness' that Luria took over the notion of *tsimtsum* with an intention to make it more *real*, or to use a contemporary philosophical idiom, to turn God's contraction into a real *event*: not so much a change of aspect (or a *Gestaltswitch*), which still keeps the divine Infinity intact within the folds of its self-concealment, as change within the Infinite itself, resulting in a *true* beginning of time and history, spun between creation and redemption.

In Luria's elaboration, *tsimtsum* is no longer a concealment of God, a switch of aspects: it becomes a real 'contraction' conceived as a radical transformation of God's ontological status. The purpose is to square the circle of the creaturely nature of being as simultaneously *different* from God and yet *linked* to him by the very fact of creation. *Tsimtsum*, God's self-reduction, is to account for this paradox and present nothingness (*'Ayin*) not as a divine attribute of self-concealment, but as God's first creative act: the first event in the series of happenings creating the world as an essentially *historical* entity. In the beginning, therefore, *God created nothing*: 'in the reduction of the divine essence which, instead of acting outwards (as in the Thomistic formula of *processio dei ad extra*), acts towards its inside, there emerges nothingness' (Scholem 1991: 104).

Only when God withdraws from himself 'for real', there emerges a place of a possible separation, a room for something else:

> Creation out of nothing, from the void, could be nothing other than creation of the void, that is, of the possibility of thinking of anything that was not God. Without such an act of self-limitation, after all, there would be only God – and obviously nothing else. A being that is not God could only become possible and originate by virtue of such a contraction, such a paradoxical retreat of God into himself. By positing a negative factor in Himself, God *liberates* creation.
>
> (Scholem 1976b: 283; emphasis added)

Scholem's description of Luria's *tsimtsum* accentuates the moment of God's self-effacement, which suggests affinities with Christian *kenosis*, especially in Hegel's treatment: the divine sacrifice, self-emptying and self-exteriorizing that condition the emergence of the world as the Other.[14] Scholem defines Luria's *tsimtsum* through the reversal of its original Talmudic meaning where it is occasionally used in reference to *kodesh kodashim*, the Holiest of Holies, in which God concentrates his presence (*Shekhinah*) into a single point:

> Here we have the origin of the term *tsimtsum*, while *the thing itself is the precise opposite of this idea*: to the Kabbalist of Luria's school tsimtsum does not mean the concentration of God *at* a point, but his retreat *away* from a point [...] One is tempted to interpret this withdrawal of God into his own Being in terms of Exile, of banishing Himself from His totality into profound seclusion [...] *The first act of all is not an act of revelation but one of limitation.*
>
> (Scholem 1995: 260–1; emphasis added)

The significance of this reversal cannot be overemphasized. We can imagine God's autoreduction as withdrawing into the circumference or even as God's withdrawal from being (as in Emmanuel Levinas's concept of *autrement qu'être*, 'otherwise than being'), but the most important aspect here indeed appears kenotic: *tsimtsum* is not a concentration of the divine presence, but the disappearance, deactivation and weakening of God's power to be and to reveal himself.

Scholem's understanding of Luria's *tsimtsum* is tendentious. He selects only one possible meaning of God's compression as withdrawal: *away from the point*, so that God can make room – *nothingness* – for the world to emerge as the truly separated other of God. This solution was favoured by Hayyim Vital, the founder of the 'Eastern School' in Lurianic Kabbalah. In *Ets Haim* (The Tree of Life), Vital interpreted the oral teachings of his master on *tsimtsum* as the voluntary act of the Infinite One who first gathers in himself and only then vacates himself, by evacuating to the circumference and creating a vacuum in his midst:

> And when it arose in the Simple Will to create worlds [...] then the Infinite *tsimtsem* [contracted] itself at the central point within itself, at the exact centre of its light, and *tsimtsem* that light, and withdrew to extremities surrounding the central point, and then a vacant place and environment, and an empty space remained.
>
> (Vital 1999: 3)

But in Israel Sarug's version, which founded the 'Italian School' of the Lurianic Kabbalah, the movement of *tsimtsum* is simpler and more mechanical than intentional: it is the cathartic compression of the Infinite which, by using the wrathful power of *Din*, the *sephira* of Judgement, withdraws into itself in order to release the 'irritant' and impure elements that disturb its inner bliss, and thus creates the opposition of inside and outside – the self-contracted transcendence which has gathered itself in itself, on the one hand, and the dispersed immanence made of the rejected 'alien' substance, on the other. Sarug tends to see *tsimtsum* merely as a metaphor and not as a literal *event* marking a true crisis in the Godhead. For him, God does not create nothingness as a free space for another being, but maintains his presence in the creation as a superessential nothingness (*'Ayin*); the decision, therefore, to conceive *tsimtsum* in a metaphorical manner indicates a step back towards the traditional Neoplatonic model of emanation.[15]

Thus, even though both hereditary lines talk about God's contraction in the traditional midrashic sense of the word *tsimtsum*, it is only Vital's variant which contains also its reversal, so strongly emphasized by Scholem; here, if God gathers himself into the point, it is only for the sake of giving himself away in the final movement. God pulls himself together from the vast expanses of the Infinite in order to give up on himself *as* God – the deiform omnipotent and omnipresent Absolute – and marginalize himself as nothing more than a 'circumference'. He thus contracts in his divinity *only* in order to create a non-God, and then to lend this non-divine otherness of the world all his substance. It is precisely this variant of *tsimtsum* – a benign self-limitation of power or 'diminution of lights' which allowed the world to come to the fore – that wandered into the Hegelian system, in the form of *kenosis* in creation.

Hans Jonas's adventure of becoming: Hegel without safety nets

But Hegel's speculation is not the last word: the latest chapter (so far) has been written by Hans Jonas in his 1984 essay 'The Concept of God after Auschwitz', where the 'Lurianic myth' is used in order to present creation as truly liberated, i.e. free from the divine providence and omnipresence, and God as always already withdrawn and thus not accountable for the adventures of becoming, even as disastrous as the Shoah. Here, *tsimtsum* serves as a strong argument against traditional theodicy: if God truly let the world be, He cannot be responsible for anything that happens within it. Freedom thus comes with a price; but without paying that price, there would simply be nothing at all.

Scholem's classical account of the Lurianic *tsimtsum* is still ambivalent and hesitant; torn between his role as a historian of Jewish thought and his unhistorical speculative temper, he wishes to remain faithful to the original doctrine. But Hans Jonas's 'frankly speculative theology' (Jonas 1996: 131), based on the Lurianic myth, is free from the Gnostic pessimism which overshadows Luria's teaching, especially in its dark Sarugian variant. What Jonas offers is a Lurianic myth reworked according to the requirements of the 'modern temper' which asserts finite existence and rejects immortality, any ahistorical vision of the cosmos, and divine providence. He thus interprets *tsimtsum* as the self-limitation of the divine which deliberately gives itself over to chance and the risk of becoming. God, emptied and contracted, reduces here to an immemorial arche-trace; always already there in the distant moment of creative decision, but no longer retrievable in the present state of creation. Jonas's *tsimtsum*-inspired apology of the 'unprejudiced becoming', where there are no safety nets, no metaphysical guarantees, just an unpredictable sea of possibilities, is one of the strongest paeans to contingency modern philosophy ever offered:

> In the beginning, for unknowable reasons, the ground of being, or the Divine, chose to give itself over to chance and risk an endless variety of becoming. And wholly so: entering into the adventure of space and time, the deity held back nothing of itself: no uncommitted or unimpaired part remained to direct, correct, and ultimately guarantee the devious working-out of its destiny in creation. On this unconditional immanence the modern temper insists. It is its courage or despair, in any case its bitter honesty, to take our being-in-the-world seriously: to view the world as left to itself, its laws as brooking no interference, and the rigor of our belonging to it as not softened by extramundane providence. The same our myth postulates for God's being in the world. Not, however, in the sense of pantheistic immanence: if world and God are simply the same, the world at each moment and in each stage represents his fullness, and God can neither lose or gain. Rather, in order that the world might be, and be for itself, God renounced his being, divesting himself of his deity – to receive it back

from the odyssey of time weighted with the chance harvest of unforeseeable temporal experience: transfigured or possibly even disfigured by it. In such *self-forfeiture of divine integrity for the sake of unprejudiced becoming*, no other knowledge can be admitted than that of *possibilities*, which cosmic being offers in its own terms: to these, God committed his cause in effacing himself from the world.

(Jonas 1996: 134)

We already know this motif from Hegel: 'This sacrifice [*Autoopferung*] is the externalization in which Spirit displays the process of its becoming Spirit in the form of *free contingent happening*, intuiting its pure Self as Time outside of it, and equally its Being as Space' (Hegel 1977: 492; emphasis added). Jonas, however, is more radical in his acceptance of 'unprejudiced becoming' and its total contingency. For Hegel, the immanent History proceeds according to strict laws which secure – sooner or later – the resurrection of the Spirit in the form of Absolute Knowledge. But for Jonas, this 'odyssey of time' is as adventurous and uncertain as it was for Ulysses: there is no transcendent guarantee that all shall be well or that the deity will have 'received back' its deiform nature. There are only *possibilities* and the risk in the divine self-forfeiture is enormous: the deity may just disperse in matter, never regaining its integrity. Thus, even if *tsimtsum* stands behind both Hegel and Jonas, the visions of history which they inspire are quite different: Hegel remains a Trinitarian thinker, for whom the reconciling activity of the Holy Spirit is metaphysically assured; but Jonas treats the historical process in terms of the 'theology of risk', which operates in the conditions of extreme incertitude.

The only fact that diminishes this uncertainty is that the transcendence, which has 'entered into the adventure of space and time', left in it an indelible trace: a *stake* that is a future re-emergence of the Divine. Jonas' 'unconditional immanence' must thus be strictly differentiated from 'pantheistic immanence', precisely because the latter, although affirmative, is void of any normative position.[16] Jonas' purpose is to combine immanence with a dynamic normativity, which can organize the oceanic movement of beings and push it into a direction, thus bestowing it with a *sense* (which, etymologically speaking, derives precisely from the vector of orientation or non-indifference in homogeneous space). This *tropos* emerges for the first time with the beginning of life which, for Jonas, marks 'a hesitant emergence of transcendence from the opaqueness of immanence':

And then the first stirring of life – a *new language of the world*: and with it a tremendous quickening of concern in the eternal realm and a sudden leap in its growth toward recovery of its plenitude. It is the world accident for which becoming deity had waited and with which its prodigal stake begins to show signs of being redeemed. From the infinite swell of feeling, sensing, striving, and acting, which ever more varied and intense rises above the mute eddyings of matter, eternity gains strength, filling with content after content of self-affirmation, and the awakening God can first pronounce creation to be good.

(Jonas 1996: 134)

The site of the awakening of God within immanence is the living soul: finite, singular, vulnerable, exposed, struggling and not knowing the ultimate outcome of the struggle. The living is thus by definition mortal; mortality is a necessary price life has to pay for exiting the world of indifferent being and stony permanence. As for Hegel, so also for Jonas, life is the privileged site of the awakening of the Spirit in the vast expanses of the inorganic matter. *Pace* Hegel, however, who sees the pain of all precarious living beings as reflecting Christ's Passion of the Cross, Jonas is more affirmative towards mortality and its discontents, accepting it as a part of the reality made possible by the act of *tsimtsum*:

> But note that with life together came death, and that mortality is the price which the new possibility of being called 'life' had to pay for itself. If permanence were the point, life should not have started in the first place, for in no possible form can it match the durability of inorganic bodies. It is essentially precarious and corruptible being, an adventure in mortality, obtaining from long-lasting matter on its terms – the short terms of metabolising organism – the borrowed, finite careers of individual selves. Yet it is precisely through the briefly snatched self-feeling, doing, and suffering of finite individuals, with *the pitch of awareness heightened by the very press of finitude*, that the divine landscape bursts into color and *the deity comes to experience itself.*
>
> (Jonas 1996: 135; emphasis added)

For Jonas, death is the price worth paying for the intensity of life in which the self-forfeited deity begins his ascension towards *restitutio in integrum*. Jonas' endorsement of finitude echoes Scholem's description of the 'liberated creation' – separated from God and made free at the price of mortality – as well as the last lines of Schiller's poem, with which Hegel ends the story of the 'Golgotha of Absolute Spirit', from its emptying out into material nature to its refinding itself in the 'community of finite spirits': 'Only from the chalice of this realm of spirits foams forth for Him his own infinitude' (Hegel 1977: 493). Jonas thus offers a Lurianic-Hegelian metaphysics of finitude in which it is precisely the community of finite living souls that presses towards the messianic finale: the re-emergence of the Godhead, yet not in its original infinitist form, but as a *Gestalt* composed of the single awakened sparks or the Lurianic *kneset Israel*. Yet, at the same time, Jonas rejects Hegel's 'unerring cunning of reason' and his version of teleology based on the 'metaphysics of success', which tells the 'self-guaranteed success stories of Being, stories that cannot go amiss' (Jonas 1996: 189). He proposes instead a subtler – open and hazardous – dialectics in which positivity (life's testimony of hope) clashes with negativity (life's taking risks with matter), with the outcome as yet unknown. In Jonas' modernized variant of *tsimtsum*, the loss of God may indeed be final: 'the deepest anguish, the feeling of complete irretrievability, the annulling of everything that is elevated, are *bound up* with this thought' (Hegel 2006: 465).

Conclusion

Depending on how we define *kenosis*, it is either close to or far from the Lurianic idea of *tsimtsum*. When *kenosis* is understood as a divine self-limitation which touches upon the very essence of God, then the Hegelian manoeuvre, which pushes *kenosis* back to the moment of creation, is fully justified: if, as Gorman argues, the Christian deity is always already and essentially *cruciform*, the act of creation cannot be conceived as a display of absolute omnipotence, but only as a self-sacrifice. This chimes well with the notion of *tsimstum* taken literally as in Hayim Vital and Hans Jonas: it is not an eruption of God's power *ad extra* that makes the world emerge out of nothing, but rather a withdrawal that creates nothing as the empty place in which the world can assert itself as an independent separate entity. Yet, despite those affinities (as well as historical mutual influences), these two paradigms of the divine self-restraint produce different results. While both creative *kenosis* and *tsimtsum* lead to the endorsement of the metaphysical significance of time, the Christian *Heilsgeschichte* retains a Neoplatonic anchor and guarantee, in the eternal life of the Trinity, whereas the Lurianic history opens itself to infinite risk, where nothing can warrant the messianic advent of *tikkun ha-olam* (redemption of the world, as well as the Godhead in its new dei-form).

Yet, if Scholem is right that Luria's innovation announces a break with Neoplatonism, then the 'analogical' interpretation of *kenosis*, strongly invested in the participatory model, builds a stark contrast with the concept of *tsimtsum* taken literally. For Rowan Williams, Christ incarnate is the very 'heart of creation', filling the finite world with the strong presence of the 'infinite agency'; for Isaac Luria, to the contrary, the heart of the world is the void and the absence of God. Williams' 'analogical' *kenosis*, in which Word becomes Flesh, strengthens the participation of the divine in the material reality; *tsimtsum*, in which God withdraws for the sake of the world as the divine other, consists in a radical break that separates and distances the two. In the act of *kenosis*, God makes the world to be *himself* and this lifting of finitude to the level of 'communication' with the infinite constitutes God's greatest gift of love; in the act of *tsimtsum*, God makes the world to be *itself*, letting it be in its non-divine otherness. In the former case, there is no 'collision' between the infinite and the finite; in the latter, the 'negative factor' in God plays a principal role, for the infinite 'element must be denied, qualified or diminished' in order for finitude to establish itself in its separate mode of being (Williams 2018: xii; 56). But if Scholem is wrong and *tsimtsum* should rather be conceived figuratively, as in Israel Sarug, then the difference between it and the 'analogical' *kenosis* rapidly diminishes: in both cases, the Neoplatonic scheme of *methexis* (participation of the world in the divine) takes the upper hand.

My purpose has been to prove that the specific place of the concept of the divine self-restraint within monotheistic theologies determines their respective conceptions of God's power. Where it is central, the divine power is never absolute: it is precisely in its self-limitation that God's ability to create can realize itself. Where it is more marginal, God is imagined as an absolutist hyper-being that retains the traditional attributes of omnipotence and omnipresence. This instability is inscribed into the very nature of monotheistic faith which from its beginnings has pondered the enigma of the divine *potentia*. For the absolutist camp, the idea 'that power should restrict itself is absurd'; for those, however, who see the specific difference of monotheism in either *kenosis* or *tsimtsum*, self-restriction constitutes the primary manifestation of God's power.

Notes

1. Schmitt comments here on Gregory Nazianzus' famous thesis that the Trinity is in the state of *stasis*, 'civil war': 'The One is always in rebellion against itself [*stasiazon pros heauto*]' (Blumenberg and Schmitt 2007: 41).
2. 'Das Wort *sein* bedeutet im Deutschen beides: Dasein und Ihmgehören' (Kafka 2006: 46).
3. The paradigmatic *tsimtsum*, in which God 'takes in his breath' and restricts his glory for the sake of something else to emerge, derives already from Isaiah, as described by Wolfson in his interpretation of one of the bahiric texts:

    > The notion of withdrawal, itself withdrawn and thus not stated overtly, is a secret exegetically derived from the verse *lema'an shemi a'arikh appi u-tehillati ehetam lakh le-vilti hakhritekha*, "For the sake of my name I will postpone my wrath and my glory I will hold in for you so that I will not destroy you" (Isa. 48:9). The plain sense of the prophetic dictum relates to divine mercy expressed as God's long-suffering, the capacity to restrain his rage. The expression *tehillati ehetam*, literally "my glory I will hold in," is parallel to *a'arikh appi*, "I will postpone my wrath." One may surmise that at some point in ancient Israel the notion of a vengeful god yielded its opposite, the compassionate god who holds in his fury.
    >
    > (Wolfson 2006: 132–3)

4. Quot. in Balthasar (1990: 15).
5. On the Cappadocian Trinity as the theologico-political model, see also Giorgio Agamben who, in *The Kingdom and the Glory*, attempts to deconstruct the double bind or 'secret solidarity' of 'a single political paradigm, which manifests itself, on the one hand, through the assertion of the necessity of civil war, and on the other, through the assertion of the necessity of its exclusion' (Agamben 2015: 4).
6. One of the most outspoken advocates of kenotic Christianity today is John D. Caputo who emphasizes the 'folly' of *kenosis* as going against the monotheistic logic of absolute power: 'The internal logic of the kingdom is the alogic – the folly – of

the cross. Its dynamics are the movements of a kenotic abdication of supreme power of a Supreme Being for the powerless power of mercy and compassion' (Caputo 2015: 105).

7. In *Truth in Aquinas*, Milbank and Pickstock claim that 'analogy is predicated upon the metaphysics of participated being' which 'is only comprehensible for Aquinas in terms of his neoplatonic ontology of participation in Being, which surpasses Aristotelianism in seeking to do justice to the doctrine of Creation' (Milbank and Pickstock 2001: 40; 90).

8. Quot. in Cross (2002: 322).

9. In *Von Konzilis und Kirchen*, Luther meditates on the hymn of Johann Richter: 'O Traurigkeit,/ O Herzeleid!/ Ist das nicht zu beklagen?/ Gott des Vaters einig Kind/ Wird ins Grab getragen./ O grosse Not!/ Gott selbst ist tot,/ Am Kreuz ist er gestorben,/ Hat dadurch das Himmelreich/ Uns aus Lieb' erworben. Luther's teaching, however, was not fully accepted by the Lutheran orthodoxy who soon decided to neutralize the revolutionary potential of the phrase 'Gott selbst ist tot' and replaced it with a more acceptably Trinitarian one: 'Gotts Sohn liegt tot' (Asendorf 1982: 152).

10. In the fifth chapter of *Liber introductorius* to *Expositio in Apocalypsim*, composed in 1186, Joachim da Fiore formulates the outlines of his famous prophecy of the three ages, neatly summarized by the historian of the Franciscan reform: 'The first [age] is in the servitude of slavery, the second in the servitude of sons, the third in freedom. The first in fear, the second in faith, the third in love. The first is the status of bondsmen, the second of freemen, the third of friends' (Benz 1964: 26). The enormous vitality of Joachim da Fiore's prophecy is well attested by Karl Löwith in his *Meaning of History: The Theological Implications of the Philosophy of History* (Löwith 1957), mostly devoted to the future transformations of Joachim's teaching and its influence on Lessing, Schiller, Schlegel, Kant, Hegel, and, last but not least, Marx.

11. Theodor Adorno sums up the defining moment of modern dialectics in a succinct epigram: 'No theological content will last untransformed; every single one will have to face the test and enter the sphere of the profane' (Adorno 1969: 608). What is particularly interesting in our context is that Adorno's remark refers both to the Hegelian legacy and to the historical effects of the kabbalistic notion of *tsimtsum*.

12. A similar metaphysical intuition combining the two terms, *tsimtsum* (concentration) and *kenosis* (descent), emerges in another great representative of German Idealism, Schelling. In the notes to his Stuttgart Lectures in 1810, he also draws on Goethe's authority, but using his quote against Blumenberg's defence of unlimited power:

> A passive limitation is indeed a mere insufficiency or a relative lack of power; however, to limit oneself, to concentrate oneself in one point, yet also to hold on to the latter with all one's might and not to let go until it has been expanded into a world, such constitutes the greatest power and perfection. As Goethe says: "Whoever wills greatness must concentrate himself/ Only in self-restriction is the

artist revealed" […] *Concentration, then, marks the beginning of all reality.* For this reason, it is the concentrating rather than the expanding nature that possesses a primordial and grounding force. Thus the beginning of creation amounts indeed to a *descent of God*; He properly descends into the Real, contracts Himself entirely into the Real. Yet such an act does not imply anything unworthy of God but, in fact, it is this descent that marks the greatest act for God and, indeed, for Christianity as well.

(Schelling 2021: 75)

The kenotic self-emptying of the Godhead as the condition of the emergence of the Real is also the focus of the contemporary 'theology of the death of God', most of all Thomas Altizer according to whom the knowledge of the death of God 'known by the Christian as occurring in the Crucifixion' is revolutionized by Hegel who 'realizes it as a universal absolute negativity. *This is that pure negativity that is the source of an absolute self-negation or self-emptying, one apart from which God would not and could not truly be God, and one apart from which the world would finally be inactual and unreal*' (Altizer 2002: 78; emphasis added). The extreme self-limitation of the Godhead, therefore, not only testifies to its original 'cruciformity', but also makes possible the very act of creation.

13. In the section on Isaac Luria, Scholem writes:

> At the same time, side by side with the Gnostic outlook, we find a most astonishing tendency to a mode of contemplative thought that can be called "dialectic" in the strictest sense of the term as used by Hegel. This tendency is especially prominent in attempts to present formal explanations of such doctrines as that of *tsimtsum*, the breaking of the vessels, or the formation of the *partsufim*.
>
> (Scholem 1978: 143)

On the kabbalistic background of German Idealism, see also Bielik-Robson 2017.

14. On the affinities, but also differences, between *tsimtsum* and *kenosis*, especially in the context of Moltmann's theology, see Podmore (2020).
15. On the history of the concept of *tsimtsum* and its various interpretations, see Schulte (2023).
16. Against Spinoza Jonas voices the objection 'that a purely immanent pantheism and panpsychism – one, therefore, without a transcendent criterion of the good – can be just as much a pandemonism, indeed a pandiabolism': Jonas, *Mortality and Morality*, 185.

References

Adorno, Theodor W. (1969), *Stichworte*: *Kritische Modelle 2*. Frankfurt am Main: Suhrkamp.

Agamben, Giorgio (2015), *Stasis. Civil War as a Political Paradigm (Homo Sacer II, 2)*, trans. Nicholas Heron. Stanford, CA: Stanford University Press.

Altizer, Thomas (2002), *The New Gospel of Christian Atheism*. Aurora, CO: The Davies Group.
Asendorf, Ulrich (1982), *Luther und Hegel: Untersuchung zur Grundlegung einer Neuen Systematischen Theologie*. Wiesbaden: Franz Steiner Verlag.
Balthasar, Hans-Urs von (1990), *Mysterium Paschale: The Mystery of Easter*, trans. Aidan Nichols OP. San Francisco, CA: Ignatius Press.
Benz, Ernst (1964), *Ecclesia spiritualis: Kirchenidee und Geschichtstheologie der franziskanischen Reformation*. Darmstadt: Wissenschaftliche Buchgesellschaft Darmstadt.
Bielik-Robson, Agata (2017), 'God of Luria, Hegel, Schelling: The Divine Contraction and the Modern Metaphysics of Finitude', in Simon Podmore (ed.), *Mystical Theology & Continental Philosophy*. London and New York: Routledge, pp. 30–52.
Blumenberg, Hans, and Carl Schmitt (2007), *Briefwechsel 1971–1978*. Frankfurt: Suhrkamp.
Caputo, John D. (2015), *The Folly of God: A Theology of the Unconditional*. Oxford: Polebridge Press.
Cross, Richard (2002), *The Metaphysics of the Incarnation: Thomas Aquinas to Duns Scotus*. Oxford: Oxford University Press.
Gorman, Michael J. (2009), *Inhabiting the Cruciform God: Kenosis, Justification and Theosis in Paul's Narrative Soteriology*. Grand Rapids, MI: William B. Eerdmans Publishing.
Hegel, G. W. F. (1977), *Phenomenology of Spirit,* trans. A. V. Miller. Oxford: Oxford University Press.
Hegel, G. W. F. (2006), *Lectures on the Philosophy of Religion (The Lectures of 1827 – One Volume Edition)*, trans. R. F. Brown. Oxford: Oxford University Press.
Jonas, Hans (1996), *Mortality and Morality: A Search for the Good after Auschwitz*, ed. Lawrence Vogel. Evanston, Chicago: Nortwestern University Press.
Kafka, Franz (2006), *The Zürau Aphorisms*, trans. Michael Hoffman. London: Harvill Seeker.
Löwith, Karl (1957), *Meaning of History: The Theological Implications of the Philosophy of History*. Chicago, IL: University of Chicago Press.
Milbank, John, and Catherine Pickstock (2001), *Truth in Aquinas*. London and New York: Routledge.
Moltmann, Jürgen (2001), 'God's Kenosis in the Creation and Consummation of the World', in John Polkinghorne (ed.), *The Work of Love: Creation as Kenosis*. Grand Rapids, MI: Wm. B. Eerdmans.
Podmore, Simon (2020), '*Abyss Calls unto Abyss*: Tsimtsum and Kenosis in Jewish and Christian Struggles with the Mystery of Evil', in Agata Bielik-Robson and Daniel H. Weiss (eds.), *Tsimtsum and Modernity. Lurianic Heritage in Modern Philosophy and Theology*. Berlin: de Gruyter: 311–38.
Schelling, F. W. J. (2021), *The Schelling Reader*, ed. Benjamin Berger and Daniel Whistler. London: Bloomsbury.
Scholem, Gershom (1976a), *Über einige Grundbegriffe des Judentums*. Frankfurt am Main: Suhrkamp.

Scholem, Gershom (1976b), *On Jews and Judaism in Crisis: Selected Essays*, ed. Werner Dannhauser. New York: Schocken.
Scholem, Gershom (1978), *Kabbalah*. New York: Meridian.
Scholem, Gershom (1991), *The Messianic Idea in Judaism*. New York: Schocken.
Scholem, Gershom (1995), *Major Trends in Jewish Mysticism*. New York: Schocken.
Schulte, Christoph (2023), *Zimzum: God and the Origin of the World*, trans. Corey Twitchell. Philadelphia, PA: University of Pennsylvania Press.
Vital, Hayyim ben Joseph (1999), *The Tree of Life: Chayyim Vital's Introduction to the Kabbalah of Isaac Luria – The Palace of Adam Kadmon*, trans. Donald Wilder Menzi and Zwe Padeh. Northvale, NJ, and Jerusalem: Jason Aronson.
Weil, Simone (1957), *Intimations of Christianity among the Greeks*, trans. Elisabeth Chas Geissbuhler. London: Routledge Kegan Paul.
Williams, Rowan (2018), *Christ the Heart of Creation*. London: Bloomsbury.
Wolfson, Elliot (2006), *Alef, Mem, Tau: Kabbalistic Musings on Time, Truth, and Death*. Berkeley, CA: University of California Press.

13

Philosophy and African art: Léopold Sédar Senghor and the philosophy of emotion and rhythm

Victor Emma-Adamah

'I am convinced that art is the supreme task and the truly metaphysical activity of this life …': so said Nietzsche famously in *The Birth of Tragedy*. The status of African philosophy as 'philosophy' remains fiercely contested. Not only does the very notion of 'philosophy' elude a univocal determination, but the designation 'African' is an unstable concept, impossible to universalize ethnographically, geographically, or by cultural practice and experience. This instability famously drove the Beninois African philosopher, Paulin Hountondji, to problematize attempts to speak of an *African* philosophy, where this 'Africanity' is refracted through an ethnographic prism that imposes an artificial unity of 'primitivism' and otherness of the African mentality relative to a European one. In his rejection of 'ethnophilosophy', he calls into question the approaches of such writers as Alexis Kagame[1] and Placide Tempels[2] on the basis of their presumptuous reduction of difference to an artificial, singular 'African' discourse. This 'ethnophilosophy', then, fails to define African philosophy and falls into the trap of being an 'exotic' production, packaged primarily for the consumption and the habits of thought of non-Africans.[3] This critique brought another African philosopher, D. A. Masolo, to characterize African philosophy in its very practice as a quest for an African identity,[4] or, with Kwasi Wiredu, a 'self-definition' of Africanity.[5]

Hountondji's definition of African philosophy, in its bid to formulate a discourse that immediately and primarily speaks to Africans and their existential concerns, was as follows:

> By 'African philosophy' I mean a set of texts, specifically, the set of texts written by Africans and described as philosophical by their authors themselves. […] African

philosophy does not lie where we have long been seeking it, in some mysterious corner of our supposedly immutable soul, a collective and unconscious world-view which it is incumbent on us to study and revive, but ... consists essentially in the process of analysis itself, in that very discourse through which we have been doggedly attempting to define ourselves – a discourse, therefore, which we must recognize as ideological and which it is now up to us to liberate, in the most political sense of the word, in order to equip ourselves with a truly theoretical discourse which will be indissolubly philosophical and scientific.[6]

These considerations shift the question of African philosophy from delimiting in advance the conditions and scope of its 'philosophical' *content* to simply placing it within the *intention* of the African philosopher to do philosophy. This frees African philosophy from the constraints of an ethnographically determined exoticism and allows for the often-thorny question of *sources* of African philosophy to include whatever sources the African philosopher would employ in his task. The heart of the question then becomes who is primarily being spoken to and spoken for, and what measure of methodological rigour is brought to bear. But Godfrey Tangwa provides needed nuance to Hountondji's position by opening the possibility of 'considering the work of an African philosopher as not being African philosophy or for considering the work of a non-African as African philosophy'.[7]

What is truly at stake is not so much deciding ahead of time what constitutes an African philosophy, specifying its boundaries and deciding its possibilities, especially vis-à-vis some global basket of discourses on philosophy in general and metaphysics in particular. For, to phrase the question this way, one runs into several impasses, not least the challenge of purism, for which the authenticity of an African discourse would be reckoned as compromised by any perceived cross-pollination of ideas or inspiration from other sources. This creates the danger of a discourse so insular and recondite as to escape any possible universality or generalizability. This danger is aggravated because the present state of the debates around African philosophy concedes too much ground, uncritically, to the exclusive determination of philosophy as reason grounded in the transparency of the concept. As such, it leaves unquestioned the very status of reason, and having assumed such a thin meaning of reason, finds it difficult to bring within the orbit of philosophical discourse African forms of religious practice, art, societal institutions and spiritual life.

Though largely in agreement with the thrust of Hountondji's assessments, I shall not follow him all the way to the wholesale rejection of all 'ethnophilosophy' because in critiquing the motivation for the discourses of Tempels and others, he by the same gesture abandons what could be an *empirical* observation of characteristic features of 'African' philosophy (whatever 'African' comes to designate). It is certainly possible that the 'thought of the Africans', and an identification of certain specificities of difference, is an ethnographic construct. However, this need not also be an underlying essentialist construct. It is also possible that, *empirically*, for whatever factors, certain people groups show the predominance of particular forms of thought or habits of practice, some of which are attenuated among other peoples.

It was the Senegalese philosopher, poet and politician, Léopold Sédar Senghor (1906–2001) who most powerfully argued that the determination and content of an African philosophy were to be found in the analysis of its various creative-artistic forms. Here he stands out from previous and later efforts in their attempts to 'distil' philosophical categories from ethnographic and anthropological explorations of Africa.[8] Hence Souleymane Bachir Diagne's comment is apt: 'Art is the proof of African philosophy and, conversely, we reach the full intelligence of African arts only through the understanding of the metaphysics from which they proceed. This metaphysics, to present it in one word, is that of *rhythm*, which according to Senghor is at the heart of the African thought and experience.'[9] Senghor (in)famously stated that 'emotion is black to the same extent that reason is Hellenic'. By this he did not set up emotion and psychological sentimentality of any kind against the would-be superiority of ratiocination, as he has very wrongly been interpreted. Instead, in context, he advanced that what reason represents to Hellenic thought and its Western heritage is analogous to the function of 'emotion' in *African art*. Emotion here is understood in a strictly Bergsonian sense, recovering the original etymology, as the movement or motion that goes 'outward'. Thus, where knowledge by way of reason encapsulates a paradigm in which the subject of knowledge stands over against the object, knowledge by way of emotion produces an alternative gesture of knowing reality by an *ek-static* movement or activity where the knower moves towards and achieves unity with what is to be known. It is precisely a union of rhythmic resonance. Senghor thus sees in African art a privileged site for the phenomenality of this emotive paradigm of knowledge and of the relation to the real.

Thus, the position of Hountondji on the inadmissibility of an 'ethnophilosophy' serves as the springboard for a further deconstruction of a philosophy used to constrain the possibilities of an *African* philosophy. African philosophy would discover itself, in this deconstruction of philosophy as a purely negative enterprise – as concerned with being as the analysis of the subjective *a priori* conditions of knowledge – and would move towards a positive philosophy, in the exploration of the raw facticity of existence (thus beyond Hegel to later Schelling[10]).

This chapter therefore follows Senghor in thinking the priority of African art as the site of an African philosophical imagination – as concerns both being and knowledge. Senghor's intuitions on African art open the terrain for a philosophical methodology on African art and philosophy, which this chapter specifically develops as a philosophy of emotion and of the union of the knower and known, as well as a philosophical account of rhythm as distinctive of an African vision of reality. I begin with the question of the status of philosophy by showing its opening to a 'positive philosophy' (to follow Schelling) beyond reason and, consequently, the opening of philosophy to the dynamism of reason. Secondly, I explore Senghor's philosophy of art through a consideration of the notion of 'emotion' and of rhythm as the philosophical expressions of African art.

Philosophy beyond the foundations of reason

The question, 'what is an *African* philosophy?' necessarily raises the question, 'what is an African *philosophy*?' The problem of a conceptualization of African philosophy is a special instance of the problem of the identity and possibilities of philosophy itself. (This question, 'what is philosophy?', is itself doing philosophy.) Hegel perhaps did the most to bring to its denouement the history of Western as rational philosophy, formalized as a science of the 'concept', determinative of thought and being, and of their interpenetration. For Hegel, 'the Concept is totality; thus, in its identity with itself it is what is in and for itself determinate'.[11] But this well-known determination of philosophy by the negative, together with Schelling's later reaction with his insistence on a positive philosophy, still lies at the heart of a crucial task for philosophy today: as a defining part of its enterprise, philosophy must positively think *that* without which it cannot think – being in its givenness or pure facticity, beyond the preconditions of thinking.

Those who reject the sources of African philosophy in myths, proverbs, songs, legends and sources of orality often do so with the argument that such sources do not meet the criteria of philosophy as a purely rational science. As a result, this account of philosophy naturally precludes the entry of any African discourse that fails to meet this a priori definition – not least African artistic expression and the understanding of being that it encapsulates.

Yet, it is precisely this meaning of 'reason' that is at issue. For, as Merleau-Ponty argued, philosophy must decide whether part of its task involves following the dynamism and progress of reason itself. If philosophy follows the movement of reason, it will be defined thus: 'the willingness to apply reason to what passes for the irrational is itself a progress of reason.'[12] Similarly, Deleuze and Guattari affirm: 'The non-philosophical is perhaps closer to the heart of philosophy than philosophy itself, and this means that philosophy cannot be content to be understood only philosophically or conceptually, but is addressed essentially to non-philosophers as well.'[13] The 'non-philosophical' here is philosophy par excellence to the extent that philosophy aims at the unfolding of being, in all its non totalized/totalizing fulness. As is well-known of Deleuze in particular, the heart of this unfolding of being is not limited to the horizon of temporality but involves pure, unpredictable creation – that is, along the same Bergsonian lines that Senghor used in developing his reflections on African art as the unprecedented making-visible of forces in spontaneous, creative expression. Thus, prior to conscious reflection, we must inhabit what Schelling called the 'unprethinkable', and within the unfolding of this process lies the very dynamic expansion of reason. As Merleau-Ponty would further argue:

> When it comes to defining philosophy vis-à-vis its relation to Oriental thought or to Christianity, we would have to ask ourselves whether the name philosophy would belong only to doctrines that translate into concepts, or whether we could not extend it to experiences, to wisdom traditions, to disciplines that do not reach up to this degree and aspect of consciousness. And thus are we met with the problem of the concept of philosophy and of its nature.[14]

Merleau-Ponty argues against the 'myth of a pure philosophy' that would invent a pure discourse of the concept, abstracted from the movements and realism of life. But at the same time, he pushed back against a 'philosophy' defined as a sum of social and socio-historical contingencies and their interconnections, or as a history of ideas.

So if philosophy is not delimited by reason already closed in on itself as a particular 'rationality' but integrates the order of pure creation and movement, it remains the case that there are spontaneous expressions of this non-reason, which are not *against* reason but can come into reason. It is in the determination of philosophy by *this* kind of dynamic reason that there is a possibility for the entry of art in general, and African art in particular, into philosophy. This is not merely for the benefit of African art (to make African art *philosophical*) but for the sake of philosophy itself – to bring philosophy closer to its deepest sources and to place within it a more robust operative notion of reason. To pave the way, let us first give a brief description of the aesthetic aspects of African art and sculpture.

African art and sculpture

Sources for the analyses of African art and sculpture abound, richly varying in their approaches, including the historical, socio-religious, aesthetic, ethnographic, psychological and archaeological, among others.[15] For our purposes, it is particularly useful to briefly consider the qualities of an African sculpture to illustrate the philosophical themes to be drawn out further below. I have argued, with Senghor, that in the practices of African art lies the expression of an African philosophy, and that the instance of this African philosophy is itself a critique of a narrow account of 'philosophy' as a negatively rational project. The African mask tradition particularly embodies aspects of this thesis. The mask tradition of sub-Saharan Africa is known for its features of high abstraction, its deep embeddedness within religious traditions and secret societies, its depiction of mythical figures, the mingling of human and animal features as well as the highlighting of exaggerated, overall unnatural human features. As many commentators have noted, in African sculpture the predominance of the movement of force and of interiority over form and exterior representation controls the distribution of the material mass of the sculpture. This animating force, understood primarily as an unseen, spiritual, vital energy, lends the sculpture its dominant animistic character.

The features of the *kpelie* mask (see Figure 1) of the Senufo tribe in Mali and northern Côte d'Ivoire illustrate this. Used primarily at special festivals and in the context of tribal rituals, it is worn by authorized members of secret societies after the appropriate ritualistic preparations and then used to perform dances. The mask itself combines human and animal features, having the overall outline of a human face flanked by inverted animal horns jutting out from the sides. Symmetry is of minimal concern, as in the asymmetrical protrusion and dominance of the forehead in the human facial outline. A common feature of African sculpture, this disproportion of the forehead was meant to emphasize the powers of the spirit and their residence in the head. The lines of scarification on the face and their convergence around the very centre of the forehead further capture this concentration of the life force in the head. Carved from a single piece of wood, one can notice the organization of the mass along a vertical plane, even though that flow seems interrupted by horizontally moving protrusions of the horns. The narrow slits that serve as the eyes, together with the aloof arching of the eyebrows, and the expressionless smooth polish of the face convey almost no emotion except one of impassioned serenity. And yet, this sense is punctuated by a certain vicious hideousness of the mouth and a tooth sticking out of it. Unlike the mouth in classical Greek sculpture, for example, which is used to convey emotive parsimony and distance, here the mouth conveys an appetitive voraciousness even within an outlook of serenity. This is the quest for the interior balance and harmony of opposing forces within the embodied unity of the creative medium, even when the exterior forms of the sculpture appear superficially contradictory. The mask itself materially dramatizes and resolves these ontological tensions. This harmony is further seen in the very ritual employment of the mask; at the climax of the frenetic rhythmic drumming and ritualistic dance ceremonies at which the mask was worn, there was a certain slippage or transmutation of the performer who takes up and is subsumed by the spirits of the mask. Thus, the supposed rigid ontological distinctions between the dancer's person and the reality of the mask – tensions already enacted in the sculpted unit – become absorbed in the reality of a more originary unity that blurs the demarcation between the animalistic and the human, between spirit and material, and ultimately plays out the continuous animation of both by the same productive life force. Thus, in this perspective, art not merely imitates nature but more essentially dramatizes the participation of realities in the same creative forces that birth and sustain nature in its movement.

The essential characteristics of African sculpture therefore embody and dramatize a certain way of Being, which warrants philosophical reflection. Munro and Guillaume identify some features of interest:

> Every part in a typical, fully realized [African] statue functions as an element in plastic design; an embodiment, a repetition in rhythmic, varied sequence, of some theme in mass, line or surface. To be transformed into a design, the human figure must be regarded in a way quite different from that of ordinary life and of most sculpture. It must not be seen as an inviolable whole, treated as one unit and merely posed in this attitude or that. The figure must be dissociated into its parts, regarded as an aggregate of distinct units: the head, limbs, breasts, trunk and so on, each by itself. So distinguished and usually marked off by a surrounding groove or hollow, each part can be moulded into a variation of some chosen theme – a sharp, slender projection, or perhaps a smooth, bulbous swelling – never exactly the same as its neighbours, for that would be monotonous; never too far from nature, or completely abstract, for that would destroy its interest as representation, its relevancy to the world of human experience. In the same figure an artist may introduce two or more radically different shapes, perhaps repeating and slightly varying each one. Such contrast gives, as in music, an arresting and interesting shock to the observer. It carries with it a possible loss of unity; the whole piece may seem to fall apart, to be confusingly unrelated. Then the genius of the artist consists in finding means to weld the contrasting themes together by some note common to both.[16]

In considering African art in general, it is important not to privilege the representational as the structure of the aesthetic experience. With African plastic arts, it is unfruitful to be guided by the questions: 'What is this figure an instance of?' 'How successfully (or not) does it capture its model?' 'What forms and aesthetic instruments does the artist deploy to achieve his purpose?' Rather, as Ladislas Segy has commented, 'the deep significance of African art lies in the incorporation and expression of the emotional states of man at the stage of his awakening as individual. Through it we can rediscover and set in vibration, with an organic, emotional shock, our own dawning impulses as a human being.'[17]

The inspiration of rhythmic movement, then, means literally that the African sculptor is understood as giving original creative life to a sculpture by allowing it to express an elemental anima through the mediation of his craft. Thus, Segy comments further, 'an African sculptor's belief that he created life was incomparably greater in its assurance than the 'symbolic' or 'representational' approach of the Western artist to his work'.[18] The *animism* at work here is not simply a belief in the ensouled nature of objects but *also* a creative act of enlivening things in novel material-spiritual instantiations. Segy defines the mask as 'the "figure", the "thing done", created with direct, spontaneous gestures to contain what man senses to be beyond form. [...] a structure of expressive forms, fused with a secret life of its own … born of a style unaware of itself'.[19] Thus, the African mask is a kind of creative incarnation, a giving body to the invisible and formless.

Along with this animism, we can highlight the aspect of the *impersonal* or non-subjectivist expression in the animism of the African mask tradition. The mask makes it difficult to project into it a subjective, personalist interiority or human psychology. It underscores that a creative intuition (of the artist) lies at the heart of this making visible of an intuited spiritual world in the materiality of the artistic medium. This is not simply a generalized animism, and it is particularly unhelpful to characterize this as 'superstition'. Rituals and sacred performances often served as technologies of control over the capriciousness of the unknown, to tame the unpredictability of nature and better the human condition. The disparaging moniker of 'primitive superstition' – often used carelessly, under ethnographical inspiration – not only misses the more interesting phenomenon at work but also fails to recognize the strong affinity between the impulse behind material technology and spiritual practices to order and harmonize the forces of the unknown.

Philosophy and African art: Emotion and a philosophy of rhythm

'Emotion is negro, as reason is Hellenistic' (*L'émotion est nègre, comme la raison est hellène*).[20] This formula, written in 1939 by Senghor in an early article famously titled '*Ce que l'homme noir apporte*' (what the Black man contributes), was envisaged by the young poet, co-founder of the *Négritude* movement and later president of Senegal, to make explicit the unique contribution of an African (and more globally 'Black') sensibility to life and ways of seeing the world. He was convinced that the African mind individuates and 'weaves' universal forces in a way that constitutes an original African consciousness:

> People will say that the spirit of the Civilization and the laws of Negro-African's Culture, as I have exposited them, are not exclusively valid for the Negro-African, but are shared by other peoples. I do not deny it. Every people unites on its face the various features of the human condition. But what I say is that we find nowhere these features together united in this equilibrium, under this light; nowhere has rhythm reigned so despotically. Nature did well in making sure that each people, each race, each continent has cultivated, with a particular dilection, certain virtues of Man; which is what constitutes its originality.[21]

But what is it for 'emotion' to constitute the original Black contribution to a universal human spirit, and what is it for 'reason' to be Hellenic? The phrase occasioned much controversy and misunderstanding, not least for the suggestion, if only on the surface, of a mutually exclusive opposition between emotion and reason, and the seeming implication that the latter escapes a Black mentality. Senghor's phrase was understood to ascribe to the Black mentality an 'emotionalism' expressed in the spontaneity and exuberance of its various cultural expressions (festivals, dance, singing, plastic arts), and devoid of discursive reason and logic.

Years later, in 1956, Senghor modified the statement to bring further precision: 'European reason is analytic in its use, negro reason is intuitive by participation' (*la raison européenne est analytique par utilisation, la raison nègre intuitive par participation*).[22] This second formulation shows that what was initially envisaged by Senghor as 'emotion' pertains to a particular order of *reason* identified as 'intuitive reason', and that its *other* (without conceding any relation of opposition and mutual exclusion between them) is 'analytic reason'. Secondly, while analytic reason is executed by '*utilisation*', that is, analogically to the way a subject deploys a tool, intuitive reason operates by way of '*participation*', which implies a certain becoming and being-taken-up of the subject into a different order of being and knowing. Thus, emotion and reason would specify orders of reality, and various depths and intensities of the patency of the real.

Later still, Senghor would come to acknowledge the many misinterpretations of his initial proposal and further clarify it in the following way:

> I know that the enemies of Negritude, who claim to be Marxists, accuse me of having written: 'Emotion is Negro as reason is Hellene'. And they have concluded that I deny Negroes every power of reasoning and of reason. But how would they know what I wanted to say by isolating a sentence from its context? For, evidently, here 'emotion' means 'intuitive reason', in a similar way as African Americans use the word '*soul*'; and 'reason', European reason here means the 'discursive'.[23]

The obvious ambiguities of Senghor's formula aside, the misrepresentations of it seem so agenda laden as to see him affirming a patently objectionable position: 'Africans have no reason.' Thus, Senghor's strong rejection: 'the Negro is not void of *reason*, as they have wanted to make me say.'[24] But this rejection brings us back, positively this time, to the status and meaning of emotion as distinctive of an African spirit. What exactly was meant by it and how might we understand its constitutive role in an African philosophical thinking?

In his resourceful study on the Bergsonian sources of Senghor's thought, Souleymane Bachir Diagne comments that the African philosopher particularly receives from Bergson

> the way he opens new possibilities of thinking outside a philosophical tradition which, at a point in history, took a particular turn, so that what was *logos*, understood as comprehending the unity of life, became distended into a *ratio* or, in other words, an intelligence that, in order to know its object, detaches it from itself and divides it into parts that are only mechanically linked – that is, that which extends in space.[25]

Thus, Senghor's 'bergsonism' is established as a quest for the recovery of a fuller meaning of the very *logos* of philosophy. But as Diagne further notes, this is not merely a critique of philosophical reason but the positive proposal of a way out of the constitution of knowledge as *ratio* to a new determination of *philosophy* in 'non-philosophy' through a vital knowing of the real. Senghor particularly sees African art as the manifestation of this knowing in 'the access to the sub-reality of visible things'.[26] This connection to African art as the manifestation of this major gesture within philosophy itself, mediated through Bergson, is decisive for Senghor's thought, which can be 'distilled to a reflection upon African art'.[27]

This centrality of African art as a primary manifestation of the African spirit and therefore of philosophical thought is established in what Senghor understood by 'emotion'. According to Bergson, 'emotion is the source of great creations of art, of science and of civilisation' not only because it is a driving impulse to this activity but more originally because emotion pertains to the depths of being. 'An emotion is an affective stirring of the soul, but a surface agitation is one thing, an upheaval of the depths another.'[28] This is both an understanding of emotion as a reactive and responsive affect, and the more primary sense of emotion that Bergson exposits as belonging to 'feeling' (*sentiment*), or better, to the intuition of the heart. For, 'beneath intelligent activity, forced in fact to choose between its own interests and those of others, there lies *a substratum of instinctive activity*, originally implanted there by nature, where the individual and the social are well-nigh indistinguishable'.[29] This obscure activity lying beneath intellectual activity, this activity of the deepest interiority of the heart (*sentiment*), which Bergson saw as in-forming the activity of all being, necessitates that the very means of knowing involves a 'sympathetic' chiming with the rhythm of being – a being-taken-up where new emotions are not simply introduced into us, but we are introduced into them, 'as passers-by are forced into a street to dance'.[30]

Thus, underneath the infrastructure of representation, and differing from art that is primarily representational, there is another perception that involves 'entering' the emotion or creative force that inspires a work of art. Bergson concedes that certain productions of the intelligence, by the right combinations of ideas and forms, can produce emotional effects. However, emotion 'in this second sense' is *cause* and not effect: it defines a 'supra-intellectual' order of knowing, where there is an experience that is more original and pertains to the ontological.[31] This is the distinction between an 'infra-intellectual' knowing and a 'supra-intellectual' one. We are faced, as Emmanuel Levinas would describe it in a critique of the so-called 'primitive mentality' of Lévy-Bruhl's ethnography, with the 'difference that separates two depths of the soul, rather than with two souls'.[32] Thus, Bergson articulates a double-tiered consideration of reason: 'Alongside the emotion which is a result of representation, and which is added to it, there is the emotion which precedes the image, which virtually contains it, and is to a certain extent its cause.'[33] Moreover:

It is emotion which drives the intelligence forward in spite of obstacles. It is emotion above all which vivifies, or rather vitalises, the intellectual elements with which it is destined to unite, constantly collecting everything that can be worked in with them and finally compelling the enunciation of the problem to expand its solution. And what about literature and art? A work of genius is in most cases the outcome of an emotion, unique of its kind, which seemed to baffle expression, and yet which *had* to express itself.[34]

Thus, the work of art pertains to the purest expression of this movement of emotion. African thought must therefore fully emerge from the long shadow of ethnology and its operative theories of primitivism to embrace the working of other aspects of reason.

African art as philosophy

Senghor's thesis remains that the creative intuition expressed in African art *is* philosophy. It is not merely that a philosophy can be distilled from it or, worse, that one should philosophize *upon* African art. Rather, it is the affirmation that the creative impulse – the creative *e-motion* – that expresses itself in African art, when the artist has been seized by a pure creative intuition, *is* the very ground of philosophy. Following Bergson's formula adopted by Senghor in his reading of African art, 'emotion alone [is] productive of ideas' or concepts of the intelligence. For Senghor, African art is supremely expressive of the vitalism of this movement of emotion and encapsulates a certain ontology of rhythm.[35]

Before turning to the philosophical import of rhythm, let us briefly explore this philosophical expression of African art. Placide Tempels, for all the criticism levelled at his enterprise in its claims to a 'Bantu philosophy', had identified the essence of Bantu 'wisdom' or way of life and thought in 'the penetrating vision into the nature of beings and forces'. In other words, this is a 'philosophy of forces', a metaphysics that is defined and traversed through and through by Force in all its complex hierarchies and dynamisms, from the so-called inanimate, through the biological, to the most sublime cadres of the spiritual and invisible.[36] Thus, 'being' *is* force, and the 'to be' is only intuited in the apperception of activity, movement, and resistance. Senghor would agree with the essence of Tempels' proposal and further elaborate on this 'existential ontology' of force as the matrix of any African thinking.

Furthermore, the German ethnologist and archaeologist, Leo Frobenius (1873–1938), who would have an important influence on Senghor, was one of the earliest to identify an African aesthetic with a defining rhythmic movement of force that takes precedence over an analytic combination of forms and points of view.

> This is the character of the African style. Anyone who has come close to it enough to get a real understanding of it will recognise that it prevails *throughout Africa* as the very expression its being. It manifests itself in the movements of all Negro peoples as much as in their plastic art; it speaks in their dances and in their masks, in their religious sentiment as well as in their ways of living, the nature of their State and their destiny as a people. It lives in their fables, fairy tales, sagas, myths.[37]

Another thinker, Pierre Baye-Salzmann, who strongly influenced Senghor's position,[38] in the same vein, and on a Bergsonian register, argues that the source of all creative endeavour lies in a fundamental tension defined by an experience of the interior tragedy of our expulsion (a kind of Neoplatonic *exitus*) from the originary ground of being, the experience in duration of our resistance to death, and the possibility of reconnection with the origin (*reditus*) only by way of participation in an eternal creation.[39] This originary source, he maintains, expresses itself differently among various people groups. For, where the mind of the Occident firmly holds on to the abiding role of a conscious subjectivity and its hypostatic persistence qua *sub*stance, which thus de-emphasizes experiences of the undoing of the self or of 'desubjectivation' that is more visible in practices elsewhere, the African sensibility, for its part, seeks to enter into the 'flow' of a mystical return to the originary and uses its art to express or capture the forces of the instinctual. Thus, 'the Black takes intuitive sensibility as objective and draws from it the religious and poetic expression of the beyond and its thousand points of interrogation. Thence the deaf dynamism of his art, emerging directly from pure mystical passion.'[40] On this basis, African art necessarily has a 'spiritual' essence, not because of a modern determination of the spiritual against a would-be 'natural' order, but rather by a spontaneous expression, a creative experimentation with the mystical experience of instinctual forces of the originary.

Senghor brings these considerations together in a robust conceptualization of African art and its philosophical import:

> The ordering force that constitutes Negro style is *rhythm*. It is the most sensible and the least material thing. It is the vital element par excellence. It is the first condition and the sign of art, like the breath of life; the breath which rushes or slows down, becomes regular or spasmodic, following the tension of being, the degree and the quality of the emotion. Such is rhythm primitively, in its purity, so it appears in the masterpieces of Negro art, particularly in sculpture. It is made up of a theme – sculptural shape – which is opposed to a kindred theme, the way inspiration is opposed to expiration, and it resumes itself. It is not symmetry which generates monotony; the rhythm is vivid, it is free. Because resumption is not repetition, nor is it duplication. The theme is resumed in another place, on another plane, in another combination, in a variation; and it produces another intonation, another tone, another accent. And the whole effect is intensified, but not without nuances. And so rhythm acts upon what is the least intellectual in us, despotically, to make us penetrate into the *spirituality of the object*; and this attitude of surrender that we have, is itself rhythmic.[41]

This surrender to the rhythmic forces undoes the despotism of the subject by a mystical experimentation that brings it closer and closer to an originary experience of the impersonal.[42] This desubjectivizing experience undoes the logic of art by representation, which depends on the persistence of the subject and its conscious self-presence. This means that the 'philosophical' in African art, as Senghor envisages it, is deeply connected to spiritual exercise and mystical experience. Such experience signifies entry into more bare forms of life and of existence, more universal in scope and more wildly creative in manifestation. Senghor's philosophy is thus profoundly influenced by Bergson who writes:

> In this way, intuition will be able to bring the intellect to recognize that life fully enters neither into the category of the many nor into that of the one, and that neither mechanical causality nor finality offer a sufficient translation of the vital process. Then, through the sympathetic communication that it will establish between us and the rest of the living beings, through the dilation that it will obtain of our consciousness, intuition will introduce us into the domain of life itself, which is reciprocal interpenetration and indefinitely continuous creation.[43]

This meant for Senghor that what is originally expressed in an 'African style' of art and life is not *un*philosophical but is *otherwise* philosophical. Senghor does not make a big deal of the colonialist and paternalistic overtones often implied in the designation of African art as 'primitive'. For him, African art is and remains 'primitive' in the original sense of the Latin *primitivus* – the primal, the original and originary fount, and thus the creative impulse from which artistic expression springs. Rather, primitive African art stands as a critique of the European tradition. For, in not being close to its primitive, originary impulses, in exchanging the chthonic vital forces for empty aesthetic forms, art loses the primal and the rhythmic force of being. African ('Negro') art thus remains 'tied to the cosmos, close to the vital sources of *emotion*, of the psychic depths of ancient cities. Close to the gods, close to God'.[44]

So what is rhythm?

> It is the architecture of being, the internal dynamic conferring form, the system of waves given off towards the *Others*, the pure expression of the life-force. It is the vibrating shock, the power which, through the sense, seizes at the roots of our *being*. It finds expression through the most material and sensual media: line, surface, colour, volume in architecture, sculpture and painting; accent in poetry and music; movement in the dance. But, in doing this, it directs all this concrete material towards the light of the *Spirit*. For the Negro-African, it is only insofar as it is incarnate in sensuality that rhythm illuminates the Spirit.[45]

When Senghor discerns the essence of African art (and sculpture in particular) as rhythm, he means that rhythm is the very grammar of being. It constitutes the structure and meaning of being, and the very means by which being expresses itself. By rhythm, Senghor means not merely the metric, quantified units of time as ordered to a certain pulse of continuity. Rather, more radically, he has in view something closer to Bergson's determination of being as duration (*durée*).⁴⁶ As is well known of Bergson's chief philosophical breakthrough, the temporality of being is not measured or quantifiable, spatialized time. Rather, time *qua* duration expresses a fundamental, indivisible, continuous unity and is the site of invention, creation and the emergence of novelty. Being as duration escapes the pre-given determinacies of forms but speaks to the *becoming* proper to a creative force. It is in this sense, then, that rhythm is the expression of being; it is the very movement of creative emergence. The temporality of rhythm that Senghor associates ontologically with African artistic expression is therefore that of *duration* as explored by Bergson:

> The universe endures. The deeper our study of the nature of time, the more we will come to understand that *durée* signifies invention, the creation of forms, and the continuous development of the absolutely new. […] It is necessary to distinguish between two opposing movements within the universe itself: one that 'descends', another that 'ascends'. The first does nothing but unroll a ready-made roll. This movement could in principle happen in an almost instantaneous way, such as when a spring is released. But the second, which corresponds to an inner work of maturation or of creation, essentially endures, and thereby imposes its rhythm on the first movement, which is inseparable from it.⁴⁷

This Bergsonian account of a double movement, especially the second movement of creation with which he associates rhythm and duration, is present in Senghor's imagery of a dynamic 'wave' of a life-force – a wave of troughs and crests, intimately interrelated, and informing the rhythm of spirit and materiality in African sculpture.

Rhythm, we have seen, is the expression of force. As Leo Apostel summarizes the elements of what Tempels had referred to as 'Bantu philosophy', the very *thisness* of a thing, the individuation and existence of anything are the result of force and rhythm. Thus, '"Something exists" means that something exercises a certain force. [… and] What constitutes the individuality of a given force is its rhythm'.⁴⁸ This 'architecture', as Senghor expresses it, or as Apostels further comments, this 'hierarchical and pluralistic energetism that is described as Africa's most original contribution to philosophy […] should find its expression in African art'.⁴⁹ But as we have argued earlier, the philosophical interest of such an account lies in the fact that it says something universal about being, through the particular instance of an African experience. To this extent, 'the harmonious combination of rhythms in a work of art depends on a force-rhythm that orders the whole into an indivisible organic unity'.⁵⁰ (There is perhaps a distant echo in all this of a very different metaphysics – the Chinese *Dao* and its fundamental principles of *qi* and *li*? See Chapters 2 and 3 in this volume.)

The implication of this identification of force-rhythm with the essence of African art can be taken even further. As a creative intuition that expresses the rhythm of force, especially in its sculpture and masks, the African artistic expression captures Paul Klee's famous formula: *not to render* the *visible, but to render visible*. But what is to be rendered visible? In the formulation of Nietzsche, it is the primordial 'chaos', the chthonic, originary depth from which an ordered plane of sensibility arises and into which order disaggregates and returns to anonymity and indifference. What Klee called the 'Void', Paul Cezanne called 'Chaos'. Hegel gestured in the same direction by speaking of the night of the concept, that is, the 'creative secret' which the concept cannot as such penetrate but from which there would be the 'birth' and emergence of the concept into luminosity.[51] Chaos as the site of the 'non-concept', of 'nothingness', of undetermined obscurity has always been the background and ever-present origin of philosophy itself.[52] This lies behind the identification by Deleuze and Guattari, in *What Is Philosophy?*, of the philosopher, the artist and the scientist, in their respective ways, as carrying out the same enterprise of casting planes of intelligibility and of protective shielding over the chaos of 'madness and hysteria':

> What the philosopher brings back from the chaos are variations that are still infinite but that have become inseparable on the absolute surfaces or in the absolute volumes that lay out a secant plane of immanence: these are not associations of distinct ideas, but reconnections through a zone of indistinction in a concept. The scientist brings back from the chaos variables that have become independent by slowing down, that is to say, by the elimination of whatever other variabilities are liable to interfere, so that the variables that are retained enter into determinable relations in a function: they are no longer links of properties in things, but finite coordinates on a secant plane of reference that go from local probabilities to a global cosmology. The artist brings back from the chaos varieties that no longer constitute a reproduction of the sensory in the organ but set up a being of the sensory, a being of sensation, on an anorganic plane of composition that is able to restore the infinite.[53]

In his essay, 'The Aesthetic of Rhythms' ('*L'esthétique des rythmes*'), Henri Maldiney would identify two moments in this struggle: first, a response of overwhelming disconcertion in the face of Chaos, caused by the undoing of a subjective centre of sense, of the situatedness of place, and of the consistency of the world.[54] The second moment is rhythm – the very point where the overwhelming vertiginous experience becomes the site of an emergence from chaos. 'In the beginning was rhythm.' Maldiney here thematizes rhythm as the expression of an impulse that itself emerges from the force of the primordial.[55] It was Paul Klee who elaborated this notion of rhythm as an emergence from Chaos in his description of the 'grey point having the double function of being both chaos and at the same time a rhythm insofar as it dynamically jumps over itself'.[56] The notion of the 'grey point', for Klee, represents the non-oppositional co-existence of Chaos and Cosmos; the state of the virtual, between coming-into-being and passing-away. This immanent virtuality is a cosmogenesis, and for Klee explains all the stages of artwork coming-into-being. When the artist turns his attention to things in the world, it is to discern the immanent movement of their cosmogenesis; when he constructs a work, it is out of an intuition of the same cosmogenesis and movement from chaos. As Deleuze and Guattari further elaborate, 'art indeed struggles with chaos, but it does so in order to bring forth a vision that illuminates it for an instant, a Sensation. [...] Art is not chaos but a composition of chaos that yields the vision or sensation, so that it constitutes it, as Joyce says, a chaosmos, a composed chaos – neither foreseen nor preconceived.'[57]

Deleuze, in his study on Francis Bacon, insisted upon the radical shift in ways of perceiving that are required by some creative productions. Chiefly, the reality of rhythm means that the ground of the unity of senses and of sense is not in the unity of the biological organization of the forms as seen in the *organism*. The aesthetic experience of the face, for example, usually expects of the artistic expression various physiological and psychological causes, structural unities and emotional processes extrapolated from the experience of the biological face. There is a decisive disruption of this experience in African art, especially the mask tradition. In place of this, as we have seen, the emotive, rhythmic flow of force organizes the material mass according to criteria of movement.

In this rhythm, the raw movement of creative forces of becoming imposes its own dynamic 'organizing', its own way of *in*-forming.[58] This was what Deleuze, following Antonin Artaud, conceptualized as a 'body-without-organs'. It is body as liberated from the forms and limits of the organism but opened to the influence of forces to which it gives expression. It is the body as the site of a manifestative 'vital emotion'. The body without organs is the conceptualization of a state of the body that has 'No mouth. No tongue. No larynx. No oesophagus. No belly. No anus.'[59] To the extent that this body is not constituted in its essence by the unity of forms and aggregation of organic parts, the artistic expression of the body-without-organs is not one of representational forms, of the aesthetic repetition of a biological unity of forms, but of forces acting on, in and through the body. As Deleuze further comments, 'when sensation is linked to the body in this way, it ceases to be representative and becomes real; and *cruelty* will be linked less and less to the representation of something horrible, and will become nothing other than the action of forces upon the body, or sensation'.[60] This body then escapes the limitations of the forms of flesh and deprioritizes the formal consistencies by which the fleshly mass is supposed to gather itself. Rather, the logic of sensation that continually in-forms the body-without-organs consists in an 'intensive reality, allotropic variations', 'axes and vectors, zones, kinematic movements', etc. In this sense, art is, according to Marcel Duchamp, 'a road which leads towards regions that are no longer governed by time and space'.[61]

The vitalism implied in this account of an emotive sensibility over an intellective one, therefore, envisages a different account of spatiality, one that in a way 'collapses' the separation between interiority and exteriority, between a cogitative 'inside' and the 'external' world that must be connected to by a representational act. Senghor envisaged emotion as a movement that creates its own kind of spatiality of continuous in-folding and out-folding. An emotive intuition comes to perception by way of an intuitive apperception. As a result, space is not a matrix of indifference, a milieu given in advance to situate objects, nor is it an operator of the boundedness of objects and their differentiation from each other. Instead, in an account of creative force, spatiality (as well as temporality) is constituted in the very production or expenditure of forces of movement. Deleuze explains it when he affirms that the essence of movement, before any external differentiation, is a creative actualization that creates its own space and time.[62] 'For in the dynamic order there is no representative concept, nor any figure represented in a pre-existing space. There is an Idea, and a pure dynamism which creates a corresponding space.'[63]

Figure 1 *Kpélié* mask, Senoufo-Dioula, Côte d'Ivoire. Wood and pigment. Owned by The Art Institute of Chicago, Chicago. Reproduced with permission.

Conclusion

After thinking along with Senghor and expanding his intuitions on African art and philosophy, we can therefore conclude that at the heart of this relationship is the very critique of philosophy itself. Senghor's philosophy of African art is a philosophical endeavour precisely in its opening of new horizons upon philosophy. Thus, philosophy would be a reckoning of the elemental, the originary movement of force expressed in emotion and rhythm. African art, in its aesthetic qualities, and supremely in the spontaneous, creative inspiration that informs its production, is thus a fundamental expression of being. To this extent, philosophy is pushed towards thinking the unthought of artistic experience. The phenomena of e-motion and of rhythm, then, are the privileged sites of thought in an African philosophy. This is the guiding thesis of Senghor's proposal, as elaborated and extended above. Two theses on African philosophy are thus advanced: first, that African philosophy, and philosophical discourse itself, involves mining the originary creative emotion of which philosophy itself is *one* mode of discourse. Secondly, African philosophy involves an engagement with thinkers who are self-consciously involved with any discourse that is inspired by, pertains to and is concerned with Africa and its heritage. But in the very particularity of this tradition, something of the universal is preserved; the artistic inspiration and expression of African art speak not only of Africans but of being.

Notes

1. Kagame (1956).
2. Tempels (2013 [1945]).
3. Hountondji (1996).
4. Masolo (1994).
5. Wiredu et al. (2004).
6. Hountondji (1983: 20–5, 20).
7. Tangwa (2017): 19–33, 31.
8. Mbiti (1970).
9. Diagne (2007: 51–68, 53).
10. For a summary of this distinction, see Dews (2023).
11. Hegel (1991: §160, 236).
12. Merleau-Ponty (2014[1946]: 64).
13. Deleuze and Guattari (1994: 41).
14. Merleau-Ponty (2000: 154).
15. For example: McClusky (2002); Bacquart (1998); Nicolas, Martin, and Kerchache, (1997); Blier (1995); Sasser (1995); Segy (1976); Segy (1975); Thompson (1974); Laude (1973).

16. Guillaume and Munro (1926: 36–7).
17. Segy, *African Sculpture Speaks*, 110.
18. Segy, *African Sculpture Speaks*, 8.
19. Segy, *Masks of Black Africa*, 10.
20. Senghor (1977: 24).
21. Senghor (1964: 216). Quoted and translated in Diagne (2007: 51–68, 63).
22. Senghor, *Liberté I: Négritude et Humanisme*, 202.
23. Senghor (1977: 283).
24. Senghor, *Liberté I: Négritude et Humanisme*, 203.
25. Diagne (2020: 12). (Translation is mine).
26. Diagne, *Bergson postcolonial*, 12.
27. Diagne, *Bergson postcolonial*, 23.
28. Bergson, *The Two Sources of Morality and Religion*, 43.
29. Bergson, *The Two Sources of Morality and Religion*, 36 [emphasis added].
30. Bergson, *The Two Sources of Morality and Religion*, 40.
31. Bergson, *The Two Sources of Morality and Religion*, 44.
32. Lévinas (1957: 556–69, 557).
33. Bergson, *The Two Sources of Morality and Religion*, 47.
34. Bergson, *The Two Sources of Morality and Religion*, 46.
35. For an elaboration of Senghor's philosophy of African art and the defining 'rhythmic attitude' of this art, see Diagne (2019: 43–81).
36. Tempels (1949: 49–51).
37. Frobenius (1936: 16).
38. Diagne, *Léopold Sédar Senghor, l'art africain comme philosophie*, 100. Cf. Hymans (1971).
39. Baye-Salzmann (1992: 300–1).
40. Baye-Salzmann, 'L'art nègre, son inspiration, ses apports à l'Occident', 301.
41. Senghor (1967: 6–9 +52, 9). I have used the translation of this pericope provided by Diagne (2007: 51–68).
42. This has important resonances with the (non)philosophical experimentation on the impersonal described by such authors as Maurice Blanchot, or with Emmanuel Levinas on the depersonalization of subjectivity in *there is* (*il y a*), or indeed with the questions of desubjectivation explored by Michel Foucault and Gilles Deleuze.
43. Bergson (2023: 159–60).
44. Senghor (1967: 6–9+52, 7).
45. Senghor, 'L'esthétique négro-africaine', in *Liberté I*, 211–12. [Taken from Diagne, 'Rhythms: L.S. Senghor's Negritude as a Philosophy of African Art', 59.].
46. Senghor's connection to Bergson is known. He considers his thought, especially vis-à-vis his philosophy of art, as an off spring of the 'revolution of 1789' that was Bergson's *Essai sur les données immédiates de la conscience* [trans. *Time and Freewil: An essay on the immediate data of consciousness*]. See Diagne (2020).
47. Bergson, *Creative Evolution*, 17.
48. Apostels (1981: 26–9).
49. Apostels, *African Philosophy: Myth or Reality*, 325.

50. Apostels, *African Philosophy: Myth or Reality*, 29.
51. Hegel (2017: 398).
52. Heidegger (1991: 82–97). For the history of nothingness in Western philosophy, see Laurent and Romano (2010).
53. Deleuze and Guattari, *What Is Philosophy?*: 202–3.
54. Maldiney (1973: 147–72).
55. Maldiney (1973).
56. Klee (1961).
57. Deleuze and Guattari (1994: 204).
58. Deleuze (2004: 39). 'This ground, this rhythmic unity of the senses, can be discovered only by going beyond the organism. The phenomenological hypothesis is perhaps insufficient because it merely invokes the lived body. But the lived body is still a paltry thing in comparison with a more profound and almost unliveable Power [*puissance*]. We can seek the unity of rhythm only at the point where rhythm itself plunges into chaos, into the night, at the point where the differences of level are perpetually and violently mixed.'
59. Deleuze, *Francis Bacon*, 39–40.
60. Deleuze, *Francis Bacon*, 40.
61. Duchamp as quoted by Guattari (1995: 101).
62. Deleuze (1994: 214).
63. Deleuze, *Difference and Repetition*, 20.

References

Apostels, Leo (1981), *African Philosophy: Myth or Reality*. Ghent: Story-Scientia.
Bacquart, Jean-Baptiste (1998), *The Tribal Arts of Africa*. New York: Thames and Hudson.
Baye-Salzmann, Pierre (1992), 'L'art nègre, son inspiration, ses apports à l'Occident', in *La Revue du Monde Noir 1931-1932*. Paris: Jean-Michel Place.
Bergson, Henri (1977), *The Two Sources of Morality and Religion,* trans. R. Ashley Audra and Cloudesley Brereton. Notre Dame, IN: University of Notre Dame Press.
Bergson, Henri (2001), *Essai sur les données immédiates de la conscience*. Paris: PUF.
Bergson, Henri (2023), *Creative Evolution,* trans. Donald A. Landes. Abingdon, Oxon; New York: Routledge.
Blier, Suzanne P. Preston (1995), *African Vodun: Art, Psychology, and Power*. Chicago, IL, and London: University of Chicago Press.
Deleuze, Gilles (1994), *Difference and Repetition*. New York: Columbia University Press.
Deleuze, Gilles (2004), *Francis Bacon: The Logic of Sensation*. Minneapolis, MN: University of Minnesota Press.
Deleuze, Gilles, and Felix Guattari (1994), *What Is Philosophy?*, European Perspectives. New York: Columbia University Press.

Dews, Peter (2023), *Schelling's Late Philosophy in Confrontation with Hegel*. New York: Oxford University Press.

Diagne, Souleymane Bachir (2007), 'Rhythms: L. S. Senghor's Negritude as a Philosophy of African Art', *Critical Interventions* 1 (1) (January): 51–68.

Diagne, Souleymane Bachir (2019), *Léopold Sédar Senghor, l'art africain comme philosophie*. Pépites. Paris: Riveneuve.

Diagne, Souleymane Bachir (2020), *Bergson Postcolonial*, Biblis 218. Paris: CNRS éditions.

Frobenius, Leo (1936), *Histoire de la Civilisation Africaine*, trans. H. Back and D. Ermont. Paris: Gallimard.

Guattari, Felix, (1995), *Chaosmosis: An Ethico-aesthetic Paradigm*, trans. Paul Bains and Julian Pefanis. Bloomington, IN/ London: Indiana University Press.

Guillaume, Paul, and Thomas Munro (1926), *Primitive Negro Sculpture*. New York: Harcourt, Brace.

Hegel, G. W. F. (1991), *The Encyclopaedia Logic*, trans. Suchting and Harris Geraets. Cambridge, MA: Hackett.

Hegel, G. W. F. (2018), *Georg Wilhelm Friedrich Hegel: The Phenomenology of Spirit*, trans. Terry P. Pinkard, The American Society of Missiology Series, No. 55. New York: Cambridge University Press.

Heidegger, Martin *Nietzsche*. II, trans. David Farrell Krell, 2 vols. San Francisco, CA: HarperSanFrancisco.

Hountondji, Paulin (1983), 'On African Philosophy', *Radical Philosophy* 35 (Autumn): 20–5.

Hountondji, Paulin (1996), *African Philosophy: Myth and Reality*, 2nd ed, African Systems of Thought. Bloomington, IN: Indiana University Press.

Hymans, Jacques Louis (1971), *Léopold Sédar Senghor: An Intellectual Biography*. Edinburgh: Edinburgh University Press.

Kagame, Alexis (1956), *La Philosophie Bantu-Rwandaise de l'Être*. Brussels: Académie Royale des Sciences d'Outre-Mer.

Klee, Paul (1961), *Notebooks. Volume I. The Thinking Eye*, ed. Jürg Spiller. Lund, Humphries, London: Georg Wittenborn.

Laude, Jean (1973), *The Arts of Black Africa*. Berkley and Los Angeles, CA: University of California Press.

Laurent, Jerome, and Claude Romano (2010), *Le néant: contribution à l'histoire du non-être dans la philosophie occidentale*, 2e éd, Épiméthée. Paris: Presses universitaires de France.

Lévinas, Emmanuel (1957), 'Lévy-Bruhl et la Philosophie Contemporaine', *Revue Philosophique de la France et de l'Étranger* 147 (4): 556–69.

Maldiney, Henri (ed.) (1973), 'L'esthétique des rythmes', in *Regard, Parole, Espace*. Lausanne: Éditions L'Âge d'Homme.

Masolo, D. A. (1994), *African Philosophy in Search of Identity*. Bloomington, IN: Indiana University Press.

Mbiti, John (1970), *African Religions & Philosophy*. Garden City, NY: Doubleday.

McClusky, Pamela (2002), *Art from Africa: Long Steps Never Broke a Back*. Princeton, NJ: Princeton University Press.
Merleau-Ponty, Maurice (2000), *Éloge de la Philosophie: Et Autres Essais*. Paris: Gallimard.
Merleau-Ponty, Maurice (2014 [1946]), *Le primat de la perception*. Paris: Verdier.
Nicolas, A., J.-H. Martin and J. Kerchache (1997), *African Faces, African Figures*. New York: Museum for African Art.
Sasser, Elizabeth Skidmore (1995), *The World of Spirits and Ancestors in the Western Sub-Saharan Africa*. Lubbock, TX: Texas Tech University Press.
Segy, Ladislas (1975), *African Sculpture Speaks*. New York: Da Capo Press.
Segy, Ladislas (1976), *Masks of Black Africa*. New York: Dover Publications.
Senghor, Léopold Sédar (1964), *Liberté I: Négritude et Humanisme*. Paris: Éditions du Seuil, pp. 216.
Senghor, Léopold Sédar (1967), 'Standards Critiques de l'Art Africain', *African Arts* 1 (1): 6–9 and 52.
Senghor, Léopold Sédar (1977), 'L'esthétique négro-africaine', in *Liberté I: Négritude et Humanisme*. Paris: Seuil.
Senghor, Léopold Sédar (1977), *Liberté I: Négritude et Humanisme*. Paris: Seuil.
Senghor, Léopold Sédar (1977), *Liberté III*. Paris: Seuil, pp. 283.
Tangwa, Godfrey (2017), 'African Philosophy: Appraisal of a Recurrent Problematic', in Adeshina Afolayan and Toyin Falola (eds.), *The Palgrave Handbook of African Philosophy*. New York: Palgrave Macmillan.
Tempels, Placide (1949), *La Philosophie Bantoue*. Paris: Présence Africaine.
Tempels, Placide (2013 [1945]), *La Philosophie Bantoue*. Paris: Présence africaine.
Thompson, Robert Farris (1974), *African Art in Motion*. Berkley and Los Angeles, CA: University of California Press.
Wiredu, Kwasi (ed.) (2004), *A Companion to African Philosophy*, Blackwell Companions to Philosophy 28. Malden, MA: Blackwell Pub.

14

The non-human in African metaphysics

Elvis Imafidon

Introduction

The discourse of metaphysics in conventional Eurocentric academic circles is human-centric. Metaphysical and ontological questions of the nature, essence(s) and categories of reality or the fundamental nature of being, whether as be-ing present (a substance ontology or a metaphysics of presence) or as be-ing in process, are approached from human-centric perspectives: first, because metaphysical and ontological questions are presumed to be asked only by humans. It is in the very onticness of the human being to ask questions and formulate answers about being and reality. This is the foundational point made by Martin Heidegger, who can rightly be said to have taken up the task of deconstructing and rewriting the history of metaphysics in the twentieth century in his existential, fundamental and process ontology, primarily developed in his magnum opus *Being and Time*. In his words:

> From which entities is the disclosure of Being to take its departure? ... to work out the question of Being adequately, we must make an entity – the inquirer – transparent in his own Being. The very asking of this question is an entity's mode of Being; and as such, it gets its essential character from what is inquired about – namely Being. This entity which each of us is himself and which includes inquiring as one of the possibilities of Being, we shall denote with the term '*Dasein*.' If we are to formulate our question explicitly and transparently, we must first give a proper explication of an entity (*Dasein*) with regard to its Being.
>
> (Heidegger 1985: 27)

And he adds:

> If to interpret the meaning of Being becomes our task, *Dasein* is not only the primary entity to be interrogated; it is also that entity which already comports itself, in its

Being, towards what we are asking about when we ask this question. But in that case, the question is nothing other than the radicalization of an essential tendency-of-Being which belongs to *Dasein* itself.

(Heidegger 1985: 35)

One could argue that the human mode of being (*Dasein*) is treated here by Heidegger not as the sole focus of a fundamental ontology but as a crucial 'departure point' and thus, not entirely human-centric. But anyone familiar with Heidegger's ontology which nicely sums up the history of European metaphysics knows it is a human-centric ontology and that it sustains the long-standing dichotomy between humanness and thingness in the history of European metaphysics.

Secondly, questions asked and theories formulated in the dominant history of metaphysics are essentially human-centric due to the categorial dichotomy in the treatment of thingness in relation to the human. There is a subtle but firm dichotomy between the metaphysics of a human and of a thing. We find this, for example, in the distinction in existential ontology between a being that exists and a being that simply is (existence and isness), and between conscious human beings and non-conscious beings in the Cartesian distinction between thinking substance and extended substance (Descartes 1991).

Thingness, the search for the essence and underlying substratum of things, becomes the dominant category for thinking about all other-than-human entities. Thus, there is a flourishing discourse of the human being, its nature, essence and categories of being in metaphysics, as evident from such themes as fatalism, personal identity, the mind-body problem, the afterlife discourse, the metaphysics of freedom and so on; but the same cannot be said about the discourse of thingness or other-than-human realities and their interwovenness with the human. Hence, the history of metaphysics cannot boast of a rich and robust discourse of environmental or animal metaphysics or ontology. Even when there are theoretical traces of the non-human, they emerge essentially as accidents in the discourse of the human. Thus, a genuinely inclusive and holistic metaphysical discourse that theorizes the relational, solidaristic and interdependent natures of being (human and non-human) is rare in the dominant European academic philosophy. It is crucial therefore, it seems to me, to look beyond Europe to non-Western metaphysical systems to redress this ontology of exclusion.

But academic philosophy in general and metaphysics in particular across the globe is dominated by the Western narrative, linguistic and conceptual powers and by the politics of knowledge. Non-Western philosophies such as Chinese philosophy, Indian philosophy, Mexican philosophy and African philosophy are caught in the web as they shape their identities and develop their philosophical thoughts, often as a defensive response to Western hegemony, but doing so within and rarely outside of the philosophical categories of the West. To be admitted into the hall of philosophy, it seems, involves showing that one has similar credentials to the gatekeepers. It is thus not surprising that we do non-Western philosophies in ways quite similar to Western philosophy. With the particular case of metaphysics in mind, while African metaphysics clearly shows potential for theorizing an ontology of the non-human, the dominant themes in African metaphysics since its much-felt presence in academia in recent times have centred on the human. Themes such as personhood, destiny, the problem of evil, the nature of being, the question of the afterlife, personal identity and ideas of rebirth (Adeofe 2004; Agada 2023; Gbadegensin 2004; Imafidon 2012; Ozumba 2004; Wiredu 1992) provide space for exploring non-human ontologies but are often discussed from a human-centric perspective.

In the following, I intend to decentre the human, and inclusively and equitably discuss it in relation to the non-human. For in African metaphysics, the be-ing of the human cannot be conceived separately from that of the non-human. African metaphysics provides an account of being and reality in which the non-human transcends thingness and is fundamental for the existence of the human. In this intensely relational account, African communitarian metaphysics interweaves all beings in a fluid (not lineal) flow of time where the past, present and future are constantly intersecting. A clear illustration is the idea of ancestors that permeates sub-Saharan Africa – of their relationship with future generations in the idea of rebirth, and with the present in the idea of causality. I will develop two theses: (a) the ontological relationality of being embedded in the concept of Ubuntu and similar concepts in other African places establishes and sustains equilibrium among all beings, human and non-human; and (b) the fluidity of personhood, in the way both humans and nonhumans can gain, lose or increase their status as persons, allows for the flourishing of human and non-human persons. I conclude by exploring the relevance of African metaphysics in understanding our duties to the environment.

African metaphysics and the relationality of being

We begin this section by addressing the elephant in the room: the usage of the term 'African'. When philosophy is linked with a place – as we find, for example, in Western philosophy, Anglo-American philosophy, Indian philosophy, Chinese philosophy, Mayan philosophy, African philosophy, and so on – there is a sense in which this is a positive strategy in that it affirms and exposes a geography of reason (Gordon 2011). This is particularly useful when a strategy based on the geography of reason is compared with silencing the role of place in philosophy – a strategy which dominates academia, research and pedagogy, and which treats philosophy as a view from nowhere (cf. Nagel 1986). This results in sustaining and promoting the colonization of philosophical knowledge by the dominant place, the Western place. Affirming the geography of reason acknowledges the epistemic importance of place and the positionality and situatedness of knowledge. Thus, the use of 'African' in African philosophy is in no way meant to present a narrative that there is a homogeneous and unified body of philosophical thought from such a diverse and large place that can be labelled African – any more than the use of 'Indian', 'Western', 'Chinese' or 'American' implies homogeneity of thought in those places. Rather, it acknowledges as African the place and geography of reason wherefrom diverse yet shared philosophical thoughts emerge: an African place, a geography that transcends the physics of place to include multi and intersectional layers of memory, history, shared lived experiences, culture, meaning-making, personal narratives, and the topophilic and topophobic embodiments of place (Janz 2017).

Thus, African metaphysics is used here to acknowledge the place from which reasoning about reality and being emerges. I write specifically of the sub-Saharan African place in which l am not only positionally and reflectively situated but to which I also have a strong topophilic affinity. There is obvious diversity in thought about metaphysical issues in sub-Saharan African places, as can easily be gleaned, for example, from the protracted discourse on the ontological features of a human person in Yoruba and Akan thought, leading to dualistic, tripartite and pentachotomistic theorizations (Ekanola 2006; Gyekye 1984; Onah 2002). But I focus here on the manifestly shared features of sub-Saharan metaphysics or ontologies, namely the emphasis on the relationality and fluidity of being and the implications for the non-human. I will begin in this section with the first – relationality. In doing so, I expand on two main theses: (i) in sub-Saharan African metaphysics, there exists an active and lively community of beings interconnected by a life force or cosmic energy; and (ii) the existence and survival of a being (human or non-human) fundamentally depend not on autonomously possessed ontic qualities but on building and sustaining relationships with other beings, both human and non-human. I will then instantiate these two points by focusing on the perception of specific plants and nuts, and on ancestors in sub-Saharan African places.

The African philosopher Polycarp Ikuenobe provides an apt description of the understanding of reality in African metaphysics:

> In the traditional African view, reality ... is a continuum and a harmonious composite of various elements and forces. Human beings are a harmonious part of this composite reality, which is fundamentally a set of mobile life forces.
>
> Natural objects and reality are interlocking forces. Reality always seeks to maintain an equilibrium among the network of elements and life forces .... Because reality or nature is a continuum, there is no conceptual or interactive gap between the human self, community, the dead, spiritual or metaphysical entities and the phenomenal world; they are interrelated, they interact, and in some sense, one is an extension of the other.
>
> (Ikuenobe 2006: 63–4)

In an African community, beings are interwoven and interlocked through a shared ontological energy of being that has been labelled variously as vital force (Tempels 1959), phenomenon aura (Okafor 1982), cosmic energy or mobile life forces (Ikuenobe 2006). The need to name this fundamental energy that interweaves beings in the community is clearly reflected in the linguistic schemes of sub-Saharan African peoples. In the ancient Benin Kingdom of Southern Nigeria, words like *etin*, *etinosa*, *orion* and *oria*, which translate as strength, the strength of the Supreme Being, life-force and a living person respectively, permeate everyday conversations; it is not uncommon for a dead person to be described as someone whose life-force departed from him/her (*orionlen kpa*). These beings that share a common essence of life force include both visible and invisible beings interlocked in a web of relationships without which the existence of a being cannot be possible and without which realities and events in the community cannot be explained. Beings in the community include visible beings such as plants, animals, landscapes and human beings, and invisible beings such as ancestors, deities, manipular forces and the Supreme Being.

Some of these beings possess an active form of shared energy or life force making it possible for them to act and be acted upon; others possess a passive form of the shared life force, such that they would require another being acting on them to emit their energy. Thus a human being (a being with an active life force) somewhere in West Africa boils or squeezes out the juice of the plant, *vernonia amygdalina*, commonly called bitter leaves (a being with a passive life force), in order to cure an ailment. The key point remains that both human and non-human beings are all fundamental parts of a community. It is not uncommon to see care and health givers or medicine men and women in African societies speaking with a plant, tree or body of water as they would to a human being during the healing process. Another clear affirmation of the being and life force of non-human plants is seen in the treatment of Kola nuts in many parts of West Africa. Ceremonies such as marriages, child naming ceremonies, funerals, ceremonies marking the beginning of new seasons, and other festivities begin with the breaking of the Kola nut, accompanied by prayers and blessings. While the kola nut is held in hand to be broken, one of the key declarations would be 'the person that brings kola brings life'; the kola nuts are then broken by the eldest in the gathering and shared with all (Achebe 1969; Kammampoal and Laar 2019). The proverbial declaration that the one that brings kola brings life affirms the life-giving force of the kola nut in terms of its health benefits, and signifies the simplicity but profound impact of hospitality in the sustenance of well-being.

The human and non-human beings in an African community come into existence by partaking of the shared life force but sustain that existence through relationships with other beings in a reciprocation of energy. In a community of Beings A, B, C and D, A's continuous existence co-depends on B, C and D and is dependent on forming relationships with them. This co-dependency means that it is not the case that A's existence is significantly more important than that of B, C or D. This relationality of being is what has been aptly captured in the philosophy of Ubuntu. The philosophy of Ubuntu translates simply as 'a person is a person through other persons' or 'a being is a being through other beings'. It is an ontological and existential Afro-communitarian philosophy of relationality, solidarity, co-dependency and cooperation. The interwovenness, harmony and solidarity that are embedded in Ubuntu as relationality and in the idea that a person is a person only through other persons emphasize the interconnectedness of all beings, human and non-human. All beings, human, the environment, ancestors, deities and so on are in an interlocked web of relationships such that there is no conceptual or interactive gap between the human self, the physically dead, the phenomenal world and intangible entities. Existing beings need one another to thrive and lead meaningful lives such that the quest for solidarity and harmony is essential and non-negotiable for general well-being.

A palpable example of the relationality of being in African communities between the human and the non-human is the relationship with ancestors. Ancestors are members of the African community who have properly departed the physical realm of existence to the non-physical. They are those who have completed the physical part of their life course and have taken on higher forms of being, a more intense energy. To be properly departed would involve a number of factors, such as living a community-accepted lifestyle and building community, having offspring, dying of natural causes and being properly buried. Being properly buried implies that the ancestor depended on the human to initiate the process of transition from a this-worldly to an other-worldly existence; this implies that the coming-to-be of the ancestor depends on humans performing the necessary rites and rituals. Once a being becomes an ancestor, he or she remains intrinsically interwoven with his or her kin. The existence of an ancestor becomes crucial to causally explain events and occurrences in the family from which the ancestor has physically departed as well as in the larger community. The Congolese philosopher, Benezet Bujo, puts this succinctly:

> The relationship between those living on earth and the ancestors is very close, since the living owe their existence to the ancestors from whom they receive everything necessary for life. On the other hand, the living dead can "enjoy" their being ancestors only through the living clan community. In this way, a kind of "interaction" – hierarchically organised from top to bottom and vice versa – is created …. The goal of this interaction is the increase of vitality within the clan.
>
> (Bujo 1998: 16)

Thus, all beings in an African community – humans, ancestors, plants, forests, animals and so on – have an equal stake in being in the community. The human is not the centre of existence, neither is he or she the margin. The human, like the non-human, exists in a web of relationships.

African metaphysics and the fluidity of being and time

A fluid being is a being that can through time take up new forms of being or status of personhood other than the ontological status it is known to possess *but yet retains an enduring identity*. A being A with an enduring identity x is fluid because it can become B, C or D while still retaining x. Thus, the fluidity of being is used here in a strictly ontological sense rather than the often sexualized sense to describe the fluidity of gender (Diamond 2020). In an African community of beings, the fluidity of being results from (i) the life force a being possesses at a given time, and (ii) the relational mode and status of a being at a given time. The fluidity of being is always linked to temporality and finitude since to be fluid invariably means being something else at different times and, as we shall see, being able to take up different forms of being at the same time. The fluidity of being or, in other words, the presence and acknowledgement of it permeates African societies. In what follows, I explore the clustered fluidity of being human, being an ancestor and being an animal.

Let us begin with the first, being human. There is clear and substantial evidence in existing literature that to be human in sub-Saharan African communities, a being must fulfil the required ontological and normative conditions. The ontological conditions consist of possessing the required ontic features that define a human being. These ontic features would include material and immaterial substances such as the physical head, the inner head (destiny) and a human life force that is specifically human due to its potentialities, say, the potential of upgrading to the status of an ancestor at some stage in the life course which does not end with death. For example, among the Yoruba people, the ontic features of a human being fundamentally include the *ara* (body), *emi* (life force or vital principle) and *ori* (destiny) (Oyeshile 2006). The normative or social condition is relationships; a human being only becomes a person if they build and sustain relationships with other human and non-human beings, relationships that are fundamental in sustaining ontological equilibrium and the well-being of the community of beings. Having the ontological features alone does not guarantee being human; normatively speaking, one cannot be a person without a community. This also implies that personhood may not be the same at all times; it can be acquired, lost and regained through time. One who acts irresponsibly and in ways that disrupt community life would be a non-person logically. In the Esan community in Southern Nigeria, for example, the following expression is often used to refer to someone who acts in ways not permissible in the community (especially habitually): 'You act like a goat. You don't act like a person.' This simply means the human being at the time of his or her misbehaving is not acting the way human beings do in the society, the socially accepted way and, hence, in terms of constituent parts of a person, is a non-person normatively at this point in time. This means that, normatively, a human being can be a person or non-human person at countless times through his or her life (Imafidon 2012). Bujo (1998: 117) adds that 'there is no end to the process of becoming a person in the Black African community. Not even entrance into the community of the deceased ancestors bestows a completed personal existence.'

Thus, in one's earthly life-course, one could flow several times between being a human and a non-human being due to actions that build or disrupt community. Yet the identity of this fluid being remains the same, enduring even when this human being successfully attains a higher form of being, a non-human one, becoming an ancestor.

An ancestor as a non-human being with more vitality and powerful life force than that of the human not only emerges from being a successful human but retains the potentiality of being a human – in fact, several humans. This is often captured with the concept of reincarnation; but I, along with a number of African philosophers, struggle with the adequacy of using the concept of reincarnation as it resonates in Western and Asian philosophical discourse to capture this fluid lived experience. The Nigerian philosopher Bolaji Idowu explains the human potentiality of the ancestor in the context of what I would preferably call rebirth thus:

> [I]n spite of this … [rebirth], the deceased continue to live in After-life. Those who are still in the world can have communion with them, and they are there with all their ancestral qualities unimpaired. Secondly, it is believed that they do reincarnate, not only in one grandchild or great grandchild, but also in several contemporary grand children or great grand children, who are brothers and sisters and cousins, aunts and nephews, uncle and nieces, ad infinitum.
>
> (Idowu 1968: 194)

What Idowu is asserting here can be stated as follows:

> A being P is a non-human being, an ancestor, at time X.
> At the same time X, P is also the physically living daughter's newborn child Q (a human being).
> At the same time X, P is also the grown-up son R (a human being) of the physically living son.
> Therefore, P can be a non-human (P) and several humans (Q and R) at the same time X.

Anyone who has lived in a sub-Saharan African place would quickly notice people speaking about the presence of their dead elderly ones (as ancestors) and yet speaking about the same dead parents as being in several children born after their death. Such realities are reflected even in names given to children. Common names among the Yoruba people attest to this. Babatunde, a typically male name translates as 'My father has returned' while the names Yetunde and Iyabo, typically female names, both translate as 'My mother has returned'. This obviously defies the Western logical law of non-contradiction as it holds that a being is a non-human being and a human being at the same time. The Nigerian philosopher Innocent Onyewuenyi (1996), who also problematized the use of the term 'reincarnation' within the African context, is perhaps the best-known contemporary African philosopher to aptly explain the logic of this reality:

> The vital force of an ancestor is comparable to the sun, which is not diminished by the number and extent of its rays. The sun is present in its rays and heats and brightens through its rays; yet, the rays of the sun singly or together are not the sun. In the same way the "vital force" which is the being of the ancestor can be present in one or several of the living members of his clan through his lifegiving will or vital influence, without its being diminished or truncated. Just as the sun is the causal agent of heat, so is the ancestor a causal agent of his descendants who are below him in the ontological hierarchy.
>
> (Onyewuenyi 1996: 40)

In a sense, the dead leaves traces of themselves in the present and in the potential future; and more broadly, the past is interwoven with the present and the future in this back-and-forth flow of human and non-human energies.

We find similar fluidity in the being of animals. The non-human animal lacks certain ontic features of being human such as destiny and a personal identity that endures and is transferable from one state of being to another. So, while death is a passage to another state of being for the human, it is the complete end for the animal. It is on this basis that the justification of an omnivorous diet can be theorized in African thought and perhaps why one will not easily find vegans, vegetarians or fruitarians in indigenous African communities. Nevertheless, one can also easily find in each sub-Saharan African community some specific animal whose status of being non-human has been elevated or even deified. The reasons for this vary but are often associated with duties performed by the animal on behalf of the community, a unique relational display of care for the community or specific beings in the community. This would explain the quite totemic treatment of specific animals in different communities in Africa. In some cases, it becomes forbidden to kill or eat such animals and they can earn a different non- human status that is revered by humans.

Concluding thoughts: Rethinking relationships with the non-human

The foregoing presents an African relational and fluid account of reality in which each being has an equitable stake in existence and in which no being can autonomously sustain its existence without dependence on other beings. Human beings contribute fundamentally to such an ontological structure but so do non-human beings in the environment. Within an African ontology, there is a fundamental interrelatedness and interdependence of all beings; recognition, acknowledgement and acceptance of this interrelatedness of all beings have been crucial for maintaining ontological balance, providing causal explanations for events, and promoting an existential or ontological ethic in terms of the duties each being has towards other beings to promote collective well-being and survival (Imafidon 2014). The harmonious interaction among beings, Polycarp Ikuenobe explains, provides the 'basis for explaining causal phenomena with respect to various events or occurrences. Harmony in interaction among forces brings about good events and lack of harmony brings about bad events such as death and disease. Human actions in relation to community and nature are central to the ability to create harmony' (Ikuenobe 2006: 63). And the South African Nobel Laureate Desmond Tutu aptly captures the ethical import of this ontological co-dependence among beings when he writes that 'Harmony, friendliness, community are great goods. Social harmony is for us the *summum bonum*—the greatest good. Anything that subverts or undermines this sought-after good is to be avoided like the plague. Anger, resentment, lust for revenge, even success through aggressive competitiveness, are corrosive of this good' (Tutu, 1999: 35). By implication, a sub-Saharan African ethic or moral theory defines as good and permissible actions those that promote harmony among beings and reduce discord and as impermissible those actions that disrupt community, create ontological disequilibrium and fail to develop community (Metz 2007).

This ontologized ethic provides a basis for rethinking our relationship with our co-beings, human and non-human, in the communities in which we find ourselves. It is a shift from thinking of ourselves as the legitimate beings in existence as against all other things around us including the environment. Indeed, the failure of the conventional human-centric ontology to acknowledge and accept a relational ontology has led to the present disequilibrium in our relationship with other forms of being in the environment, leading to the current climate and environmental crisis. Thus, African environmental ethicists have developed a more inclusive environmental ethical theory of duties to our environment from African ontology. The key idea in African environmental ethics and philosophy is that all beings that have a life force, and therefore, in an African ontology, all beings deserve moral consideration and are owed duties and obligations (Behrens 2014; Kelbessa 2005; Murove 2004; Sindima 1990; Tangwa 2004). The South African philosopher Kevin Behrens summarizes this point thus:

> This notion of life as a single texture, a web or a fabric of interdependent, interrelated entities provides an attractive construct for understanding moral considerability. It is not just each individual living organism that counts morally, it is the web of life itself, with all of its complex interactions. What is morally considerable is anything that is part of this complex web of life. Thus, it is possible to include communities,

families, species, and ecosystems as morally considerable. It is also possible to include rivers, mountains, forests, ocean currents, winds, and even the atmosphere as morally considerable because they are natural things that play a systemically important role in the flourishing of other (inanimate) natural objects.

(Behrens 2014: 88)

An African metaphysics, therefore, provides a robust ontological basis for shifting our focus to the non-human without ignoring the human and for exploring ethical, equitable and inclusive ways of thinking about the non-human such as the natural environment, future generations and planetary beings, in ways that recognize and promote the relational, fluid and interwoven web of life forces we are immersed in.

References

Achebe, C. (1969), *Things Fall Apart*. New York: Ballantine Press.

Adeofe, L. (2004), 'Personal Identity in African Metaphysics', in L. M. Brown (ed.), *African Philosophy: New and Traditional Perspectives*. Oxford: Oxford University Press, pp. 69–83.

Agada, A. (2023), 'God's Existence and the Problem of Evil', in E. Imafidon, M. Tshivhase and B. Freter (eds.), *Handbook of African Philosophy*. Cham: Springer, pp. 555–574.

Behrens, K. G. (2014), 'Toward an African Relational Environmentalism in African Traditions', in E. Imafidon and J. I. A. Bewaji (eds.), *Ontologized Ethics: New Essays in African Meta-ethics*. Lanham, MD: Lexington Books, pp. 95–112.

Bujo, B. (1998), *The Ethical Dimension of Community: The African Model and the Dialogue between North and South*. Nairobi: Paulines Publications.

Descartes, R. (1991), *The Philosophical Writings of Descartes,* trans. J. Cottingham, et al. Cambridge: Cambridge University Press.

Diamond, L. M. (2020), 'Gender Fluidity and Nonbinary Gender Identities among Children and Adolescents', *Child Development Perspectives* 14 (2): 110–15.

Ekanola, A. B. (2006), 'Metaphysical Issues in African Philosophy', in O. Oladipo (ed.), *Core Issues in African Philosophy*. Ibadan: Hope Publications, pp. 61–78.

Gbadegensin, S. (2004), 'An Outline of a Theory of Destiny', in L. M. Brown (ed.), *African Philosophy: New and Traditional Perspectives*. Oxford: Oxford University Press, pp. 51–68.

Gordon, L. R. (2011), 'Shifting the Geography of Reason in an Age of Disciplinary Decadence', *Transmodernity* 1 (Fall): 95–103.

Gyekye, K. (1984), 'The Akan Concept of a Person', in R. A. Wright (ed.), *African Philosophy: An Introduction*. Lanham, Maryland: University Press of America, pp. 101–122.

Heidegger, M. (1985), *Being and Time*, trans. J. Macquarrie and E. Robinson. Oxford: Basil Blackwell.

Idowu, B. E. (1962), *Olodumare: God in Yoruba Belief*. London: Longman Green.

Ikuenobe, P. (2006), *Philosophical Perspectives on Communalism and Morality in African Traditions*. Lanham, MD: Lexington Books.

Imafidon, E. (2012), 'The Concept of Person in an African Culture and Its Implication for Social Order', *Lumina* 23 (2): 1–19.

Imafidon, E. (2014), 'On the Ontological Foundation of a Social Ethics in African Traditions', in E. Imafidon and J. I. A. Bewaji (eds.), *Ontologized Ethics: New Essays in African Meta-Ethics*. Lanham, MD: Lexington Books, pp. 37–54.

Janz, B. (2017), *Place, Space and Hermeneutics*. New York: Springer.

Kammampoal, B., and S. Laar (2019), 'The Kola Nut: Its Symbolic Significance in Chinua Achebe's Things Fall Apart', *International Journal on Studies in English Language and Literature* 7 (8): 26–40.

Kelbessa, W. (2005), 'The Rehabilitation of Indigenous Environmental Ethics in Africa', *Diogenes* 52 (3): 17–34.

Metz, T. (2007), 'Toward an African Moral Theory', *The Journal of Political Philosophy* 15 (3): 321–41.

Murove, M. F. (2004), 'An African Commitment to Ecological Conservation: The Shona Concepts of Ukama and Ubuntu', *Mankind Quarterly* 64 (3): 195–215.

Nagel, T. (1986), *The View from Nowhere*. Oxford: Oxford University Press.

Okafor, S. O. (1982), 'Bantu Philosophy: Placide Tempels Revisited', *Journal of Religion in Africa* 13 (2): 83–100.

Onah, G. I. (2002), 'The Universal and the Particular in Wiredu's Philosophy of Human Nature', in Olusegun Oladipo (ed.), *The Third Way in African Philosophy: Essays in Honour of Kwasi Wiredu*. Ibadan: Hope Publications, pp. 91–108.

Onyewuenyi, I. C. (1996), *African Belief in Reincarnation: A Philosophical Reappraisal*. Enugu: Snaap Press.

Oyeshile, O. A. (2006), 'The Individual-Community Relationship as an Issue in Social and Political Philosophy', in O. Oladipo (ed.), *Core Issues in African Philosophy*. Ibadan: Hope Publications, pp. 105–118.

Ozumba, G. O. (2004), 'African Traditional Metaphysics', *Quadlibet Online Journal of Christian Theology and Philosophy* 6 (3): (Accessed 01/15/2005) from http://www.Quadlibet.net.

Sindima, H. (1990), 'Community of Life', in C. Birch, W. Eaken and J. McDaniel (eds.), *Liberating Life*. New York: Orbis Books.

Tangwa, G. (2004), 'Some African Reflections on Biomedical and Environmental Ethics', in K. Wiredu (ed.), *A Companion to African Philosophy*. Malden, MA: Blackwell Publishing, pp. 387–395.

Tempels, P. (1959), *Bantu Philosophy*. Paris: Presence Africaine.

Wiredu, K. (1992), 'Death and after Life in African Culture', in K. Wiredu and K. Gyekye (eds.), *Person and Community: Ghanaian Philosophical Studies*. Washington, DC: The Council for Research in Values and Philosophy, pp. 137–152.

15

The divine names: The human role in the construction of the cosmos in the Maya *Popol Vuh* and Ibn ʿArabī's *Fusus al-Hikam*

Alexus McLeod

In a number of philosophical traditions, we find the position that human activity plays a fundamental role in bringing about the cosmos. This often involves the notion of the transformation of a mind-independent transcendent unity into multiplicity through human acts of imagination and action. This is understood as bringing new things to be in some sense, while at the same time representing a manifestation of a pre-existent substrate. The tangible, intelligible world is not the result of a completely mind-independent process that we simply discover. Positions maintaining that humans are at least partially responsible for the construction of the world range from the relatively modest to the radical. The most widely accepted position is the most modest – the view that it is human society, including social institutions, artefacts, norms, arts, sciences and the like, that humans create. Other positions, including the ones considered here, hold that more fundamental components of the world that we often take to be mind-independent are at least partially constructed by humans, including time, space or other key components of the cosmos.

In the texts, art and practices of the Maya tradition, particularly in colonial period texts such as the K'iche' *Popol Vuh*, we find a general view that the knowable and tangible world is constructed through human activity and conceptualization from a preconceptual and transcendent ground of being. We find discussion in Maya tradition of the capacities of humanity that allow humans to play this role, and of how humanity itself is linked to the ground of being out of which we fashion a cosmos. The accounts in Maya texts such as the *Popol Vuh*, or the *Chilam Balam* books of

Yucatan, however, are not theoretical discussions drawing on familiar philosophical concepts. Instead, they rely on a host of specifically Maya and Mesoamerican concepts, images, and stories. Thus, it is often unclear to Western or contemporary readers just what is going on in these texts.[1] In addition, certain aspects of the discussion of human creation of the cosmos are left implicit, largely because they depend on certain widespread and widely accepted ideas in precolonial Maya thought, which can be understood through artwork, recounting of practices by Maya and non-Maya sources in the early colonial period, related texts, and post-colonial practices and views retaining elements of earlier ideas.

There are important parallels with the Maya vision in some works of the Greco-Abrahamic world, however. We find in the thought of the twelfth/thirteenth century CE Islamic mystical philosopher Muhammad Ibn al-ʿArabi (more commonly known as Ibnʿ Arabī), developed in his *Fusus al-Hikam* (Bezels of Wisdom), a theoretical apparatus that approximates that of the Maya position and offers a specific account of the nature of human activity that brings about the cosmos. Understanding Ibnʿ Arabī's position in light of the Maya view sheds light both on what is going on in Maya understandings of the human construction of the cosmos and on Ibnʿ Arabī's likely motivation for developing his position as he did.

Humanity, in both the *Popol Vuh* and the *Fusus al-Hikam*, plays a fundamental creative role in completing the cosmos, alongside the work of the gods (for the Maya) or God (for Ibnʿ Arabī). This view does not, for either, undermine the existence of a mind-independent creation or a mind-independent source. Neither text endorses anything like an idealist view in which all things are created and constituted solely by mind. The role of the transcendent, foundational source or ground of being is crucial in both. And in both texts, humanity itself is created by this mind-independent source. Humanity thus serves as an intermediary between the transcendent ground of being and the cosmos. We find in these texts ways of thinking about the human role in constructing aspects of the world or even the divine itself, through thought, imagination and ritual activity, that can give us a more robust understanding both of how such views develop and of how we might make sense of such accounts.

In the *Popol Vuh*, the processes of ritual performance and manifestation of essence through substitution (*k'ex*) are central to the creation and completion of the cosmos. In the case of Ibnʿ Arabī, the cosmos and aspects of God, the divine names, arise through particular forms of relationship between humans and God, the creative power of the human imagination, and particular forms of conceptualizing and understanding God and the world.

We find the views discussed here in other works of both Ibnʿ Arabī and Maya thinkers,[2] but the particular formulations of these views in the *Popol Vuh* and *Fusus al-Hikam* give us clear articulations and line up well alongside one another. Thus, they are natural comparators. While the human role in divine construction is more pronounced in the case of the *Popol Vuh*,[3] we also find the position in the *Fusus al-Hikam* that distinguishable and conceptualized features of God come about as such through the operation of (and God's reflection through) human imagination.

Human construction of the cosmos in the *Popol Vuh* and Maya thought

The Maya philosophical tradition emerged in the southern part of Mesoamerica, roughly corresponding to the contemporary nations of Guatemala, Belize, southeastern Mexico (including the Yucatan peninsula) and the Western parts of Honduras and El Salvador, in the first few centuries CE. This period, known commonly as the 'Classic Period', stretched from the third to tenth centuries. During this period many of the well-known features of precolonial Maya culture developed in their most familiar forms, such as the widespread use of the 'Long Count' calendar, the concept of the *ahau* (the ruler, also in this period associated with shamanic power), and the majestic art and architecture of such city centres as Tikal, Copan, and Palenque.[4] Many of the available precolonial texts, written on stelae, architecture and pottery, date to this period. While the Maya had paper books, most of the books from the precolonial period are lost – falling victim to destruction, theft and decay in the humid tropical environment.[5]

What we know of precolonial Maya metaphysics comes from these precolonial sources, as well as from colonial period texts written in Maya languages in Latin script, such as the *Popol Vuh* of the K'iche' (one of the numerous Maya groups of Mesoamerica, in the southern highlands of Guatemala) and the *Chilam Balam* books of the Maya of northern Yucatán.[6] It is in the colonial period texts that we find the most robust discussion of metaphysical issues. While all of these texts were written in their current forms after the arrival of the Spanish in Mesoamerica in the sixteenth century CE, these texts contain mainly thought originating in earlier periods. Of the colonial period texts, *Popol Vuh* is the most clearly precolonial in nature – with Christianity and the Spanish mentioned only at the very beginning and end of the text, to explain the reasons for its writing, to preserve K'iche' ideas in the face of Spanish persecution and the spread of Christianity.

Many scholars have concluded that the bulk of the *Popol Vuh* likely existed in an earlier glyphic form prior to the colonial period, but was lost during the colonial period, as many of the glyphic texts of the Maya were.[7] We find an enormous amount of evidence from precolonial imagery and text consistent with and including stories from the received *Popol Vuh*. Using this text along with the aid of other sources such as precolonial glyphic texts, archaeological evidence of performances and other activities, and ancestral practices and stories of contemporary Maya people, we can locate important philosophical positions of the precolonial Maya.

Two discussions with contemporary K'iche' Maya people in Guatemala recounted by the Mayanist scholar Allen Christenson show us that the view that performance of characteristic activity manifests or constitutes the essence and identity of a person or thing is still held to this day in the Maya region. This view can be found in texts pre-dating the *Popol Vuh* and Spanish contact as well, and in iconography concerning rulers, gods and those who substitute them.[8]

In the introduction to his translation of the *Popol Vuh*, Christenson recounts a conversation with a number of K'iche' Maya in a village in Guatemala. After reading them some passages from the *Popol Vuh*, an old man said to Christenson that 'you make them [the ancestors] live by speaking their words'.[9] Christenson goes on to write:

> The word [the old man] used was *k'astajisaj*, meaning 'to cause life', or 'to resurrect'. [...] When the words of the ancestors are read, or spoken aloud, it is as if that person had returned from death to speak again. Reading ancient texts is therefore a very delicate matter, filled with peril if the words are not treated with sufficient respect.[10]

In many areas of Maya thought, we find the view that the characteristic activity of individuals and performances of this activity can manifest the essence of that person, in terms of the recurrence of their actual person. One can perform characteristic activities of an ancestor, and thus manifest the essence of that ancestor, literally *becoming* them, allowing them to be seen. In this sense the *Popol Vuh* itself is understood as an *ilb'al* (means for seeing),[11] a word that in contemporary use can refer to such tools as a magnifying glass or eyeglasses. The text itself, or rather its performance, manifests and allows us to view the otherwise hidden activity of the continual creation of the cosmos. In the performance, we see the role of the gods, the other creatures in the world and also crucially of humans. In the account of the origins of the K'iche people late in the *Popol Vuh*, we find the self-referential claim about the text itself:

> There was an instrument of sight (*ilb'al*) – there was a book. Popol Vuh was their name for it.[12]

The notion of the text as the means for seeing is echoed in the last lines of the *Popol Vuh*, explaining that the tool – the text and performance based on it – has been lost.[13]

In Maya thought, the concept of seeing or vision is generally connected with that of knowing.[14] What is seen through the Popol Vuh is the continual creation of the.cosmos, the various origins discussed, the ancestors and the gods. Through reading or performing the words in the book, a person or community brings about the actions described. In another conversation with Christenson, a man in the Maya highlands explains: 'to read the words of one who is dead is to make that person's spirit present in the room and give him a living voice'.[15] Christenson later writes, discussing the Maya view:

Events associated with the creation of the world are repeated again and again in times of conflict through the living priest-shamans who carry out ancient rituals established by the first ancestors. When a Maya priest-shaman performs a ritual at the proper time and in the proper manner, he is able to re-create the world just as it was at the first dawn of time.[16]

Christenson describes the ceremony of a Tz'utujil Maya shaman he observed in Santiago Atitlan:

> As part of the ceremony, the *nab'eysil* [priest-shaman] extracts the garments of the deity from a sacred bundle and wears them as he dances to the four cardinal directions to re-create the limits of the cosmos. Following the performance of this dance, the *nab'eysil* sought me out to ask if I had seen 'the ancient ancestors giving birth to the world.' He explained that they had filled his soul with their presence as he danced, guiding him in his steps, and now everything was new again. In the eyes of the *nab'eysil* the dance was not a symbol of the rebirth of the cosmos but a genuine creative act in which time folded inward upon itself to reveal the actions of deity in the primordial world.[17]

Such performances, like the *Popol Vuh* itself, are 'means for seeing/knowing' because they allow the observer to see and thus know the gods, ancestors, and substituted entities themselves – not a recounting, description or impersonation, in the way we think about what an actor or orator does. There are of course a number of questions concerning this notion of substitution and 'embedded identity', questions that are beyond the scope of this chapter, but which I discuss in more depth in other work.[18]

One issue, though, is crucial to answering a question about the human role in construction of the cosmos. There is a potential problem that arises from the idea that the performance of, for example, an ancestor brings that ancestor back into existence, such that the performer becomes *identical with* the ancestor. If there is identity at this time between the performer and the ancestor who is being substituted, how does the performer fail to take on all of the features of the ancestor? Perhaps the performer engages in the characteristic activities and utters the words of the ancestor, but the performer fails to have numerous other features of the ancestor. But this problem is no more pressing for the case of substitution than it is for personal identity over time. We might ask the same question of a woman of fifty years old, for example – how is it that she can be identical to the ten-year-old girl from forty years ago? Manifesting the essence or taking on the identity of a thing is not a matter of taking on all its characteristics. Otherwise continued identity of anything through time would be impossible. One embeds the identity of another within one's own when one performs the *characteristic* or defining activities of another. Those activities associated with the essence of a particular ancestor, god or other individual can be sufficient for the manifestation of that ancestor, god or individual.

Even thought can be sufficient for such substitution. It all depends on the nature of the characteristic action of the individual we are trying to substitute, and the relationship between this individual's features and the community (a crucial element discussed below). For something to be a key individuating feature of an individual and a part of their essence, it must be a feature possessed by the individual *and* socially recognized as such. This often has to do with features associated with their role in the wider community. Within closer communities such as families, it may have to do with common features family members recognize. Private and socially inaccessible thoughts or behaviours cannot be marks of the essence of the individual, as the social context is not created for the construction, recognition and performance of the individual through these features. Some thoughts, however, *can* be the basis of substitution or embedded identity – in particular where thoughts are shared. Even in the case of thought, therefore, we find that it is primarily social accessibility and relationship that allow for sharing or fusion of essence. We see an example of this in the *Popol Vuh*, in the story of the fathers of the Hero Twins.

The fathers – called Seven Hunahpu and One Hunahpu – of the Hero Twins Hunahpu and Xblanque, who play a major role later in the Popol Vuh, were summoned to the underworld (Xibalba) by the lords of death, where they were ultimately overcome and sacrificed. Seven Hunahpu was buried, while One Hunahpu's head was removed and placed in a calabash tree, with the rest of his body buried with Seven Hunahpu. The Hero Twins came to be through the actions of this disembodied head of One Hunahpu (which was also the head of Seven Hunahpu). The head, still animated, able to think and speak, impregnated a woman from the underworld by spitting into her hand. The text explains that this saliva can be understood as carrying the essence of One Hunahpu (and Seven Hunahpu), such that his children can be understood not only as new entities derived from One Hunahpu, but as literally the continuation, the substitution, of One (and Seven) Hunahpu. It also explains that One Hunahpu and Seven Hunahpu think and act together through the head:

> After that, his son is like his saliva, his spittle, in his essence, whether it be the son of a lord or the son of a craftsman, an orator. The father does not disappear, but goes on being fulfilled. Neither dimmed nor destroyed is the face of a lord, a warrior, craftsman, orator.[19]

The head of One Hunahpu, which is now referred to as the head of One *and* Seven Hunahpu (despite Seven Hunahpu having been buried whole without his head removed), goes on to say 'thus be it so'. The following text is unclear but seems to entail that the gods give One and Seven Hunahpu these words, although it also seems plausible that what is stressed here is the thought of One and Seven Hunahpu, as explanation for the head representing *both* One and Seven Hunahpu, rather than One Hunahpu alone. Either way, this is clearly a joint action and a joint thought of the two brothers, who then become the dual father of the hero twins, Hunahpu and

Xbalanque. Whether it is the shared thought that makes them identical in the form of the head, the action of impregnating the girl of Xibalba, or some other reason, the fact remains that they are at this point one and the same – their identities have both been embedded into that of the head in the calabash tree.

This turns out to be a specific instance of human ritual activity constructing and reconstructing things in the world. If we look to other parts of the *Popol Vuh*, we find other ways in which human ritual activity plays a fundamental creative role in the continual creation of the cosmos at every moment, including of individual humans and the gods themselves. Like the occasionalist metaphysical systems of al-Ghazali or Malebranche, in which God continually creates the world anew with each change, explaining causation as successive creation of one state following another, a common Maya view in texts like *Popol Vuh* holds that there is such continual creation but that humans also play a role in it. Not just in terms of causation through will – in fact not *primarily* in this way, but through the performance of ritual with implications for the community that substitutes and thus brings about things in the cosmos.

One of the most interesting parts of the *Popol Vuh*, and one that proves an important structural parallel to the views found in IbnʿArabī's work, is the story of the gods' creation of humans that begins early in the text. There are a number of interesting and difficult interpretive issues involved in the section recounting this story, some of which I discuss here. Part of the issue, in translating the K'iche' text to English, is the implications of the English words and concepts used, and their ability or inability to express the richness of the K'iche' ideas.

Early in the *Popol Vuh*, there is a discussion between the gods about the creation of humanity, and the role of humanity in keeping the rituals that ensure the manifestation of the days of the gods, thus completing a crucial aspect of the cosmos. The gods attempt to create humans with this goal in mind. They initially create the animals, but the animals prove unable to speak and engage in the proper rituals, and their status is demoted to becoming servants and food. The gods then create beings of mud, but end up destroying these beings when they too prove unable to perform the crucial tasks. After a number of failed attempts (including constructing beings of wood), the gods hit on the right formula, creating humans from the maize plant. These humans are able to engage in the crucial ritual of 'daykeeping', as well as being able to substitute, that is to take the role, through performance, of the gods themselves.

The term used for 'daykeeping' or 'bringing about the day' is *q'ijarisaj*. The gods are clearly in need of this, and because of the inability to engage in this activity of the early beings they created, the gods condemned the animals to serve and be food, destroyed the failed people of mud, and reduced the failed people of wood to nothing. Christenson translates *q'ijarisaj* as 'worship'.[20] The idea is that it signifies either honouring the days associated with certain gods in calendric rituals, or to honour them like the sun, a central and powerful aspect of the world. 'Worship' seems a bit of an odd choice here, given the conceptual baggage of this term in English. The concept generally entails honour, adoration and devotion to the worshipped thing, and usually also subordination. It is far from clear that these things are intended in the *Popol Vuh*'s use of *q'ijarisaj*, or if they are to some extent, there is certainly more going on here as well. The gods enjoined the beings they created to speak their names. This is crucial: the act of naming, of speaking, is a fundamental element of conceptualization in numerous philosophical and cultural contexts (as we will see it is in the thought of Ibn'Arabī; see also Part 2, Chapter 4 of this volume).

Speaking the words, performing the characteristic activities or speaking the name of a certain thing (all of which are actions performed in the *Popol Vuh*) are identity-making actions – actions that bring about the manifestation or substitution of a particular thing in the world. In being enjoined to speak the names of the gods, then, and to 'bring about the days', the creatures the gods have created are being instructed not just to worship or show devotion to the gods, but to actively create, to help play a role in the continual construction of the world, including crucially *the gods themselves*. Recall above the contemporary Maya idea that reading or saying the words of the ancestors brings the ancestors again to life. Likewise, it appears in the *Popol Vuh* that speaking the words of the gods brings them (more fully) into existence.

In Tedlock's translation of the *Popol Vuh*, this sense of *q'ijarisaj* is brought out more clearly, though it retains the element of praise. While Christenson translates the command of the gods to the animals, '*kixch'awoq! Kojisik'ij! Kojiq'ijila!*' as 'Speak! Call upon us! Worship us!', Tedlock translates it: 'Speak, pray to us, keep our days.'[21] This 'keeping of days' is often enjoined alongside honouring and glorifying the gods in this section of the *Popol* Vuh; so it is unlikely that the three commands are simply enjoining the beings the gods have created to worship them in three different ways – to speak (in worship), to call upon them (in worship) and to worship them. Rather, it is far more plausible (because also consistent with what we find heavily throughout the *Popol Vuh* and other areas of Maya thought and even more widely in Mesoamerican thought in general) that the gods require *sustenance*. They require human ritual activity for their completion and for assistance in completing the continual construction and reconstruction of the cosmos and of the gods themselves. The gods, while they have the ability to create, are not fully gods without the assistance of humans.

We find strong parallels with this view in related Mesoamerican traditions (which may have received this view from the Maya). These parallels are quite different from what we find in Abrahamic traditions (even in the thought of Ibn'Arabī, who will understand human construction in a cleverly different way even while echoing Maya thought). In Nahua (Aztec) thought, for example, it is well known that the gods, including the central and important sun god, required sustenance from humans, provided through ritual, for their continued existence and thriving, and for the maintenance of order in the cosmos. The sacrifice of bloodletting, including well-known executions (generally of prisoners captured in warfare), was primarily for this purpose of sustaining the gods.[22]

Sources in Maya thought can be found for this idea as well. The bloodletting ritual had a key importance in precolonial Maya culture.[23] Not only and not primarily the human sacrifice that figures so prominently in breathless early Spanish accounts of Mesoamerica, but far more frequently the auto-sacrificial drawing of blood by rulers and other nobles. The speaking of the names of the gods, the formulation of their words and the recounting of their actions are also crucial ritual functions of human beings.

This is what is meant by 'keeping of days'. This notion of daykeeping can still be found in contemporary Maya communities. The *ajq'ij* (daykeeper) in Maya communities in Guatemala is not only in charge of calendrics, but something more like a general advisor, sage and keeper of cultural knowledge.[24] The daykeeper is able to perform the rituals that maintain the community, and on a deeper level, the cohesion of the cosmos. The daykeeper relies on the community to assist in the performance of these rituals, through recognition and accompaniment, just as the gods rely on humans for completion through their performance. Thus in the *Popol Vuh*, and Maya thought more generally, humanity plays a fundamental and pivotal role in the construction of the cosmos.

Human construction of the cosmos in the *Fusus al-Hikam* of Ibn ʿArabī

> 'Even the names "the One," "the Unique" and the like are not descriptions of Allah with respect to Himself, but with respect to his creation.'[25]

How we square the view that humanity constructs and maintains the cosmos with the view that a mind-independent reality both exists and ultimately grounds and causes human existence itself is a question not explicitly taken up in the *Popol Vuh* and other Maya texts. It is clear that these texts do hold that both of those things are the case, but they are not given an explanation other than a suggestive one. I suggest here that Ibn ʿArabī's explanation of this very idea seems to be close to a position that the Maya texts rely on or assume, even while they do not explicitly offer theory in the way Ibn ʿArabī does.

The role humanity plays in Ibn ʿArabī's ideas of the divine names, their grounding in relationships between humanity and God, and the role of imagination in the anthropomorphic construction of the cosmos and manifestation of God are central in his works. These ideas feature prominently in his most well-known and most accessible work, *Fusus al-Hikam* (Bezels of Wisdom), as well as in his masterwork, the enormous *Futuhat al-Makkiyah* (Meccan Revelations).

IbnʿArabī's consideration of this issue begins with what we might think of as a difficulty for the view that humans play a role in creation – that is, the idea that everything in the cosmos is created directly by God. In the first chapter of the *Fusus al-Hikam*, on the prophet Adam, IbnʿArabī offers an explanation of the role of the human in the cosmos, with Adam as the archetype of the human, given his role as first human. At the beginning of the chapter, IbnʿArabī explains that God created the entirety of the cosmos out of the desire to see his divine names manifest:

> [A]s they really operate, or if you wish, say to see his Essence, in an all-inclusive being containing all of them and qualified by existence. Through this being, His mystery will be revealed to Him. That is, because one's self seeing is not like one's seeing oneself in another, which serves as a mirror for the seer.[26]

We see here right at the opening of the first chapter of the *Fusus*, that while God is ultimately responsible for the creation of the cosmos, God's creation of his names comes through the reflection of his essence through the mirror of nature, which is humanity itself. Thus, while God creates, God creates through the medium of human imagination, through which God experiences and sees himself. IbnʿArabī writes: 'If such a substrate does not exist and does not appear to the seer, he cannot see himself.'[27]

For this reason, the human being is called the *khalifa* (viceregent) of God, suggesting the assistance of humanity in the structuring of this cosmos created by God. IbnʿArabī discusses the relationship between God and humanity in the following way:

> [His humannness] derives from his comprehensive structure and his comprising of all the realities, because the human being relates to God (*al-haq*)[28] as the pupil relates to the eye, and through the pupil seeing occurs.[29] Hence he is called human/pupil (*insan*), because through him God (*al-haq*) looks at His creatures and has mercy on them.[30]

According to IbnʿArabī, God's essence is transcendent and fully unknowable. This essence is single and unchanging, so cannot be represented in the multiplicity of features such as the divine names or characteristics at all. The names and other features of God become manifest by the creation of what IbnʿArabī refers to as the 'mirror' of things in the world, through which God may then be manifest in a multiplicity distinct from his essence, with numerous features. This manifestation cannot happen without the creation of things in the world to serve as this mirror, this tool with which God can in a sense bring into creation his own multiple features (which cannot belong to his essence as such).[31]

We find a clear statement of the human creative role in the formation of the cosmos in the first chapter of *Fusus al-Hikam*. IbnʿArabī here makes a direct claim about the human role in the creation of the cosmos, which at first appears to contradict his earlier claim that God creates all things in the cosmos, but which he explains in a way that eliminates this difficulty (although interestingly not through eliminating all *contradiction*, which is essential to understanding the human role as *barzakh* ('limit') between God and nature).[32] He writes:

> This human being is both created in time and is eternal, coming into being and living forever. He is both the separating and unifying principle. The world owes its existence to him. His relation to the world is like the relation of the bezel of the seal ring to the seal ring. The human is the tool and the sign by which the King seals his treasure. Because of this function God calls him the viceregent, for through him God preserves His creation, as the seal ring preserves the treasures. [...] So long as the Perfect Human Being remains, the world will not cease to exist. Do you not see that when he disappears and the seal of the treasure of the world is broken, nothing of what God (*al-haq*, the real/true) preserved in the treasure will remain.[33]

Given this view, the question for Ibn ʿArabī becomes how humans play this role of creation, or rather of completion of divine creation as tools of God. To understand the ways humans contribute to the construction of the cosmos, and even the divine properties themselves, we must understand Ibn ʿArabī's views of human (and divine) imagination, the nature of the divine names, and the situation of the human as the 'limit' or 'isthmus' (*barzakh*) between God and the world.

The key distinction between Ibn ʿArabī's view and the Maya view outlined in the previous section is that insofar as there is a conventional and changeable structure of things in Maya philosophy, it is real and actual, no less so than what we might call the 'ground of being' itself – a result of the correlative nature of Maya thought. For Ibn ʿArabī, on the other hand, the changing and multiple world is connected to non-existence and lack of reality, insofar as it is combined with the ultimately real, the eternal, changeless, transcendent God. Thus, while in both views we find a constructive role for the human in the characterization and even creation of the world, the nature of this creative act is somewhat different. This difference does not however undermine the fact that the process and the human role in it seem to be structurally the same for Ibn ʿArabī and the Maya authors. While the world itself may be treated differently on both accounts, the creative process that according to Ibn ʿArabī does this work, human imagination, seems to capture the nature of the process suggested in Maya texts.

For Ibn ʿArabī the human imagination, which has an essential creative role in bringing out things in the world, does so as a function of the divine imagination itself. The human imagination can then be associated with or understood as a manifestation of the divine imagination. As Henry Corbin writes, 'our manifest being *is* the divine Imagination; our own Imagination *is* Imagination in His Imagination'.[34] This in part explains why for the 'perfect person' (*al-insan al-kamil*), the activity of the human is the activity of God. Corbin describes the active imagination of humans playing a role in creation as also coextensive with the divine imagination and intention – our imagination itself as theophany, as manifestation of God. He writes:

> '[I]t is thanks to the Active Imagination that the multiple and the other exist, in short, that theophanies occur, so that the Active Imagination carries out the divine intention, the intention of the "Hidden Treasure" yearning to be known, to appease the distress of His Names. Any purely negative critique of the Imagination would be untenable, for it would tend to negate this revelation of God to Himself and to drive Him back into the solitude of no knowledge, to refuse His Names the assistance they have expected of us since pre-eternity.' [….] 'Without the Active Imagination the infinite exaltations provoked in a being by the succession of theophanies which that being bestows on himself would be impossible.'[35]

God here forms the ground and necessary being, on which humans must operate in order to generate theophany, to generate knowledge of God. Without a knower, there is nothing to which God can be known. This echoes the *Popol Vuh*'s statement of the gods suggesting that humans are needed to keep the gods in memory, to assist the gods through ritual in being manifest and known. This focus on the creative act connected to perception and knowledge makes the knowing of God, of the gods, of the ground of being, itself a creative imagination that brings about things in the world. One way we can describe the world, on both accounts, is as the engendering of things through human perception of and attempt to know the ground of being itself. This exchange between God/the gods and humanity, between being and non-being (on Ibnʿ Arabī's view), creates the multitude of relations that form the world of our experience.

The *Popol Vuh* and Maya thought, like that of Ibnʿ Arabī, takes this creativity and the nature of things as fundamentally relational. A thing is what it is, not by having some intrinsic substantiality – this is where Ibnʿ Arabī parts ways with the Aristotelians – but through its relation to the source of being and to other things (appearances, theophanies) in the world. The essence of a thing on the Maya view, likewise, is understood as in its relation to other things in the world, including the ways it can be transformed into those other things, manifest them, and be altered through human concerns, uses and concepts.

On Ibnʿ Arabī's view, according to Corbin, even God insofar as God appears with certain characteristics via theophany, is as such based on the human imagination. In a sense, then, humanity completes not only the world, but God. This formulation would likely not have been used by Ibnʿ Arabī himself, or perhaps it would be sidestepped in saying that insofar as human imagination completes God, it is human imagination manifest as the divine imagination, thus God is completing God. This comes very near a kind of constructionism about God, in which the human mind creates God. There are two distinct features of this, however, that distinguish it from such a constructivist view. First, while the human imagination might bring about the particular characteristics of God in terms of the divine names, it does not bring about nor does it grasp the essence of God as singular, unchanging, transcendent. God as nameable, with characteristics, comes about due to this human imagination. God as the transcendent ground of being is not constructed by imagination, nor can it ever be known (as what can be known can be characterized). Secondly, the act of human imagination, in its creative capacity, always *is* as such the divine act. Inherently, according to Ibn'Arabī, the divine imagination and the human imagination are one, the source of all creativity. Not all individual humans come to realize or perfect the imagination, so as to perfectly manifest the divine imagination. One who has attained this is the 'perfect person' (*al- insan al-kamil*), whose imagination becomes merged with the divine imagination, and whose will thus becomes merged with and a manifestation of the divine will. The possibility of perfected personhood, according to Ibn'Arabī, is what makes sense of the institution of prophethood. The acts and words of the prophets manifest the acts and words of God, allowing us to glimpse, to access, the divine nature and will. Because the actions of the perfect person do not diverge from the divine will, such a person serves as a visible model of this will.

Because the human imagination is necessary to complete or characterize God, a complete understanding of God requires an understanding of one's own mind, of one's imagination. One of the key features in Ibn'Arabī's system is that the constructed and imagined are not thereby the artificial or false. To see it as such would be to hold there to be a fundamental gap or distinction between human imagination and God's imagination – but because only God truly is, there can be no source or identity of the former other than the latter. Our own contemporary English term 'imaginary' shares many features with Ibn'Arabī's *khayāl*, which can be 'imagination' or 'make believe'. When we call something 'imaginary', it means that the thing has been invented by our minds, created by us rather than the world. While Ibn'Arabī accepts that the imagination is creative – indeed, its creativity is primarily what defines imagination, he does not draw the distinction between mind and world, between imagination and reality, that contemporary usage assumes. Imagination is not measured by some kind of independent reality, rather imagination *creates* reality. It does not create reality *ex nihilo*, however. Imagination accesses God, and based on its relation to God, it creates the myriad characteristics of God, who in his essence is fundamentally uncharacterizable, and thus all the things in existence.

The human imagination, on Ibn'Arabī's view, manifests theophany; it reveals aspects of the divine nature, in part creatively. The fact that imagination constructs, based on access, conceptualization and determination of things, does not undermine the veridicality of what is accessed and created through imagination. This is because there is no distinction between the veridical and non-veridical products of imagination – there is nothing grasped through imagination that is more true or more real than another thing. It can be helpful to contrast here Ibn'Arabī's approach with that of Descartes.

According to that view, while images created or attained through imagination are not in themselves veridical, judgements based on those images can be veridical. One may have an image of a floating castle, in itself not a matter of veridicality.[36] When one judges that the castle exists in reality or the world, however, one then can be right or wrong. On Ibn'Arabī's view, this is not so – because what we gain through the imagination is always the image of the ultimately real, that is, God himself. The image of a floating castle, or of a tree standing before us, are equally images of the divine, theophanies of God in different manifestations. Indeed, the imagination itself, associated with the isthmus (*barzakh*) standing between God and world, is itself a manifestation of the divine, itself a theophany. Thus, although we might distinguish between different kinds of image and the results of imagination, we cannot distinguish between them in terms of judgements concerning which of them corresponds to the world and which are merely inventions of the mind not corresponding to the world. All imagination corresponds to reality – to God, in which it originates. What we perceive, what we experience, what we imagine and create – all of this is ultimately God. Any differing products of imagination, as the imagination itself, are different theophanies of the same one ultimately real – just as in the Maya case, all things are ultimately transformable to one another because in possession of the same fundamental essence. On Ibn'Arabī's view, the creativity (*himma*) of the individual human in manifesting a particular theophany is also at the same time, as Corbin writes, 'the Creator's theophanic Imagination at work in the heart of the gnostic'.[37]

One crucial shared feature of Ibn'Arabī's thought and that of the *Popol Vuh* is the idea of *continual creation*. This seems to be necessitated by the idea of the creative imagination bringing things into existence, and is a key reason that Ibn'Arabī's account of the operation of human imagination fits consistently with Maya accounts of creation and re-creation through the *Popol Vuh* and other texts. Creation, on both accounts, does not happen at a moment, a beginning time in which the components of the cosmos are created. Rather, the world is being continually renewed, shaped, brought into new forms, through the creative imagination of those conceptualizing this world. Both views understand this creation in terms of the duality between decay and generation – each requiring the other. Corbin explains this for Ibn'Arabī thus:

> At every break of the 'sigh of divine compassion' (*nafas al-rahman*) being ceases and then is; we cease to be, then come into being. … An eternal hexeity takes on one existential determination after another, or changes place, yet remains what it is in the world of Mystery.'[38]

This 'world of mystery' to which Corbin refers is this ground of being, the divine essence which cannot be directly known, but which is revealed through the variety of determinate manifestations created through the imagination, through the particular capacities of humans. God, as the eternal thing in itself, in his unknowable essence, takes these numerous forms, moment to moment, and at the same time, wherever there is change, wherever there is the act of imagination. Thus, while God as the ground of being is himself eternal, changeless, transcendent, inaccessible – ultimately mysterious – God as manifest in the world is continually changing and revealed in different ways. The world of multiplicity and change can be understood as itself the unfolding variety of theophanies of the divine nature, brought to completion by the imagination.

According to William Chittick, the manifestations of the features of the divine are themselves 'anthropomorphic', but this human construction of the features of God (in their relation) is itself also 'theomorphic', insofar as humans themselves are a creation of and manifestation of God. Chittick writes:

> In one sense, the divine attributes are all anthropomorphic, which is to say that we conceive of them in terms of ourselves. They must be anthropomorphic, because we can only conceive of things in terms of ourselves. In a more profound sense, however, human attributes are theomorphic. God, after all, is the truly real, and human beings are real only inasmuch as they possess a reality given to them by God.[39]

The way in which things in the cosmos and even features of God himself in the variety of different manifestations come to be is through *both* God's emanation and manifestation *and* through the human imagination in manifesting particular theophanies. But because the human imagination is itself a result of and follows from divine manifestation, we can say that the variety of theophanies are not *merely* human creation, but also God's manifestation of himself, through us. Thus, as Chittick writes:

> [T]he designation of His names and attributes depends in an important sense upon our knowledge of ourselves and, following upon that knowledge, our knowledge of God. This knowledge of God is, of course, knowledge of God's Level in relation to us, not knowledge of His Essence.[40]

One of the keys here is that the divine names become manifest *relationally* – that is, based on humans and our distinct relationships to the divine, the variety of names become completed and manifest in the world. In the *Fusus al-Hikam*, it seems to be just this idea that Ibn ʿArabī is trying to capture by associating each successive prophet, beginning with Adam and ending with Muhammad, with some characteristic that can be associated with a divine name and a feature of God captured by that name.

The relations between humans and God that create these names and thus complete the features of God that can be known by humans and are manifest in God (although at the same time standing in front of and obscuring God's unknowable essence itself) create and constitute the intermediary between the unknowable essence of God, the transcendent ground-of-being, and the visible, multiple and changing cosmos. The individual imagination, creative in itself and thus linked to God, also envisions God through itself, in a way associated with God's own self-manifestation, the theophany through which he becomes apparent to each individual, in accordance with that individual's own mind. The very final passage in the last chapter of the *Fusus*, which closes the text, discusses a *hadith* of the prophet included in the collection of Bukhari,[41] in which Muhammad recounts God telling him *ana 'inda dhanni 'abdi bi* ('I am as my slave imagines me to be').[42]

Ibn'Arabī writes that this means that God manifests himself to the individual in the particular way the individual imagines him, which will be dependent on the imagination of the individual. He explains what he takes to be the inner meaning of this *hadith*:

> [T]hat is, I manifest myself to him only in the form of his belief; if he wishes, he will make my self-manifestation unlimited, and if he wishes, he will make it limited, for the God of beliefs is limited, and hence He is the God whom His servant holds in his heart, because the unlimited God cannot be comprised by anything, for He is the essence of things and of Himself.[43]

In the final expression of the *Fusus al-Hikam*, Ibn'Arabī returns to this crucial issue of the central role of human imagination and the human construction of the cosmos and completion of God's characteristics. It is the human imagination that makes the hidden, transcendent, unknowable essence of God visible, knowable, accessible.

And this is at the heart of both the *Popol Vuh* and the *Fusus al-Hikam*. The fundamental question they aim to answer is how we distinguish humans from God, the gods or nature itself, while at the same time recognizing that all things are ultimately dependent on and in an important sense one with that source?

For Ibn'Arabī, the question is: How do we accommodate the view that the nature of humanity is ultimately of one shared identity with the nature of God, without violating the view of the distinctness of God, the oneness of God (*tawhid*) and the disassociation of any created thing from God – ideas at the very core of Islam itself? Ibn'Arabī's answer embraces the fundamental contradiction at the heart of mystical experience in numerous traditions. Humanity is both God and other than God, both of the divine nature and lacking it, as other things in the world. Humanity's sameness with God in terms of the imagination, which is the power of creation,[44] also creates or completes things in the world, which include and are linked to the divine names, which while they characterize God, also serve as a veil (*hijab*) hiding his essence.[45] Humanity can be understood as that part of the world which uniquely takes part in the creation of the world. It is this creative capacity that marks humans as distinct.[46]

Ibn'Arabī's account of the creative imagination in the process of manifesting features of the transcendent mind-independent ground of being gives us a model for also making sense of the way human thought and activity operate to create the cosmos through ritual such as daykeeping and substitutive performance in the *Popol Vuh* and other Maya texts. While the Maya had no conception of a transcendent God as in the Abrahamic tradition, something akin to Ibn'Arabī's model of human imagination, taken to inform the idea of continual creation in Maya texts, is consistent with and can help explain the human creative power in those texts. In addition, regardless of how these historically disconnected texts, thinkers and traditions arrived at their strikingly similar of the human role in construction of the cosmos,[47] we can also learn something valuable about the development of the idea of humanity's role in the construction of our world as we find it across a variety of philosophical traditions.

Notes

1. For contemporary Maya thinkers as well, who occupy a very different intellectual culture than their precolonial and early colonial ancestors, one heavily influenced by the imposed systems of Europe, this position can be difficult to grasp. Despite massive shifts in Maya intellectual culture since the seventeenth century, however, certain fundamental ideas can still be found from Maya and Mesoamerican thought more broadly in what came to be known as 'Latin American Philosophy', and the position discussed here of the precolonial Maya will not seem as foreign to contemporary Maya as they will to many non-Maya in North America or Europe.
2. For Ibnʿ Arabī, particularly in his voluminous masterwork *Futuhat al-Makkiyah*.
3. And even more so in colonial period Yucatec Maya texts such as the *Chilam Balam of Chumayel*, as I argue in the forthcoming 'The Creation of Dios: Continual Creation and Divinity in the Yucatec Maya *Chilam Balam of Chumayel*'.
4. The later Postclassic Period would see the rise of city centres in the northern Yucatan such as Chichen Itza, Uxmal and Mayapan.
5. The oldest paper text, the *Códice Maya de México*, dates to the eleventh century. Texts known to us on stone and pottery and wall murals go back much further than this, as far as the second century BCE.
6. The name 'Maya' itself originally refers to this people and language of the Yucatan peninsula, and was applied by scholars as a term to refer to the culturally and linguistically interrelated people of the wider region.
7. See Tedlock (1992).
8. The concept of substitution (*k'ex*) is the idea of the ability of one thing to represent or stand in for another. This happens through a literal adoption of the identity of the substituted thing. A person who becomes the substitute for a god in a ritual performance, for example, becomes identical to the god. This identity, interestingly, does not undermine a person's previous identity. I refer to this idea as 'embedded identity'. See McLeod (2017: chapter 4).
9. *Popol Vuh*, Christenson (2007: 6).
10. *Popol Vuh*, Christenson (2007: 6).
11. *Popol Vuh*, Christenson (2007: 25).
12. *Popol Vuh*, Christenson (2007: 287).
13. *Popol Vuh*, Christenson (2007: 285).
14. See McLeod (2023: chapter 7).
15. Christenson (2001: 4).

16. Christenson (2001: 24).
17. Christenson (2001: 24).
18. McLeod (2017: 79–82).
19. *Popol Vuh,* Tedlock (1996).
20. *Popol Vuh*, Christenson (2007: 63).
21. Tedlock (1986: 67).
22. Miguel Aguilar-Moreno describes the Aztec view thus:

> [A] variety of sources indicate a fundamental Aztec belief that envisioned a shared cosmic energy between all living things – plants, animals, humans, and gods – that need to be exchanged regularly. This energy was transported from humans to the gods through various forms of sacrifice, human and otherwise. The gods returned it in the form of light and warmth (from the Sun), water and food, especially maize. The Sun was the supreme recipient in this exchange of energy, for the Sun provided the key elements to the sustenance of life.
>
> (Aguilar-Moreno 2007: 173)

23. See Foster (2005: 191), who also associates this bloodletting with 'sustenance of the gods'.
24. See Fitjar (2014: chapter 1).
25. Yousef (2011: 277).
26. *Fusus al-Hikam*, Abrahamov (2015: 16).
27. *Fusus*, Abrahamov (2015: 16).
28. *Al-haq*, literally 'the truth', is one of the traditional names of God in the Islamic tradition, and Ibnʿ Arabī's use here points to God as manifestation of reality. As I discuss below, each of the features encapsulated in the divine names originates with the vision and relationship between God and the divine imagination of humanity.
29. Ibnʿ Arabī is using a play on words here in the Arabic, given that the term *insan* can have the meaning of 'pupil' and 'human being'.
30. *Fusus,* Abrahamov 2015: 18.
31. The influence of Neoplatonist views here is clear, going back to Plotinus' consideration of the One as generative source, through intermediaries.
32. See Bashier (2004: ch. 1).
33. *Fusus*, Abrahamov (2015: 18).
34. Corbin (1969: 190–1).
35. Corbin (1969: 193–4).
36. Descartes, *Meditations on First Philosophy*, Second Meditation.
37. Corbin (1969: 198).
38. Corbin (1969: 201).
39. Chittick (1997: xviii).
40. Chittick (1997: xviii).
41. Bukhari (7405; 97:34).
42. There is of course disagreement on what this quote means. Ibnʿ Arabī reads it, as he tends to read such texts, in an ideosyncratic way. Many discussions of this *hadith*, connected to the rest of the passage, understand it to be about the individual's

understanding of the ways God will *act* – in essence, a claim that God will do what the individual human imagines that God will do, given their knowledge of his ways. Ibn'Arabī reads this in a metaphysical way. Of course, these two readings need not rule each other out. It is a well-known feature of Sufi interpretations of scripture that there are multiple layers of meaning within a text, in particular the *dhahir* (literal, or manifest) and the *batin* (hidden) meanings, among others. See Abdel-Latif (2020: 655), Ali and Leaman (2008: 138).
43. *Fusus*, Abrahamov (2015: 182).
44. *Fusus,* Abrahamov (2015: 72). 'All existence is imagination within imagination'.
45. Chittick (1990: 61). Chittick writes: '[E]ach entity displays a perfection of Being, thus veiling and revealing It and one and the same time.'
46. *Fusus*, chapter 27, Abrahamov (2015: 173).
47. And it turns out they are not the only ones, as we find somewhat similar views in early China.

References

Abdel-Latif, Sara (2020), 'The Development of a Sufi Anti-Curriculum: Politics of Knowledge and Authority in Classical Islamic Education', in Sebastian Günther (ed.), *Knowledge and Education in Classical Islam: Religious Learning between Continuity and Change*. Leiden: Brill.

Abrahamov, Binyamin (2015), *Ibn Al-Arabi's Fusus Al-HIkam: An Annotated Translation of 'The Bezels of Wisdom'*. London: Routledge.

Aguilar-Moreno, Miguel (2007), *Handbook to Life in the Aztec World*. Oxford: Oxford University Press.

Ali, Kecia, and Oliver Leaman, (eds.) (2008), *Islam: The Key Concepts*. London: Routledge.

Bashier, Salman (2004), *Ibn al-'Arabi's Barzakh: The Concept of the Limit and the Relationship between God and the World*. Albany, NY: SUNY Press.

Chittick, William (1990), 'Ibn al-'Arabi and His School', in Seyyed H. Nasr (ed.), *Islamic Spirituality: Manifestations*. New York: Crossroad.

Chittick, William (1997), *The Self-Disclosure of God: Principles of Ibn Al-'Arabi's Cosmology*. Albany, NY: SUNY Press.

Chittick, William (1999), 'The Paradox of the Veil in Sufism', in Elliot Wolfson, (ed.), *Rending the Veil: Concealment and Secrecy in the History of Religions*. New York: Seven Bridges Press.

Chiu, Wai Wai (2018), 'Zhuangzi's Knowing-How and Skepticism', *Philosophy East and West* 68 (4): 1062–84.

Christenson, Allen (2001), *Art and Society in a Highland Maya Community*. Austin, TX: University of Texas Press.

Christenson, Allen (2007), *Popol Vuh: The Sacred Book of the Maya*. Norman, OK: University of Oklahoma Press.

Christenson, Allen (2009), 'Who Shall Be Our Sustainer? Sacred Myth and the Spoken Word'. Expedition 51 (1): 9–16.

Corbin, Henry (1969), *Creative Imagination in the Sufism of Ibn ʿArabī*. Princeton, NJ: Princeton University Press.

Descartes (2017), Meditations on First Philosophy, ed John Cottingham: Cambridge, Cambridge University Press.

Fitjar, Daniel (2014), *Balancing the World: Contemporary Maya ajq'ijab in Quetzaltenango, Guatemala*. Lausanne: Peter Lang.

Foster, Lynn (2005), *Handbook to Life in the Ancient Maya World*. Oxford: Oxford University Press.

Knysh, Alexander (1998), *Ibn ʿArabī in the Later Islamic Tradition: The Making of a Polemical Image in Medieval Islam*. Albany, NY: SUNY Press.

McLeod, Alexus (2017), *Philosophy of the Ancient Maya*. Lanham, MD: Lexington Books.

McLeod, Alexus (2023), *An Introduction to Mesoamerican Philosophy*. Cambridge: Cambridge University Press.

Tedlock, Barbara (1992), 'Mayan Calendars, Cosmology, and Astronomical Commensuration', in Elin Danien and Robert Sharer (eds.), *New Theories on the Ancient Maya*. Philadelphia, PA: University Museum, University of Pennsylvania.

Tedlock, Dennis (1996), *Popol Vuh: The Definitive Edition of the Mayan Book of the Dawn of Life and the Glories of Gods and Kings*. New York: Touchstone.

Yousef, Mohamed Haj (2011), Ibn ʿArabi- Time and Cosmology. London: Routledge.

16

Philosophy as a way of life: Metaphysics, ethics and spiritual exercises

Sajjad Rizvi

The idea of philosophy as a therapy, as an intellectual and spiritual cognate to the craft of the physician, is venerable in different traditions. The late antique Neoplatonist Porphyry (*c.* 234–305) wrote to his wife Marcella:

> Wisdom and knowledge have no part in chance. It is not painful to lack the gifts of chance, but rather to endure the unprofitable trouble of vain ambition. For every disturbance and unprofitable desire is removed by the love of true philosophy. Vain is the word of that philosopher who can ease no mortal trouble. As there is no profit in the physician's art unless it cures the diseases of the body, so there is none in philosophy, unless it expels the troubles of the soul.
>
> (Porphyry 1986: 57)

This approach to philosophy assumes that there is a self, that we can investigate its states and provide a diagnosis, and that we can cure and transform that self.[1] The diagnosis of the self and its therapy are discussed in a number of Neoplatonic texts, especially theurgic ones, in which wisdom descends from the divine and the soul ascends to its origins through the praxis of ritual and theurgy; thus, diagnosis and cure is paralleled by philosophy and theurgy to transform the self (Iamblichus 2003: 1.2–4, 9– 21; Damascius 1999: §4, 79–81; Alcinous 1993: 152.1–153.24, 3–4; see also Uždavinys 2014: 5–41, 229–49). Texts play a critical role in that transformation; to draw upon an analogy evoked by Sara Rappe, they constitute switches that activate the dynamic of the self towards its theurgic ascent; enacted as ritual they connect the material with the spiritual, the human with the divine, and symbols with their correspondences (Rappe 2000: 191–5, see also Shaw 1995: 127–228). Parallel to the Platonic traditions, one also finds therapeutic approaches to philosophy among the

Epicureans, Stoics and other Hellenistic thinkers. Nussbaum cites Cicero (106–46 BC) from *Tusculan Disputations* 3.6:

> There is, I assure you, a medical art for the soul. It is philosophy, whose aid need not be sought, as in bodily diseases, from outside our selves. We must endeavour with all our resources and all our strength to become capable of doctoring ourselves.
>
> (Nussbaum 1994: 14)

This therapeutic approach sees philosophy as activity and engagement. But the Hellenistic conception is rather introspective and, under the later Neoplatonists, steeped in the community of ritual and theurgy.[2] The turn from therapy of the self and philosophy as a way of life to intellectual inquiry and method in European philosophy is usually associated with Descartes (1596–1650), whose *Meditations* is not only a form of askesis but also the establishment of an apparatus for debate and introspective inquiry (Hadot 2002a: 263–5, 272; McGushin 2007: 195–6; Ogunnaike 2020: 4–5). As Foucault puts it in the *Hermeneutics of the Subject*:

> The transition from spiritual exercise to intellectual method is obviously very clearly in Descartes. I do not think we can understand the meticulousness with which he defines his intellectual method unless we have clearly in mind his negative target, that from which he wants to distinguish and separate himself, which is precisely these methods of spiritual exercise that were frequently practiced within Christianity, and which derived from the spiritual exercises of antiquity, and especially from Stoicism.
>
> (Foucault 2005: 294)

In recent decades, however, philosophy as a way of life (PWL) has seen renewed interest, in the study of the history of philosophy and of what philosophy is, cutting across different traditions and epochs. This is partly due to dissatisfaction with a philosophical guild which seems to have forgone the study and practice of the philosophical life in favour of more precise and narrower concerns and which seems to have imbibed the notion that the study of philosophy need not concern itself with aspects of either history or the socially embedded nature of the philosophical life (Collins 1982: 1–3; Kitcher 2023: 2–25). This may be something of a caricature of analytic philosophy as uninterested in big questions, in broader social relevance or even in the history of its craft. But even analytic philosophers can feel frustration with the absence of solutions to the problems of the present (MacBride 2014). Aligned with the professionalization and compartmentalization of philosophy as a discipline, this conception of a bounded intellectual pursuit poses a challenge in these post-colonial times when there is a growing awareness of the need for global and intercultural philosophy. And it poses the question: how can we best practice philosophy and produce philosophical communities in neo-liberal institutions like universities, or perhaps at least establish 'third institutions' that work in parallel to our institutional homes? (Kramer 2021: 100–14). The project of a third university is predicated on the idea that universities are transformative and that the pursuit of the humanities transforms us and our world through our ontology and praxis (paperson 2017: xiii–xxv). A concern with the social, with the world and with doing philosophy – and not just talking about philosophy – means that we cannot restrict ourselves to the highly particularized aspects of a particular culture or context; rather what is global can only emerge from the intersections of diverse ways of life.

PWL is therefore necessarily broad and holistic, covering all aspects of philosophy based on the fundamental intuition that philosophy is more than just an intellectual, introspective pursuit, more than the ethical concern for the self and for self-cultivation, and more than mere training in a particular cosmology and metaphysics or in a particular form of argument. PWL draws upon the distinction between discourse about philosophy as theoretical discourse about philosophy and as a philosophical mode of life. As an intuition about the study of philosophy, PWL began with the work of Pierre Hadot on ancient philosophy (especially the Stoics and the Neoplatonists) but has been extended to the study of Buddhism, Islamic philosophy, medieval philosophy, Wittgenstein, Foucault and much beyond. Other distinguished contributions have come from thinkers such as André-Jean Voelke (1925–91) on Stoic and Hellenistic philosophy (especially his *La philosophie comme thérapie de l'âme*), Juliusz Domański (b. 1927) on medieval philosophy and his *La philosophie, théorie ou manière de vivre?*, Jean Greisch (b. 1942) and his *Vivre en philosophant*, and Alexander Nehamas on ancient and modern philosophy, especially *The Art of Living*. Nehamas, for example, suggests that the widespread assumption that philosophy is normatively a theoretical discipline disengaged from the life of activity needs to be problematized. In his approach to the care of the self and the construction of the self, like some other post-structuralists including Foucault, he conflates the act of philosophizing with other forms of literary and artistic production in which personal self-fashioning lies at the heart of the result, a form of what we now call positionality (Nehamas 1998: 2–15). But in his focus on the Socratic, Nehamas places less emphasis on spiritual exercises than others – and especially Hadot – do, while Foucault's fashioning of the self as an aesthetic expression is surely too narrow. Cooper considers Hadot's position on spiritual exercises to be exaggerated and not justified by the textual evidence (Cooper 2012: 18–19; Hadot 1995: 206–13; see also Chase in Chase et al 2013: 263–5). Nussbaum's work on Stoic ethics as therapy of the soul is a fellow traveller; but by restricting PWL to ethics, it does not have the same scope as Hadot. Eli Kramer's ongoing trilogy uses PWL as an approach to what he calls intercultural modes of philosophy predicated on three levels: philosophical community, because in much pre-modern and arguably modern European philosophy (especially in the so-called continental traditions) no philosopher is a solitary thinker working in isolation; the reflective, a journey away from rehearsing arguments and settled dogmas towards disruptions; and finally systematic inquiry into the philosophical life (Kramer 2021: 3–4). The emphasis on community is an attempt to hold on to the idea that philosophers can transform not only themselves but their societies and cultures, for which he draws upon ancient Hellenic norms, medieval and renaissance Europe, the community in India and Tibet, the *shuyan* as well as the imperial academies in Confucian China, and the Buddhist monasteries (Kramer 2021: 31–99). But the best way to start an exploration of PWL is with Hadot himself:

> Philosophy was a way of life. This is not only to say that it was a specific type of moral conduct … Rather, it means that philosophy was a mode of existing-in-the-world, which had to be practiced at each instant, and the goal of which was to transform the whole of the individual's life.
>
> Philosophy was a way of life, both in its exercise and effort to achieve wisdom, and in its goal, wisdom itself. For real wisdom does not merely cause us to know; it makes us 'be' in a different way.
>
> (Hadot 1995: 265)

Two further elements in Hadot's thought are worth mentioning: first is the philosophical way of life and philosophical discourse:

> It is perhaps necessary to have recourse to the distinction proposed by the Stoics, between discourse about philosophy and philosophy itself. For the Stoics, the parts of philosophy – physics, ethics, and logic – were not, in fact, parts of philosophy itself but parts of philosophical discourse … Philosophy, itself – that is, the philosophical way of life – is no longer a theory divided into parts but a unitary act, which consists in living logic, physics, and ethics.
>
> (Hadot 1995: 266–7)

Secondly, for Hadot, philosophy as a way of life, an art of living and a way of being, was a constant from the ancient Greeks through until the medieval period, until Christianity subordinated it to theology (rendering it theoretical) and the monastic life replaced the philosophical way of life (Hadot 1995: 269). A central feature for Hadot of PWL is spiritual practice and living in the present:

> Philosophy in antiquity was an exercise practised at every instant. It invites us to concentrate on each instant of life, to become aware of the infinite value of each present moment … in the lived experience of a concrete, living, and perceiving subject.
>
> (Hadot 1995: 273)

Hadot's approach to the inner life and the ascent to the spiritual through philosophizing is already clear in his early work on Plotinus, especially drawing on the doffing metaphor of *Enneads* IV.8.1 (Hadot 1998a: 25–8). Already here we have the notion that philosophy is something one does. Therefore, PWL provides us with not only a potential method for studying a particular philosophical tradition in its own context, but also with the possibility of comparative metaphysics that allows us to read across traditions with certain key themes and motifs in mind, without lapsing into false comparisons or the problem of incommensurability.

In this chapter, I examine Hadot's contribution and method in some detail and then consider their extension to some other philosophical traditions, including a selective reading of Buddhist philosophies and Islamic philosophies. Before concluding, I consider some objections to the paradigm, and how, those objections notwithstanding, PWL can constitute a productive approach to comparative metaphysics, seeing metaphysics as a holistic and connected philosophical framework that takes into consideration our embodiment and place in the cosmos and our mutuality with others.

Philosophy as a way of life and Pierre Hadot

Hadot's work put forward a number of critical insights for the study of ancient philosophy that may be extended to the study of other traditions of philosophy. Perhaps the most important is the notion of spiritual exercises; but we should begin with questions of the nature of the study of the history of philosophy, models of wisdom and happiness and their articulation within a school or community, and the cultivation of philosophy as a means to transformation, following a sage and seeking sagehood.

The history of philosophy

The history of philosophy develops in a series of leaps, contextual and felicitous mistranslations, misreadings and creative mistakes. Thus, for example, we should not read Mullā Ṣadrā on Aristotle and compare it to the Aristotle that we know from the (often analyticizing) study of Aristotle in philosophy and classics departments, but the Aristotle that he read, received and creatively manipulated, a thoroughly Islamicized and Neoplatonized Aristotle with elements of Plotinus, Porphyry and even Ibnʿ Arabī – an Aristotle who spoke Arabic. It is this process that makes commentary literature such a creative force in philosophy and impels us to read philosophy as the product of particular school traditions (e.g. Wisnovsky 2004). Philosophy takes place within a tradition; reading the text is not a simple dialogue across time but a practice rooted in a school tradition and the commentary culture associated with key texts and significantly with concomitant spiritual practices. In his inaugural lecture as professor at the Collège de France, Hadot said:

> Each school, then, represents a form of life defined by an ideal of wisdom. The result is that each one has its corresponding fundamental inner attitude […] but above all every school practises exercises designed to ensure spiritual progress towards the ideal

state of wisdom, exercises of reason that will be, for the soul, analogous to the athlete's training or to the application of a medical cure [...]

It seems to me, indeed, that in order to understand the works of the philosophers of antiquity, we must take account of all the concrete conditions in which they wrote, all the constraints that weighed upon them: the context of the school, the very nature of *philosophia*, literary genres, rhetorical rules, dogmatic imperatives, and traditional modes of reasoning. One cannot read an ancient author the way one does a contemporary author [...] in fact, the works of antiquity are produced under entirely different conditions than those of their modern counterparts.

(Hadot 1995: 59–61)

An important corollary is that there is a difference between reading a contemporary philosophical text and one from the past (Hadot 2001: 93–6), because of the privileging of the oral in the latter and the nature of the teaching imparted, and hence because the professional contexts of the two are quite distinct (Dillon 2005). The history of philosophy therefore is a series of practices of reading within communities and traditions that develop over time.

Models of wisdom within a community and practices of dialogue

Secondly, training in philosophizing is to inculcate practices of dialoguing. Philosophy is primarily an oral exercise and requires engagement: merely reading a written text will not allow one to understand the hermeneutical rules and methodology of the school, which is unwritten in the treatises (Hadot 2002b: 272). The written word is an *aide-mémoire* for the spoken word, based on the logocentrism inherent in the philosophical tradition and predicated on the idea of philosophy as revealed word, encoded in a sacred book, and requires a spiritual master to initiate and explicate it (Athanassiadi 2006: 31–70; Carruthers 1992). The dialoguing basic to the Socratic method is a learned practice within a community, an externalization of the need to inculcate an examination of the self, an inner dialogue and attention to and care of the self – to know oneself as the Delphic maxim has it, and as the famous saying articulates it in the Islamic context: 'whosoever knows his self knows his Lord' (*man 'arafa nafsahu fa-qad 'arafa rabbahu*) (Hadot 1995: 89–93, 2002b: 41).

In what sense can we consider dialoguing to be a spiritual exercise? Hadot answers that dialoguing involves a conversion of the self from the sensible and an orientation to the Good (Hadot 1995: 93). Dialogue is thus a mode for the expression and emergence of the self, in dialogue with the teacher but also with the text, insofar as reading the text is designed to effect and activate 'switches in the soul' that take it along the path of transformation through the mode of non-discursive pedagogy

(Rappe 2000: 3–23). Discourse is thus taken here in two rather different senses: the former is addressed to a disciple or the self and linked to an 'existential context, a concrete praxis', while the latter is formal and has an intelligible content (Hadot 1995: 26). It is the former that amounts to a spiritual exercise. Significantly, this spiritual exercise must be conducted within a tradition and community. Dialoguing – and indeed philosophy – only exists within traditions and communities (Hadot 2002a: 3). The question for historians and contemporary thinkers is whether the *madrasa*, the monastery and the university constitute such communities. And indeed, whether they continue to do so.

And what about other, newer, forms of traditions and communities such as enhanced reality and virtual reality, which as Chalmers (2022) has argued are forms of reality and interpersonality?

The cultivation of philosophy, transformation and sagehood

The cultivation of philosophy purports to have an effect on the soul of the seeker so that they may not only think but orient themselves in the world, with the goal of becoming a sage. The process of philosophy is thus the forming of the individual and not just informing that self (Hadot 1995: 60). At the heart of Hadot's thought is a particular anthropology of the ancient philosopher: humans need to understand and live in this world but also recognize their ability to make their world (Hadot 2002b: 343). The sage of antiquity is a philosopher whose practice allows him to be embedded in this world.

That rootedness makes us cosmic and hence provides the possibility of making and humanizing our world (Hadot 2002b: 355–6).

Thus the sage not only affects the world he inhabits but also is capable of creatively reconfiguring how we understand reality. The sage is more than just a modern scientist investigating phenomena. Sagehood involves the acquisition of three states: peace of mind and inner tranquillity (*ataraxia*), inner freedom and independence (*autarkeia*), and the view from above of the cosmic consciousness, which he draws from the Stoic tradition and from Marcus Aurelius (Hadot 2010b: 248–51; 2020: 194–7). The sage realizes in himself the unity of the inner life of the person as well as his role in everyday life (with its social and political elements) and in the cosmos (with its metaphysics). This notion of the sage as one who makes the world is a common Sufi trope related to the idea of the realized Sufi as the perfect human (*al-insān al-kāmil*), in the image of God, who participates in the divine names and deploys divine attributes. Such a sage in the Islamic tradition thus becomes the face of God (Corbin 2008). A similar case could be made for the sophianic understanding of divine humanity in some modern Orthodox Christian philosophies (Berdyaev 2009; Bulgakov 1994). These align well with the notion of the sage as one who has achieved godlikeness in the Platonic tradition. But Hadot does not really speak much of *theosis*. He acknowledges that godlikeness is an end of becoming a sage but does not really develop the notion as it is normally discussed in Platonic literature (Hadot 2010b: 237–42; 2020: 188–9; 2014: 103–4).

Spiritual exercises

The central notion of PWL is spiritual exercises; philosophy involves an *askēsis*. Hadot first used the term in a work on Marcus Aurelius in 1973 but its germ lay in his earlier work on Wittgenstein in which he tried to see how one could apply 'language games' to the study of ancient philosophy (Sharpe and Ure 2021: 3–4). Philosophizing requires spiritual exercises which are more than just intellectual and contemplative but entail a mode of living, a way of life; citing the *Seventh Epistle of Plato*, Hadot describes spiritual exercises as a way 'to really do philosophy' that entails a more totalizing 'ethics of dialoguing' involving the whole individual (Hadot 1995: 66–9). One issue here is whether Hadot casts the body aside in this process and focuses too much on the spirit and the self, following Plotinus (Sharpe and Ure 2021: 113–20). The extent of the embodied nature of the spiritual exercises needs to be considered, and his partner Ilsetraut Hadot does discuss acts of disciplining the self and self-mortification including frugality, ascetic practice and vegetarianism (Hadot 2019: 352). Philosophizing is therefore not just about pedagogy or learning how to learn but also a training and guiding of the soul, a learning how to live and become. Theoretical knowledge is insufficient; it needs to become present to the mind and a 'habitus of the soul' (Hadot 1995: 23). Thus, Hadot argues that spiritual exercise takes one beyond the acquisition of philosophy as theory:

> The philosophical act is not situated merely on the cognitive level, but on that of the self and of being. It is a progress which causes us to be more fully, and makes us better. It is a conversion which turns our entire life upside down, changing the life of the person who goes through it. It raises the individual from an inauthentic condition of life, darkened by unconsciousness, and harassed by worry, to an authentic state of life, in which he attains self-consciousness, an exact vision of the world, inner peace, and freedom.
>
> (Hadot 1995: 83)

Thus, philosophy is therapy for the soul: knowing is being and becoming. Philosophy does not just cause one to know but causes one to be in a particular way (Hadot 1995: 265; see also Nussbaum 1994; Sorabji 2000). But it is insufficient to associate spiritual exercises with ethical living alone, since ethics is but one of the three parts of philosophy: in ancient philosophy, the distinction between theory and practice applies to the physics and the metaphysics as well (Hadot 1995: 24).

What sorts of spiritual exercises might there be? The first is *askēsis* as a form of disciplining and transforming the self. It is a process of connecting the I to the self. The problem here is the lack of actual details. Hadot suggests that the old Greek notion of athleticism is extended from the body to the soul as a care of the self, and he mentions certain actions that later traditions would call meditative such as breath and spirit control (Hadot 2002a: 180–8). Part of *askēsis* concerns certain forms of contemplation including thinking of death, or *memento mori,* the preparation for which recalls one of the aspects of philosophy in the Platonic tradition (Hadot 2002a: 190–1; 1995: 93–101).

The second form of spiritual exercise is philosophical reading and writing, understanding the logos (Hadot 1995: 101–9; 1998b: 48–53). Practice of reading involves training in forms such as rhetoric, argumentation, systematic doctrine (rehearsing and understanding of the dogmas of the school) and dialectic (the dialoguing discussed above) (Hadot 2002a: 103–8). This involves a certain hermeneutical approach predicated on the notion that reading and learning concern the acquisition of a 'method for contemplating how all things transform themselves into one another' (Hadot 2002a: 136). Texts such as handbooks, textbooks, commentaries and epitomes were the main conduit for the inculcation of the method, arranged around the way in which the sage teacher would engage with disciples (Hadot 2002a: 149–53). Writing for Hadot is never for its own sake but rather a practice insofar as it provides material support for oral learning and speech – with the clear notion that the structure and language of the writing will once again return to speech (Hadot 2010b: 209–11; 2020: 58). It is a reflection of the philosopher's meditation; Hadot cites Marcus Aurelius' *Meditations* I, 1, 25 on the need to write every day about one's spiritual exercises; this need is related to the self's watchfulness (Hadot 1998b: 50). He argues that the philosopher's primary job in ancient times was not to write works constructing a system; in fact, he argues that it is a feature of modern philosophy to write in order to construct an architecture of ideas (Hadot 2010b: 213; 2020: 56–8).

Contrary to Foucault, Hadot does not think that philosophical writing in itself creates a spiritual self (Hadot 2002a: 210). Writing might be useful for the disciple but for the aspirant sage, it is oral teaching that is paramount (Hadot 2010b: 217; 2020: 69).

The third form of spiritual exercise is the accounting of the self and examining one's conscience. This state of watchfulness and introspection that reflects where one is and takes into consideration one's historical self has a number of parallels in different traditions to which we will return (Hadot 2002a: 198–202). The fourth spiritual exercise is practising the self in the world, a form of its ascent, its dilation into the cosmos in order to become cosmic consciousness (Hadot 2002a: 202–6; 1995: 251–63). The end of this spiritual exercise is precisely to obtain 'the view from above' (Hadot 1995: 238–50; 2023: 41–6). Thus physics as well as ethics and politics can be spiritual exercises. The fifth exercise is about choice – choosing the sage to follow and emulate, and the way of life in order to inculcate within the self-happiness, freedom and the contemplation of the cosmos that arises from cosmic consciousness (Hadot 2002a: 221–9). The final exercise is living in the present, where Hadot draws upon Goethe's notion of the 'present alone being our happiness' and the contemplation of living, a *memento vivere*, and not just dying (Hadot 1995: 82–9, 218–37; 2002a: 279; 2023: 5–6, 27–8). There are clear parallels to all this in Sufism and other traditions.

What this list suggests is that spiritual exercises are not just intellectual ones; they are multi-faceted. They involve numerous genres including dialogues, poetry and gnomic sayings. They often reflect our embodiment and engage with craft, initiation, governance of self and others. The holistic nature is brought together once we realize that the end of spiritual exercises reflects the three features of sagehood: peace of mind, inner freedom and cosmic consciousness. Is *askēsis* a better term to use than spiritual exercises (Harter in Firodalis 2018: 154)? While various examples are given in Hadot, the broad sense of spiritual exercises seems vague and three critical questions remain (before we venture into the question of the historically gendered nature of the sage): does he neglect the body and somatic elements of practice? Does spiritual exercise tend to exaggerate the soteriological and play down the argumentative nature of ancient philosophy? In the absence of strong evidence of the contexts and the sociology of philosophical models of living in many traditions, what can we really say about PWL and spiritual exercises beyond the broad notion of an abstract ideal?

Conception of philosophy as a way of life and spiritual exercises: Hadot and beyond

Extending our discussion of PWL and spiritual exercises, I want to consider two examples: the thought of the Safavid sage Mullā Ṣadrā Shīrāzī (d. 1636), and some traditions of Theravāda and Mahayāna Buddhism.

In the case of Mulla Sadra, I focus on three themes: philosophy as a way of life and of discourse, philosophy as a spiritual exercise, and the concept of philosophy as an act within a community. Hadot seems content to use the term 'philosophy' to describe those practices that he considers to constitute the philosophical life; philosophy is the discipline that he defines. Mullā Ṣadrā offers a definition of *ḥikma* – wisdom, the standard term used for philosophy in the broadest sense in the later tradition in Islam – that suggests that the pursuit of philosophy as a love of wisdom requires more than ratiocination: it needs a heavy dose of intuition, even mystical experience, and an exegesis of the ways in which God discloses himself.

Consider two examples. The first is the definition in the *Four Journeys*, his major work:

> Know that *ḥikma* is the perfecting of the human soul through cognition of the realities of existents as they truly are, and through judgments about their being, ascertained through demonstrations, and not grasped through conjecture or adherence to authority, according to what is humanly possible. One might say that it [philosophising] ascribes to the world a rational order understood according to human capability so that one may attain a resemblance to the Creator.
>
> The human emerges as a mixture of two: a spiritual form from the world of command [the intelligible world] and sensible matter from the world of creation [the sensible world], and thus he possesses in his soul both attachment [to the body] and detachment [from it]. *Ḥikma* is sharpened through the honing of two faculties relating to two practices: one theoretical and abstract and the other practical, attached to creation ...
>
> The theoretical art ... is the *ḥikma* sought by the lord of the messengers [Muḥammad] – peace be with him – when he sought in his supplication to his lord when he said: 'O My Lord, show me things as they truly are', and also [sought] by the intimate of God [Abraham] when he asked: 'My lord bestow upon me judgement (*ḥukman*)' [Q. Sūrat al-Shuʿarāʾ v. 82]. Judgement is verifying the existence of things entailed by conceptions.
>
> (Shīrāzī 2001–2004, I: 23–4)

This definition makes it clear that philosophizing is more than a ratiocinative discourse but is in fact closely associated with the practice of theosis (*taʾalluh* in Arabic) central to Neoplatonic conceptions of philosophy as a theurgic practice that seeks to invoke the divine through magical practices to understand reality. It also closely relates this practice to a prophetic inheritance and connects philosophizing to the Qurʾānic notion of wisdom.

This theme is made more explicit in the second definition that derives from his exegesis on the Qurʾan in which he collates an exegetical philosophy with a philosophical anthropology. He writes:

> Know that the human is the most noble of beings; he was at the beginning of his generation in the very limits of baseness and imperfection that arise out of the nature of the elements and components [that formed him] like all other species of animals, and his nature was in degrees of baseness in relation to other substances and entities, except that he had in his essence a faculty of progression to the very limit of perfection and progress to the lights of the transcendent Origin and the active Sustainer, stripped of evil and calamity, becoming one of the inhabitants of the world of light, bestowed with the bounty of the afterlife and with bliss; it does not behove divine providence to allow him (the human) to wallow in the grazing grounds of the passions like insects and worms ...

> For it is known that everything has a perfection that is specific to it, for which it was created, and an act that completes it that is appropriate [to it]. The perfection of the human is through the perception of divine stations and partaking of divine intelligible knowledge by stripping away material sensible attachments and renouncing base worldly matters and being saved from the impulses of passion and freed from the bonds of carnal, concupiscent desires.
>
> All this is not made easy except through guidance and learning and disciplining and steadfastness.
>
> (Shīrāzī 2010, I, 4)

Returning to the themes in Hadot's work, one finds philosophy as both theory and practice in Mullā Ṣadrā, practice as a way of discourse but also as a way of mystical experience and insight. The pedagogy of training souls requires spiritual masters, sages who can inculcate virtues and guide the initiate in the pursuit of the good (Shīrāzī 2001–4, I: 18). Philosophy is thus a religious commitment that requires some divine grace for success and attachment to divine providence (Shīrāzī 2001–4, I: 13).

But what about the spiritual practices? Dialogue in the Socratic method is a given of *madrasa* practice in which it is often called the *mubāḥatha* or discoursing during which students repeat, rehearse and critique arguments learned in class; he makes it clear that the rehearsal of discourse and dialogue is critical to philosophizing (Shīrāzī 2001–4, IX: 146). In the narrower sense of quasi-theurgic practices or Sufi disciplining of the soul, philosophy for Mullā Ṣadrā cannot forsake it. It is precisely these practices and the cultivation of a mystical method that mark out his philosophical method from Avicennism and indeed from a more ratiocinative Aristotle (even if Azadpur 2011 has argued for a PWL approach to Avicenna).

For Mullā Ṣadrā, PWL without ethical and religious commitment would be meaningless; the practice of spiritual exercises while it may well include those that Hadot discusses would necessarily also involve devotions, litanies, acts of remembrance and memorialization, as well as rituals such as prayer. Spiritual practice and discourse, that is conscious and self-reflective, require a sage as guide and mentor. This further entails a clear idea of what a sage is. In the *Four Journeys*, Mullā Ṣadrā explains the qualities of a sage:

> The sage possesses the qualities of generosity, good humour, fine judgement, pronounced taste and experiences of spiritual insight.
>
> (Shīrāzī 2001–4, VI: 6)

Such a sage is a (late antique) holy man, the hieratic engaged in theurgy. This leads us to the final issue: the nature of the community in which philosophizing is practised and led by the sage as Hadot required. Unfortunately, we have little by way of direct accounts of the teaching and practice of philosophy even by Mullā Ṣadrā. The history of the practice of philosophy in Safavid Iran and indeed in the world of Islam has still to be written, a history that would be more sociologically attuned to practices of knowledge production, formation and dissemination. Mullā Ṣadrā is clear that there is a community, a *qawm*, which practises philosophy, a circle centred on texts and sages who define that practice. One needs to know who is not worthy of that community and companionship:

> It is incumbent upon one who wishes to traverse the way of the people of reality and certainty, after purifying his soul from the vicious character traits, to set aside the company of the deniers (of God) and the astray because there is a seal set upon their hearts and their audition and their sight yet they do not understand, and also (set aside) the company of the innovators who are astray because when the prophets came to them with clear proofs, they delighted in what knowledge they possessed and they embraced them but mocked them [the proofs of the prophets].
> (Shīrāzī 2010, I: 5)

Even if we do not have much on the details of the community – and of course, any *madrasa* is a community by definition and we know that his *madrasa* in Shiraz (the Madrasa-yi Khān) where he taught was founded for the purposes primarily of teaching philosophy – we know that the community is bounded and closed to those not worthy of it. In the *Four Journeys*, he says:

> It is forbidden for most people to set out to acquire these complicated sciences and join the community because the worthy are rare and exceptional. Guidance to philosophising is an act of grace from God.
> (Shīrāzī 2001–4, III: 560)

But the exact nature of the particular spiritual exercises involved is not set out.

Turning to Buddhism, we start with the question of *askēsis* and spiritual exercises in the Abhidharma and Theravāda tradition, before considering some elements of the Mahayāna tradition.

What sort of wisdom traditions are involved in Buddhism? How does *askēsis* work? A central problem that we face when we consider Buddhisms – just as we did with Mullā Ṣadrā – is the simple fact that the dichotomy of philosophy and religion is particular to modern European history and its sensibilities (Kapstein in Chase 2013: 101). What if PWL cannot make sense without recourse to notions of faith, myth, devotion and ritual? This is as true of the Mahayāna tradition – for example, in the cases of Śāntideva and Buddhaghosa – as it is for Theravada and early Buddhism (Kapstein in Chase 2013: 113). Collins considers two ways in which a Buddhist education and spiritual practices work for PWL: the narrative, and more abstract reflection.

The first relates to seeking wisdom centred upon acquiring excellence through narrative practices, in particular the Jātakas or birth stories of the Buddha prevalent especially in the Theravāda tradition and Abhidharma (Collins 2020: 1–3). The birth stories include moral tales and legends and pious sayings but also jokes, fables, romances and fairy tales (Collins 2020: 17–19). These tales orient us towards the everyday social order through social justice and the five precepts of moral order (Collins 2020: 7–9). He gives a number of examples of themes in these narratives: friendship (Story of the Present), filial piety (*Sāma jātaka*), justified violence (Story of the Crane – *Baka Jātaka* – and Story of the Cat – *Bilāra Jātaka*), and comedy – Kacchapa Jātaka on the story of the Turtle (Collins 2020: 30–7). The narrative approach mirrors the more abstract and reflective insofar as it is also concerned with the quest for reality and things as they truly are beyond conventional reality and truth (Collins 2020: 55–7).

The second more abstract approach, especially in Mahāyana works, includes the acts of monasticism and asceticism. Collins cites the Path of Purification of Buddhaghosa on types of meditative subjects (*kammaṭṭhāna*), of which there are seven (Collins in Fiordalis 2018: 38–9): first, ritual practices and objects; secondly, contemplation of the virtues or divine abidings such as friendship, compassion and joy; thirdly, recollections or memorialization of the Buddha, the faith (*dharma*) and death (which recalls the Platonic tradition and Hadot); fourthly, a focus on the sources of suffering, which is linked to the recollection of death; fifthly, meditation on the carnal, with a focus on the 'foulness' of food; sixthly, contemplation of the four elements and the constituents of the cosmos; and finally, metaphysics, the immaterial and cosmology (Collins in Fiordalis 2018: 124–39). Overall, we can see in this text the abstract intersecting with meditative practices and focuses: the aim is to end suffering, practice emptying, and to come to knowledge of the truth (Collins in Fiordalis 2018: 45). And that truth is ineffable. Alongside this path of wisdom, there are other kinds of practices associated with the monastic life: chanting, devotions and paying respect; social location and bodily comportment; forms of spiritual direction and friendship; and monastic rules on forms of restrictions (Collins 2020: 109–12, 112–19, 119–24). For Collins, these constitute what Foucault calls spirituality, namely, 'the pursuit, practice and experience through which the subject carries out the necessary transformations on himself in order to have access to the truth' (Foucault 2005: 15).

Śāntideva's text *Bodhicaryāvatāra* follows a similar approach in which the meditation upon the text is a spiritual practice. It involves the same homiletic to alleviate suffering through foregoing pleasures of the body and acts of self-mortification to become a healing person by adopting the 'awakening mind' (*bodhicitta*) (Śāntideva 1995: 6–14). Reflecting on texts is an important element of the spiritual exercises, as are devotion to the Buddha and obedience to the sages (Śāntideva 1995: 34–5, 119). The meditative absorption in the world as well as the vigilance of the awakening mind is recognizably similar to Hadot's living in the present and seeking the view from above (Śāntideva 1995: 25, 88–104). As an approach, the text is holistic and clear about the broader context of being with a teacher and in a community in order to achieve mindfulness through spiritual exercise:

Mindfulness comes easily to those fortunate people who practice wholeheartedly through the instruction of their preceptor, because they live with their teacher, and out of fear.

(Śāntideva 1995: 36)

The concept of fear here recalls the restrictions of the sangha and the Sufi idea of the disciple placing himself in the hands of the master like a corpse being washed and shrouded for burial. The Mahāyana tradition tends to see the practice of philosophy as essentially ethical and soteriological. Yet, while these texts are meditative, they are also rather abstract and theoretical.

Before concluding, it is worth putting forward some reservations. Hadot's approach to the study of ancient philosophy can be a fruitful way of reading Mullā Ṣadrā. But one wonders about basic issues of commensurability. Hadot's own work stresses the need to pay careful attention to context without reducing the practice of philosophy to historicism. Safavid Iran may share values, ideas and even some contextual parallels to late antiquity but basic notions of competing communities of religious and philosophical commitment were not common in seventeenth-century Iran. Not that late antiquity was devoid of imperial fiats in areas of doctrine and philosophy or that heretication and objectification of heterodoxy were absent (Athanassiadi 2005 and 2010). But the Shi'i context of Safavid Iran is a particularity distinguishing Mullā Ṣadrā from an Iamblichus. Even if they shared notions of dialogue, practices of discourse or mysticism, notions of the centrality of spiritual exercises, and even the notion that philosophizing requires not just a spiritual master but also a community, this does not necessarily mean that these concepts sufficiently overlap. Mystical practices and theurgy in pagan late antique philosophy cannot be identical to Shi'i Sufism. As Collins also suggests, it can be difficult to derive a phenomenology merely from texts which are often lacking context (Collins 2020: 151–3). Most importantly, I am not suggesting that we should set aside other approaches and adopt Hadot as a singular, totalizing hermeneutics for studying Safavid philosophical texts. Rather, I propose a more open approach that is worth testing. Philosophical practice even within the study of Islamic thought perhaps needs more of an experimental turn, not a conversion from one absolute and closed reading of the text to another. This would be very much consonant with Mullā Ṣadrā's own distrust of closure and his condemnation of imitation and the mere mechanistic rehearsal of doctrine.

What about PWL as a religious commitment? At one level, the question for PWL is cognate to the Platonic ideal of the quest for godlikeness that draws on the famous quotation of *Theaetetus* 176a–b: 'One should strive to escape from here to there as quickly as possible. Now the way to escape is to become as nearly as possible like to God; and to become like God is to become just and pious, with the accompaniment of intelligence' (Alcinous 1993: 181.19–182.13, 37–8; see also O'Meara 2003: 31–9; Annas 1999: 52–71; Uždavinys 2014: 67–70). That Platonic tradition was quickly taken up in both Christian and Islamic philosophical traditions by aligning the way of life and the spiritual practices with the rituals and cultic practices of those traditions. The Church fathers associated Christianity and Christ with the truth and the pursuit of godlikeness, with the end of felicity conflated with happiness in the afterlife (Karamanolis 2014: 48–59) – see Part 1 Chapter 11.

There is an assumption that PWL and spiritual exercises might confuse our modern distinction between philosophy and religion, which no doubt makes some people uncomfortable. It also seems to cede – in the area of global philosophy – too much to the non-West that has traditionally since the enlightenment been seen as an abode of religion and mysticism but not of philosophy (Bernasconi 1997; König-Pralong 2019: 9–55; King 1999: 1–41; Park 2013: 51–96, 113–2). Or might PWL simply be outdated since it rejects the naturalistic revolution in thought (Cottingham in Chase 2013: 150–3) and because it valorizes those aspects of the ancient tradition broadly neglected in the modern period and neglects other aspects such as logic and precise argumentation? Yet the search for meaning and the hermeneutics of the self at the centre of many philosophical inquiries surely cannot be separated from the religious (or the noumenal) (Garfield 2002: 251–60).

Hadot's approach seems to focus on the metaphysical and the pursuit of becoming a sage. Different traditions have differing emphases on disciplines, and one can see how they might overlap with Hadot's broad notion of spiritual exercises. But, as Collins suggests, what about narratives that people share and the everyday – for which his example is the jataka tradition of the Buddha's birth? Furthermore, Hadot's approach pays rather thin attention to institutions and the broader sense of the community (Collins 2020: 159–61). Thus, the sociological dimensions as well as the quotidian context seem to be absent, even if recognizing that not every askesis is transformative and not every text soteriological. In short, the very notion of spiritual exercises as central tends to a reductionist approach to all ethical development (Harter in Fiordalis 2018: 169). Are we expecting too much?

Conclusions

For any project of comparative metaphysics, the question of method is paramount. Philosophy as a way of life is an insight drawn from evidence in the history of European philosophy in antiquity that has been successfully but critically extended to the study of other philosophical traditions, European, Buddhist or Islamic. As a method, though, it may occlude by a somewhat simple rejection of the alternative – or rather dominant – modes of doing philosophy in the Eurocentred traditions, which Hadot rejects for lacking any clear notion of human destination or a soteriology, or indeed for simple speculative manipulation of reason: he dismisses modern philosophers from Kant onwards as mere 'artists of reason' (Hadot 2002a: 266–7).

There are risks and possible false friends involved in the process: the very notion of spiritual exercises is rather broad and somewhat vague: for many philosophical traditions, we may not be able to discover corresponding concepts and practices. Similarly, the context often required to make sense of the philosophical life may not be available beyond the limited evidence of the texts – a point famously made by Jonardon Ganeri about Indian philosophies (Ganeri 2011: 63–73). A totalizing approach to method almost inevitably runs into the problem of incommensurabilities and exceptions. Should philosophy *necessarily* be spiritually sublime and soteriological? On the other hand, an approach that begins with an acknowledgement of diverse possibilities is rather more conducive to creative interpretations. PWL thus can be an approach that brings together diverse traditions in a critical manner, while acknowledging inner diversities; for example, it may work for some of the more mystically inclined traditions and for the school of Mullā Ṣadrā and others in Islamic Safavid thought, but perhaps not so much for earlier traditions of *falsafa* including Averroes. It may work as part of a decolonial turn in the study of philosophy. But it is important to hold on the critical, the argumentative, and the reflective and discursive. A return to the 'big questions' need not set up a false binary of spiritual exercise and praxis on one side and critical, intellectual reflection on the other. The philosophical quest indeed does not come to an end – even if one suspects the triumphalism of the analytic tradition in an earlier period has given way to greater humility and openness. Perhaps we should therefore end with Hadot:

> Another danger, the worst of all, is to believe that one can do without philosophical reflection. The philosophical way of life must be justified in rational, motivated discourse, and such discourse is inseparable from the way of life. Nevertheless, we have to reflect critically on the ancient, modern, and oriental discourses which justify a given way of life. We must try to render explicit the reasons we act in such-and-such a way, and reflect on our experience and that of others. Without such reflection, the philosophical life risks sinking into banal vapidity, 'respectable' feelings, or deviance. To be sure, we cannot wait until we have read Kant's *Critique of Pure Reason* in order to live as philosophers. Nevertheless, living as a philosopher also means to reflect, to reason, to conceptualise in a rigorous, technical way – or, as Kant used to say, 'to think for oneself'. The philosophical life is a never-ending quest.
>
> (Hadot 2002a: 280)

Notes

1. While the term 'self' is more common in later philosophical traditions, I use it interchangeably with soul, the latter having a more religious connotation.
2. The idea of philosophy as therapy is also found in a number of non-European traditions. Early Buddhism and Abhidharma: Kalupahana (1992: 85–9, 144–59);

Tantric Buddhism: Williams (2000: 192–244); Zen Buddhism: Izutsu (1977: 3–7); the theurgic and the divinatory aspects of the therapy in ancient Babylonian thought: Van De Mieroop (2016: 87–140); therapy and Nepantla-process in Aztec philosophy: Maffie (2014: 479–529).

References

Alcinous (1993), *The Handbook of Philosophy*, trans. John Dillon. Oxford: The Clarendon Press.
Annas, J. (1999), *Platonic Ethics, Old and New*. Ithaca, NY: Cornell University Press.
Arnold, D., C. Ducher and P-J. Harter, (eds.) (2019), *Reasons and Lives in Buddhist Traditions: Studies in Honor of Matthew Kapstein*. Boston, MA: Wisdom Publications.
Athanassiadi, P. (2005), *La lutte pour l'orthodoxie dans le platonisme tardif: De Numénius et Plotin à Damascius*. Paris: Les Belles Lettres.
Athanassiadi, P. (2010), *Vers la pensée unique: La montée de l'intolérance dans l'Antiquité tardive*. Paris: Les Belles Lettres.
Azadpur, M. (2011), *Reason Unbound: On Spiritual Practice in Islamic Peripatetic Philosophy*. Albany, NY: State University of New York Press.
Berdyaev, Nicholas (2009), *The Divine and the Human*, trans. R. M. French. San Rafael, CA: Semantron Press.
Bernasconi, R. (1997), 'Philosophy's Paradoxical Parochialism', in K. Ansell-Pearson, B. Parry and J. Squires (eds.), *Cultural Readings of Imperialism*. London: Lawrence & Wishart, pp. 212–26.
Buddhaghosa (1975), *Visuddhimagga*, trans. Bhikku Ñāṇamoli as *The Path of Perfection*. Kandy: Buddhist Publications Society.
Bulgakov, Sergii (1994), *Sophia, the Wisdom of God: An Outline of Sophiology*. Hudson, NY: Lindisfarne Books.
Chalmers, D. J. (2022), *Reality +: Virtual Worlds and the Problems of Philosophy*. London: Allen Lane.
Chase, M., S. R. L. Clark and M. McGhee, (eds.) (2013), *Philosophy as a Way of Life: Ancients and Moderns. Essays in Honor of Pierre Hadot*. Oxford: Wiley Blackwells.
Collins, S. (1982), *Selfless Persons: Imagery and Thought in Theravāda Buddhism*. Cambridge: Cambridge University Press.
Collins, S. (2020), *Wisdom as a Way of Life: Theravāda Buddhism Reimagined*, ed. Justin Mcdaniel. New York: Columbia University Press.
Cooper, J. M. (2012), *Pursuits of Wisdom: Six Ways of Life in Ancient Philosophy from Socrates to Plotinus*. Princeton, NJ: Princeton University Press.
Corbin, Henry (2008), *Face de Dieu, face de l'homme: Herméneutique et soufisme*. Paris: Entrelacs.
Cusinato, Guido (2023), *Periagoge: Theory of Singularity and Philosophy as Exercise of Transformation*, trans. Rie Shubuya and Karen Whittle. Leiden: Brill.

Damascius (1999), *The Philosophical History*, ed. and trans. P. Athanassiadi. Athens: Apamea Cultural Association.

Davidson, A., and F. Worms, (eds.) (2010), *Pierre Hadot, l'enseignement des antique, l'enseignement des modernes*. Paris: Éditions ENS rue d'Ulm.

Dillon, John (2005), 'Philosophy as a Profession in Late Antiquity', in Andrew Smith (ed.), *The Philosopher and Society in Late Antiquity: Essays in Honour of Peter Brown*. Swansea: The Classical Press of Wales, pp. 1–17.

Domański, J. (1996), *La philosophie, théorie ou manière de vivre?*. Fribourg: Éditions Universitaires de Fribourg.

Fiordalis, D., (ed.) (2018), *Buddhist Spiritual Practices: Thinking with Pierre Hadot on Buddhism, Philosophy, and the Path*. Berkeley, CA: Mangalam Press.

Foucault, M. (2005), *The Hermeneutics of the Subject: Lectures at the Collège de France, 1981–82*, trans. G. Burchell, ed. A. Davidson. New York: Palgrave Macmillan.

Ganeri, J. (2011), *The Lost Age of Reason: Philosophy in Early Modern India 1450–1700*. Oxford: Oxford University Press.

Ganeri, J. (2012), *The Concealed Art of the Soul: Theories of Self and Practices of Truth in Indian Ethics and Epistemology*. Oxford: Oxford University Press.

Garfield, J. (2002), *Empty Words: Buddhist Philosophy and Cross-Cultural Interpretation*. New York: Oxford University Press.

Gowans, C. W. (2021), *Self-Cultivation Philosophies in Ancient India, Greece, and China*. Oxford: Oxford University Press.

Greisch, J. (2015), *Vivre en philosophant: Expérience philosophique, exercices spirituels et thérapie de l'âme*. Paris: Éditions Hermann.

Hadot, P. (1992), *La citadelle intérieure: Introduction aux Pensées de Marc Aurèle*. Paris: Fayard.

Hadot, P. (1995), *Philosophy as a Way of Life*, ed. A. Davidson, trans. M. Chase. Oxford: Blackwells.

Hadot, P. (1997), *Plotin ou la simplicité du regard*. Paris: Gallimard.

Hadot, P. (1998a), *Plotinus, or the Simplicity of Vision*, trans. M. Chase. Chicago, IL: University of Chicago Press.

Hadot, P. (1998b), *The Inner Citadel: The Meditations of Marcus Aurelius*, trans. M. Chase. Cambridge, MA: Harvard University Press.

Hadot, P. (1999), *Plotin, Porphyre: Études néoplatoniciennes*. Paris: Les belles lettres.

Hadot, P. (2001), *La philosophie comme manière de vivre: Entretiens avec Jeannie Carlier et Arnold I. Davidson*. Paris: Albin Michel.

Hadot, P. (2002a), *What Is Ancient Philosophy?*, trans. M. Chase. Cambridge, MA: Belknap Press, Harvard University Press.

Hadot, P. (2002b), *Exercices spirituels et philosophie antique*. Paris: Albin Michel.

Hadot, P. (2004), *La voile d'Isis: Essai sur l'histoire de l'idée de nature*. Paris: Gallimard.

Hadot, P. (2010a), *Wittgenstein et les limites de langage*. Paris: Vrin.

Hadot, P. (2010b), *Études de la philosophie ancienne*. Paris: Les belles lettres.

Hadot, P. (2011), *The Present Alone Is Our Happiness: Conversations with Jeannie Carlier and Arnold I. Davidson*, trans. M. Jaballah and M. Chase. Stanford, CA: Stanford University Press.

Hadot, P. (2014), *Discours et mode de vie philosophique*. Paris: Les belles lettres.
Hadot, P. (2016), *N'oublie pas de vivre: Goethe et la tradition des exercices spirituels*. Paris: Albin Michel.
Hadot, P. (2019), *La philosophie comme éducation des adultes: Textes, perspectives, entretiens*. Paris: Vrin.
Hadot, P. (2020), *The Selected Writings of Pierre Hadot: Philosophy as Practice*, trans. M. Sharpe and F. Testa. London: Bloomsbury Academic.
Hadot, P. (2023), *Don't Forget to Live*: *Goethe and the Tradition of Spiritual Exercises*, trans. M. Chase. Chicago, IL: University of Chicago Press.
Iamblichus (2003). *On the Mysteries*, trans. Emma C. Clarke, John M. Dillon and Jackson P. Hershbell. Atlanta, GA: Society of Biblical Literature.
Izutsu, Toshihiko (1977), *Toward a Philosophy of Zen Buddhism*. Tehran: Imperial Iranian Academy of Philosophy.
Kalupahana, David J. (1992), *A History of Buddhist Philosophy*: *Continuities and Discontinuities*. Honolulu, HI: University of Hawaii Press.
Karamanolis, George (2014), *The Philosophy of Early Christianity*. London: Routledge.
King, R. (1999), *Indian Philosophy*: *An Introduction to Hindu and Buddhist Thought*. Washington, DC: Georgetown University Press.
Kitcher, P. (2023), *What's the Use of Philosophy?* New York: Oxford University Press.
König-Pralong, Catherina (2019), *La colonie philosophique: Écrire l'histoire de la philosophie aux XVIIIe et XIXe siècles*. Paris: Éditions EHESS.
Kramer, E. (2021), *Intercultural Modes of Philosophy, Volume One*: *Principles to Guide Philosophical Commentary*. Leiden: Brill.
MacBride, F. (2014), 'Analytic Philosophy and Its Synoptic Commission: Toward the Epistemic End of Days', *Royal Institute of Philosophy Supplement* 74: 221–36. doi:10.1017/S1358246114000095.
Maffie, James (2014), *Aztec Philosophy*: *Understanding a World in Motion*. Boulder, CO: University Press of Colorado.
McGushin, E. F. (2007), *Foucault's Askesis*: *An Introduction to the Philosophical Life*. Evanston, IL: Northwestern University Press.
Nehamas, A. (1998), *The Art of Living*: *Socratic Explorations from Plato to Foucault*. Berkeley, CA: University of California Press.
Nussbaum, M. C. (1994), *The Therapy of Desire*: *Theory and Practice in Hellenistic Ethics*. Princeton, NJ: Princeton University Press.
Ogunnaike, O. (2020), *Deep Knowledge*: *Ways of Knowing in Sufism and Ifa, Two West African Intellectual Traditions*. University Park, PA: Pennsylvania State University Press.
O'Meara, D. J. (2003), *Platonopolis: Platonic Political Philosophy in Late Antiquity*. Oxford: Clarendon Press.
Paperson, la (2017), *A Third University is Possible*. Minneapolis, MN: University of Minnesota Press.
Park, P. K. J. (2013), *Africa, Asia, and the History of Philosophy: Racism in the Formation of the Philosophical Canon, 1780–1830*. Albany, NY: State University of New York Press.

Porphyry (1986), *Letter to Marcella*, trans. Alice Zimmern, rpt. Grand Rapids, MI: Phanes Press.

Rappe, S. (2000), *Reading Neoplatonism: Non-Discursive Thinking in the Texts of Plotinus, Proclus, and Damascius*. Cambridge: Cambridge University Press.

Śāntideva (1995), *The Bodhicaryāvatāra*, trans. K. Crosby and A. Skilton. Oxford: Oxford University Press.

Sharpe, M., and M. Ure (2021), *Philosophy as a Way of Life: From Antiquity to Modernity*. London: Bloomsbury Academic.

Shaw, Gregory (1995), *Theurgy and the Soul: The Neoplatonism of Iamblichus*. University Park, PA: Pennsylvania State University Press.

Shīrāzī, Mullā Ṣadrā (2001–2004), *al-Ḥikma al-mutaʿāliya fī-l-Asfār al-ʿaqlīya al-arbaʿa*. gen ed. Sayyid Muḥammad Khāminihī, 9 vols. Tehran: Sadra Islamic Philosophy Research Institute.

Shīrāzī, Mullā Ṣadrā (2010), *Tafsīr al-Qurʾān al-karīm*, eds. Muḥammad khājavī et Alii, 8 vols. Tehran: Sadra Islamic Philosophy Research Institute.

Sorabji, Richard (2000), *Emotion and Peace of Mind: From Stoic Agitation to Christian Temptation*. Oxford: Oxford University Press.

Uždavinys, Algis (2014), *Philosophy & Theurgy in Late Antiquity*. Kettering, OH: Angelico Press.

Van De Mieroop, Marc (2016), *Philosophy before the Greeks: The Pursuit of Truth in Ancient Babylonia*. Princeton, NJ: Princeton University Press.

Voelke, André-Jean (1993), *La philosophie comme thérapie de l'âme: Études de philosophie hellénistique*. Fribourg: Éditions universitaires de Fribourg.

Williams, Paul with Anthony Tribe (2000), *Buddhist Thought*. London: Routledge.

Wisnovksy, Robert (2004), 'The Nature and Scope of Arabic Philosophical Commentary in Post-Classical (ca. 1100–1900 AD) Islamic Intellectual History: Some Preliminary Observations', in Peter Adamson et al. (eds.), *Philosophy, Science and Exegesis in Greek, Arabic and Latin Commentaries*, vol. 2 London: Institute of Classical Studies, pp. 149–91.

Part 2

1

Suchness

Lucia Dolce

Comparative philosophy has mostly unfolded as a parallel history of ideas, which provides a space for contributions from traditions other than Western philosophy, but effectively retains the conceptual framework developed in Western philosophy and, more often than not, takes its cue from a particular problem common to Western philosophy, assuming that the object of comparison is the same concept in the traditions that it compares.[1] Few attempts have been made to focus on concerns which originate from a non-Western tradition. Yet these may have received extended and sophisticated philosophical analysis in that tradition and might engender closer comparison with other non-Western traditions. Thus to take one such concern and use it as both an analytical category and a methodological position opens new avenues to reconsider familiar conceptualizations. It allows us to explore the possibilities of an alternative articulation of reality, based on different premises and expressed in a language that may find resonances with, but is fundamentally different from, that inherited through European languages.[2] The thrust of this exercise is not only to begin our thinking from another type of assumption, but also, and perhaps most importantly, to probe the consequences of taking that standpoint as standard, rather than exceptional.

This chapter tests this possibility by reconsidering some of the questions posited by the metaphysical pursuit and dealt with in the present volume, through the lens of a central idea indigenous to what I will for convenience call 'Buddhist metaphysics'. I here use the term 'metaphysics' with inverted commas because the term per se does not belong to the tradition of thought I take my cue from, and therefore it may belie the very purpose of the analysis undertaken here. I have also put 'Buddhist' in inverted commas because, as a pan-Asian philosophical tradition that developed through many centuries and across different cultural geographies in complex and heterogeneous ways, Buddhism cannot be subsumed under a single, uniform mode of thinking – there is no Buddhist metaphysics as such, just as there is no normative 'Western' metaphysics.[3] Writing in English, the concept of 'metaphysics' can function as a general rubric under which to gather the multiple, at times contradictory, notions and interpretations that Buddhists engendered of reality, being and the invisible world 'beyond'.

The concept at the centre of this reflection is 'Suchness'. In making use of this Buddhist notion, my aim is to envisage the possible articulations of a metaphysical position which emphatically asserts this world and values the present, but which is formulated in a non-substantialist language that avoids both reification and apophaticism. The framework in which the notion of Suchness develops is that of a non-dualistic system which yet does not completely reject dualism.[4] Recentring the metaphysical discourse on such a notion thus means not only to move away from the centrality of transcendence as *the* model to approach ideas of reality, but also to set aside the certainty of distinct essences and to put ambiguity at the core of the metaphysical inquiry. If paradox is a challenge in a transcendence-focused metaphysics, here it is the norm. Considering suchness as a meta-category also interrogates the inextricable relations that metaphysics maintains with other sub-spheres of philosophical practice, in particular what has been called ontology, epistemology and soteriology, which have often been understood as separate from metaphysics, and it provides a perspective from which to reconsider its boundaries.

To begin with, it is necessary to understand the meaning of Suchness within the philosophical tradition in which it emerged. Given the impossibility of making sense of the entirety of Buddhist interpretations, I shall explore the concept drawing on the discrete discourses produced by a current of Mahayana Buddhism that developed in East Asia and was disseminated through the medium of the Chinese language: the Tiantai/Tendai school. This tremendously influential intellectual tradition intersected with other currents of Buddhism, in particular Huayan in China and the Tantric schools in Japan, and the nuances that these interactions introduced in a metaphysical discourse informed by Suchness contributed to shaping a sophisticated and extensive philosophy of reality. Historically, the Chinese and Japanese thinkers whose interpretations I will bring into play cover a period which spans from the sixth to the thirteenth centuries CE and embody specific moments in the articulation of the idea of Suchness.[5]

What is Suchness?

'Suchness', or 'thusness', are the somewhat awkward English terms used to translate the idiom through which Buddhists identify the nature of reality as what is 'truly as it is' (Ch. *zhenru*/Jp. *shinnyo* 眞如; Skt. *tathatā*).[6] Suchness embodies the Reality (with a capital R) which for convenience I call 'ultimate' reality, a reality which is 'such', or 'such-like' (*rushi*/*nyoze* 如是) because it is beyond predication and change.

In basic Buddhist understanding, the ultimate is a non-conditioned type of existence. It is characterized by equality and lacks differentiation. Depending on the specific type of Buddhism, it may identify the existence of the Buddha, or the realm of enlightenment where the nature of reality is correctly perceived; it may be a synonym of emptiness (*kong/kū* 空; Sk. *śūnyatā*), the fundamental Mahayana notion that sees the true nature of the world as devoid of self-being. Buddhist thinkers contrasted this Reality with the reality we perceive and experience as ordinary beings. This is conditioned, in the sense that it is the result of a confluence of causes and conditions, which Buddhists call co-arising (*yuanqi/ engi* 緣起 or *yinyuan/innen* 因緣; Sk. *Pratītya – samutpāda*). It is denoted as 'conventional', because it is characterized by differentiation: when we experience things, we give them conventional designations, that is, different names.[7] By being named, we and the things around us 'exist' provisionally. However, the Buddhist thinkers discussed here posited Suchness as what is in absolute terms and yet appears in front of our eyes, conflating the two dimensions of reality.

The meaning of Suchness is explicated through a net of significations, a methodological approach that proceeds through associations and contrasts, rather than explicit definitions. Thus, Suchness is the 'truly real' (*zhenshi/shinjitsu*眞實) or the way things are, 'the real marks of all things' (*zhufa shixang /shohō-jissō* 諸法實相) – a popular expression which encapsulates the apparent ambiguity of being at once the true forms (in contrast to a deluded perception of the conventional world) and the marks, namely, the identifying characteristics 相 of the conventional world.[8] Suchness is also understood to be synonymous with other Buddhist terms pointing to a world 'beyond:' Buddha-nature (*foxing/busshō*佛性), dharma-realm (*fajie/hokkai*法界), dharma-body (*fashen/hosshin*法身), the principle (*li/ri*理) of reality. These terms, taken together, at first suggest a hierarchy between the reality encompassed by Suchness and the conventional reality of ordinary being, whereby the first is the most relevant. If the emphasis is placed on the inexplicable nature of Suchness, these associations point to a status which is not immediately discernible by nor belongs to ordinary beings: 'things as they are' would then refer not to the 'as it is' of the everyday, but to what it is in the origin and needs to be unveiled. In this case, the term 'true' denotes an epistemological concern for a level of cognition which is based on direct perception of Reality rather than discriminatory cognition. If Suchness is identified with the Buddha or with Buddhahood, one may even detect a transcendental entity, while the terms 'nature' and 'principle' signal an inherent 'grounding' of the ever-changing existence.

Seen in this light, it seems that one can take Suchness as a parallel idiom to express the beyond, in its transcendent or immanent form: that something which justifies our world and gives it sense. Thus one might read these Buddhist articulations as similar to the many elaborations of the relation between being and the beyond in Western/Western-oriented metaphysics. These correspondences, however, are misleading and constrain the potential of the notion of Suchness. Besides the perceived hierarchy, to which I will return, they precipitate Suchness into a status of permanent substance and attribute to it a degree of self-being. But is Suchness a thing to be acquired? Buddhist thinkers had been wary of the danger of substantialist interpretations of reality from the very beginning. Indeed, this was one aspect which distinguished Buddhism from the preceding Indian philosophical systems. The question they were concerned with was not only how to speak of the ultimate, but how to do it without making it into an object. The discourse on Suchness developed within the Tiantai/Tendai school represents solutions that were formulated to overcome this risk. They open the way to a radical conception of ultimate reality, which has consequences for the meaning of being and becoming.

Reconsidering the metaphysical paradox: Beyond duality/with duality

I shall take the lead from Zhiyi (538–97), putative father of the Tiantai school. Zhiyi used the model of Mādyamika logic to develop a theory of a threefold truth, according to which three metaphysical positions are possible: that of emptiness (*kong/kū*空), where existences are seen as empty and nonsubstantial in themselves; that of convention (*jia/ke*假), where phenomena nevertheless exist provisionally as nominal designations; and that of the middle (*chong/chū*中), which is the ultimate reality of all existences. While the Mādyamika understanding, shared by other Mahayana schools, remained at the logical/epistemological level, where it signified the impossibility of discussing reality as either negative or affirmative, for Tiantai thinkers the notion of the middle gave sense to reality in positive terms. Zhiyi applied the position of the middle to the metaphysical/ontological question and argued that the meaning of the middle is that reality, as it is, possesses emptiness and conventionality at once. Emptiness, thus, does not express the ultimate, contrary to the position of other Buddhist schools; it is not the 'beyond'.[9] In the system that Zhiyi conceived ultimate reality is not only undifferentiated, it is *both* dual *and* non-dual. The 'mundane' made of everyday experiences and the 'real', that is, the way things are, are neither one nor two, neither completely different nor totally the same: 'nondual yet not distinct' (*weier weibie / muni mubetsu* 無二無別), 'not-two yet two, two yet not-two' (不二而二二則不二), 'neither merged nor scattered' (*buhe bisan/fugō fusan* 不合不散), 'neither vertical nor horizontal' (*buzong buheng/ fujū fuō* 不縱不橫). 'One should not seek an essence separate from these shared names', Zhiyi cautions.[10] Suchness does not exist apart from everything.

This notion of middle subverts one of the pillars of Aristotelian metaphysics, the principle of the excluded middle, according to which there cannot be an intermediate between contradictions, but of 'one subject we must either affirm or deny any one predicate'.[11] Zhiyi's metaphysical middle creates a space where Suchness is posited as complex: Reality is one yet many, threefold yet united. This position makes redundant the difference between (metaphysical) Reality and (ontic) reality, and posits these two possible spheres as in an essential relationship.

One of the most compelling articulations of this Reality/reality may be found in the idea that 'three thousand realms [are contained] in a single moment of thought' (*yinian sanqian/ichinen sanzen* 一念三千). Later identified as the central idea of Tiantai philosophy (although it may have not been intended as such in Zhiyi's *Mohe zhiguan,* where it first appeared), this notion would become particularly influential in Japan. It is a complex way to point at the totality of existence in relation to an individual being, which expresses itself in a single act of thought. It states, paraphrasing the terser Chinese, that the thoughts that arise from one moment to the next in the mind of a being carrying on their conventional existence are each endowed with all states of existence, represented by the six destinies of reincarnation, namely, hell dwellers, hungry ghosts, animals, asuras, humans and gods, and the four types of noble beings, śrāvakas, pratyekabuddhas, bodhisattvas and buddhas.[12] These are called the 'ten dharma realms'. Each of these realms contains the other nine within itself – another fundamental principle in Tiantai/Tendai metaphysics, known as the mutual encompassing of the ten realms (*shijie huju/jikkai gogu* 十界互具). Thus, existents not only depend on each other, they also include each other. The individual mind at each moment is endowed with a hundred dharma realms. Each of these dharma realms also possesses ten 'suchlike' characteristics or modes in which Suchness unfolds: appearance (outward form), nature (inner quality), essence, power (potential), function (the outward display of that power), cause, condition, recompense and the ultimate integration of the initial and final Suchness.[13] Furthermore, each dharma realm is also understood as endowed with three categories of existents (*shijian/seken*世間): sentient beings, that is, individuals distinguished by specific names; the five aggregates, namely, the physical and mental constituents that come together temporarily to constitute individual beings; and the space that living beings occupy (the land). In short, the individual mind of an ordinary being, at each moment, is endowed with the whole of existence.[14] The relation between the partiality of one moment of mental activity, discrete from the next moment, and the totality of reality, is one of equality:

> If there is even an ephemeral thought, this includes three thousand [realms]. But we cannot say that the single thought has prior existence, and that all phenomena exist later, nor can we say that all phenomena have prior existence, and that the single thought exists later.[15]

This structure of reality may appear fluid and paradoxical at different levels. Yet, here the paradox is postulated on philosophical arguments and precedents that make the paradox normative in its fluidity. Furthermore, such integrated reality is not presented as a condition to be obtained in a kind of mystical experience of union with the absolute. (I shall come back to this point.) The arguments put forward to constitute this reality have important consequences for establishing the meaning of 'beyond' from a position other than classic Western metaphysics, or early Buddhist understandings. Of particular significance is that the starting point lies in the conventional existence of sentient beings rather than in the 'absolute'.[16] Equally critical are the two points noted above, the emphasis on multiplicity and the non-hierarchical relation between the diversity and temporaneity of existence and the totality of Reality. It is clear that a concept of reality expressed in these terms reverses the focus put in early Buddhism on the need to escape from this world, which is often perceived to be the standard Buddhist position. Rather, it affirms this world and ordinary existence exactly as it is, without even the need to transform it. While early Buddhism places temporal causality at the core of a Buddhist understanding of reality and liberation, the notion of non-duality and the connected ideas of buddha-nature and original enlightenment deny causality. In recent years, scholars from within the Japanese Buddhist tradition caused a sensation arguing that this stance, long regarded as representative of East Asian Buddhism, is not at all Buddhist if considered from the perspective of early Buddhism.[17] The radical articulations of Chinese interpreters contrast with the more apophatic perspective of Indian Mādyamika and its insistence on what reality is not because of the limitation of language. A shift can be observed towards pluralistic and affirmative formulations ('one and many', instead of 'one and none'). It has been suggested that this may even be a consequence of the Chinese language, which does not make explicit distinctions of plural and singular.[18]

A comparative outlook within the broader Buddhist tradition calls attention to the importance of cultural contextualization, which is not generally of concern to philosophical analysis. Undoubtedly, other Chinese assumptions on the constitution of Reality have played an important role in the Tiantai understanding of Suchness. One can detect resonances with the idea of Oneness found pervasively in Chinese thought, whether one calls that *dao* or *yi* and whether one understands it as the underlying source of reality or the original unity of the ultimate, as we have seen in the chapters by Yao, Bunnin and Li in this volume.[19] The conceptualization of ultimate reality as an undifferentiated oneness triggers the problem of how individualized reality comes to be and how it can be distinguished from the whole. It may be questioned, however, whether one should understand undifferentiated Reality as the 'grounding' of immanent reality in the terms of Aristotelian metaphysics. While the notion of grounding highlights the relation between the two realities, it also attributes different degrees of fundamentality to Reality. Yet, once one takes the stance that there are no independent substances, where can this reality be grounded? Seemingly, the lack of a qualitative difference between the absolute and phenomenal beings engenders questions of identity and action.

From the broader perspective of comparative metaphysics, the notion of Suchness accentuates the difficulty of using philosophical rubrics that originate in other distinct intellectual contexts. Is the interdependent reality a total unity? Or is it a total affirmation of distinctions? If Suchness, the 'true aspect of all things', the 'principle', consists of the acknowledgement that Reality and reality are always non-dual and yet mutually inclusive, should Suchness be understood as epitomizing a monistic reality? Or does it encapsulate an immanentist view of reality? Neither of these positions accurately conveys what Zhiyi and other Chinese thinkers have pointed to. Or perhaps we need to qualify both monism and immanentism and consider expressions such as 'radical monism', 'radical pluralism', or 'radical immanentism' to alert ourselves to the ambiguity of these categories when filtered through the Western philosophical experience, and to indicate the possibility of a Reality where no complete subsuming into a single entity nor elimination of all differences occurs, and there is no pantheistic multiplicity either.[20] The possibility which these ideas open up is that of a non-monolithic non-dualism: things retain their distinctiveness while at the same time maintaining identity with others and with the whole – like water and waves, to use an analogy widespread in East Asian Buddhism. What counts are the relationships that are established between them.

Identity

What are the implications of this metaphysical position for the meaning of 'identity'? This is another key concept that one needs to grasp in order to be able to apply the category of Suchness. Once again we are faced with the problem of transposing terminology from one context to another based on different suppositions. Let us consider the Sinitic character that encompasses this concept, 即 (*ji /soku*). This term does not denote personal identity; it signifies the relationship that exists between two entities defined in mutual opposition or two contradictory properties. It may be understood as 'identicalness' or 'sameness', as one finds in Tiantai pronouncements such as 'the identity of emptiness, conventionality, and the middle'. It is often translated with the verb 'to equal', or with a predicative copula, as in established Mahayana expressions of non-duality: 'afflictions are awakening' (*fannao ji puti /bonnō soku bodai* 煩惱即菩提), 'saṃsāra is exactly nirvāṇa' (*shengsi ji niepan / shōji soku nehan* 生死即涅槃), 'ignorance equals dharma-nature' (*wuming ji faxing / mumyō soku hosshō* 無明即法性). These statements may be regarded paradoxical when considered from a perspective that separates the world of conventional existence from the real world of buddhahood. Yet in a conceptual framework defined by the notion of Suchness analysed above, the self-contradiction is caused only by the challenge of the translation. In fact, *ji* does not imply complete, total equivalence. A more accurate rendition of the expressions above would be some technical term such as 'indivisible from', as Swanson suggests in his introduction to the translation of Zhiyi's *Mohe zhiguan*. This awkward expression can convey the idea that opposites are co-related and intertwined, and do not make sense on their own. This does not mean that opposites are mathematically identical, that there is no difference between the two opposites or that they are totally interchangeable. Rather, what is put forward through enunciations that appear as paradoxes is their necessary coexistence: 'They lack meaning apart from each other, but they are not exactly overlapping equivalents'.[21] In other words, they share mutuality: they can be distinguished but cannot be separated; in their identity there is difference. Zhiyi explained this through a set of 'six types of identity' (*liuji* /*rokusoku* 六即), which may be read as six indivisible aspects of reality and, at the same time, function as six levels of attainment of insight into this reality.[22]

Such concept of identity is intimated in notions, such as 'the interpenetration of the ten realms' (where the lowest realm is hell and the highest is the Buddha), or 'three thousand realms [contained] in a single thought-moment'. Another expression that emerges from the discourse on *ji*/*soku* is 'the equality of the first stage and the last stage (of attainment)'. These pronouncements reinforce the ultimate lack of hierarchies between opposite positions. Other Buddhist schools that share this view of reality echo this language. Huayan thinkers use the analogy of a coin which has two sides, distinct and yet complementary. Tantric Buddhism, which draws on the notion of 'mandala' to convey the idea of Suchness as integrated reality, articulates a notion of bodily identity between the Buddha and the practitioner (*jishen chengfo*/ *sokushin jōbutsu* 即身成佛). I shall return to this point.

Thus, to postulate that 'all dharmas are exactly (*ji*/*soku*) Suchness' means that Suchness as the nature of all phenomena is shared by the Buddha and sentient beings, as well by nonsentient existence. Suchness is not only the privileged image of the undifferentiated and ultimate. Suchness is none other than the forms of all dharmas unfolding as they mutually encompass and pervade one another. It is this reasoning that leads to a specific mode of affirmation of the phenomenal world: if individual dharmas are not other than the Buddha, then concrete phenomena, *just as they are*, equal the nondifferentiated Reality.

Dynamic relations

The relation of the whole and the parts is a standard metaphysical problem. It usually implies stable correlations between the two. Yet Suchness is not fixed, therefore it can render this relation in a non-static mode. Let us consider Suchness expressed in terms of buddha-nature. Zhiyi tells us that buddha-nature is threefold (*sanyin foxing* 三因佛性): it is direct or primary cause, that is, the inherent, transformative potential common to all being; conditional cause, that is, practice, which allows this potential to be realized; and complete cause, that is, realization, in other words, wisdom that becomes aware of buddha-nature as primary cause.²³ This interdependence shows that Suchness/buddha-nature is not a status of (ultimate) existence, but implies transformative action. This is another way to avoid reifying buddha-nature, for it works by incorporating causation and emphasizing the contingency of practice.

Other Buddhist schools debated the way in which Suchness expresses the subsuming and simultaneous coexistence of apparently antagonistic realms. In the Huayan reading, shaped by the centrality of dependent origination, all dharmas arise out of Suchness. Suchness is dissected into two types, 'Suchness as an unchanging principle' (*bubian zhenru* / *fuhen shinnyo* 不變眞如) and 'Suchness as conditioned movement' (*suiyuan zhenru* / *zuien shinnyo* 随緣眞如). Later Tiantai Chinese and Japanese interpreters drew on this hermeneutical pattern as an alternative to Zhiyi's central idea of reciprocal endowment (*xingju/shōgu* 性具). Saichō (767–822), the founder of Japanese Tendai, understood Suchness as at once embodying a principle (identical to itself) and as manifesting the phenomenal world in accordance with the conditions in this world. He emphasized this dynamic aspect of Suchness, which he called 'buddha-nature in action' (*gyō busshō* 行仏性). Suchness in both aspects is universal, and this means that the realm in which Suchness acts is the same as its principle, the ultimate reality. As principle, Suchness is the essential nature of all things, which is unchanging, although the phenomena of the actual world may change. At the same time, Suchness is exactly the diverse forms of the phenomenal world, because it responds to causal conditions and manifests itself.²⁴

Annen (841–89?), influential systematizer of the Tendai and Tantric schools in Japan, also maintained that not only does Suchness underlie the workings of the world, but that the world itself is the activity of conditioned Suchness. If one applies this understanding to the status of human beings, this means that ordinary beings, deluded as they may be, exist as part of conditioned Suchness. Because of this origin they can seek liberation. Suchness thus is the nature of being and the force behind sentient beings' aspiration to grasp that nature (which is the meaning of awakening). This is a radical understanding. It does not mean, for instance, that individual attainment of buddhahood is absorbed into a unified principle of Suchness, because conditioned Suchness is seen not only as the single principle that integrates all things, but also as the principle that expands in diverse forms and recognizes and positively values all existences for their very differences. Drawing on Zhiyi, Annen articulated this conception of suchness in a fourfold categorization of 'oneness' (*shi'ichi* 四一): all buddhas, times, places and teachings are the one Buddha (*ichibutsu* 一佛), one time (*ichiji* 一時), one place (*issho* 一處) and one teaching (*ichigyō* 一教).²⁵ Annen's position cannot be defined simply as monistic. Once again one may note the resonances with broadly shared notions of reality in non-Buddhist Chinese metaphysics, which understand all things to be interconnected and constantly changing, arising spontaneously from an ultimate source that resists objectification.

This poses again the question of the adequacy of the language we use when we indicate such all-encompassing status as monistic.

Being: Being fluid, being plural

I now address the questions analysed above from the perspective of 'being'. What does 'being' mean in a philosophical framework which conceives reality in terms of relational existence? How is 'being' constituted?

As I pointed out at the beginning of this reflection, the basic Buddhist position is that beings have no self-determining essence, 'own-being' 自性, nor 'own-becoming'. Accordingly, to posit a single, distinct, individual ('I') would be paradoxical at different levels. Being is to be more properly understood as 'existence' in the sense that nothing *is* in absolute terms; everything *exists* in time and space and in relation to others. Being is referential, not substantial, and provisional. Thus, it cannot exist without the space/world. What we denote as 'self', i.e. the individual being, is not a finite entity, but rather a process or a happening, engendered by the interaction of mental and physical factors, and never identical to itself. Because all things are empty of permanent substance, they are not independent. Because they are provisional existence, they are temporary. Time is a property of conventional reality. One may say, then, that 'being' *is* the form or name that an entity takes at a specific moment. Being is subjected to continuous transformation; what 'is' is always *in fieri*, dynamic rather than static. Being is 'being-time' (*uji* 有時), to borrow a well-known expression by the medieval Japanese Zen thinker, Dōgen (1200–53).[26] Thus, impermanence (*wu chang / mujō* 無常), the characteristic of being particular, becomes the ontic condition of relational existence. This condition is not understood in negative terms, and in fact, Japanese philosophers and poets alike valued and celebrated its ephemeral beauty. Impermanence is not an obstacle to liberation. It is the True Reality of everything, as Dōgen emphatically maintains:

> Grasses and trees, as well as thickets and forests, are impermanent and, accordingly, they are Buddha Nature. It is the same with the human body and mind, both of which are impermanent and, accordingly, they are Buddha Nature. The mountains and rivers in the various lands are impermanent, so, accordingly, they are Buddha Nature. Supreme, fully perfected enlightenment is Buddha Nature, and hence it is impermanent. The Buddha's great entry into nirvana was impermanent, and hence it is Buddha Nature.[27]

If fluidity is a constitutive category of being, being also means to be plural. This stance has consequences for the definition of an individual existence in this world. How can we speak of 'self' and 'other'? The stress on impermanence seems to imply that the very identity of existences is complex: two identities may be present at the same time without losing their specificity. Let me illustrate this view with two case studies, drawn from the Japanese Buddhist tradition, of existences perceived as other or opposite. The first case concerns the relation between Buddhist deities and Shinto deities, called kami. The second addresses the position of human beings vis-à-vis the Buddha.

The relation between buddhas and kami, or if one wants to use more abstract terms, Buddhism and Shinto, is a huge topic that has been at the centre of much analysis in Western scholarship, perhaps because of the difficulties in explaining it if one does not depart from an Aristotelian and monotheistic perspective. Associations between Buddhist and local gods may be found in all Asian cultures where Buddhism took root, in a variety of combinatory patterns. Originating in different mythological or philosophical contexts, the buddhas (a comprehensive name for the diverse kinds of beings included in the Buddhist pantheon) embody universal entities, while local gods are considered to be existences in the karmic realm (one of the ten realms in the Tiantai system), which often function as protectors of Buddhism. In Japan, in particular throughout the medieval period (eleventh to sixteenth centuries CE), these associations developed further into a sophisticated ontology of identity and distinction, whereby the buddhas and the kami are at once regarded as discrete beings and yet as one and possibly interchangeable. The kami are deemed to be 'expedient means' of the Buddha, which 'soften the radiance [of Buddhism] and identify with the dust' to allow all beings to grasp the meaning of Buddhist doctrine. Borrowing the language of the Tiantai interpretations of the *Lotus Sutra* and the discursive articulation of identity (*soku*) discussed in the preceding sections, Buddhist thinkers theorized the relation of kami and buddhas as origins (or roots, *honji* 本地) and manifestations (or traces, *suijaku* 垂跡). The model is offered by the Lotus scripture, where the nature of the Buddha is revealed to be at once one and yet multiple and changing: a Buddha is the principle of being the Buddha (buddhahood) and, simultaneously, all the buddhas, each with its name, who have appeared in the world through the ages. Similarly, kami are buddha-beings (the origins) and beings abiding in Japanese territory (the traces). This double identity was not only posited in conceptual terms, but given concrete form in narratives, rituals, material objects and the physical space. These traditionally 'non-philosophical' expressions provide irrefutable evidence of the conception of a multiple being: statues of kami have their simultaneous identity as Buddhist and Shinto deities carved in the wood of which they are made; pictorial images portray the same kami assuming Buddhist guises at one time and retaining their identity as kami at other times; temples (i.e. buildings dedicated to the buddhas) and shrines (i.e. structures dedicated to the kami) share the same space and enshrine each other's deities.[28] The icon of a Sannō deity in Figure 2 eloquently epitomizes this conception: Jūzenji is imagined at once as a kami (*suijaku*), dressed in monastic robes, and as its essence (*honji*), embodied by the bodhisattva drawn within a circle above his head. In the upper section of the painting the Sanskrit seed-syllables manifesting the Buddhist forms of all seven Sannō deities are inscribed in seven circles. Yet this is not a syncretistic movement which blends Buddhist and local deities, as it is often misunderstood. Syncretism implies a vertical relation of power between a pure 'religion' and weaker, popular cults that are absorbed in the larger system. In Japan, however, the correspondence of kami and Buddhas is predicated on the basis of the equality of essence and individual being, which governs

Figure 2 Mandala of Jūzenji and the Sannō deities of Hiei. Kamakura period (fourteenth century). Hanging scroll, colour on silk. Owned by Shinnyo-en Shinchōji, Tokyo. Reproduced with permission.

the relation between universal principle and conventional manifestation: as conveyed in the Tiantai vision of the interdependence of the ten realms, the buddhas are not higher essences than the gods; buddhas and gods are ontically the same, and therefore can be interchangeable.

This dynamic provides a compelling alternative to the exclusivistic language informed by monotheistic points of view, according to which the two types of divine beings described above, with acknowledged different origins, should be identified through the binary model of either Buddhist or Shinto. The being of the Japanese kami urges us to search for a different vocabulary to express the logic underlying their correspondences to Buddhist deities and to overcome the ambiguity that their double identity poses. One may think of this identity as analogical, and of their being as rhizomatic. This stance further reveals that the articulation of the 'other' is affected by a non-substantialistic view of reality as much as the definition of the 'self' is. The Japanese development of a combinatory cultic system provides a metaphysical rationale to conceive of 'relative otherness', and to create a hermeneutical paradigm that employs plurality and inclusiveness as its guideline rather than the exception. Can this metaphysics of the double become the template for an alternative way of doing 'dialogue' (including interreligious dialogue), making use of the potential that the fluidity of forms affords?

The second case study considers how the same logic is applied to the identity of a human being vis-à-vis that of a Buddha. I have already pointed out that in the Tiantai system, the notion of identity reiterates the indivisibility of buddhas, mind and sentient being.[29] This stance is also present in other Buddhist traditions, although it may be articulated in different terms. In Tantric Buddhism, a remarkably influential tradition in Japan, the multiplicity of Reality is embodied by the mandalic existence of the Buddha: the mandala, a material form where different types of venerable beings are gathered, is posited as the true, single body of the Buddha, epitomizing the indivisibility of what is differentiated from the undifferentiated.[30] In fact, in Japanese interpretations, this mandalic existence of the Buddha is more accurately instantiated not in a single but in a pair of mandalas, which function as contrasting yet symbiotic poles to assert duality as a necessary condition to realize oneness. How in this context does an ordinary being construct their non-dual identity with this Buddha? The Tantric model envisages that a practitioner imitates the Buddha in his physical attributes, gestures and utterances and inscribes the mandala on his/her body: ordinary beings reproduce the sonic, bodily and mental activities of the Buddha through their body and in doing so they are 'transformed' into the perfected body of the Buddha. Yet they do not lose their status of being in a transient body made of flesh and bones. They encompass both conditions at once. This process of mandalization of the ordinary body is what is conveyed in the expression 'becoming a buddha in one's own body' (sokushin jōbutsu).[31] This is not a mystical union, but the possibility of acquiring the identity that was in the origins through ritual enactment.[32]

What makes this 'becoming' possible is the ontic continuity between the individual being identified by an ordinary body and the totality of Reality epitomized by the perfected body of the Buddha. The structures of being and ultimate Reality are the same. Kūkai (774–835), eminent thinker and representative of the most important Tantric school in Japan, argued that the constituent elements of the phenomenal world, earth, water, fire, wind, space and consciousness, are also the essential 'materiality' of the ultimate reality, i.e. the constituents of the dharma-body of the Buddha (another synonym of Suchness). Thus, here Suchness consists of the six elements (*rokudai* 六大) penetrating each other, mutually unhindered, in the Buddha as well as in ordinary beings. This provides the basis for a physiopsychic mutual correspondence, by which the principle of the equality of ordinary being and Buddha is established. These notions are part of a broader discourse on form. The mandala is not an abstract cosmogram; it is understood as both the ontic expression of the ultimate reality and the agency for its actualization. Tantric Buddhist thinkers explicitly contended that a formless essence of buddhahood is of necessity instantiated in material, sonic and visual forms; the insistence on presenting any aspect of material reality as one of the 'bodies' of the Buddha serves this purpose.[33] Indeed, Kūkai made perhaps the most compelling statement on the possibilities of metaphysical materiality, once again shifting the emphasis towards the phenomenal world:

> 'Suchness is beyond form, but it is depending on forms that it can be realised'.[34]

Being beyond the human: Nonsentient beings

These ideas of Suchness also prompt a rethinking of the boundaries within which we apply the concept of being. As the ten types of existence described by Tiantai indicate, 'being' is not restricted to humans, but extends to other forms of existence, such as the realm of animals. Eventually, it would become a broad category which encompasses all living beings (*shujō* 衆生; Skt. *sattva*), as well as nonsentient beings and inanimate objects. Sentient beings may be distinct by the fact that they possess a mind, but East Asian interpreters emphasize that the mind cannot be the discriminating element that sets them apart from plant life and inanimate matter. Saichō, for instance, asserts that

> Sentient and nonsentient [beings] are originally nondual. If one says that they are two, it would mean there are dharma apart from the mind … But [to say that] a single moment of thought [contains the three thousand worlds] means that person and environment are nondual.[35]

Environment, here, literally the 'circumstantial cause of retribution' (*ehō* 依報), is the space in which we abide as a result of our karma. Sentient beings do not occupy a privileged position outside the world in which they exist. Space is not an empty abstraction in which things are situated.

Kūkai reiterates the Tiantai stance, which breaks down the hierarchy between sentient beings and nonsentient beings:

> One cannot say that the mind is prior and all dharmas are subsequent, nor that all dharmas are prior and the mind is subsequent. If one says that all dharmas arise from the one mind, then that is a vertical relationship. If one says that all dharmas are at once contained within the mind, that is a horizontal relationship. […] The mind is all dharmas and all dharmas are the mind. Therefore, their relation is neither vertical nor horizontal; they are neither the same nor different.[36]

The lack of hierarchies that characterizes the world of Suchness pushes these assumptions further. Chinese and (even more) Japanese thinkers articulated a complex discourse on inanimate beings, going beyond the received Buddhist episteme. These theories come under the general rubric of the 'attainment of the vegetal world' (*caomu chengfo/sōmoku jōbutsu* 草木成仏).[37] Mahayana Buddhism in general does not consider trees and plants to be capable of sensation and places them on a par with tiles and stones.[38] Yet in East Asia both Tiantai/Tendai and Tantric Buddhism upheld the idea that the nonsentient world is endowed with and can attain Buddhahood. Not only did these traditions highlight the universality of buddha-nature, which one finds in other Mahayana traditions, and which allows the world of insentience passively to partake in such nature. Rather, they established non-conditioned nature as both ontologically constitutive of the nonsentient world *and* epistemologically attainable by it. This is quite different from Indian and Tibetan interpretations of Buddhism, where only sentient beings can possess buddha-nature. Once this equal status was attributed to inanimate beings, then the question that concerned East Asian thinkers was how it is possible for entities such as plants and trees to engage in Buddhist practices and *attain* buddhahood, which implies volition (aspiring to enlightenment), practice and accomplishment.

Nonsentients are endowed with the same virtues and capabilities as sentient beings because they are grounded on the same ontic premises. The buddhahood of grasses and trees came to be a concern precisely because human beings and plants were thought of as being with the same attributes. According to Annen, for instance, no clear distinction between sentient and nonsentient could be posited, because at the root of the heart-mind of sentient beings (*shin* 心, or *shittashin* 質多心, Skr., *citta*) is the fleshy bodily organ that the Buddhist called *karidashin* 汗栗駄心 (Skt., *hṛdaya*); this is the same as the heart of trees and grasses, and it is through this that buddhahood is attained.[39]

The extraordinarily nuanced discourse on the being of the nonsentient developed in Japan cannot be explored fully here.[40] We can, however, identify two major positions, both extensively articulated by Annen.[41] One, first advanced in China by Zhanran

(711–82) and upheld by Saichō, employs the principle of conditioned Suchness to argue that trees and rocks are sentient beings. In this case, however, the attainment of buddhahood by nonsentient beings is contingent upon that of sentient beings.[42] When a sentient being attains buddhahood, the whole environment becomes the Buddha realm. According to the principle of non-duality between karmic being and karmic environment, a sentient being's existence, which comes to be as an effect of past karma ('direct cause', *zheng bao*/*shōbō* 正報), causes the environment ('circumstantial cause') to arise, too. Environment is dependent on individual existence; hence, when a sentient being attains buddhahood, so do nonsentient beings. This means that grasses and trees fulfil their aspiration to liberation through others' agency. Yet, the argument also postulates that sentient beings, in virtue of their relational existence, cannot attain liberation separately or outside the environment.

The second position, more broadly shared in Japan both by Tendai and Tantric thinkers, propounds that nonsentient beings can attain buddhahood through their own agency, i.e. individually. Annen argued:

> Even though plants die, their material essence does not. It pervades every place without the least mutation over time. This being the character of their nature, Suchness constitutes its essence. Since Suchness is its essence, they always have the capability of awakening, and because they have the capability of awakening they arouse the desire for enlightenment and become buddhas.[43]

According to Annen, plants engage in cultivation through practice (*shushō* 修生). Later treatises produced within a current of medieval Japanese Tendai Buddhism known as Original Enlightenment Thought elaborated on this point and argued that the very coming into existence, abiding, changing and perishing of grasses and trees parallel the four phases of human life, from birth to death, and constitutes the aspiration, practice and nirvana of plants.[44] The awareness that plants have of the cycle of seasons and their growing branches and leaves at specific times attests to their ability to realize buddhahood. Natural change is seen to be the form of the Buddha in itself.

These theories make clear that the concern for the status of the inanimate and the equal potential it expresses cannot be read through the lens of a primordial form of animism, as is often done. Rather, the articulation of the activities and accomplishments of the vegetable world is yet another consequence of the radical positing of the world as at once immanent and completely unconditioned. Once again, these ideas did not remain confined to the scholarly world, but permeated society and were expressed in theatre, poetry and art. I find a painting by the celebrated artist Itō Jakuchū (1716–1800) one of the most poignant illustrations of this thinking: *Vegetable Nirvana* reproduces a famous motif in Buddhist representation, the demise of the Buddha Sakyamuni (which is in early Buddhism the moment of his *paranirvana*), but places at the centre of the depiction a large white radish, surrounded by turnips, gourds, mushrooms and a host of other vegetables[45] (Figure 3). Seen in the light of the Buddhist debate on being, the painting is more than a parody or a metaphoric image. It makes a visual statement on how Suchness is actualized in the world of insentience, overturning any anthropocentric exceptionalism – almost a manifesto for our current posthumanistic concerns.

Figure 3 *Vegetable Nirvana.* Edo period (*c.* 1792). Hanging scroll, ink on paper. Formerly owned by Seiganji temple, Kyoto. Kyoto National Museum. Reproduced with permission.

Practice: Becoming

The potential of the radical non-dual-and-yet-plural system is ultimately revealed in the actualization of Reality effected through practice. This I would see as the counterpart of the notion of becoming in Western metaphysics. Whether expressed as awareness of reality or realization of bodily buddhahood, such actualization has a performative dimension unfolding in the space and time that constitute the phenomenal world. The notion of buddhahood encompasses both the *idea* of the ultimate and the *attainment* of identity with the ultimate. Because this accomplishment does not engender 'leaving this world', but changing the perception of the world within the world itself, the everyday is charged with the potential to experience the ultimate Reality. Zhiyi, for instance, asserts:

> All [phenomena experienced through] the aggregates and senses are thusness 如; therefore there is no [substantial] suffering that needs to be removed. Since ignorance and the exhausting dust [of passionate afflictions] are indivisible from wisdom, there is no origin [of suffering] to be severed. Since the extreme [dualities] and false [views] are [indivisible from] the Middle and what is right, there is no path to be cultivated. Since [this cyclic world of] samsara is [indivisible from] nirvana, there is no extinguishing [of craving] to be realized. Since suffering and its causes do not exist [substantially], there is no mundane world [to be transcended]; since the path and the extinction [of craving] do not exist [substantially], there is no transcendent world 出世間 [to be gained]. There is purely the single true mark [of reality-as-it-is]; there are no separate things outside this true mark.[46]

In this perspective, even apparently trivial conventional actions, such as cleaning the garden or preparing food, may be meaningful actions that have the same value as meditative or ritual actions (i.e. actions purportedly aiming at perceiving the way things are): they are significant because they are endowed with the same ultimate Reality. This assumption stands on the metaphysical position that individual, concrete phenomena, just as they are, manifest the nondifferentiated Reality. A particular action thus becomes the embodiment of the total Reality in a specific/the present moment.

These dynamics are perhaps most explicit in the elaboration of medieval Japanese Tendai, in particular in Original Enlightenment Thought. For example, a twelfth-century treatise known as 'The Contemplation of Suchness' argues that attainment means to see oneself and others as identical to Suchness in the midst of one's daily activities:

> Clergy or laity, male or female, all should contemplate in this way. When you provide for your wife, children, and retainers, or even feed oxen, horses, and the others of the six kinds of domestic animals, because the myriad things are all Suchness, if you think that these others are precisely Suchness, you have in effect made offerings to all Buddhas and bodhisattvas of the ten directions and to all living beings, without a single exception.[47]

Here practice is not posited as the cause but as the effect of realization. This is a radical inversion of the causal relation between practice and attainment: buddhahood is not a future achievement but inherent from the outset, and practice is not a means to realize buddhahood but its paradigmatic expression. In this sense, there is no becoming, if one understands becoming as succession of before and after. Liberation is becoming what you already are.

In a similar logic, albeit with different terminology, Tantric thinkers considered ritual practices, which bear the visible marks (*youxiang/usō* 有相) of the phenomenal world, to be the expression of the ultimate reality. I have always found it compelling that the Sinitic character used to denote ritual action in the Tantric context, *shi/ji* 事 (or *shixiang/jisō* 事相), is the same character that denotes the phenomenal world, in Chinese thought seen as counterpart of principle/Reality (*li/ri*). Ritual actions thus are understood to be not only the forms or the means through which the truth can be accessed, but the very physical actualization of this truth. This gives a metaphysical significance to practice.

Conclusion

The issues briefly analysed in this chapter have shown that focusing on the notion of Suchness as a category to articulate the meaning of Reality and being affords a linguistic and conceptual shift away from a metaphysics that centres on the beyond and assumes it as qualitatively different from the reality of being and becoming.

As a kind of meta-theory, Suchness engenders the possibility of positing both unity and diversity, sameness and difference, as proper modes of the True and Real. It establishes ambiguity as a positive, dynamic status, full of potential. It points to a process-oriented metaphysics that privileges positive expressions of the ultimate and gives value to the concrete world of change and to the embodied reality of the present. In this sense, a theory of Suchness generates a conceptual field that complicates and ultimately goes beyond the notions of immanence and transcendence (existence and essence) as self-contained modes.

The discursive practices of Suchness make available an alternative language to think about reality. Can this language be applied to metaphysical inquiries that start from the distinction of subject and object, Being and being? Suchness provides a sophisticated model for thinking of the world as interconnected and ultimately made of the same components, where ('creative') agency belongs not only to gods and humans, but also to things. This model resonates with other (non-Western) ideas of reality, in East Asia, or, for instance, in Africa.[48] Interestingly, Suchness-informed 'Buddhist metaphysics' finds a compelling counterpart in views of reality suggested by contemporary science, from quantum physics, with its theories of indeterminacy and complementarity, to the discovery in biology and chemistry of the life of plants as entities that know and are able to remember.[49] Similarly, the Buddhist ontology of the nonsentient echoes the extension of the concept of person which we have witnessed in the provision of the status of legal person to natural elements.[50] In this sense, theorizing reality from the perspective of Suchness also opens up and makes the metaphysical question relevant to other fields of inquiry.

Finally, in methodological terms the discursive positions engaged in this chapter pose the question of the boundaries of metaphysical inquiry: the equivalence of Suchness and Truth that Buddhist thinkers assumed, on the one hand, and the correspondences between metaphysical inquiry and practices of liberation, on the other, reflect the overlapping of epistemology and metaphysics, metaphysics and ontology and metaphysics and transformative insights.[51] Does it then make sense to speak of metaphysics?

Acknowledgement

I am grateful to Shinnyo-en, Tokyo, and to the Kyoto National Museum for granting permission to publish the material in their holdings, and to Reiko Hori and Melissa Rinne for facilitating access to the material. I gratefully acknowledge the support of a Nichibunken Visiting Research Fellowship which helped me in completing this chapter.

Notes

1. Chakrabarti and Weber (2017) make a similar point.
2. This can then shed a different light on notions that either are not significant in Western framed thinking, or are misunderstood as similar. It does not mean to think as, let us say, a contemporary Chinese thinker. As Ma and van Brakel (2016) have pointed out, the language of Western philosophy has penetrated also the current Chinese intellectual field.
3. Comparative studies have been carried out of individual figures in Western philosophy with Daoism or Buddhism. This seems to me misleading because it takes as a term of comparison the entirety of an Asian tradition, as if it were a static and homogeneous thought.
4. To speak of a 'system' here seems appropriate as it is a systematic and comprehensive conceptualization of the topic, constructed coherently in reference to other views. This does not mean that the system is stable and closed.
5. There is no space in this chapter for historical contextualization of these thinkers. I note, though, that these individual figures should be seen as agents of a more collective discursive production which is accomplished through oral delivery (lectures and debates), scribes and copyists, and where individual authorship is more often attributed than verified.

6. I have given both the Chinese and Japanese pronunciation of the Sinitic characters because my analysis considers concepts that were formulated in both cultural areas. I have occasionally added the corresponding Sanskrit term, when this is more generally known.
7. 'Conventional' here is a technical term which has three interconnected meanings: worldly, namely, our mistaken understanding of reality, obscured by deluded view; co-dependent arising, that is, the mutual interdependence of all phenomena; discriminative and ordinary language. For the sources of this term see Swanson (1989: 2–5).
8. This expression has its canonical basis in the *Lotus Sutra*, an important scripture in East Asia, where it recurs frequently. See, for instance, the opening section of Chapter Two, 'Expedient Means' (T.9: 5c; English translation in Hurvitz (1976: 22).
9. This position is taken consciously and reflectively against earlier understandings. For instance, in the *Mohe zhiguan* one reads: "The Tripitaka teaches that the names [of phenomena] are conventional, but that the dharmas [themselves] are real, and you realise emptiness by analysing this reality, like realizing emptiness by removing all the pillars [that support substantialist thinking]. Now, the meaning of 'essence' in Mahayana is that both the names and the [supposed] reality [underlying the names] all are only conventionally existent. Their 'own marks' [that is, their self-identifying characteristics] are empty [of independent existence] and are fundamentally quiescent. [This emptiness] is like [the reflection of] a pillar in a mirror; fundamentally [the reflection] is not, by itself, a pillar. [The reflection] is empty [of self-existence] even without waiting for the pillar itself to perish". (*Mohe zhiguan,* T.46: 32 b-c; English translation in Swanson (2017: 542–43.)
10. *Mohe zhiguan*, T.46: 23c20; Swanson (2017: 450).
11. Aristotle, *Metaphysics*, Book IV; translation by W. R. Ross (1924).
12. *Āsuras* are semigods of Indian origin; *śrāvakas* and *pratyekabuddhas* are the practitioners of non-Mahayana Buddhism who attain inferior forms of liberation (from the Mahayanist perspective).
13. The notion of Ten Suchnesses (*shi rushi/jūnyoze* 十如是), too, has its origin in Chapter Two of the *Lotus Sutra*, 'Expedient Means', as one reads it in Kumarajiva's translation (T.9: 5c11–13; English translation in Hurvitz (1976: 22–3). Kumarajiva's translation on this point differs substantially from the extant Sanskrit version of the scripture. Zhiyi gives detailed readings of the passage in his commentary to the *Lotus Sutra, Fahua xuanyi* (T.33: 693b; English translation in Swanson (1989: 179–81) and in *Mohe zhiguan* (T.46: 53a–54a; Swanson (2017: 804–15). For a contextual analysis, see Swanson (1989: 130–34).
14. *Mohe zhiguan*, T.46: 54a; Swanson (2017: 815).
15. *Mohe zhiguan*, T.46: 54a; Swanson (2017: 815).
16. Zhiyi speaks of the three thousand worlds in a single moment of thought when discussing conventional reality. See also Swanson (2017: 816) (notes).
17. Matsumoto Shirō and Hakamaya Noriaki, scholars of Indian Buddhism affiliated with the Zen school, initiated a movement known as Critical Buddhism (*hihan bukkyō* 批判仏教). On this polemic, see Hubbard and Swanson (1999).

18. Swanson (2017); Ziporyn (2016).
19. This does not mean that *dao* and Suchness are the same notion, just as the Buddhist concept of emptiness (*kong/kū* 空) is not exactly the same as the Daoist concept of nothingness (*wu/mu* 無). Interestingly, Zhiyi discussed the dissimilarities between the Dao and his idea of reality in several sections of the *Mohe zhiguan*.
20. See Ziporyn (2000: 112–98). The Japanese scholar Tamura Yoshirō used a similar expression: *zettai funi* 絶対不二 (absolute non-duality) and *zettai ichigenron* 絶対一元論 (absolute monism). See, for instance, Tamura (1975: 202–9).
21. Swanson (2017: 56).
22. *Mohe zhiguan*, T.46: 10b7–10c24; Swanson (2017: 229–39). The six types of identity are: 1. identity in principle; 2. verbal identity; 3. identity in contemplative practice; 4. analogical identity (i.e. resemblance in appearance); 5. identity in partial realization; 6. ultimate identity.
23. This idea of buddha-nature is reiterated in several places in *Mohe zhiguan*. See, for instance, T. 46: 126c; Swanson (2017: 1490). For a discussion of the notion, see Swanson (1990).
24. 'The ten thousand things are none other than Suchness, because they are immutable. Suchness is the ten thousand things, because it responds to conditions' (*Chū Kongōbeiron*, DZ 4:17. Saichō here draws on Zhanran's *Jingang pi*, see n. 44). This is the metaphysical basis on which Saichō argued that all beings can realize Buddhahood, in a famous debate against Tokuitsu, exponent of a current of the Hossō school (Yogācāra) which argued that Suchness did not manifest itself in the world. For a discussion of Saichō's position in English, see Asai (2014).
25. Annen, *Kyōjigi*, T.2396.75:374a. Cf. Zhiyi, *Fahua xuanyi*, T.33: 692a–693a; Swanson (1989: 171–7). On Annen, see Sueki (1994) and Dolce and Mano (2011).
26. Being-time, 'Uji', is the title of one of the chapters of Dōgen's masterpiece, *Shōbōgenzō*. The concern with impermanence seems to anticipate the stress that modern continental philosophy has placed on temporality, and comparisons have been made between Heidegger and Dōgen. Abe Masao, however, has argued that there are fundamental differences between the two. In his reading, Heidegger does not conceive of time and Being as completely belonging together, nor does he deem past, present and future to be interchangeable, as they are in Dōgen, who claimed their simultaneity. See Abe (1992).
27. *Shōbōgenzō*, 'Busshō', T.82: 95a-c; translation by Nearman (2007: 257).
    On Dōgen's dynamic view of impermanence, see Raud (2015). The pervasiveness of images that convey the unparalleled virtue of the fleeting moment has made of impermanence a quintessential characteristic of Japanese culture.
28. See, for example, the thirteenth-century statue of a male deity from Takagi shrine in Ōiso, wearing a Buddhist robe over layman clothes (Kanagawa kenritsu shiryō hakubutsukan (2006), no. 8); the many variations of the mandalas depicting the Sannō deities, protectors of Tendai Buddhism, where the deities appear either as *honji* or as *suijaku*, or as both (Shinbutsu imasu Ōmi jikkō iinkai (2011), nos. 34–63 and Fig. 1); the Kumano temple-shrine complex in Nachi.

On the relation between kami and buddhas, see Dolce (2009) and Dolce and Mitsuhashi (2013).

29. This point is continuously reiterated in Zhiyi's *Fa hua xuan yi*, which cites the sentence 'The buddha, the mind and sentient beings are not different' from the *Avatamsaka Sutra*, T.9: 465c29. See, for instance, T.33: 693a and 696a and Swanson (1989: 179 and 197–9).
30. For a discussion of the nature of the Buddha as interpreted by Kūkai, the initiator of Tantric Buddhism (aka Esoteric Buddhism) in Japan, see the chapter by Pascal and Kaufman in this volume.
31. To translate the term *jō* 成 with the verb 'to become' may be misleading. The Sinitic character, read in Japanese *naru*, has also the meaning of 'to be'.
32. For examples of ritual attainment of an innate body, see Dolce (2022).
33. The four types of mandala instantiating the body and activity of the Buddha are discussed in the *Sokushin jōbutsugi*, attributed to Kūkai.
34. Kūkai, *Goshōrai mokuroku*, T.55: 1064b; Hakeda (1972: 145).
35. *Tendaishū miketsu*, DZ 5:44.
36. *Jūjūshin ron*, T.77: 351b. In the *Mohe zhiguan* Zhiyi uses the terms 'vertical' and 'horizontal' over and again to explain the integrated nature of reality.
37. There are important differences between Chinese and Japanese articulations, which are documented in the Tang period exchanges known as *Tōketsu*. Sueki Fumihiko has suggested that the rubric focuses on plants, rather than other elements of the nonsentient world, because in Japan nature was thought in terms of plants and even human beings were in early chronicles referred to as people-grass (*hitogusa*). By contrast, in China traditionally the expression 'tiles and stones' was used to indicate nonsentient existence. See Sueki (2015: 139–44).
38. Schmithausen (2009).
39. Annen, *Bodaishingishō*, T.75: 454b–455c. Here Annen draws on the *Mohe zhiguan*, which speaks of three types of mind: the reflective and cognitive mind (*xin*); the physical organ, which is called the 'heart' (i.e. core) of grasses and trees (*hanlituo*); and the core of the collective aggregates that make up a being. (T.46: 4a; Swanson (2017: 138–9).)
40. An extensive treatment of the question is in Rambelli (2007) and Sueki (2015).
41. *Shinjō sōmoku jōbutsu shiki*, in Sueki (1995: 705–24). In this work one finds the first mention of the phrase 'plants and trees, countries and lands, all become buddhas' (*sōmoku kokudo shikkai jōbutsu* 草木国土悉皆成仏) frequently found in Japanese literature and the arts.
42. *Jingang pi*, T.46: 781–6, translated in Penkower (1993: 382–556). Zhanran's work is often considered the first explicit assertion of the enlightenment of the vegetal world.
43. *Bodaishingishō*, T.75:487b; translated in Rambelli (2007: 36).
44. *Sōmoku hosshin shugyō jōbutsu ki*, an eleventh-century work attributed to Ryōgen (912–85); cited in Rambelli (2007: 39). For an extensive analysis of Original Enlightenment Thought, see Stone (1999a).
45. For a comprehensive reading of the painting see Shimizu (1992).
46. *Mohe zhiguan*, T 46, 1c–2a; Swanson (2017: 100–1) (slightly amended).

47. *Shinnyokan*, Stone (1999b: 208).
48. For examples of agency in African thought, see Imafidon's chapter in this volume.
49. On plant behaviour and memory, see Karban (2015); Mancuso (2017).
50. In New Zealand the Te Urewera National Park was granted personhood in 2014.
51. On the relation with practices of liberation, see Sajjad Rizvi's chapter in this volume.

References

Abbreviations

T.   *Taishō shinshū daizōkyō*. 100 vols. Takakusu Junjirō et al., eds. Tokyo: Taishō Issaikyō kankōkai, pp. 1924–35.

DZ   *Dengyō daishi zenshū*. 5 vols. Heizan senshūin ed. Tokyo: Sekai seiten kankō kyōkai, 1989.

Primary sources

Bodaishingishō (full title: *Taizō kongō ryaku mondōshō*), by Annen. T.2397.75: 451–559.
Chū Kongōbeiron, by Saichō. DZ 4: 1–46.
Fahua xuanyi (full title: *Miao fa lian hua xuanyi*), T.1716.33: 681–814; partial English translation in Swanson (1989).
Goshōrai mokuroku, by Kūkai. T. 2161.55: 1060–6. Partial English translation in Hakeda (1972): 140–50.
Jingang pi, by Zhanran. T.1932.46: 781–5.
Jūjūshin ron (full title: *Himitsu mandara jūjūshinron*), by Kūkai. T.2425.77: 303–62.
Kyōjigi (full title: *Shingonshū kyōjigi*), by Annen. T.2396.75: 374–450.
Lotus Sutra, see *Miao fa lian hua jing*.
Metaphysics, by Aristotle. English translation by W. R. Ross, Oxford: Oxford University Press, 1924.
Miao fa lian hua jing, T.262.9: 1–62. English translation in Hurvitz (1976).
Mohe zhiguan, T.1911.46: 1–140. English translation in Swanson (2017).
Shinjō sōmoku jōbutsu shiki, by Annen. In Sueki (1995): 705–24.
Shinnyokan. In *Tendai hongaku ron*, *Nihon shiso taikei* 9, Tada Kōryū et al, eds. Tokyo: Iwanami shōten, 1973: 119–49. English translation in Stone (1999b).
Shōbōgenzō, by Dōgen. T.2582.82: 7–310. English translation by Hubert Nearman Mount Shasta, California: Shasta Abbey, 2007.
Sokushin jōbutsugi, attributed to Kūkai. T.2428.77: 381–4. English translation in Hakeda (1972): 225–34.
Sōmoku hosshin shugyō jōbutsu ki, *Dainihon bukkyō zenshō* 24: 345–6.
Tendaishū miketsu, DZ 5: 43–8.

Secondary sources

Abe, Masao (1992), 'The Problem of Time in Heidegger and Dogen', in his *A Study of Dogen: His Philosophy and Religion*. Albany, NY: SUNY, pp. 107–44.

Asai, Endō (2014), 'The Lotus Sutra as the Core of Japanese Buddhism: Shifts in Representations of its Fundamental Principle', *Japanese Journal of Religious Studies* 41 (1): 45–64.

Chakrabarti, Arindam, and Ralph Weber (2017), 'Introduction', in Chakrabarti and Weber (eds.), *Comparative Philosophy without Borders*. London: Bloomsbury, pp. 1–33.

Dolce, Lucia (2009), 'Duality and the *Kami*: Reconfiguring Buddhist Notions and Ritual Patterns', *Cahiers d'Extrême-Asie* 16 (special issue on 'Medieval Shinto'): 119–50.

Dolce, Lucia (2022), 'The Abhiṣeka of the Yogin: Bodily Practices and the Interiorization of Ritual in Medieval Japan', in Fabio Rambelli and Or Porath, (eds.), *Rituals of Initiation and Consecration in Premodern Japan: Power and Legitimacy in Kingship, Religion and the Arts*. Berlin: DeGruyter, pp. 275–320.

Dolce, Lucia, and Mitsuhashi Tadashi, (eds.) (2013), *Shinbutsu shūgō saikō [Rethinking Syncretism in Japanese Religion]*. Tokyo: Bensei shuppan.

Dolce, Lucia, and Shinya Mano (2011), 'Godai'in Annen', in Charles Orzech general (ed.), *Esoteric Buddhism and the Tantras in East Asia*. Leiden: Brill, pp. 768–75.

Fumihiko, Sueki (1994), 'Annen: The Philosopher Who Japanized Buddhism', *Acta Asiatica* 66: 69–86.

Fumihiko, Sueki (1995), *Heian shoki bukkyō shisō no kenkyū: Annen no shisō keisei o chūshin toshite*. Tokyo: Shunjūsha.

Fumihiko, Sueki (2015), *Sōmoku jōbutsu no shisō*. Tokyo: Sangha.

Gimello, Robert M. (1978), *Chi-yen (602–668) and the Foundations of Hua-yen Buddhism*. Ann Arbor, MI: UMI.

Hakeda, Yoshito (1972), *Kūkai: Major Works*. New York: Columbia University Press.

Hubbard, Jamie, and Paul Swanson, (eds.) (1999), *Pruning the Bodhi Tree: The Storm Over Critical Buddhism*. Honolulu, HI: University of Hawai'i.

Hurvitz, Leon (1976), *Scripture of the Lotus Blossom of the Fine Dharma (The Lotus Sūtra)*. New York: Columbia University Press.

Kanagawa kenritsu shiryō hakubutsukan (ed.) (2006), *Kamigami to deau: Kanagawa shintō bijutsu*. Tokyo: Benridō.

Karban, Richard (2015), *Plant Sensing and Communication*. Chicago, IL: University of Chicago Press.

Ma, Lin, and Jaap van Brakel (2016), *Fundamentals of Comparative and Intercultural Philosophy*. Albany, NY: State University of New York Press.

Mancuso, Stefano (2017), *Plant Revolution: Le piante hanno già inventato il nostro future*. Milano: Giunti.

Penkower, Linda (1993), 'T'ien-t'ai during the T'ang Dynasty: Chan-jan and the Sinification of Buddhism', Ph.D. diss., Columbia University.

Rambelli, Fabio (2007), *Buddhist Materiality: A Cultural History of Objects in Japanese Buddhism*. Stanford, CA: Stanford University Press.

Raud, Rain (2015), 'Dōgen's Idea of Buddha-Nature: Dynamism and Non-Referentiality', *Asian Philosophy* 25 (1): 1–14.

Schmithausen, Lambert (2009), *Plants in Early Buddhism and He Far Eastern Idea of the Buddha-Nature of Grasses and Trees*. Lumbini: Lumbini International Research Institute.

Shimizu, Yoshiaki (1992), 'Multiple Commemorations: The Vegetable Nehan of Itō Jakuchū', in James H. Sanford, William R. LaFleur and Masatoshi Nagatomi (eds.), *Flowing Traces: Buddhism in the Literary and Visual Arts of Japan*. Princeton, NJ: Princeton University Press, pp. 201–33.

Shinbutsu imasu Ōmi jikkō iinkai, (ed.) (2011), *Shinbusu imasu Ōmi*. Kyoto: Shibunkaku.

Stone, Jacqueline I. (1999a), *Original Enlightenment and the Transformation of Medieval Japanese Buddhism*. Honolulu, HI: University of Hawai'i Press.

Stone, Jacqueline I. (1999b), 'The Contemplation of Suchness', in George Tanabe (ed.), *Religion of Japan in Practice*. Princeton, NJ: Princeton University Press, pp. 199–204.

Swanson, Paul L. (1989), *Foundations of T'ien-t'ai Philosophy: The Flowering of the Two Truths Theory in Chinese Buddhism*. Nanzan Studies in Religion and Culture. Berkeley, CA: Asian Humanities Press.

Swanson, Paul (1990), 'T'ien-t'ai Chih-i's Concept of Threefold Buddha Nature: A Synergy of Reality, Wisdom, and Practice', in Paul J. Griffiths and John P. Keenan, (eds.), *Buddha Nature: A Festschrift in Honor of Minoru Kiyota*. Reno, NV: Buddhist Books International, pp. 171–80.

Swanson, Paul (2017), *Clear Serenity, Quiet Insight: T'ien-t'ai Chih-i's Mo-ho chih-kuan*, 3 vols. Honolulu, HI: University of Hawai'i Press.

Tamura, Yoshirō (1975), *Nichiren: junkyō no nyoraishi*. Tokyo: Nippon hōsō shuppan kyōkai.

Ziporyn, Brook (2000), *Evil and/or/as Good: Omnicentrism, Intersubjectivity, and Value Paradox in Tiantai Buddhism Thought*. Cambridge, MA: Harvard University Press.

Ziporyn, Brook (2004), *Being and Ambiguity: Philosophical Experiments with Tiantai Buddhism*. Chicago, IL: Open Court Press.

Ziporyn, Brook (2016), *Emptiness and Omnipresence: The Lotus Sutra and Tiantai Buddhism in Contemporary Philosophical Perspective*. Bloomington, IN: Indiana University Press.

2

Beyond, being and becoming

Agata Bielik-Robson

What is the *beyond*? In the Greek, it is the subject of metaphysics as the science of *meta-physis* or what lies *beyond* the physical world of nature. The word *beyond*, therefore, can mean anything metaphysical, from the primordial impersonal *arche* to the personal God of Abrahamic revelation, and as such is discussed in every chapter in this book. But in the narrower sense, which will be my concern here, the word *beyond* signifies a *transcendence*: something – or, perhaps, not a thing at all – that exceeds the order of being so radically that it cannot be captured by terms deriving from the physical realm of experience. Although the term 'transcendence' was invented late, only in the nineteenth century in the Protestant milieu of German philosophy of religion – together with its counterpart, 'immanence', deriving from the Latin *immanere* meaning 'to dwell in' – the intuition of the true origin as belonging to the realm of radical *beyond* is almost as old as the metaphysics itself.

A short history of transcendence

Almost, because the intimation of the radical *beyond* does not yet appear in the prehistoric origins of mankind: it has its history which – as we will see presently – is also the beginning of history as such. It emerges, in a mysterious synchronicity, in a similar period in very different cultural and religious formations, from China, through India and Egypt, to Greece – a period which, precisely because of that sudden switch of metaphysical perspective, was called the 'axial age'. The concept of the axial age was coined by Karl Jaspers, but the elements of the axial theory can be found already in the writings of Max Weber in his studies on the relation between religion and economy in various world cultures.[1] Yet, it was with Shmuel Eisenstadt and his school of comparative philosophy of religions and civilizations that it acquired a broader meaning, able properly to encompass the non-Western traditions.

In Jaspers' original account, the axial breakthrough occurred between the ninth and the fifth century BCE, in the Mediterranean region, ranging from ancient Israel to Greece (later on he also was willing to add India and what he called 'the Buddhist revolution'). Jan Assmann, the Egyptologist fascinated with the Egyptian monotheism of Akhenaton, which was introduced during the Amarna Reform long before the period postulated by Jaspers, famously criticized him for defining the Axial Age as an *age* located more or less precisely located in time. According to Assmann – and Eisenstadt seconds him on that – the axial turn is an evolutionary potentiality of possibly all human cultures, which also creates a cautious form of a universal history of mankind.[2] The contrastive split between transcendence and immanence could thus potentially occur anywhere and anytime, given the right conditions, because it consists in creating a structural contrast conceived in terms of a tension rather than a rigid dualism – hence the controversial axial status of the ancient 'Iranian religions', where the original divide between the forces of good versus the forces of evil does not mirror exactly the axial divide between the transcendent and the immanent (Arnason, Eisenstadt, Wittrock 2005: 3). It is precisely this *tension* which constitutes the most productive normative element of the Axial Religions: the otherworldly Godhead and this-worldly dimension of *being* (as well as *becoming* which dynamicizes the ontological order) must eventually come closer to one another and find a moment of reconciliation. Thus, having in mind Assmann's critique of the axial turn based on strict chronology, the authors of *Axial Civilizations and World History* postulate that, instead of talking about the 'Axial Age, it seems better to conceive of the *axial syndrome* as a crucially important component in the history of human societies, which develops in different ways in different contexts, giving rise to different, multiple axialities which interact continually among themselves and with non-axial civilisations in the shaping of different patterns of world history or histories' (Arnason, Eisenstadt, Wittrock 2005: 5).

Eisenstadt's comparative scheme is free – or, at least, attempts to be free – of the Western biases that can be detected in Jaspers and Weber. The defining feature of axial religion is the 'invention of the transcendence', which evacuates the sacred from the world and locates it in the otherworldly Godhead, either personal (as in religions of revelation) or impersonal (as in Plato's Form of Good, lying *epekeina tes ousias*, 'beyond being', or as in Daoism). According to Benjamin Schwartz, whom Eisenstadt quotes at the beginning of his magisterial work, *Comparative Civilizations and Multiple Modernities*:

> If there is nevertheless some common underlying impulse in all these 'axial' movements, it might be called *the strain towards transcendence* […] What I refer to here is something close to the etymological meaning of the word – a kind of *standing back and looking beyond* – a kind of *critical, reflective questioning of the actual and a new vision of what lies beyond* […] In concentrating our attention on those transcendental breakthroughs we are of course stressing the significance of changes in man's conscious life. What is

more, we are stressing the consciousness of small groups of prophets, philosophers and wise men who may have had a very small impact on their immediate environment.
(Schwartz 1975: 198; emphasis added)

In Eisenstadt's approach, the decisive axial breakthrough consists not so much in the invention of transcendence as such, as rather in shaping a new dynamic *relation between transcendence and immanence* or between *beyond and being*. This relation can take many different forms and it is precisely those fundamental differences within one Axial Model that are most intriguing from the comparative perspective. While the Axial Model delivers a general framework making possible comparisons and juxtapositions, the particular ways in which the 'transcendental turn' is interpreted offer the most convincing map of differences. It also allows for fruitful mediation between abstract metaphysical structures and concrete socio-historical conditions in which those structures evolved: while it is philosophically sophisticated and non-reductive, it nonetheless keeps the balance with the concrete histories of various social evolutions.

What Eisenstadt calls the *basic tension between the transcendental and the mundane orders* constitutes the decisive difference between mythic and post-axial metaphysical systems. While the former are 'homologous', that is, imagine the higher order as a stronger but also continuous version of the mundane one – the latter are 'heterologous', that is, imagine the higher order as essentially different and transcending the worldly one:

> These conceptions of a *basic tension between the transcendental and the mundane orders* differed greatly from the 'homologous' perceptions of the relation between these two orders which were prevalent in so-called pagan religions in those very societies and civilisations from which these post-axial-age civilisations emerged. Certainly, the transmundane order has, in all human societies, been perceived as somewhat different, usually higher and stronger, than the mundane one. But in the pre-axial-age 'pagan' civilisations this higher world has been symbolically structured according to principles very similar to those of the mundane or lower one. Relatively similar symbolic terms were used for the definition of God(s) and man; of the mundane and transmundane orders – even if there always was a continuous stress on the difference between them. In most such societies the transmundane world was usually equated with a concrete setting, 'the other world', which was the abode of the dead, the world of spirits, and not entirely unlike the mundane world in detail. These pagan societies, of course, always recognised the moral frailty of man; the failure of people to live up to the prevalent social and moral ideals. However, a conception of an autonomous, distinct moral order which is qualitatively different from both this world and 'the other world' developed only to a minimal degree. Such *homologous conceptions of the transmundane and mundane worlds* were very often closely connected with some mythical and cyclical conception of time in which the differences between the major time dimensions – past, present and future – are only mildly articulated. By contrast, in the axial-age civilisations, the perception of *a sharp disjunction between the mundane*

and transmundane worlds developed. There was a concomitant stress on the existence of a higher transcendental moral or metaphysical order which is beyond any given this – or other-worldly reality. The development of these conceptions created a problem in the rational, abstract articulation of the givens of human and social existence and of the cosmic order. The root of the problem lies in the fact that the development of such conceptions necessarily poses the question of *the ways in which the chasm between the transcendental and the mundane orders can be bridged.*

(Eisenstadt 2003: 199–200; emphasis added)

The question of how to overcome the tension between the transcendent and immanent orders is one of *salvation*. While the initial condition of being is marked by the stark contrast between the perfection of the *beyond* and the imperfection of the this-worldly dimension, the soteriological process aims at bringing the lower strata of existence to the level of the transcendent ideal:

> Another major distinction lies in the focus of the resolution of the transcendental tensions which, in Weberian terms, is salvation. Here the distinction is between purely this-worldly, purely other-worldly and mixed this- and other-worldly conceptions of salvation. It is probably no accident that the 'secular' conception of this tension was connected, as in China and to some degree in the ancient world, with an almost wholly this-worldly conception of salvation, or that the metaphysical non-deistic conception of this tension, as in Hinduism and Buddhism, tended towards an other-worldly conception of salvation, while the great monotheistic religions tended to stress combinations of this- and other-worldly conceptions of salvation.
>
> (Eisenstadt 2003: 215)

The issue of salvation is closely linked to the emergence of a new type of human subjectivity as the individual soul that can be either saved or damned. The rise of the individuated soul, deeply aware of the ethical difference between good and evil, reflects the normative tension between the ideal *beyond* and the this-worldly non-ideal order of being. It also creates 'a new type of elite':

> The development and institutionalisation of the perception of basic tension between the transcendental and the mundane order was closely connected with the emergence of a new social element. Generally speaking it was a new type of elite which was cited as the carrier of models of cultural and social order. Examples would include the Jewish prophets and priests, the Greek philosophers and sophists, the Chinese Literati, the Hindu Brahmins, the Buddhist Sangha and the Islamic Ulema. It was the initial small nuclei of such groups of intellectuals that developed these new 'transcendental' conceptions. In all these axial-age civilisations these conceptions ultimately became institutionalised. That is, they became the predominant orientations of both the ruling as well as of many secondary elites, fully embodied in their respective centres or subcentres.
>
> (Arnason, Eisenstadt, Wittrock 2005: 201)

For Eisenstadt, those elites are formed on the basis of a new ideal model of human personality, which embodies and simultaneously anticipates the moment of salvation, where the two dimensions – transcendent and immanent – no longer collide, but potentially come together:

> The attempts at re-ordering of the world developed in most spheres of human existence and activity. Such reorganisation of the world has far-reaching implications for the formation of the human personality and of personal identity in terms of the model of the ideal man. In the societies in which the perception of the tension between the transcendental and the mundane orders has been institutionalised, this personal identity and the definition of man was taken beyond the primordial givens of human existence, and beyond the various technical needs of daily activities. Purely personal virtues, such as courage, or interpersonal ones such as solidarity, have been taken out of their primordial framework and are combined, in different dialectical modes, with the attributes of resolution of the tension between the transcendental and the mundane orders. In this way a new level of internal tensions in the formation of personality is generated.
>
> (Arnason, Eisenstadt, Wittrock 2005: 202)

With transcendence, therefore, there also appears an individual *subject* as a reflexive unit, possessing an inwards dimension, potentially universal, and engaged in the normative pursuit of perfection offered by the transcendent ideal. This 'enhanced reflexivity' leads to 'a broadening of horizons, or an opening up of potentially universal perspectives, in contrast to the particularism of more archaic modes of thought; an ontological distinction between higher and lower levels of reality; and a normative subordination of the lower level to the higher, with more or less overtly stated implications for human efforts to translate guiding principles into ongoing practices' (Arnason, Eisenstadt, Wittrock 2005: 2).

The findings of the Eisenstadtian school are widely confirmed by other twentieth-century philosophers of religion. According to Jacob Taubes, who applied the Jaspersian model in his analysis of the Hebrew 'prophetic age', the invention of subjective inwardness or a 'deep self' closely mirrors the invention of transcendence. Taubes locates the axial turn in the Book of Ezekiel, where 'radical inwardness' giving rise to the new understanding of human subjectivity emerges as a *tselem* (image and likeness) of the transcendent God: the infinite depth of the singular soul corresponds to the infinite distance of the transcendent *beyond*. Just as the Godhead can gain distance from the immanent here and now, so the new subject can step back from the flow of life, retreat inwards and become reflexive. And just as transcendence offers a vantage point to see the world as a totality, perhaps also criticize it, so does the soul equipped with the 'deep inside': she too can call the Maker *de profundis* – out of the depths – and, like Job, the paradigmatic axial hero, not only inspect her own wrongdoings, but also challenge the whole order of being as essentially unjust. In his essay 'On the Current State of Polytheism', written in a fierce polemic against Francois Lyotard and Odo Marquard, who famously defended the postmodern individual against the tyranny of the monotheistic narrative, Taubes demonstrates that without this very narrative there would never have emerged a concept of the individual, and that the polytheistic Greeks, still immersed in the 'mythic consciousness', failed to develop a strong enough concept of individuation:

> Ezekiel 18 marks a turning point in the history of religion. It is indeed a constitutive chapter in the 'ur-history of subjectivity' because in the prophet's speech the power of the mythical nexus of guilt and atonement within the chain of generations is broken and the mythic horizon of consciousness is decisively transcended [...] When the mythic spell is broken, humans acquire what since Ezekiel we have called a 'soul': his ego.
>
> (Taubes 2009a: 306–7)

The awakening of deep subjectivity, therefore, also spells the beginning of the metaphysics of ethical concern which will be most characteristic for Judaism and, to some extent, for Christianity as the late child of the axial revolution. Proper individuation commences when the soul discovers that she is solely responsible for her sins. Thus, when Ezekiel says: 'The one who sins is the one who will die' (Ezek. 18.3-4), we should read it as *Only* the soul who sins shall die, to indicate that the soul can be solely responsible for those evils she herself committed, not the wrongs that do not belong to her (like the Greek *Ate*, the tragic fate transmitted from generation to generation). This line of interpretation has been very strongly recommended by Hermann Cohen who, in *Religion of Reason*, inaugurated a new reading of Ezekiel, later on reflected in Taubes' description of the crucial turn:

> Thus the new man is born: in this way the individual becomes the I [...] In the recognition of his own sin, man becomes an individual. Through the power to create for himself a new heart and a new spirit, he becomes an I [...] One should think that henceforth the main emphasis was firmly placed on the religion of the heart, since through Ezekiel, particularly, repentance became the inward substitute for sacrifice.
>
> (Cohen 1995: 193; 194; 27)

Cohen perceives Ezekiel not as a prophet of zealous righteousness and godly fear, but as an inventor of moral inwardness and individuation, which – to quote Harold Bloom's title of honour, originally applied by him to Shakespeare – makes him a true 'inventor of the human' (Bloom 1998). It is only with the emergence of the singularized subject that the issue of salvation or damnation can be properly raised. For, only the soul that sinned and is thus accountable for her sins, can also be saved, that is, redeemed from her sinful status, or eternally damned, that is, consigned to the 'second death'.

Salvation: Multiple potential modernities

The most significant contribution of Eisenstadt's school is the concept of salvation translated into multiple potential modernities, that is, various strategies of redemption/modernization undertaken by cultural elites, formed by the new type of human subjectivity. This new type of social praxis is the direct consequence of the contrastive dynamics between transcendence and immanence, ranging from the Gnostic pattern of extreme dualism to 'this-worldly transcendentalism' in Daoism. Eisenstadt's Axial Model thus offers a theory of the *esoteric origins of modernization* which are potentially present in all axial traditions, Western and non-Western. The combination of transcendence and reflexive deep inwardness of the 'awakened' subjectivity creates an elite of new subjects who claim to represent both simultaneously. Opposed to – or ill at ease with – the simple dimension of everyday life, the esoteric elites put a pressure on this-worldly reality, by demanding that it conform to the transcendental ideal. The potential modernity actualizes itself when this demand takes a *dialectical* form, that is, when it does not content itself with simple condemnation of the fallen world – as in the case of the Iranian-Gnostic dualism, which sees no chance of redemption for the immanent reality, forever marked with evil – and chooses instead a 'spiritual investment in this world'[3] – but only on the condition that it can eventually develop according to the transcendent ideal, until it *becomes* fleshed out at 'the end of history'. Potential modernity, therefore, emerges whenever and wherever the new priestly elite translates devotion to the transcendent *beyond* as the ideal of goodness and justice into social practice – and attempts to mould the recalcitrant material reality according to its high standard. It thus enforces a similar change, which first formed the priestly elite, on the rest of the society, by demanding that it too becomes individualized and focused on the exacting norms of the new ethical piety.

In this manner, with the concept of potential modernity, there also emerges the *metaphysics of time* – time conceived as Holy History (*Heilsgeschichte*): the temporal dynamics of salvation necessary to lift the world to the level of transcendence in a purposeful process of *becoming*, to complete the goal of worldly redemption. In Eisenstadt's illuminative account, the new esoteric elites are usually split into two warring camps, divided on the issue of the very possibility of 'mending the world' according to the high standards set by the transcendent ideal. One camp is characterized by a deep scepticism and disbelief in any attempt to raise immanence to the level of transcendence: these are the 'apocalyptic fundamentalists' who await the end of history as the catastrophic event that would put an end to the scandal of worldly existence (as, for instance, late Taubes who, disappointed with the Western model of eschatological historiosophy, famously claimed that he no longer had a 'spiritual investment in the world as it is'). The other camp is characterized by a deep belief that radical transformation of the world, bridging the gap between transcendence and immanence, is indeed possible: these are the 'messianic reformists' who insist on the perfectibility of material existence (the best example is Hegel with his redemptive vision of ultimate reconciliation of the two orders at the end of history). This opposition comes to the fore most explicitly in the history of Western modernity, but can also be witnessed in other parts of the axial time-space, sometimes equally openly, sometimes tamed or merely *in nuce*:

> The religious (more specifically sectarian) roots of modernity [...] find a very strong resonance in the utopian sectarian traditions of other Axial civilisations.
> (Eisenstadt 2003: 46)

Eisenstadt's Axial Model delivers a link between the purely theological account of the *beyond* as transcendence, on the one hand, and the social-cultural evolution which it sets in motion, on the other. Apart from offering an 'esoteric' insight into the matrix of potential modernities, it also offers a unique *metaphysical definition of potential modernity* as an attempt to decrease the tension between transcendence and immanence, positively evaluating the historical process of *becoming* as the essential transformation of the order of being. It is worth noticing that this is the very opposite of the more popular Nietzschean understanding of modernity as secularization which frees immanence from divine power: the Nietzschean 'death of God' leads towards atheism and the demise of metaphysics as an obsolete system of thought destined to die with the disappearance of the last 'shadow' of the *beyond*.[4] According to Eisenstadt's 'esoteric' definition, which does not restrict modernization only to Western culture, modernity is not an effect of atheisation, but an integral element of the metaphysics of transcendence: it occurs whenever there appears a soteriological attempt to transform immanent reality in accordance with a transcendent ideal of goodness and justice.

The Eisenstadtian motif of multiple potential modernities allows us to introduce a general comparative rule: the greater the original tension between the transcendent *beyond* and the order of *being*, the more dramatic the process of *becoming* as the potential modernization of the latter. Within the Abrahamic paradigm, with its strong inclination towards maximal difference, the tension can lead to violent upheavals, according to the equation proposed by early Taubes for whom 'revelation is revolution'.[5] Millenarian movements, pre-reformation peasant uprisings, radical formations like the Münster circle, messianic sects like the Jewish Sabbatians, or, in a secularized form, the Jacobins (Eisenstadt generally calls all those revolutionary answers to the challenge of modernity 'Jacobin': Eisenstadt 1999) – all follow the Taubesian understanding of transcendence as a radical counter-principle to the World (*Gegenprinzip der Welt*) which has revolutionary consequences. But when the tension between transcendence and immanence is presented in a less dramatic manner – as, for instance, in Hegel – then modernity expresses itself in *reform*: literally, a thorough working-through of the ontological *status quo* in order to give it a new form, re-formed and thus conforming to the divine Notion of freedom and a free association of beings in a metaphysical community of 'all-in-all'. A similar axial pattern can also be found in Buddhism which seems to replicate the difference between the two camps of the religious elites defined by Eisenstadt: the *satori* wisdom of withdrawal from the world, on the one hand, and the Bodhisattva teaching of return to the world to reform it, on the other. We can also assume that when the tension between transcendence and immanence is kept minimal – as, according to Eisenstadt, in Chinese Daoism and Confucianism – there will be hardly any metaphysical grounding for either violent revolution or a fervent reformist spirit. In less antagonistic models of the relation between transcendence and immanence, as in the Chinese one, the former is seen less as a 'counter-principle' to imperfect worldly reality, and more as an agency of 'letting-be' and 'paving-the-way' for the order of beings which are allowed to *become* with no definite *telos* set in front of them as a historical ideal:

> China [...] was characterized by a visibly weak stress – as compared to other post-Axial Age Civilizations – on the tension between the transcendental and the mundane order; a strong this-worldly focus of overcoming this tension; a very weak conception of an historical-transcendental time dimension; a cyclical time dimension; and a relative openness in its formulation as well as accessibility of the broader strata to the social and cultural orders as indicated by the Confucian literati.
>
> (Eisenstadt 2003: 230)

Not at all accidentally, a similar intuition concerning Dao emerged in the post-war philosophy of Martin Heidegger. In his critical reflections on Western onto-theological metaphysics, strongly informed by the maximal contrast between the highest being and the lower worldly beings, Heidegger attempted to overcome the 'principle of violence', which, as he argued, necessarily follows the original opposition between transcendence and immanence (Heidegger 1977). While the transcendent order does violence to the mundane one, being too ideal to tolerate anything less perfect than itself – the immanent order of beings does violence to the divine origin, by trying to forget it (according to Heidegger, *Seinsvergessenheit*, the forgetting of Being, culminates precisely in the Western ontotheology). In late Heidegger, disappointed with the violent, decisionistic and will-oriented thought of the Nazi period and seeking an alternative inspiration in Daoism and Japanese Zen, Being (*das Seyn* as *beyond* beings, *die Seiende*) is not the religious ideal transcendence violently confronting the non-ideal world, but a gentle principle of *Seinlassen* or 'letting-be', which simply gives being without expecting anything in return: Being does not create beings in its more or less perfect image, but only lets them be through the act of metaphysical gift (*es gibt*).[6] As the principle of 'letting-be' it paves the way or even, as in Daoism, becomes a Way – a Path for beings emerging in the Open of the world as a realm of fluid change and possibility – and as such opposed to the necessitarian-deterministic concept of the 'highest ground' which rules everything to the point of depriving its subjects of free will.[7] The Eisenstadtian question, however, would be: can such minimal tension be a matrix of 'potential modernity' too – or is it too pacified to create a reformist movement within the world? Certainly, that was Heidegger's anti-modernist intention when he reached for Chinese and Japanese wisdom: to stop the violent madness of reform, of tinkering with the 'sendings of Being' which should be peacefully accepted by beings, naturally grateful for the gift of being and 'released' from the obligation to match any divine ideal and reconcile itself with it in the course of the Holy History. Heidegger's choice of the Eckhartian term, *Gelassenheit*, as the catch-phrase of his late post-war period, meant to cover all those connotations: non-violence in relation between Being and beings, redefined not in terms of the strong creationist paradigm, but as a gentle procedure of 'letting be'; 'releasement' from the hierarchy of high transcendence and low immanence, now regarded much more horizontally; and, last but not least, peaceful acceptance of one's finitude, no longer to be judged according to the absolutist standards of the eternal infinite.

The *beyond* today: An ongoing debate

Although flexible and comprehensive, the Eisenstadtian model does not cover *all* possible aspects of the relation between the *beyond* and the order of being; as some participants in our project objected, it is still biased, in that it takes the Western history of transcendence as its basic criterion in assessing other potential modernities. Our basic goal has been to avoid a monological perspective that would thwart the very project of comparative metaphysics – with the main concern about the Western perspective, being that it has already created comparative categories in its abstract philosophical discussions of the relation between the beyond and the order of being.

These lend themselves as a deceptively suitable canvas for the translation of metaphysical intuitions of non-Western systems of thought. In order to remain faithful to our collective enterprise, this chapter is also written in response to the live dialogue of experts representing different traditions, with no ambition to create one universal model of the *beyond* that would either sublate all the differences or state them in a language that would stifle other – less philosophically oriented and more poetic and imaginative – approaches. This chapter is thus a record of living ongoing debate: of doing comparative metaphysics in dialogic practice, with no pre-established goal of *consensus*.

The first systematic issue that comes to the fore once the motif of the *beyond* is introduced is the status of the relation between the transcendent and this world – the aspect which the Axial Model indeed holds as the defining one. Is this a contrast or a co-existence? Is this a relation at all – if the *beyond* and the order of being cannot be said to exist on the same plane? Is the *beyond* the only truly existing unconditional – a 'necessary being' – while worldly phenomena are merely conditioned and thus weaker in their mode of existence, or, perhaps, when regarded in contrast with the transcendent, almost non-existent at all and 'close to nothing'? Or, alternatively, is the *beyond* a 'no-thing,' radically transcending the realm of being, while 'beingness' can only be attributed to the 'things' in this world? What is real – and what is an illusion? Can both, the *beyond* and the worldly realm of being and becoming, be equally real? Or is one more real than the other?

In all traditions belonging to the Axial Model, these questions are asked, debated – and, depending on the answers, determine the different paths of evolution not only between various cultural formations, but also within them. In Indian thought, the relation between the *beyond* conceived as a primal consciousness and the worldly order of being can be pictured as reducing the latter to a merely epiphenomenal 'veil of Maya' – but it can also be described as positively constitutive, granting the phenomena a real status, as real as suffering itself.[8] In Christianity, depending on the relation to its double origin in 'Athens and Jerusalem', this question can be answered in the Platonic manner, which privileges the hierarchical ontological solution, where only the *beyond* has a status of the ultimate reality – but it can also follow the Hebrew source, where God creates the world as a solid entity, by elevating it from the 'no-thingness' of the primary chaos, and describes it as good (*ki tov*).[9] Similarly in Islam, where God, as in all Abrahamic religions, is perceived as the powerful creator of something real: yet, when his power is conceived as absolute (as in the Asharite *kalam*), it begins to endanger the ontologically separate status of the created world, then regarded as a mere limitation to the divine *potentia absoluta*. Daoism seems to be most immune to this metaphysical oscillation, in which 'realness' of the world is granted and then withdrawn, but it also retains a tension which is incipient in the relation between the *beyond* and the immanence: Dao as a 'path of things', can never be thought in separation from what it makes possible – unlike, e.g. the Islamic-Asharite God possessing absolute power which does not need the world as its counterpart – but it is never reduced to the phenomena which it conditions. The relation between the *beyond* and the order of being is thus based on the *fundamental asymmetry* between what is primary and what is only secondary: the former, which founds, conditions or creates, cannot be thought as equal with the latter as *merely* founded, conditioned or created.

This essential asymmetry immediately translates into another universal problem in the Axial Model: the relation between the original One and the immanent Many.

The *beyond* is thought here as the primordial undivided source which, the moment it creates/conditions beings, *becomes* multiple and manifests itself in a variety of the worldly phenomena. The very formulation of this problem immediately reveals a major methodological dilemma: in what sort of language to approach it – via the mystical apophatic idiom of the Supreme Paradox or via the meta-philosophical idiom which insists on explaining paradoxes? One of the advantages of the 'meta-history' or the 'transhistorical approach' – to use terms introduced by Toshikiko Izutsu in his comparative study of Daoism and Sufism (Izutsu 1983: 2) – in the comparative enterprise is that it does not want to take *paradoxa* at face value: it may not be as firm in rejecting them as simple contradictions, as in Western philosophy based on the Aristotelian rule of the excluded middle, but it nonetheless attempts to solve them – or, at least, explicate them. From the mystical point of view, however, which privileges the apophatic approach, the relation between the One and the Many is a mystery to be rather contemplated than solved – hence the Supreme Paradox as the favourite mode of expression.[10] The contemplative mystic, therefore, will say that 'the Many is nothing but One' and, vice versa, that 'One is nothing but Many', and will live with the aporia, convinced that if mundane language approaches the highest mystery, it can do so only in negation and putting itself in doubt. A 'meta-historical' philosopher would never stop at that: for him, the mystical paradox constitutes the most serious challenge for thought. Hegel, the first Western 'meta-historical' *avant la lettre*, whose dialectics, forming a non-binary type of thinking, were designed specifically for tarrying with the paradoxical, defined his philosophy as a sublation of religious paradoxical images (*Vorstellungsdenken*) into an explanative discourse.[11] The 'mystics', however, defending their apophatic and contemplative mode of thinking, would strongly disagree, claiming that all is lost with such a sublation-translation, and insist on their own extra-logical methods of approaching the *beyond*.

The problem of the One and the Many then inevitably leads to the next one, already signalled by the Axial Model: *the metaphysics of time* – the temporality in which the paradox or the tension between transcendence and immanence is to be resolved – or, at least, decreased – by the 'spiritual investment in the world' as the realm of purposeful *becoming*. The historical metaphysics of the world-invested Spirit is firmly turned towards the worldly as the 'earth without heaven': instead of the atemporal static metaphysics of the Neoplatonic 'everlasting cycle', it offers a metaphysics of time, where secular history becomes inscribed into *die Heilsgeschichte*, the future-oriented grand narrative in which traditional transcendence is replaced with the eschatological *telos*. According to Taubes' *Occidental Eschatology*, all these new characteristics point to a revolutionary break with the Greco-Christian cosmos of the Neoplatonic harmony – 'as above, so below' – ruled by the sublimated principle of Eros:

> In the Copernican view of the world there is an earth but no heaven. The earth mirrors no heaven, and the reality of the world is gained by Copernican man, not by having

the world emulate a superior archetype, but by revolutionising the world in terms of an ideal that lies in the future. The Ptolemaic world is ruled by the Platonic concept of Eros, which attracts the lower sphere to the upper sphere. The Copernican world is ruled by the spirit, which invariably presses ahead. The ethics of the Copernican man is an ethics of the future [...] The Platonic relationship of image and archetype, which Origen and Augustine set up between earthly history and heavenly guidance, is transformed for Joachim [da Fiore] into a powerful chain of events within history: the Kingdom of Heaven becomes the final realm of the spirit.

(Taubes 2009b: 88–9)

The passage from Eros to Spirit is also called by Taubes the 'transition from analogy to dialectics' or 'leaving the Realm of the Paradox' where the latter stands for the divine *coincidentia oppositorum* which contains all the opposites – being and becoming, infinity and finitude, Heaven and Earth – in a static manner (Taubes 1953/1954). According to Taubes, the birth of modern historiosophic metaphysics repeats the foundational passage from *mythos* to *logos* as a transition from faith to knowledge (*de fidei ad rationem*) due to the seminal substitution which replaces the mystical contemplation of the Supreme Paradox with the dynamic mode of dialectical thinking that attempts to resolve the heavenly paradoxa in the temporal sequence of dramatic transitions – precisely as was done by the precursor of the Hegelian dialectics, Joachim da Fiore, who temporalized Trinity in order to transform its static inner *coincidentia* into a historical denouement of subsequent epochs: the era of the Father, of the Son, and – the coming – era of the Spirit:

A theology that has lost the cosmological basis for the principle of analogy but nevertheless continues with the method of analogy becomes purely metaphorical. In a Copernican universe a theology that takes its symbols and presuppositions seriously can only proceed by the method of dialectic.

(Taubes 2009a: 171–2)

Yet, although a rationalization of the mystical paradoxa, dialectics does not announce a total break with *fides*: it rather transforms it, shifting attention from the supreme mysteries of God towards the world as the realm on which those mysteries are not only reflected (as in the Neoplatonic scheme of analogy), but also *enacted*. The secular world becomes a *stage* for the acts of Spirit which cannot but invest in the worldly domain that, no longer spellbound by the analogical 'bonds of love', gains ontological autonomy. This autonomy is strictly bound with the new appreciation of time: the world's emancipation manifests itself mostly in its openness towards the Event – a 'temporal other' which breaks through the confines of the 'everlasting circle' and its eternal archetypes in order to create something *new*. The Spirit, therefore, invests in the world's *future* which, for the first time in the history of metaphysics, is a real future, open and unpredictable, to be intimated only in the mode of prophecy – like the one of Joachim da Fiore, the paradigmatic modern case of the 'spiritual investment in the world'. In Taubes' *Occidental Eschatology*, the potential modernity of the Western axial religions becomes actual once the time is taken seriously as a metaphysical agent of the spiritual transformation of the world – a dynamic made possible only by the demise of the Neoplatonic atemporal metaphysics.

Yet, even within the Western, most openly historiosophic and time-oriented metaphysical paradigm, the issue of temporality is far from settled: in the classical strains of Christian Neoplatonism (from Augustine, through Erich Voegelin, to today's Radical Orthodoxy of John Milbank), time still does not matter on the ultimate plane of things, formed by the 'eternal structures of being'. If the divine *beyond* tends to be conceived as a divine Absolute, subsisting in an eternal and hence atemporal realm, the time of the world – *becoming* – remains a merely relative phenomenon, a tainted Platonic 'mirror of eternity'. The concept of the Holy History, implicating transcendence in the historical process, thus goes very much against any theological absolutism, which is firmly poised against any processual form of deity. The absolutization of the *beyond*, which became a dogma in certain forms of Christianity and Islam, rejects time as a metaphysical factor and invests instead in the eternity of the 'everlasting cycle'. When the *beyond* is regarded as the *arche* of the eternal structures of being, time and becoming are irrelevant and merely epiphenomenal. When, however, the *beyond* is conceived as a processual model-ideal for the worldly reality, time and becoming step into the middle of the metaphysical story – as, precisely, the Holy History.[12]

The discussion on the status of the 'spiritual investment in this world' (or its lack) leads directly to the problem of ethics. The concept of the *beyond* cannot be reduced to the ontological dimension solely: it must also – or perhaps even primarily – be interpreted in normative terms. This was precisely the perspective of Emmanuel Lévinas in his 'ethics as the first philosophy'. For Lévinas, the modern representative of one of the oldest axial religions, Judaism, immanence or 'totality' needs transcendence or 'infinity' for ethical reasons: the sameness of being needs the radical otherness of 'otherwise than being', because without such a vantage point, it could never be criticized, doubted or put in question – as it was done paradigmatically in the Book of Job. For Lévinas, therefore, transcendence is above all the transcendental possibility of the critique of being as such (or what he calls 'ontologism') – which forms the polemical opposite of the metaphysical view of Nietzsche and Heidegger who both rejected the Jewish mode of ethical criticism as the resentful manifestation of the 'spirit of revenge':

> This 'beyond' the totality and objective experience is, however, not to be described in a purely negative fashion. It is reflected within the totality and history, within experience. The eschatological, as the 'beyond' of history, draws beings out of the jurisdiction of history and the future; it arouses them in and calls them forth to their full responsibility. Submitting history as a whole to judgment, exterior to the very wars that mark its end, it restores to each instant its full signification in that very instant: all the causes are ready to be heard [...] The eschatological vision breaks with the totality of wars and

empires in which one does not speak. It does not envisage the end of history within being understood as a totality, but institutes a relation with the infinity of being which exceeds the totality. The first "vision" of eschatology (hereby distinguished from the revealed opinions of positive religions) reveals the very possibility of eschatology, that is, the breach of the totality, the possibility of a signification without a context. The experience of morality does not proceed from this vision – it consummates this vision; *ethics is an optics.*

(Lévinas 1991: 23; emphasis added)

Without the idea of transcendence as exempt from the harsh – and inherently immoral – ways of the world, where all beings egotistically struggle for self-preservation, the questions of Job, putting into doubt the ontological arrangement of the order of being, could never be asked (which, as already indicated, is the point of Heidegger's intervention: to stop the very possibility of such questions and accept being as it is, that is, as simply 'given'). This, obviously, implies the problematic issue of defining transcendence as 'otherwise than being' and, in this manner, not responsible for the wrongs of the created order. Indeed, Lévinas' theology is without God the Creator – perhaps even without creation at all. God's true divinity manifests not in his creationism, but in offering a true *beyond* as the ethical counter-principle, but also an ideal for the world to emulate: the possibility of the ethical judgement over the totality of creation. Lévinas' thought forms thus an alternative line of ethical Judaism – where it is not *bore olam*, the Creator of the World, which forms the essence of the transcendence, but the divine justice. Following Job, the paradigmatic subject of the Axial Age (reflexive, critical, bestowed with inwardness), humans emulate God precisely in his ethical opposition to the world *as it is*: as Lévinas states, 'man is an irruption of God within being' and 'the place through which transcendence passes' (Lévinas 1981: 142; 145). This ethical irruption, going against the grain of all other beings simply following their *conatus*, is the only sign of transcendence within the immanent: a radical moral intuition according to which 'it is not righteous to be' (Lévinas 2001). While to be means to bend to the rules of self-preservation, transcendence – 'otherwise than being', as Lévinas translates the Platonic *epekeina tes ousias* – does not have to bend or compromise and because of that can serve as the absolute ethical ideal of justice.

Such extremely pronounced ethical priority in conceiving the relation between transcendence and immanence seems to be a highly specific feature of the 'Joban' form of Judaism, deeply concerned about individual suffering in the essentially unjust world. It does not have clear equivalents in Christianity, Greek Neoplatonism or Islam: from the point of view of the Muslim theologians, Lévinas' anti-creationist image of the purely ethical Absolute could be even regarded as blasphemous. But it bears a resemblance to the radical ethics of Buddhism, which also focuses on the suffering creature in the midst of the phenomenal reality, shaped by the antagonistic rule of *samsara* as the cruel 'wheel of fate'. In those radically ethical variants of the Axial

Model, the *beyond* serves as the respite from the hardships of a this-worldly reality which is too deeply ingrained into the order of being itself to be reformed by a purposeful becoming. This disbelief in any reparability-perfectibility of being is also shared by the Gnostic perspective, representing the most dualistic pole of the axial continuum: the true *beyond*, not to be confused with the minor deity or the Archon who created this world, the miserable *cellula creatoris*, offers the promise of redemption as the ultimate escape from the 'creaturely prison'.[13]

The Axial Model therefore allows us, in doing comparative metaphysics, to see a certain dynamic pattern operative in all systems of thought related to it, which could be imagined in mathematical terms as a tensor correlating the three crucial variables: *beyond*, *being* and *becoming*. As the term itself suggests, the *tensor* is all about the *tension*: a non-indifferent multilinear relation between the three factors, that may vary from maximal to minimal, but never disappears completely. The way we conceive and value the *beyond* impacts the way we conceive and value the order of *being*, which then immediately reflects on the way we conceive and value the process of *becoming*. In static models, based on the absolutized transcendence as the foundation of the 'eternal structures of being', time and becoming will be reduced to a minimal significance. In dynamic models, based on the contrary vision of the *beyond* as critical of and antithetical to the order of being, time and becoming will be increased in their value as the 'history of redemption' – either the possibility of repairing the world and lifting it to the transcendent ideal or the apocalyptic awaiting of the end of the world as unworthy of any 'spiritual investment'. The elements of both models, the static and the dynamic, can be detected in all axial traditions: Abrahamic, Indian and Chinese.

Notes

1. See Jaspers (1978), as well as Weber (1996).
2. See Assmann (2000: 290–2). 'Assmann's conclusion is that we are not dealing with an epochal threshold (*Epochenschwelle*), but with a cultural transformation, and that chronology is external to it' (Arnason, Eisenstadt, Wittrock 2005: 11).
3. This phrase derives from Taubes' *The Political Theology of Paul*: 'I can imagine as an apocalyptic: let it go down. I have no spiritual investment in the world as it is' (Taubes 2003: 103).
4. See the aphorism nr 108 of *Gay Science*: 'After Buddha was dead, they still showed his shadow in a cave for centuries – a tremendous, gruesome shadow. God is dead; but given the way people are, there may still for millennia be caves in which they show his shadow. – And we – we must still defeat his shadow as well!' (Nietzsche 2001: 109).
5. According to Taubes, revelation is revolution pure and simple because it marks a radical turn (*Wende*) in the history of mankind, and this revolutionary revelation

inaugurates the understanding of time in terms of Holy History (*Heilsgeschichte*) the aim of which is the development of human freedom. God, therefore, is most of all the 'God of Exodus', that is, a counter-principle to the natural world (*Gegenprinzip*) that helps mankind to get out from the bondage of nature and everything natural. He is the God of liberation, whose proper element is history: the time of initiation and new beginnings, which breaks with the pagan glorification of natural life and its timeless origin (Taubes 2009b: 88–90).

6. See the comment of Eric Nelson: 'Heidegger's fascination with Laozi and Zhuangzi occurs while he is assessing the dangers of decision, self-assertion, and the will (concepts that he employed in his early support of National Socialism) and, in his Daoist reflections on a defeated Germany in 'Evening Conversation: In a Prisoner of War Camp in Russia, between a Younger and an Older Man' (1945) published in *Country Path Conversations*, adopting a more radical language of letting (*lassen*) and releasement (*Gelassenheit*) in relation to the Zhuangzi (mediated through the translations of Martin Buber and Richard Wilhelm) in addition to German sources such as Meister Eckhart and Schelling'. (Nelson 2019: 520). In 'A Dialogue on Language between a Japanese and an Inquirer', written in 1957, Heidegger, disguised as the 'Inquirer', interrogates his Japanese visitor about 'east Asian' modes of metaphysical thinking which involve a concept of the path: 'I: I am amazed by your insight into the nature of the paths of thinking. J: We have rich experience in the matter; only it has not been reduced to the form of a conceptual methodology, which destroys every moving force of the thinking steps' (Heidegger 1971: 21). Earlier, the interlocutors exchange their thoughts on the nothingness from which everything emerges: 'I: That emptiness then is the same as nothingness, that essential being which we attempt to add in our thinking, as the other, to all that is present and absent. J: Surely. For this reason we in Japan understood at once your lecture "What is Metaphysics?" when it became available to us in 1930 through a translation which a Japanese student, then attending your lectures, had ventured. – We marvel to this day how the Europeans could lapse into interpreting as nihilistic the nothingness of which you speak in that lecture. To us, emptiness is the loftiest name for what you mean to say with the word "Being" …' (Heidegger 1971: 19).
7. On the pitfalls and limitations of translating Dao as the 'way' or 'path', see Xinzhong Yao in Part 1, Chapter 2. On the interplay of necessity and possibility in the Chinese philosophy in juxtaposition with Spinoza's concept of freedom, see Nicholas Bunnin in Part 1, Chapter 5.
8. On the issue of reality versus irreality of the mundane order in Hinduism and Buddhism, see Gavin Flood in Part 1, Chapter 8.
9. On the defence of the mundane reality as bestowed with non-illusory being in Byzantine Christianity and Japanese Buddhism, see Ana-Maria Pascal and Paulus Kaufmann in Part 1, Chapter 11; and Lucia Dolce in Part 2, Chapter 1.
10. On the apophatic approach to transcendence, see Ana-Maria Pascal and Diwakar Acharya in Part 1, Chapter 10.
11. 'So if we say now that philosophy ought to consider religion, then these two are likewise set in a relationship of distinction in which they stand in opposition to

one another. But on the contrary it must be said that the content of philosophy, its need and interest, is wholly in common with that of religion. The object of religion, like that of philosophy, is the eternal truth, God and nothing but God and the explication of God' (Hegel 1984: 152).

12. This rejection of time, however, especially in the context Christianity, cannot be accepted without some significant provisos: what complicates the absolutist perspective is the problem of the Incarnation as the crucial dynamic moment in the relation between transcendence and immanence, characteristic of the second-generation axial religions. On this topic, see again my Chapter 12 in Part 2.
13. All these terms derive from the teachings of Marcion, the second-century CE representative of Christian Gnosticism. In his study on Marcion, published in 1924, Adolf von Harnack described him as 'the only thinker in Christianity who took fully seriously the conviction that the Deity who redeems one from the world has absolutely nothing to do with cosmology and cosmic teleology' (von Harnack 1990: ix).

References

Arnason, Johann P., Shmuel N. Eisenstadt and Björn Wittrock, (eds.) (2005), *Axial Civilizations and World History*. Leiden and Boston, MA: Brill.

Assmann, Jan (2000), *Herrschaft und Heil: Politische Theologie in Altägypten, Israel und Europa*. München: Beck.

Bloom, Harold (1998), *Shakespeare: The Invention of the Human*. New York: Riverhead Books.

Cohen, Hermann (1995), *Religion of Reason: Out of the Sources of Judaism*, trans. Simon Kaplan. Atlanta, GA: Scholars Press.

Eisenstadt, Shmuel N. (1999), *Fundamentalism, Sectarianism and Revolution: The Jacobin Dimension of Modernity*. Cambridge: Cambridge University Press.

Eisenstadt, Shmuel N. (2003), *Comparative Civilizations and Multiple Modernities*. Leiden and Boston, MA: Brill.

Harnack, Adolf von (1990), *Marcion: The Gospel of the Alien God*, trans. John E. Steely and Lyle D. Bierma. Jamestown, NY: Labyrinth Press.

Hegel, G. W. F. (1984), *Lectures on the Philosophy of Religion (One-Volume Edition)*, trans. and ed. Peter Hodgson. Berkeley, CA: University of California Press.

Heidegger, Martin (1977), 'The Turning', in William Lovitt (trans.), *The Question Concerning Technology and Other Essays*. New York: Garland Publishing.

Izutsu, Toshihiko (1983), *Sufism and Taoism: A Comparative Study of Key Philosophical Concepts*. Berkeley, CA: University of California Press.

Jaspers, Karl (1978), *The Origin and Goal of History*. New Haven, CT: Yale University Press, 1953.

Lévinas, Emmanuel (1981), *Otherwise than Being or beyond Essence*, trans. Alphonso Lingis. The Hague: Martinus Nijhoff.

Lévinas, Emmanuel (1991), *Totality and Infinity: An Essay on Exteriority*, trans. Alphonso Lingis. Dordrecht: Kluver Academic Publishers.
Lévinas, Emmanuel, (2001), *Is It Righteous to Be?: Interviews with Emmanuel Lévinas*. Stanford, CA: Stanford University Press.
Nelson, Eric S. (2019), 'Introduction to the Special Theme: Heidegger, Politics, and Chinese Philosophy', *Frontiers of Philosophy in China* 14(nr 4/ 2019): 519–22.
Nietzsche, Friedrich (2001), *Gay Science*, trans. Josefine Nauckhoff. Cambridge: Cambridge University Press.
Schwartz, Benjamin I. (1975), 'The Age of Transcendence in Wisdom, Doubt and Uncertainty', *Daedalus* (Spring): 3–4.
Taubes, Jacob (1953/1954), 'The Realm of Paradox', *Review of Metaphysics* 7 (7): 482–92.
Taubes, Jacob (2003), *The Political Theology of Paul*, trans. Dana Holländer. Stanford, CA: Stanford University Press.
Taubes, Jacob (2009a), *From Cult to Culture: Fragments towards a Critique of Historical Reason*, trans. Aleida Assmann. Stanford, CA: Stanford University Press.
Taubes, Jacob (2009b), *Occidental Eschatology*, trans. David Ratmoko. Stanford, CA: Stanford University Press.
Weber, Max (1978), *Economy and Society: An Outline of Interpretive Sociology*. Berkeley, CA: University of California Press.
Weber, Max (2019), *Die Wirtschaftsethik der Weltreligionen: Hinduismus und Buddhismus*, in Max-Weber-Gesamtausgabe Band I/20. Tübingen: J. C. B. Mohr.
Zachhuber, Johannes (2022), 'Transcendence and Immanence', in Daniel Whistler (ed.), *The Edinburth Critical History of Nineteenth-Century Christian Theology*. Edinburgh: Edinburgh University Press.

3

Persons, selves and metaphysics

Ana-Maria Pascal and Gavin Flood

Inferring general metaphysical principles from the particular histories of philosophical inquiry is beset with difficulties because the kind of language entailed in any one tradition is not easily translatable into the categories of another without doing injustice to those primary categories.[1] Furthermore, the very enterprise of seeking common principles might be questionable in that it already presupposes what it seeks to establish: namely a commonality of metaphysical structures. And yet there is a prima facie case for a comparative metaphysics because of the parallelism of concerns in some areas, in particular, about the nature of the human person. While this is not always on the syllabus for Western philosophy courses in metaphysics,[2] all the metaphysical systems addressed in Part 1 offer some account of what it is to be a human being although they might have widely diverse answers to that question. Moreover, the pre-modern metaphysical systems discussed in this book make claims about the nature of the person in relation to others, in relation to a wider cosmos and in relation to a putative transcendence. Our task here is to illustrate differences and common features among some traditions, with a view to demonstrating how diverse historical systems address this question of the relation of human person to society, cosmos and transcendence. Our argument is that we can identify types of claim about metaphysical ground or foundation, that this corresponds to particular conceptions of person and that the pre-modern metaphysical systems we have examined all present a view of person as integrated within a wider cosmos, in spite of such diverse metaphysical claims about foundation. Indeed, in all pre-modern metaphysical systems human persons need to be understood in the context of a wider cosmos and such an understanding has consequences for the ways in which people conduct their lives.

Let us begin with a reflection by Thomas Merton. Merton observes in a note: 'I consider that the spiritual life is the life of man's real self'.[3] This seems to be a common belief in many traditions considered in this book; this chapter looks particularly at

Christian, Buddhist and Hindu perspectives in exploring the nuances of that common ground and reflecting on what they might tell us about the topic.

A good starting point in any exploration of what it is to be human in the Christian tradition is Andrew Louth's remarkable insight about Bishop Kallistos's teachings on the *Philokalia*[4] – namely that, when he explores the Patristic terminology in order to help us deepen our understanding of the human nature, the Bishop uses the same sources he would when explaining the spiritual journey (through the hesychastic prayer of the heart) to deification. Louth reflects on the association, concluding that:

> This is, maybe, not very surprising, as what it is to be human – how we are constituted – is bound up with the purpose for which we were created, which is union with God, deification, which is effected through prayer, most fundamentally.[5]

This deification – the possibility of becoming united with God – is seen as due to an already existing link between the human self and divinity. This notion is present in all three traditions (Christian, Hindu and Buddhist), albeit in very different forms – ranging from the idea of Christ's presence in each of us (expressed in the notion of a *person*), to the notion that the individual self is, at the core, the same as the universal consciousness, in some Hindu and Buddhist worldviews.

Key concepts

We are immediately faced with a terminological problem regarding the categories 'human being', 'person' and 'self'. While not perfect synonyms, their meaning overlaps considerably, to the extent that they are often used interchangeably, without much explanation. The category of the person, for instance, has a long history across disciplines (including theology) and there have been attempts to secure a comparative history in both the social sciences and philosophy.[6] Whether the 'individual' is an invention of the West as Mauss thought or whether such a notion is shared across civilizations is a complex question. It could be that while all metaphysical systems have a concept of the person, individualism as a cultural value could be the product of a modernity that assumes the negation of much of the traditional metaphysics described in Part 1.

We cannot adequately address this question here, but wish to account for different kinds of discourse about the categories 'human', 'person' and 'self' in the systems we have looked at. There are two concerns fundamental to the concept in the traditional metaphysical systems we have described: the relation of the category of person to a metaphysical ground (whether in ontological or theological terms), and secondly its relation to cosmology. These ontological and cosmological concerns are related, although sometimes they appear to be in tension. The idea of metaphysical foundation also covers the claim in Buddhism of non-foundation, a meontology.

Other nuances, such as the link with an onto-theological notion of truth (*aletheia*) in Christianity, and that of the non-self as an ethical category, in Hinduism, will be briefly mentioned, without detailed discussion.

The search for metaphysical foundation

The search for foundation has been a concern of metaphysics in ancient Greece, India and China. There are three conceptions of metaphysical foundation: the first claims that such a foundation is identical with the self – this is the Brahmanical tradition of the Upaniṣads; the second – Buddhist – view is that there is in fact no foundation, that the person and phenomenal world are without substance; and the third is theism, which posits the metaphysical foundation as a transcendent theistic reality. This generally takes two forms, the Indian or 'Hindu' version of theism and a theism that comes to dominance in the Abrahamic religions of Judaism, Christianity and Islam, although there are significant metaphysical differences among them.

   a   The self as metaphysical foundation. Early Indian thinking as represented by the Upaniṣads identified the metaphysical foundation of the world with the self (*ātman*), as the basis of the human person, deeper than the empirical sense of self or ego (*ahaṃkāra*) and deeper than the mind (*manas*) and intellect (*buddhi*). The human person is in essence this unchanging foundational reality that supports the empirical person or is the necessary condition for it. This foundation of the individual person is identified with a universal foundation of reality itself, *brahman*, absolute reality as foundation of the world. The identification of self with absolute reality is a characteristic of Brahmanical thinking in this early period (from around 800 BCE into the early centuries CE) and is the basis for non-dualist philosophy of Advaita Vedānta as advocated by Śaṅkara (see Part 1, Chapter 8). But we must not forget the important strand of Brahmanical thinking that rejected such foundational conceptions, namely the Mīmāṃsā that understood the human person in transactional rather than substantive or in essentialist terms. Also, the Nyāya-Vaiśeṣika system of philosophy considered the self to be ontologically distinct, although in the liberated state, not conscious, having become stone-like. This realist and particularist system, that we do not have space to explore here, presented arguments against both Advaita Vedānta and Buddhism.

   b   Buddhism rejected such foundationalist thinking. Early Buddhist philosophy recognizes that reality has three characteristics: suffering, impermanence and no-self (*anātman*/*anatta*). The person has no underlying metaphysical support but can be analysed as a process of flux driven by causes and conditions. This way of thinking developed into the early centuries CE with the Mahāyāna and the emphasis on emptiness (*śūnyatā*), particularly in the Perfection of

Wisdom texts (Prajñāparamita sūtras) and in the Madhyamika school or śāstra, especially of Nāgārjuna. Not only is the selfempty of essence or own-being (*svabhāva*) but the world itself is empty and true cognition of this emptiness is a liberating cognition. Although the Buddhist picture is complicated by the emphasis on mind-only in the Yogācāra tradition, arguably emptiness, as Murti argued,[7] is the central philosophy that moves into China as Ch'an and so to Japan as Zen. This is a non-foundational metaphysics in which person is an ephemeral dream.

c Rejecting the non-dual foundationalism of the earlier Upaniṣadic tradition and rejecting the rejection of foundation in Buddhism, theism began to emerge in India. Early texts bear witness to this such as the *Bhagavad-gītā* and, inspired by that book, the *Śvetāśvatara-upaniṣad*. This trajectory posited a transcendent, theistic source of the world and the support of the self. In this view, God is the Supreme Person (*puruṣottama*) who creates, maintains and destroys the cosmos over and over. Here the metaphysical foundation of the world is a transcendent God upon whose being persons and world depend. The major traditions of what became known as Hinduism promote and develop this kind of view. The tradition focussed on Viṣṇu or Kṛṣṇa is a theism that presents God as the source and destination of the world. Likewise, the tradition focussed on Śiva presents a similar idea, adding to the list of God's functions that he conceals and reveals himself too as an act of grace. There is a non-dual version of this (called 'Kashmir' Śaivism although the tradition extended beyond Kashmir) that presents a non-theistic view of absolute consciousness. The Goddess tradition of the Krama is within this trajectory (see Part 1, Chapter 9).

d The Abrahamic religions are uncompromisingly theistic, which means that the transcendence of God is emphasized, and metaphysical speculation comes to be focussed on the nature of this transcendent reality. Avicenna, for example, regarded the intellectual object of metaphysics to be God as known through his effects. In contradistinction to Judaism and Islam, Christianity develops a conception of God as three persons (*hypostases*) in a single substance, or essence (*ousia*) along with the theology of the incarnation of the Second Person of this Trinity. While Islamic and Judaic theologians have argued that the oneness of God is compromised by this trinitarian doctrine, Christian theologians have for the most part maintained it down the ages (see Part 1, Chapter 11). One of the features that mark out Abrahamic metaphysical theism is that God creates *ex nihilo* in contrast to the Hindu God who acts upon pre-existent matter. Furthermore, for Abrahamic metaphysics creation has a purpose, a telos (although what that purpose is lies beyond human comprehension), in contrast to the Hindu theism in which the universe itself has no purpose other than being the expression of God's play (*līlā*) or the expression of God's freedom (*svatantra*) and nature (*bhāva*) for the purpose of enabling souls to be liberated.

Yet cutting across these diverse metaphysical positions, there is a common idea – arguably common to all pre-modern civilizations – that the human person must be understood in terms of a cosmos. Human beings are embedded within a cosmos, we are the consequence of cosmos, and in some worldviews, we are trapped by a cosmos. Whether the system's metaphysics is conceptualized as a plenum/essence (as with the early Upaniṣads and Advaita), whether it is conceptualized as a vacuum devoid of essence/emptiness (as in Madhyamaka Buddhism), or whether metaphysics is conceptualized as a transcendent source beyond the cosmos (as in Hindu and Abrahamic theism), all systems have a conception of how person relates to the wider cosmos. Even if this is understood as a lower level of truth, all pre-modern metaphysical systems have been cosmological, understanding the human person in relation to the wider cosmos.

The role of the human in the hierarchy of the cosmos

A common feature of pre-modern understandings of the cosmos that we find in all pre-modern civilizations is that they present a view of the cosmos as a hierarchical structure within which living beings are located. In this structure, the material world is the most solidified whereas 'above' this are more subtle worlds where beings live without material bodies (although possessing more subtle embodiment). Furthermore, this structure has soteriological consequences for human persons, for the journey to redemption is often conceptualized as a journey through this hierarchical cosmos.[8] In medieval Christianity, we have the hierarchy of the cosmos with God at the top and ranks of angels below, with human beings below that. We see such a structure portrayed on the facades of medieval abbeys and cathedrals and described in both popular and theological writings from the anonymous fourteenth century *The Monk of Eynsham* to Dante's *Purgatorio*. Although this view comes to be attenuated with the Reformation and the rise of science, especially in the sixteenth century with the retreat of religion from cosmology, it never completely dissipates and the idea of life as a journey or pilgrimage to redemption is still present in texts such as Bunyan's *Pilgrim's Progress*. Let us take two examples to illustrate the notion and the place of the human within it.

Theologians of the early church, inspired by Greek philosophy, presented a general cosmological framework that – while sometimes rejected – was very influential, especially on the history of mysticism and monasticism. One interesting figure was Evagrius Ponticus (c. 345–99) who articulated an ascetic theology inspired by one of the first theologians, Origen (184–254). Although his theology was condemned at the Fifth General Council of Constantinople in 553 for espousing the views of Origen, his work was influential on later thinking, especially on John Cassian

(c. 360–430), the link between eastern and western monasticism and even on the important Orthodox theologian Maximus the Confessor (c. 580–662). Evagrius sets out his vision in a letter to an interesting ascetic in Jerusalem, Melanie the Ancient and in his *Kephalaia Gnostica*, in which he presents a complete picture of creation and human restoration.

He agrees with Origen about the pre-existence of souls and the twofold nature of creation. God created beings with reason, the *logikoi*, but they turned away from God which necessitated a second creation of matter to house them. In this theology, a soul is an intellect that, because of sin, has descended into matter, the second creation. Our bodies for Evagrius contain a kind of memory of our situation as *logikoi* for Christ has traced this wisdom onto us, as children trace letters on their tablets.[9] There is a hierarchy of beings mapped onto the hierarchy of the cosmos, thus following Origen, angels have bodies of fire while demons are cold. With angels there is a predominance of fire and intellect (*nous*), with humans a predominance of earth and concupiscence (*epthumia*) and with demons a predominance of air and anger (*thumos*).[10] There is a hierarchy of beings arranged along the hierarchy of the cosmos. The general idea developed by later thinkers is that the soul needs to ascend the hierarchy of the cosmos back towards God in a process of becoming God-like, a process called *theosis*. This model of ascent comes to be common not only in the East[11] but in Western Christianity and Sufism[12] too, and the ladder of divine ascent comes to be a standard metaphor in mystical theology. The journey back to God, to redemption enabled by Christ, is a journey through the hierarchical cosmos from this earthly realm to higher spiritual realms. There are many examples of this from Hugh of St Victor's *The Mystic Ark* (*De arca Noe mystica*) to Bonaventure's idea of the mind's journey into God in which the mind rises higher into the being of God.[13]

In this model of divine ascent, the human person is understood as being located within the hierarchy and as being privileged in having the capacity to ascend through the cosmos back to the creator. The same basic idea is found in the Indian material, both Hindu and Buddhist. In the medieval religion of Śiva called the Śaiva Siddhānta that had a large canon of revealed scriptures and commentary, the cosmos – as for its European contemporaries – was a hierarchical structure divided into the pure creation (*śuddha-sarga*) and the impure creation (*aśuddha-sarga*). The pure creation is created directly by Śiva; within it beings dwell who are without impurity (*mala*). From within these deities Śiva appoints a regent, Ananta, who then creates the lower order of the impure creation. This is to enable souls who have not yet been liberated to be reborn and so to work out the consequences of their action in previous lives and to gain eventual redemption through being initiated in the religion and following a regime of daily rites.[14] While this hierarchical structure operated in exoteric religion, the idea is also present in the esoteric Goddess religion. Within the Krama sect, the ineffable reality of consciousness, the nameless Goddess, comes to appearance as the sky of consciousness (*cidgagana*) and the practitioner becomes open to this sky realizing his identity with it as a liberating cognition (see Part 1, Chapter 9). This notion of a hierarchical cosmos goes back a long way in India: the Vedic cosmology of sky, atmosphere and earth populated by different deities; and in early Buddhism, levels of the cosmos are identified with levels of meditational attainment. As is the state of consciousness (*citta*) so is the world of experience (*loka*).[15]

Examples of this fundamental idea could be multiplied. But the point is that there is a shared principle in the Buddhist and Hindu texts and also in medieval Abrahamic religious texts, that an account of the human person is bound up with the structure of the cosmos in a hierarchy of layers and that the world a being encounters is partly determined by the quality of consciousness. For Evagrius, angels perceive worlds of light because of the quality of their awareness while demons perceive darkness and anger; in Brahmanical cosmology, deities in higher worlds have bodies of subtle sound whereas beings with animal or human material bodies are restricted in the kinds of interaction they can experience. This model holds true to some extent in East Asia, although there the reception of the Indian cosmological material underwent change and the meditational hierarchy of early Buddhism with its levels of absorption or *dhyāna/ jhāna* is somewhat forgotten in favour of a view of enlightenment as an immediate experience in the here and now, as we find with Chan and Zen Buddhism. But nevertheless, mediation remains an important idea even within Zen, with great reverence for relics, holy places and pilgrimage forming an important part of the cultural landscape.[16]

Commonalities and divergences

So far, we have suggested that diverse metaphysical systems share certain features in common and a general typology might be created concerning the relationship of person to metaphysical foundation. We have suggested that the views represented in Part 1 fall into a threefold typology: a non-dualist metaphysical foundation, a rejection of metaphysical foundation and a theistic metaphysical foundation. Furthermore, in spite of these profound conceptual divisions, there is a common cosmological theme that the human person finds her or his place within a wider cosmos as participative within a wider structure. The specific details of these cosmologies are diverse, and yet human persons seem to be located within a cosmology, always hierarchical, with the material world being the most solidified layer of a structured, subtle hierarchy. In this section, we look more deeply at the divergencies and commonalities in order to present a more textured or nuanced picture for a comparative metaphysics. To do this we will discuss two categories of the *self* and the *person*.

The concept of the self

One of the important nuances in the metaphysical systems we have looked at in Part 1 concerns the metaphysics of the *self*: between the Christian self as rooted in divinity (that, which is deeper in you, than yourself) and the notion of no-self in Buddhism and some Hindu philosophies.[17] This fundamental divergence is worth exploring because it brings out the difficulties of locating common foundations across civilizations and sharpens the concepts of the self and person that are being used in these traditions. In so doing, we focus our comparison on two sources, Buddhaghosa's *Path of Purification* (*Vissudhimagga*) and Augustine's conception of self. These are quite close to each other in terms of time frame and their texts are fine exemplars of the traditions out from which they emerge, namely Theravāda Buddhism and Latin Christianity.

Buddhaghosa, in the fifth century CE, went to Sri Lanka and composed his magnum opus as a summary of the Buddha's teaching and a commentary upon two verses of the Pāli canon. The book clearly accedes to the Buddhist doctrine of no-self and yet is focussed on the development of the solitary practitioner along the Buddha's path to enlightenment (*bodha*) or cessation (*nibbāna*). The book follows the division of the Buddha's path into the cultivation of virtue (*sīla*), concentration (*samādhi*) and wisdom (*paññā*). Wisdom is the culmination of the path and is arrived at through the meditation practice of insight (*vipassanā*) into the three characteristics of existence, namely that all life is suffering (*dukkha*), impermanence (*anicca*) and no-self (*anatta*). The whole systematic edifice constructed by Buddhaghosa, the carefully charted map for the practitioner to follow, ends in the realization of non-substantiality. This is a pure doctrine of no-self and a metaphysics that argues against any foundation to self or world.

But what is meant by 'self' here? Buddhaghosa is not presenting an idealism in which the material world is nothing but mind or mental stuff (as in later Yogācāra). Indeed, he is presenting a realism in which he does not deny the reality of the world but claims that it is constantly changing and contains nothing that is unchanging, there is no essence to the world. When we apply that insight to ourselves, we realize that we have no essence either and that the person is simply an amalgam of constantly changing constituents, held together in a causal process. These constituents are body or form (*rūpa*), feeling (*vedanā*), sense-perception (*saṃjñā*), impulses or latent tendencies (*saṃskāra*) and consciousness (*vijñāna*). All of these are impermanent and constantly changing. We have a body that enables us to interact with a world that grows old and is subject to decay. We have feeling, which in a Buddhist context means three possible reactions to the world: attraction, turning away or indifference, themselves constantly changing. Feeling responds to our encounter with world through the senses, through sense perception that comprises six senses for Buddhism, the five plus the mind. Impulses or latent tendencies could be from previous lives that impel current experience, and consciousness is the result of the causal chain evoked by the process of engaging with the world. All of these are impermanent, even consciousness. Indeed, consciousness is the most impermanent of them all, being subject to constant change every thought moment (*cittakhanna*). The process of enlightenment is the gradual deconstruction of the causes and conditions that keep the process of the constituents carrying on through time. Once the constituents have dissolved and no further latent tendencies are produced, enlightenment is achieved, and the practitioner will not face further rebirths (even though no self is reborn, but it is simply that a process carries on).

Buddhaghosa is in line with early Buddhist thinking in rejecting the idea of a permanent self. This is probably a generally Upaniṣadic idea of the self (*ātman/atta*). The self is not the person but a notional underlying substratum or basis that is the true subject of experience in early Brahmanic thinking. The Buddha and his faithful follower reject this notion completely. But they do not deny the reality of the empirical person and world. The world is real, and we are real as beings within it, but it is simply that we are made up of more basic constituents that are thrown together through a process of causation. All actions performed lay seeds or latent tendencies in the deep memory that will come to fruition in a future birth, even though there is no constant substance in which those memories or tendencies are held. This was one of the main bones of contention with Hindu thinkers. Abhinavagupta, for example, argues against the Buddhists that there must be a basis, a foundation or receptacle which holds memories and past experiences, and this holder of past experiences is what is called the self (*ātman*). There is potentially a problem here regarding morality. If the future person down the line of the causal chain that I currently identify as an 'I' is not real, then why should I be concerned about that person in the future? Buddhaghosa can only respond to this through the idea of compassion, that we should be compassionate to all living beings, as the Buddha was, and so compassion for the person that we will become is motivation enough to follow the Buddha's path and seek the cessation of future becoming.[18] Later Mahāyāna Buddhism was to emphasize this. The Perfection of Wisdom texts present the message that all is empty: in his wisdom the Bodhisattva, the one on the way to enlightenment, knows that there are no beings to save, but in his compassion, he vows to save all beings. Buddhaghosa has not yet articulated this paradox, but it is arguably incipient in this Theravādin work.

Were Augustine able to speak with Buddhaghosa, they would have fundamentally diverged on the metaphysics of the self. Augustine uses the term 'soul' or *animus* to indicate the essence of the person that survives death and that is the bearer of moral qualities. The soul can become good through an act of will and can only become good by turning to something outside of itself, which is different from it. This is God that becomes the object of desire and love, and which is an unchanging good.[19] This is quite distinct from Buddhaghosa whose journey to enlightenment is devoid of such an external power. In Augustine's view, the soul must turn towards the good, which is

God, and cling to the good through love. God is the supreme good and other goods – such as good food conducive to health, the just person and even the stars, the moon and the sun – are lesser goods and only gain goodness because of their proximity to and participation in the supreme good that is God.[20] The soul can cling to the good, to God, and so realize its true nature as being wholly reliant on the good. The soul can adhere to the good 'to which it is indebted for being a soul' (*a quo habet ut animus sit*).[21]

There is meaning in creation and moral quality is intertwined with the nature of the soul. To be good is for the soul to participate in the good and to move towards God. Such movement is not only love but knowledge too; for we can only love what we know at least partly, and we partly know God because he has left an image within the human, within the soul, the *imago dei*. This image of God is in fact an image of the trinity which is reflected in human cognition and action, specifically in our memory, sight and love or, in another formulation, in our memory, understanding and love.[22] This idea of the *imago dei* lies at the heart of Augustine's understanding of the soul and how we can journey to God. Indeed, this image is in the inner man (*homo interior*) and because of it, we can have some knowledge of God and so love God who is, moreover, the inner master (*magistrum interiorem*) that we can access through memory (*memoria*) that embraces the idea of God as well as moral values and reason.[23] The image of God within us allows us to contemplate the vision of God, which is also to become 'like him'.[24] This is an important idea often neglected in Christian Western metaphysics:[25] the trinity within us allows us to participate in the divine trinity that exceeds us and is beyond us.

For Augustine, the work of redemption of fallen selves is the realization of the *imago dei* within us through will and through grace. The soul has to be prepared for its ascent to God. In fallen humanity, the image of God has become distorted but is the necessary condition for our future perfection and participation in the divine. Our fallen humanity is incomplete and in our very being we lack something, such that we both participate in being and yet are also non-being: the person 'is and is not' (*est non est*).[26] Augustine is inspired here by Neo-Platonism, but his vision is not Neo-Platonic because of his Christian view of creation as good and the necessity of a political vision of the human community, ordered towards the good. For Augustine there is no Demiurge who created the world from which we must escape. Through the correct ordering of desire, because of the *imago dei* within us, we can move towards an eschatological future in which there is a correct political ordering of human affairs in accordance with divine will. It is not simply that the soul achieves salvation through becoming god-like; rather, the human community moves towards a condition of eschatological hope and anticipation of the city of God established finally on earth. The *imago dei* allows us to recognize our god-like quality and is the necessary condition for establishing a harmonious world. The world is good because created by the good, and creation itself contains the imprint of God upon it, the *vestigia dei*, that allows us to recognize nature as good, a good that is so because of its participation in the supreme good, which is God. Augustine thus has both an individualistic view of salvation in the sense that each soul bears within it the *imago dei* through which to participate in the divine being, and also a strong collective, political vision of redemption in which the human community is well-ordered in accordance with divine command and ordered through grace rather than through sin.

Augustine's and Buddhaghosa's visions of metaphysics and of what it is to be a person are quite distinct. For Buddhaghosa, there is no metaphysical foundation: through analysis we understand how the person functions and what is to be done to achieve freedom from suffering and rebirth. For Augustine, there is a metaphysical foundation, which is the trinitarian God, and the person is incomplete because of sin but moves towards perfection because of the *imago dei* within. But while they do not have a common metaphysics, they do share the view that human life is a journey to perfection and that this life is set within a wider cosmos. Indeed, the journey to perfection is imaged as ascent up through levels of meditation, for Buddhaghosa, and through elevation to the trinity, for Augustine. The vertical axis of cosmological structure is shared. For both, the moral life matters – although its role is very different. For Augustine it orientates our lives towards leading a good life, participating in the good; for Buddhaghosa it orientates our lives to skilful thought and action, driven by compassion, such that we develop skilful states of mind (*kusala-citta*) conducive to eventual enlightenment.

The notion of no-self can also have ethical connotations in some Hindu philosophies, for example, when Swami Vivekananada talks about selflessness, or self-sacrifice. 'In his interpretation, the Gita's 'selflessness', which there connoted 'non-self', a contemplative condition devoid of identity, becomes an active ethical aspiration' (Mangala Frost 2017: 189–90). This creates a common space for Christian and Indian spirituality, where the focus is not on whether the self exists (whether as absolute atman, individual consciousness or not at all); rather, it is an exercise in humility and virtue, which can lead to both ethical and soteriological gain. Indeed, the Christian ideal of deification presupposes a stage of transformation (metanoia, return to God) which could be interpreted as selflessness, in the sense of a deep transformation of the self through the grace of God.

The concept of the person

The core of the Christian self is its likeness to God. This gives it the unique character of a person (rather than a mere individual), as personhood also characterizes God himself. This notion stands at the core of trinitarian theology, which stipulates that God is one entity in three hypostases (or Persons): the Father, the Son and the Holy Spirit.

For Fr Dumitru Stăniloae (one of the better known Orthodox theologians of our time), there is a difference between the *person* of Jesus (which is one and the same) and its two *natures* (human and divine). The person is present in the divine Word – the Logos, which has always been divine and has also acquired human nature, becoming an individual self (through incarnation). Human nature dwells not in itself but in Logos; together, they form one of the hypostases of the holy trinity.[27] So the person (or the self, in this deeper understanding) is different from mere human nature; grounded in a deeper reality, it is a 'divine shard'. Fr Stăniloae emphasizes the relational nature of the human person: for supreme being itself is interpersonal.[28]

Zizioulas explains the uniqueness of personhood (indeed, what distinguishes it from individuality) by the fact that it brings two apparently contradictory aspects together – particularity and communion. A person can only be imagined in the context of their relationships; indeed, a person shows their particularity through community; this makes it 'the horizon within which the truth of existence is revealed' (Zizioulas 1985: 105–6).

The philosophical counterpart of this view is what is sometimes referred to as personalist phenomenology, represented by Emmanuel Mounier, Husserl's disciples Edith Stein, Roman Ingarden and Karol Wojtyła, as well as contemporary philosophers like Emmanuel Housset and Robert Sokolowski.[29] A key element in all these philosophies, which are relevant for the link with the Christian framework, is the relational aspect of personhood. The sense of purpose (or even destiny) is also important: in Christianity – as well as for many personalists – a person fulfils her destiny when she becomes who she really is (that 'deeper in us than ourselves'). And there is also a link to the notion of truth understood in Heideggerian terms (as *aletheia*). Zizioulas puts it explicitly – the roots of the iconological language of the Fathers is not in Platonism (with its focus on truth as a connection of the soul to the pre-existing world of ideas); rather, the Patristic tradition 'presents truth not as a product of the mind, but as a "visit" and a "dwelling" (cf. Jn. 1:14) of an eschatological reality entering history to open it up in a communion-event' (p. 100). This link between icon, truth and person goes to the core of Patristic theology (where beauty and the good are intricately connected).

The commonality with Indian metaphysics lies in the non-dualistic view of the self and the world – where the true nature of the former is pure light and reflexive consciousness (of a non-dual nature), undifferentiated into subject v. object (Flood 2013: 143sq). This core (the light of consciousness) is different from the empirical self, which is subject to change and time. In Christian language, this would be expressed as the divine energy within us.

The analogy doesn't end there. Uptaladeva and Abhinavagupta (Indian mystics from the tenth and eleventh centuries), unlike other Indian philosophers, believed in the actual personal aspect of the human self, and that it is deep in this inwardness that one discovers the light of consciousness; indeed, at its core, it is one and the same. What Metropolitan Kallistos calls 'the *total person*' consisting of soul and body intertwined (and referring back to the mystery of Jesus's dual nature, complete in Godhead and in humanity), Abhinavagupta calls 'the human world' – a self-experience that makes the experience of pure consciousness possible. 'Thus the functioning of the human world –which stems precisely from the unification of cognitions … would be destroyed if there were no Mahesvara who contains within himself all the infinite forms, who is one, whose essence is consciousness, possessing the powers of knowledge, memory and exclusion' (Uptaladeva, cit. by Flood 2013: 145).

The difference lies in the language used, and the nuances it carries. Where the Indian mystics use the language of ultimate reality, consciousness and its object, Christian theologians revert to concepts anchored in their trinitarian framework. Bishop Kallistos addresses the topic of the Christian self in terms of the 'continuing mystery of our human personhood',[30] emphasizing the role of practice in Christian life and suggesting that it is through some form of discipline that we can better know ourselves and the divine spark within us. We have seen this illustrated in Gregory Palamas and the hesychast tradition (see Part 1, Chapter 11). Kallistos also talks about the Jesus prayer as an ascetic practice that, alongside fasting and prostrations, can lead to self-knowledge. And he emphasizes the role of *the heart* in Christian ascetic discipline; this, he explains, denotes much more than a physical organ: 'It is to use the Hindu term, a chakra, a centre of spiritual energy … regarded as the directing centre of the total human person'. One should, of course, be careful about using the term 'chakra' in the context of the Christian 'heart' because the Sanskrit term entails a bodily system that the Christian view does not and the heart functions in a different way, in the Christian worldview. But the fact that both traditions have ascetic disciplines centred around the core of the human person remains significant.

Conclusions

In making general claims about metaphysical systems we need on the one hand to avoid reducing them to a level of abstraction where difference is eroded: they clearly do not make the same claims. Yet, on the other hand, we need to avoid a problematic relativism according to which diverse metaphysical systems make such incompatible claims that they are in effect closed worlds. We have argued that underlying these different metaphysical claims in relation to person and/or self is a shared understanding of person as contextualized within a wider cosmos. Metaphysical positions in three broad traditions (Abrahamic, Buddhist, Hindu) share concepts of person in connection with a broader cosmology. Our comparative reflection suggests there is a multi-layered ground of commonalities and differences, which sustain each other. The difference in nuances of personhood, between the Christian and the Hindu frameworks, for example, feeds into the deeper common platform about the essential link between the human self, cosmos and the divine: this relationship is a constant feature of metaphysics as presented here. What varies is the degree of association with other concepts invested with theological significance – such as beauty of a divine source (comprised in the notion of the icon) and the onto-theological meaning of truth.

Notes

1. There have been many attempts to do this with varying success. One of the most important and sophisticated has been Hick's 2004 (1989). But whether this successfully negotiates the issue is open to question: what Hick calls 'the real' as a catch-all for concepts from the Trinity to the Buddhist Dharma-kāya (272–75) loses the ability to discern the function of those terms within their own metaphysical systems. For a fine discussion, see Hedges (2013: 113–37).
2. Some anthologies list the topic of the self under 'Identity' and talk, for example, about 'personal identity' as in Derek Parfit, or human versus animal identity as in P. Snowdon (see Crane and Farkas (2004)); others (like Lowe (1998); Marmodoro and Mayr (2019)) don't mention it at all.
3. Merton (1955: ix).
4. Louth (2015: chapter 21) – 'Metropolitan Kallistos and the theological vision of the *Philokalia*' (332–48).
5. Louth, *Modern Orthodox Thinkers*, 345.
6. For example, Marcel Mauss' developmental idea of the person in 'Le concept du soi'. See the important collection of papers responding to Mauss: Michael Carrithers, Steven Lukes and Steven Collins, eds. (1985), *The Category of the Person*. Cambridge: Cambridge University Press.
7. Murti (1955).
8. This can be contrasted to Daoism and Chinese metaphysics more generally, where Dao (which remains untranslatable) is often referred to as the origin of all things, but doesn't have a beginning itself; in fact, it is more like a principle, which enables cosmic generations, while remaining in clear contrast to formed physical entities or phenomena. For a detailed account of the various understandings of Dao in Chinese metaphysics and culture, see Part 1, Chapter 2 of this volume.
9. Evagrius Kephalia Gnositica 1.57 in Guillaumont (1958: 121).
10. Guillaumont, *Les Six Centuries*, 1.68, 149.
11. The Orthodox East has followed the Patristic tradition in this, and many other respects, more closely than the Latin West. Eastern theologians often refer to Christian life and practice as a theology of *theosis* – a process of deification that entails purification of the soul and contemplation of the divine, aimed at unification with God. Important sources on this are Evagrius, *Gnostic Problems* (Berlin 1914); Theophanis the Monk, *The Ladder of Divine Graces*, in *Philokalia* vol 3; John Climacus, *The Ladder of Divine Ascent*; Dionysius the Areopagite, *The Mystical*

Theology etc. There are, however, scholars in the West who wrote extensively on desert spirituality – see, for instance, Thomas Merton's *Courses*, and his *Ascent to Truth*. The latter, for instance, explores the mystical journey both apophatically and cataphatically – in Merton's terms, a theology of light and a theology of darkness – represented by St Augustine, St Bernard, St Thomas Aquinas on the one hand, and St Gregory of Nyssa, Pseudo-Dionysius, St John of the Cross on the other (Merton 1958: 25).

12. In Islam, the Prophet Muhammad's ascent through the heavens is considered the prototype of the mystic's spiritual ascension, one that brings the believer, through prayer, into the immediate presence of God – where he is said to have had a vision of God (see Schimmel 2011: 27, 41).
13. Turner (1995: 102–17).
14. See Goodall (2004: chapter 5).
15. Collins (1998).
16. See Faure (1991).
17. See, for instance, Part II 'The doctrine of not-self' in Steven Collins, *Selfless Persons: Imagery and Thought in Theravada Buddhism*, CUP, 1982; Lama Yeshe Losal Rinpoche, *From a Mountain in Tibet: A Monk's Journey*, Penguin, 2020; Gavin Flood, 'Inwardness without Self' in *The Truth Within*, OUP, 2013; and Mangala Frost (2017: 189–90) about the notion of selflessness in Swami Vivekananda.
18. Heim (2015: 171–89).
19. Augustine (2002: 8).
20. Augustine, *On the Trinity*, 7–8.
21. Augustine, *De Trinitate*, 9.
22. Augustine, *De Trinitate*, 14.2, 140.
23. Hart, *L'image vulnerable*, 126.
24. Augustine, *De Trinitate*, 14.19, 164–5.
25. In the Eastern Orthodox tradition, there has always been interest in the notion of the human having been created in the image of God, and its implications – for ars sacra, as well as Christian practice (the role of the icons therein). St John Damascene is the one who not only defended the cult of the icons, but actually explained their theological significance (see his section on the attack on the heresy of iconoclasm in *The Fount of Knowledge*, 370–3). Thereafter, the whole of Orthodox Christianity embraced the view that 'the incarnation makes it not merely possible, but quite unavoidable, to understand truth in the manner of an icon', because 'ικων ways means something *real* and as true αληθεια' (John Zizioulas 1985: 99). Given this onto-theological significance of the sacred icon, it is unsurprising that Paul Evdokimov describes desert spirituality and the whole patristic tradition as a theology of beauty (2011).
26. Augustine, *Confessions* XII, 6.
27. Stăniloae (1993: 108sq) (my translation).
28. Stăniloae (1993: 22sq) (my translation).
29. See, for instance, Housset's 'La dramatique de la personne ou l'ipséité comme paradoxe' (*Les études philosophiques*, 2007, 215–33), and 'L'invention de la personne

par saint Augustin et la métaphysique contemporaine' in *Questio*, 6 (2006), 463–82; and Hans Urs von Balthasar, 'On the Concept of Person' in *Communio: International Catholic Review*, 13 (Spring): 18–26.

30. Ware (1999: 57–79).

References

Augustine (2002), *On the Trinity,* ed. Gareth B. Matthews, trans. Stephen McKenna. Cambridge: Cambridge University Press.

Carrithers, Michael, Steven Lukes and Steven Collins (eds.) (1985), *The Category of the Person.* Cambridge: Cambridge University Press.

Collins, Steven (1982), *Selfless Persons: Imagery and Thought in Theravada Buddhism.* Cambridge: Cambridge University Press.

Collins, Steven (1998), *Nirvana and Other Buddhist Felicities.* Cambridge: Cambridge University Press.

Crabbe, James, (ed.) (1999), *From Soul to Self.* London and New York: Routledge.

Crane, Tim, and Katalin Farkas (2004), *Metaphysics: A Guide and Anthology.* Oxford: Oxford University Press.

Damascus, St. John of (2012), *Writings: The Fount of Knowledge: The Philosophical Chapters, on Heresies, the Orthodox Faith,* trans. Frederic H. Chase, Jr. Washington, DC: Ex Fontibus.

Evdokimov, Paul (2011), *The Art of the Icon: A Theology of Beauty,* trans. Fr. Steven Bigham Pasadena. California: Oakwood Publications.

Faure, Bernard (1991), *The Rhetoric of Immediacy: A Cultural Critique of Chan/Zen.* Princeton, NJ: Princeton University Press.

Flood, Gavin (2013), *The Truth Within.* Oxford: Oxford University Press.

Frost, Christine Mangala (2017), *The Human Icon: A Comparative Study of Hindu and Orthodox Christian Beliefs* Cambridge: James Clarke, pp. 189–90.

Goodall, Dominic (2004), *The Parākhyatantra: A Scripture of the Saiva Siddhanta.* Pondichéry: Institut Français.

Guillaumont, Antoine (1958), *Les Six Centuries des 'Kephalia Gnostika' d'Evagre le Pontique.* Paris: Frimin Didot.

Hart, Kevin (2018), *L'image vulnerable: Sur l'image de Dieu chez saint Augustin.* Paris: PUF.

Hedges, Paul (2013), *Controversies in Interreligious Dialogue and the Theology of Religions.* London: Hymns Ancient and Modern.

Heim, Maria (2015), 'Buddhaghosa on the Phenomenology of Love and Compassion', in Jonardon Ganeri (ed.), *The Oxford Handbook of Indian Philosophy.* Oxford: Oxford University Press, pp. 171–89.

Hick, John (2004 (1989)), *An Interpretation of Religion: Human Responses to the Transcendent,* 2nd ed. New Haven, CT: Yale University Press.

Housset, E. (2006), 'L'invention the la personne par saint Augustin et la métaphysique contemporaine', *Questio* 6: 463–82.

Housset, E. (2007), 'La dramatique de la personne ou l'ipséité comme paradoxe', *Les études philosophiques* 81 (2): 215–33.

Louth, A. (2015), *Modern Orthodox Thinkers*. London: SPCK.

Lowe, E. J. (1998), *The Possibility of Metaphysics: Substance, Identity, and Time*. Oxford: Oxford University Press.

Mangala Frost, Christine (2017), *Human Icon: A Comparative Study of Hindu and Orthodox Christian Beliefs*. Cambridge: James Clarke.

Marmodoro, Anna, and Erasmus Mayr (2019), *Metaphysics: An Introduction to Contemporary Debates and Their History*. Oxford: Oxford University Press.

Merton, Thomas (1951), *The Ascent to Truth*. New York: Harcourt, Brace.

Merton, Thomas (1955), *No Man Is an Island*. Tunbridge Wells: Burns and Oats.

Merton, Thomas (2017), *A Course in Christian Mysticism*, ed. Jon Sweeney. Collegeville, MN: Liturgical Press.

Merton, Thomas (2019), *A Course in Desert Spirituality,* ed. Jon Sweeney. Collegeville, MN: Liturgical Press.

Murti, T. R. V. (1955), *The Central Philosophy of Buddhism*. London: George Allen and Unwin.

Rinpoche, Lama Yeshe Losal (2020), *From a Mountain in Tibet: A Monk's Journey*. London: Penguin.

Schimmel, Annemarie (2011), *Mystical Dimensions of Islam*. 35th anniversary ed., Chapel Hill, NC: University of North Carolina Press.

Stăniloae, D. (1993), *Iisus Hristos sau Restaurarea Omului*. Craiova: Omniscop.

Stăniloae, D. (1993), *Sfânta Treime sau La început a fost Iubirea*. Bucuresti: Editura Institutului Biblic.

Turner, Denys (1995), *The Darkness of God: Negativity in Christian Mysticism*. Cambridge: Cambridge University Press.

von Balthasar, Hans Urs (1986), 'On the Concept of Person', *Communio: International Catholic Review* 13 (Spring): 18–26.

Ware, Kallistos (1999), 'The Soul in Greek Christianity', in James Crabbe (ed.), *From Soul to Self.* London and New York: Routledge, pp. 57–79.

Zizioulas, John D. (1985), *Being as Communion: Studies in Personhood and the Church*. London: Darton, Longman and Todd.

4

Names, naming, unnamed, unnameable

Nicholas Bunnin and Sajjad Rizvi

This chapter reflects on naming, regarding both what is in the world and the transcendent. Nicholas Bunnin surveys the uses of naming in Part 1 and reflects on his own journey of exploration into names. Sajjad Rizvi explores various approaches to the questions posed by naming the transcendent, with particular reference to Islamic traditions of thought.

Nicholas Bunnin

Several chapters in Part 1 illustrate how comparing conceptions of naming is fundamentally important to comparing metaphysical attempts to make sense of things. Some chapters focus on comparing texts by different individual authors; others compare different traditions in which individual authors and their writings were embedded. Several chapters explore the metaphysical significance of contrasting what can and cannot be named, known and said.

Yao Xinzhong (Part 1, Chapter 2) pays close attention to the claims in the *Daodejing* that *Dao* cannot be named and its discussion of what to do if forced to give it a name. Jana Rošker (Part 1, Chapter 4) explores contrasting resolutions to logical paradoxes of time and motion offered by Hui Shi and Zeno of Elea. Both Hui Shi and Zeno employed logical insights to propound a range of paradoxes in their attempts to undermine terms, names or notions crucial to conventional understandings of the world. Both Zeno's and Hui Shi's use of logic predated formal systems of logic, such as that devised by Aristotle in Greece or the Buddhist logic imported into China from India.

Alexus McLeod (Part 1, Chapter 15) compares the human role of creating and maintaining the world of experience through naming Mayan gods in the *Popol Vuh* and using divine names in the works of IbnʿArabī. In my view, dealing with the constantly precarious world through human ritual agency in the *Popol Vuh* contrasts with Malebranche's occasionalism, where divine causal agency bears this burden. It also recalls the attempts of the later Platonists to bring divine agency to bear in the cosmos through theurgic ritual. For IbnʿArabī, imagination as a faculty that connects the human to the divine enables the use and understanding of divine names drawn from the experience of divine manifestations to perform the human role in completing the construction of the world.

My comparisons of Xunzi and Maimonides (Part 1, Chapter 5) and Spinoza and Wang Bi (Part 1, Chapter 7) attend to contrasting conceptions of names in a metaphysics of substance and of change. Those comparisons pose questions: if, for example, human languages are the locus of names, what powers, faculties or capacities must humans have in order to give names? Are names best understood as expressing sharply defined concepts distinguishing kinds of things according to their essences or as functioning in a world of shifting differences within inclusive balances of opposites? Are correct names purely descriptive or also evaluative? How are names in the discourse of ordinary people related to names understood by the metaphysically learned? Is '*Dao*' a name if *Dao* is not a thing? Is 'God' a name if humans cannot know the simple infinite essence of God?

Indeed, several chapters explore the place of names in what can and cannot be known and said about God according to apophatic traditions and negative theology. Ana-Maria Pascal and Diwakar Acharya (Part 1, Chapter 10) provide a typology of apophatic approaches ranging over the impossibility of naming or knowing God, the knowing and unknowing of God through divine manifestations, the suspension of judgement according to which God is neither effectively known nor entirely unknown, and the non-cognitive mystical personal relationship with God. They then turn to comparative examination of the possibility or impossibility of using divine names within the approaches distinguished.

Ana-Maria Pascal and Paulus Kaufmann (Part 1, Chapter 11) compare the mystical practices of the Japanese Buddhist monk Kūkai and the Byzantine Greek theologian Gregory Palamas as ways of proceeding beyond the negative theological consequences of intellectual approaches to the Absolute.

Agata Bielik-Robson (Part 1, Chapter 12) alludes to speculations that '"nothingness" is a secret name of the Infinite which is beyond being as we know it, and thus is a superesse, a hyper-being which can be known to us only as nothing'. This finds a parallel in various middle period Neoplatonic approaches that often seem to present the ultimate reality as both part of a singularity of being (identified by consciousness) and as beyond being. In the Sufi tradition, this is expressed by the notion of the Unseen or the infinite cloud that is beyond limitation or determination of names.

Gavin Flood (Part 1, Chapter 9) explores the interplay between the goddess Kālī, who is identified with the deepest selves of her worshippers, and the ineffable 'supreme secret which cannot be named, the system of the Goddess', an esoteric reality underlying the manifest world emanating from it. Flood also explores parallels between the intentionality of consciousness in this account and Heidegger's modern phenomenology of openness and clearing as a state of mind through which we can come to know ourselves.

These chapters in Part 1 thus provide intriguingly diverse examples of metaphysical reflections on names and naming and on what can and cannot be named. The texts explored were composed at different times, in different languages and in different cultures by individuals founding, reviving, conforming to, innovating within or rebelling against the traditions and circumstances in which they lived. Some contemporary readers will discover their own resonances with the metaphysical issues raised and the solutions explored in some or all the chapters. Other readers may challenge the priority given to metaphysics and pursue questions about names by giving priority to other philosophical domains, such as epistemology, logic, philosophy of mathematics, philosophy of language, philosophy of science, philosophy of history, ethics, philosophy of mind, political philosophy or poetics and rhetoric. But it is important to recognize that different philosophical domains have developed and continue to develop their own ranges of internally contestable methodologies that guide their followers to some insights and blind them to others.

The same is true within the complex diversity of the domain of metaphysics. My own fascination with metaphysical questions about names has been shaped through reflecting on works by writers distant from one another in time, language, tradition, and broader cultural context. The following five principal examples of works that have inspired me might help readers to assess my own insights and blind spots.

My first example is Plato's *Cratylus*, which is entirely devoted to issues concerning language. The dialogue begins with Socrates raising the possibility that names might be true or false like the propositions or statements of which they are parts. This question struck me as being comparable with the distinction between true and false names initiated by Confucius and developed by Xunzi. The dialogue ends with Plato having Socrates change focus by musing that ancient legislators might have given names that were true for a world of flux but false for a world of permanence, and that by using a proper method of dialectic, philosophers might replace these received names with names true in a Platonic world of permanence. The distinction between true and false names in the worlds of flux and of permanence strengthened my conviction that there was value in comparing the dialogue and the Chinese discussions of correct naming in terms of their metaphysical settings. A more extended account of my reading of *Cratylus* is available in my paper 'The Theory of Names in Plato's *Cratylus*' (2009).

My second example is Laozi's sparely compelling founding text of Daoism, the *Daodejing*, which can be translated as 'The Way and its Virtue'. I focus on ambiguities of crucial terms in its title and its Chapter 1, which sets out contrasting ways of taking '*Dao*' and the question of whether *Dao* can be named or is nameless. It also justifies taking '*de*' as virtue in ways capturing the creative power of *Dao*. The chapter distinguishes two ways in which we can engage with *Dao*, the deep and the deepest. In the two and a half millennia since the composition of *Daodejing*, interpretations have been proposed and contested without achieving a settled consensus over the meaning of text. For similar reasons, all translations have been open to controversy. I invite readers to begin sharing my perplexed fascination by reading two excellent contemporary English translations of Chapter 1. The first is taken from Gia-fu Feng and Jane English, *Lao Tsu, Tao De Ching* (1973):

> The Tao that can be told is not the eternal Tao.
> The name that can be named is not the eternal name.
> The nameless is the beginning of heaven and earth.
> The named is the mother of ten thousand things.
> Ever desireless, one can see the mystery.
> Ever desiring, one can see the manifestations.
> These two spring from the same source but differ in name;
> this appears as darkness.
> Darkness within darkness.
> The gate to all mystery.

The second is taken from Wang Keping, *Reading the Dao: A Thematic Introduction* (2011):

> The Dao that can be told is not the constant Dao.
> The Name that can be named is not the constant Name.
> The Being-without-form is the origin of Heaven and Earth;
> The Being-within-form is the mother of the myriad Things.
> Therefore it is always from the Being-without-form
> That the subtlety of the Dao can be contemplated;
> Similarly it is always from the Being-within-form
> That the manifestation of the Dao can be perceived.
> These two have the same source but different names,
> They both may be called deep and profound.
> The deepest and most profound Is the doorway to all subtleties.

My third example is Kant's Appendix to the Transcendental Analytic in his *Critique of Pure Reason*: 'The Amphiboly of Concepts of Reflection arising from the confusion of the empirical with the transcendental employment of understanding'. My engagement with Kant's account of amphiboly enriched my recognition in Part 1 Chapter 5, of the importance of Maimonides's use of amphibolous meaning which bears an ancestral relation to Kant's later discussion of amphibolous concepts of reflection. Kant's move from his account of concepts of reflection in the first *Critique* to his account of our power of reflective judgement in his third *Critique* is featured in my paper 'A Moral Metaphysics and a Metaphysics of Morals: Xunzi and Kant' (2022). I was also influenced by Kant's fourfold division of the 'concept of *nothing*' along with his view that a division of [the concept of] '*something*' directly followed from it. For Kant, the division of nothing and the division of something followed the division of four kinds of pure concepts of the understanding comprising the fundamental categories of his metaphysics (quantity, quality, relation and mode). Although alleged links between these categories and the division of nothing remain obscure, the division of Nothing itself is nonetheless impressive:

>   ***ens rationis*** is an empty concept without object (noumena, for example) to which no possible intuition corresponds but which is not therefore to be deemed impossible.
>   ***nihil privativum*** is an empty object of a concept (like darkness, cold or silence).
>   ***ens imaginarium*** is an empty intuition without a concept (like pure space and time which are forms of intuition but not themselves objects which are intuited).
>   ***nihil negativum*** is an empty object without concept (like a two-sided rectilinear object, which is impossible because its concept is self-contradictory).

This analysis by Kant contributed to my own worries about how alignment or non-alignment between concepts and objects might help to understand names and what they name and the distinction between what can and cannot be named. Kant clearly did not banish terms falling under the different kinds of nothing; indeed, space, time and the distinction between noumena and phenomena were crucial to his whole project. This encouraged me to attend to different conceptions of nothing in other metaphysical contexts, especially where an alleged reality and agency of nothing come into play. In our time, conceptions of nothing are vitally important to the ongoing string theoretical investigations of basic particles and to the metaphysical setting of quantum cosmology (see Li Chenyang's discussion of a Confucian framework for this in Part 1, Chapter 3).

My fourth example is Wittgenstein in *Tractatus Logico-Philosophicus* and *Philosophical Investigations*. Viewed narrowly, the first work can be taken as an internal dissenting response to the views of his co-founders of analytic philosophy, Frege and Russell. The second work was profoundly self-critical of his own earlier views. I have long been intrigued by the transition from 'logical form' in the *Tractatus* to a humanly general 'form of life' in the *Investigations*. Wittgenstein used the shared logical form of propositions, distinguished by their capacity to be true or false, and states of affairs, about which propositions can be true or false, to explain how propositions can be about states of affairs and how words or names within propositions can be about objects. He also held that 'the limits of my language mean the limits of my world' and that the metaphysical subject 'I', unlike the man, human body and human soul, is the limit of my world rather than part of the world. Wittgenstein excluded both nonsense (comparable to Kant's *nihil negativum*) and the senseless (comparable to Kant's *ens rationis*) from identifying anything within the limits of the world. These claims are related to his distinction between what can be said and what cannot be said. But the latter ultimately included the contents of the *Tractatus* itself; at best these puzzlingly could be shown, not said.

Much followed from Wittgenstein's shift of attention to a general human form of life in the *Investigations*. The priority of the logical meaning of language gave way to the priority of the human practical social use of language as the fundamental context in which to approach language. Private language knowable only to the single individual using it gave way to the need for publicly sharable criteria of meaning for language to be meaningful to anyone. An object mediated through shifts in aspect challenged the rejection of ambiguity in the unmediated relations between names and objects in the *Tractatus*. The metaphysical 'I' as a limit of the world moved to the centre of the world in the *Investigations*. Nevertheless, the status of 'I' as a name was open to challenge by showing that it functioned in some other way, perhaps as an indexical term (like here or now indicating a point of origin). In any case, there remained a problem of relating first person and third person discourse about a person. I have been influenced by Wittgenstein's rejection of sharply bounded conceptual determination of what does or not fall under names and his preference for a looser determination through family resemblance held in place by the reality of human participation in varieties of what he called language games. Rather than seeking to provide a philosophical theory of language, his preferred approach was to assemble reminders drawn from the immense variety in the actual use of terms in language to rebuff any proposed philosophical theory.

My fifth and final example is Emmanuel Lévinas in *Totality and Infinity: An Essay on Exteriority* and *Otherwise than Being, or Beyond Essence*. In these works, he critically responded within phenomenology to the writings of his main predecessors Edmund Husserl and Martin Heidegger. He rejected both Husserl's epistemology and Heidegger's ontology as the grounding concerns of phenomenology and sought to persuade readers to grasp that a fusion of metaphysics and ethics was phenomenology's first philosophy. In some ways, he sought to accomplish this by conversion through a gestalt switch of aspect rather than by the conclusion of argument. Fundamental to Lévinas were relations between the self and the other and the absolute otherness of the other. Starting with the self and taking all others as being both like oneself and like each other placed all of us in an unethical form of totality in which like selves were mutually replaceable, a view enabling totalitarian atrocity. By starting with the other and taking all others and oneself as being absolutely different from one another placed all of us in a metaphysical and ethical framework of infinity in which no self was replaceable by another self, a view enabling the possibility of peaceful stability of living together in the world. I have also been influenced to celebrate the infinite otherness of individual philosophers from one another and to prefer reading their works without the deadening effect of first taking them as representatives of -isms, ideologies or doctrinal schools.

Lévinas also included God among those infinitely other from the self. But he endorsed neither a negative theology concerning God nor a negative anthropology concerning human others. That would have followed if God had a humanly unknowable divine essence or if human others and a human self each had a human essence unknowable to the self. Rather, Lévinas held that God and humans were in a sense otherwise than being and therefore beyond essence. He gave priority to the active flow of saying, where communicating did not invite a search for essence, over the static said where a search for essence seemed inevitable.

My five examples do not exhaust the list of philosophers, teachers, colleagues, students and friends who have influenced my thinking about metaphysics and names, but they might help readers to assess what I grasp and what I miss. The five examples cannot be merged to form a single homogeneous super-example because there are ineliminable tensions within and among the texts I specified. They might better be seen as contributing to a critically inclusive comparative philosophical approach to multifaceted truth about metaphysics and names, conforming to the method introduced in my paper co-authored with Yu Jiyuan 'Saving the Phenomena: An Aristotelian Method in Comparative Philosophy' (2001).

I conclude by raising three questions. First, what in general is necessary in order to be a name-giver? Candidates in chapters in Part 1 include sacred and human name-givers. In monotheistic religious texts, a divine being initially gives names to things and is depicted as conversing directly in human languages with individual or communal followers or indirectly through divine messengers. There is also divine communication with human prophets, expressed by them in human languages. Similar depictions are possible in polytheistic religious settings where diverse deities are taken to be mutually independent or to be humanly available representations of attributes of a single deity. Some chapters examine whether or in what sense understanding the divine as a single simple infinite intellect is compatible with deeming that divine being to have the capacity to be a name-giver. Other chapters have different grounds for shifting the burden of name-giving to humans, or indeed take human name-giving as fundamental. Human name-giving can be assigned to ancient or contemporary communal practices or to one or more individual initiators, reformers or the exemplarily wise, engaged with the practical problems of their place and time. I am particularly interested in the human renewal or reform of names, if meanings of crucial names grow stale, change, decay or are entirely evacuated of meaning. In *After Virtue*, Alasdair MacIntyre diagnosed changes over time in the meaning of moral terms culminating in their collapse of meaning in modern times. He controversially proposed returning to Aristotelian virtue ethics to cure what he saw to be this dangerous modern malaise.

Secondly, what psychological or psychology-like resources are necessary to be a name-giver? I start with Christian controversies between Monophysite claims that Jesus and Christ have one nature and Dyophysite claims that, although in some sense combined, Jesus has a human nature and Christ a separate divine nature. Questions regarding unity and difference also appeared in Christian controversies over the three persons of the Trinitarian God. These controversies raise problems in deciding the number and subjects of psychological or psychology-like investigation. These problems wane if we take seriously stories of God or Gods acting and conversing with us in human-like ways, but wax if we take the nature or personhood of God or Gods as entirely different from the nature or personhood of human beings. It is baffling how, if at all, we could investigate the psychology of a divine name-giver that is absolutely other than our human selves. The problem radically diminishes if the psychology of human others is just as unavailable to each of us as is the psychology of God. However, it is not at all clear whether or how this would follow from Lévinas's placing relations between the self and both human and divine others within a framework of infinity rather than of totality.

Bafflement might be eased in another way by examining accounts of the human psychology of name-giving found in Part 1. The chapters generally ascribe varieties of powers, capacities or faculties to human psychology, including intellect or reason; emotion, passion or affect; sensibility, imagination and desire. Xunzi and Wang Bi understood the heart-mind (*xin*) as encompassing and unifying their capacities by avoiding dichotomous distinctions among them and thus explained the capacity of sages to be name-givers. Maimonides balanced intellect and imagination in his account of names but rested his account of prophecy on Moses's human intellect somehow engaging with God's divine intellect. Ibn ʿArabī held that imagination was fundamental to the human capacity to give divine names. Apophatic mystical thinkers rejected intellectual attempts to name God, instead seeking a non-cognitive nameless personal relationship with God. Spinoza gave priority to intellectual cognition and condemned the corrupting role of imagination.

Among these, the accounts of human psychology offered by Maimonides's rendering of Moses as prophet, and Spinoza's rendering of the crucial role of intellect in achieving the pinnacle of human freedom, come closest to aligning human psychology with what can be taken as an intellect-based divine psychology. Nevertheless, neither Maimonides's Moses nor Spinoza's free individual could communicate their human insights to other human beings without drawing on other aspects of their human psychology to be name-givers. Finally, the human intellectual intuition fundamental to both accounts faces the powerful retrospective criticism offered by Kant in his arguments that intellectual intuition is unavailable to human beings.

Thirdly, what can we say concerning what cannot be named? For example, if names exhaust language through their relation to things and if things singly or in combination exhaust the contents of reality, then the bleak answer to this question is 'nothing'.

But chapters in Part 1 explore varieties of metaphysical settings and conceptions of language in which nothing has a crucial active role underlying the workings of the world in which discriminating among mundane things is possible. Heidegger's 'nothing noughts', scorned as nonsense by logical positivists nearly a century ago, seems to fit in very well with some of the radically different understandings of nothing and nothingness examined in these chapters. It is also worth considering examples of struggling to express in language thoughts and feelings about our engagement with the natural and human world. In some cases, the words are there within ourselves to discover, but in others we seemingly must create rather than discover ways of capturing in language what is there non-linguistically in our experiences.

Sajjad Rizvi

Complementing the discussion so far, I focus on the question of divine names and how thinkers in the Islamic tradition, in particular, took up the challenge of engaging with them while recognizing the limitation posed by the incommensurability of human and divine language (acknowledging that the very application of language to the divine is analogical).

The divine names articulated in scriptures and liturgical practices pose a problem of how we make sense of them and their ontological and epistemological status. The Neoplatonic tradition's Abrahamic inheritances posed a multi-level problem (Boulnois 1999). First, 'God' as such, transcendent, ineffable, beyond being and beyond the grasp of the human intellect, was not a name but a manifestation in its disclosure to humans. Secondly, scripture provided certain names for 'God' but those did not pick out what God is. Thirdly, the multiplicity of names did not violate divine simplicity and singularity or indeed the 'non-dual' nature of reality. Finally, humans' agency of naming God was the theurgic inculcation of divine agency in the cosmos and a process of becoming what one names and participating in divine agency.

This scheme posed three possibilities of philosophical-theological response. The first is a cataphatic approach, subsuming divine names into the broader category of names as labels that pick out features of an entity, based upon a commonality that allows for the use of analogy. Even if one holds that 'God' is unchanging, impassible, existent and singular (designators that reveal the somewhat irreducibly Aristotelian nature of much theological language), that approach suggests that speaking of God's mercy recalls how we conceive of mercy, but with the understanding that divine mercy is either the limit case of intensity in that concept or unknowably far beyond it. The mechanism for understanding is the notion of analogy, or what the Islamic traditions from Avicenna onwards called 'modulation' (*tashkīk*), in which a concept may have multiple instances with an overlapping focal sense and in which the many senses within the concept are arranged in modulating levels of intensity, or at the very least 'more or less' (Bonmariage 2007: 53–74; Rizvi 2009: 38–53). Such a position recognized the polysemy of language and the possibilities of literal and figurative discourse.

A critical question is whether the divine names have any independent reality – whether they are ontologically or merely conceptually distinct from the divine essence, a question at the heart of Islamic rational theological debates. For example, the Sunni Ashʿarī theologian Ghazālī (d. 1111) argued that the names are real and not mere synonyms for the divine reality; in fact, names indicate various aspects of the divine and of divine agency – they might indicate properties to be predicated of God as well as negated of God, or relations within the godhead and with the cosmos; fundamentally they are indicators for divine attributes (*al-ṣifāt*) that are real and conceptually distinct from the divine essence (*al-dhāt*) (Ghazālī 1995: 159–62). The multiplicity of objects of knowledge in the 'mind' of God – just like the multiplicity of Platonic Forms – does not entail a real composition within a singularity; similarly a multiplicity of divine names and attributes does not violate God's unity (Ghazālī 1995: 165). Thus, his position indicates a mixture of a cataphatic alongside a more negative approach to naming God, which was distinct from his opponents, philosophers and Muʿtazila, especially Shiʿi thinkers, who held that names were conventions given in scripture, but that God possessed a single divine attribute of necessary existence.

The second possibility is the apophatic approach in which there is negation of the names and indeed the expression of being unable to grasp the names. The Ismaili tradition in Islam in particular resisted the solution of modulation because for them 'God' or the ultimate reality was beyond being – in fact, 'God' and other divine names were ciphers for the second-order entities responsible for the creation of the cosmos such as the *nous*. Hence, petitionary prayer was not an attempt at influencing an impassible God but a means for connecting to higher intelligible beings involved in the cosmos which did not possess the absolute perfection of the ultimate reality (Sijistānī 2000: 81–99). A medieval Ismaili refutation of Avicennian metaphysics went as far as to argue that 'modulation' and the language of existence that encompasses the Necessary and the contingent would render existence as a genus and implicate the ultimate reality into a composition violating monotheism (Shahrastānī 2001: 36–42). A further expression of their apophasis was to assert the double negation that 'God' does not exist and also does not not-exist (Sijistānī 2000: 72–3). Calling upon God through the divine names and understanding God through the signs of the cosmos is, for the Ismailis, not a direct grasping of the divine nature but of the possibility of oneness and non-duality. Apophasis in other Shiʿi traditions is more conditional. Certain things such as having volume and extension, being in space and time, passibility, perceptibility, ability to know are negated of God. And names which are positively predicated of God do not have reality; they are conventions – like knowing, powerful, alive, willing and perceiving – which pick out the divine essence (Ḥillī 2021: 214–53). The classic expression of the relationship of names, attributes and divine essence is the formulation in a famous oration attributed to ʿAlī, the cousin of Muḥammad and first Shiʿi Imam:

> Sincerity to God is achieved by negating all attributes ascribed to him, by the testimony of every attribute that is separate from the thing described, and by the testimony of everything described that is separate from the attribute. To describe God is to ascribe associates to him. To ascribe associates to him is to ascribe duality to him. To ascribe duality is to divide him. To divide him is to undervalue him. To undervalue him is to depict him. To depict him is to circumscribe him. To circumscribe him is to quantify him. To ask, 'In what?' is to confine him. To ask 'On what?' is to make another space empty of him. God is a being but not by coming into being. He is existent but not after non-existence. He is with all things but not by association. He is other than all things but not by detachment. He is an agent but not by movement or instrument.
>
> (Raḍī 2024: 107)

Apophasis can lead, as a third possible response, to a more restrained theology associated with Sunni traditionalism in Islam: suspension of judgement about the names – in particular the position known as *bilā kayf*, of 'affirming' names without asking about the nature of their modality and causality (Kars 2019: 195–234). Such a position also bears within it possibilities ranging from what seems like an anthropomorphic literalism through 'anti-interpretivism' to a more radical non-cognitive insistence on silence.

Alongside these ways of understanding the divine names, we find the Neoplatonic model of the role of the divine names in the cosmogonic procession of the universe from the One and in its theurgic reversion to its origins. This is predicated on the model of creation in Plato's *Timaeus* in which the demiurge fashions the cosmos from the *paradigm*, or the Platonic forms in the 'mind' of God, animating matter through what the *Chaldean Oracles* call the 'connectors' (Brisson 2003). It is then the role of theurgy and ritual to effect the soteriological return of souls and the cosmos to its Origin. Similarly in the pseudo-Dionysian corpus, the divine names are the agency of manifestation that produces the cosmos since the Superunknowable, transcendent One is beyond being and knowing; it is the role of prayer and the invocation of the divine names (not least the Trinity) – names taught by scripture as one cannot ascribe divine names from reason alone – to inculcate the divine presence and allow for the possibility of realizing spiritual union (Pseudo-Dionysius 1987: 51–3, 68–71). In Ibn ʿArabī, the divine names as the self-manifestation of the ultimate reality produce the cosmos and act as its controller; while God and the names that he intellects in his mind are singular and undifferentiated, at the next level of the names that project outwards, so to speak, their differentiation accounts for phenomenal multiplicity in the cosmos (Ibn ʿArabī 1981: 78, 125, 148). The theurgic use of the names in the human imagination to construct and remake the world and to effect the reversion to the One is the primary agency of the divine names in much of the tradition of Ibn ʿArabī and Sufism – as is most clear in Iskandarī's *Key to Salvation*, a treatise on the invocation of the divine names that is about the reversion as an act of union (Iskandarī 1996).

In conclusion, I return to the nature of names as tokens of knowledge and ontological items taught to Adam. Divine names are relations and self-designations of the ultimate reality usually given in scripture to designate God's sempiternity, omnipresence and providential existence. But the names taught to Adam descend from the transcendent level of God to the level of divine agency in the cosmos and levels of manifestation of that ultimate name, God. The divine names that we may utter are tokens of those names – what the Ibn ʿArabī tradition calls the 'names of names'; if one can grasp the ultimate name, sometimes conceived as an occult formula or entity, the spiritual traditions see this as the internalization of the creative agency of the demiurge and the power of articulating 'be and it is'. Thus, naming is an act of becoming and producing – on one side theology and the metaphysics of what is and can be named, and on the other the act of prayer and praise (Soskice 2023: 229). Is this a peculiarly human privilege (for scriptures talk of the praise and naming of the divine by all manner of creatures)? Mullā Ṣadrā considers these issues in his exegesis of God teaching Adam all the names and presenting 'them' to the angels and testing the angels on their knowledge, which of course falls short (Shīrāzī 2010, III: 754ff). The name is not presented to the angels to capture a certain meaning or some sort of predicate; rather, it denotes a sign or manifestation that calls to the mind a reality pertaining to the divine essence, names, and agency. God's creation of Adam as primordial human makes humans capable of perceiving and understanding three classes of objects: sensible, intelligible and imaginal. God's teaching of the names to Adam therefore bestows the names as realities of these three types of objects. So divine naming not only produces the cosmos but also through teaching gives humans the capacity to make sense of their reality and of metaphysics and indeed make their world. In Platonic fashion, Mullā Ṣadrā concludes:

> The divine names are the ground of the essences of contingent beings and the world of divine names is the ground of this world including all the forms and images of the cosmos such that those forms are shadows and reflections of the higher forms. Perfect saints and those of true insight can witness the forms of the higher world through the light of the inner selves in their true hierarchy and how they in turn effect order and hierarchy in this world.
>
> (Shīrāzī 2010, III: 761–2)

References (Nicholas Bunnin)

Bunnin, Nicholas (2009), 'The Theory of Names in Plato's *Cratylus*', *Journal of Chinese Philosophy* 36 (4) (December): 531–40.

Bunnin, Nicholas (2022), 'A Moral Metaphysics and a Metaphysics of Morals: Xunzi and Kant', *Journal of Chinese Philosophy* 49 (2) (July): 174–80.
Bunnin, Nicholas, and Yu Jiyuan (2001), 'Saving the Phenomena: An Aristotelian Method in Comparative Philosophy', in Bo Mou (ed.), *Two Roads to Wisdom? Chinese and Analytical Philosophical Traditions*. Chicago, IL: Open Court.
Feng, Gia-fu, and Jane English (1973), *Lao Tsu, Tao De Ching*. London: Wildwood House.
Kant, Immanuel (1928), *Critique of Pure Reason*, trans. Norman Kemp Smith. London: Macmillan Publishers.
Keping, Wang (2011), *Reading the Dao: A Thematic Introduction*. New York: Continuum.
Lévinas, Emmanuel (1991), *Otherwise than Being, or beyond Essence*, trans. Alphonso Lingis. Dordrecht, Boston, MA, and London: Kluwer Academic Publishers.
Lévinas, Emmanuel (1991), *Totality and Infinity: An Essay on Exteriority*, trans. Alphonso Lingis. Dordrecht, Boston, MA, and London: Kluwer Academic Publishers.
MacIntyre, Alasdair (1981), *After Virtue: A Study in Moral Theory*. London: Duckworth.
Wittgenstein, Ludwig (1967), *Philosophical Investigations*, 2nd ed., trans. G. E. M. Anscombe. Oxford: Basil Blackwell.
Wittgenstein, Ludwig (1974), *Tractatus Logico-Philosophicus*, revised edition, trans. D. F. Pears and B. F. McGuinness. London: Routledge and Kegan Paul.

References (Sajjad Rizvi)

Bonmariage, Cécile (2007), *Le réel et les réalités: Mullā Ṣadrā Shīrāzī et la structure de la réalité*. Paris: Vrin.
Boulnois, Olivier (1999), *Être et representation*. Paris: Presses universitaires de France.
Brisson, Luc (2003), 'Plato's Timaeus and the Chaldean Oracles', in Gretchen Reydams-Schils (ed.), *Plato's Timaeus as Cultural Icon*. Notre Dame, IN: University of Notre Dame Press, pp. 111–32.
Ghazālī, Abū Ḥāmid (1995), *The Ninety-Nine Beautiful Names of God: Al-Maqṣad al-asnā fī sharḥ asmā' Allāh al-ḥusnā*, trans. David B. Burrell and Nazih Daher. Cambridge: The Islamic Texts Society.
Ḥillī, Ibn al-Muṭahhar (2021), *Clearing the Soul for Paradise (Taslīk al-nafs ilā ḥaẓīrat al-quds)*, ed./trans. Jari Kaukua. Birmingham: Al-Mahdi Institute Press.
Ibn ʿArabī, Muḥyī'l-Dīn (1981), *The Bezels of Wisdom: Fuṣūṣ al-ḥikam*, trans. R. J. Austin. New York: Paulist Press.
Iskandarī, Ibn ʿAṭāʾ Allāh (1996), *The Key to Salvation & the Lamp of the Souls (Miftāḥ al-falāḥ wa-miṣbāḥ al-arwāḥ)*, trans. Mary Ann Danner. Cambridge: The Islamic Texts Society.
Kars, Aydogan (2019), *Unsaying God: Negative Theology in Medieval Islam*. New York: Oxford University Press.
MacIntyre, Alasdair (1981), *After Virtue: A Study in Moral Theory*. London: Duckworth.

pseudo-Dionysius (1987), *The Complete Works*, trans. Colm Luibheid. New York: Paulist Press.

Raḍī, al-Sharīf (compl.) (2024), *Nahj al-balāghah: The Wisdom and Eloquence of ʿAlī*, ed./trans. Tahera Qutbuddin. Leiden: Brill.

Rizvi, Sajjad (2009), *Mullā Ṣadrā and Metaphysics: Modulation of Being*. London: Routledge.

Shahrastānī, ʿAbd al-Karīm (2001), *Struggling with the Philosopher: A Refutation of Avicenna's Metaphysics. A New Arabic Edition and Translation of Kitāb al-Muṣāraʿa*, eds./trans. Wilferd Madelung and Toby Mayer. London: I. B. Tauris.

Shīrāzī, Mullā Ṣadrā (2010), *Tafsīr al-Qurʾān al-karīm*, ed. Muḥsin Bīdārfar, 8 vols. Tehran: Sadra Islamic Philosophy Research Institute.

Sijistānī, Abū Yaʿqūb (2000), *Kitāb al-iftikhār*, ed. Ismail Poonawala. Beirut: Dār al-gharb al-islāmī.

Soskice, Janet M. (2023), *Naming God: Addressing the Divine in Philosophy, Theology and Scripture*. Cambridge: Cambridge University Press.

Afterword: Continuing to do metaphysics in a diverse world

There are no closed systems or complete revelations. The essence of (human) being is exploration, which will not cease. But the end will not just be to know where we started from for the first time. Once we leave our islands, literally, digitally or metaphorically, they are not the same if and when we return – though they are still there, transformed in themselves by time and because we are transformed by the journey.

The journey thus far has taught us three things about the way forward. First, and most generally, it is a recurring theme in this volume that openness without constraint to the wisdom expressed in the other should be at the heart of the philosophical endeavour.

Secondly, this conversation with the other is not just about 'philosophy': the philosophical challenge and opportunity come not only from the recognizably philosophical but from very different forms of expression too – from poetry, art, music, rhythm and movement. This implies, thirdly, that philosophy has to engage with other discourses (whether historiographical, psychological, sociological, anthropological, religious or aesthetic) even though it is not reducible to them. To repeat, therefore: the terrain is limitless.

Limitless, but not featureless. We can discern outcrops which attract our attention and draw us towards them. These are where we may wish to go next. In this volume, for instance, we have not explored the thought worlds of Latin America in which vibrant literary creativity has been a prominent vehicle of philosophical ideas in postcolonial times. Moreover, African expression is as diverse as that huge continent is: we have focused on two particular African traditions – but there is plainly much more to be explored. And there is also more to discover – with the eye and ear of philosophy, not just anthropologically – about the non-urbanized (or not yet radically urbanized) expressions of metaphysical reflection which are still the lived experience of at least some people in every continent of the world. Whether or not they continue to flourish in an increasingly connected world through the coming decades, they have much insight to offer to the wider world as our planetary environment comes under more and more stress.

Furthermore, once it is accepted that 'institutional' academic borders are in fact highly porous, the texts and artefacts that become available are enough to last many lifetimes. The great epics of the world (from Gilgamesh onwards), the great plays of the world (from the Greek tragedians onwards), the great poetry of the world (from the Vedic texts and the Hebrew Bible onwards), the great novels of the world (from the Tale of Genji onwards), visual art (from the caves of the ice ages onwards), music (from the Hurrian songs of Ugarit onwards): all of this is available for potential *philosophical* encounter.

For reasons set out in the Introduction, we believe that this continuing work of exploration matters, and that it can only be done these days in cross-cultural conversation. Our exercises in comparative metaphysics will bear fruit to the extent that they encourage further creative explorations and conversations across cultures. We set out these brief reflections on where the conversations might be taken next, in the hope that others will share in the pleasure of such conversations as well as sharing our belief in their importance.

Stephen Green

Index

Abhinavagupta 155–7, 159, 168, 170, 369, 372, 373
African art 9, 19, 33, 237, 239–47
African sculpture 241–3, 250
  as philosophy 237–53
Analects 20, 45, 50, 52, 67
ancestors 49, 264–7, 274–5
animism 243–4, 330
Annen 323, 329–30
apophaticism 26, 181–3, 185, 187, 193, 195, 205–7, 316
Aquinas, Thomas 154, 158, 221
ʾArabī, Ibn 32, 272, 278–87
Aristotle 17, 20, 34, 44, 74, 105, 132–3, 295, 302
Artaud, Antonin 252
ascent, mystical 185–8, 192–5, 205, 207, 291, 294, 299, 366, 370–1
ascetic theology 365
asceticism 146, 304
askēsis 193, 292–300, 303, 306
Assmann, Jan 342
ātman 147, 149–50, 184, 363, 369, 371
Augustine 36, 353–4, 369–70, 375
Aurelius, Marcus 297–9
Avicenna 36, 365, 387
Axial Model 343, 347–8, 351–2, 356

Basil the Great 185, 208
Baye-Salzmann, Pierre 248
becoming 28, 63–75, 172, 223, 228–30, 250, 252, 274, 328, 332–3, 341, 347–8, 352–6, 366, 369–70, 387, 390
  being and 28, 175, 298, 318, 351
Behrens, Kevin 268
Bergson, Henri 34, 245–6, 249–50

beyond, the 191, 248, 317, 333, 341, 348, 350–2, 354, 356
Bhagavad-gītā 150–2
Bi, Wang 17–18, 39, 52, 131–3, 136–44, 386
Big Bang 72–3
Blumenberg, Hans 217
Bo, Shi 66
brahman 26, 28, 149–53, 182–4, 188–9
Brahmanas 182, 193
Buddha 52, 153–5, 189, 199–204, 212, 303–4, 317, 322–3, 325, 327–30, 369
buddha-nature (*foxing*) 201, 317, 320, 322–4
Buddhaghosa 303–4, 368–9, 371
Buddhism 46, 53, 146, 148, 151–3, 155–6, 160, 200–1, 203, 293, 303, 315, 317–18, 320, 325, 329, 344, 349, 355, 362–4, 367–8
  Abhidharma 154, 303
  Madhyamaka 365
  Mahāyāna 212, 300, 316, 329, 369
  Sanron 200
  Shingon 204
  Tantric 322, 325
  Tendai/Tiantai 316, 318–19, 323, 329–30, 332
  Theravāda 300, 368
  Yogācāra 148
  Zen/Chan 308, 324, 349, 364, 367
buddhology 199–201, 212
Bujo, Benezet 264, 266

causation 74, 145, 154, 277, 323, 369
Cezanne, Paul 251
chaos 69, 72, 83, 123, 131, 138
China 46, 50, 53, 64, 82–3, 98, 145, 177, 200–1, 294, 316, 329, 341, 344, 349, 363–4, 379

Christ 204, 206, 210, 218–21, 231, 306, 366, 386
   Body 210
   death of 221–2
   divinity of 207
Christianity 16, 181, 183, 205–6, 211, 218, 222–3, 234, 273, 292, 294, 306, 346, 351, 354–5, 363–6, 368, 372
Chrysostom, John 208
Cicero 292
civilization 128, 244
Clement of Alexandria 181, 184–5
Cohen, Hermann 346
communism 3
Confucianism 51, 53, 83, 116, 118–19, 125–7, 160–1, 349
   Neo- 53, 145
Confucius 45, 50–3, 56, 67, 98, 126, 132, 137–8, 381
consciousness 149, 151–7, 160, 170–7, 190, 241, 244, 249, 298, 328, 343, 367–8, 371–2, 381
   absolute 364
   cosmic 247, 299, 300
   mythic 346
   primal 351
   pure 375
   sky of 168–70, 176, 177
   universal 170–2, 362
Constantinople, Council of 205, 365
constraint 156–7, 173, 393
constructivism 30, 117–18
   Kantian 117
   metaethical 116, 118, 120, 127–8
conversation 4–7, 10, 22–3, 274, 357, 393–4
Corbin, Henry 281–2, 284

Damascene, John 181
dao 26, 28, 43–57, 70–1, 97, 100–4, 109, 119, 131–2, 137, 139–44, 250, 320, 349–50, 379, 382
Daodejing 20, 26, 71, 379, 382
Daoism 50–1, 160–1, 347, 349–52, 382
Davidson, Donald 17
death 54, 73, 104, 125, 147, 170, 182, 185, 201, 204, 218–23, 230, 234, 248, 265–8, 274, 276, 299, 304, 346, 348, 365

deification (*theosis*) 205–7, 209–11, 362, 371, 374
Deleuze, Gilles 240, 251–3
   and Guattari 240, 251
democracy 111, 219
Derrida, Jacques 33–4
Descartes, René 132–3, 152–3, 159, 161, 260, 283, 292
dharma 147–8, 176, 202–4, 319
dharmadhātu 204
dharmakāya 201–3, 328
Dharmakīrti 154
Diagne, Souleymane Bachir 245–6
dialectics 80, 230, 352–3
Dōgen 324
dualism 152–3, 159, 188, 209, 212, 221, 316, 343, 347
   non- 150, 170, 321
Duchamp, Marcel 252

education 48, 51–2, 56, 65, 100, 105, 110–1, 159
eidos 28, 47
Eisenstadt, Shmuel 341–5, 349
emanation 167, 169–70, 182, 218, 224–5, 227, 285
emotion 131, 137, 140, 211, 237, 239–40, 242, 245–9, 252, 254, 386
emptiness 103, 109, 121, 140, 144, 154–6, 173, 193, 317–18, 321, 363–5
epistemology 6, 48, 133, 193, 316, 334, 381, 384
epoché 18
essence 48, 74, 86–7, 92, 108, 124, 134–5, 147, 153, 155, 160, 169, 171, 173, 184–6, 195, 199–200, 203, 206–13, 218–20, 226, 231, 247–53, 259–60, 263
   and energy of God 205
   human 124, 385
ethics 10, 17, 48, 56, 64, 73, 83, 117, 131, 133, 142, 205, 268, 291, 294, 298–9, 353–5, 381, 384–5
   metaethical constructivism 116–18
   Stoic 293
'ethnophilosophy' 237–9

Europe 20, 24, 29, 78, 80, 82–3, 158, 175, 177, 280, 294
Evdokimov, Paul 209
evolution 43, 63, 69, 72, 74–5, 152, 348, 351

family resemblance 16, 86, 384
feeling 102, 131, 229, 246, 368
Foucault, Michel 133, 292–3, 299, 304
friendship 63, 126, 304

Garden of Eden 57, 108
God 7–10, 46, 52, 97, 104–9, 132–6, 140–5, 153–6, 160, 169, 181–95, 200–12, 217, 219–20, 222–32, 249, 272–3, 277, 279–86, 297, 303, 305, 345, 355, 362–71, 380, 387–90
  arguments for 157–8
  death of 348
  personal 187–91, 341
  unknowability of 185–6, 193, 205
  withdrawal of 226–7, 231
Goddess 146, 167–77, 194, 381
Goethe, J. W. von 218, 233
Gospels 35
Gregory of Nyssa 184–5, 188

Hadot, Pierre 293–302, 304–7
happiness 295, 300, 306
harmony 15, 28, 53, 63–75, 110, 139, 158, 242, 264, 268, 352
Hawking, Stephen 73
heart/mind (*xin*) 27–8, 66–7, 97, 99–104, 121–2, 125, 137, 140–3, 147, 168, 173, 187, 329, 386
  prayer of the heart 188, 194, 286, 362
Heaven 46–8, 50–5, 101–2, 116, 120–4, 127, 137, 139–43, 147, 352–3, 382
  tian 46, 49–50, 53, 116, 119
Hegel, Georg 30, 34, 94, 221, 223–4, 228–30, 240, 251, 348–9, 352
Heidegger, Martin 33, 175, 259–60, 349, 384
hell 222, 319, 322
Heraclitus 65
hesychast tradition/hesychasm 188, 194, 204–5, 211, 373
Hinduism 159–60, 167, 182, 194, 344, 363–4

Hountondji, Paulin 237
Hugh of St Victor 366
human nature 51, 53, 99, 362, 372, 386
humanity 16, 48, 51, 55, 57, 75, 126–7, 136, 139, 143, 159, 210, 271–2, 279–80, 282, 286, 370, 373
Husserl, Edmund 18, 20, 30, 150, 384

Ikuenobe, Polycarp 262, 268
imagination 69, 93, 106–7, 134–6, 140, 143, 187, 271–3, 279, 280–6, 386
incarnation 205–7, 221–3, 244, 364, 372
India 38, 83, 145, 160–1, 167, 175, 182, 201, 294, 341–2, 363–4, 367, 379
interconnectedness 26, 81, 85–6, 89, 264
  textual 29
Islam 104, 158, 286, 300, 303, 351, 354–5, 373, 388–9

Jainism 146
Jakuchū, Itō 300
Japan 200, 316, 319, 323, 325–30
Jaspers, Karl 341–2
Joachim da Fiore 353
Jonas, Hans 30, 228, 231

Kabbalah 218–19, 221, 224–7
Kafka, Franz 217
Kālī 167–8, 381
Kant, Immanuel 133, 143, 306–7, 383, 386
karma 148, 323, 330
kenosis 217, 219–21, 223–4, 226–7, 231, 252
Klee, Paul 251
Krama 167–77
Kṣemarāja 168, 170–3
Kūkai 26, 199, 200–4, 211–2, 328–9, 380

language 19, 22, 26–33, 44, 48, 83, 88–9, 93, 97–9, 102, 104–5, 108–13, 126, 132–3, 147–51, 168, 171, 184, 186, 191–2, 200–2, 208, 221, 299, 315–16, 320, 324, 327, 333, 361, 373
  analysis of 148
  philosophy of 133, 381
  theistic 157, 160

Legalism 53–4, 83
Levinas, Emmanuel 246, 354–5, 384–5
Lévy-Bruhl, Lucien 246
li 28, 46, 137–9, 250, 317, 333
light, uncreated 205, 207, 209
light of apophaticism 205–7
Locke, John 68
logos 28, 46–7, 57, 145, 245–6, 299, 353, 372
Louth, Andrew 186, 362

MacIntyre, Alasdair 16, 385
Maimonides 17, 26, 97, 104–13, 380
Maldiney, Henri 251
Mandanamiśra 150
Mauss, Marcel 362
Maximus the Confessor 181, 188, 194, 206, 208–9, 366
Maya philosophical tradition 271–4, 278–82
mean, doctrine of 45, 51, 53, 75
meditation 18, 146, 153, 155, 187–8, 190, 191, 194, 204, 211, 222, 299, 304, 368, 371
memento mori 299–300
Mencius 52–3, 56, 98, 119, 122
Merleau-Ponty, Maurice 241
Merton, Thomas 361
method 44, 55, 79–82, 85–6, 92–3, 111, 131, 139–40, 183, 188–90, 201, 211, 252, 294–6, 299, 302, 306–7, 381
  Aristotelian 385
  mystical 302
  philosophical 302
  Socratic 302
methodology 44–5, 84, 110, 239, 296
Milbank, John 354
Mīmāṃsā 146–9, 151, 158, 160
mind 19, 54, 70, 81, 124, 135–6, 152, 156, 173, 176, 184, 186, 190, 192–4, 202–4, 209, 211–2, 219, 244, 248, 261, 271–2, 279, 282–6, 292, 294, 297–8, 300, 319, 324, 327–9, 366, 368, 371–2, 381, 389
  body, speech and 202
  of God 388
  mind only 155, 364
  mind-body problem 260
  pure 185

Mishnah 104
modernity 20, 110, 161, 223, 347–50, 353, 362
Mohism 53, 83, 119
monasticism 304, 365–6
monotheism 217–18, 232, 342, 388
morality 46, 64, 116–17, 121, 126, 355, 369
  moral intuitionism 116
  moral judgement 115–16, 118
Moses 108–9, 185, 188, 192, 194, 205–6, 208, 225, 386
Mozi 54, 83–4, 92, 102
Muhammad 285–6, 301, 389
mystical experience 190, 192–3, 195, 206, 258, 286, 300, 302, 320
mystical union 184, 187, 327
mysticism 182, 305–6, 365
  brilliant darkness 185, 188, 191–2
  via negativa 185, 192

Nāgārjuna 151, 154, 189, 200, 364
names 21, 83–4, 98–104, 110, 183–6, 189, 266, 279–80, 317, 319, 379–90
  divine 186, 272, 278–80, 283, 285–6, 297, 380, 387–90
nature 200, 244, 281
  biological 127
  God and 134–5
Nazianzus, Gregory 194, 219
Neoplatonism 206, 225, 231, 354–5
Nietzsche, Friedrich 33, 237, 251, 354
nirvāṇa 212, 321, 324, 330, 332
normativity 115–16, 121, 124, 128, 229
nothingness 46, 137, 146, 174, 224–7, 387
noumenon 47
Nussbaum, Martha 64, 292, 298
Nyāya 158–60, 363

objectivity 116–17, 127, 148, 170, 173
  moral 64, 115–18
ontology 56, 88, 133, 148, 247, 259–61, 268, 293, 316, 325, 333–4, 384
Onyewuenyi, Innocent 267
Origen 181, 218, 353, 365–6
ousia 207, 364

Palamas, Gregory 26, 188, 199, 204–9, 210–2, 373, 380
Parmenides 35, 88–9, 181
personhood 30, 152, 261, 265, 283, 371–3, 386
persons 132, 137, 143, 146, 157, 170, 175–7, 211, 261, 264, 361, 365, 367, 371
phenomenology 168, 171, 174–6, 305, 372, 381
Philokalia 210
philosophy 15–16, 18–21, 25, 27–34, 44, 64, 80, 83, 118, 133, 138, 184, 186, 205, 223–4, 237–40, 260–1, 316, 341, 349, 354, 364, 381, 384, 394
    African 238–54, 260–9
    analytic 387
    as way of life 291–307
    Chinese 44, 46, 74, 83, 141, 260–1
    comparative 132, 315, 384
    Confucian 65, 67, 74
    Daoist 48, 50–1, 57, 84
    European 89
    Global 79
    Indian 145, 161
    political 112–13, 116
    pragmatist 109
    transcultural 80
Plato 35, 47, 64, 67, 88, 381
Plotinus 135, 158, 161, 294–5, 298
polytheism 217, 346
Ponticus, Evagrius 365–7
Popol Vuh 32, 35, 271–87, 380
Popper, Karl 64–5, 67
Porphyry 291, 295
prayer 181–2, 186, 188, 191, 194, 204–9, 211, 302, 362, 373, 389–90
    contemplative 191, 210
    Jesus/of the heart 188, 194, 210
    petitionary 388
Proclus 181
Pseudo-Dionysius 181, 185–7, 389
puruṣa 152–3, 184, 189

qi 47, 67–9, 71, 73, 137, 139, 142–3, 250
Quine, Willard 17, 33–4
Qur'an 20

Rawls, John 97, 109–10, 112–13, 116–17
reading 15–34, 106, 111–2, 136, 192, 207, 247, 274, 295–6, 299, 305, 346, 385
realism 116, 241, 368
reason 28–31, 46, 56, 72, 83, 92, 99, 101, 103, 131–4, 137, 140, 142, 144–5, 171, 186, 188, 200, 230, 238–41, 244–6, 261–2, 277, 280, 284, 296, 306–7, 366, 386, 389
redemption 160, 226, 231, 347, 356, 365–6, 370–1
reincarnation 146–7, 150, 155, 159, 173, 266–7, 319
relativism 16, 89, 373
religion 16, 50, 167, 176, 303, 306, 326, 341, 346, 265
rhythm 210, 237, 239–40, 244, 246–50, 393
    philosophy of 244–52, 254
Rigveda 105, 149, 182, 192
ritual 46, 99, 120–6, 147–9, 159, 176, 200, 203, 207, 211–2, 242, 275, 277–9, 282, 286, 291–2, 303, 380, 389

sacrifice 52, 146–7, 149, 169, 221, 224, 226, 229, 231, 278–9, 346, 371
Sadra, Mulla 36, 295, 300, 302–3, 305, 307, 390
Saichō 323, 328, 330
salvation 51, 57, 155, 160, 193, 218, 344–7, 370–1
Sāṃkhya 151–3, 156
saṃsāra 150, 212, 321, 332, 355
Śaṅkara 150–1, 343
Śāntideva 303–4
Schelling, Friedrich 239, 241
Schmitt, Carl 217, 219
Scholasticism 145
Scholem, Gershom 224–6, 231
self 17, 113, 144, 146, 148–53, 155–7, 159–60, 172–3, 186, 188–90, 229, 264, 291–3, 296–9, 306, 324, 327, 362–4, 367–71, 372–3, 384–5
    no-self 152–3, 363
Senghor, Leopold Sedar 237, 239–41, 244–50, 252–3
Shi, Hui 17, 79–93, 379

Shinto 325, 327
Socrates 29, 44, 49, 88, 381
soul 147, 160, 170, 182, 191–4, 206–7, 209–12, 230, 238, 245–6, 275, 291–3, 296–9, 301–3, 244–6, 366, 369–73, 383
   ascent of 205
   purity of 194
speech 98, 106, 136–7, 184, 187, 299, 346
Spinoza, Baruch 131–6, 139–44, 173, 380, 386
Spivak, Gayatri 34
Stoicism 292
Stoics 292–4
sublation, method of 79–82
substance 28, 48, 68, 89, 102, 131–2, 142, 145, 148, 170, 207, 227–8, 248
   mysterious 46
   necessity and 133–6
   ontological 51
   thinking and extended 260
suchness 184, 315–34
Sufism 300, 305, 352, 389
symbol 50, 206–7, 209, 275

Tangwa, Godfrey 238
Tantras 155, 167
Taubes, Jacob 345–6, 347–8, 352–3
Tempels, Placide 238, 247, 250
theophany 282–4, 289
Torah 104, 111
transcendence 103, 141, 145–6, 149, 160, 166, 172, 174, 186, 191, 193, 199, 206, 208, 211, 222, 227, 229, 316, 333, 341–50, 354–6, 361, 364
   and immanence 159, 209, 349–50, 352, 355
translation 26–8, 142, 191, 219, 249, 274, 278, 321–2, 350, 352
Trinity 194, 209–10, 217, 219–20, 223, 231, 253, 370–2, 389
tsimtsum 174, 217–19, 221, 224–32
Tutu, Desmond 268

Ubuntu 261, 264
Udayana 158
Upanishads 20, 146, 148–51, 182, 184–5, 188–90, 363, 365
Utpaladeva 156

Vairocana 201–2, 204
Veda 20, 145–6, 149–50, 158
Vedanta 146, 149–53, 156, 159–60, 186, 189–90, 363
vitalism 247, 252
Voegelin, Erich 354

Weber, Max 11, 16–17, 21, 29, 341–2
Weil, Simone 218
Williams, Rowan 209–11, 220, 222, 231
wisdom 15–16, 35, 49, 86, 186, 203–4, 241, 247, 272, 291, 294, 298, 300–1, 303, 322, 332, 349–50, 366, 368
   Perfection 153, 369
withdrawal from the world 51, 349
Wittgenstein, Ludwig 293, 298, 383–4

xiang 71
xīn 28, 137, 386
Xunzi 17, 26, 31–2, 35, 53, 85, 97–104, 109–10, 113, 115, 120–7, 380, 383

Yangming, Wang 18
yi 44, 69, 83, 121, 139, 320
Ying, Yan 66–7
Yi Jing (Book of Changes) 46–7, 69–71, 83, 89, 102, 132, 136

Zeno of Elea 17, 79, 82, 85–93, 379
Zhiyi 36, 318, 321–2, 332–3
Zhuangzi 31, 36, 50, 84–5, 118–20, 127
Zhuxi 18–20, 53
Zizioulas, John 372
Zongsan, Mou 103